# Loving, Parenting and Dying:

## The Family Cycle in England and America, Past and Present

by

Vivian C. Fox and Martin H. Quitt

Psychohistory Press, Publishers
New York, New York, U.S.A.

LOVING, PARENTING AND DYING:
The Family Cycle in England and America, Past and Present

Cover: William Franz

Cover photo: William Dobson (1610-1646)
      *Portrait Group, probably of the Streatfield Family*
      oil on canvas
      42 x 49½ in. (106.75 x 125.75 cm.)
      Yale Center for British Art, Paul Mellon Collection

ISBN 0-914434-15-2

Library of Congress Cataloging in Publication Data

Main entry under title:

I. Fox, Vivian C. II. Quitt, Martin H.
  Loving, parenting, and dying.

  Bibliography: p.
  Includes index.
  1. Family—England—History. 2. Family—United States—History. 3. Life cycle, Human—History.
HQ615.L68 1981     306.8 '0942     81-1722

ISBN 0-914434-15-2

*To Debbie,*
*to Sandy,*
*with love*

# Table of Contents

PART ONE

UNIFORMITIES AND VARIATIONS IN THE ENGLISH AND
AMERICAN FAMILY CYCLE: THEN AND NOW
*Vivian C. Fox and Martin H. Quitt*

## PART TWO

## THE ANGLO-AMERICAN FAMILY CYCLE, 1500-1800

# PREFACE

This book is divided into two parts. Part I is our essay, "Uniformities and Variations in the English and American Family Cycle: Past and Present." It describes our six-staged model of the family cycle. Using this model, we compare family life in early modern England and America with family life in those two countries today. This essay is fully annotated.

Part II of this book consists of a stage by stage analysis of the early modern family cycle, 1500 to 1800. It compares developments on both sides of the Atlantic as well as regionally within each side. Each of the six chapters in Part II includes an introduction by us followed by edited selections from previously published scholarship, with two exceptions: the essays by Mary Ann Glendon and Alan Macfarlane, which have not been published elsewhere. It is for this reason that we have included their footnotes. We have eliminated the footnotes which were part of the original materials from which the edited selections in Part II have been excerpted. At the end of Part II is a short bibliography for references in our chapter introductions. There is of necessity some overlap between these introductions and our essay in Part I. Thus, while both parts complement each other, they can be read separately.

While this book is intended primarily for college students in family history and sociology courses, we have composed it with the research interests of family historians, sociologists, anthropologists and psychologists in mind. Current problems related to family life have captured the attention of the population in general and even of governmental officials. Accordingly, we hope that the overview we have undertaken in Part I will not only be helpful to students and scholars, but will also provide a meaningful perspective to everyone who has wondered about the past, present, and future of the family.

During the recent years when our interests and research have focused more fully on family history, we have been generously assisted by many people. This book itself has evolved out of our jointly taught course, The Family in Early Modern Times. We have profited from the insights that our students have regularly provided us both from their own familial experiences and from their interaction with the materials presented in class.

The book has been a principal project of the Center of Family Studies at Boston State College. From the outset we have been supported by Special Projects Grants from the Massachusetts State College System. Many peo-

1

ple in the Central Office of the System and in the administration at Boston State have facilitated and encouraged our efforts over the past half dozen years. We are especially grateful to the following: Dr. John R. Rothermel, President Kermit Morrissey, Dr. James P. Jones, William T. Morrissey, Herbert Regan, Peter Donko-Hanson, Dr. William Haas, Dr. Baheej Khleif, and Ann Marie Carroll. In addition, Dr. John C. Weston and our colleagues in the History Department have been most cooperative.

During the Spring of 1977 we benefitted from a series of six Family Development Workshops when colleagues from various Massachusetts State Colleges intensively analyzed an early version of this book from the perspective of their respective disciplines: David Haughey (Psychology), Baheej Khleif (Sociology), Winston Langley (Political Science), William Barker (English Literature), P. Brad Nutting (History), A. Gibbs Mitchell (History), and Robert LaSota (History).

In addition, we profited from the opportunity of discussing our approach with a special meeting of the Institute for Psychohistory held at Boston in December, 1977. We are grateful to the Research Associates who attended: Lloyd deMause, Alice Eichholz, David Beisel, Patrick Dunn, Henry Lawton, Jacques Szaluta and Paul Elovitz.

The initial Special Projects Grant from the Massachusetts State College System enabled us to travel in England and America during 1975 to collect source materials for the Center and to consult with specialists in family history and related fields. We were enormously helped and stimulated by the opportunity to attend classes and lectures and to have private discussions with specialists on both sides of the Atlantic. During the entire time spent conceiving and writing this book we have been aware of this important experience. We would like to extend our genuine appreciation to the following: in England, Alan Macfarlane, Peter Laslett, Joan Thirsk, Christopher Hill, Cecily Howell, Charles Phythian-Adams, Paul Slack, K.M.V. Davies, C.S.L. Davies, Isabel Kendrick, and John Yudkin; in America, Lloyd deMause, Mary Ann Glendon, Joseph Illick, Philip Greven, Richard Lyman, Norman Barka, Cary Carson, Dr. Thomas Cone, Jane Carson, John Demos, Daniel Pershonak, and Mary K. Matossian. To Professor Herbert Moller, we want to extend our special appreciation for the great care with which he read our manuscript and for the recommendations which we found so helpful.

We would also like to express our gratitude to the staffs of the following institutions for their generous assistance in providing us with access to and selected reproductions of their holdings: in England, the British Museum (Library), the Bodleian Library at Oxford University, the library at Nottingham University, the Public Record Office and Museum, Wellcome Institute for the History of Medicine, the Geffreye Museum, Bethnal Green Museum, London Museum, the National Gallery, and the Museum of Childhood in Edinburgh; in America, Metropolitan Museum of Art (esp.

2

Roberta Paine and Gordon Stone); Abbey Aldrich Rockefeller Folk Art Collection, Colonial Williamsburg (esp. Beatrix Rumford and Barbara Luck); Department of Collection, Colonial Williamsburg (esp. Mrs. Gill); Research Library, Colonial Williamsburg (esp. Harold Gill); Pennsylvania Historical Society (esp. Peter Parker); New York Historical Society (esp. Thomas Cummings); Archives Div., New York Public Library; National Gallery; Archives Div., Library of Congress; Rare Books Div., Boston Public Library; Alderman Library, University of Virginia; American Philosophical Library; Virginia State Library; and the New England Historical and Genealogical Society.

We would also like to thank our typists, Ann Strodder and Claire Murray. And John Lang's help facilitated the last stage of work.

Through our years of joint teaching, thinking, and writing, we have become increasingly aware of how much our own family experiences have shaped our approach. Our feelings and thoughts have been influenced and enriched by our respective parents. Our perseverance has been strengthened by the loving patience, advice, and editorial assistance of our spouses as well as the presence of our own children. Throughout all, they were there and with understanding.

## PART ONE

# UNIFORMITIES
## AND
# VARIATIONS
## IN THE
# ENGLISH
## AND
# AMERICAN
# FAMILY CYCLE:
## THEN AND NOW

# Introduction

## i. Family Life Cycle Model: An Explanation

When the two of us began to plan an undergraduate course on the Anglo-American family in early modern times, we decided to organize our study within the frame of a family cycle model. The model we conceptualized consists of six stages: Courtship to Marriage, Preparenthood, Childbearing, Childrearing, Post Childrearing, Spouse Loss. This model is primarily a logical construct that builds upon our own value system and that of our students. The cycle delineated in it involves a progression through which we expect to proceed in our own respective family histories and, as we discovered, through which most of our students expect to proceed in theirs. Equally important, moreover, is the congruity between the model and the actual experiences of most early modern Englishmen and Americans. It does not by itself, as no model can, fully describe the reality of family development in the early modern era. But it has fulfilled one of our original requirements for a family cycle model: namely that it be flexible enough to describe families which did not fully conform to its idealized progression. Indeed, the value of the model, as we conceived it, would be tested by its contribution to our ability to compare and differentiate family history at various times and various places. The model, then, was and remains a heuristic device for integrating the information available on past family life into a framework that is meaningful to us and our students today.[1]

Use of a cyclical model reflects the view that the family is a dynamic institution that involves its members in a series of altered situations, each of which poses its own peculiar stresses, options, and opportunities. It reflects the conclusion that all basic family matters (e.g., the control of property, the structure and size of households, the status of women, parental relationships with children, the interaction between nuclear families and other kin, the relationships between households and the community, and state involvement in family affairs) vary, sometimes subtly, sometimes sharply, from stage to stage in the family cycle. Accordingly, a cycle model requires us to avoid generalizations about the family that fail to consider variations by developmental stage. For example, our cyclical approach has forced us to diverge from the general belief that married women in the past were in-

4

variably dominated by their husbands. As we shall see, pregnant women enjoyed, potentially at least, a position of control and manipulation which was not granted them otherwise.[2] The demographic fact that childbearing was an ongoing part of the early modern family cycle suggests, then, that married women had a regular and continuing opportunity to exert control over their husbands, despite the norm that relegated them to an inferior and deferential status in the household.

There are at least two potentially valuable ways of utilizing our family cycle model. One is to view the developmental process as a whole by exploring the possible connections between various stages. For example, if parental influence over courtship is high, if the participants are brought together by parental matchmaking for socio-economic reasons, what are the consequences for later stages of the newly created family? Are there predictable correlations between such arranged marriages and spouse relationships during childbearing or childrearing modes or post-childrearing patterns of interaction between the generations? Are survivors of spouse loss likely to be better off materially if economic considerations have received a high priority during the courtship to marriage formation period? Conversely, will a marriage founded on romantic love lead to a highly affectionate childrearing mode which in turn will produce grown up children who will voluntarily take care of their elderly parents? This application of our family cycle model would require an intensive study of one family or one group of families. Only after this kind of developmental study of the family is made respectively for various groups and periods will comparisons of the whole family cycle over time and space be possible. At present such comparisons can best be served by a second application of our model, that is, by comparing each stage separately in chronological, socio-economic, and geographic terms. Accordingly, in this book we compare segmentally the six stages of the family cycle over time (from 1500 to 1800 as well as between the early modern period as a whole and the present), over space (between England and America as well as from region to region within both entities), and socio-economically (from class to class). In fact, we believe that this second application is indispensable for providing a framework in which the more narrowly focused developmental studies can proceed. For only after the researcher has acquired comprehensive historical understanding of each developmental stage, as can be derived from a broadly conceived comparative treatment of each, is he then prepared to investigate how the six stages interact with each other, within any particular family or group of families.

Of the various levels of comparison we are undertaking in Part I of this book, perhaps none requires as much justification and explanation as that between the early modern period as a whole and the present. As professional historians, our main scholarly expertise lies in the past, not the contemporary family. Yet during the years of our collaborative teaching and research, we have found ourselves continuously drawing upon our own familial experiences and those of our students to gain insight into family life of the past. Family history has evoked this kind of self-conscious involvement on our part and on the part of our students as has no other area of historical research in which we have been engaged. Although there is always the danger that a researcher will project upon his subject his own values or motives, by entering into our comparisons quite self-consciously we have at least tried to guard ourselves against false projections onto early moderns. At the same time, as we have come to realize how complicated our contemporary motives and values are, as reflected in our own decisions to get married, our relationships to our own parents and children, our own expectations regarding marriage, and our own respectively male and female experiences during childbearing, we have become more sensitive to the inherent complexity of the issues we are trying to examine for the people of the past.

If our scrutiny of some contemporary family experiences has contributed to a less simplified and less distorted understanding of family dynamics in the past, our comparison has also provided a much needed historical perspective to the trends that are occurring today. Change is a constant dimension of family life. But its meaning depends upon the yardstick we use for measuring it. When an older generation contrasts the behavior of the younger generation to itself the differences usually appear to be great and (often) alarming. When the younger generation's behavior is placed against a longer yardstick, however—that is, when it is compared to the behavior of many previous generations—the change it represents may be regarded as less dramatic. As Philippe Aries has written: "History enables us to put in their correct place *and in their correct order* facts which contemporary observers, who live with them, tend to believe are unique or extraordinary. By linking them to other facts in the story of development thus reconstituted, the historian can dedramatise them and make their import clearer."[3]

## ii. Value Of Comparative Overview

The primary historical focus of this book will be on family life in England and America from 1500 to 1800. These early modern centuries loom large in the new history of the family for three reasons: (1) our earliest systematic records of vital family events (marriages, births, and deaths) for whole localities date from these years;[4] (2) much of the pioneering work in family history has been done by specialists in that period;[5] and (3) there is much scholarly agreement that several of the features of contemporary family life (e.g., close parent-child bonding, romantic or at least affectionate marriages, and weak kinship ties) either originated in or have per-

6

sisted since the early modern era.[6]

The value of a comparative overview of both English and American family history in early modern times would seem to be self-evident, but perhaps a few words of explanation are in order.

In the past several years, students of early America increasingly have been expected to develop a sophisticated understanding of English history so as to be better able to ascertain what is distinctive in the American past and what represents an English transplantation. This expectation reflects the realization that if we are to gauge more accurately the impact of American environmental conditions on the values, institutional forms, and behavioral patterns of immigrants, we have to become more intimately familiar with the societies from which they came. Students of English history can profit as well from this kind of comparative approach, for a knowledge of family life among the English in America will enable them to draw inferences for application to areas of family life in England where direct evidence is lacking. Some English family scholars have drawn on French family studies to suggestively compensate for gaps in the English records. Analogies to the experience of the English in America would seem to be more tenable.[7] Moreover, one way of measuring the vitality of various features in English family life is to determine their persistence, modification, or disappearance in the American environments.

## iii. Broad Historical Background

Before we move to our comparative study of the early modern family cycle, we believe it would be valuable to sketch in the larger historical background of those centuries. For the broader perspective that is thereby gained can serve as a corrective against the possible distortions that can ensue from a too narrow focus on the private issues of family life.

Between 1500 to 1800 the English people transformed their own nation and founded another three thousand miles across the Atlantic. In their economic activities, in their political arrangements and rearrangements, in their geographic and social mobility, in their material culture, in their ideas, their values, and even their feelings, in the rhythms of their daily lives, English men and women as a whole developed a new energy and spirit that accompanied several remarkable transformations. Some were lasting, others short-lived; all testified to a comparatively vital, inventive, masterful people. They had not always been such.

Economically in 1500 England was a backward country. She was backward not because she was a pre-industrial society for the world was still pre-industrial. Rather it was because she was underdeveloped commercially in comparison to some of her Continental neighbors. Hers was a semi-colonial relationship to the rest of Europe. Between 40 to 50% of her overseas trade was in the hands of foreign merchants.[8] Her leading exports were raw wool and an unfinished wool cloth that had to be finished in Flanders. "In the production as well as the consumption of wealth, in industrial technique and scientific skill, she was markedly behind her nearest neighbors on the Continent."[9]

Englishmen were chronically "underemployed," in the countryside and in the towns. Work was seasonal and punctured by innumerable days off. To modern eyes production was lamentably low. In the early 16th century the English Protestant ethic and the spirit of capitalism were not yet widely at work. In the view of contemporaries and some modern historians, 16th-century Englishmen were an idle and lazy lot.[10] As is sometimes the case with phlegmatic people, energetic leaders were able to aggrandize their authority.[11] The early Tudors expanded the monarchy's control over the central government and extended its reach over local administration. In the 1530s "Henry VIII seemed more powerful than any English king, before or since, and he used Parliament for his government purposes."[12] It might be added, however, that the territory over which the Tudors reigned was as narrowly confined as at any time since the Conquest. Sixteenth-century England was an independent island, unimaginably remote from the empire of which it would soon become the center.

All of this and more would change deeply before 1800. From about the middle of the 16th century, English merchants began to reverse the semi-colonial position they had been in vis-à-vis Continental traders. The 17th century became the heroic age of English commerce. First the Spanish, then the Dutch were aggressively removed as rivals to English overseas trade and colonization. With her American colonies serving initially as a source for raw materials and later as a major market for her manufactured goods, England by 1700 established the primacy of her empire for Europe's economy. London was already the entrepôt for the Continent's colonial produce.[13] England's new wealth was fueled by her imperial expansion, but it was by no means solely derived from her overseas possessions. The early modern era was also the heroic age of English agriculture, for, as recent scholarship has measured it, the revolution in farming that enormously increased the food supply was well under way before 1700.[14] Without this early capacity to produce more food than was required to feed her population, England would not have been able to enlarge her urban populations sufficiently to provide an adequate home market and labor force for an industrial revolution. The 17th century was also the heroic age of politics, when the aggrandizing tendency of the monarchy was permanently limited. After the civil war of the 1640s, men of property, in both the countryside and the cities, would be freer to govern their own interests, through the instrument of Parliamentary legislation, than ever before. Indeed by the 18th century the English Constitution would be celebrated by theorists on the Continent as a model of Enlightenment.[15] Whereas his ancestor of 1500 had been often deemed as idle and lazy, the Englishman of 1700 was praised for his ingenuity, inventiveness, and push. New forms of commercial and financial organization, such as the joint stock company and the Bank of England, new legal instruments for estate and business management, such as the strict settlement, the trust, and limited liability for shareholders, and new techniques for cultivating previously fallow or marginal land contributed to economic growth and testified to the innovative spirit in the population as a whole.[16] In the second half of the 18th century, England became the first nation to cross the threshold into the industrial age. In view of her comparative economic and technological position in 1500, England's leadership in industrialization by 1800 itself represents perhaps the most unpredictable and revolutionary transformation of early modern Europe.

Two caveats should be attached to this necessarily brief and cursory summary of England between 1500 and 1800. First, while growth was an unmistakable theme, as measured in such areas as the food supply, consumer goods, the spread of literacy and knowledge, technical skill, national unification, overseas territories, naval strength, international prestige, the volume of trade, the accumulation of capital, urbanization, communications and transportation, and medical science, it usually did not occur along an unbroken line of advancement. For example, in 1800 England possessed the greatest empire among European powers, but it was smaller than what it had been before the American colonies successfully revolted a quarter-century earlier. The food supply was more constant from season to season than it had been before the Agricultural Revolution, but periods of dearth would recur for portions of the population, as evidenced by the food riots of the 1790s.[17] Nevertheless, if growth was not always steady it was persisting, for the English people of 1800 clearly possessed more wealth, more mastery over nature and the world, more national pride, prestige, and influence than their ancestors of 1500 could have even fantasized about. A second caveat must be added. Growth did not always mean an across the social spectrum improvement in the quality of life. Adversity as well as prosperity is an inevitable concomitant of growth, and the two conditions are never distributed evenly. Moreover, those who prosper must lose something, those who suffer must gain something. These truisms are particularly applicable to generations living through periods of deep change, when the conditions of their lives are profoundly altered.[18] Much of the growth between 1500 and 1800 that we have broadly charted was incremental. It did not result in the abrupt transformation of individual lives. But some elements of growth were experienced intensely and involved people in dramatic shifts within a single lifetime. Enclosures are a well known example. Although three-fourths of enclosure may have taken place by 1700, it was a movement that continued to affect some rural families throughout the three centuries of our study.[19] A concentration in ownership brought a more intensive and efficient use of the land, and a growth in agricultural output. It also brought a profound dislocation to those peasant families who were fenced out from previously common fields or who were squeezed off their noncompetitive smaller holdings. Their status and lifestyle as small, independent landowners or customary tenants could be suddenly transformed into that of rackrented tenants or servile wage-earners. And as such, their access to the fuller and more regular food supply that was gained from enclosure may have been precarious.[20] Those who left the countryside altogether and took up jobs in the new factories of the later 18th century must have found industrial growth to be a very mixed blessing. On the one hand, their wages would be more steady and higher than they had been on the farms. On the other hand, the pace of work would also be steadier, more highly regimented, and more monotonous.[21]

Still, if growth did not bring improvement without distress, the drive for improvement became a hallmark of the English people during these centuries. This is the point of our summary that we should bear in mind as we approach the early modern family cycle. For we must assume that there was an intimate connection between their individual family life and the ongoing quest for improvement that the English displayed in their collective economic, political, and cultural activities. It is not Whiggish hyperbole to say that they became an extraordinarily striving and achieving people between 1500 and 1800. And no account of their family history during that time can ignore these qualities without becoming distorted or merely trivial. When we are considering their attitudes towards marriage and mate selection, their thoughts about bearing and rearing children, their interaction as husbands and wives, their transfer of property and authority across the generations, and their provisions for surviving spouses and children, we should keep in mind that they were on the whole not a people who resignedly let things be or who simply allowed nature to take its course. Rather they generally, in these centuries, challenged nature and the status quo, they attempted to master their environment and to control their own destiny, they tended to exert their will against fate. The "they" we are talking about were members of early modern families.

If this characterization is valid for the English people at home, how much more so is it for those who founded and settled colonies in America during the 17th century. The evolution of these small, disparate immigrant societies into an independent nation in less than two centuries is surely one of the great events in Western history. And if our rhetorical style in alluding to it substitutes a grandiloquence one associates with 19th-century Whig history for the sober analysis of current historiography, it is done intentionally to remind ourselves that the new interest in topics that the older history regarded as trivial should be pursued without trivializing the people whom the older history described in perhaps overly lofty terms. If family history is to become a significant field of inquiry, it must explain, not reduce, the lives of people in the past.

# Stage I
# Courtship To Marriage Formation

In the early modern era marriage was the most consequential transition point in both the family cycle and in individual life history because it normally involved the transfer of property across the generations and, therefore, usually determined what the social and economic status of the younger generation would be. Moreover, it was generally believed that the ingredients which went into the formation of a marriage would bear significantly on the quality of the marital relationship and on the welfare of the family that would be created. In a sense, then, the stage of courtship to marriage formation was to the family cycle in the early modern view what childhood is to the individual in today's view: the base that shapes formatively later stages of development.[22]

We have divided courtship to marriage formation into three parts that we shall discuss separately: (1) the decision to marry (2) criteria for mate selection, and (3) courtship practices. The longest of these sections will be on the criteria for mate selection, for these are very difficult to ascertain and historians continue to disagree about them. We should note that our division of courtship to marriage formation into these three separately discussed segments is not entirely an artificial construct designed to serve our analytical needs. For in the early modern period people usually first decided when it was time to get married, then concerned themselves about choosing a mate, and, finally, entered into courtship practices that were customary in the social groups they and their prospective mates belonged to.

## i. The Decision To Marry

Family watchers today have expressed alarm over the future of the family. They point to the growing number of people who are living together out of wedlock, the delayed age at first marriage, the postponement of childbearing, and the rising incidence of divorce as converging signs that mar-

11

riage is being rejected.[23] There are indeed some important changes current-ly unfolding that may differentiate marital patterns in the last third of this century from those that prevailed during the first two-thirds. But when some of these trends are viewed against a longer historical background, their meaning appears to be not that marriage is being rejected, but that at-titudes toward it are changing

## ii. Rate Of Marriage

The act of getting married is not taken for granted these days as an in-evitable step in every individual's life history as it was for most people a generation ago. Young people today often express an unwillingness to marry.[24] But the surest test of their choice cannot be made until they reach the later stages of their lives. In this connection, it is well to keep in mind that while the proportion of people under thirty who married declined be-tween 1960 and 1974, the proportion over thirty who did so increased.[25] In fact, all behavioral indices point to a marriage rate of well over 90% con-tinuing for both men and women.[26] This would represent a higher marriage rate than what generally obtained during the early modern era, when be-tween as few as 1/15 to as many as 1/4 of the various English and American populations studied appear never to have married.[27] Indeed, one of the most significant findings of historical demography has been the com-paratively high proportion of Western European peoples who never mar-ried between the early modern era and the middle of the 20th century.[28] In short, we have a paradox: while they may be the first generation to widely entertain the desirability of never marrying, the trend indicates that more of today's youth will eventually marry than generally has been the case with generations of the past.

Young people today are not rejecting marriage but rather are delaying it to an older age than what was normative for their parent's generation. American women born in the 1950s have been entering their first marriage at the median age of 21.2 years in comparison to the 20.0 median age of their mother's generation. A similar increase has occurred in men who are marrying at a median age of 23.6 in comparison to the 22.5 of their father's generation.[29] While the most recent groups of men and women have been postponing their first marriage significantly beyond the median age of their parent's generation, they are approximating the experience of their grand-parents' and earlier generations. Indeed, a delayed age at first marriage (of at least 23 for women) has generally characterized Western Europe since the 16th century and America since the 18th.[30] The anomaly has been in the pattern displayed by men and women who married in the middle of this cen-tury, the parental generation of today's youth. They were the youngest Americans to marry since the 17th century.[31]

While their rate of marriage and age at first marriage is not dissimilar to that of early moderns, today's young people approach the decision to marry within a different atmosphere from that which existed at any time before. They know that to remain single will not incur the social stigma that their own parents and grandparents would have experienced had they not married. Bachelorhood and spinsterhood are respectable options today. In fact because of the pejorative connotations that those terms evoked in the recent past, unmarried adults today are usually referred to as "singles" instead.

Although a higher proportion of early modern Anglo-American groups did not marry than is the case today, it is not clear whether the status of being unmarried was socially creditable in the past. Certainly the written opinions of the times enjoined marriage as the natural and socially desirable stage in everyone's development. As a rite of passage marking one's transition into adulthood, marriage appears to have been considerably more critical then than now. Both in terms of the well-being and maturation of the individual as well as the well-ordering and perpetuation of society, marriage was regarded as a necessity.[32] The unmarried young adult was generally distrusted as a potential source of social disruption, and apparently with good cause. One historian has suggested that the large bachelor population in Virginia during the 1670s contributed to the breakdown of social order and the eruption of a civil war.[33] In England, poor laws were enacted in part as a response to the growing fear of young male vagabonds.[34] Some communities, particularly New England towns, required unmarried people to live with families. The single person household, which has become a commonplace today for both young adults and elderly people, was usually viewed with suspicion then.[35] Still, we cannot infer that the unmarried man or woman was invariably subjected to extreme social pressures to marry. Even in New England towns, where the family was considered as the crucible of social cohesion and stability and where effective instruments of community pressure could be brought to bear on the non-conforming individual, everyone did not marry. In Andover, Massachusetts less than 10% never married, but in Barnstable on the South Shore 16 to 20% of the various men and women did not marry.[36] Here the unmarried rate appears to have had less to do with sex ratios than with economic strictures. People who did not think they could afford to marry did not, and apparently were not expected to do so. Marriage was desirable, but it was better to remain single than build a union on a soft material foundation.

## iii. Economics Of Getting Married

The economic advantages and disadvantages of getting married are not always the same for both parents and children. For parents the marriage of children was doubtlessly a greater economic burden in earlier times than it is today because those with property were expected to provide both their sons and daughters with the wherewithall to set up house. Newlyweds expected to live separately under their own roof, and usually that could be achieved only by dint of parentally transferred property. Proportionately the cost to parents of endowing a daughter or settling real estate on a son was considerably more than the increasingly optional practice of parents today to pay for a daughter's wedding, which is virtually the only economic obligation that their children's marriage imposes upon contemporary mothers and fathers.[37] Today parents can in fact anticipate their children's marriage as bringing them financial relief, for newlyweds are expected to support themselves. Whether or not they will be able to is not certain, for marriage today is not always an economic advantage for the participants the way it usually is for their parents.

In contrast, early modern marriages appear to have been generally advantageous for the participants. Before the advent of the factory system, the household was a productive unit in both rural and urban areas. And a husband and wife invariably could produce more together than either could alone. Their joint standard of living would be higher if the wife did no more than simply care for the garden that provided their diet than if either lived alone. The modern household, on the other hand, is a consumption unit in which marriage often proves to be an economic liability unless both partners are able to hold jobs. A working man can obviously do better alone financially than if he marries a non-working woman. Yet working adult males continue to marry women who do not work post-nuptially. In such cases clearly the desire to head one's own family, or to rear children, or to have a long-term companion outweigh the economic calculations.

## iv. Sex Ratios

The availability of age-compatible members of the opposite sex was frequently a problem for early moderns who otherwise would have married. The sex ratio in fact has been regarded generally as the most significant variable that accounts for the differing proportions of unmarrieds in the early modern groups thus far studied. An uneven sex ratio appears to have characterized particular colonial populations, especially in the initial years of settlement.[38] Virginia and Maryland in the 17th century experienced a severe shortage of women. The result there was that men who lived long enough might eventually find a widow, but at any one point in time a majority of unmarried adult males probably could not find age eligible single females.[39] Moreover, if colonial wars took as high a toll of New England men as has been recently suggested, then the demographic consequences of war, including its impact on the sex ratio and marriage patterns, may have to be studied for the whole early modern period.[40] In 18th-century England, especially in London, there was a large surplus of marriageable women.[41] A predominantly male immigration to the colonies and the series of wars England engaged in during the century may have been the major contributors to this female surplus.

Today, although a young person generally need not anticipate the possibility of not finding a person of the opposite sex to marry, demographic phenomena still can shrink the pool of age desirable persons of the opposite sex. For example, in the 1960s there was a so-called "marriage squeeze" when nubile girls belonging to the extraordinarily large post-World War II birth cohorts outnumbered age desirable (older) boys belonging to the smaller birth cohorts conceived before the end of the war. The result was that some girls delayed marriage while others married men more their own age.[42] The projection for the 1980s is for a reversal in which men will feel the squeeze from a slight shortage of age desirable females.[43]

## v. Personal Motives In The Decision To Marry

Once we have examined and compared the demographic, economic, and social factors affecting the decision to marry, the fact remains that no matter how conducive to marriage the sex ratio, social pressures, and material advantages may have been, a significant portion of men and women in America and Europe (in western Europe generally) have always chosen to remain unmarried for reasons that can only be described as personal. While it may be possible for family historians to explore these reasons on the basis of some individual case studies, it seems worth emphasizing that in many societies individuals have apparently not been free to remain unmarried.[44] To the extent to which the decision to remain unmarried has been a personal one in England and America, these societies throughout the early modern era as well as today have allowed room for individuality that other cultures have not.

## vi. Criteria For Mate Selection

Perhaps at no other point in the family cycle have family historians described a deeper contrast between the early modern period and the present than on the matter of how people choose their mates. We find that the differences between them then and now are less stark than they sometimes have been made out to be.

Neither of the archetypes that are sometimes contrasted in the historical literature represents the reality of either period. The unfeeling couple whose match was arranged from afar by socio-economically minded parents did not typify marriage formation in the early modern period; and the infatuated young boy and girl who marry without parental consent solely on the compulsion of their physical attraction do not represent the normal mating experience today. Each type is a simplified abstraction, bordering on caricature, that does embody some of the central *tendencies* of its age. But the actual process of choosing a mate was and is more complex than either archetype suggests. The question of mate selection involves three considerations: (1) the weight attached to a prospective partner's group identity (2) the acknowledged degree of parental influence; and (3) the personal qualities consciously valued in prospective mates.

*Group Identity*

Group identity is the most complex component in marital choice because every individual, past or present, holds in the eyes of his contemporaries a variety of identities that derive from group memberships. The more enduring group identities in England and America over the past 400 years have been based upon religion, socio-economic class, geographic residence, occupation, schooling, and race. In the early modern era, however, group identity was generally a much more controlling and pervasive influence than it is today. Then, it could count heavily in an individual's access to political office, to prestige, to justice, to friends, and to marriage partners. Indeed, an older but still suggestive scholarly way of differentiating the early modern from the modern period in Western Civilization is to consider the former as more closely resembling the model of a corporate society, in which a person's political, legal, and social standing are determined solely by the groups to which he belongs; and the latter era as more closely conforming to the model of a civil society, in which a person's position depends solely upon his individual qualities.[45] The latter model has been celebrated as an ideal since the American and French Revolutions, while the former was the dominating model in prescriptive writings before the age of democratic revolutions.

In the context of marital choice the matter of group identity is usually discussed by sociologists and anthropologists in terms of endogamy and exogamy, and for the sake of facilitating an interdisciplinary approach we shall use those terms here.

*Endogamy*

The rules governing endogamy are considerably looser today than they were generally during the early modern era, but it is not clear how divergent the practice actually is. Racial endogamy, for example, was prescribed by law in the South beginning in the 1660s. By 1750 all the plantation and two northern colonies legally prohibited miscegenation. Occasional intermarriages occurred, but in general "the weight of community opinion was set heavily against the sexual union of white and black, as the longstanding statutory prohibitions indicated."[46]

Since 1967, all legal impediments to interracial marriage have been removed and community opinion is less overtly hostile. Yet the incidence of racial exogamy remains negligible. In 1970 only 7/10 of 1% of American married couples reported themselves to be interracially married.[47] In England neither social nor ethnic exogamy was prohibited by law, "but in practice both were strongly disapproved of. As a result . . . even in colonies with highly unbalanced white sex ratios, like India in the 18th century, it was normal to take a native mistress but unthinkable to marry her."[48]

The importance of class identity, or what is usually referred to as the degree of social or status endogamy, has been the central problem of assessment for students of marriage formation. In the early modern era, the publicly-sanctioned pattern was for people to select spouses from their own socio-economic groups. At no point before 1800 would an Englishman or an American have had to feel defensive about openly admitting his desire to find a mate from his own class, as would be the case for either person today.[49] Yet certain kinds of social exogamy were considered creditable. In England, where the social pyramid was much higher and more clearly demarcated than in America, opinion appears to have tolerated if it did not unreservedly approve of marriage between persons of adjacent classes. The rule seems roughly to have been, the further removed their classes from each other the less acceptable was intermarriage between them. It was inconceivable, for example, for the son or daughter of a peer to marry someone from the propertyless poor.

At the higher levels of English society interclass marriages appear to have been more deliberately discouraged during the 18th century. By 1800, writes Lawrence Stone, "cross-class marriages were universally condemned in theory and very rare in practice."[50] The increased rigidity of upper class barriers in England during the 18th century has been observed by various political and social historians who have described it respectively in such terms as "the growth of oligarchy," "aristocratic resurgence," or "patrician hegemony."[51] After 1753 boys and girls who were under their legal age of majority certainly found it less possible to marry exogamously against their parents wishes, because the aristocratically-sponsored Hardwicke Act of that year for the first time declared unions involving minors who lacked parental consent to be null and void. Previously, clandestine marriages, while in violation of canon law, had been upheld as valid.[52] Nevertheless, while the law gave parents new leverage over their under-age children, external restraints were not generally necessary for upper-class parents who wanted to enhance the likelihood of their children choosing mates from homogamous socio-economic backgrounds. In the 18th century, class identity was more internalized and less dependent on external restraints and symbols than it had been a century earlier.[53] This may explain why social endogamy could persist and even intensify in England after 1700, while at the same time direct parental control over marital choice diminished, and the personal qualities participants valued in their prospective mates could shift from instrumental to more affective considerations.[54]

The importance of group identity in marital selection has not concerned colonial scholars to the extent that it has English family historians. At this point, therefore, an impressionistic generalization may prove useful as a guide and a possible stimulus for further research as long as its suggestive and limited purpose is borne in mind: Social endogamy became more self-consciously practiced over time as the American social pyramid itself was transformed from an amorphously delineated and relatively flattened structure in the 17th century into a more deeply stratified and highly elongated one by the Revolutionary Era. The case for increasing social consciousness in marriage formation over time appears to be especially strong for the American South. An upper class of Virginia families, for example, do not even become visible to us until the end of the 17th century, when we can identify a group of families that possessed the symbols of superior class location (conspicuous wealth in land, servants or slaves, and major political office) at least for two successive generations. It is not really possible to talk of the First Families of Virginia (FFVs) until the late 1690s.[55] The pattern of intermarriage whereby FFVs fortified their relationships with each other and enhanced the growth of an American-style aristocracy is an 18th-century story that in fact deserves to be retold from the perspective of the new family history.[56] While 17th-century Virginia and Maryland colonists may have considered social background to have been a critical component in mate selection, the severely imbalanced sex ratio, the fact that three quarters or more of the immigrants had arrived as servants, and the comparatively blurred lines of social distinction among the free population, mean that for the great majority of people class identity could not be a relevant concern as yet. Indeed, in a relatively undifferentiated social structure social endogamy is less of an issue than a fact of life.

Among the Puritan settlers of early New England, however, endogamy was very much an articulated concern from the outset. The rule prescribed equals to marry equals, and this extended to considerations of church membership, wealth, rank and education. Religion and wealth appear to have been the factors repeatedly stressed, with ministers asserting the primacy of the former and parents often pressuring in behalf of the latter.[57] In 17th-century Hingham, Massachusetts, for example, what John Waters calls "an early American oligarchy" was formed when wealthy families set aside some important differences between themselves and had their children intermarry.[58]

The importance which English and colonial Americans ascribed to socioeconomic status as a factor in marriage formation would seem to have been integrally related to the kind of social structure in which they lived. It was one matter to have valued social status in a small rural town where everyone was engaged in subsistence farming and the range of property ownership was too narrow to result in dramatically divergent standards of living; it was quite another in a commercially thriving city where the extremes between rich and poor were conspicuously manifested in contrasting residential neighborhoods.[59] The northern colonies of the 18th century had many more commercially oriented urban centers and a higher proportion of their people living within these highly graded social structures than had been the case a century before.[60] In these highly populous, heterogeneous areas, the group identity of a daughter's suitor or a son's possible choice may have been even more important as a screening mechanism for concerned parents than was the case in the more homogamous small towns, where the personal qualities of individual candidates may have been the more valued differentiating principle. One scholar has identified four types of social structure in the northern colonies by the middle of the 18th century: the large urban centers, the commercial farm societies, the subsistence farm communities, and the frontier societies.[61] The emphasis placed upon group identity in marriage formation and the long-term trends with regard to intra-class marriages may well have varied along lines of this typology.

Group identity was and still remains an important screening mechanism for the establishment of lasting personal relationships, be they friendships or marriages. Even in our age where the primacy of individual qualities is self-consciously asserted, we invariably form relationships with people from socio-economic, religious and racial groups similar to our own.[62]

The difference between the early modern era and today is that groups were arranged hierarchically in the mentality of the age, and therefore individuals who wanted to cross group boundaries in forming intimate relationships risked overt censure from their own groups, while today crossing group boundaries is consistent with our self-conscious egalitarianism, and therefore the pressures against it tend to be subtle and minimal. The similarity between then and now, however, should not be forgotten: most people formed and still form their friendships and marriages with individuals from within their own or socially proximate groups.

With these variations in mind it is still possible to suggest that group identity in mate selection became a more important differentiating factor generally for Americans after 1700 than had been the case earlier. Class membership became more important as class differences became more pronounced. A result was that in the formation of marriage colonial practice in the 18th century came to more closely resemble that of the mother country.

19

## vii. Parental Influence In Mate Selection

Students of marriage formation have usually assumed a direct correlation between parental control and social endogamy. The inclination of parents to press their children to marry persons of the same background has been taken as a universal in Anglo-American society for the past five centuries and there would seem to be sufficient empirical data to support this premise. Even today, when class identity is not explicitly stressed as a criterion for mate selection, sociologists find that where parental influence is high, as when both parties to the couple live at home during courtship, status homogamy is extraordinarily high, whereas it is significantly lower when parental influence is more remote, as when neither party lives at home.[63]

Direct parental control over marriage appears to have lessened measurably among the English upper classes beginning in the late 17th century.[64] They were most affected by what was unquestionably a new sensibility regarding marital choice by the 1700s. Forced marriages were widely discredited, even for those archetypal practitioners, the English nobility. Plays and novels caricatured the father who would arrange a loveless match for his son or daughter. Advice literature denounced the parentally arranged marriage as forcing the parties into a kind of legal prostitution. The main thrust of 18th century literary comments, in short, was to push the feelings of the participants ahead of the preferences of the parents.[65]

As important as this ideological change was, perhaps more influential in marital selection was the shift away from the threat of disinheritance that landed families had earlier been able to bring to bear on their children's marital choice. After 1660, the increasingly widespread adoption of the strict settlement had the apparently unintended effect of reducing patriarchal power over marriage formation. A new legal device designed to preserve the family patrimony over three generations, the strict settlement stipulated the property arrangements for the current owner at the time of his marriage as well as for his unborn children. Thus the current owner would not be able to use his previously forfeited control over property as a clout over his children when they reached their marrying time.[66]

In the lower classes, however, parental involvement may always have been minimal. This was probably due to a high degree of parental death prior to children reaching the age of marriage as well as to the probability that many lower-class children left their parental home permanently during their adolescent years.[67]

The decline of direct parental control over marriage among the English propertied classes by the 18th century appears to be a roughly parallel development to what was occurring in some of the American colonies. But the comparison must be carefully drawn, for the English studies of parental power have been more broadly cast and have focused largely on class patterns, while the American studies have been local in scope. The former has resulted in broadly delineated class trends while the latter suggest conspicuous regional variations.

In Massachusetts towns the long-term trend between 1650 and 1800 appears to have been in the direction of less parental manipulation of property as an instrument of intergenerational control generally and of marriage formation in particular. For example, the third generation of families that founded Andover displayed a substantially greater willingness than their parents to transfer outright ownership of the land to their sons at a younger age than when they had inherited it. But whether this significantly earlier attainment of economic independence by fourth generation sons reflected a commensurate autonomy with regard to mate selection has not been demonstrated in Andover, although it would seem to be a plausible inference.[68]

In Hingham, Massachusetts, various statistical indices, ingeniously devised by Daniel Scott Smith, led him to conclude that parental power over the spouse selection of both sons and daughters waned after the middle of the 18th century.[69] On the other hand, Peter D. Hall's study of Massachusetts merchant families between 1700 to 1900 indicates that while the pattern of endogamy changed after the Revolution, parental influence over marital choice persisted in those families that maintained their commercial success.[70]

In the Colonial South it is not yet clear whether the attitude towards parental control over marriage changed over time. What does seem certain, however, is that in the 17th century fewer parents were living when their children reached their marrying age than would be the situation in the 18th century, when adult mortality declined.[71] In contrast, 17th-century New England mothers and fathers normally lived to see most of their children come of age. Because the great majority of Virginia and Maryland children undoubtedly lost their natural fathers before reaching adulthood, and were therefore able to take control of bequeathed property no later than their twenty-first birthday, we can infer that marital selection was largely a matter of their personal choice. Certainly this was true of the sons of property-owning fathers, whose early decease enhanced the sons' likelihood of early economic independence.[72] Daughters, on the other hand, presumably benefited from the severely imbalanced sex ratio and could demand some independence in the matter of choosing a husband. There are in fact some famous examples of daughters from elite Chesapeake families as early as the late 17th century who spurned suitors their fathers would have chosen for them. Comparable examples exist for the 18th century.[73] It may well be that low parental control remained a continuing feature of Southern marriage formation throughout the colonial period.

## viii. Personal Qualities Valued In Prospective Mates

Are the personal qualities valued in prospective mates different today? Many scholars believe so. In fact, if there is a consensus among family historians regarding any facet of their subject it is on the matter of sexual attractiveness as a criterion for marital selection. They agree that whereas sexual attractiveness has become the dominating factor in marriage formation today, before 1700 neither in England nor the American colonies was sexual attractiveness widely considered to be a creditable reason for choosing a spouse.[74] Where the influence of family, kin and friends was felt, the individual would be inclined to marry someone who belonged to the appropriate groups and whose personal qualities ideally would include, if a man: piety, sobriety, diligence and humility; if a woman: piety, obedience, cheerfulness and diligence.[75] If one could love someone who possessed these objectively identifiable group and personal characteristics, so much the better. In fact, prescriptive writers enjoined the development of love as a marital duty. The assumption was, however, that marital love could evolve only if the couple had chosen each other for the right reasons. Moreover, perhaps because the desired group and personal qualities were objectively identifiable, it was believed that parents were in a better position to judge the suitability of marriage partners for their children than were the children themselves who were apt to follow the inclinations of their hearts rather than their minds. Here is perhaps the distinguishing element in the early modern approach to marriage formation, namely, the emphasis upon rationality. Reason, not emotion must govern one's choice of a mate. This was the ruling paradigm in the 16th and 17th centuries among English people on both sides of the Atlantic.[76]

By the early 1700s, however, converging quantitative and impressionistic evidence points to a different attitude emerging among certain groups in England and America regarding the role of sexual attractiveness in mate selection. Most people still believed that romantic love was not a solid base on which to build a marriage. And since marriage was still for keeps, with divorce now a more possible but still remote refuge from an unhappy marriage, reason remained the most dependable guide to choosing a spouse. The 18th century saw a good many of the older dikes against excess remain standing but it was unable to contain an overflow of emotional enthusiasm, be it in the area of marriage formation, religion, the arts, or politics. Whether there was an integral connection between the legitimation of romantic love, the awakening of religious revivalism, the romantic movement in music and poetry, and the feverish political activity of urban mobs along the Atlantic seaboard and London is not for us to speculate upon. It is worth noting, however, that some historians have observed the shift from rational control to emotional expression as occurring earliest in matters touching the family, such as mate selection, husband-wife relations, and childrearing—all of which converged in the late 17th century.[77]

A critical figure here was John Locke, whose "sensational" psychology would be integrated into the theology of Jonathan Edwards, the great defender of the Awakening in New England, whose political writings would enjoy such wide currency among the American revolutionaries. Locke's reflections on familial issues and individualism have been used by recent historians as an indication of the changing sensibility that was expressed by the end of the 17th century.[78]

No one recommended marriages to be formed on the basis of erotic passions. Rather what an 18th-century English moralist called "rational love" was first preached in England and was then "elevated to a social ideal" on the Continent.[79] The difference between this rational love of the 18th century and what prevailed earlier is not adequately described by any such polarities as interest vs. affection or sexlessness vs. eroticism or materialism vs. emotionalism or instrumental vs. sentimental impulses. Any such polarity posits an extreme contrast that risks reducing either marriage pattern to a caricature. The differences over time appear to us to have been subtle and a matter of emphasis rather than of kind.

The role of sexuality in marriage formation during the early modern era, we believe, has been treated too often in terms of these polarities. One of the (perhaps unintended) results is that in some discussions sexuality suddenly appears as a factor in heterosexual relationships for the first time in the 1700s.[80] Now it may well be that sexuality was in fact a generally less urgent drive among English people before the late 1600s. Sexual feelings are affected by a variety of psychobiological influences, including diet, childhood experiences and diseases. Each of these factors did change significantly for different groups between the 17th and 18th centuries. We will describe the changes in childhood later in this essay. But as yet the causal connection between these specific factors and early modern sex drives have yet to be demonstrated. Thus, unless evidence is produced to indicate that psychobiological sources of sexuality were significantly different in the 16th and 17th centuries from what they would become in the 18th, we must begin our analysis with the assumption that men and women were sexually attracted to each other with the same degree of urgency and frequency over time. When we keep this assumption in mind, we are forced to be more cautious about taking at face value the 17th-century prescriptions that relegated passion outside the compelling criteria for mate selection. While the prescribed and individually admitted attitude towards sexual attractiveness in marriage formation did change and must be explained, the underlying role it actually played in marital selection may have been more persisting.[81]

At no time in these centuries was unbridled passion considered a sufficient ground for choosing a husband or wife. "Lust," or sexual attractiveness alone, was not considered by adults as the same thing as "love."

The difference between 17th and 18th century parents was that the latter appear to have been more willing than the former to allow sexual attractiveness to be considered along with the traditionally valued personal qualities (piety, diligence, humility, etc.). Since sexual attractiveness could not be objectively identified, they were more willing than their predecessors to grant their children a prominent role in the selection process. Still, children were not to be permitted to choose unwisely, that is, solely upon the basis of sexuality, or emotion. As long as it was bounded by the presence of traditionally-valued group and personal characteristics, a prospective candidate's emotional attractiveness to one's child was now recognized as respectable. If an 18th-century youth would find his parents more receptive when he spoke of his feelings for a would-be spouse, he still could not admit to lust.[82] Sexuality as a frankly-mentioned basis for attraction did not become respectable until the 20th century.

## ix. Courtship Practices

Having discussed the decision to marry and the criteria for choosing a spouse, we will close this section with a few words comparing courtship in the past and present. It seems appropriate to discuss courtship last, because in the early modern era courtship generally appears to have followed the decision to marry and the selection of a suitable candidate. As the word itself meant, courtship was an instrumental process with marriage as the end to which it was directed. There was no early modern counterpart to the practice of dating whereby young men and women, especially teen-age boys and girls, could participate as heterosexual couples in a social life initiated and arranged solely by themselves or their peers and which carried with it no long-term commitments between the partners. Dating seems to have been a "spontaneous invention" of the early 20th century in America that quickly became the dominant pattern of premarital social intercourse between the sexes.[83]

We should note that most of the information we have about early modern attitudes towards courtship derive from upper and middle class sources. The lower classes, without the imperatives of property to regulate their behavior, may have had what one historian calls a "tradition of promiscuity" for centuries.[84] Certainly eroticism was not a new component in the premarital relationships of Europeans prior to 1700, even though respectable classes in Anglo-American society only now began to make some allowances for it. But the evidence of premarital erotic behavior before 1700 thus far comes mainly from France and other parts of the Continent. We can only infer the possibility that English villagers engaged in similar activities.[85]

In the 1970s another pattern has emerged, especially on the college campuses, where heterosexual residence and dining groups pair off as a seemingly natural extension of their daily activities without formally going out on dates. This pattern is a variation of the dating system and should not be viewed historically as marking a departure from it.[86] The two characteristics of the 20th-century premarital, heterosexual socialization system that distinguish it most sharply from early modern courtship are its noncommital facet and the emphasis it places upon participant control.

In the early modern era, according to writings by or about the upper and middle classes, it was not altogether honorable for a man to woo a woman for any purpose other than determining her suitability for marriage. Still, intrigues or affairs were tolerated and even considered respectable in certain circles in England, but only when one of the parties, usually the man, was married.[87] In America, fornication and adultery were universally condemned by law and there appears to have been no widely-practiced counterpart to the English patrician style with mistresses and paramours.

On both sides of the Atlantic, moreover, young unmarried people were expected to interact with their opposites only within a ritualized pattern which aimed not at a general heterosexual socialization but rather at the culmination of marriage between the participants if their parents and they themselves agreed to the match. In short, courtship was inseparably connected to marriage formation, whereas today dating and its variations are viewed as a self-contained developmental stage that is worthwhile whatever the marital outcome.

# Stage II
# Preparenthood

Preparenthood is a critical time in the relationship between newlyweds today. The most typical interval between first marriage and divorce in the U.S. today is 2 or 3 years. While the arrival of the first child is enormously stressful and often is the precipitating event prior to early marital break-up, a high proportion of marriages dissolve before the couple become parents. About 40% of all divorces in U.S. and one-third in England are between couples without children. Clearly, then, the statistics alone indicate, first, that the way in which a couple adjusts to each other during the preparenthood period affects the durability of a marriage and, second, that a high incidence of marital maladjustment occurs during preparenthood today, as measured by the high frequency of early marital break-up.[88]

## i. Marital Adjustment In The Early Modern Era

During the early modern era the transition to married life appears to have been much smoother than has been the case recently, for the preparenthood period seems to have been marked by a quick adjustment by the couple to their new relationship and setting. The early modern couple was more likely to work out an effective, lasting *modus vivendi* between themselves during preparenthood than the average newlyweds today, in good part because divorce was not as readily available to them as it was to become in modern times. Still, we should bear in mind that both husbands and wives could escape from unbearable unions by routes that varied from place to place, from time to time, and from class to class. These will be discussed in the last section. Suffice it to note here that nothing more complicated than the act of running away was a possibility for the propertyless while the well-to-do could always afford whatever form of legal dissolution was available, and some form always was.

Nevertheless, the legal impediments to voluntary marital break-up were great, and probably most couples who were maladjusted resigned themselves to sticking it out until death terminated their union. A famous example was the case of the Virginia councillor, John Custis (1678-1749), who had himself remembered on his tombstone thusly:

> Aged 71 years, and yet lived but seven years, which was the space of time he kept a bachelor's home at Arlington on the Eastern Shore of Virginia.

## ii. Reasons For High Marital Adjustment

If marital adjustment during preparenthood was largely forced upon early modern couples by legal obstacles to dissolution, it was at the same time facilitated and reinforced by a number of economic, social-psychological, ideological and demographic circumstances that, taken together, smoothed the transition into marriage: (1) Each party was less likely to depress his or her short-run economic condition as a result of marriage than is the case today, say, with a working wife whose husband is a full-time student or the working husband whose wife is a housewife. The careful consideration of the economic viability of the marriage had usually preceded its formation, whereas today participants often proceed without economic calculations. On the other hand, where both parties are working at the outset of marriage today, the preparenthood period usually means a period of heightened material comfort that may be lowered, with accompanying stress, with the birth of the first child and the mother's partial or complete withdrawal from income producing work.[90] (2) The act of setting up house in the early modern era did not mark as radical a departure from the immediately prior experience of the couple as it has in recent times. Early modern men and women usually moved from one heterosexual household into another when they married. With the exception of a handful of boys who, for example, had lived in a college residence house or who had been to sea, they had spent their entire premarried lives eating, sleeping, working, socializing and doing much of their learning within the orbit of heterosexual households. This is in contrast to the experience of the majority of newlyweds in modern times, who have usually spent several years prior to their marriage living in sex-segregated college dormitories, single-person households, households made up of persons of the same sex or army barracks. In the 1970s the popularity of co-ed dormitories and the practice of living together before getting married is believed to have eased the problem. (3) The articulated ethos in the early modern era enjoined the couple to worry about how each could contribute to the marriage rather than how the marriage could contribute to their individual needs. That is, the institution counted more in the publicly sanctioned scheme of things than did the individual, so that marital adjustment was openly valued regardless of the personal cost on which it might rest. (4) Men who are over 25 when they marry, as was the norm then, are statistically more likely to form enduring marriages today than are men who marry in their early 20s, as has been the norm for the past century.[91] To the extent that one recognizes as universally applicable any contemporary model of individual development, this demographic fact suggests that the later age at first marriage of early modern men was an important psychological stabilizer that facilitated rapid marital adjustment. Contemporary studies of adult stages seem to concur that a man of 26 or 27 is likely to be better able to forge a mutually satisfying intimate relationship with a woman than is a man of 22 or 23.[92] (5) Parental approval usually preceded early modern marriages and this removed a potential source of early marital instability. Sociological studies of modern marriages have identified parental disapproval as a major source of tension in the first years of marriage.[93] (6) Objectively identifiable personal qualities had been stressed in matchmaking rather than subjectively rooted feelings, and thus the potential for sudden disillusionment after marriage would seem to have been markedly low. (7) The group identities of the couple were more narrowly defined and more closely matched than today. This tighter fit of group identities diminished the likelihood of incompatability stemming from divergent religious and socio-economic backgrounds. (8) Most important, perhaps, the economic role of the early modern household forced the newlyweds to work out quickly a *modus vivendi* that would enable them to cooperate in the daily tasks that were their joint responsibility. Marital adjustment was an urgent matter of daily necessity because the household was the all-encompassing center of their lives. In contrast, modern newlyweds spend only a small portion of their waking days within the orbit of their home. For them the task of making mutual adjustments may be avoided for most of the day and may therefore be put off or not directly confronted at all.

## iii. Setting Up A Nuclear Household: Three Implications

The immediate task of setting up house has faced nearly all newly married couples in England and America at least over the past four centuries. A striking finding of historical demography has been the ubiquity of the nuclear household in the early modern and modern West with the concomitant likelihood that newlyweds normally moved into their own quarters following their wedding.[94] The origins of this custom is not known. But some of its implications are readily perceived. It symbolized a measure of autonomy on the part of the married couple. The fact that the couple would live by themselves after marriage always meant that their compatibility had to be factored into the process of marriage formation, no matter how much parents wanted to intercede. The parent's child, not the parents, would have to live with his mate selection. Conversely, among those families where forced marriages were not uncommon, namely among the English aristocracy, newlyweds, especially eldest sons, frequently spent their first year or so of marriage with the parents until a new home could be built for them.[95] In these cases the parents had an immediate stake in their child's choice of partners, because they would all have to live together for a time. Thus, while we find a greater degree of parental influence over marriage formation in the early modern era than today, we should keep in mind that the common pattern of separate households for newlyweds has placed a premium on the compatibility of the participants and some need to consult their wishes.

A second implication of nuclearity was that the couples usually did not marry until they or their families could afford to set up an independent household for them. At a time when sons were heavily dependent upon the receipt of their father's property in order to be successful in an agrarian economy, it was not uncommon for marriage and the concomitant establishment of a separate household to be postponed until the death of a father, when inheritance of his land would be forthcoming. This pattern doubtlessly contributed to the older age at first marriage of early modern men.[96]

A third implication was that in most instances early modern husbands and wives would be in charge of their daily household activities. Even where they lived on property owned by their parents or in close proximity to a parental home, as was the case in Andover, Massachusetts, the newlyweds were expected to work out their new relationship in private without the presence of intermediaries from the older generation. As is the case today, no matter what the role of parents, kin and friends in courtship and marriage formation, after the wedding the married couple was given virtually complete autonomy over their daily lives.

## iv. Roles Of Husbands And Wives

The roles of husbands and wives before 1700 in all classes, and thereafter mainly among the less affluent classes, were diffuse in much the same manner as has become the pattern with an ever increasing percentage of the married population since World War II. By the diffusion of roles we mean the conjugal overlapping of different *categories* of function. Especially noteworthy is the comparable economic functions jointly performed by early modern couples and their very recent counterparts. But whereas today the diffusion of roles is in harmony with the new ideology of sexual equality, in the early modern era there was a sharp divergence between the conception of a husband's and wife's proper places and the actual practice. The ideology prescribed a hierarchical, not an egalitarian relationship in the home. Husbands were expected to rule over their households and their wives. Wives were advised to be docile, obedient helpmates.[97] This inequality was pegged to a prescribed system of separate duties. But the distinctions articulated in the ideal were modified by the conditions of life. Because the household was the focal point of both the family's sustenance as well as its living area, husbands and wives often had to perform functions that in the ideal were held to belong to the other. A farmer's wife, for example, might be called upon to help him in the fields, especially if he could not afford paid labor. This was most common at the beginning of rural marriages among the poorer couples. The early marital field work of a planter's wife in the 17th-century Chesapeake sometimes enabled him subsequently to buy an indentured servant or slave who could release his spouse full-time for in-house chores, such as preparing food and mending or even making clothes.[98] It was, in fact, in household manufacturing and commerce rather than in field work that wives played their most prominent economic role on farms and in towns, on both sides of the Atlantic. They spun, knitted, or stitched cloth, sold produce on house to house routes, rented rooms and fed boarders, ran taverns or shops attached to the home, and generally were indispensable partners in managing the economic activities of middle, lower-middle, and lower class households.[99] Only the extremely well-to-do families could afford to have their wives detach themselves from the household economy, and even in these families this practice did not become commonplace until the end of our period, when the household itself was increasingly removed from the center of economic life.[100]

The division of labor between husband and wife was as much affected by the practical demands of running an efficient household as it was by the theoretical requirements of gender specialization. Whereas the latter assigned particular tasks to each sex, often it was more practical for the couple to share some duties or to have one partner assume responsibilities which theoretically lay within the sphere of the other. Thus the farm wife who toiled occasionally in the fields or the shopkeeper's wife who kept the books might rely on her husband to order furnishings for their home or to help rear the children by instructing them in reading and writing, catechising them regularly, or teaching them the skills that would prepare them to help out in the household economy. The individual inclinations and skills of particular husbands and wives influenced the assignment of household tasks within the limits permitted by the general theory of gender specialization.[101]

It may in fact be anachronistic to talk about a theory of gender specialization in the early modern era, for there was no rigidly adhered to standard of differentiation between male and female functions in the family. What appears to have concerned them was more the power relationship than the division of specific functions. As long as the superiority of the husband was recognized, the couple could cross over each other's work boundaries apparently without raising eyebrows.

This was not an age that readily abstracted human activity into general categories. In politics, for example, the whole doctrine of the separation of powers (e.g., executive, judicial and legislative) appears not to have been conceived of in the Anglo-American world until the 1640s and then it did not gain wide currency even among theorists until the Frenchman, Montesquieu, popularized it in the middle of the next century.[102] Similarly, family commentators did not separate the responsibilities of husbands and wives in a doctrinaire way. Instead they assigned specific tasks to each, all the while emphasizing the general supremacy of the husband's word.[103] Thus, for households involved in a multitude of tasks, the variable intermingling of specific duties between husbands and wives from household to household by itself did not represent a flagrant violation of the value system; even though from our perspective it would not appear to have done so, because role diffusion today goes hand in hand with an ideology of sexual equality.

## v. The Ideology Of The Double Standard

The ideology of early modern marital relations has been described as that of the double standard, an ideology that persisted until very recently. Nowhere was the view more sharply focused than in Thomas More's otherwise egalitarian 16th-century *Utopia*. The *Utopia* clearly advocated a patriarchical family model where a wife was to demonstrate deference and obedience to her husband in the same way that children were to behave towards their parents. Although such a model was an anomaly in the context of other utopian values, More appears to have shared with his times the assumption that a patriarchical family was essential to a well-ordered society.[104]

The inequality between man and woman which More assumes in *Utopia* reflected an idea that was accepted by all religious denominations and social groups and was strengthened by the law of the 16th and 17th centuries.[105] In its most ideal form the double standard postulated feminine docility, passivity and subservience in contrast to masculine strength, dominance and superiority.

Double-standard ideology was interlaced with such terms as "mutuality of comfort" and the "sacred condition of equality" between the spouses. But writers and preachers during the early modern era did not mean these phrases to imply that husbands and wives should be on equal footing. Rather these were dictums of advice on ways to achieve harmonious households within a double standard context. If a happy marriage were to be achieved, they contended, spouses should be solicitous to one another, thus providing a mutuality of comfort, and this could be attained only when the couple shared similar social backgrounds and ages, or the "sacred condition of equality."[106]

It can be suggested, therefore, that an important difference in spouse relationships between the past and the present lies in the inconsistency between what was preached as the ideal of the double standard and what was actually practiced in many households. Today this inconsistency is lessening perceptively.[107] Then, despite the inconsistency within the context of the double standard, a harmonious relationship could certainly be achieved. This indeed was the goal of the advice literature and, as we have suggested, was promoted by the circumstances of household duties. On the other hand, the philosophy underlying the double standard could encourage abusive behavior, mistrust between the spouses, and an attitude toward women which underscored their inferiority. Some wives, however, who were of high social status or who had some economic independence could enter their marital relationships with greater self-assurance of spouse solicitude. But because of the inequality in the law and because the mores supported wifely subservience, women in the main were more vulnerable to the behavioral patterns of their husbands. Today this kind of vulnerability has been assuaged largely by the decline of the double standard.

## vi. The Honeymoon And The Matter Of Mutual Intimacy

The relationship between husband and wife that we have just described was established during the preparenthood stage. Perhaps nothing better reflects the different expectations of early modern couples from those of the 19th century and later than the institution of the honeymoon, which is a modern invention.[108] The most distinguishing characteristic of the modern honeymoon is the immediate post-nuptial isolation of the couple. They are isolated both from family members and friends as well as from the workaday world of their eventual household. This removal from familiar people and environs is designed to enable them to devote themselves entirely to their mutual intimacy and pleasure for a period ranging from a few days to a few weeks. Whatever the motives for their union, be they prudential or romantic, by going on a honeymoon they assume as their first marital responsibility the fulfillment of each other's emotional needs for sexual satisfaction and intimate companionship. Clearly this is to be a primary, ongoing responsibility for each partner with the initial honeymoon serving as a reminder and a building block. Their isolation from family and friends during the honeymoon indicates as well that this responsibility is to be theirs alone. Parents may help the new couple out financially; nurses, babysitters and teachers will help out later with the tasks of childbearing and child-rearing; but the responsibility of providing intimate companionship cannot be shared with others. This is the implication of the modern honeymoon. Nothing really comparable to it marked the preparenthood period of newly-weds before 1800. The early modern couple was usually expected to take up their household responsibilities immediately following their marriage. A honeymoon, with its exclusive preoccupation with pleasure and feelings, would not be compatible with the temperament of those early modern people who denied or distrusted their inner selves, who tried to eradicate or control their appetites, who renounced or moderated the promptings of the flesh. A modern honeymoon requires a different temperament, one that seeks to give free play to inner feelings.

In his evocation of three Protestant temperaments in early America, Philip Greven found no personality that deliberately sought to explore and express his deepest strivings, as is not uncommon today. Only those people whom he describes as genteel were more comfortable with their emotions, but even then not self-consciously so. The genteel temperament was outwardly directed, preoccupied with activity for its intrinsic pleasure rather than for its symbolic expression of the inner life. Greven found examples of this temperament only among the well-to-do, mainly among the American gentry in the 18th century.[109] In England, on the other hand, evidence for a genteel lifestyle, if not a genteel temperament, dates at least from the 16th century, when men and women from the wealthy classes increasingly took pleasure in social discourse, displaying learning, traveling abroad, acquiring more luxury goods for their homes, and, in short, living well.[110] And not surprisingly perhaps it was among the English upper classes that the prototype of the modern honeymoon first appeared. This was the "marriage tour," whereby the newlyweds went off on a holiday for some weeks, but always accompanied by bridesmaids and groomsmen.[111] This practice would seem to be reflective of a genteel temperament, that is, one in which the desire to enjoy oneself could be pursued within a context of pleasant company rather than in isolation, where a level of self-consciousness would be unavoidable.

The comparative importance of the modern couple's responsibility of mutual intimacy is suggested finally by a quantitative index, the interval between marriage and the birth of their first child. Today, the preparenthood period is considerably longer than what it was during the early modern era, when the average couple became parents within a year of their wedding. Since the end of the 19th century the typical American couple has had their child slightly more than a year and a half after their marriage.[112] The longer interval has provided modern couples with a little more time to develop their companionship in private. It also has given many couples needed time to determine whether their relationship is compatible enough to warrant their entering the stage of parenthood together. In the past decade the preparenthood interval has declined to 1.3 years.[113] In part this may be due to the increase in the number of couples who have married only after ascertaining their compatibility of living together prior to marriage. In the early modern era, childbearing does not appear to have been deliberately postponed in order to enhance the early marital adjustment of the couple. Just as the couple did not go on a honeymoon but rather immediately took up the task of setting up their household, they proceeded to procreate, subject only to involuntary biological and epidemiological causes of delay.

# Stage III
# Childbearing

## i. Childless Marriages

Today the option of remaining a childless couple has become as socially acceptable as remaining unmarried. Effective birth control has of course made the option much more realistic than it was during the early modern era, when *coitus interruptus* appears to have been the most widely available instrument for family limitation. Yet, just as a higher proportion of men and women is marrying today than was generally the case before 1800, so too is a higher proportion of today's wives becoming mothers. Indeed, there has been a remarkable decline in the childless rate of all women (married and unmarried) to a range of 9 to 14% during the past forty years from a range of 21 to 26% during the previous forty years.[114] This dramatic change has been attributed to the decline in child mortality resulting from medical advances. No study that measures the proportion of childless couples in the early modern era has yet been done.* The circumstantial evidence, however, would seem to suggest that, like the unmarried rate, it was much bigger than it is now or is likely to be in the projected future, when only 4.4% of the youngest cohorts of ever-married women are considered likely to remain childless.[115] The level of perinatal mortality was undoubtedly much higher before 1800 than it is today. The causes of infertility were not as well known and thus could not be treated effectively. Moreover, there were couples who wanted to limit the size of their families and some who did not want any children. We do not know about the experience of these childless couples in the past. We can only guess that they were more common than they are now and suggest that they deserve some investigation.

We do not even know what the public attitude was towards marriage without children. The majority of ever-married women bore children in the early modern era, but whether the majority of marriages passed through the childbearing stage cannot yet be certain. For the number of married couples included those with partners who had previously been married and whose childbearing days were over as well as those with infertile first-timers. Marriages between previously married partners with children from their former marriages could experience childrearing without childbearing. Thus, when we describe childbearing as a stage in the early modern family cycle, we are referring to a normal stage in unions where both partners were marrying for the first time, and a stage through which most men and women who ever married shared with at least one partner. But it was not a stage through which a majority of marriages necessarily passed.

## ii. Husbands And Wives During Pregnancy

There are some commonalities to the human experience that no amount of historical specificity of cultural differentiation should be allowed to obscure. One such commonality is the intense emotional involvement of parents in childbearing. The period of pregnancy and the moment of childbirth are recognized as vital events and evoke special behavioral patterns from the participants.[116] The actions and expressed feelings of early modern fathers and mothers-to-be are for the most part easily understood and empathized with by today's parents. One connecting line across the centuries is the matrix of ambivalence.

---

*In an article published after this book was typeset, Lloyd Bonfield calculates that among the peerage, childless marriages ranged from 17 to 18% during the years 1625-1699. To the extent that wealth and health went together, we can assume that their childless rate was among the lowest of the time. "Marriage Settlements and the 'Rise of the Great Estates,' The Demographic Aspect," *The Economic History Review,* 2nd ser., xx11:4 (1979), 486 n.

Hope and fear: Will the mother survive the birth? Will the child be stillborn or defective? Will it be a he or a she?

Asset or liability: Can the couple afford to do without the wife's labor in the household economy or her extra-household job during the later stages of her pregnancy and her post-partum recuperation? Will a son's eventual contribution to the family's work force and perhaps to the couple's care in old age be offset by the cost of bringing him up? Will a daughter's eventual dowry be a dreaded prospect?

Paternal pride and humility: His wife is about to bear the fruit he planted successfully but he cannot control its cultivation and cannot even participate in its harvesting. He was banned from the delivery room then and may sit by only as a spectator today.

Maternal pleasure and pain: The wife may feel psychological elation at her ability to experience motherhood and at the same time the physical discomfort and distress that come with pregnancy; the pleasure of reaching the end of term is mixed with the pain of labor and delivery. The hope of bearing a healthy child mingles with the fear of producing a deformed one.

The ambivalence in parents was reflected in the range of childbearing patterns in the population as a whole. At one extreme there were early modern couples who scrupulously went by the latest advice book, with the pregnant wife following the prescribed regimen of diet and exercise and her husband dutifully satisfying her every whim and trying generally to be solicitous.[117] These couples, whatever their reservations, knew they wanted a successful childbirth for both the mother and the offspring and they were determined to do whatever the best wisdom of the times advised to enhance their prospects. Towards the other extreme were couples whose apprehensions about childbearing weighed more heavily. They might ignore the rules of diet, exercise, and husbandly solicitude and thereby let nature take its course unaided by themselves. Or some might secretly apply various abortifacents. Or, as we now know, some might resort to infanticide once the child was born.[118] A similar range of approaches to childbearing characterizes the population today. Ambivalence in individual couples and in the whole society has been a commonality to the Anglo-American experience with parenthood.

The role of husbands during their wives' pregnancy, both in theory and practice, was not dissimilar to what it is today. Solicitude to their wives was and remains the essential contribution expected of husbands. Early moderns seem to have been as concerned with the psychological state of pregnant women as are their post-Freudian successors, although the language they used to express their concerns did not carry the weight of theoretical significance. A pregnant woman's mood was deemed crucial to her own welfare and that of the child-to-be. Accordingly her husband was enjoined to demonstrate sympathy by using kind words and providing her with whatever she wanted.[119] Thus Ralph Josselin, a 17th-century English minister, searched for special food his pregnant wife desired, while his contemporary in Massachusetts, Cotton Mather, comforted his wife by praying for her.[120] Childbearing was in fact a time when wives might effectively reverse their normal position of subordination to their husbands, for if husbands failed to make their wives happy during pregnancy, they might have to bear some responsibility for any eventual mishaps before term.[121] The fact that married women tended to become pregnant throughout their fertile years, rather than segregating childbearing to a limited period as is the current practice, meant that early modern wives had a regular opportunity to make special demands in which their husbands were expected to acquiesce. The subordination of husbands during childbearing was further signified by their exclusion from the delivery room, which occurred invariably in the home. Although the presence of male physicians became more common after the invention of the forceps in the late 17th century, before 1800 probably the great majority of deliveries were an exclusively female affair, with the midwives, relatives and neighbors in attendance.[122] Indeed, as late as 1910 at least 50 percent of all births in U.S. were attended by midwives.[123] In the past, then, one of the vital events in family life remained largely under the power of women, a point that has been insufficiently appreciated by students who have dwelled on spheres of male dominance.[124] Today the ideology of sexual equality has paralleled a slight alteration in the role of husbands in childbearing. If they wish, husbands today may accompany their wives into the delivery room of a hospital. Some husbands have in fact learned how to serve as midwives to some wives who have natural childbirths. But for the most part, the role of husbands appears to be essentially the same as it was in the early modern period.

If women were able to retain a controlling hand over childbearing, it was an important counterweight to claims of male superiority and domination. In fact the sickness and suffering that accompany childbirth was cited by early modern moralists as evidence of the natural inferiority of women.[125] This was an old argument advanced by men who may have been rationalizing their own sense of impotence during this stage of the family cycle.[126]

# Stage IV
# Childrearing

The new scholarship on the history of childhood has stressed the differences between past and present to the nearly complete exclusion of the commonalities. Having been thereby conditioned to expect only differences, we have understandably been surprised and impressed by certain commonalities that show up in the primary sources from the early modern period. But there are indeed important differences, and we shall try to review them as well.

## i. Values And Evidence

A seemingly inescapable problem in describing childrearing practices derives from one's value judgments. Perhaps no other subject evokes such immediate and deep feelings on the part of family historians as the treatment of children. The most dispassionate observer of family life cannot easily remain neutral when seeing children even of the very distant past treated in a way he regards as abusive. Thus the words "brutal," "neglectful" and the like are replete in the recent descriptions of past parenting even in works that are otherwise free of such blatantly evaluative adjectives. The problem is not how to do away with these terms and the feelings they reflect. For value judgments and the historian's passion can add enormous relevance and vitality to our understanding of the past. Rather the problem is how we can express our own values without distorting the past. We want to analyze, not moralize. We can only state our awareness of the problem, for we have no ready formula to resolve it.

We shall take a three-pronged approach to our comparison of early modern and contemporary childhood. We shall try to examine the attitude and behavior of parents, the perspective of children, and the expectations and advice of society. Too often in the literature the views of society, as registered in laws, social commentaries and advice manuals, are taken to represent the actual practice of parents. Similarly, too often children are considered to be the fully malleable instruments of parental and societal expectations. By treating each separately, perhaps we will gain a more accurate albeit less uniform overview.

Our inquiry is cast in the form of questions. Regarding parents, we want to know:

1. Did early modern parents try to please their children?
2. Did they consciously think of their children as economic assets or liabilities?
3. Did they believe that their treatment of their children during childhood would greatly affect them later as adults?

Before we pursue these questions, we should note that the kind of evidence upon which comprehensive answers could rest is simply not obtainable for the early modern period. Our most reliable sources are the extant private papers and publically printed memoirs of a fraction of the literate population, which itself was usually a minority. The representative character of this evidence simply cannot be measured. Yet, we should remember that even in our own over-documented, computerized age only rough approximations can be made on many crucial problems, such as how many children are being physically and emotionally abused.[127] Contemporary social scientists must depend ultimately on intelligent estimates and impressions. With even sparser information, we must rely on similar methods.

## ii. Parental Attitudes

Did early modern parents try to please their children? This was not a question that they were likely to ask about themselves, especially before the 18th century. For if there was a common denominator in parental attitudes towards childhood before 1700 (and in most circles before 1800 as well), it was that it was better for children to be pleasing than pleased. The inverse proposition has become the first principle of childrearing only in our own day. Yet if we could magically transcend time and put the question directly to early moderns, it is unlikely that they would greet us with bewilderment or derision. For they were most serious and articulate about the inclination of many parents to indulge their children. They regarded the temptation as natural but dangerous, with pernicious consequences resulting for the over-gratified child.[128] They did not worry, as we do, that an unpleased child would be unredeemed in the eyes of God or unpleasant in the eyes of the world. The interpersonal context of life was always more pervasive in the thinking of early modern people than it has become in our time. The happy child is a powerful ideal in current parenting, for the quest for a private personal happiness has become a central theme in the ethos of modern man and has acquired a paramount if not obsessive importance with many adults today. In contrast, even in the 18th century when happiness became "a constant preoccupation," its pursuit was intimately connected to society. To be happy oneself, one had to promote the happiness of others. To be pleased, one had to be pleasing.[129]

Whatever their inclinations, the great majority of early modern parents faced conditions that militated against the indulgent treatment of children. When life is hard and day to day survival a matter of continuing struggle, rare is the parent who would express his concern for his children in terms of pleasing them. Throughout the early modern period, even in the 18th century when consequences of the agricultural revolution and the promises of industrialism were felt, the majority of people on both sides of the Atlantic were confronted with issues in their daily lives that do not press on the majority of Englishmen and Americans today. Illness and pain were so widespread and frequent that one can justifiably wonder if good health were a curiosity before 1800.[130] By our standards, the death rate was extraordinarily high and did not markedly discriminate by age or class, although the very young and the poor appear to have been most vulnerable. Despite the improvements in diet and medical science, Englishmen at the end of our period could not expect to live much longer than their ancestors three centuries earlier.[131] Economic hardship was pervasive and outright destitution was probably much more commonplace than it is today. Inflation was a periodic occurrence that could have a choking effect on families that were already squeezed. Artisans and laborers in Boston and Philadelphia, for example, had to allocate 55 to 60% of their household budgets for food in normal times well into the 19th century.[132] When food prices soared, as during the years of the Revolution, their decline in living standards could be debilitating. In England the rise in food prices often meant no bread on the table for the poor, who rioted.[133] The French historian Fernand Braudel, in fact, believes that the standard of living of "the common people—the majority"—across Europe deteriorated from where it had been between 1350 and 1550.[134] To the extent that concern for instantaneous happiness is a luxury for those who do not have to worry about their daily bread, then, it would seem that unlike the situation today only a small portion of Anglo-American parents before 1800 placed a premium on the immediate gratification of their children. The physical and spiritual well-being of their children were more pressing obligations to early modern parents than to their more affluent and secular descendants today.

Did they consciously think of their children as economic assets or liabilities? For the common people the exigencies of life were overriding considerations, and the economics of childrearing could not be ignored. The labor of children was taken for granted and counted upon in ways we cannot easily understand. The four hands of a poor farming couple were sometimes so strained to sustain three stomachs that they put their three-year-old's hands to work tending livestock or helping with the spinning.[135] Child labor did not become disreputable until the 19th century, when the increasing presence of working children in the new factories and mines became a scandal.

Whether the work of children generally contributed to the early modern household economy the equivalent of what they consumed, let alone an excess of their own consumption, is not known, but it does seem unlikely. If their entire childhoods were tabulated, children undoubtedly cost their parents much more financially than was ever recouped for their labor, as is the case today. Perhaps the question should be not whether parents viewed their children as economic liabilities, then, but rather how did early modern parents cope with the economic burdens of childrearing? The most common method of coping was by placing children in service with families who could afford them. So common was this practice in England, that it has been suggested that a majority of boys and girls in pre-industrial settlements spent some time in service prior to marriage.[136] As late as the early part of this century, in fact, servants constituted the largest single occupational group in England.[137] In America children were put out into other people's households as servants or apprentices throughout the early modern period. There was no consistent age at which a child was first placed in service, but rarely was it before his seventh year, unless he was orphaned.[138] In addition, adolescent farm boys were often sent away to work during the winter months, when their most visible activity in the rural household was eating. This seasonal pattern of homeleaving and homecoming might facilitate a poorer family's ability to sustain itself.[139]

The wellspring of behavior is complex, and we cannot be sure whether parents who put out their children were consciously thinking of only the economics involved. The practice of "putting out" was not uncommon among families which could well afford to keep their children home.[140] Some parents may have felt, unconsciously perhaps, a need to distance themselves from their own children, some may have genuinely believed that their children would be better prepared for society if they served a time in other people's homes, and some no doubt saw a tempting way to reduce the number of mouths they had to feed. As in most critical decisions people face, a variety of reasons (and rationalizations) were probably at play and will forever remain beyond our reconstruction. What seems likely, however, is that early modern parents were probably freer to admit the economic considerations that affected their actions toward their children than parents today, just as they appear to have been less restrained than we about openly considering the economic pluses and minuses of marriage and mate selection. The instrumental aspects of human relationships, even intimate ones, were not as morally troublesome as they seem to have become in the post-Freudian age.

Having said this, we do not have to leave the impression that early modern parents necessarily loved their children less than moderns do.[141] Instrumental considerations, be they between courting couples or parents and children, do not preclude affection, as the "either . . . or" school of analysis sometimes implies. Man's capacity to hold contradictory ideas and emotions may be illogical but it is real. Be they rich or poor, country gentry or urban laborers, early modern parents could on the one side calculate the pluses and minuses of keeping their children at home or placing them in service, or sending them to work or to school, or allowing them to play or requiring them to perform household chores, while, on the other side, feel an intense affection for them. Love and self-interest are not mutually exclusive. And though we possess virtually no direct evidence about how the poor felt towards their children in the early modern era, we must keep this human potential in mind instead of assuming that the material circumstances of their lives necessarily circumscribed their capacity for feelings.[142]

Did early modern parents believe that their treatment of their children during childhood would affect them later as adults? The answer is unequivocally yes. Modern psychology did not discover the relevance of childhood to adult development, and neither did early modern theorists. The understanding of the individual's life history as a developmental process whereby preceding stages influence succeeding stages can be easily traced at least as far back as the Greeks.[143] Indeed, the process would appear to be so self-evident as to make the reader wonder why we bothered to raise the question, why we would think there would be any question about early moderns believing there was a connection between childhood and adulthood. The reason is simply that modern psychology has so monopolized our view of childhood and its connections to adulthood that some of us occasionally look rather parochially and patronizingly upon the ideas of people who reared children before Freud. This is unfortunate for two reasons. First, we are apt to distort their attitudes by prematurely and presumptuously thinking that they lacked our insight because they did not use our Freudian-derived vocabulary. Second, we may deprive ourselves of valuable advice that earlier generations had to offer about the nature and treatment of children.

Much as the case today, most parents of the early modern era appear to have worried about the kind of adults their children would become. This concern with the developmental importance of childhood underlay many of the childrearing modes that have been identified. Lloyd deMause has done the pioneering work in conceptualizing and documenting various childrearing modes in the past; he delineates four as having evolved in the West by 1800, six by today.[144] Lawrence Stone finds in England between 1500 and 1800 six childrearing modes, each of which he associates predominantly with particular social groups.[145] Philip Greven describes three types among American Protestants between 1600 and 1850 or so, and he associates each with a different type of Protestant temperament.[146] Whether it is "the child-oriented, affectionate and permissive mode" of "the upper Bourgeoisie and squirarchy," "the child-oriented but repressive mode" of the same classes, "the egocentric intrusive mode" of the "pious nonconformists," "the brutal but careful mode" of "the cottager and artisan," the will-breaking mode of the "evangelical" Protestants, or the will-bending mode of the "moderate" Protestants, it reflected a parental view that childhood was consequential for adulthood and that parents had a major responsibility in shaping what their children would become as men and women. What distinguishes one of these modes from another was the technique adopted and the sense of anxiety parents had about the whole process. Ironically, it has been claimed by Stone and Greven that the parents who were least anxious about the kind of adults their children would turn into were to be found both at the top and at the bottom of society. (deMause finds evidence of his six modes in all social classes.) At the top of English society was the aristocracy, to whom Stone attributes "the negligent mode" of childrearing.[147] At the top of American society, especially in the southern colonies, was the gentry, primarily among whom Greven finds the "genteel" temperament and corresponding "indulgent" mode of childrearing.[148] Despite the differences in their taxonomic terms, Stone and Greven describe essentially similar modes of parenting for these wealthy groups. They spent comparatively little time with their children, whom they turned over to such surrogates as nurses, tutors and servants from infancy on. Many of these parents could enjoy their abbreviated hours with their children in an indulgent manner while the formative tasks of instruction and discipline were relegated to others. It may be that these upper crust parents did believe that childhood was a crucial time for the eventual growth of their children into responsible adults; but also felt that they could count on a proper developmental outcome resulting without their close, personal involvement being required. Thus they could enjoy their children as children without worrying about developmental issues. At the bottom of society were "the mass of the very poor" to whom Stone attributes "the indifferent and exploitative mode" of childrearing.[149] If many of them treated their children in a present-minded (what we might call short-sighted) way without regard for developmental implications, they may have been reflecting an outlook so constricted by poverty that it had no room for future considerations.

While most early modern parents recognized connections between childhood and adulthood, they did not generally share with moderns the same sense of urgency about the long-range consequences of the first few years of life. Physical survival was a more immediate problem facing parents with infants than was psychological conditioning, although Puritans in particular and evangelicals in general do appear to have stressed the lasting impact of these years for the character and soul of their children. Others, however, appear to have taken a less anxious approach to parenting until their children reached the age of six or seven. It was not that parents viewed their seven-year-olds as miniature adults, as has been suggested, but that they believed from that age forward a child's experiences would be crucial to his eventual development as an adult.[150]

## iii. The Perspective Of Children

Having regarded childhood from the vantage point of parents, we now want to view it from the perspective of children. That is an extremely difficult if not impossible task, for the children of the past remain almost entirely inarticulate to us. We cannot assume that they were the completely malleable receptacles of adult wishes and behavior. How they internalized adult actions cannot usually be known. Indeed, we cannot be certain today how children interpret many of their parentally controlled stimuli. We do know that they often do not fulfill the expectations of the most self-consciously manipulative, psychologically knowledgeable parents. With this in mind, we ask the following answerable questions:

1. Was childhood a nightmarish or happy time for children?
2. Did children believe or feel themselves to be neglected or cared for by their parents?
3. Were children effectively prepared to become functioning members of their society?

Only the last question might have struck early moderns as worthy of their attention. It is unlikely that many could have even thought up the first two questions. For what the child would become when he grew up was much more important to them than what he experienced when he was young. Except among certain social groups in the 18th century, it was adulthood, not childhood, that was celebrated in those centuries.[151] Reaching adulthood could not be taken for granted, and that sad demographic fact itself may explain their preference for adult ways. Parents who dressed children in adult fashions were not so much forcing premature expectations on their young as they were reflecting a value system that ranked adult status, adult tastes and adult standards unequivocally above those of children.[152] The bottom line for successful parenting then, therefore, was not the happy child or the secure child but the child who survived to become an effective adult.

But the first two questions do interest us for several reasons. First as bumper stickers proclaiming "Children are people too" indicate, our sensibility mandates that we consider childhood not only as a stage of becoming but as a state of being as well. The quality of a child's life concerns us for its own sake as much as it does for its developmental consequences.[153] Second, influenced by modern psychology, we are apt to be more concerned with the feelings of children than with their skills or attitudes. Unlike most early moderns, we generally believe that the key to effective adulthood lies in the child's sense of happiness and nurture. Accordingly, a third reason for our interest in these questions is our assumption that in the answers lie important clues to the motives and behavior of early modern adults. As we pursue the answers to all three questions, however, we should be prepared to let the evidence modify our assumptions.

Although the stuff of which a sense of happiness is made may vary from individual to individual, let alone from period to period, the evidence indicates that a happy childhood was neither the common goal of early modern parents nor necessarily the uncommon experience of their children. Since children did not leave written accounts of their feelings, the most direct evidence we have are the necessarily selective recollections by adults of their childhoods. Often these memoirs were offered as sources of instruction by personal example, and it would not advance their paradigmatic purpose to portray a carefree, happy childhood. Still, they confirm what other sources suggest, namely that the recurring themes that dominated childhood in most God-fearing families were the inculcation of piety and obedience, the cultivation of parental authority, the punishment of misbehavior, and the struggle to control or repress natural inclinations.[154] If happiness consisted of freedom to spend their days without adult supervision or in an uncontrolled environment, fewer early modern children were as happy as their medieval counterparts. For perhaps a pervasive theme in childhood during this period was the involvement of parents or parental surrogates in self-consciously regulating the behavior of children. Indeed, if there has been a linear development in any facet of the history of the family over the past half-millenium or so, it may be, as Philippe Ariès, Lloyd deMause and Lawrence Stone have respectively suggested, in the increasing awareness of and concern for childhood.[155] Increasing concern has meant increasing adult supervision, intervention and structure. Whether the accompanying lessening of freedom has brought an increase or decrease in the happiness of children is unclear. But certainly the sense of being cared for must have increased generally over what it had been.

A recent theme in contemporary childrearing advice has suggested that particular childrearing techniques are less consequential for the child's sense of well-being and his development into an effective adult than his sense of being wanted and cared for by his parents.[156] Early modern children in England and America do appear to have received more attention from their parents and the adult world generally than had been the case before, and, as we indicated at the beginning of this essay, as adults the English peoples in these centuries displayed a remarkable capacity for innovation and achievement. Early moderns appear to have been more self-confident adults than were medieval men and women. They may have had good reason to be so. They had on the whole themselves received more attention as children. Moreover, they had been given new skills. They benefited from the flood of books that the invention of moveable type in the 15th century unloosened.[157] They went to schools in unprecedented proportions, as middle-class philanthropy and new commercial society's need for trained men stimulated an educational revolution in Tudor-Stuart England. These emotional and cognitive dimensions of childhood were experienced unevenly across society and over time. But they appear to have been of sufficient impact to contribute to the transformation of English and English colonial societies in these centuries.

## iv. Didactic Literature

Having looked at childhood from the perspective of parents and children, we now want to consider briefly the attitudes of influential outsiders, whose ideas may not be traceable directly to internal family developments but which nevertheless formed an inescapable background against which parent-child relations were played out. Largely didactic in nature, the written reflections of early modern clergymen, humanists and philosophers regarding proper childrearing, if not evidential of the actual behavior parents adopted, reveal a prescribed code of parenting against which many mothers and fathers could measure their own mode of upbringing.[159]

Two themes in early modern writings about childrearing are strikingly familiar to modern readers. First, throughout the three centuries under study commentators stressed the formative role of childhood in shaping adult character. "Childhood shows the man, As morning shows the day," wrote Milton in 1671.[160] No one ever suggested in print that childrearing could be ignored or neglected without consequence. Second, childrearing practices, like morals, invariably drew the critical eye of social observers. We cannot think of an early modern writer who expressed unqualified approval of what he discerned to be the prevailing mode of parenting. Rather they continuously exhorted parents to alter their ways of raising children. The price of literacy, then as now, was for informed parents to be anxious over the method of childrearing they had adopted.[161]

Yet if they tried to follow the prescriptions of the day, early modern parents could more easily assess their success or failure than can their modern counterparts. For the yardstick of effective parenting then was visible. The early modern sensibility was more closely attuned to how people acted than to what they felt. Accordingly, it was the behavior of children that preoccupied writers. From the 16th through the 18th centuries English and American children were expected to demonstrate "respect" for their elders, to exhibit "civility" or good manners, and to display "piety." These were the key words in childrearing manuals that reflected the attention given by early moderns to the externals of childhood.[162]

In contrast, today's parents and teachers are flooded with specialist advice not to crush the child's "psyche" or "self-esteem" but rather to promote his "self-expression," "self-reliance," and "creativity." The modern emphasis on the inner life of the child has been accompanied by a shift in training techniques. When behavioral modification was the principal aim of rearing, corporal punishment was deemed an appropriate means of achieving the desired results. External ends could be achieved by external instruments. Writers who eschewed physical punishment believed that influencing the mind of the child would lead to more certain and more lasting results. But before 1800 results were defined in terms of conduct, and writers did not tarry long over the inner consequences of psychological conditioning as long as it eventuated into proper behavior. Today behavior is considered less as an end in itself than as an index of the inner state. The child's feelings are the primary concern of contemporary advice manuals; therefore the efficacy of instruction and discipline is measured less by their effect on a child's conduct than on his motives. Since motives remain normally invisible, the success of modern childrearing methods is not easily determined. Understandably parents who read widely in the current literature find less agreement and certainty than was possible among the behaviorists of the early modern era.

# Stage V
# Post-Childrearing

We define post childrearing as that stage in the family cycle when all of a couple's surviving children have reached adulthood. For at that point we can say the couple's childrearing responsibilities have terminated, although they continue in their role as parents to their now adult children. But what do we mean by adulthood? Is it attained once the legal age of majority is reached? Does it involve primarily economic independence? Is it achieved when one feels oneself to be independent; that is, is it an emotional state? Is it attained only upon marriage? Do both parents and children agree on the same criteria for determining when adulthood has been reached, or do parents persist in treating their children as children when the latter believe themselves to have become adults and therefore beyond the rearing responsibilities of the former? As the questions imply, the concept of adulthood may vary considerably from person to person today and probably even more so between people of early modern times and today. Although the people of any given complex society probably never share the same notion of adulthood, it seems safe to assume, as Modell, Furstenberg, and Hershberg have done,

> that both in the past and now, becoming as adult involves a *series* of changes in status which moves an individual from economic dependence upon parents or their surrogates to economic independence (or dependence upon a spouse) and from participation in the family of orientation to the establishment of a family of procreation (or, far less commonly, to move out of the family of orientation into lifetime roles as spinster or bachelor). These events may not universally announce adulthood, but they certainly bear an overwhelming and apparent association with participation in the adult world.[163]

Modell, Furstenberg, and Hershberg select five events as keys to the modern transition from youth to adult status: exit from school, entrance to the work force, departure from home, marriage, and establishing a

46

separate household. They conclude that the overall process of becoming an adult is more compressed, more uniform, and occurs earlier in the individual life history of American youth today than was the case a century ago. Their finding significantly undermines the commonly repeated belief "that growing up in contemporary America has become more problematic because it takes a longer period of time or because the expectations for becoming an adult are more blurred than was once the case."[164]

When modified, the Modell, Furstenburg, and Hershberg model can be useful in comparing the passage into adulthood during early modern times with the process more recently. Then as now, we would agree, the achievement of economic independence and the movement away from the family into which one was born bore "an overwhelming and apparent association with participation in the adult world." But the five steps which they have identified as critical in signaling the achievement of economic independence and removal from the family of orientation during the 19th and 20th centuries are not all the same as those which were taken during the early modern period. Three of the steps are the same. Marriage and the setting up of a separate home were critical determinants of adult status then as now. So, too, was departure from home, although we would add the modifier "permanent," for both early modern and contemporary children and youth are periodically removed from their homes on a temporary basis, either as servants and apprentices then or as students or summer campers today. But exit from school and entrance to the work force were not commonly crucial signposts on the route to adulthood before 1800, especially in the farming areas where most people lived. Control of land was the preindustrial equivalent of these two events as an indicator of a man's readiness to participate in the adult world. This was clearly true among all levels of property owners. Indeed, control of land was normally a prerequisite to getting married and setting up a separate household, just as completion of one's schooling and getting a job usually precede marriage and the establishment of independent households today. Control of land did not necessarily mean absolute ownership, for one could sustain a rural family as a tenant farmer. But the eventual ownership of the land one worked seems (and our conclusion is admittedly impressionistic) to have been even more important psychologically to early moderns as evidence of their full autonomy than is homeownership to young marrieds today.

If control of land, permanent departure from the home, marriage, and the setting up of a separate household, taken together, completed the passage from childhood to adulthood before 1800, then it would appear that few early modern parents survived together to see all of their children reach full adulthood. Post childrearing was rarely a fully realized stage in the family cycle of early modern couples. Three factors combined to produce this result. First, a higher proportion of children failed to experience *all* of the critical events that marked the transition to adult status then than

47

do so today. For example, as we indicated in the first section, a greater percentage of males and females never married then than has been the case in present times. Yet, as Peter Laslett has observed, "you had to be married in that society to be accepted as fully grown up."[165] Second, the typical early modern mother could expect to bear her last child at the age of 38 or 39.[166] She would have to have lived well into her 60s for the possibility to see all of her children fulfill the conditions of adulthood. But, as it was, most mothers before 1800 could not expect to live a dozen years or so past the birth of their last child.[167] And even if she did live much longer, the chances were slim that the father of her children would survive with her into the post childrearing period. For early parental mortality was the third factor that militated against the achievement of a completely post childrearing stage by the average early modern couple. After 1800 mothers would finish their childbearing at an increasingly earlier age and they and their husbands would live considerably longer. Not until the second half of the 19th century, however, did a post childrearing period become commonplace as a realized stage in the English and American family cycle.[168] Today, if they do not divorce, the average Anglo-American couple can expect to live together after their last child becomes a full-fledged adult almost as long as the average modern marriage itself lasts.[169] In sum, the infrequency and limited duration of post childrearing as a fully realized stage in early modern families is the most salient difference between then and now as measured in terms of our family cycle model.

Still, while they invariably had dependent and semi-dependent offspring whose rearing was incomplete, early modern parents usually had some adult children with whom they had to establish a relationship. Unfortunately, we do not yet know very much about the daily patterns of interaction between surviving couples and their grown-up, married children. As Peter Laslett has summed up the state of our present knowledge: "We are certainly in no position to estimate how much money was transferred, how often children visited their parents and how frequently and strenuously they exerted themselves to live near them or to find accommodations which would enable parents themselves to come within easy reach. The most likely conjecture from what we know is that they behaved very much as we behave now in these respects, no better and no worse."[170]

Our knowledge about the relationship between adult children and their parents becomes fuller for crisis situations, particularly for when one of the parents died. We shall discuss this in the last section of this essay, Spouse Loss.

# Stage VI
# Spouse Loss

### i. The Demographics

Increased life expectancy has made modern marriages the most durable in history. The typical married couple can expect to stay together for upwards of thirty years, or more than 50% longer than the average couple survived in the early modern era.[171] The comparatively high mortality levels in England and America before 1800 made any marriage that lasted more than twenty years exceptional.[172] In some areas, such as the early Chesapeake, the death rate was so heavy as to make a ten-year marriage extraordinary.[173]

Today death is also the major cause of marital dissolution, although it is increasingly rivaled by divorce. Still, the rising incidence of divorce in recent years should not obscure the fact that the average married person has a far likelier chance of becoming a widow or widower than she or he does of being divorced. Indeed, the high frequency of remarriage among divorced persons enhances their chances of experiencing spouse loss by death at some point in their lives.[174] Moreover, today women are much more likely than men to bury a spouse, because of greater life expectancy and their younger age at marriage.[175] Women also appear to have survived most early modern marriages.[176] Then and now the average woman could expect to experience widowhood as a stage in her life history. Successive widowhoods were undoubtedly much more common in the past, however, although comparative figures are not available.[177]

Children are, of course, the other major survivors of spouse loss, or what is better described from their perspective as parental loss. The loss of one parent due to death was a commonplace of early modern childhood. The lower the child in the birth order, the higher his chances of being orphaned. Hard statistics are not available for enough localities to support a numerical overview for the whole period. From studies of local areas we know that three-fourths of the children in one Virginia county during the 17th century lost at least one parent before reaching adulthood and more than one-third lost both.[178] But, outside of the Caribbean islands, early maternal mortality was probably more pervasive in the early Chesapeake than anywhere else in the Anglo-American world.[179] In New England, which appears to have enjoyed the highest longevity in that world, the average child could expect to have both his parents alive when he entered his twenties. In one New Hampshire town in 1680, in fact, 90% of the children had at least one grandparent still living and first- or second-born children there could expect to have a grandparent alive until they reached their twenty-fifth birth-day.[180] In England the typical experience appears to have fallen in between these two demographic extremes. It has been estimated that from 40 to 67% of English girls in pre-industrial times lost their fathers by the time of marriage.[181]

Today orphanhood is rare. In the United States only 4% of all children need fear the loss of one parent by death before reaching the age of 18. They are much more likely to be affected by the departure of one parent from the home due to marital separation or divorce. Between 12 and 15% of American children under 18 have experienced this kind of parental loss.[182] In England the divorce rate today is lower than in the U.S., and therefore the percentage of children experiencing all forms of parental loss is lower as well.[183]

## ii. Divorce

Divorce and other forms of spouse abandonment were not unknown in the early modern era, although they were negligible in comparison to spouse loss by death. Divorce as we understand it, involving the legal dissolution of a valid marriage with the right of both parties to remarry, was a Protestant innovation. But in England for more than a century and a half after the Reformation divorce remained an unacceptable practice that the Anglican Church, which retained jurisdiction over marriage, refused to recognize.[184] The New England colonists were the first Englishmen to legitimize divorce. In Massachusetts divorce was a clearly established civil process well before 1660.[185] In England divorce with the right to remarry could be obtained only through a special decree of Parliament, and this expensive route did not become available until the late 17th century.[186] Still, on both sides of the Atlantic the weight of community opinion was that whether one viewed the marriage contract as sacramental or civil, it was binding and should not be voluntarily abrogated except for extraordinary circumstances, such as adultery, incest, impotence, bigamy, or desertion.[187] Wives could initiate divorce proceedings in New England from the beginning, but could not do so in England until 1801.[188] A double standard mentality persisted in New England as well, however, for while husbands had been able to sue successfully for divorce on the sole charge of their wives' adultery since the 17th century, women petitioners did not succeed on these grounds until the Revolutionary era.[189]

Where divorce was unavailable or simply too expensive and complicated to be a reasonable alternative, husbands and wives could escape from unbearable matches by literally running away. Eighteenth-century newspapers in the southern colonies, where divorce was not granted by law, are replete with advertisements for runaway wives.[190] Southern courts provided maintenance in cases of separation, but separated spouses who

50

wanted to remarry would have to commit bigamy, a not uncommon practice among the poor in England or the colonies.[191] The sale of wives was another extra-legal method of marital dissolution that appears to have been practiced among the poor in certain areas in England.[192] Wife sale has yet to be discovered in early America.

These expedients of desertion, bigamy, and wife sale were not reasonable options for people with property and with children to whom they felt bound. For the middle classes outside of New England, death was the only likely route of departure from an unhappy marriage.[193] Indeed, it may be more than a tantalizing coincidence that in New England, the one region where husbands and wives could expect to have their spouses live long lives, divorce was a well-established and comparatively accessible safety valve.

By the early 17th century in England some radical Protestant sects openly talked about the possibility of divorce and even polygamy.[194] During the Interregnum, John Milton advocated divorce as a logical outcome of the Puritan conception of marriage as a civil contract. But the great Puritan poet could not persuade the Commonwealth government to legalize divorce.[195] Upper class aristocratic families in England, however, always had access to "legal separations" from unhappy marriages, and in some instances with the sanction of the church could have their marriages declared invalid if a legal loophole could be found.[196]

Today the theological and ethical underpinnings so long associated with marriage and divorce in the West have almost vanished. With the emergence of "no-fault divorce" we are closer to the ancient Roman view that divorce, like marriage, simply requires the agreement of both parties than we are to the prevailing ethos of the early modern era. Moreover, the social status of the divorced person today seems to be considerably different from what it was two centuries ago, indeed, from what it was until quite recently. The divorced woman was particularly subjected to social scorn, especially since in most cases resulting in divorce decrees, the husbands were the petitioners and wives were accused of divorceable offenses.[197] The emergence of no-fault divorce reflects the modern assumption that both parties are usually equally responsible for marital instability and that marital dissolution should not result in either being stigmatized for having caused the break-up.

## iii. Conditions Of Widowhood

While the status of divorced persons has changed dramatically from what it was in the early modern era, it is not so clear how the condition of widowhood has changed. Certainly some of the problems facing the widow have remained fundamentally the same: Did she and her husband adequately plan for the contingency of widowhood or is she totally unprepared

51

for it? Did her husband leave her enough property to enable her to be economically independent? Can she rely upon her children for either material or emotional support? Will she have to turn to extra-familial agencies for financial assistance? Should she live alone as the head of a solitary household, should she have some of her children move into her home where she can maintain her role as household head, or should she move into the home of married children and thereby assume a dependent or inferior role within the household hierarchy? Should she remarry and, if so, how long should she wait to do so? As the way in which we have phrased her problems implies, the widow, then and now, has faced the necessity of choosing among various options that were and are available to her. Perhaps this is the most remarkable commonality to the experience of widowhood in the early modern and modern periods.

For most women widowhood has brought a sense of loss at several levels of experience. First, the widow has suffered the psychological pain of being bereaved of her closest companion and partner. Second, unless from the wealthy classes, she has faced the strong likelihood of economic hardship or, at the least, a lower standard of material well-being. Third, she has had to adjust to a different if not reduced status in the eyes of her friends, neighbors, and family.[198] These three levels of psychological, economic, and status loss have been common denominators to the stage of widowhood across the centuries. Family historians, however, have so far focused almost entirely upon the economics of widowhood in the past, while ignoring its psychological and social dimensions.

What follows, therefore, are tentative suggestions intended more as guides for further investigation rather than as firm conclusions with regard to these psychological and social components. It would seem that whether romance played a primary or prominent role in the formation of the marriage, or whether the couple's union had been more instrumental than affectionate, most husbands and wives ate together daily, slept together nightly, and necessarily evolved a mutually dependent relationship that could not help from becoming psychologically dislocating when it was severed irreversibly and involuntarily. Today we have come to learn a good deal about the psychological distress that normally accrues to both parties when they have mutually agreed to terminate their marriage.[199] The pain that accompanies bereavement appears to be much greater.[200] While the impact on children from parental loss may be the same whether it is due to death or divorce, as Laslett has suggested (although we are not yet persuaded that it is), the psychological consequences of divorce and of bereavement would seem to be profoundly different for the surviving spouses.[201] Since divorce usually occurs much earlier in the individual's life history, it can be more easily felt to be the beginning stage, a time of promise and hope. The death of a spouse, in contrast, usually occurs late in one's life and is a powerful reminder of the survivor's own approaching end. Indeed, the psychological strain of a spouse's death has been pointed to in recent studies which find that "the incidence of death among the recently widowed is higher than among married persons of the same age."[202] The increased risk occurs mainly within the first six months after bereavement. Moreover, widowers are at higher risk than widows.[203] Similar quantitative indices could be constructed to measure the psychological impact of spouse loss in the past. Historians have dug into the reactions of some early modern parents to the death of their children. They have found examples of deeply aggrieved mothers and fathers as well as parents who displayed a seeming insensitivity, an insensitivity that has been explained as an adjustment to the high infant and child mortality rates that parents of the past had to cope with.[204] And while it may have been possible for some parents to have coped by cultivating a callousness towards the loss of young offspring, we cannot assume that they were able to maintain a similar emotional resiliency in the face of spouse loss. The death of a child did not result in the need to rearrange one's daily routine, as did the departure of one's wife or husband. Life could go on much the same after the child died, but it changed dramatically after one's household partner was gone, whether one felt a great deal of affection for the deceased mate or not. Moreover, whatever their capacity for emotional attachment, early modern couples were directed to love each other more than they did their children or any other person.[205] Presumably they felt the loss of each other more than they did that of their children. Still, the psychological dimensions of widowhood remains an important area of future research.

## iv. Status Of Widows

If the ethos of modern society directed single adults to marry, was there a corollary belief that widows should not remain solitary? The Protestant Anglo-American world did not appear to harbor the guilt about remarriage that some Catholic countries experienced and that may have existed in England during the centuries it was Catholic. Although canon law allowed Catholics to remarry, the church did not give a couple who were remarrying a benediction, and the community expressed social disapproval towards the couple after the marriage. In 16th-century France, for example, adolescent boys would bang on pots and pans outside the houses of newlyweds in cases of second marriage for either party. This *charivaris*, albeit harmless, reflected the ambivalence of the community toward remarriage. While social disapproval was expressed in the *charivaris*, afterwards the couple was left alone. Indeed remarriage was a necessity in a society with a high death rate.[206]

By the 17th century, Protestant England and America entertained more secular views about marriage, marital dissolution and remarriage. Marriage could be ended by divorce which, *de facto*, removed its previous sacramental element. What remained after the theology was an attitude toward marriage, especially on the part of the middle and upper classes, that matrimony should last for the lifetime of the spouses.[207] This attitude became embedded in the ethics of Victorian England and America. Only in the 20th century, and then not until quite recently, has this final link to the sacramental view been socially and morally rejected.[208] For most of these past centuries when divorces were discouraged, the only sanctioned route to remarriage followed widowhood. From the perspective of Protestant society the widow's decision to remarry became a personal one unimpeded by theological restraints. Moreover, society might encourage poorer widows to remarry in order that they not become a burden to their community. On the other hand, the poorer widow would find it more difficult to find a man willing to marry her especially if she had young children or if she were old. But widows with some money and property were viewed as "good catches," especially by young men who had little or no wealth with which to establish themselves on their own. It appeared to be a relatively common practice for insolvent younger men to marry widows who often were older than their suitors.[209]

Society found the young, wealthy, attractive widow a source of moral concern. Several comedies written during the 16th and 17th centuries revolved around the widow. One might show how rogues tried to trap helpless widows into marriage in order to control their fortunes. Another might portray the widow as a lustful, sexually experienced woman in quest of sexual gratification. These antithetical views reflected the ambivalent attitude widows evoked and the uncertain status they held.[210]

Widowers, on the other hand, seemed to have been placed in a far less precarious position. Literature and drama offered few caricatures of the widower as they did of the widow. The sexual longings of a widower did not arouse special concern for a society in which the double standard operated. Furthermore, it was believed that men required less protection physically and financially and were better able to care for themselves. In fact this was not the case, for widows outlived widowers.[211] But it would take a long time for the double standard mentality to accept the implications of demographic reality.

Age was and remains an important factor in a widow's decision to remarry. As we might expect, the younger a widow the more likely she was to remarry, especially if she had young children to rear. In the Chesapeake colonies, where a high adult mortality rate was combined with a severely imbalanced sex ratio, second and third marriages were the rule for women.[212] This occurred especially in the 17th century. In New England, where wives did not become widows usually until they were in their 50s or 60s and their children were nearly all grown-up, remarriage was the exception.[213]

Because today in England and America widows constitute a much older group than they did during early modern times, most remain alone. For many this is their preferred status.[214] In contrast to the older double standard view that women need male protection, this new enlarged group of widows has acquired a reputation of being able to manage in the main by themselves. Moreover, the sex ratio among older people reinforces the likelihood of widows remaining unmarried. As in the past, wives outlived husbands and widows continue to outlive widowers.[215] And widowers die before married men of their own age.[216] Such facts should bury the double standard myth of greater male self-reliance and superiority.

The status of these surviving widows would seem to be less ambivalent today than it was in the past.[217] They have forged a collective identity with other "senior citizens" and thereby have been able to provide themselves with social and psychological support. Senior citizen groups have also been able to press government for special services. The older widow today is less dependent upon her children than was her early modern counterpart and enjoys a more independent status.[218] Status, however, is connected in important ways to economics, which we shall now explore.

## v. Economic State Of Widowhood

Unless a wife has been amply provided for by her husband or even by her own family, her financial condition will deteriorate upon her widowhood. In contemporary society when a husband retires, his pension usually becomes central to his and his wife's maintenance. But after his death many wives do not continue to receive this benefit even though their basic expenses remain what they had been.[219] Rents, mortgage payments, property taxes, utility and fuel bills are not reduced by the death of one's spouse; on the contrary, because of inflation they are steadily increasing. In the early modern era, when no pension system existed, widows along with orphans and the disabled were the most frequent recipients of charitable relief for the poor.[220]

While we do not know the measure of economic loss that early modern families typically experienced following the death of a husband, it would seem that his passing resulted in at least a temporary reduction of his widow's economic condition, and often a permanent one. For her principal contribution to the economy of the household had been inside the house.[221] Accordingly, she rarely was equipped to take over the operation of a farm by herself after her husband died. The typical farmer's wife might cultivate a vegetable garden and feed the livestock, but she had little experience in overseeing the field work required for commercial crops. On a commercial farm, therefore, the crop cultivated by the husband's own hands for market might be lost forever if his widow could not afford to hire a laborer to do her late husband's work. Even then she would not receive the same level of return after paying a live-in hired hand. Her plight, moreover, became increasingly difficult when she had small children to look after.[222]

If a widow had a fully grown bachelor son who lived at home, she probably could maintain her previous standard of living. For the son would simply succeed her late husband as economic head of the house, and she could retain her status as mistress of the household, unless and until her son married. At that time new household arrangements would of necessity take into account the position of the son's wife as mistress. Often the deceased husband's will took this development into account, directing his son to grant his mother entitlements such as living space, food and clothes. Living with married children would assure a widow of her material welfare; but inevitably such an arrangement brought a loss of status within the family hierarchy, for she no longer would be the head of the household.

Economically the widow who was left with small children, with little or no endowments, or with not enough material well-being to hire a servant would most likely be classified as a pauper. She and her young dependents might constitute too onerous a burden to be taken in by relatives. Relatives provided potentially one of the most important support services for indigent or dependent widows.[223] But the growing reliance upon institutions such as the workhouse (which first appeared in English parishes during the 1630s and American cities in the next century) may have reflected a decline in the willingness of kin to assume responsibility for extra-nuclear relations. Indeed, widows and fatherless children do appear to have become an increasing burden on the public and on private charities as the early modern era progressed.[224] Perhaps this increase reflected a decline in kinship charity, or it may have been due to the sheer size of a rising population.[225] In any case, public and private charities were far from ample even when first organized, and as we move closer to the industrial age, we find that local authorities in England and America became increasingly hostile and reluctant to care for dependent persons.[226]

Between the impoverished and the wealthy widows there existed a group of women who may not have suffered great economic hardship upon the death of their spouses. Some of these women had worked alongside their husbands in their shops or inns, and, if they were not disabled, could continue in their husband's place. Similarly, those women who had belonged to guilds while married could retain their positions when they became widows, and they could work as long as they desired since there was no mandatory retirement age. Indeed, it is possible to suggest that these women acquired a new position of power since they were now in control of the wealth from their husband's property which had been legally denied them during their marriage, although they lacked the freedom to sell (alienate) the dower land which by common law had to be passed on the the family heir. Women who inherited their husband's businesses might also attain great economic liberty during their widowhood.[227]

It should come as no surprise that older widows and widowers constituted one of the most economically depressed groups in the early modern period just as they often do today. Now we have a relatively well-defined group of elder people, our "senior citizens," who are retired and are recipients of governmental programs to ease their loss of income. Early moderns would not understand the concept of a specific retirement age, although they did understand the idea of retirement and had a good idea of what it was to be old.[228] Although the lack of any mandated retirement age allowed them to work as long as they wanted, many continued to labor because they lacked the security of institutionalized support systems such as social security, food stamps, housing for the elderly, and so on. Only moral pressure was put on employers to assist their former workers, who were now old and incapacitated; there were no legal requirements to compel them to do so. Rather, it was believed that the children of the old should look after their parents.[229] The English Poor Law of 1601 codified this sentiment, stating that children should provide relief for their parents. But the law did not include the requirement to shelter them in their own household.[230] Even the provision requiring relief was hard to support. Evidence exists that some English children disdained all responsibility, while others assumed it.[231] In America most children were required by their fathers' wills to feed, clothe and shelter their widowed mothers. But there, too, as some data from New England suggests, some children may not have responded to this maternal need.[232]

Demographic studies reveal that between one-third to one-half of the widows lived alone, but in America the number of such women living alone appears to have been small.[233] The annals of the first American Congress in 1790 stated that "there were few female solitaries without families, and the ease of procuring subsistence removed all apprehensions in old age."[234] Despite this congressional belief, much more study is still needed before a final assessment can be made on the way Anglo-American children treated their elderly or widowed parents, especially when they were poor.

Some good evidence exists that the most honored and cared for surviving spouses were those with financial means of their own. Grandparents with sufficient wealth in old and New England were visited and entertained by their children and even took care of (and in some cases took charge of) their grandchildren, and some affection between these generations has been shown to have existed. Perhaps grandparents in the past found it easier to give their unstinted love to their grandchildren than to their own children, as many grandparents today claim they do.[235]

Respect was accorded such elderlies not only because their age bespoke wisdom, but also because they retained a certain status as a result of their economic independence. In fact, old age when not accompanied by some wealth has rarely been the basis for deference.[236] Perhaps widows and widowers have long realized the importance of financial independence, even from their adult children. Laslett sums up the prevailing ethos among the elderly that crosses the centuries:

> the conclusion might be that then, as now, a place of your own, with help in the house, with access to your children, within reach of support, might have been what the elderly and the aged most wanted for themselves in the pre-industrial world. This was difficult to secure in traditional England for any but fairly substantial people.[237]

## vi. Widow's Benefits And The Law

In the early modern age married women were accorded few legal rights. Among the few that they had was the right of dower, which by common law entitled a wife upon her husband's death to the income and control of part of his estate.[238] It has been suggested that dower rights represented a recognition of the wife's "role in contributing to (her husband's) property, whether by the property she had brought to the marriage or by the labor she performed in the household."[239] Common law dower in England, which was accepted in the colonies, obliged a husband to arrogate his wife a one-third life interest in all of his real property that was possessed at any time during their marriage. The wife acquired her rights of dower upon marriage and neither the husband (through making a will or otherwise), nor his creditors, nor a purchaser of this land could effect the wife's interest.[240]

During the husband's lifetime, the wife's interest in his land was "inchoate," "that is, it was capable of becoming possessory only in the case of the wife's surviving her husband." Once he died her dower interest became "consumate."[241] These limitations imposed upon her husband's financial flexibility by inchoate dower were recognized so that unless the wife released her claim to any part of her husband's real property with her consent, her proprietary claim to the land constituted a "cloud on the title" which might discourage a potential purchaser. Thus a husband's freedom to negotiate any business related to land sale could be significantly impeded.[242]

To offset these financial encumbrances a variety of devices was utilized. One was a cash sum that was brought to the marriage in the form of a dowry or portion. This money could be used for investment on the property, the purchase of new property, or the payment of family debts. In aristocratic families the portion was of considerable size so that the bride's father was allowed to pay this out in installments. By the 17th century, fathers might be charged interest on any remaining part of the portion should they be late on payment.[243]

Another device for circumventing some aspects of dower rights was the "jointure" arrangements agreed upon by the families of both the bride and bridegroom. A jointure was an estate usually settled upon the wife in a pre-marital agreement in order to supersede her dower interest. If, however, a settlement was agreed upon after marriage, the wife was able to choose between dower or jointure. Jointure settlements arranged prior to the marriage were advantageous to the husband because they did not have to conform to the fixed amount of one-third; and "the jointure could be whatever proportion of landed income the bridegroom's father chose to assign."[244] However, should the agreement be less than the provisions of common law dower, a signature to the marriage contract by the future wife or her guardian was necessary.[245]

Since the form of jointure payments often was an annual allowance to the widow that began upon the death of her husband, great consideration was given by the bridegroom's family as to how the estate could undertake to bear these costs. Among the considerations taken into account was the size of the cash portion, an estimate of the future value of the land, and the amount of future debt that might become attached to the land. The ratio between the jointure and cash portion, however, constituted the major issue for negotiation between the two families. [246]

The concern with dower rights, jointures and portions included in the pre-marital and post-marital settlements indicates how much widowhood was a contingency that early modern propertied families anticipated and planned for assiduously. These settlements also took into consideration the financial arrangements for future offspring which thereby affected later stages of the family cycle.

As their lives together unfolded, husbands and wives could modify some of these earlier arrangements and even substitute new ones. Their planning for widowhood could take into account post-marital developments that could not have been fully anticipated in the marriage settlements. The number and ages of their children, the acquisition or loss of property, the developing relationships between the husband and wife and between them and their children would all affect their post-marital thinking about spouse loss. The extent to which they jointly considered the contingency is not yet clear. But normally the husband was expected to plan for his wife's widowhood by drawing a testamentary will. For the less wealthy, wills were the most common form of settling their property, when their children were under age.[247] But not enough research has been undertaken on either side of the Atlantic to determine if wills always tended to adhere to the principle established by common law dower, of the one-third life interest to the widow. Moreover, we know even less about testamentary benefits for widows from those groups without landed wealth, such as the urban poor and the landless peasants for whom common law dower did not apply. We are not yet in a position, therefore, to confirm that colonial American widows were more advantaged than their English counterparts, as had frequently been suggested.[248] Indeed, preliminary research on actual widows' benefits undertaken for sections of England and America point to a great deal of variation, both within the colonies and England and between the Anglo-American world. For example, in the middle of the 17th century Chesapeake widows were likely to receive land in fee simple but by the end of the century they were increasingly limited to a life interest, as was the established practice in 18th-century Woburn, Massachusetts.[249] While some upper class widows may have claimed and received both their jointure and dower benefits, in two of three Cambridgeshire villages studies for the late 16th and early 17th centuries, lower ranked widows lost their life-interest in their husband's estate. In these villages the husbands had specified in their wills, perhaps without the knowledge of the law, or possibly even with the wife's consenting signature, that the new heir to their estate need only provide shelter and support for his widowed mother.[250]

We should not infer from these Cambridgeshire wills, however, that the husbands were indifferent to the welfare of their surviving wives. In fact, our strong impression is that with few exceptions the wills of early modern husbands reflected a genuine desire to care for both surviving wives and children. Differences in testamentary stipulation could be clues to a variety of circumstances that the testator had considered, such as the age of his children, the number and character of nearby kin, the value of his property, and the customs of the community. Our impression is that husbands tried to do well by their spouses.[251]

The extent to which widows needed to draw upon the law or actually did so in order to offset unfair treatment at the hands of their deceased husbands is not known. What is clear, however, is that the law was geared to make certain that a husband's property would be used to support his wife during her widowhood. When widows received less than their due from their husbands or if their husbands died intestate, wives could sue in court for their dower. But under the common law her dower right was only a lifetime-interest amounting to one-third of her husband's real property, not an outright ownership. She could not sell or transfer title to it, for upon her death it would be incorporated into the inheritance of her husband's blood heir. Thus the laws of dower sought to provide security for the widow during her life and, to maintain the property that supported her as a family preserve across the generations.[252]

It may be that English and American spouses have generally enjoyed a more secure position in regard to their deceased spouses' estates than did their offspring. According to Macfarlane, English landowners as far back as the 13th century could not only disinherit their children but also had the legal right to sell their land.[253] Only the widow could not be denied her dower rights from her husband's estate; similarly a husband could not be denied his right (of courtesy) to his deceased wife's property should they have a living child. Although these entitlements shared the similar characteristic of lasting solely for their holders' lifetimes, they nevertheless provided them with security sanctioned by the law and by judges' decisions.[254]

Despite the long tradition and the judicial enforcement of a widow's dower rights, criticism against them existed in the early modern era and mounted in the 19th and 20th centuries. The criticism was broadly based, representing the business perspective as well as the personal ones of husbands and wives. For example, not only were husbands required to obtain their wives' signatures should they want to sell their real property, but purchasers of land had to search titles on it to see if inchoate dower were attached. Further, sometimes wives were put in the untenable position of having to choose between present security and future protection. For if their husbands needed to sell their property most wives would not deny their required signatures; but by relinquishing this claim to dower, wives put in jeopardy their future security. In addition, the relevance of dower came under question as property became increasingly differentiated during the industrial and technological revolutions of the 19th and 20th centuries. Wealth became less and less identified solely with land and more associated with other forms of property, such as securities and bonds. Wives whose husbands possessed little or no real estate, but who owned a great deal of stocks and bonds, were not protected by common law dower.[255]

In 1833 the English widow lost the protection of dower rights and could, in fact, be disinherited. It was not until 1938 that a new legal protection was re-instituted so that if a husband disinherited his wife the widow could go to court. There the judge would decide what would be a reasonable provision for her that took into account the other natural obligations of the deceased.[256] In the U.S., in contrast, widows never lost legal protection. Should a wife be disinherited, American judges would, under the law, give the widow one-third of the estate, a situation not legally mandated in England, where judges have discretion.[257]

In intestate cases in England today the usual practice in court is for the judge to award the widow an established amount of the estate plus a fraction. In most moderate estates this sum will consist of almost the entire estate. In the U.S. the many problems associated with dower have led states to abolish it or to provide other protective devices along with dower.[258] These devices, such as homestead, dower, family allowance and indefeasible share, have assured her a great deal of protection. In the main, we can conclude that English and American widows' benefits are immeasurably better today.[259]

# Conclusions

The most obvious conclusion that follows from our comparative analysis of the family cycle is that there was enormous variability in the family life of early modern Englishmen and Americans. Although obvious, the point needs to be stressed because so often people speak of family life in the past as if there were a single pattern against which the present could be compared. But as we have seen, whether we look at the motives for marriage, childrearing methods, the role of women, or any component of family living, there were variations according to class, time and place.

Take parental power in marriage formation as an example. We cannot simply say that parents in the past generally exercised greater control over the spouse choice of their children than they do today. The variations were such as to require us to be fairly specific about the socio-economic, geographic, and chronological location of the families of the past that we are referring to. Generally parents with property and high status were more likely to influence directly the marital selection of their children than were parents without property. Children of poorer folk may have been completely free of parental influence in the matter of marriage. In addition to this variation *by* class, we must consider variations over time *within* each class. In the 18th century, for instance, upper-class parents were granting their children greater latitude in spouse choice than they had earlier, but still not as much as was available to children of parents without property. Finally, there was variation by place. In New England parents with property were likely to live long enough to influence their children's marital choice directly; while in the Chesapeake colonies early parental mortality was likely to give children with property as much independence as was enjoyed by those without property.

Once we have particularized past families by class, time, and place, we must then take account of variations related to their developmental stages in the family cycle. The family was not a static structure; the relationships, roles, and statuses of its members varied along different points of its cycle. Take the status of married women as an example. We cannot generalize about their position even within particular households without regard to variations by developmental stage. For instance, even in matches arranged by patriarchally-minded aristocratic families, wherein the brides were expected to cultivate a subservient relationship to their husbands, there were

62

opportunities for wives, potentially at least, to gain a measure of dominance over their mates. As we have seen, husbands were enjoined to be solicitous and acquiescent towards their wives during pregnancy or they would have to bear the guilt should a miscarriage occur. Thus, the distribution of power between wives and husbands could vary within a marriage according to its point in the family cycle.

Similarly the role of married women as mothers was not static. During the infancy and early childhood stages of her sons, a mother usually held a more influential position than did her husband. When each son matured to about the age of seven, however, her husband would normally assume control over his training and the planning of his future education, while the mother became a less conspicuous director of his growth. Later in the family's cycle, the mother might even become a dependent on one of her sons after her spouse died.

The relationship between fathers and daughters also seems to have varied cyclically. For example, historians have observed early modern fathers, especially the heads of aristocratic families, to have been largely uninvolved in the upbringing of their daughters, who were left mainly to the charge of their mothers or surrogates. If these upper-class fathers were cold and distant towards their daughters during childhood, they involved themselves very much in their daughters' courtship. And if a daughter entered into an economically and socially advantageous marriage, during this new post childrearing stage the father-daughter relationship might well be close and warmer than it had been during her childhood. For people who valued adulthood more than childhood, as was the case with early moderns generally, it was possible to develop a bond with a grown-up, married daughter that had not existed when she was a young dependent who was not highly esteemed.

If an awareness of variations must be at the forefront of our thinking about early modern families, there were some commonalities in English and early American family life that we can point to. On both sides of the Atlantic the family was regarded as being of fundamental importance to the well ordering of society; and the heads of households were accorded a respect and position in their communities that were denied to single men. On both sides the nuclear household structure predominated through most of the family cycle; and newly-weds were expected to live separately under their own roofs. On both sides a European marriage pattern of late marriages and a significant proportion of unmarrieds generally prevailed, especially in the 18th century. Indeed, there were probably greater uniformities between the family lives of Englishmen and Americans in the 18th century than had been the case in the 17th, when the unusual demographic conditions of some frontier settlements could make for anomalous family patterns. Even the range of variations within each society became more alike over time. The comparatively flattened social structure in 17th-century

America meant that there were few, if any families, that resembled the English extremes, the aristocratic families at the top or the vagabonds or cottagers at the bottom. But by the 1750s, as colonial stratification widened, America too, had ostentatiously wealthy families and visibly impoverished ones. And if America's upper crust lacked the hereditary distinctions of English nobility, England's lowest orders did not form a caste like America's slaves.

There are several noteworthy similarities that cut across the centuries between then and now as well: the diffused roles of husbands and wives within the household; the turnover of household members, due to geographic mobility, marriage, and spouse desertion, divorce, or death; the numerical predominance of widows over widowers; the frequent assumption of responsibility by children of elderly parents; the current resumption of the European marriage pattern (more or less); the value attached to marriage; the decision of most married couples to have children and thereby to experience the later stages of the family cycle as we have described it.

But there are also significant differences between then and now. Today husbands and (increasingly) wives both work outside the household, which has become exclusively a consumptive unit whereas it was essentially a productive one during the early modern period. The growing similarity in the economic activities of husbands and wives outside the home has been accompanied by a more self-conscious egalitarianism between them within the home. The double standard ideology of the past has virtually disappeared as a creditable guide to husband-wife relations today. Children are more likely to be cherished for their own developmental traits today than they were when adulthood was a more highly valued time of life. In addition, today the state interferes far more in the lives of families as evidenced in social welfare benefits, juvenile courts, child abuse hearings, and extensive legislation regulating marriage, divorce, and inheritance. We are today more romantic about marriage and more insistent that we experience personal satisfaction from our spouses. Because as we live longer and demand more pleasure from marriage, our spousal relationships appear to be more subject to psychological strain than those of the past. And while the early modern centuries experienced profound transformations in economic, social, political, and cultural developments, the pace of change has surely accelerated in our own time with resulting strains and readjustments being forced upon contemporary family relationships that seem to us to be even more intense. Yet the continuing high rate of marriage and remarriage after divorce as well as the continued bearing of children within marriage suggest not only the resiliency of the family cycle but its capacity to evolve new relationships as it repeats itself across the generations.

# FOOTNOTES

FOOTNOTES

1. Although the particular six part model we are using here is our own, our interest in a cyclical approach to the family was vitalized by others, especially Lutz K. Berkner, "The Stem Family and the Development Cycle of the Peasant Household: An Eighteenth-Century Austrian Example," *American Historical Review*, LXXVII (1972), 398-418; and Tamara Hareven, "The Family as Process: The Historical Study of the Family Cycle," *Journal of Social History*, 7 (1974), 322-329.
2. See below, Ch. 4.
3. Philippe Ariès, "La Famille," *Encounter*, XIV: 2 (1975), 7-12.
4. Valuable surveys of the extant demographic records include E.A. Wrigley ed., *An Introduction to English Historical Demography* (New York, 1966); T.H. Hollingsworth, *Historical Demography* (Ithaca, 1969); James H. Cassedy, *Demography in Early America* (Cambridge, 1969); Alan Macfarlane in collaboration with Sarah Harrison and Charles Jardine, *Reconstructing Historical Communities* (Cambridge, 1977).
5. Four pioneering studies in the new English and American family historiography were published in 1965-66: Peter Laslett, *The World We Have Lost: England Before the Industrial Age* (New York, 1965); E.A. Wrigley, "Family Limitation in Pre-Industrial England," *Economic History Review*, 19 (1966), 82-109; John Demos, "Notes on Life in Plymouth Colony," *William and Mary Quarterly*, 3d ser., 22 (1965), 264-286; Philip J. Greven, Jr., "Family Structure in Seventeenth-Century Andover, Massachusetts," *William and Mary Quarterly*, 3d ser., 23 (1966), 234-256.
6. The pivotal role of the early modern centuries in the development of these family characteristics is stressed in such major syntheses as Philippe Ariès, *Centuries of Childhood*, (Vintage pbck., 1962), Edward Shorter, *The Making of the Modern Family* (New York, 1975), and Lawrence Stone, *The Family, Sex and Marriage in England, 1500-1800* (New York, 1977). Another major synthesizer, Lloyd deMause, also describes more intense parent-child bonds as developing in the 17th and 18th centuries, but he discerns the beginnings of a significant watershed in parenting as early as the 14th century. "The Evolution of Childhood," in *The History of Childhood*, edited by Lloyd deMause (New York, 1974), esp. 51-52. Perhaps the most audacious and acute challenge to the importance of the early modern era as a time of these transformations comes from Alan Macfarlane, *The Origins of English Individualism: The Family, Property, and Social Change* (Cambridge, 1978).
7. See, for example, Stone, *The Family*, 159, 193, 642, and Martin H. Quitt's "Comment" on this book, *The Journal of Psychohistory*, 5 (1978), 600-601.
8. The putative semi-colonial dependence of England on foreign merchants at the outset of the 16th century is a commonplace in much of the literature. The formal removal of the Venetian and the North Germanic Hanseatic merchants in 1587 and 1598 respectively are taken as symbols of the upsurge of Tudor commerce. See, for example, Christopher Hill, *Reformation to Industrial Revolution*. (Pelican pbck.; 1969), 74; W.E. Minchinton (ed.), *The Growth of English Overseas Trade in the 17th and 18th Centuries* (London, 1969), 2-3; Roger Lockyer, *Tudor and Stuart Britain, 1471-1714* (New York, 1971), 147. But W.G. Hoskins places the amount of English trade in the hands of foreigners to be from 40 to 50% at the beginning of the 16th century. *The Age of Plunder: The England of Henry VIII 1500-1547*. (Longman pbck., 1976) esp. chapters 7-8. See also E.M. Carus-Wilson, *Medieval Merchant Venturers*, second edition. (London, 1967), xv-xxxiv, esp. xxvii.
9. J.B. Black, *The Reign of Elizabeth, 1558-1603*, 2nd. ed. (Oxford, 1959), 236.
10. Edmund S. Morgan, *American Slavery-American Freedom* (New York, 1975),

58-70; Hill, *Reformation to Industrial Revolution*, 98. On the other hand, Joan Thirsk, *Economic Policy and Projects* (Oxford, 1978), 159, 160, notes that "the productive capacity of labour was not yet being absorbed," not because of laziness but rather in relationship to "rising population and price inflation." Yet, she goes on to state: "the history of projects and projectors (in the 16th century) mirrors the undertakings of businessmen whose energies were stimulated by inflation; out of their adventures flowed the beneficial consequences of work for the poor." Harry A. Miskimin, *The Economy of Later Renaissance Europe, 1460-1600* (Cambridge, 1977) asserts, "England's industrial growth during the 16th century proceeded faster and was more broadly based than that of any other major State in Europe," 77. On the difficulty of generalizing about English farmworkers because of their variety, see Eric Kerridge, *The Farmers of Old England* (Totowa, N.J., 1973), esp. 55-66.

11. For a different view of the Elizabethans, see A.L. Rowse, *The England of Elizabeth* (London, 1964), Ch. VI, *passim*.

12. Hill, *Reformation to Industrial Revolution*, 19. See also, Mervyn James. *English Policies and the Concept of Honour, 1485-1642, Past and Present*, Supplement 3, 1978.

13. The expansion of trade was persisting but not linear. Charles Wilson, *England's Apprenticeship, 1603-1763*, (New York, 1963); Minchinton, *Growth of English Overseas Trade;* E.A. Wrigley, "A Sample Model of London's Importance in a Changing English Society and Economy, 1650-1750," *Past and Present*, 37 (1967), 44-70.

14. Eric Kerridge, *The Agricultural Revolution*, (London, 1967), esp. 347-348; Hill, *Reformation to Industrial Revolution*, 146-154; E.L. Jones, "Agriculture and Economic Change, 1660-1750," *Essays in Agrarian History*, edited by W.E. Minchinton, (Newton Abbot, 1968), 205-219; H.J. Habakkuk, "Economic Functions of English Landowners in the 17th and 18th centuries," *Ibid.*, 189-194; and Joan Thirsk, *Economic Policy*, esp. 161-167. For an informative overview see Arthur Joseph Slavin, *The Precarious Balance, English Government and Society, 1450-1640*, (New York, 1973), esp. Chapter 7.

15. The most famous and influential celebration of the English Constitution came in Montesquieu's *Spirit of the Laws*. Peter Gay, *The Enlightenment: An Interpretation*, Vol. II, *The Science of Freedom*, (New York, 1969), 469-470, 325. Voltaire also praised it in his famous *Lettres Philosophiques*, published in 1734.

16. Keith Thomas, *Religion and Decline of Magic*, (New York, 1971), 661, explains the change as "not so much technological as mental. In many different spheres of life the period [the 17th century] saw the emergence of a new faith in the potentialities of human initiatives." Some historians see a new spirit of ingenuity, burst of energy or "modern" outlook as existing in the reign of Henry VIII, if not earlier. See for example, E.A. Wrigley, "The Process of Modernization and the Industrial Revolution," *The Journal of Interdisciplinary History*, 3: 2 (1972), esp. 244. Macfarlane's central point in *The Origins of English Individualism* is that the English small landowner exhibited a "modern" outlook from at least the 13th century.

17. Alan Booth, "Food Riots in the North-West of England, 1790-1801," *Past and Present*, 77 (1977), 84-107.

18. The paradigm of "deep change" has been introduced and defined by David H. Fischer, *Growing Old in America*, expanded edition, (New York, 1978), 100, as "change in the rate of change—an alteration which is at once discontinuous in its nature and transforming in its effect. . . . It customarily happens abruptly, but its full effects are often felt very slowly on the surface of history."

19. Kerridge, *Agricultural Revolution*, 24.

# FOOTNOTES

20. The classic account of the negative impact of enclosures can be found in Thomas More's *Utopia*, Book I, which was written in 1515-16. For an effort to reach a balanced assessment of the negative concomitants of rural change, see Wilson, *England's Apprenticeship*, 141-159, 243-262. Some important recent attempts to view rural change from the bottom up, especially through the prism of 18th-century criminal justice, include Douglas Hay, et al., *Albion's Fatal Tree*, (New York, 1975), esp. Ch. 5, and E.P. Thompson, *Whigs and Hunters; The Origin of the Black Act*, (New York, 1975).

21. The impact of industrialization on the first generation of English factory workers has begun to be re-examined from the perspective of the new family history. See especially Michael Anderson, *Family Structure in 19th-Century Lancashire* (London, 1971). For an interesting analysis of the relationship between modernization and the industrial revolution, see Wrigley, "The Process of Modernization."

22. The planning that propertied families put into it, the various legal instruments that were invented to facilitate and control it, the amount of legislation that regulated it, and the measurable material and social significance modern scholarship has attributed to it, all suggest to us the validity of this conclusion regarding the role of marriage formation to early moderns. Still, our impression is exactly that, an impression that in the end may be more a reflection of the emphasis recent scholarship has given to early modern marriage making than of the actual preoccupations of most early moderns themselves.

23. Examples abound in the popular media. Typical are such cover stories as, "The American Family: Can It Survive Today's Shocks," *U.S. News and World Report* (October 27, 1975); "The American Family in Trouble," *Psychology Today* (May, 1977); "Who's Raising the Kids?" *Newsweek* (September 22, 1975). For countervailing arguments that predict a positive future, see Mary Jo Bane, *Here to Stay: American Families in the Twentieth Century* (New York, 1976); Martin H. Quitt, "The Contemporary 'Crisis' of the American Family," *The Journal of Psychohistory*, 4: 1 (1976) 101-110; Vivian C. Fox, "The Rise of Women's Equality and Mythical Decline of the Family," *Psychohistory: Bulletin of the International Psychohistory Association*, 2: 2 (1978), 23-27. For a mix of views see John A. Clausen, "American Research in the Family and Socialization," *Children Today*, 7, No. 2 (March-April, 1978), 7-10, 46.

24. Eleanor D. Macklin, "Heterosexual Cohabitation Among College Students," *The Family Coordinator*, 21: 4 (1972), 463-472, esp. 465-466.

25. Bane, *Here to Stay*, 22. Internationally, however, "during the 25 years ending in the early 1960s, the trend was toward marriage at lower ages." Hugh Carter and Paul C. Glick, *Marriage and Divorce: A Social and Economic Study*, revised edition (Cambridge, Mass., 1976), 26.

26. Arthur J. Norton and Paul C. Glick, "Marital Instability: Past, Present and Future," *Journal of Social Issues*, 32: 1 (1976), 5-20. U.S. Bureau of the Census, *Current Population Reports*, Series P-20, No. 323, "Marital Status and Living Arrangements: March, 1977" (Washington, D.C., 1978), 2, estimates that despite the continuing postponement in the age at first marriage, "as in the recent past . . . about 95 percent of all adults will ever marry."

27. Alan Macfarlane, "The Informal Social Control of Marriage in Seventeenth Century England: Some Preliminary Notes," below, Part II, Chapter I; Robert V. Wells, "Quaker Marriage Patterns in Colonial Perspective," *William and Mary Quarterly*, 3d ser., (1972), 415-442; John R. Gillis, *Youth and History* (New York, 1974), 14.

28. The seminal work here was J. Hajnal, "European Marriage Patterns in Perspective," in *Population in History*, edited by D.V. Glass and D.E.C. Eversley (London, 1965), 101-143. See also a critique of Hajnal's work in Macfarlane, *The*

*Origins of English Individualism*, 156-158.

29. Paul C. Glick, "Updating the Life Cycle of the Family," *Journal of Marriage and the Family*, 39:1 (1977), 5-13. "In 1977 the estimated median age at first marriage was 24.0 for men and 21.6 for women. . . . These figures represent an increase for both sexes of 1 full year since the mid-1960s." *Current Population Reports*, Series P-20, No. 323, "Marital Status," 2.

30. Hajnal, "European Marriage Patterns," 101.

31. The median ages at first marriage for men and women in 1956 were the lowest recorded in the history of the United States—22.5 years for men and 20.1 for women. Since that time, however, the median age at first marriage for both men and women has increased, as indicated in Note 29 above. Compare these U.S. Census computations to the higher mean age for before 1890 compiled from historians' samples, as found in Fischer, *Growing Old in America*, 279, Table VI. See also Rudy Ray Seward, *The American Family: A Demographic History*, Sage Library of Social Research, Vol. 70 (Beverly Hills and London, 1978), 55, Table.

32. Roger Thompson, *Women in Stuart England and America*, (London and Boston, 1974), 114; Lawrence Stone, *The Crisis of the Aristocracy, 1558-1641* (Oxford, 1965), 612-613; Lu Emily Pearson, *Elizabethans at Home* (Stanford, 1957), 279-361, *passim*; Edmund S. Morgan, *The Puritan Family*, revised edition (Harper Torchbook, 1966), Chapters II and VI, *passim*; Julia C. Spruill, *Women's Life and Work in the Southern Colonies* (Norton pbck., 1972), 136-137.

33. John M. Murrin, "Review Essay," *History and Theory*, XI: 2 (1972), 273.

34. Local authorities often found it difficult to distinguish between professional vagabonds and those who migrated in search of work. In either case, early moderns attested to the large amount of migrant peoples in their communities. Paul Slack, "Poverty and Politics in Salisbury," *Crisis and Order in English Towns, 1500-1700*, edited by Peter Clark and Paul Slack, (London, 1972), 165-167; Peter Clark, "The Migrants in Kentish Towns 1500-1700," *Ibid.*, esp. 138-146; Geoffrey W. Oxley, *Poor Relief in England and Wales 1601-1834* (London, 1974), esp. Chapter 6; Ivy Pinchbeck and Margaret Hewitt, *Children in English Society*, Vol. I (London, 1969), Chapters 5 and 7.

35. David H. Flaherty, *Privacy in Colonial New England* (Charlottesville, 1972), 175-179; Morgan, *Puritan Family*, 145-146. On the growth of solitary households in contemporary America, see Frances E. Kobrin, "The Fall in Household Size and Rise of Primary Individual in the United States," in *The American Family in Social-Historical Perspective*, edited by Michael Gordon, 2nd edition (New York, 1978), 69-81. Laslett contends that "almost no young men and women (were) living on their own." The exception to the relatively few who lived alone were the solitary widows. See Peter Laslett, *The World We Have Lost*, 2nd edition (London, 1971), 11. See also 262, Note 17. Elsewhere, Laslett elucidates further: "Just over 1% of the population of pre-industrial England seem to have lived as solitaries, and of them a good third (35.2%) are marked as widowed in the 78 lists containing such information." Laslett, however, believes this figure is low, that 50% would be more accurate, *Family Life and Illicit Love in Earlier Generations* (Cambridge, 1977), 199.

36. Philip V. Greven, *Four Generations: Population, Land, and Family in Colonial Andover, Massachusetts* (Ithaca, N.Y., 1970), 121, 207-208; John J. Waters, "The Traditional World of the New England Peasants: A View from Seventeenth-Century Barnstable," *The New England Historical and Geneological Register*, CXXX (1976), 3-22.

37. This of course refers only to those families who could endow their children with material wealth. We know more about such practices among wealthier families. See for example Lawrence Stone, *The Crisis of the Aristocracy, 1558-1641* (Ox-

ford, 1965), esp. 632-645. A 17th-century English Clergyman, Ralph Josselin, spent £700 or 12% of his total lifetime income on the dowries of his daughters. Alan Macfarlane, *The Family Life of Ralph Josselin* (Cambridge, 1970), 39, Table 51. Tenants living on their landlords' property could endow their children only if the landlords allowed them to. See Mervyn James, *Family Lineage and Civil Society: Politics and Mentality in the Durham Region, 1500-1640* (Oxford, 1974), 27-28. Macfarlane has a different view about the relationship of tenants to their landlords and its implications for the tenants' heirs. See his *Origins of English Individualism*, Chapter 5.

38. R. Thompson, "Seventeenth-Century English and Colonial Sex Ratios: A Postscript," *Population Studies*, 28: 1 (1974), 163-165; Herbert Moller "Sex Composition and Correlated Culture Patterns of Colonial America," *William and Mary Quarterly*, 3d ser., II (1945), 113-153.

39. Martin H. Quitt, Virginia House of Burgesses, 1660-1710: The Social Educational and Economic Bases of Political Power, (Ph.D. diss., Washington University, 1970), Appendix IV; Lois G. Carr and Lorena S. Walsh, "The Planter's Wife: The Experience of White Women in Seventeenth-Century Maryland," *William and Mary Quarterly*, 3d. ser., XXXIV (1977), 542-571.

40. The suggestion is John M. Murrin's, made at a Boston University Colloquium in Early American History and Culture (November, 1978).

41. A suggestive literary documentation of the imbalanced sex ratio in 18th-century London and its effect on the status of women is Ian Watt, *The Rise of the Novel* (Berkeley, Cal., 1957), 138-149, 154-164. In 1695 there were 87 men for every 100 women in London. D.V. Glass, "Notes on the Demography of London," *Daedalus*, 97: 2 (1968), 581-592, esp. Table 4.

42. Norton and Glick, "Marital Instability," 10; Carter and Glick, *Marriage and Divorce*, 81.

43. *Ibid.*, 82.

44. The reasons for people not marrying, both in the West and outside, have not been adequately investigated. Perhaps what has distinguished the West has been the opportunity *not* to marry. In some primitive cultures, for example, to remain unmarried is to risk calamity because the conjugal unit is so vital to the very survival of both individuals and the group. Claude Levi-Strauss, *The Elementary Structures of Kinship*, 2d. ed. (London, 1969), 38-39. See also Hajnal's discussion in "European Marriage Patterns in Perspective," esp. 105-106.

45. This schema draws on a lecture by Paul Lucas at Washington University in 1964. See also, Robert R. Palmer, "Man and Citizen: Applications of Individualism in the French Revolution," in Milton R. Konvitz and Arthur E. Murphy, *Essays in Political Theory*, (New York, 1948), 130. For an analysis of how a particular area in England developed into a civil society, see James, *Family Lineage*, esp. 177-198. For an overview see Lawrence Stone, *The Family, Sex and Marriage in England, 1500-1800* (New York, 1977), esp. Chapter 6, "The Growth of Affective Individualism." Macfarlane's recent book, *Origins of English Individualism*, offers a different perspective.

46. Winthrop D. Jordan, *White Over Black: American Attitudes Toward the Negro, 1550-1812* (Chapel Hill, 1968), 139-140.

47. Gerald Leslie, *The Family in Social Context*, 3rd. ed., (New York and London, 1976), 507. In 1967 the U.S. Supreme Court struck down state laws forbidding miscegenation and intermarriage, *Ibid*. According to the 1977 Census, as reported in *Parade*, "The number of marriages between blacks and whites increased 92% in the years 1970-77; the number of marriages between black husbands and white wives increased by 132% . . . , marriages between white husbands and black wives increased 25%. *Parade*, February 25, 1979, 17. Despite the increase, the

percentage of interracial marriages remain infinitesimally small. For a discussion of recent trends in U.S., see Carter and Glick, *Marriage and Divorce*, Chapter 5.

48. Stone, *The Family, Sex and Marriage in England*, 491.

49. In the 18th-century South, "Men discussed marriage as a means of obtaining pecuniary advantages, with surprising frankness." Spruill, *Women's Life and Work in the Southern Colonies*, 155. While Benjamin Franklin denounced mercenary matches, he saw "no harm in a realistic discussion before marriage about respective economic resources and expectations. Such discussion avoided trouble and disappointment later on." Sidney Ditzion, *Marriage Morals and Sex in America* (New York, 1953), 25. On colonial attitudes see also J. William Frost, *The Quaker Family in Colonial America* (New York, 1973), Chapter 8; and Morgan, *The Puritan Family*, 52. On English attitudes from the 16th through 18th centuries, see Pearson, *Elizabethans at Home*, 297; Thompson, *Women in Stuart England and America*, 116-117; Miriam Slater, "The Weightiest Business: Marriage in an Upper-Class Family in Seventeenth-Century England," *Past and Present*, 72 (1976), 25-54; and Stone, *The Family, Sex and Marriage in England*, 60-62, 88-89, 128, 394, 491.

50. *Ibid.*, 394.

51. The terms are used respectively by J.H. Plumb, *The Growth of Political Stability in England, 1675-1725* (London, 1967), Ch. 3; Robert R. Palmer *The Age of the Democratic Revolution: The Challenge* (Princeton, 1959), 23 and Ch. X-XIV; E.P. Thompson, "Patrician Society, Plebian Culture," *Journal of Social History*, 7: 4 (1974), 382-405, esp. 388.

52. For an excellent brief discussion of Hardwicke's Act and the history of the English laws governing marriage, see Stone, *The Family, Sex and Marriage*, 30-37. To place the English laws against a broader European perspective, see Mary Ann Glendon, "Legal Concepts of Marriage and the Family," Part II, Ch. 1, below. See also her, *State, Law and Family: Family Law in Transition in the United States and Western Europe* (North-Holland, 1977), esp. Ch. 7; Beatrice Gottlieb, Getting Married in Pre-Reformation Europe: The Doctrine of Clandestine Marriage in Fifteenth-Century Champagne, (Ph.D. Diss., Columbia University, 1974), *passim*; R. Helmholz, *Marriage Litigation in Medieval England* (Cambridge, 1957), esp. 27-31.

53. This conclusion has been suggested by varied kinds of evidence. Keith Thomas has noted, for example, that while dress functioned as a significant delineator of class identity, the coercion of conformity to the dress code ceased by the end of the 17th century, when sumptuary legislation was set aside, "Dress and the Social Order in Early Modern England," (paper read at Brandeis University, April, 1978). Differences in dress continued, only the need to externally impose them ended. At the same time historians have observed the growth of a deepening class consciousness on the part of the English aristocracy, indeed on the part of the upper classes everywhere in Europe beginning in the late 17th century. (See sources in Note 51 above.) Finally, this internalization seems to us to be a part of what Norbert Elias refers to as "the civilizing process," whereby a new code of civil behavior and self-control, first urged upon the literate classes by humanists in the 16th century, was increasingly assimilated especially by the middle and upper classes whose children were deliberately socialized in its rubrics. Proper conduct and class identity became intimately associated. *The Civilizing Process: The History of Manners* (New York, 1978). See Note 82 below, also.

54. This theme of declining parental control over marital choice in the 18th century is a central one in Stone, *The Family, Sex and Marriage*. He stresses that the evidence points toward "a trend, not uniformity of behaviour," (317). But note critics of Stone who argue for greater participant control earlier, especially but not

# FOOTNOTES

exclusively among the lower orders. J.H. Plumb, Review Essay, *New York Review of Books*, 24:19 (Nov. 24, 1977), 30-36.

55. Bernard Bailyn, "Politics and Social Structure in Virginia," in *Seventeenth-Century America*, edited by James M. Smith (Chapel Hill, 1959), 90-118; Quitt, Virginia House of Burgesses, Ch. 1.

56. The classic account of the ruling class in pre-Revolutionary Virginia is Charles S. Sydnor, *Gentlemen Freeholders* (Chapel Hill, 1952).

57. Morgan, *Puritan Family*, 55-56.

58. John J. Waters, "Hingham, Massachusetts, 1631-1661: An East Anglian Oligarchy in the New World," *Journal of Social History*, 1:4 (1968), 351-370.

59. The increasing stratification of northern metropolises, sometimes referred to as "the progress of inequality," between the 17th century and the Revolution is a common theme in recent urban historiography. James A. Henretta, "Economic Development and Social Structure in Colonial Boston," *William and Mary Quarterly*, 3rd ser., XXII (1965), 75-92; Alan Kulikoff, "The Progress of Inequality in Revolutionary Boston," *William and Mary Quarterly*, 3rd ser. XXVIII (1971), 375-412; Gary B. Nash, "Urban Wealth and Poverty in Pre-Revolutionary America," *Journal of Interdisciplinary History*, VI: 4 (1976), 545-584, and "Up From the Bottom in Franklin's Philadelphia," *Past and Present*, 77, (1977), 57-83. For a dissenting view regarding Boston, however, see G.B. Warden, "Inequality and Instability in Eighteenth-century Boston: A Reappraisal," *Journal of Interdisciplinary History*, VI: 4, (1976), 585-620.

60. Urban populations in colonial America can only be roughly estimated. The most comprehensive treatment or urban growth before the Revolution remains Carl Bridenbaugh, *Cities in the Wilderness: Urban Life in America, 1625-1742*, (pbck., New York, 1964). For his estimates on population increases in major cities, see *Cities in the Wilderness*, 6, 143, 305, and *Cities in Revolt*, 216, 217.

61. Jackson T. Main, *The Social Structure of Revolutionary America* (Princeton, 1965).

62. Leslie, *The Family in Social Context*, 505; Shorter, *Making of the Modern Family*, 152-154; John Sirjamaki, *The American Family in the Twentieth Century* (Cambridge, Mass., 1953), 66-68.

63. Leslie, *The Family in Social Context*, 505.

64. In England, Stone indicates that personal choice in marriage did exist even among the nobility in the 16th and 17th centuries, albeit in a limited group. He observes that these love-matches usually ran in families and were possible if a father were not alive or if a young man were at Court. Stone, *Crisis of the Aristocracy*, 609.

65. Stone, *The Family, Sex and Marriage*, Ch. 7. Utopian literature of the entire early modern period came out strongly against forced marriage. See Vivian C. Fox, Deviance in English Utopias, (Ph.D. diss., Boston University, 1969), 89-98.

66. H.J. Habakkuk, "Marriage Settlements in the Eighteenth Century," *Transactions of the Royal Historical Society*, XXXII 1950), 15-30.

67. See below, 56.

68. Greven, *Four Generations*, 229-231.

69. Daniel S. Smith, "Parental Power and Marriage Patterns: An Analysis of Historical Trends in Hingham, Massachusetts," *Journal of Marriage and the Family*, 35 (1973), 419-429.

70. Peter D. Hall, "Marital Selection and Business in Massachusetts Merchant Families, 1700-1900," in *The Family and Its Structure and Functions*, edited by Rose L. Coser (New York, 1974), 226-242.

71. The following "preferred estimates" of the life expectancy of different samples of Chesapeake *men* are computed by the same method, as suggested by Lorena S. Walsh and Russell S. Menard, "Death in the Chesapeake: Two Life Tables for

71

Men in Early Colonial Maryland," *Maryland Historical Magazine* LXIX (1974), 211-227.

| Sample of Men | Age | Preferred Estimated Life Expectancy |
|---|---|---|
| Maryland Immigrants in 17th Century | 22 | 22.7[a] |
| Born in Charles County, Md., 1652-99 | 20 | 26.0[b] |
| Born in Charles Parish, Va., 1665-99 | 20 | 20.8[c] |
| Born in Southern Maryland, 1690-1729 | 22 | 35.3[d] |

(a) *Ibid.*, 214; (b) *Ibid.*, 213; (c) Daniel Blake Smith, "Mortality and Family in the Colonial Chesapeake," *Journal of Interdisciplinary History*, VIII: 3 (Winter, 1978), 403-437, Table 3; (d) Allan L. Kulikoff, Tobacco and Slaves: Population Economy and Society in Eighteenth Century Prince George's County, Maryland (Ph.D. diss., Brandeis University, 1976), 439. The improvement in life expectancy during the 18th century should not be overstated. Nancy L. Oberseider, A Socio-Demographic Study of the Family as a Social Unit in Tidewater, Virginia, 1660-1776, (Ph.D. diss., University of Maryland, 1975), 294, for example, finds that 69% of the men whose deaths are recorded in the North Farnum/Lunenberg, Virginia register, 1711-1788, died under the age of 50.

72. The early assumption of adult responsibilities and autonomy by the underage sons of deceased members of the elite in 17th-century Virginia is suggested by Martin H. Quitt, From Elite to Aristocracy: The Psychodynamic Transformation of the Virginia Ruling Class, (paper read at the Second Summer Workshop of the Institute for Psychohistory at New York, July, 1976). The death of a father in general freed sons from the patriarchal influence in England as well as in Virginia. In 1771 when Thomas Weld came of age he wooed and married Mary Massey Stanley; because his father had died he did not have to gain his approval. Nevertheless, in a letter to his older brother describing his future wife it is apparent that the values of the gentry class of which he was a member had been internalized. Joan Berkeley, *Lulworth and the Welds* (Dorset, 1971), 149. See also Vivian C. Fox, *The Catholic Paternity of Thomas Weld* (forthcoming).

73. Fairfax Downey, *Our Lusty Forefathers* (New York, 1947), 13-32. Edmund S. Morgan, *Virginians at Home* (Williamsburg, Va., 1952), 34.

74. Smith, "Parental Power and Marriage Patterns;" Thompson, *Women in Stuart England and America*, 116-117. Certainly this appears to have been the parentally sanctioned view among the propertied elite, although they were exposed as well to an ideal of romantic love that was propagated by poets and playwrights. (Stone, *Family, Sex and Marriage*, 180-181.) The non-propertied may have subscribed to the value of sexual attachment, however, Christopher Hill, "Sex, Marriage, and the Family in England," *Economic History Review*, 2nd. ser., XXXI: 3 (1978), 458.

75. These personal qualities are impressed upon us from our readings of the period. They are meant to be suggestive rather than definitive. For an excellent discussion of the personal qualities that English education strived to inculcate, see Lawrence A. Cremin, *American Education* (New York, 1970), 31-79. Pearson, *Elizabethans at Home* offers a mine of literary evidence as to the personal qualities admired by the age. These desired personal qualities changed only slowly and subtly over time. In 19th-century America, for example, Barbara Welter identifies the following qualities in women's periodicals that were held up for the True Woman: piety, purity, submissiveness, and domesticity. "The Cult of True Womanhood: 1820-1860," *American Quarterly* (Summer, 1966), 151-174. Compare this true woman ideal with that uncovered by Laurel T. Ulrich, Virtuous Women Found:

# FOOTNOTES

New England Ministerial Literature, 1668-1735," *American Quarterly*, 28 (1976), 20-40.

76. Protestantism (especially Calvinism), with its emphasis on original sin, did not generally regard the passions as reliable guides to behavior. Indeed, the relationship between religious ideology before 1700 and marital selection cannot be underestimated. For example, there was an intimate connection between the Quakers' doctrine of the inner light, in which they posited the presence of God dwelling within the individual, and their stress upon the importance of love as a crucial criterion for marital choice. Frost, *The Quaker Family in Colonial America*, 14-15, 153, 162-163; Barry Levy, "Tender Plants: Quaker Farmers and Children in the Delaware Valley, 1681-1735," *Journal of Family History*, 3: 2 (1978), 116-135, esp. 121. Utopian literature throughout the early modern period also emphasized sensible choice in marital selection. Terms such as love and adoration were not part of the vocabulary of utopian families. The emphasis was on careful and rational selection of mates. Yet we should not preclude the importance of the passions. Thomas More urged couples to view each other in the nude before they married. Fox, Deviance, Ch. 3, section on "The Role of the Family." See also by the same author, "Deviance in Some English Utopias, Sixteenth to Eighteenth Centuries," *Humboldt Journal of Social Relations*, 2: 2 (1975), 14-20. Kathleen M. Davies has examined the prevailing marriage ethics in England from about the mid 15th century to the 17th and found that those among the Puritan bourgeoisie did not substantially differ from those of earlier Catholics. "The Sacred Condition of Equality—How Original Were Puritan Doctrines of Marriage?" *Social History*, V (1977), 563-578.

77. Stone, *The Family, Sex and Marriage*, Ch. 8-9. Hill argues against this view and cites Davies, "Sacred Condition of Equality," in the belief that the late 17th century did not contribute a different marriage ethic. Moreover, Peter Laslett suggests that the unusual feature of Western marriages, especially in England, was the similarity of the ages of the spouses as compared with other cultures. In Laslett's view this fostered a "companionate marriage," a characteristic identifiable for the entire early modern period. Stone, in contrast, suggests that companionate marriages is a mid to late 17th-century development. Although Laslett does not delineate this term as carefully as does Stone, nevertheless his usage is roughly similar to Stone's. (Laslett, *Family Life and Illicit Love*, 12-49.) Moreover, as we suggest below (38-39), "the fact that the couple would live by themselves after marriage meant that their compatibility had to be factored into the process of marriage formation, no matter how much parents wanted to intercede."

78. Joseph E. Illick, "Child-Bearing in Seventeenth-Century England and America," in deMause, ed., *History of Childhood*, 303-350, esp. 318-320. Stone, *The Family, Sex and Marriage*, 267, 424, 280-281. For the influence of Locke's psychology on Edward's theology, see Perry Miller, *Jonathan Edwards* (pbck. New York, 1959), 52-67.

79. Gay, *The Enlightenment*, II, 32.

80. The starkest argument comes from Shorter, *The Making of the Modern Family*, who contends that romantic love, defined "as the capacity for spontaneity and empathy in an erotic relationship," did not exist in the West before the "Great Transformation" of modernization, which began generally after 1750 but perhaps earlier in England and America (15, 21).

81. David Hunt, *Parents and Children in History: The Psychology of Family Life in Early Modern France* (New York, 1970), 60-67, stresses the importance of love in marriage formation in 17th-century France. French historians have been particularly insistent on the importance of sexuality in early times. For examples, see, J.L. Flandrin, "Repression and Change in the Sexual Life of Young People in

Medieval and Early Modern Times." *Journal of Family History*, 2: 3 (1977), 196-210; Emmanuel LeRoy Ladurie, *Montaillou: The Promised Land of Error* (New York, 1978), Ch. VIII-XI for sex and sexuality inside and outside marriage in a 14th-century French village. Some English historians have also stressed the importance of passion in marriage formation earlier. See Alan Macfarlane's review of Stone's *The Family, Sex and Marriage* in *History and Theory*, XVIII: 1 (1979), 103-126, esp. 107-108.

82. Stone, *The Family, Sex and Marriage*, 781-787. Peter Gay writes that "as the power of conscience had grown, the passions had been safer; as reason tightened its hold, sensuality improved its reputation. It was precisely the growth of the superego in Western culture that made greater sexual freedom possible," *The Enlightenment*, II, 204-205. Other historians, however, tend to interpret what Gay has identified as the growth of conscience somewhat differently. For example, Flandrin views the early modern period as more repressive sexually than earlier centuries, "Repression and Change." See also Elias, *The Civilizing Process, passim*. Keith Thomas believes that the English never had one attitude toward sex; rather different classes had very different perspectives. "The Double Standard," *Journal of the History of Ideas*, XX (1959), 195-216, esp. 206.

83. Morton M. Hunt, *The Natural History of Love* (New York, 1959), 356-358.

84. Thomas, "The Double Standard," 206.

85. See Note 81 above.

86. Leslie, *The Family in Social Context*.

87. Thomas, "The Double Standard," *passim*; Stone, *Crisis of the Aristocracy*, 662-668; Stone, *The Family, Sex and Marriage*, 281-287, 501-507; Pearson, *Elizabethans at Home*, 301-304.

88. Figures relating to divorce in the U.S. today are often cruder than the public realizes. Inferences based on available data cannot be drawn too cautiously. For a sound treatment of the use of these data, see Leslie, *The Family in Social Conflict*, 676-691. The relationship between duration of marriage and divorce remains in need of up to date treatment, *Ibid.*, 686-688, 547. See also U.S. Bureau of the Census, *Current Population Report*, Series P-20, No. 297, "Number, Timing, and Duration of Marriages and Divorces in the United States: June, 1975," (Washington, D.C., 1976), 13. In England little analysis has been carried out on marital instability or divorce. However, one study seems to indicate a different divorce pattern exists there from that of the U.S. Within one cohort of couples who married during 1960-65, divorces occurred at later stages of the family cycle, increasing more than four-fold from the fourth year of marriage through the ninth year. Robert Chester, "Divorce," in *The Sociology of Modern Britain*, edited by Eric Butterworth and David Weir, rev. ed. (Fontana Books, 1976), 59-65. On divorces between childless couples in England, see Geoffrey Gorer, *Sex and Marriage in England Today* (Panther pbck., 1971), 226.

89. Morgan, *Virginians at Home*, 48.

90. "In Britain . . . the drop in female employment still occurs at the time of childbirth and, although participation rates for mothers with children of preschool age increased from 18 to 27 percent between 1966 and 1976, it is among older married women that the increased rates have been so dramatic." Hilary Hand, "The Changing Place of Women in Europe," *Daedalus*, (Spring, 1979), 76. In America, "in 1974 the 25-54 category of wives with husbands present had a 34 percent workforce participation if they had children under 6 years, but 60 percent if they had none under 18 years . . . this general pattern holds in all capitalist nations." Gabriel Kolko, "Working Women: Their Effect on the Structure of the Working Class," *Science and Society*, XLII, No. 3 (Fall, 1978), 266.

91. According to the U.S. Census of 1970, "among persons who first married between

# FOOTNOTES

1901 and 1970, the proportion of men who were divorced after their first marriage was more than twice as high for those who married before the age of 20 as for those who married in their late 20s . . . " Norton and Glick, "Marital Instability," 9.

92. Daniel J. Levinson, *The Seasons of a Man's Life* (New York, 1978), 106-108.

93. Leslie, *The Family in Social Context*, Ch. 15.

94. The now classic work on the predominance of the nuclear household is Peter Laslett, (ed.), *Household and Family in Past Time* (Cambridge, 1972). But see Laslett's own updating of the matter of household types in his *Family Life and Illicit Love in Earlier Generations* (Cambridge, 1977), Ch. 1.

95. Stone, *Crisis of the Aristocracy*, 634.

96. Greven, *Four Generations, passim*; Smith, "Parental Power and Marriage Patterns;" Seward, *The American Family*, 57-61; Michael Anderson, "The Family and Industrialization in Western Europe," The Forum Series, FE 147 (St. Louis, 1978), 5-6. But Linda Auwers, "Fathers, Sons, and Wealth in Colonial Windsor, Connecticut," *Journal of Family History*, 3: 2 (1978), 141, finds no evidence of economic manipulation by fathers in forcing sons to delay marriage by withholding economic independence.

97. Pearson, *Elizabethans at Home*, especially Ch. 5. Morgan, *The Puritan Family*, 39-48. Gordon J. Schochet, *Patriarchalism in Political Thought; The Authoritarian Family and Political Speculation and Attitudes Especially in Seventeenth-Century England* (New York, 1975), *passim*. Not all women subscribed to their prescribed subservience. See, for example, Keith Thomas, "Women and the Civil War Sects," in *Crisis in Europe 1560-1660*, edited by Trevor Aston (New York, 1967), 332-357; Lyle Koehler, "The Case of the American Jezebels: Anne Hutchinson and Female Agitation During the Years of the Antinomian Turmoil, 1636-1640;" *William and Mary Quarterly*, 3rd ser., XXXI: 1 (1974), 55-78. Koehler concludes that while the rebellion of Hutchinson and her followers was not "directed self-consciously against their collective female situation or toward its improvement . . . antinomianism was simply an ideology through which the resentments they instinctively felt could be focused and actively expressed," (78).

98. The impact of marriage upon the mobility of small planters is described by Paul G.E. Clemens, "Economy and Society on Maryland's Eastern Shore, 1689-1733," in *Law, Society and Politics in Early Maryland*, edited by Aubrey C. Land, Lois G. Carr, and Edward C. Papenfuse (Baltimore and London, 1977), 153-171, esp. 157, 160.

99. Spruill, *Women's Life and Work*, Ch. IV; Eileen Power, *Medieval Women*, edited by M.M. Postan (New York and Cambridge, 1974), especially Ch. 3; David Levine, *Family Foundation in an Age of Transient Capitalism* (New York, 1977), *passim*; Louise A. Tilly, Joan W. Scott, and Miriam Cohen, "Women's Work and European Fertility Patterns," *The Journal of Interdisciplinary History*, VI: 3 (1976), 447-476.

100. The effect of industrialism in the late 18th and 19th centuries on women is portrayed by Eli Zaretsky, *Capitalism, The Family and Personal Life* (New York, 1976), Ch. 3; Nancy F. Cott, *The Bonds of Womanhood "Women's Sphere" in New England, 1780-1835* (New Haven, 1977), Ch. 1 and 2.

101. Pearson, *Elizabethans at Home*, Ch. VI.

102. W.B. Gwyn, *The Meaning of the Separation of Powers*, Tulane Studies in Political Science, Vol. IX (New Orleans, 1965); M.J.C. Vile, *Constitutionalism and the Separation of Powers* (Oxford, 1967), esp. Ch. II-IV.

103. Shorter, *Making of the Modern Family*, 68; Pearson, *Elizabethans at Home*, Ch. 6; Thomas, "The Double Standard."

104. Thomas More, *Utopia*, edited by Edward Surtz and J.H. Hexter (New Haven,

1965), Book II; Schochet, *Patriarchialism*, Ch. 3.

105. Eileen Power describes the legal position held by upper class women in the Middle Ages when she says: "the fact which governed her position was not her personality but her sex, and by her sex she was inferior to men." *Medieval Women*, 10. Schochet implies this position continued as patriarchalism developed and reached its highest point in 17th-century England, *Patriarchalism, passim*. See also Thompson, *Women in Stuart England and America*, 162-168; Keith Thomas, "The Double Standard," *passim*; Jeremy Taylor, *Married Life* (1653), in *In God's Name, Examples of Preaching in England, 1534-1662*, edited by John Chandes (Indianapolis, 1971), 505-511. Yet there existed an interesting contradiction in English law: An unmarried woman or widow—the femme sole—had under private law much the same rights as men. She could hold land, make contracts and carry on business, whereas once she married most of these rights became her husband's. F. Pollock and F.W. Maitland, *The History of English Law*, Vol. II, 2nd. ed. (Cambridge, 1968), 390-392.

106. Davies, "The Sacred Condition of Equality." *passim* but esp. 565, 568.

107. M. Young and P. Willmott, "The Symmetrical Family," in *The Sociology of Modern Britain*, ed. by Butterworth and Weir, 24-34.

108. Although the word honeymoon was used as early as the 16th century in England to refer to newlyweds, it did not take on its modern meaning until the 19th century, according to the *OED*.

109. Philip Greven, *The Protestant Temperament* (New York, 1977), esp. Ch. VII.

110. Elias, *The Civilizing Process*; Pearson, *Elizabethans at Home*; Jones, "English Politics and the Concept of Honour," 56-68; Joan Simon, *Education and Society in Tudor England* (Cambridge, 1967), esp. Ch. II. A.L. Rowse, *The Elizabethan Renaissance: Life of a Society* (New York, 1971) depicts a society eager for wealth, fun, and luxury as well as being enterprising.

111. Stone, *The Family, Sex and Marriage*, 334-6.

112. Paul C. Glick, "Updating the LIfe Cycle of the Family," 10. C.C. Harris points out that this is a general phenomenon in Western societies. *The Family* (London, 1969), 125.

113. Glick, "Updating the Life Cycle of the Family," 10.

114. *Ibid.*, 9-10.

115. *Ibid.*, 10. Hoffman reports that 66.2% of married women under forty who had at least one child reported that children satisfied their desire for love and the feeling of being in a family. In the cross-cultural findings for Asian countries these twin points are also dominant. Following a close second (60.1%) were the feelings of "stimulation and fun" derived from loving children. Thus it could be said that the reason why a majority of married women continue to bear children is because of their need to satisfy this kind of love as well as to be involved with a family that consists of more than a spouse. Lois W. Hoffman, "The Value of Children to Parents and the Decrease in Family Size," *Proceedings of the American Philosophical Society*, 119, No. 6 (Nov., 1975), 430-439. In England there are also a greater number of marriages and a greater number that do not remain childless than in the past. O.R. McGregor, "The Stability of the Family in the Welfare State," in *The Sociology of Modern Britain*, ed. by Butterworth and Weir, 434.

116. Most societies acknowledge childbirth in one way or another. Circumcision, baptism, and naming the child are rituals that reflect this recognition. See, Stuart A. Queen, Robert W. Habenstein, and John B. Adams, *The Family in Various Cultures* (pbck., 1961), esp. 75, 100, 124-125, 148, 196.

117. Michael K. Eshleman, "Diet During Pregnancy in the Sixteenth and Seventeenth Centuries," *Journal of the History of Medicine*, XXX: 1 (1975), 23-39; Ralph Josselin demonstrated particular sensitivity toward his wife's needs during her

many pregnancies. On June 3, 1647 he recorded: "brought my wife home some cherries." *The Diary of Ralph Josselin, 1616-1683*, edited by Alan Macfarlane (London, 1976), 96. See also Alan Macfarlane, *The Family Life of Ralph Josselin, A Seventeenth-Century Clergyman—An Essay in Historical Anthropology* (Cambridge, 1970), 84-85.

118. Robert V. Schnucker, "Elizabethan Birth Control and Puritan Attitudes," *Journal of Interdisciplinary History*, V:4 (1975), 655-667; Keith Wrightson, "Infanticide in Earlier Seventeenth-Century England," *Local Population Studies*, 15 (1975), 10-21; Lloyd deMause, "The Formation of the American Personality through Psychospeciation," *Journal of Psychohistory*, 4:1 (1976), 1-30, esp. Appendix: "On the Demography of Filicide," 16-22; William L. Langer, "Infanticide: A Historical Survey," *History of Childhood Quarterly*, I:3 (1974), 353-365; Barbara Kellum, "Infanticide in England in the Later Middle Ages," *History of Childhood Quarterly*, I (1974), 367-388; J.D. Chambers, *Population, Economy, and Society in Pre-Industrial England* (Oxford, 1972), Ch. 4.

119. R.V. Schnucker, "The English Puritans and Pregnancy, Delivery, and Breast Feeding," *History of Childhood Quarterly*, 1:4 (1974), 637-658; Spruill, *Women's Life and Work*, 50-51. See Note 117 above.

120. William Gouge in *Domestical Duties* (1634) advised pregnant mothers "to take great care to gratify their cravings for food." Quoted in Pearson, *Elizabethans at Home*, 79. For the Mather example, see *Diary of Cotton Mather*, edited by Worthington C. Ford (2 Vols., New York, 1911-12), I, 217-218. For Josselin, see Note 117 above.

121. Schnucker, "The English Puritans," 646. Gouge felt that husbands should display extreme sympathy "during travail and child bed" and that they should satisfy her "longings." Pearson, *Elizabethans at Home*, 377.

122. *Ibid.*, 640. Richard W. Wertz and Dorothy C. Wertz, *Lying In: A History of Childbirth in America* (New York, 1977), Ch. 1-2. Catherine M. Scholten, " 'On the Importance of the Obstetrick Art': Changing Customs of Childbirth in America, 1760 to 1825," *William and Mary Quarterly*, 3d. ser., XXXIV:3 (1977), 426-455, finds that between 1760 and 1825 "beginning among the well-to-do women in Philadelphia, New York, and Boston, childbirth became less a communal consequence and more a private event confined within the intimate family . . . [and] birth became increasingly regarded as a medical problem to be managed by physicians," (427).

123. Judy B. Litoff, "Forgotten Women: American Midwives at the Turn of the Twentieth Century," *The Historian*, XL:2 (1978), 235-351.

124. Anthropologists have also failed to penetrate into the ways women in peasant societies have been able to wield real power despite a public ideology of male dominance, according to Susan C. Rogers, "Female Forms of Power and the Myth of Male Dominance," *American Ethnologist*, 2:4 (1975), 726-754.

125. Schnucker, "The English Puritans," 642. This view continued and received medical support in the 19th century. Carroll Smith-Rosenberg and Charles Rosenberg, "The Female Animal: Medical and Biological Views of Woman and Her Role in Nineteenth-Century America," *Journal of American History*, LX:2 (1973), 332-356.

126. Margaret Mead noted that "in societies in which men were forbidden to see birth," she saw "men writhing on the floor, acting out their conception of what birth pangs were like." Quoted in Wertz and Wertz, *Lying-In*, 180.

127. In a recent report estimating the incidence of child abuse between 1962 and 1975 through the United States, the variations ranged from 302 to over 4 million cases. U.S. Department of Health, Education and Welfare, *1978 Annual Review of Child Abuse and Neglect Research*, DHEW Publication No. (OHDS) 79-30168, 5,

Table 1.

128. Greven, *The Protestant Temperament*, 164, 165 and *passim*; Morgan, *The Puritan Family*, 77-78. Eighteenth-century parents generally appear to have become less anxious about the adverse effects of indulging their children, but current standards of intolerable permissiveness were rarely applicable before 1800. Lawrence Stone would seem to be correct when he notes, "Some of the stories about parent-child relations in the late 18th century indicate a degree of indulgent permissiveness among parents and of spoilt arrogance among children which historically have no parallel except for conditions in the United States in the late 20th century." *The Family, Sex and Marriage*, 435-436.

129. Gary Wills, *Inventing America: Jefferson's Declaration of Independence*, (New York, 1978), 251-252; Franklin Baumer, *Modern European Thought* (New York, 1977), 142. In an interesting interpretation of the phrase, "the pursuit of happiness," Hannah Arendt suggests that its meaning can be found in the 18th-century conception that happiness required public participation in the improvement of the political community "and that men knew they could not be altogether 'happy' if their happiness was located and enjoyed only in private life." *On Revolution* (pbck. ed., 1963), 124.

130. Keith Thomas, *Religion and the Decline of Magic* (New York, 1971), Ch. 1; Pierre Gourbet, *Louis XIV and Twenty-Million Frenchmen* (pbck. ed., 1975), Part One, esp. 21-26.

131. Laslett, *Family Life and Illicit Love*, 182, Table 5.1.

132. Gary B. Nash, "Up From the Bottom in Franklin's Philadelphia," *Past and Present*, 77 (1977), 57-83, esp. 74.

133. Booth, "Food Riots in the North-West of England, 1790-1801."

134. Fernand Braudel, *Capitalism and Material Life, 1400-1800* (pbck. ed., 1975), 129-130.

135. As Robert Bremner writes about colonial America, "The labor of children was a social fact, not a social problem." Bremner, ed., *Children & Youth in America: A Documentary History* (Cambridge, Mass., 1970), Vol. I, *1600-1865*, 103. Morgan, *The Puritan Family*, 66, says: "Probably most children were set to some kind of useful work before they reached seven." Lorena Walsh notes that in early Maryland the county court authorized payment from public taxes to persons who cared for orphans without estates until they were two years old. Thereafter orphans, in theory, paid for their maintenance through their labor." Walsh, "Till Death Us Do Part, Marriage and Family in Maryland in the Seventeenth Century," in *The Chesapeake in the Seventeenth Century: Essays on Anglo-American Society*, edited by Thad W. Tate and David Ammerman (Chapel Hill, 1979), 126-152. The question of whether children were viewed as economic assets is not a simple one to answer. We suspect that class variations occurred. For example, Macfarlane believes that parents did not expect their children "to invest their labour into a 'family pool' and remain at home. Rather as soon as they were old enough to be trained, either in school, in a trade or in the household of somebody else, they left home. But Macfarlane is generally talking about those property owners who engaged in commercial farming and land sales." (*Origins of English Individualism*, 64.) On the other hand, Paul Slack shows that children of the poor did provide some income for their parents, although many of them were also put to service. "Poverty and Politics in Salisbury, 1597-1666," in *Crisis and Order in English Towns, 1500-1710*, 164-203. Still the question remains as to whether the use of children who brought in an income offset their own costs. The idea that children were not economic assets to their own parents would seem to be confirmed by the extensive use of household servants in the past, as Peter Laslett has documented. It was, he believes, the practice of the poor to send their children to

# FOOTNOTES

richer households. Laslett, *Family Life and Illicit Love*, 12-49. Further research is needed to determine to what extent children, when they could work, contributed to the subsistence of their own households or instead were sent out to contribute their labor to the households of others. That child labor existed is not in doubt. The question is to whose profit. More particularly, did parents profit from the labor of their own children? Laslett offers one perspectiye when he says, "although we shall insist that servants are not property to be described as a class, the practice of the poorer families offering up their children to the richer families at the very time when those children were at the height of their productive powers must certainly be called exploitation of one set of persons by another set." *Ibid.*, 45. The psychological ramifications for the child who is an economic asset to his parents was recently explored by Jerome Kagan, "The Child in the Family," *Daedalus*, 106:2 (1977), 33-56, esp. 43.

136. Laslett, *Family Life and Illicit Love*, 34. For a dissenting view that tries to "dispel notions of a universal early exodus from the parental household," see Richard Wall, "The Age of Leaving Home." *Journal of Family History*, 343, (1978), 181-201.

137. Laslett, *Family Life and Illicit Love*, 35.

138. Richard B. Morris, *Government and Labor in Early America* (New York, 1946), 391-392: Bremner, *Children and Youth in America*, Ch. V, *passim*. On the age gradation of children regarding work and schooling, see James Axtell, *The School Upon a Hill: Education and Society in Colonial New England* (New Haven, 1974), 97-99; Ross W. Beales, Jr., "In Search of the Historical Child: Miniature Adulthood and Youth in Colonial New England," *American Quarterly*, 27:4 (1975), 379-398. In England after 1572 vagrant and impoverished children at any age could also be placed in service. Pinchbeck and Hewitt, *Children in English Society*, I, 98.

139. Joseph F. Kett, "The Stages of Life," in *The American Family in Social-Historical Perspective*, ed. by Gordon, 171-172.

140. Morgan, *The Puritan Family*, 77; John Demos, *A Little Commonwealth: Family Life in Plymouth Colony* (New York, 1969), 73; Laslett, *Family Life and Illicit Love*, 45.

141. The growing expression of affection by parents toward their children, especially during the 18th century, is a theme in recent research. The seminal work in trying to trace parental feelings toward children over time is Lloyd deMause, "The Evolution of Childhood," in *The History of Childhood*, 1-73. He sees the 18th century as marking a significant advance in the treatment of children and in parental capacity for empathy. See also J.H. Plumb, "The New World of Children in Eighteenth-Century England," *Past and Present*, 67 (1975), 64-93; Stone, *The Family, Sex and Marriage*, Ch. 9; John F. Walzer, "A Period of Ambivalence: Eighteenth-Century American Childhood," in *The History of Childhood*, ed. by deMause, 351-382; Daniel B. Smith, "Autonomy and Affection: Parents and Children in Eighteenth-Century Chesapeake Families," *The Psychohistory Review*, VI:2-3 (1977-1978), 32-51; Fox, "Comment," *The Journal of Psychohistory*, 5 (1978), 587-597; Alan Macfarlane, Review Essay, *History and Theory*, XVIII (1979), 103-123.

142. Stone assumes throughout *The Family, Sex and Marriage* that the poor were unable to develop the same level of feelings as did the well-to-do because of their poverty. His assumptions have been challenged by several reviewers; Thomas, "The Changing Family," *Times Literary Supplement*, 1226-1227; Quitt, "Comment," 601-602; Macfarlane, Review Essay.

143. Vivian C. Fox, "Is Adolescence a Modern Phenomenon?" *Journal of Psychohistory*, V (1977), 271-290.

144. deMause, "Evolution of Childhood," esp. 51-54.

145. Stone, *The Family, Sex and Marriage*, 449-478. Stone's taxonomy draws heavily on deMause's schema.

146. Greven, *The Protestant Temperament*.

147. Stone, *The Family, Sex and Marriage*, 451-52.

148. Greven, *The Protestant Temperament*, 269-274.

149. Stone, *The Family, Sex and Marriage*, 470-478. See above Note 141.

150. The issue over the adult conception of childhood is neatly summarized and re-solved by Beales, "In Search of the Historical Child."

151. Keith Thomas, "Age and Authority in Early Modern England," *Proceedings of the British Academy*, LXII (1976), 205-248, esp. 233-236; David H. Fischer, *Growing Old in America* (rev. ed., New York, 1978), esp. Ch. 1. For a review of the recent literature, see N. Ray Hiner, "The Child in American Historiography: Accomplishments and Prospect," *The Psychohistory Review*, VII, 1 (Summer, 1978), 13-23.

152. *Ibid.*; Pinchbeck and Hewett, *Children in English Society*, I, 298-304. In the late 18th century children's clothing became the fashion to be imitated by adults. A. Hyatt Mayor, "Children Are What We Make Them," Metropolitan Museum *Bulletin*, XV:7 (1957), 181-188.

153. Henry Ebel offers an eloquent expression of this sensibility when he writes, ". . . I never like to hear childhood described in terms of levels not yet attained, as if the child were merely an incomplete adult." "The Damned," *History of Childhood Quarterly*, 3:3 (1976), 408. Hiner contends that the perspective of the child is the most important area yet to be explored. "The Child in American Historiography," 15-16. On the modern child-parent relationship and value system, see also Howard Gadlin, "Scars and Emblems: Paradoxes of American Family Life," *Journal of Social History*, 11:3 (1978), 305-327. Gadlin writes that "now the terms by which we understand people are the terms of childhood, not adulthood—change, growth and spontaneity become the criteria for judging the health of adults; openness to change becomes the new measure of personal stability; the inability to change the sign of disturbance," (318).

154. Greven, *The Protestant Temperament*, provides a mine of excerpts from these sources.

155. Ariès, *Centuries of Childhood*, 365-415, *passim*; deMause, "The Evolution of Childhood," esp. 51-54; Stone, *The Family, Sex and Marriage*, 683. Although Stone explicitly disassociates himself from deMause's evolutionary model (758n), his debt appears to be greater than he chooses to acknowledge: "The only steady linear change over the last four hundred years seems to have been a growing concern for children, although the actual treatment has oscillated cyclically between the permissive and the repressive." (683).

156. Jerome Kagan, *Infancy* (Cambridge, Mass., 1978), 29-38, stresses the certainty of "the child's perception of his value" rather than particular modes of parenting.

157. The impact of printing extended across the West and was "an *epoch-making event*." Elizabeth L. Eisenstein, "The Advent of Printing and the Problem of the Renaissance," *Past and Present*, 45 (1969), 19-89.

158. J.H. Hexter, "The Education of the Aristocracy in the Renaissance," in his *Reappraisals in History* (New York, 1961), 45-70; W.K. Jordan, *Philanthropy in England, 1480-1660*, esp. Ch. VII; Lawrence Stone, "The Educational Revolution in England, 1560-1640," *Past and Present*, 28 (1964), 41-80.

159. Among contemporary writings which outline a code for parents were: Thomas More's *Utopia*, Erasmus' "On the Civility of Children," Roger Ascham's "On Youth," William Gouge's *Of Domestical Duties*, and John Tillotson's "Of the Education of Children." The secondary literature on this subject is considerable.

# FOOTNOTES

See, for examples, Steven S. Smith, "Religion and the Conception of Youth in Seventeenth-Century England," *History of Childhood Quarterly*, II (1975), 493-516; Fox, *Deviance*, 89-97; Boyd M. Berry, "The First English Pediatricians and the Tudor Attitude Toward Childhood," *Journal of the History of Ideas*, 35 (1974), 561-577.

160. John Milton, *Paradise Regained* (1671), Book I, Line 220.

161. Aristocratic women in 18th-century England, for example, became anxious upon reading Rousseau not only because they were interested in being good mothers, but also because his advice conflicted with that of relatives. Trumbach, Aristocratic Family in England, Ch. 3.

162. Philip J. Greven, Jr., ed., *Child-rearing Concepts, 1628-1821* (Itasca, Ill., 1973), 9-78; Greven, *The Protestant Temperament, passim*; Cremin, *American Education*, 31-106; Pearson, *Elizabethans at Home*, Ch. 2 and 3; Elias, *The Civilizing Process*, 53-160, *passim*. But see an important warning and set of guidelines for the interpretation of advice manuals by Jay Mechling, "Advice to Historians on Advice to Mothers," *Journal of Social History*, 9:1 (1975), 44-63.

163. John Modell, Frank F. Furstenburg, Jr., and Theodore Hershberg, "Social Change and Transition to Adulthood in Historical Perspective." *Journal of Family History*, 1:1 (1976), 7-33, esp. 9. For an interesting discussion on biological, psychological, and physiological conceptions of adulthood, see Herant A. Katchadourian, "Medical Perspectives on Adulthood," *Daedalus*, (Spring 1976), 29-56. In the same issue the difficulty of arriving at a coherent definition of adulthood in secular law is examined by Joseph Goldstein, "On Being Adult and Being an Adult in Secular Law," 69-87.

164. Modell, et al., "Social Change and Transition to Adulthood," 19.

165. Laslett, *Family Life and Illicit Love*, 163.

166. Fischer, *Growing Old in America*, 279, Table.

167. *Ibid.* Decline in the death rate among women in Europe's ruling class, however, was an important feature during the later part of the early modern era. Sigismund Peller, "Births and Deaths Among Europe's Ruling Families Since 1500," in *Population in History, Essays in Historical Demography*, edited by D.V. Glass and D.E.C. Eversley, 87-100, esp. 96, Table 8. There are other essays in the Glass and Eversley book which bear on this point. For example, see Thomas McKeown and R.G. Brown, "Medical Evidence Related to English Population Changes in the Eighteenth Century," 285-307, esp. 300-307; T.H. Hollingsworth, "Demographic Study of the British Ducal Families," 354-378, esp. 361-364, Tables 8, 9, 10, 11, 12, 13, 15, 16. Two interesting facts emerge from these tables: (1) that mortality decreased during the middle and older years as the centuries progressed, and (2) that more females than males survived during middle and old age years.

168. Fischer, *Growing Old in America*, 279, Table.

169. "Married couples a century ago had only about a year and a half alone together before the birth of children. In contrast, couples marrying now [1976] are likely to spend nearly twenty-two years, almost half their married life, alone together with no children in the home—mostly after the children are grown." Bane, *Here to Stay*, 25. "Among two-parent families in contemporary American society . . . on average the last child leaves home when parents are in their forties, thus leaving the couple two or more decades without children in the household." Howard P. Chudacoff and Tamara K. Hareven, "From the Empty Nest to Family Dissolution: Life Course Transitions into Old Age," *Journal of Family History*, 4:1 (1979), 69-83, esp. 72. Primarily because of increased life expectancy, the average couple marrying in the 1970s can expect to live together 12.9 years past the *marriage* of their last child, as compared to 1.6 years in the case of couples marrying eighty years ago. Glick, "Updating the Life Cycle," 9.

170. Laslett, *Family Life and Illicit Love*, 180.
171. In 1960 the life expectancy of all American marriages, including those ending in divorce and later marriages, was 30.8 years. Marriages that did not end in divorce had a longevity estimate of 38.2 years. Bane, *Here to Stay*, 163, N. 11. See also C. Rosser and C.C. Harris, *The Family and Social Change* (London, 1965), esp. 160-170.
172. Stone, *The Family, Sex and Marriage*, 55, estimates "that among the bulk of the population the median duration of marriage in Early Modern England was probably somewhere about seventeen to twenty years." Laslett, *Family Life and Illicit Love*, 184, believes that the "duration of marriage in pre-industrial England was of the order of twenty years for most couples, but could last for thirty-five years or more for a fifth or a quarter of them."
173. In Charles County, Maryland, fifty percent of the marriages during the second half of the 17th century were terminated by the death of at least one spouse within seven years. Walsh, "Till Death Do Us Part," 128.
174. "About three-fourths of the women and five-sixths of the men who become divorced eventually remarry, [moreover] it is likely that somewhere between one-half and two-thirds of those who remarry will remain married from that time forward as long as both partners survive." Glick, "Updating the Life Cycle," 12.
175. In 1975 the life expectancy for a newborn male in the U.S. was 68.5 years in comparison to 76.4 years for the female. *The CBS News Almanac, 1977* (Maplewood, N.J., 1976), 247. When the life expectancy differential between men and women is juxtaposed against the approximately two year differential in age at first marriage between men and women, it is not surprising to find that in contemporary America there are 5 to 6 times as many widows as widowers in the population. *Ibid.*, 224. Understandably, the older women live the more likely they are to become widowed. U.S. Bureau of the Census, *Current Population Reports*, Series P-20, No. 312, "Marriage, Divorce, Widowhood, and Remarriage by Family Characteristics: June 1975," (Washington, D.C., 1977), 12. This has been true for some time. In Providence, Rhode Island during the late 19th century among women "widowhood increased by age in an almost linear pattern." It "reached 60 percent and above for women in the late 60s and early 70s . . . [and] seldom rose above 15 percent for men under 70." Chudacoff and Hareven, "From the Empty Nest to Family Dissolution," 73-74. In Britain, the experience seems to have been similar. In 1960, 50% of all English women over age 65 were widowed in comparison to 22% of the men over 65. Laslett, *Family Life and Illicit Love*, 189, 192.
176. *Ibid.*, 190, Table and 204-205. Walsh and Menard, "Death in the Chesapeake," 219, find that in 17th-century Charles County, Maryland, 411 marriages resulted in 221 widows and 114 widowers, mainly because women were several years younger than men at marriage, and because they lived longer. A similar pattern occurred in New England. See Alexander Keyssar, "Widowhood in Eighteenth-Century Massachusetts: A Problem in the History of the Family," *Perspectives in American History*, VIII (1977), 83-119, esp. 88.
177. Le Roy Ladurie, *Montaillou*, 161, writes that "successive widowhoods were commonplace in *ancien regime* demography." See also, Pearson, *Elizabethans At Home*, 491-516.
178. Darrett B. and Anita H. Rutman, "Now-Wives and Sons-in-Law: Parental Death in a Seventeenth-Century Virginia County," *The Chesapeake in the Seventeenth Century: Essays on Anglo-American Society,* ed. by Tate and Ammerman, 153-182.
179. On the Chesapeake, see *Ibid.*; and Smith, "Mortality and Family in the Colonial Chesapeake;" Morgan, *American Slavery, American Freedom*, Ch. 8, *passim*. On the English West Indies, see Richard S. Dunn, *Sugar and Slaves* (Chapel Hill,

# FOOTNOTES

1972), 300-334. He writes, "Everyone seemed caught up in a race between quick wealth and quick death," 333.

180. John Demos, "Old Age in Early New England," in *The American Family*, ed. by Gordon, 220-256, esp. 230-231; Maris H. Vinovskis, "Angels' Heads and Weeping Willows: Death in Early America," *Proceedings of the American Antiquarian Society*, 86, Part 2 (1977), 273-302.

181. Laslett, *Family Life and Illicit Love*, 161.

182. *Ibid.*, 161.

183. Chester, "Divorce," 59-61. Yet divorce is becoming increasingly more common in England, especially after the Divorce Reform Act of 1969, when the judges were given the right to grant divorce solely on the grounds that the marriage had broken down irretrievably. An American travelling through England today comes away with the impression that divorce is very much on the minds of Englishmen especially from the middle and professional classes. But there seems to be less publicity given to it in the newspapers and magazines than is the case in the U.S. Still, there are some studies available for those who search. See, for example, Gerald Sanctuary and Constance Whitehead, *Divorce and After* (London, 1970).

184. Glendon, "Legal Concepts of Marriage and the Family," below.

185. George E. Howard, *A History of Matrimonial Institutions* (3 Vols., Chicago, 1904), II, 331.

186. Stone, *The Family, Sex and Marriage*, 38.

187. Morgan, *The Puritan Family*, 35-37.

188. Although theoretically a wife could obtain a Parliamentary divorce (as could her husband) from about 1660, Parliament appeared reluctant to grant it to a woman even though she followed the same procedure as a man. This procedure required that she first obtain a decree from the ecclesiastical courts, and then petition Parliament. Men had been granted divorces if their wives were adulterous, but for a woman Parliament required that she prove her husband to have been dissolute or adulterous plus cruel. During the entire period when Parliamentary divorce existed only in conjunction with an ecclesiastical one, only 3 or 4 women were granted divorces. The first was in 1801. In 1857 Parliament enacted a civil divorce law. Howard, *History of Matrimonial Institutions*, 107-109; Thompson, *Women in Stuart England and America*, 170.

189. Nancy F. Cott, "Divorce and the Changing Status of Women in Eighteenth Century Massachusetts," *William and Mary Quarterly*, 3d. ser., XXXIII (1976), 586-614, esp. 601.

190. Spruill, *Women's Life and Work in the Southern Colonies*, 178-183, 341.

191. Richard B. Morris, *Studies in the History of Early American Law* (New York, 1930), 139-141; Spruill, *Women's Life and Work in the Southern Colonies*, 342-344; Oberseider, A Socio-Demographic Study of the Family in Virginia, 178-180; Stone, *The Family, Sex and Marriage*, 604, 40. In America deserted wives (often the victims of bigamy) were often declared to be femme soles, with sole rights to the property their husbands left behind. Oberseider, *op. cit.*, 179.

192. Stone, *The Family, Sex and Marriage*, 40-41.

193. Howard, *History of Matrimonial Institutions*, II, 107-108; Glendon, "Legal Concepts of Marriage," 14-15; Thompson, *Women in Stuart England and America*, 169-181.

194. Philip McNair, "Ochino's Apology: Three Gods or Three Wives," *History*, 60 (Oct. 1975), 353-73; Christopher Hill, *The World Upside Down* (New York, 1973), Ch. 14; Hill, "English Marriage," 460.

195. Howard, *History of Matrimonial Institutions*, II, 85-92; John G. Halkett, *Milton and the Idea of Matrimony* (New York, 1970); Christopher Hill, *Milton and the English Revolution* (Penguin pbck., 1979), Ch. 9.

196. Thompson, *Women in Stuart England and America*, 113-4. In Massachusetts from 1692 to 1786, more women petitioned for divorce than did men, but the latter had a significantly better rate of success in gaining decrees. Cott, "Divorce and the Changing Status of Women," 594-596, 612-613. R.H. Helmholz, *Marriage Litigation in Medieval England*, Ch. 3, *passim*; Michael M. Sheehan, "The Formation and Stability of Marriage in Fourteenth Century England—Evidence of an Ely Register," *Medieval Studies*, 33 (1971), 228-64; Stone, *Crisis of the Aristocracy*, 660-671; Gerhard O.W. Mueller, "Inquiry Into the State of a Divorceless Society: Domestic Relations, Law and Morals in England from 1660-1857," *University of Pittsburgh Law Review*, 18 (1957), 545-78. Mueller presents an interesting account of how non-divorce solutions were sought for those unable to obtain divorce.

197. Even when divorce laws were liberalized and divorce increased, public reaction was one of fear if not panic. See O'Neill, "Divorce in the Progressive Era," 208-217.

198. Marc Petrowsky, "Marital Status, Sex, and the Social Networks of the Elderly," in *Journal of Marriage and the Family*, 38, No. 4 (1976), 749-768, esp. 759, about the awkwardness experienced by widows in their social relationships after the death of their spouses. See also, Nicholas Babchuk, "Aging and Primary Relations," *International Journal of Aging and Human Development*, 9:2 (1978-79), 137-151.

199. For an interesting breakdown on how divorce affects women differently see, Purdence Brown, Lorraine Perry, and Ernest Harburg, "Sex Roles and the Psychological Outcomes for Black and White Women Experiencing Marital Dissolution," *Journal of Marriage and the Family*, 39, No. 3 (1977), 549-561. Apparently white women with a more traditional outlook suffer the most dislocation. Fathers and children also suffer dislocation. This view is suggested in, E. Mairs Hetherington, Martha Cox and Roger Cox, "Divorced Fathers," *The Family Coordinator*, 25 (Oct. 1976), 417-458.

200. Bernard Schoenberg, et al., eds., *Bereavement: Its Psychological Aspects* (New York and London, 1975).

201. Laslett, *Family, Sex and Illicit Love*, 161. See also, Notes 198 and 199 above.

202. Douglas C. Kimmel, *Adulthood and Aging: An Interdisciplinary Developmental View* (New York 1974), 431.

203. *Ibid.*, 431-432.

204. The view that parental feelings for children were constricted by the likelihood of child mortality is expressed by Ariès: "People could not allow themselves to become too attached to something that was regarded as a probable loss. . . . This indifference was a direct and inevitable consequence of the demography of the period," *Centuries of Childhood*, 38-39. Lloyd deMause reverses the causal relationship. He believes that the demography was a lamentable result of parental feelings toward children, especially their filicidal wishes, "Evolution of Childhood," 25-32. For English and American responses to child mortality, see Stone, *The Family, Sex and Marriage*, 206-215, *passim*, 246-249; Pinchbeck and Hewitt, *Children in English Society*, 301-304; Peter G. Slater, "From the Cradle to the Coffin; Parental Bereavement and the Shadow of Infant Damnation in Puritan Society," *The Psychology Review*, VI:2-3 (1977-78), 4-24; Daniel B. Smith, Family Experience and Kinship in Eighteenth-Century Chesapeake Society, (Ph.D. Diss., Univ. of Virginia, 1977), Ch. 6. Macfarlane rejects the idea that poverty and high mortality preclude deep parental grief. Review Essay, esp. 105-107.

205. There is disagreement among historians over the Puritan impact on the early modern notion of marriage. For example, James T. Johnson, "The Covenant Idea and the Puritan View of Marriage," *Journal of the History of Ideas*, XXXII (1971), 107-118, stresses the primacy of the covenant between husband and wife

among English and New England Puritans. Their mutual relationship contituted *the* central element in their notion of a good marriage. Davies, "The Sacred Condition of Marriage," *passim*, on the other hand, contends that the Puritan conception of mutuality was not original nor in fact was any of their other marital priorities, such as procreation. Earlier Christian writers had espoused similar views, she argues. Both would agree, however, that (1) 17th-century writers were overwhelmingly preoccupied with the husband-wife relationship and that (2) prescriptive writings about that relationship were suffused with an appreciation of the significance of love between the couple. Moreover, the role of love in the relationship between husband and wife was not a new idea. Charles Donohue, Jr., "The Case of the Man Who Fell into the Tiber: The Roman Law of Marriage at the Time of the Glossators," *The American Journal of Legal History*, XXII (1978), 1-53, argues that the modern emphasis on marital love was foreshadowed by the decretals of Pope Alexander III in the 12th Century.

206. For evidence of charivaris practiced on remarried French couples, see Natalie Z. Davis, "The Reason of Misrule: Youth Groups and Charivaris in Sixteenth-Century France," *Past and Present*, 50 (Feb. 1971), 40-75. Despite the social disapproval, remarriage was widespread as pointed out by Micheline Boulant in "The Scattered Family: Another Aspect of Seventeenth-Century Demography," in *Family and Society, Selections from the Annals*, edited by Robert Foster and Orest Ranum, translated by Elborg Foster and Patricia M. Ranum (Baltimore, 1976), 104-116.

207. Lawrence Stone, *The Family, Second Marriage*, esp. 37-41, on attitudes toward divorce in England during the early modern period. Nancy Cott discusses how 17th-century New England Puritans accepted divorce as a part of the view that marriage was a contract. Nevertheless, even in Colonial New England the amount of divorce by our standards was small. "Divorce and the Changing Status of Women in Eighteenth-Century Massachusetts," 589 and 592, Table I.

208. Attitudes toward marriage have undergone some fundamental changes during the past four hundred years. Glendon, "Legal Concepts of Marriage," describes how the church then the state gained control over marriage formation and break-up. When the state gained control over marriage, the law regulating marriage and divorce initially reflected the ecclesiastical moral system; conversely, when most Protestant reformers advocated that civil not ecclesiastical courts regulate marriage, they did not believe the values would be anything but Christian ones. Glendon, "Legal Concepts of Marriage and the Family." Ecclesiastical control in general was severed in America with the Revolution but not in England until 1857. When American divorces became more widespread at the end of the 19th Century, many reformers were shocked, believing healthy family life required the indissolvability of marriage. O'Neal, "Divorce in the Progressive Era," 203-217. Most recently in England and America divorce is increasingly looked upon as an individual's entitlement. According to Mary Ann Glendon, the State is increasingly retreating from taking any moral stand as to who marries whom and which marriage partner is to blame in divorce proceedings. It is clear from the amount of divorces and the moral retreat of the State that the indissolvability of marriage is now no longer a cornerstone of Western values. Mary Ann Glendon, "Marriage and the State: The Withering Away of Marriage," *Virginia Law Review*, 62:4 (1976), 663-720; Sanctuary and Whitehead in *Divorce and After* reveal that after the 1969 and 1970 Divorce Acts English judges have been concerned with two facets of divorce. The first is if the marriage has "irretrievably broken down," and second, if they have to decide the future financial arrangements of the couple. (20-22).

209. Keith Thomas, "Age and Authority in Early Modern England," *Proceedings of*

*the British Academy*, LXII (1976), 205-248, esp. 244; Laslett, *Family Life and Illicit Love*, 13 and 28; Pearson, *Elizabethans at Home*, 513. Morgan, *American Slavery, American Freedom*, 167. Morgan writes, "The man with his eye on the main chance went for the widow rather than the daughters when a wealthy Virginian died."

210. *Ibid.*; Pearson, 500-516; also Elizabeth Mignon, *Crabbed Age and Youth, The Old Men and Women in Restoration Comedy of Manners* (Durham, 1947).

211. For England, see Pearson, *Elizabethans at Home*, 494; for America, see Note 176, above.

212. Carr and Walsh, "The Planter's Wife," 560; Morgan, *American Slavery, American Freedom*, 164-165.

213. This was the case in the Woburn, Mass. sample studied by Keyssar, "Widowhood in Eighteenth-Century Massachusetts." Keyssar's findings are unexpected to students of New England Puritanism, because ministers urged survivors to limit their mourning time, to remarry, and to get on with the business of God's work. To indulge in a prolonged mourning period for a departed spouse was to risk idolatry. Morgan, *The Puritan Family*, 49. Quaker leaders, in contrast, urged a waiting period of at least a year to manifest "chastity and virtue, and temperance." Frost, *The Quaker Family*, 161.

Early modern English widows appeared to have remarried, especially if they were young and wealthy. Pearson, *Elizabethans At Home*, 491-2. Laslett notes that it was easier for a widower to remarry, especially when older. *Family Life and Illicit Love*, 200-201. Macfarlane, however, points out that historians of Medieval England have stated that a large number of widows did not remarry. *Origins*, 134. But French widows and especially widowers in the area of Paris during the 17th and 18th centuries remarried at a high rate. Boulant, "The Scattered Family," 104-116.

214. U.S. Bureau of the Census, "Marital Status and Living Arrangements," *Current Population Report*, Series P-20, No. 242 (Washington, D.C., 1972), 2; Frances E. Kobrin, "The Fall in Household Size and the Rise of the Primary Individual in the United States," 69-81; Laslett, *Family Life and Illicit Love*, 203-205, esp. Table 5, 12. In a survey taken of older people living alone in the Bethnal Green section of London, a majority indicated the desire to remain alone in their own home. Peter Townsend, *The Family Life of Old People* (London, 1957), 25.

215. Kobrin, "The Fall in Household Size," 72. See also Note 175 above. For a breakdown comparing the number of male and female widowed people in England from the 17th to the 20th centuries, see Laslett, *Family Life and Illicit Love*, 204-205.

216. Kimmel, *Adulthood and Aging*, 431-432.

217. Fischer characterizes the colonial widow as desperate. *Growing Old in America*, 62. Morgan, in contrast, views the position of Virginia widows as enviable. He describes them as "a singularly unlovely lot." *American Slavery, American Freedom*, 164.

218. David Hapgood, "The Aging are Doing Better," in *The New Old: Struggle for Decent Aging*, edited by Ronald Gross, Beatrice Gross, and Sylvia Seidman (Anchor, 1978), 345-365. Hapgood contends that elderly people or senior citizens are the best organized of the nation's "out people," better than the poor, the blacks and women. They received 52% in raises in their social security between 1970-2, lobbied for and were successful in tying social security benefits to a cost of living index and are receiving health care benefits through Medicare.

219. Recently there has been increased media coverage on the lack of pension benefits for widows. Moreover, the query as to who should receive pension benefits has been expanded to divorced couples.

# FOOTNOTES

220. Laslett, *Family Life and Illicit Love*, 200; Oxley, *Poor Relief*, 90-92. Keith Thomas claims that "the Poor Law never solved the problem of aged poverty," that private charity helped, but that throughout the early modern period institutional facilities were never adequate. "Age and Authority in Early Modern England," 241-242. Still the fact that institutions existed for the elderly contradicts Tamara Hareven's contention that when old people in the past became "dependent" they were not put in institutions. See, "The Last Stage: Historical Adulthood and Old Age," *Daedalus* (Fall 1976), 17. The most common institutional response to poverty was the workhouse. In America widows were also principal recipients of poor relief. Gary B. Nash, "Poverty and Poor Relief in Pre-Revolutionary Philadelphia," *William and Mary Quarterly*, 3d. ser., XXXIII (1976), 3-30. In one year, 1772, "637 widows and single women entered the hospital [The Hospital for the Sick Poor], the almshouse, or the workhouse, or received aid from the overseers of the poor," (28). Pre-Revolutionary Boston, despite its hard times, was a sanctuary for the poor because of its generous relief program. Widows, orphans, and the unemployed poured in. William Pencak, "Suburban Commuters and the Massachusetts Revolution," (paper read at Boston University Colloquium in Early American History and Culture, February, 1979). Virginia Bernhard, "Poverty and the Social Order in Seventeenth-Century Virginia," *Virginia Magazine of History and Biography*, 85 (1977), 141-155, mentions widows along with "the aged, the inform, and orphans as the most likely candidates for charitable relief there. (148). But in light of the special demography of the early Chesapeake, we would guess that fewer widows were in need of such help there than was the case elsewhere. A systematic investigation is still necessary, however.

221. For the role of women in the household, see Pearson, *Elizabethans at Home*, Ch. 6. For a more general earlier analysis of women's work, see Power, *Medieval Women*, esp. Ch. 3. For a 19th-century perspective the article by Joan Scott and Louise Tilly, "Women's Work and the Family," *The Family in History*, edited by Charles Rosenberg (Philadelphia, 1975), 145-178, is useful.

222. Widows whose husbands employed servants might continue to receive their assistance after their husbands died. However, since most servants were young the help would be limited. Widows over 60, on the other hand, appear to have had few servants and therefore they either would receive assistance from family, kin or neighbors or be left in a more desperate situation. Laslett, *Family Life and Illicit Love*, esp. 49, 201-202.

223. See Note 225, below.

224. In colonial America, poverty generally increased as an economic fact and a social problem in the 18th century. See sources in Note 59 above. See Bridenbaugh, *Cities in the Wilderness*, 78-85, 231-238; *Cities in Revolt*, 122-128, 319-325; Morris, *Government and Labor*, 14-16; Marcus W. Jernegan, *Laboring and Dependent Classes in Colonial America, 1607-1783* (New York, 1931), esp. 175-209 on Virginia and New England. Slack describes "the intellectual and social origins of changing attitudes toward poverty" and a governmental attempt to deal with it. "Poverty and Politics in Salisbury," 1597-1666 in *Crisis and Order in English Towns, 1500-1700*, edited by Peter Clark and Paul Slack (London, 1972), 164-203. In assessing the quality of support that was afforded the poor by public institutions, we should keep in mind what the Webbs said about the Poor Law: "Between the Statute Book and the actual administration of parish officers there was in the 18th Century only a casual connection." S. and B. Webb, *English Poor Law History*, Part I, *The Old Poor Law* (1927), 149.

225. The decline in the role of kin in the European family and the concomitant withdrawal of the conjugal family into itself over time has been developed by

Ariès, *Centuries of Childhood, passim*, but esp. 356-357, 363-364, 398; and Stone, *The Family, Sex and Marriage*, Ch. 4. The relationships between kin who lived in separate households remains an important area for research among early modern scholars. Suggestive is a study of Middlesex County, Virginia in the 17th century made by the Rutmans ("Now-Wives and Sons-in-Law"), where they find that "kinship and quasi-kinship were the essentials of the [family] system. One can even argue that they were accentuated in the society in large measure in response to the expectation of parental death and parentless children."

226. On the reliance upon and attitudes towards institutional support for the poor in colonial America, see the sources cited in Note 220 above. In addition, Clark and Slack, (ed.), *Crisis and Order*, 20; W.K. Jordan, "Social Institutions in Kent, 1480-1660," *Archaeologic Cantiana*, LXXV (1961), 42-45; Pinchbeck and Hewitt, *Children in English Society*, I, 175-197, 308-310. This hostile attitude toward indigents was even adopted by John Locke, who is generally viewed as a humanitarian. By the end of the 17th century there was the general belief that people should increasingly help themselves and not depend upon government assistance. Locke believed that this independence and work habits should be taught early when he was Commissioner of the Board of Trade and submitted a "Report for the Reform of the Poor Law" in 1697. In it he said,

"The children of the labouring people are an ordinary burden to the parish, and are usually maintained in idleness, so that their labour is also generally lost to the public, till they are twelve or fourteen years old. . . . The most effectual remedy for this, that we are able to conceive, and which we therefore humbly propose, is, that working schools be set up in each parish, above three and under fourteen years of age, whilst they live at home with their parents. . . . By this means, the mother will be eased of a great part of her trouble in looking after and providing for them at home, and so be at more liberty to work . . . and from the infancy [children will] be inured to work which is of no small consequence to making them sober and industrious all their lives after." Quoted in Pinchbeck and Hewitt, *Children in English Society*, I, 309.

227. For the independence of some medieval widows see E. Power, *Medieval Women*, Ch. 3, and Macfarlane, *Origins*, 134. For the independence of widows and why London widows were especially wealthy see, W.K. Jordon, *Charities of London, 1460-1660* (1959), 28-32; Thomas, "Age and Authority," 236; Pearson, *Elizabethans at Home*, 511, for the potential freedom of wealthy widows. Stone, *The Family, Sex and Marriage*, 25, notes that gentry and yeoman widows were given separate residences. Pearl Hogrefe, "Legal Rights of Tudor Women and the Circumvention by Men and Women," *Sixteenth Century Journal*, III:1 (1972), 97-105, notes how dower rights were well protected in the 16th century and that by circumvention widows could get more than their dower. (101-105).

228. For the idea that stages of the life cycle have become more formalized in contemporary society , see Hareven, "Historical Adulthood and Old Age," 19.

229. See Thomas, "Age and Authority," 236-7. Although it was generally assumed children and kin would take care of their aging parents, we cannot infer that they necessarily did, *Ibid.*, 236-245.

230. Laslett, *Family Life and Illicit Love*, 177.

231. *Ibid.*, 177-181.

232. Fischer, *Growing Old in America*, 61-63.

233. Laslett, *Family Life and Illicit Love*, 199, 205, draws our attention to the difficulty of assessing how many solitaries were widows, since elderly spinsters who were solitaries were counted among the widowed.

234. Quoted in Fischer, *Growing Old in America*, 61. He adds, "if the aged poor were only a small minority, their misery was great."

# FOOTNOTES

235. John Demos notes that it was likely that grandparents felt affection for their grandchildren in some New England towns, "Old Age in Early New England," 229-231. He quotes an essay by Reverend John Robinson who in the 17th century admonished grandfathers for being "more affectionate toward their children's children than to their immediates." (230). Because of the high mortality rate in the Chesapeake and in England, grandparents may have been, in John Murrin's words, "a New England invention, at least in terms of scale." "Review Essay," 238.

236. Thomas states "there is . . . no reason to look back wistfully at the aged in this period [early modern]," particularly if they were poor. "Old Age and Authority," 245. Fischer says that, "to be old and poor and outcast in early America was certainly not to be venerated, but rather to be despised." *Growing Old in America*, 60. These views contrast sharply with Hareven's nostalgic notion regarding the pre-industrial era when, she says, if old people "became 'dependent' because of illness or poverty, they were supported by their children or other kin or were placed by the town authorities in the households of neighbors, or even strangers but not in institutions." "Historical Adulthood and Old Age," 17. To be old, poor and dependent was far from idyllic. Status and security came with wealth, perhaps more in the past than today. Understandably Macfarlane notes that older parents appreciated the importance of maintaining their economic and physical independence from their grown-up children. *Origins of Individualism*, 143.

237. Laslett, *Family Life and Illicit Love*, 213. He believes there is little to the prejudice that contemporary Britons expel the really old, or fail to take care of them. Indeed he finds little difference between contemporary Britons' actions toward their elderly parents and the behavior of their early modern ancestors. (208). This view is confirmed by Fischer for modern America. He claims: "Recent research has demonstrated that most older people in America never became totally isolated. The great majority lived near their children and grandchildren and visited frequently." *Growing Old in America*, 146. These views contradict the main point of Tamara Hareven's essay, "Historical Adulthood and Old Age," which is that in the 20th century old people have become isolated from their kin because of changes in family function. (23). Hareven relies heavily on the Parsonian view of the changing family functions. (21). For an excellent critique of Parsonian sociology of the family, see Christopher Lasch, "The Waning of Private Life," *Salmagundi*, 36 (1977), 3-15.

238. For a general overview of a married woman's rights see F. Pollack and F.W. Maitland, *The History of English Law*, 2d. ed. (Cambridge, 1898), Bk. II, Ch. VII, pt. 2; also Cornelius J. Moynihan, *Introduction to the Law of Real Property* (St. Paul, 1962), esp. 55-58.

239. Carr and Walsh, "The Planter's Wife," 561.

240. Max Rheinstein and Mary Ann Glendon, *The Law of Descendents' Estates* (Mineola, N.Y., 1971), 89-90.

241. *Ibid.*, 90.

242. *Ibid.*, 94.

243. Stone, *Crisis of the Aristocracy*, 633.

244. Stone, *Crisis of the Aristocracy*, 643.

245. Rheinstein and Glendon, *The Law of Descendents' Estates*, 94.

246. Stone, *Crisis of the Aristocracy*, 643.

247. Margaret Spufford, "Peasant Inheritance Customs and Land Distribution, in Cambridgeshire from the Sixteenth to the Eighteenth Centuries," *Family and Inheritance, Rural Society in Western Europe, 1200-1800*, edited by Jack Goody, Joan Thirsk and E.P. Thompson (Cambridge, 1976), 156-176. She finds that among Cambridgeshire peasants with grown-up children, wills were atypical

because they had already helped to establish their children. (172-173). In America as well, many people who ranked low in wealth but who did possess bequeathable property failed to leave wills. The rich appear to have been much more systematic at planning their bequests. Daniel S. Smith, "Underregistration and Bias in Probate Records: An Analysis of Data from Eighteenth-Century Hingham, Massachusetts," *William and Mary Quarterly*, 3d. ser., XXXII (1975), 100-110, esp. 101, 105. A valuable guide for students of family history regarding the use of wills is Gloria L. Main, "Probate Records as a Source for Early American History," *idem.*, 89-99.

248. The classic argument comes from Morris, *Studies in the History of American Law*, Ch. 3, who has long been recognized as the authority on the matter. See, for example, Thompson, *Women in Stuart England and America*, 162-169, esp. 167. Based on their study of wills, Carr and Walsh, "The Planter's Wife," believe that Maryland widows "were favored; but the position of 17th-century English women —especially those not of gentle status—has been little explored. A finding of little difference between bequests to women in England and in Maryland would greatly weaken the argument that demographic stress created peculiar conditions especially favorable to Maryland women." (570).

249. Carr and Walsh, "The Planter's Wife," 556; James Deen, "Patterns of Testation: Four Tidewater Counties in Colonial Virginia," *American Journal of Legal History*, XVI (1972), 154-176, esp. 161; Keyssar, "Widowhood in Eighteenth-Century Massachusetts," 106.

250. Stone, *Crisis of the Aristocracy*, 642n; Spufford, "Peasant Inheritance Customs," 169-176.

251. Deen, "Patterns of Testation," 159-160, notes that while male testators preferred their male heirs, they displayed "concern that extended to all women."

252. Rheinstein and Glendon, *The Law of Descendents' Estates*, 91-92.

253. Macfarlane, *The Origins of English Individualism*, 105-130.

254. *Ibid.*, 80-93; Hogrefe, "Legal Rights of Tudor Women," 100-105; Moynihan, *Introduction to the Law of Real Property*, 52-58; Pollack and Maitland, *The History of English Law*, II, 404, 420-426.

255. Rheinstein and Glendon, *The Law of Descendents' Estates*, 90-104. Prof. Glendon has been kind enough to allow us to read an early draft of M. Rheinstein and M. Glendon, "Marriage: Interpersonal Relations," in *International Encyclopedia of Comparative Law*, edited by A. Chloros (forthcoming, 1979), Ch. 4.

256. Glendon, *State Law and Family*, 280-282.

257. *Ibid.*, 282-284.

258. *Ibid.*, 280-284.

259. Rheinstein and Glendon, "Marriage: Interpersonal Relations," Ch. 4.

≈ PART TWO ≈

# THE
# ANGLO-AMERICAN
# FAMILY CYCLE
# 1500-1800

# 1

# Courtship To Marriage Formation

## 1. INTRODUCTION

Getting married in the early modern era involved participants in a process that could be informal and simple or ritualistic and complex. It could involve a simple exchange of vows between the couple or a formal betrothal, the publication of banns, and a church ceremony. The pattern followed might vary even in the same geographical area according to the economic or religious differences of the population. Thus, while some generalizations are possible, a great deal of research at the local level remains to be done before we will be able to describe fully, let alone explain, the process from courtship to marriage.

The attitude towards marriage as an institution should perhaps be the starting point for an inquiry into the whole process of marriage formation. For unless we know what people thought about the institution we cannot go very far in explaining what they looked for in choosing a marriage partner or why they involved themselves in a simple or complex courtship to marriage process. In Tudor-Stuart England political theorists, utopists, clergymen, and religious reformers treated marriage as an indispensable institution for three major reasons: (1) the stability of society, (2) the physical well-being of individuals, and (3) the propagation of the population.

The stability of society was thought to be intimately connected to marriage formation because of its importance in the orderly transmission of property and status. Unless proper marriages were arranged, the continuity of family wealth and social position could not be assured.

The physical well-being of individuals was also thought linked to family life and particularly to a judicious marriage. In the pre-industrial past the family was the fundamental productive unit in society. It generally provided for the food, clothing, and housing of its members. Its efficiency as an economic unit depended on the division of tasks among its members and

91

especially on the respective supervisory responsibilities of the husband and wife. Thus an unmarried adult or one who did not marry wisely placed himself or herself in a precarious position with regard to the necessities of life, unless he or she could otherwise be certain of being attached to an ongoing household.

Early modern writers took for granted that procreation was properly the function only of married couples. It was not solely a matter of morality. Children born out of wedlock might eventually become public charges.

No colonial American historian has investigated attitudes towards marriage as systematically as has Edmund Morgan (1966) for New England Puritans. Drawing mainly upon the works of the great Puritan divines, he concluded that New Englanders believed that well ordered families supplied the foundation upon which a stable social order could stand. For them properly arranged marriages would enhance the transmission of piety and civility.

Recent scholarship has questioned the extent to which the attitudes and practices of New Englanders can be attributed to a systematic theological outlook. Nevertheless, Morgan's pioneering effort to locate the ideological place that marriage held for these people provides a valuable model for comparable studies that should be directed to other colonies and denominations.

While English and colonial writers emphasized the central importance of marriage for their societies, a significant number of people did not marry. Many appear to have preferred bachelorhood or spinsterhood. In our own time the decision to get married has become precisely that, a decision that people must make. The option of not getting married has become a more creditable one today than it was a generation ago. But what was the situation three hundred years ago? We cannot assume that options available to us today were not necessarily available in the distant past. The behavior of thousands of Englishmen who emigrated to Virginia in the 17th century suggests that some people did not place marriage high in their value systems. Whereas immigrants to New England usually came in family units, single males predominated in the crossing to Virginia. The result was a severely imbalanced sex ratio. This meant that a majority of men could not be monogamously married at the same time until the very end of the century. The high mortality rate there was attributed by one contemporary to the lack of wives who could care for the physical well-being of the men. And yet male immigrants continued to pour into the colony without mates and without realistic prospects of acquiring them. If they shared the attitude of English writers on the importance of marriage to social stability and physical survival, should we not expect them to have practiced polygamy? Moreover, how do we explain the phenomenon of women in the colony who remained unmarried? Given the sex ratio, it would seem that a woman who did not marry in Virginia did not because she did not want to.

# COURTSHIP TO MARRIAGE FORMATION

A large number of unmarried adults is one component of what historians have recently described as the European marriage pattern. A second component of this pattern has been the comparatively late age of men and women at their first marriage. The average age at marriage varied from place to place and from time to time. Nevertheless it fell within a range that was apparently higher than what was obtained in non-European countries. This twofold pattern of late marriages and a high proportion of unmarrieds has been the dominant one in England at least since the 16th century. It was established in America also by the 18th century, as Robert Wells' article shows.

The late age at marriage of early modern Englishmen and Americans had significant implications for their family life. It especially effected their reproductive rate, as will be discussed in Chapter 3. Indeed the desire for birth control may have been a reason for the postponement of marriages to a woman's early or mid-twenties. But the central role which prescriptive writers assigned to marriage formation in the early modern period seems at odds with the late marriage pattern. If marriage was so desirable, why postpone it? Clearly the motives behind this pattern remain to be explored.

The framework in which these inquiries into marital selection have been cast—as the readings below by Macfarlane, Habbakuk, Frost, and Smith illustrate—weighs the relative importance of romantic and material considerations in choosing a spouse. A common premise is that where parental influence was great, material considerations were asserted to the sacrifice of feelings. And the term "prudential" is often used as a synonym for "material," as if a wise choice would depend solely upon property arrangements rather than include a concern for love as well. As with most important questions that historians raise, to ask whether love or property counted more is to call for an answer that will order the past in a manner that is intelligible to us but that may distort the reality of the past. Questions that call for "either-or" answers are apt to result in reconstructions of the past that are most remote from the actualities of human decision-making. Thus we caution students to recognize in people of the past a degree of complexity comparable to our own and to bear in mind that in interpersonal relationships, especially between prospective mates, the couples themselves may not have been able to categorize and segregate their own motives as easily as historians of a later century believe they can do in retrospect. We especially urge caution towards conclusions about motivation that rely on statistical analysis to the exclusion of the feelings expressed in the words people used. Our own reading of the literary evidence impresses upon us the extent to which affection characterized intrafamilial relationships in early modern times and how parents generally realized that a suitable marriage involved emotional as well as material compatibility. Affection is not the exclusive preserve of our own times.

Thus far we have discussed three facets of the courtship to marriage process in England and colonial America: (1) the attitude towards marriage as an institution; (2) the Euro-American marriage pattern; and (3) the criteria for marital selection. A fourth facet is the procedure that was followed. It is perhaps the most important one for historians to learn about, for more certain knowledge of the procedure will enhance our understanding of the entire process whereby people got married. It involved the sequence of steps that were taken from the initiation of courtship to the exchange of vows. It also involved the time frame in which people went from wooing to wedding each other.

Despite its importance, procedure has not been subjected to much research by the present generation of family historians. Alan Macfarlane's essay below is one of the few exceptions. Most of our knowledge of procedure is, however, based on the research of an earlier group of social historians. Scholars like Arthur C. Calhoun, George E. Howard, Chilton L. Powell, Lu Emily Pearson, and Julia C. Spruill mined the traditional kinds of literacy sources to derive necessarily impressionistic accounts of the patterns leading to marriage formation.

The recent generation of family historians, equipped with such tools of investigation as family reconstitution methodology and aggregate analysis, have been able to tap previously ignored sources like birth registers, marriage registers, marriage licenses, and probate records with fruitful results for our understanding of the family. But many of the questions that concern us regarding the procedure men and women followed or were expected to follow in getting married do not lend themselves to quantitative analysis because the records are not adequate for meaningful quantification. For example, if we try to ascertain whether men generally asked permission of the fathers of the girls they wanted to court, there is no sufficient bulk of diaries, memoirs, or letters to support a conclusion that is not impressionistic. Or, if we seek to estimate the average interval between a man taking up his suit of a woman and his marrying her, we can only know what some writers prescribed and what some people say they did, but we cannot establish with certainty the behavioral pattern of a significant sample, let alone of the majority at any given time. Similarly we cannot determine numerically whether betrothals were a necessary part of the process. Even where they were prescribed, they did not necessarily reflect practice. The impressionistic literature should still be searched, then, if only to enhance the reliability of what can be impressionistic answers to these questions.

Throughout western history the most critical stage in the procession from courtship to marriage has been the exchange of vows. What has varied geographically and chronologically has been the degree of formality attached to this exchange. But whether attached tightly in a religious ceremony in a church or loosely by the fact of two people living together voluntarily for a period of years, mutual consent, which the exchange signifies, has always been the *sine qua non* for a marriage to be considered valid by western society. And where marriage conferred status, effected the distribution of property, and defined the legitimacy of children, as appears to have been the case in England and the colonies, its validity was a matter that people had to be most concerned about.

Once we have linked the exchange of vows to the issue of validity, it is clear that our understanding of the whole matter must begin with clarifying what were the public agencies that were charged with determining the validity of marriage, what did they insist upon as criteria for validity, and what sanctions did they impose when their criteria were not met. Anyone familiar with the standard works that have dealt with this subject realizes that answers to these questions require someone to disentangle the mores and customs as well as the respective norms and practices of ecclesiastical and secular authorities in the early modern period. The first selection by Mary Ann Glendon succeeds in accomplishing this complex and necessary task.

## 2. Legal Concepts of Marriage and the Family
by Mary Ann Glendon

Louis le Roy, the French historian, jurist and encyclopedic humanist, commented sadly in the 16th century that nowadays it was no longer possible to master even a single discipline, not to mention a whole encyclopedia.[1]

Twentieth-century scholars must experience a special anguish in reading Le Roy's lament. Armed with only a partial knowledge of our own ever-expanding fields, we lawyers and historians are compelled at times to forage in each other's territories. For historians, laws and legal records of various kinds, and legal documents such as wills and contracts, are highly important (often the only) evidence of the social life of the past. Like any other kind of evidence, however, legal artifacts can be tricky, ambiguous and misleading. For lawyers, our occasional efforts to make use of historical methodology and materials intensify the discomfort we already feel being in a profession which tends to attract individuals who love order and certainty but which offers them a generous share of chaos and doubt. Yet the two disciplines are related, and should be drawn together on the occasions when they need each other by the fact that the careful, skeptical sifting and weighing of evidence is an essential part of the work of both.

These notes are offered, therefore, in the hope of making the way somewhat smoother for those historians whose travels take them into the area of Anglo-American family law, in particular those who may wish to explore the relationship of law to actual family behavior, and to ideas or ideals concerning family behavior.

Any interdisciplinary discussion of this sort must begin with a recognition of the difficulties posed by the fact that words such as "family," "marriage," and "law" are and have been used in many different ways. What lawyers mean when they use these words to refer to legal concepts is often quite different from what social scientists mean when they use the same terms to describe social phenomena. Furthermore, lawyers themselves use and have used such terms in a number of ways. Therefore, it is desirable to begin this essay by separating out some of the concepts that often are lumped together indiscriminately under these key terms. "Law" was usefully defined by Max Weber as that set of norms which is sanctioned by the probability that the enforcement staff of some social group, specialized for the purpose, will go into action to bring about conformity with the norms or punish violations.[2] Law can be and is defined in many other ways, but the foregoing definition has the virtue of helping to bring out three important points for interdisciplinary family studies.

In the first place, "law" is only *one* of the social norm systems regulating or purporting to regulate human conduct (others, for example, can be the norms of convention, custom, ethics or religion). Two special features of *legal* norms, of particular interest for present purposes, are that they appeared on a large scale only rather late in history and that their effectiveness has varied greatly from time to time and from place to place.[3] This is especially true of those legal norms of which the family law of England and the United States (and indeed all Western Europe) is composed. Family law appeared quite late, relatively speaking, and there has always been skepticism about its effectiveness.

The second important point for family history suggested by Weber's definition of law is that the set of norms embodied in the legislatively enacted or judge-made family law of a given society has no necessary relationship to, and never exactly corresponds to, the reality of family relationships within that society. The two sets vary in their relationship to each other and have resembled each other more at some times than at others.

Third, since the concept of law, as defined above, excludes those legislative or judicial pronouncements which have no sanctions, it helps us see that one of the distinctive characteristics of that field which lawyers call "family law" is *not* really "law" in Weber's sense. This fact in turn leads to the realization that much of what passes and has passed for family law, is merely symbolic language, expressing ideals of behavior, rather than a command whose violation will be punished. Needless to say, one has to be very careful about the way in which one uses this type of legal material as evidence of actual family behavior in society.

The best examples of this kind of legal pronouncement can be drawn from the elaborate manner in which the great 18th- and 19th-century European codes purported to regulate by law matters which are highly resistant to any type of regulation—the personal relationship of husband and wife, the roles of family members and the family decision-making process. The Prussian General Code of 1794 probably represents the extreme in its minute regulation of such matters as when marital sexual intercourse may be rightfully refused.[4] To this group of legal pronouncements belongs also code provisions declaring that "The husband is the head of the family;" or that the wife must "love," or "love and obey," or merely "obey," her husband.[5]

In general no consequences attached to the violation of such norms established in the codes.[6] Yet such legal materials do give us as close a look as we can get at the symbols through which the legal order confers approval on certain types of conduct, and changes in these symbols are significant as indicators of changes in the ideology being communicated through the family law. The question is, of course, whose ideology? Here it takes the resources of both lawyers and historians to ascertain in any given case the extent to which such symbols reflect the behavior or ideals and aspirations widespread in a given society; or those of a dominant group within society; or those of an enlightened monarch or an intellectual elite; or perhaps just behavior or ideology of some earlier time which no one has thought important to bring up to date. Before going any further along these lines, however, we must return to some problems of terminology, in particular, those posed by the use of such words as "husband," "wife," "marriage" and "family" which can describe a variety of legal and/or social relationships.

From what has been said so far about law, it should be apparent that the correspondence is imperfect between the institutions which a particular legal system may classify as "families" or "marriages" and that type of social conduct which an anthropologist or sociologist might call family or marriage behavior. For analytical purposes it is useful to make this distinction even though it may not be possible to proceed to a precise definition of either the legal or social institutions of family and marriage. Within a single legal system these terms often have a variety of meanings; and it is harder still to identify what constitutes marriage or family behavior in society.[7] In spite of these difficulties, the utility of drawing a distinction between legal and social phenomena can be demonstrated by using "marriage" as an example.[8]

Let there be a set of men and women married to each other according to the rules of the legal system to which they are subject. Call this Set A. Now, let there be a set of men and women cohabitating with each other in unions entered with some idea of duration and openly manifested to the relevant community. Call this Set B.

Note that in Set A marriage is whatever the legal system says it is. The contents of Set B call for more lengthy comment. In constructing Set B as the set of heterosexual unions which are undertaken with some idea of duration and in which the partners attest formally or informally to the relevant social environment (relatives, neighborhood, clan, community, sib, or society at large) that they consider themselves as belonging together, I have

97

attempted to include within it behavior that a social scientist might describe as "marriage behavior." The element of intended duration does not mean that the unions in Set B are necessarily permanent or even enduring, nor, as this set is constructed, need the unions it contains be sexually exclusive or even monogamous. I am here following the family sociologist René König in using the factors of intended duration and attestation to help to get over the difficulty of defining what turns a sexual relation into "marriage."[9] The fact that the imprecision of these terms leaves some cases that will be hard to classify does not destroy the utility of the model. Thus constructed, Set B includes a wide variety of formal and informal unions, some of which are recognized by the legal system and some not.

Now notice, that the two sets (of *de jure* marriages on the one hand and of *de facto* marriages on the other) overlap. The intersect of Sets A and B is the set of *de facto* unions which are stamped as legal marriages by the State (which in modern Western societies is the social control organization with a juridical monopoly of marriage and divorce). The part of Set A which does not intersect with Set B contains those men and women between whom a legal marriage bond exists, but who are not in a *de facto* union with each other. In modern everyday experience, then, this would include separated but legally undivorced couples and those couples between whom the *de facto* union, but not the legal bond, has been terminated by what was once called "poor man's divorce," i.e., absenting oneself without procuring a legal death certificate for the marriage.[10].

That part of Set B which does not intersect with Set A includes all those *de facto* unions as defined above which are not recognized as legal marriages by the legal system. In modern everyday experience this would include cohabitation without compliance with the formalities established by the State for formation of a legal marriage, both by those who have no interest for one reason or another in complying with formalities, and by those who are not eligible for one reason or another to comply. In this group, for example, we would not only find those cohabitants who find that legal marriage has no advantages to offer them, but also those cohabitants who are prevented from forming a legal marriage because of the existence of a prior undissolved legal marriage of one or both of them. Set B would also include persons cohabiting after religious marriages not recognized as legally valid by the State, for example, in countries like France and West Germany where civil marriage is compulsory.

Today, the overlap between Sets A and B is considerable. Most marriage behavior still takes place within the framework of legal marriage. Ease of divorce helps keep that part of Set A which does not intersect with Set B small. But this was not always so, as the following brief historical survey will demonstrate.[11]

In Western Europe prior to the Reformation, there was no set of legal marriage bonds created in compliance with secular norms of the State.

Rather, we would have to speak of those marriages recognized as such by other social norms. Looking back, we may well wonder how it came about that in the Western world the innovations of *law*, ecclesiastical or secular, became to a great extent, our marriage customs. How, for instance, did marriage in the West become indissoluble in principle, or dissoluble only for serious cause? How did the Church and State succeed in gaining social acceptance of rules that persons had to pass before an official in order to be married or unmarried? To what extent *did* they succeed?

In primitive society, law, in Weber's sense, is absent. Social relationships are regulated by custom, convention, ethics and religion, including magical beliefs and taboos. When government developed, that is, in archaic states, kinship group relations were still left to be determined by non-legal norms. This was the case, for example, in classical Rome, Confucianist China and even Meiji Japan.[12] In the late Roman Republic and in Imperial Rome, two people were held to be married, not because they had gone through any particular ceremony, but because they in fact lived together as man and wife. Just as marriage began with the setting up of life in common, so it ended when the community of life was broken by either spouse.

The fact that in Roman times, and among the Germanic peoples by whom the Roman empire eventually was overrun, marriage was not regulated as such by norms of law does not mean, however, that there was no community or kinship group interest in mating. On the contrary, early forms of rank and status were derived from marriage and birth. "Marriage" existed in the sense of being a definite social status. The wedding, or marriage rite, itself seems to have been important only under special circumstances, in particular where property was exchanged. Among the early Germanic peoples, marriage was different from other sexual unions only in that the wife and children of the marriage enjoyed a more secure position in relation to the husband and his kinship group than other women with whom he cohabited and their offspring. The distinction between marriage and other unions which, though not disapproved, are of lower status appears not only in primitive systems, but also in Roman law and in pre-Tridentine canon law, and in the civil law of France until the 16th century. Only the "wife" shared the social rank and status of her husband. So we can say that while marriage itself was not regulated by law, it was a social institution which produced legal effects.

In the widespread custom of high status families to give away their daughters only on assurances of preferred status for the daughter and her children, Max Weber saw the origin of the earliest *legal* characteristics of the legitimate marriage: dowry, the agreement to support the wife and to pay her compensation upon abandonment, and the successoral position of her children.[13] From a sociological point of view, the significance of the legitimate marriage is that it enables the family to function as a status-conferring institution. But it was only in the comparatively recent past that legitimacy, expressed in social norms, became "legality," expressed in rules of positive law.

In cultures where marriage is simply the decision of the partners to live together and raise common children, and involves no exchange of property, it tends to be dissolved simply by desertion and separation. But as marriage formation becomes more complex, the procedure for dissolving it does too. The emphasis on procedures for formation and dissolution seems to vary with the importance of rank and property. Where these are important, there is a need to clearly distinguish which sexual relationships will give rise to rights. The need to justify the dissolution of marriage and to furnish reasons to neutralize the objections of relatives appears.

König has postulated that the complexity of divorce rituals bears a direct relationship to the elaborateness of the marriage rite.[14] Where the marriage rite is attended with great pomp and ceremony, the chances are the reverse rite, divorce, will be also. What social factors are characteristically associated with elaborate marriage and divorce rituals? König tells us that where there is a high degree of family involvement in and control of marriage formation, it is usual to find the practice of producing arguments and reasons for its termination. Similarly, he notes that emphasis on property exchange before a marriage and property relations during marriage is characteristically associated with elaborate procedures for undoing such arrangements.

At the close of the Roman period, however, such rituals and procedures had not yet been juridified. It can be said that the law still took little notice of the social institution of marriage. Marriage itself was formless so far as the law was concerned; the idea of legal regulation of marriage formation or the conduct of married life was unknown; legal regulation of marriage dissolution had been attempted only to a very limited degree by the legislation of the Christian emperors which implicitly accepted the premise of the essential dissolubility of marriage.[15] To find out how marriage became formal, indissoluble and subject to far-reaching state regulation, we must turn to another legal system which, at the time of Christian Roman legislation, was not a legal system at all but only an evolving body of doctrine: the system of Roman Catholic canon law.

After the Roman Empire in the West broke down in the course of the 5th century A.D., the Christian Church not only remained intact but became stronger than ever. The Church was able to exercise great influence over, and was closely associated with the secular power of, the new Visigothic kings, and the later Merovingian and Carolingian dynasties. Even so, the establishment of the doctrine of indissolubility of marriage and of ecclesiastical jurisdiction over matrimonial matters took centuries.

The Church's claim to exclusive jurisdiction over marital causes and the novel idea that marriage was indissoluble were both closely connected to the new Christian idea that marriage was a sacrament. But the idea of the indissolubility of marriage did not easily gain a foothold in the early medieval world, where among the Anglo-Saxons, the Franks, the other Germanic tribes and the Romans, marriages were dissoluble, (without the intervention of any judge) by mutual consent or by unilateral repudiation, sometimes with payment of a penalty. For centuries, when all the Church had to work with was its disciplinary power over Christians, it had to exercise a great deal of tolerance. To some extent, it even accepted divorce and remarriage.

Ecclesiastical authority over matrimonial causes and the rudiments of a canon law system were established in what is now France and the Germanies by the end of the 10th century, and in England by the middle of the 12th century. In the rise of church jurisdiction over marriage, we begin to find the answers to the questions of how marriage came under any official regulation at all, how it became the subject of legal norms, and how it came to be indissoluble. But this is only the beginning, for there is abundant evidence that marriage continued to be considered as basically a private matter even after ecclesiastical jurisdiction was established and canon law had fixed the norm of indissolubility. In other words, even when the Church's authority was successfully asserted *vis-à-vis* the political authority (which had never regulated marriage as such anyway), its norms had not yet fully penetrated the mores. The Church bided its time, winning social acceptance of its norms in much the same way as it had gained jurisdiction, through a long patient process of action and interaction with social life. Meanwhile, canon law took the form which was to be of crucial importance for the future, even where and when the authority of the Church much later had been eroded.

Once the rule of indissolubility had been established, an important consequence followed. It had to be spelled out in minute detail exactly which unions were of the type that now could not be dissolved, and outside of which all sexual intercourse was forbidden. "Marriage" had to be defined with more precision than ever before. Out of this need came the whole complex canon law system of marriage impediments and prohibitions, and banns, and the law of nullity. The principle of indissolubility was considerably mitigated by these rules. This proliferation of grounds for annulment has been variously interpreted as: following from the necessities of intrinsic logic; related to money and power in the sense that annulments gave the Church a source of revenue and a certain amount of control over families; a humane response to the need of some individuals to escape from intolerable situations and to remarry; and a "safety valve," substituting for the necessary but missing institution of divorce. No doubt each of these factors played its role.

The Church's own records, according to recent English and French studies, show the continuation of the habit of contracting marriages informally, and the stubborn persistence of older notions of marriage as a private matter.[16] Helmholtz concludes, on the basis of his study of 13th-through 15th-century marriage litigation in Church courts in England, that it took a long time for the idea to disappear that people could regulate marriage for themselves. At the same time, he was able to trace a process, equally gradual, of social assimilation of the Church's standards, and to demonstrate considerable room for variety and growth as the canon law itself adapted to social behavior.

The Church mitigated the harshness of its indissolubility rule in other ways besides through the many causes for annulment. It provided for judicial separation in situations where one spouse had committed adultery, apostasy or heresy, or had deserted or seriously mistreated the other. But unlike annulment, judicial separation did not give rise to permission to remarry. Thus, apart from the avoidance of sin, the main interest in judicial separation must have been in connection with property concerns such as the assignment of support rights to a blameless spouse and denial of them to a blameworthy one. But separation is of great interest to us because it explains the origin of that divorce law which we have come in Western societies to take for granted. Foreshadowed itself by the grounds of justifiable repudiation[17] in the imperial Roman decrees, the canon law of judicial separation prefigures and is in fact the model for that doctrine of divorce as a sanction for marital misconduct which reappeared in the ideas of the Protestant reformers and which did not come to dominate Western divorce law until the 1970s.

So far we have not answered the question of how the *formation* of marriage came to require, in nearly all Western legal systems, the presence of an official. Up to the Council of Trent, the Church had shown its interest in this subject only by making a blessing in church a religious duty sanctioned by penance or censure. The idea that a couple must pass before a priest in order to be validly married, was established quite late in canon law—by the Tridentine Decree *Tametsi* in 1563. Until that time, canon law had recognized private and informal marriages as fully valid. Indeed the theological "purists" at Trent were opposed to making the presence of a priest as a witness a condition for the *validity* of marriage. *Tametsi* must be understood as an outgrowth, not of ecclesiastical doctrine, but of the pressures and events of the secular world.

In England, the Anglican Church, which had taken over the exclusive jurisdiction of matrimonial causes from the Roman Church in 1534, continued to recognize informal marriages as valid until 1753. But in continental Reformation Europe, the stress under which the Church found itself, combined with social and economic changes which in certain levels of society pressed for family control over the shifts of wealth and power which marriages could produce, prepared the way for a modification of the time-honored doctrine that Christians formed their marriages by consent alone. This doctrine, it should be noted, had had the beneficial side effect of liberating the individual from constraints which parents, kinship groups or political authority might try to impose on the choice of spouses. But it was this very liberating effect which began to be troublesome in 16th-century Europe, in those circles where increasing amounts of money were changing hands upon marriage. These were not negligible factors in the politics of the Council of Trent. The Decree *Tametsi* aided families at least to keep up with the marriage plans of their children, and thereby perhaps to exercise some control over marriages. Secular versions of *Tametsi* turned up all over continental Europe. Typically, they went further than the Tridentine legislation by requiring parental consent to marriages. It is questionable whether these legal innovations were evidence of anything more than a concern with the marriage practices of the dominant classes, whose property interests are reflected in the laws they alone were in a position to influence. Even in these circles, and in spite of the pressures operating in favor of parental authority and the maintenance of class lines, Professor Hunt has found a persistent

> . . . conflict between public legislation on the one hand and generally accepted popular custom and usage on the other. The edicts and ordinances clearly show that legists recognized the strength of the tradition they were trying to uproot: the continuing belief that cohabitation, simple mutual consent, made a marriage.[18]

The history of canon law up to the Council of Trent shows how marriage became subject to a kind of official regulation, namely that of the Church courts, applying canon law. It also shows the origin of the idea of legal indissolubility and the beginning of compulsory ceremonial marriage. But how did these matters become concerns of the secular State which previously had been largely indifferent to them?

From the 16th to the 18th century, in great parts of Western Europe, the Catholic Church lost its jurisdiction over marriage: in Protestant regions as a consequence of the Reformation, and in France in connection with Gallicanism and the progress of the monarchy. In Protestant areas, when the Roman Church lost its monopoly over matrimonial causes, the State acquired jurisdiction more or less by default. But to a great extent it simply took over the ready-made set of rules of the canon law, the prior law on judicial separation and maintenance becoming the model for the new secular divorce law. Although Luther and others had claimed that marriage was a proper subject for the civil courts and not subject to exclusive ecclesiastical control, they little dreamed that marriage would one day be regulated by the State according to other than Christian principles. While the reformers held that marriage was not a sacrament, they thought that secular regulations should conform to Christian teaching. Christian teaching was of course reinterpreted by them to permit divorce as a punishment for grave violation of marital duties, for adultery in particular, but gradually for other causes as well. This well-known instance of departure from Roman Catholic doctrine should not, however, obscure the fact that Catholic canon law was still widely applied. Nor should the importance of the introduction of divorce itself be exaggerated, for it was accompanied by a tightening up of nullity which the Roman Church had at times offered rather freely. Protestantism did not return divorce to the private order by any means: no divorce by mutual consent was recognized and divorce for cause had to be granted by an official. Only in the Enlightenment did a true antithesis to the Roman Catholic attitude appear.

The effects of the Protestant Reformation take us further toward understanding how marriage formation and dissolution came under the jurisdiction of the secular State, and thus how much modern law of marriage formation and dissolution took shape. However, we have yet to learn how the State came to apply its own secular, as opposed to ecclesiastical, norms of law.

In addition, we still have no answer to the question of how the secular law came to regulate or at least to purport to regulate a matter from which even canon law had abstained, namely, the organization and conduct of married life. To understand the evolution of this branch of law, account has to be taken of two developments for which the Protestant reformers cannot be held responsible, although in a sense they helped pave the way. These developments are the appearance of the humanistic and individualistic thought of the Enlightenment and the rise of the absolutist State.

The developments occurred in different fashion in France and the various regions of Germany, but resulted eventually in unprecedented comprehensive regulation of family relationships there. England, on the other hand, remained in some ways a special case, and so, in consequence, did the United States.

Rulers like Frederick II of Prussia, Joseph II of Austria, Napoleon, and their legal scholars and bureacratic administrators felt the need for a clear and complete codification of all private law. Further, these rulers were in a position to impose their own ideas as rules of positive law in their Codes. In the great codifications the law intervened in the smallest details of the most intimate relationships in a way unknown to the Roman and Canon law. Sometimes these extremes of juridification seem to be in the furtherance of some interest of the State (as with population-related provisions), or of dominant groups in society (as with the paternal authority over children). Sometimes they seem to be merely the result of that urge for completeness so evident in other aspects of, say, the Prussian General Code of 1794.

As has already been mentioned, England remained a case apart in some ways. Ecclesiastical jurisdiction over marriage survived the Reformation without real disruption until 1857. Briefly, under Cromwell, it seems civil marriage was available and divorce may have been permitted. But civil marriage did not reappear in England until 1836 and then only as an optional system. Informal marriages were valid in England until Lord Hardwicke's Act in 1753 which, like the Decree *Tametsi*, made an ecclesiastical ceremony compulsory and required publication of banns. Divorce was available after 1660 but only by special Act of Parliament, and then only for adultery. This procedure was expensive, complicated, and rarely used. Judicial divorce became available only by the Matrimonial Causes Act of 1857, effective in 1858. Secularization occurred earlier in America where no ecclesiastical courts on the English pattern had been established in the colonies.

But in many ways, Anglo-American law was marked by influences broadly similar to those just described as affecting continental European law. The uncodified English case law developed sets of legal rules which were analogous to those of French and German law, particularly so far as family hierarchy and family property relationships were concerned. It did not, however, develop the heavy component of symbolism and ideology, the "non-law," about marriage that distinguishes the continental family law.

The chief characteristic of English law concerning marriage which has constantly differentiated it from the French and German modes of regulation, is not any particular provision, but its past and present relative restraint in dealing with the whole question. English law had no such elaborate system of family control of or participation in the marriage decision as did the Prussian General Code and French Civil Code. Also, in contrast to the situation in continental Europe, the English common law, which became the law of the United States,[19] did not attempt to regulate all family relationships neatly and systematically. Since the common law developed case by case, its family law was more limited in scope and less heavily symbolic than the family law of the sweeping European codifications. Until the 1960s and 1970s, Parliament in England and the state legislatures in the United States acted only occasionally in the family law area to remedy glaring anachronisms, such as the legal position of the married woman. Change and innovation were by and large brought about by the courts in a gradual process of adaptation to changing social conditions. There are a number of factors that kept this process of adaptation slow, diffuse and incomplete. Chief among these is the fact that a court, unlike a legislature, cannot act until a point has been raised in litigation. The highest courts cannot speak with their own special authority on a subject unless such litigation is carried up to them on appeal. Appeals are costly and, thus, in the family law field, (as opposed to commercial law, for example) were rare until legal services became widely available in the 1960s.

As mentioned above, until Lord Hardwicke's Act, a valid marriage could be contracted in England by an informal present change of consents. But in fact by then it had long been customary for marriages to be celebrated in the

Church and for the Church authorities to require consent of parents of parties under 21. These customs became legal requirements in 1753 when Lord Hardwicke's Act was passed, partly in response to the concerns of parents of daughters. The common law rule that a wife's personal property vested in her husband immediately upon marriage had made such families vulnerable to valid informal marriages, particularly as personal property came to rival and replace real property as a source of wealth and power.

Lord Hardwicke's Act was not, however, completely effective in putting a stop to marriages without parental consent. Many couples evaded it simply by marrying in Scotland. Also, Engels undoubtedly had a point when he observed, commenting on the relative leniency of English marriage law, that there is more than one way to influence a child's marriage decision: in England, although a child could succeed in marrying without parental consent, his parents were legally free to disinherit him; in France and Germany on the other hand, where parental consent was required, children could not, in principle, be disinherited.[20] So long as English property law permitted and even facilitated indirect control of the marriage decision by such devices as the strict family settlement, it was unnecessary to establish direct legal control through the marriage law itself.

Like English law, American law developed without an elaborate legal framework for direct family participation in or control of the marriage decision. The characteristic American abstention from regulation of the organization or conduct of the on-going marriage, and from embodying any express ideology of marriage or family in the law has to be attributable in part to the fact that by the time of the War of Independence rapid growth and diversity were already transforming colonial society. As Lockridge has put it, by 1776 the democracy of pluralism had already begun to replace the democracy of homogeneity.[21] This process prefigured a characteristic trait of modern American society and gave rise to problems which persist in American family policy and law.

Those areas of the United States settled by Puritans had divorce laws from early times, while those with a strong Anglican influence initially had no divorce at all. Legislative divorce survived in many states into the 19th century. The Western frontier states were more liberal, so that by 1860 migratory divorce had already appeared. With the English background of valid informal marriages until 1753, and, in the Southwest, with the indulgence of the canon law, informal marriage became an established legal institution in some places. "Common law" marriages are still recognized in some 13 states and the District of Columbia.

So far as the property relationships of husband and wife were concerned, on the eve of the Industrial Revolution, it could be said that the legal systems for regulating marital property relationships in England, France, the United States and in the various regions of Germany differed in legal techniques but were similar in their basic characteristics. The husband had the power to manage all the family property, including the property of the wife. He was expected to provide for the material needs of the members of the household; the wife was expected to care for the household and the children. Since some of the family property might have been brought into the marriage by the wife, all the traditional systems were characterized, by the early 19th century, by the development of legal techniques to protect the wife and the wife's blood relatives from the consequences of mismanagement by the husband, and to assure that title to land remained in the family from whence it came.

These traditional systems were transformed in the late 19th and early 20th centuries as the law adjusted to changes in society. As rural families moved to cities, the wages of privates in the industrial army rarely were sufficient to meet the needs of whole families. The wives and children often had to seek employment outside the home or to take in work to be done at home. The model of bourgeois marriage enshrined in the 19th-century laws developed for the propertied classes was inappropriate for the wage-earning classes whose voices were increasingly coming to be heard in political life. Gradually the double-earner marriage began to find recognition in the law, first in some of the American states, then in England, then in the German Civil Code of 1896, and finally in the French Law of 13 July 1907, with the rest of the American states falling into line along the way. The technique chosen in each system was to give married women the right to dispose freely of at least their own earnings and whatever assets might have been given to them *inter vivos* or by will under stipulations that the assets were to remain subject to the wife's separate control. These innovations were really no more than an extension to the entire population of devices which had been worked out by solicitors for the wealthy and incorporated into marriage settlements (in England) and marriage contracts (on the continent) and of exceptions which had appeared early for the special case of the married woman merchant. It is probable that the appearance of the first Married Women's Property Acts, starting as early as 1839 in the United States, is related to the fact that marriage settlements were never used in the new country to the extent that they were in England. Thus the need for change appeared earlier in the United States among sectors of the population who were in a position to do something about it.

The processes of secularization and statization of marriage law which have been broadly outlined here coincided with certain trends in legal thought which were to reach their high point in the 19th century. In 19th-century English and American case law and doctrine legal norms and concepts were formalized and expressed in a highly conceptualistic way. Legal rules, which often were but the expression of moral value judgments or the resolution of conflicting interests, came to appear to have life of their own, producing "logical" and "necessary" consequences. At the same time, as Max Weber noted, the notion of legitimacy had come to be identified with that of "legality."[22] Conduct came to be oriented to norms of positive law, rather than to ideas of legitimacy expressed in customs, convention and religion, (although, as Weber was quick to point out, the fact that conduct may be oriented to legal norms does not necessarily mean the norms are obeyed.) As we have already mentioned, family law appeared relatively recently in history. Yet, once it appeared, it interacted with the mores and eventually even acquired the force of tradition. Thus, rules of law, to a certain extent, became themselves the matrimonial customs of the modern Western world.

However, we are only beginning to discern the extent to which the image of the family contained in "family law" has been the creation of the State and its laws made for fine ladies and gentlemen or prosperous burghers. Historical research has made enormous strides in recent years shedding light on what the life of other travellers through this world may have been like.

While the chief desire of historians in confronting the family law artifacts of past societies may be to make them speak about the family life of the past, the lawyer's preoccupation is apt to be with whether and how they might have affected ideas or behavior. But these two concerns—with law as evidence of social conduct and with law as a motivating force in social conduct—are not really separate. They are just two ways of trying to penetrate and understand the complex and reciprocal interaction of behavior, ideas and law. In the area of family studies, however, one cannot begin to approach these very difficult problems without appreciating first how stubbornly the forms of behavior involved in family law follow their own patterns independently of what the legal systems say they should be doing. For this we need the help of anthropologists and probably even ethologists. Thus, although Louis le Roy's pessimism was undoubtedly justified, and though it is less likely than ever in the 20th century that we can succeed where he forecast failure, the study of family law or of family history requires us to sail into the wind: we must become encyclopedists.

FOOTNOTES

1. D. Kelley, *Foundations of Modern Historical Scholarship: Language, Law and History in the French Renaissance* 84 (Columbia 1970).
2. M. Weber, *Law in Economy and Society* 5 (M. Rheinstein ed., Harvard 1954).
3. Id. at 35.
4. *Allgemeines Landrecht für die Preussischen Staaten von 1794 II* §§ 178-180 (A. Metzner, Frankfurt and Berlin 1970).
5. See generally, M. Rheinstein and M. Glendon, "Marriage: Interspousal Relations," in *International Encyclopedia of Comparative Law* Ch. 4 (A. Chloros ed. to be published in 1977).
6. In a legal proceeding for divorce, separation or separate maintenance, these norms technically could be relevant on the question of whether a spouse had committed marital "fault."

7. We can learn from the anthropologists that it is useful to distinguish further between "marriage" and the "family," since the importance of marriage, as a highly individualized heterosexual relation is quite variable, while the same cannot be said of the family as a social group which includes more persons than the marriage partners (if any). Marriage, as distinct from other sexual relationships, is said to be barely visible in some societies, and, in others, irrelevant to family formation. The fact that the family is the primary institution does not exclude the fact that the family has existed in a variety of forms. Indeed, it seems that no society known to us has had only one family type. On the other hand, the range of family types and, for that matter, of the forms of marriage has not precluded a constant process of change which results in the development and emergence of family forms new at least to the societies in which they emerge. But this process of change is slower in the case of family forms than it is for marriage forms.

8. The following analysis is adapted from M. Glendon, *State, Law and Family: Family Law in Transition in the United States and Western Europe,* Ch. 1 (North-Holland 1977). It does not apply, in this form, to marriage in non-Western countries.

9. R. Konig, Sociological Introduction, in *IV International Encyclopedia of Comparative Law* Ch. 1 (A. Chloros ed. 1974).

10. Just as marriage is both a legal and a social phenomenon, so is marriage termination. A man or woman who ceases to live in a formal or informal marriage has "dissolved" that marriage. There has never been a society where divorce, or some functional equivalent (such as simple departure of a spouse) did not exist. As with legal marriage, legal marriage termination (divorce, annulment) overlaps but does not exactly coincide with the social phenomenon it purports to regulate.

11. The evidence upon which the following overview is based, and documentation thereof, can be found in Chapter 7 of M. Glendon, supra n. 8, where the subject is treated at greater length.

12. M. Rheinstein, Motivation of Intergenerational Behavior by Norms of Law, in *Social Structure and the Family: Generational Relations* 241-266 (E. Shanas and G. Streib eds. Prentice-Hall 1965).

13. Weber, supra n. 2 at 134.

14. König, supra n. 9.

15. That this is so has been convincingly demonstrated by Noonan, in Novel 22, in The Bond of Marriage: An Ecumenical and Interdisciplinary Study 41 (W. Bassett ed. 1968).

16. B. Gottlieb, Getting Married in Pre-Reformation Europe: The Doctrine of Clandestine Marriage and Court Cases in Fifteenth-Century Champagne (unpubl. Ph.D. dissertation, Columbia University, 1974); R. Helmholz, *Marriage Litigation in Medieval England* (Cambridge 1975).

17. That is, cases in which a spouse could be repudiated without payment of a penalty or incurring some other sanction.

18. D. Hunt, *Parents and Children in History: The Pychology of Family Life in Early Modern France* 63 (Basic Books 1970).

19. In some parts of the United States, the Spanish influence has to be taken into account as well. See generally the excellent study by Baade, "The Form of Marriage in Spanish North America," 61 *Cornell L. Rev.* 1 (1975).

20. F. Engels, *The Origin of the Family, Private Property and the State* 136 (Leacock ed. 1972; orig. publ. 1882).

21. K. Lockridge, *A New England Town: The First Hundred Years. Dedham, Massachusetts 1636-1736* at 171 and 174 (1970).

22. Weber, Supra n. 2 at 4.

## 3. The Informal Social Control of Marriage in Seventeenth–Century England; Some Preliminary Notes[1]

by Alan Macfarlane

It is obvious that a detailed study of the control of marital and sexual relations can only be made after a more general study of marriage patterns in a particular society. No such general study exists for pre-industrial England.* (New York, 1977). All that can be attempted here is a very general sketch which blocks in some of the few known facts and leaves blank the vast areas of unexplored problems. The major topics in the ensuing discussion will be age at marriage; proportion ever married; courting, betrothal and the degree of contact between future husband and wife; the extent to which marriages were arranged by parents; exchange of wealth at marriage; patterns of residence after marriage and the actual patterns of marriage choice measured by geographical and social distance. The major aims of this study will be to discover firstly the general extent to which marriage was controlled in Tudor and Stuart England, and secondly, whether there were any important endogamous groups.

On the basis of analyses of the occasional census and of work on parish registers, we now know that the age at marriage in Tudor and Stuart England was, compared to that in modern pre-industrial societies, extremely high. Without going into too much detail, the (mean) average age of brides at first marriage was usually between 20 and 30, of grooms between 25 and 30.[2] Wrigley has shown that ages at marriage fluctuated quite considerably during the sixteenth and seventeenth centuries, but they remained within these general limits. For example, the (mean) average age at first marriage for brides at Colyton.in Devon fluctuated between 25.1 and 29.6 years.[3] This delay for a number of years after puberty is so unusual in human societies as a whole that it has earned the title of the "European marriage pattern" and has been described as "unique or almost unique in the world."[4] Little is known about when it originated, nor have the possible reasons for its existence been ascertained. The fact that it entailed a gap of some ten years between puberty and marriage is obviously of considerable significance for the historian of sexual and marital practices. The other feature of this "European marriage pattern" is also very important. This was a considerable rate of never-married persons.

In the majority of pre-industrial societies almost 100% of those aged over 35 have been, or are, married.[5] Those who do not marry are often derided and scorned unless they are deformed and hence unable to marry.[6]

*Editor's note: Since this article was written, Lawrence Stone has written a general study of pre-industrial England. *The Family, Sex and Marriage in England 1500-1800,* (New York), 1977.

This may have been the case in medieval England if Pollock and Maitland are right in saying that "early Medieval law never seems to have contemplated the existence of an unmarried woman of full age."[7] Even in the later period it has been said that "Elizabethans who wished to remain single felt bound to defend themselves,"[8] and there were not a few who believed that the unmarried life would automatically lead to "sin and iniquity."[9] Another writer warned people not to marry because of social pressure: "let not a fond conceit, that it is a reproach to thee to continue so ancient a Maid or Batchelor" force one into marriage.[10] Yet, in the cases where we have any statistics, it appears that, as in modern Italy,[11] only a certain proportion of the population could expect to marry. From the very crude figures so far available it appears that up to 25% of men and women might remain unmarried.[12] Among the questions this poses are: in what way did the marriage market function in order to ensure that certain people married and others remained unmarried; did the existence of a considerable body of unmarried men and women at all ages have any repercussions on the attitudes to, or rate of, sexual offences?

Although historians have made some general descriptions of courting customs,[13] there is still much to be learnt about the process by which a bride was chosen. A short extract from the most famous account of such customs will indicate the nature of the general descriptions, upon which investigators have based most of their conclusions.

> Usually the young man's father, or he himself writes to the father of the maid to know if he shall be welcome to the house, if he shall have futherance if he come in such a way or how he liketh of the notion . . .If the motion be thought well of, and embraced, then the young man goeth perhaps twice to see how the maid standeth affected. Then if he see that she be tractable and that her inclination is towards him, then the third time that he visiteth, he perhaps giveth her a ten-shilling piece of gold, or a ring of that price; . . . then the next time, or the next after that, a pair of gloves of 6s.8d. a pair . . . They visit usually every three weeks or a month and are usually half a year, or very near, from the first going to the conclusion.[14]

This description of formal, spaced, visits accords with the descriptions we have of actual wedding negotiations among the English nobility.[15] The exchange of gifts also seems to have been widespread. For instance we find in the ecclesiastical court records of the county of Essex for 1639 that a man gave a woman "a peece of money and a paire of gloves with silver fringe as tokens of love and affection." When the engagement was broken off such gifts were demanded back: thus a man asked back for his ring, silver whistle and handkerchief.[16] The events leading up to marriage clearly passed through a series of demarcated stages, each with its own ritual and legal significance and each bringing the feature partners together and severing them from their previous relationships. Such a process can be studied, for example, in the courtship of Ralph Josselin, an Essex clergyman of the mid-seventeenth century who left behind a detailed Diary.[17] On October 6th he saw his future bride in Church and was immediately physically attracted to her. By December 13th he was so much enamoured that he rejected his uncle's offer of a living in Norfolk on account of her. On January 1st they first proposed to match "one to another" and some three weeks later on the 23rd undertook their "mutual promise." This was their private contract, and to make it completely binding they made a public contract on September 29th. Then the banns were called and a month later on October 28th they were wed. The usual interval between meeting and marriage seems to have been about six months.[18] Among the stated reasons for this delay were the necessity for the bride's father to gather together her marriage "portion" and because, as contemporaries pointed out, it was important for future bride and groom to gain an intimate knowledge of each other's habits; how they ate, walked, worked.[19] There is some evidence to show that the engaged couple were allowed to meet alone and, in certain areas and in certain periods, to have sexual intercourse.[20]

The final culmination of the creation of a new social unit was the wedding. The cost of weddings and their importance as a form of conspicuous consumption;[21] the rituals at the actual wedding; the range of people present at the wedding, showing the effective range of bride and groom's social ties, all these problems need further study. Why, for example, were there sometimes two wedding feasts, one at the bride's father's house, and then another at the bridgegroom's home a month later?[22] How common was the custom of taking a large-scale collection from the wedding guests which, for example, raised £56 at one of the weddings attended by Josselin?[23] These and many other questions need answering before we have a reasonable picture of the nature of Tudor and Stuart weddings.

It was a saying of the seventeenth century that a father should marry his children betimes lest they marry themselves.[24] This brings us to the general problem of the degree to which marriages were controlled by people other than the married couple. Since marriage drew together two hitherto unrelated sets of kinsmen and friends, and since these kinsmen and friends were invited, so to speak, to invest in the new family in the form of dowries, gifts and general goodwill, it is not surprising that they should expect to have some say in the timing and choice of marriage partners. Moreover it was through the opinions and acts of such kinsmen and neighbours that wider economic pressures were mediated. Little study has been made so far of the degree to which marriages were affected in England by harvest fluctations and epidemics. We need to know, for example, the extent to which poor harvests would mean that families would have too little capital to found a new unit. In theory the degree of control might vary between completely arranged marriages, as in many parts of the modern world, or as described by Thomas Becon who wrote that "many there be of that order which make open sale of their children, as the butcher doth of his calves"[25] and those in which the future marriage partners chose their own mates.[26]

The ideal in this period was clear. Parents, friends and the young couple should all give their consent to the union, none of them should be forced. Becon, Perkins, and the ecclesiastical injunctions all stressed that parental consent was absolutely necessary before a wedding took place.[27] But the same authorities also warned that parents should not force their children to marry against their wishes.[28] In practice, however, the slight evidence so far unearthed suggests that parental consent, though useful, was not absolutely necessary. The idea that all marriages were arranged and based mainly on economic motives seems to be a myth created by historians. There is certainly evidence for the arrangement of marriage among the gentry and upper classes [29] and it may be true, as sociologists have suggested, that the control of marriage becomes tighter and more extended as one ascends the social hierarchy.[30] Yet contemporaries were well aware that children often married without their parents' consent. Becon noted this [31] and John Stockwood deplored the tendency of the younger generation "making matches according to their own fickle fantasies, and choosing unto themselves, yoke-fellowes after the outward deceivable directions of the eie."[32]

There is the problem of whether, in fact, the degree of parental control was changing—for instance with the change in age of marriage, growing possibility of earning a living outside the family holding. In a later period it would be possible to investigate the effects of industrialization on the control of marriage.[33]

There is considerable evidence, for example, in the ecclesiastical court records, to show that the "goodwill" of friends was thought very important in a marriage; for instance a man argued that it was necessary for him to "obtain his friends and her friends goodwill" before he could marry a girl in 1592.[34] Yet there is also contrary evidence that such goodwill was often not obtained, yet the marriage occurred.[35] The same is true of parental consent. On the one hand we have depositions such as the following in 1578 when a man said to his prospective wife,

> Ellen, I pray you be careful what you do and thinke that it is no iestinge or triflinge match (i.e. to plight troth and then to break it because) for fear of yo(u)r parentes you be forced to denie that wh(i)ch you have promised (as I ensure you I feare they will doe what they can to keepe us asonder if there good wills be not first requested.[36]

On the other hand we know that, for example, many of the Martindale family married against their parents' wishes.[37] The essence of the difficulty lay in the fact that it was extremely difficult, since many children seem to have left home before the age of 15 and to have spent the ten years before marriage elsewhere, for the parents to exert complete control.[38] Parents' main lever, however, was a strong one: it was the withholding or transferring of wealth in the form of a dowry to girls, or a house and property to a son.

When two people married they were, in effect, setting up a small corporation, a property-owning and productive unit large enough to support future children. For this, capital was needed. The question was, who would finance this venture? Various societies have suggested a number of methods: the partners themselves contribute by saving in the form of a trousseau woven by the girl or property accumulated by the man; or the girl's parents may pay a dowry to the husband or his family as an advance on the girl's inheritance and to be held in trust for the children;[39] or the man's kin may pay a "brideprice" to the girl's kin. In English society, as far as can be seen in an area where so little research has been carried out below the level of the gentry,[40] it seems that each family contributed one member and an equal amount of property.[41] The wife's family might contribute cash and husband's land, or *vice versa*. It is usually easier to assess the size of the girl's dowry for it is often carefully stipulated in the negotiations which occur before a wedding. We know that such portions were often very large among the upper classes: Evelyn, for example, mentions sums of £3,000 or £4,000 being paid.[42] Yet we know practically nothing about their size, over how long a period they were paid, how they varied over time, or anything else about them at the village or artisan level.[43] The way in which the marriage is financed will clearly influence the degree of parental control, the age of marriage, inheritance systems and much else.

Another fact it influences, and influencing it, is residence after marriage. Broadly speaking the young couple may either live with one set of parents or the other or by themselves. If they live with either set of parents this means living in the same house or the same village. What actually happens in a society is extremely important: for instance if the young married couple live with their parents this may mean that they remain under parental control for years after marriage and that the whole family acts as one economic unit. Behind all the arrangements there is a tension between the two founding families who may both wish to retain their offspring. The logical result of this, as among some Irish islanders at the present time, is that husband and wife live apart, visiting each other occasionally at night.[44] Little research has been done on this problem so far in its seventeenth-century context, but it seems likely that new households were set up immediately after the wedding and that these tended to be either in the bridegroom's village or in a town or village foreign to both sets of parents. Contemporaries thought that if two married couples lived in the same house there would be friction—for example William Whately wrote that "the mixing of governors in an household, or subordinating or uniting of two Masters, or two Dames under one roofe, doth fall out most times, to be a matter of much unquietness to all parties."[45]

The analysis of household sizes has shown that this ideal was followed.[46] The slight evidence so far analysed suggests that the newly married couple moved more often into the husband's village than into that of the wife.[47]

The problem of residence after marriage is clearly related to that of the geographical distance which separated the engaged couple before marriage. This is also relevant to the question of incest since it is likely that a high rate of village endogamy will lead to technically incestuous marriages. In many of the societies studied by anthropologists where kinship is a basic organizing principle, there is also a very limited geographical range within which marriage partners may be found. The situation may vary from hamlet endogamy as in some Balinese villages,[48] or matched pairs of villages who exchange marriage partners,[49] to groups of 25 or so villages which form an endogamous unit, as in Ceylon.[50] It would be possible to parallel the maps and diagrams analysing this topic produced by anthropologists, in a study of Tudor and Stuart England, but, so far, little work has been published on this subject.[51] Studies of French communities in the seventeenth and eighteenth centuries have shown that between 60 and 95% of the marriages involved people from the same parish.[52] It seems likely that this high rate of village endogamy was also characteristic of pre-industrial Ireland.[53] Historians have tended to assume that people married within the village or into neighbouring villages in pre-industrial England.[54] This seems to be true for at least certain regions in the medieval period,[55] and it may have continued to be true in certain areas of England during the sixteenth and seventeenth centuries. There is some evidence to show that, in certain areas, marriage partners were usually found within 15 miles.[56] Yet there was probably considerable variation both by region and by social status. In the village of Wrangle, Lincolnshire, for example, the evidence for marriages in the late seventeenth century which shows that only a small proportion of the marriages were between two partners from the same village, has been summarized as follows. "It is clear that the idea once held that there was persistent in-breeding in the villages is not borne out by the facts as far as Wrangle is concerned."[57] It also seems likely that the geographical range might increase with social level. Again as in Bali, or the Vendée, distance of marriage would be related to social status,[58] Certainly we know that the geographical range of marriages involving the nobility was very wide and, it has been argued, increasing, throughout the period.[59] Another problem needing analysis is the "social distance" between marriage partners, that is the degree to which different occupational and status groups intermarried. We know practically nothing about intermarriage between different social groups below the level of the gentry in Tudor and Stuart England. William

Perkins probably spoke for the majority of his contemporaries when he argued that husband and wife should come from the same social level,[60] but whether they did or not, we do not yet know. There is plenty of evidence that each occupational group *had* its level, and that it should marry within this level. For instance, the Earl of Clarendon argued that it was a sign of the confusion of ranks caused by the Civil War that some noblemen's daughters had married clergymen: waiting-women were supposed to be about the social level to make good cleric's wives.[61] The most detailed work on people at the lower social levels has been undertaken for the Vendée (in the eighteenth century) by Charles Tilly. He has shown that certain occupational groups were linked, commercial bourgeois and winegrowers for example, while others, like farmers and industrial artisans, were not. But the figures need breaking down even further, into male and female for example.[62]

Although the English gentry have been studied assiduously their intermarriage rates have been little investigated. This is not for lack of evidence. Marriage licences of the period give the occupation and rank of both husband and wife and it would be possible to do a study of intermarriage on a large scale. The sort of analysis that might emerge is shown by preliminary work by Peter Laslett. Taking a sample of some fifty bridegrooms and sixty brides described as "gentry" in Lincolnshire between 1612 and 1617 he shows that

> almost a third of the men and over two-fifth of the women married outside their social order. When clergy and the obviously bourgeois occupations are taken into account the indication of social mobility is rather less; only about 20 per cent in the case of men though still over a third of the women married outside . . . the ruling segment. Nearly a quarter of the women and over 15 per cent of the men married into yeomen's families.[63]

One of the facts that emerges most strikingly from the historical material is that in a system where wealth and blood flowed predominantly through the eldest male, the other males tended to marry downwards, if they married at all. Lawrence Stone said of younger sons that "Almost always poorly endowed, they either did not marry at all, or married late and relatively humbly."[64] Stone also supplied diagrams and statistics on the intermarriage of the peerage class. His conclusion is that "Between 1485 and 1569 over half the marriages of titular peers and their heirs male were within the peerage class, but between 1570 and 1599 the proportion fell to a third."[65] The reason suggested for changes in rates, by Stone, is that the aristocracy needed new money: changes in the financial and economic structure of Tudor England forced a widening of perspectives in the marriage market.

The same process of aristocratic marriage into the moneyed classes has been studied in eighteenth-century France by Elinor Barber.[66] She shows a fluid situation where husbands with wealth could buy themselves into the old nobility. There was a similar process in fifteenth-century England, according to J.H. Hexter, and this may have meant that merchant capital was drained off into land-purchases rather than being re-invested in trade and industry.[67] The methods used to control the marriage market, especially at the village level, need further research. It seems likely that there was already a great amount of marital mobility, centering on the London marriage sorting house.

As far as can be discovered, no historical studies have been made to show to what extent marriage linked families that were already linked by ties and kinship. We cannot tell, for example, whether that was any parallel to the situation among modern Greek shepherds where, of 121 marriages, 52 were contracted between families already linked by kinship ties. [68] Although no indications have been given by contemporary literature that there were preferential rules of marriage based on kinship, until analyses of a number of villages have actually been made we will not know whether, in practice, people married, for example, their cross-cousins. All that can be said at this stage is that the reconstruction of the kinship ties and marriages in the parish of Earls Colne in Essex for the period 1560-1660 has not shown any significant rate of intermarriage between families already linked by marriage or blood.

One final problem in the general field of marriage also needs more research. This is the degree of emotion generated before and after the wedding: the presence or absence of the "romantic love complex." This emotion will be interlinked with all the other phenomena already discussed. For instance, its absence may help to account for the late age of marriage; if it was generally true that people did not become attracted into marriage but took a conscious decision at a certain point that they ought to marry,[69] this would fit the necessity to delay marriage. It is extremely important to know whether the seventeenth-century situation was closer to that of a modern bilateral system where there is a complete lack of emotion before marriage,[70] or that of some other pre-industrial societies where the choice of marriage partners is based on spontaneous physical attraction.[71] The situation in our period is complicated by the fact that there were probably enormous shifts occurring, both in ideology and practice. For example, it has been suggested that the Puritan ethic fostered "romantic love" and helped to break down the tight control of marriage choice by parents and kin.[72] Certainly there is enough evidence in contemporary records for an investigation of this important topic. Ecclesiastical court cases provide some evidence. Two servants in Essex were described as "falling in love togethers," and a woman refused to marry a suitor because "she could not find in her to love him."[73] The wider problems of how far such an ideology

# FOX & QUITT

is a necessary part of a nuclear-family system[74] and of its part in mate selection, cannot be discussed here. Future historical researchers, however, will find these sociological and anthropological discussions cited above a constant stimulus to further research in the records.

FOOTNOTES

1. This essay is an almost unchanged version of chapter 3 of my dissertation on "The Regulation of Marital and Sexual Relationships in Seventeenth Century England, with Special Reference to the County of Essex" (London School of Economics, M.Phil., 1968). A future work on *Sex, Marriage and the Family in Tudor and Stuart England* will incorporate results of studies published since 1968, and of extensive further research on local sources along the lines sketched in this short paper. Place of publication of books cited in the notes is London, unless otherwise specified.
2. Figures are given in P. Laslett, *The World We Have Lost* (1965), p.83; J. Hajnal, "European Marriage Patterns in Perspective" in D.V. Glass and D.E.C. Eversley (eds.), *Population in History* (1965), p.110; E.A. Wrigley, "Family Limitation in Pre-Industrial England," *Economic History Review,* 2nd ser., xix, no. 1 (1966), pp.86-8.
3. Wrigley, *Family Limitation,* p.86. Figures for aristocratic marriages are given in L. Stone, *Crisis of the Aristocracy, 1558-1641* (Oxford, 1965), pp.652ff.
4. J. Hajnal in Glass and D.E.C. Eversley (eds.), *Population in History,* p.101.
5. European patterns are summarized by Hajnal in Glass and Eversley (eds.), *Population in History,* pp.101ff. M. Nag, *Factors Affecting Human Fertility in Nonindustrial Societies* (Yale University Publications in Anthropology, 66, New Haven, 1962), p.182, indicates ages in percentages in pre-industrial societies. Tikopia, with a high age at marriage, seems to be an exception (R. Firth, *Essays on Social Organization and Values* (1964), p.91).
6. Examples of social pressure are J.K. Campbell, *Honour, Family and Patronage* (Oxford, 1964), pp.128, 150; P. Stirling, *Turkish Village* (New York, 1965), p.42.
7. Quoted in G.G. Coulton, *Medieval Panorama* (Fontana, 1961), ii.281.
8. L.E. Pearson, *Elizabethans at Home* (Stanford, 1957), p.289.
9. E.S. Morgan, *The Puritan Family* (Harper Torchbook, 1966), p.145.
10. William Whately, *A Care-cloth or a Treatise of the Cumbers and Troubles of Marriage* (1624), p.64.
11. J.W. Cole, Economic Alternatives in the Upper Nonsberg, unpublished paper, Canterbury Conference, 1966. Similarly in Ireland (K.H. Connell, "Peasant Marriage in Ireland: its Structure and Development since the Famine," *Econ. Hist. Rev.,* xiv no. 3 (1962), p. 502).
12. Figures are given in Glass and Eversley (eds.), *Population in History,* pp.102, 113, 114. One contemporary in the late seventeenth century commented "I believe there are more bachelors now in England by many thousands than there were a few years ago" (quoted in H.J. Habakkuk, "Marriage Settlements in the Eighteenth Century," *Trans. Roy. Hist. Soc.,* xxxii (1950), p. 24 note 1).
13. For example Laslett, *Lost World,* p. 142; G.C. Homans, *English Villages of the Thirteenth Century* (New York, 1960), ch.xxi.
14. The whole account is quoted in Laslett, *Lost World,* p.96.
15. Stone, *Crisis of the Aristocracy,* pp.649ff.
16. Essex Record Office, Chelmsford, Essex (hereafter E.R.O.), D/ACD/5 (in a separate folder); D/AED/1 fol.11.
17. A fuller description of Josselin's courtship and marriage appears in A. Macfarlane, *The*

*Family Life of Ralph Josselin* (Cambridge, 1970), pp.95-7.

18. For instance M. Campbell, *The English Yeoman under Elizabeth and the Early Stuarts* (New Haven, 1942), p.402.

19. As stressed by John Dod and Robert Clever, *A Godlie Forme of Household Government* (1612), p.109.

20. Samuel Pepys, *The Diary of Samuel Pepys, from 1659 to 1669,* ed. Lord Braybrooke (no date), p.248, stated that it was suggested that an engaged couple be left alone together. Further evidence for this is contained in Percival Moore, *Marriage Contracts or Espousals in the Reign of Queen Elizabeth* (Associated Architectural Societies' Reports and Papers, xxx part 1 (1909)), p.275.

21. The huge expenses at noble weddings are discussed and analysed in Stone, *Crisis of the Aristocracy,* pp.633, 651.

22. Henry Best, "Concerninge our Fashions at Our Country Weddinges" in *Rural Economy in Yorkshire in 1641,* ed. C.B. Robinson (Surtees Soc., xxxiii, 1857), p.117. A similar phenomenon was described and analysed in Campbell, *Honour, Family and Patronage,* pp.52,60, 136.

23. Josselin, *Diary,* 8 July 1647.

24. W. Notestein, *English People on the Eve of Colonization* (Harper Torchbook edn., 1962), p.57, cites this saying.

25. Thomas Becon, *The Worckes of T. Becon* (1560), i.sig.DCXXXI$^V$ (the foliation is erratic; the passage comes *after* sig.DCL). ·

26. Many illustrations of the wide range of degree of control of marriage by kin or other groups, from arranged marriage to 'romantic love,' are summarized in E. Westermarck, *The History of Human Marriage* (5th edn., 1921), ii.ch.xxii.

27. Becon, *The Worckes of T. Becon,* i.sig.DCXX$^V$; William Perkins, *Christian Oeconomie* (1609), p.76; W.P.M. Kennedy and W.H. Frere (eds.), *Visitation Articles and Injunctions of the Period of the Reformation* (Alcuin Club Collections, xv, 1910), ii.275.

28. Miles Coverdale, *Christian State of Matrimony,* p.23$^V$; Kennedy and Frere (eds.), *Visitation Articles and Injunctions,* ii.50.

29. For example *The Diary and Correspondence of John Evelyn, F.R.S.,* ed. William Bray (no date), pp.374-5; *The Apologia of Robert Keayne,* ed. Bernard Bailyn (New York, Harper Torchbook edn., 1964), p.33.

31. Becon, *The Worckes of T. Becon,* i.sig.DXXXii (foliation out of order, just *before* DCX-Lii).

32. Quoted in Campbell, *English Yeoman,* pp.283-4.

33. Margaret Mead, *Male and Female* (Pelican edn., 1962), p.15, for example, briefly discusses this subject.

34. E.R.O., D/AEA/16 fol.70$^V$. Other similar cases are cited in W.J. Pressey, "Essex Affairs Matrimonial," *Essex Review,* xlix (1940), p.89.

35. An instance is described in Moore, *Marriage Contracts or Espousals in the Reign of Queen Elizabeth,* p.296.

36. Consistory Court Depositions, 1578, fol. 56 (Guildhall Library, London). Another example of the necessity of parental consent is quoted in Moore, *Marriage Contracts,* p.270.

37 Described in Campbell, *English Yeoman,* p.286.

38. There is a discussion of this phenomenon in Macfarlane, *Family Life of Ralph Josselin,* Appendix B.

39. Discussions of the dowry and its functions may be found in Goode, *The Family,* pp.41-2 ; Jack Goody and S.J. Tambiah, *Bridewealth and Dowry* (Cambridge, 1973); Westermarck, *History of Human Marriage,* ii. ch.xxiii.

40. On gentry dowries and those of the nobility there is Stone, *Crisis of the Aristocracy,* pp.632ff and H.J. Habakkuk, "Marriage Settlements in the Eighteenth Century," p.21.

41. This appears to be the principle in the bilateral kinship system of Greek shepherds, (Campbell, *Honour, Family and Patronage,* p.45).

42. *Diary and Correspondence of John Evelyn,* pp.375, 499. The size and increases in aristocratic dowries are discussed in L. Stone, "Marriage Among the English Nobility in the 16th and 17th Centuries", *Comp. Stud. in Soc. and Hist.,* iii no. 2 (1961), pp.184, 189.

43. W.G. Hoskins, *The Midland Peasant* (1957), pp.123-4, cites two instances from bonds. Cases before the ecclesiastical courts are quoted in Moore, *Marriage Contracts,* pp.294-5.

44. As described in R. Fox, "Tory Island" in B. Benedict (ed.), *Problems of Smaller Territories* (1967), pp. 129-130.

45. Whately, *A Care-Cloth or a Treatise of the Cumbers and Troubles of Marriage,* sig. A6$^V$. Other quotations on the same subject are cited in Pearson, *Elizabethans at Home,* pp.296-7.

46. Much of the evidence showing little change in household size between the sixteenth and nineteenth centuries in England, is summarized in P. Laslett and R. Wall (eds.) *Household and Family in Past Time* (Cambridge, 1972), ch.4. For the medieval period some of the evidence is summarized in J. Krause, "The Medieval Household: Large or Small?" *Econ. Hist. Rev.,* 2nd ser., ix no. 3 (1957), pp.420-432.

47. A few figures are given in H.E. Hallman, "Some Thirteenth-Century Censuses," *Ec. Hist. Rev.,* 2nd ser., x no. 3 (1958), p.356; P.E.H. Hair, "Bridal Pregnancy in Rural England in Earlier Centuries," *Population Studies,* xx no. 2 (1966), p.238.

48. C. Geertz, "Form and Variation in Balinese Village Structure," *American Anthrop.,* 61 (1959), p. 997.

49. As among the Garos of Assam (R. Burling, *Rengsanggri* (Philadelphia, 1963), p.217).

50. E.R. Leach, *Pul Eliya - A Village in Ceylon* (Cambridge, 1961), p.23.

51. Useful model maps and diagrams are provided by Leach, *ibid.,* pp.81-3 and Stirling, *Turkish Village,* pp.201-7.

52. P. Goubert, *Beauvais et le Beauvaisis de 1600 a 1730* (S.E.V.E.P.E.N., 1960), i. 66; C. Tilly, *The Vendée* (1964), p.89.

53. Connell, "Peasant Marriage in Ireland," p.519.

54. For instance Campbell, *English Yeoman,* p.283, and Hoskins, *The Midland Peasant,* p.196.

55. Hallam, "Some Thirteenth-Century Censuses," p.356, shows that all but one of 53 women married within 11 miles of their natal home.

56. E.A. Wrigley (ed.), *An introduction to English Historical Demography* (1966), pp.22, 41 (note 22), 64. Hair, "Bridal Pregnancy in Rural England," p.238, gives figures which imply a limited geographical range.

57. F. West, "The Social and Economic History of the East Fen Village of Wrangle, 1603-1837," p.65.

58. Geertz, "Form and Variation in Balinese Village Structure," p.997; Tilly, *The Vendee,* p.90.

59. Stone, *Crisis of the Aristocracy,* p.623.

60. Perkins, *Oeconomy,* p.64.

61. Clarendon, cited in T.B. Macaulay, *History of England* (Everyman edn., 1957), i.246-7

62. Tilly, *The Vendee,* p.97.

63. Laslett, *Lost World,* p.191.

64. Stone, *Crisis of the Aristocracy,* p.599.

65. Stone, *ibid.,* p.627. Statistics are presented on p.789.

66. Barber in William J. Goode (ed.), *Readings on the Family and Society* (New Jersey, 1964), pp.66-7.

67. J.H. Hexter, *Reappraisals in History* (1961), p.95.

68. Campbell, *Honour, Family and Patronage,* p.132.

69. A situation described for seventeenth-century New England (Morgan, *Puritan Family,* p.54). Hajnal in Glass and Eversley, *Population in History,* p.132, also draws a connection between emotion at, and age at, marriage.

70. Campbell, *Honour, Family and Patronage,* p.66.

71. E.G., C. Fürer-Haimendorf, *Morals and Merit* (1967), p. 19. Other examples of physical attraction and personal choice are given in Westermarck, *History of Human Marriage*, ch.xxii.
72. Argued, for instance, by M. Walzer, *Revolution of the Saints* (1966), p.194 and Stone, *Crisis of the Aristocracy*, p.615.
73. E.R.O., D/AED/1 fols.7$^V$, 10.
74. For an argument concerning the 'necessity' of romantic love see Goode, *The Family*, p.39.

# 4. Marriage Settlements In The 18th Century

by H.J. Habbakuk

There were important changes of substances in the eighteenth century in marriage settlements which originated independently of changes in form. The most significant of these was the change in the relation between the size of the portion or dowry which the wife brought with her from her father, and the size of the jointure, the annual income which her husband settled on her to provide for her in case she survived him. The size of the provision which a man made for his wife's possible widowhood was naturally dependent on the amount of money she brought into the family, but the degree of the dependence differed at different times. In marriage settlements made in the early eighteenth century the portions are normally substantially larger, in relation to the jointures, than in settlements made a century earlier.

In the early part of the century the general average of portions, in relation to jointures, is somewhat lower; when Sir Edmund Verney married the daughter of Sir Thomas Denton in 1612, a portion of £2,300 was matched against a jointure of £400 a year, and when, about the same time, Sir John Farmer married a daughter of Sir Henry Compton, a portion of £4,000 matched a jointure of £800 a year. These were typical of the proportions among substantial squirarchical families. The most popular book of precedents at the opening of the sixteenth century gives, in the case of a marriage to a widow—and widows were able to command favourable terms—a portion of £620 for a jointure of £100.

What is the significance of this change? Does it mean that the terms on which marriages between landowning families were made were becoming progressively more favourable to the husband, that a larger share of the burden of maintaining the wife was being borne by her father?

Contemporaries were apt to attribute the rising scale of portions to the greater competition in the marriage market of the daughters, especially the heiresses, of merchant families. Thus, towards the end of the century, Sir William Temple, whose own marriage negotiation had been difficult, wrote that he thought he remembered

> within less than fifty years, the first noble families that married into the City for downright money, and thereby introduced by degrees this public grievance which has since ruined so many estates by the necessity of giving great portions to daughters.

Calculations of material interest have played an important part in marriages between propertied families in almost all periods. But there is evidence that in the early eighteenth century they were more important than for the early seventeenth century and for most of the sixteenth century, and that the material interests involved were more exclusively a matter of wealth.

There is first a strong general presumption that, in a period when political power was becoming more dependent on the possession of landed wealth, men sought the extension of their estates more continously than in the sixteenth and early seventeenth centuries, when political power depended more on royal favour; and that they bent marriage—always a most effective method of acquiring more property—more systematically to the accumulation of landed wealth.

There is secondly contemporary opinion which, though necessarily subjective, appears to confirm the general presumption. To a contemporary observer like Temple it appeared not only that material considerations over-rode all other considerations but that this was a relatively recent development.

> These contracts would never be made, but by men's avarice, and greediness of portions with the people they marry, which is grown among us to that degree, as to surmount and extinguish all other regards or desires: so that our marriages are made, just like other common bargains and sales, by the mere consideration of interest or gain, without any love or esteem, or birth or of beauty itself, which ought to be the true ingredients of all happy compositions of this kind, and of all generous productions. Yet this custom is of no ancient debate in England . . .

Temple clearly exaggerated the novelty of the development. But that his emphasis was right seems clear from the more objective evidence of the portions. For during the seventeenth century there was not only an increase in the size of the average portion in relation to the jointure; there was also the growth of a more uniform ratio between the portion and the jointure; or, more precisely, the deviations from the average ratio were fewer and smaller in the late than the early seventeenth century. In the later seventeenth century the standard ratio was £100 jointure for every £1,000 of portion. This did not mean that this ratio would be observed in every case. The position was well put by Lord Chancellor Hardwicke:

> The law has entrusted the parents with the care of the marriage of their children; there are many considerations, which may induce them, besides strict equality in settlements—inclination of the parties—rank and quality of the person—convenience and propriety in families—bringing together and uniting different parts of the same estate; all these are proper reasons.

If the bride was young and beautiful, if her husband was much in love with her, if there was a prospect of her becoming an heiress, if she was of social status superior to his, the husband might accept a portion which, in relation to the jointure he settled on her, was below the standard ratio. In the reverse of any or all of these conditions he might be able to demand an abnormally large portion. But the standard ratio was clearly recognized as the basis for the bargaining.

The development of this conformity to a standard ratio suggests that the marriage market was becoming more perfect in one or both of two senses. Information about prospective brides may have become more widely diffused. Considerations other than the relative wealth of the parties may have become less important. That the first had some effect cannot be ruled out; as more estates became subject to settlement, an increasing amount of knowledge about marriage prospects became concentrated in a few London conveyancers. But the strong probability is that the second factor is more important, and that this development reflects a situation in which the acquisition of wealth was becoming the primary object of an increasing number of marriages.

This probability is strengthened by the changes in the jointure over the same period. The jointure was, in origin, the substitute, in the case of lands held under uses and subject therefore to equitable jurisdiction, for the widow's common law right to one-third of the real estate of her husband. In the early seventeenth century the jointure, in a large number of settlements, was about one-third of the value of the estates which were settled on the husband. The notion that this was the proper proportion persisted strongly at the end of the century. When a landowner's settlement omitted to empower him to raise a jointure for his wife, and he sought to remedy this omission by private Act of Parliament, he was normally empowered to grant a single jointure up to one-third of the income of his settled estates. The proportion was, indeed, not an arbitrary one; it bore some relations to the maximum which, in normal circumstances, an estate could be expected to bear during a widowhood without encroaching unfairly upon the interests of the children.

But marriage settlements in the later seventeenth century increasingly departed from this proportion. This may have been because, once it was certain, as earlier it has not been certain, that provision for the children would not fall upon the widow, there was less reason to provide her with so high a proportion of the income of her husband's estate. But it is difficult to avoid the impression that the increasing flexibility of the jointure in relation to the husband's income is another consequence of the increasing subordination of marriage to the accumulation of wealth. A man who was particularly anxious to make an advantageous marriage was apt to persuade himself that he could, without impairing the provision for other members of his family, offer much more than one-third of his estate. Thus when Louis de Duras sued for the hand of the daughter of Sir George Sondes, he offered a jointure equivalent to the whole of his annual income. Naturally enough the jointures tended to be smallest, in relation to the husband's income, in the case of the very greatest landowning families for whom, in normal circumstances, wealthy marriages were both less urgent and easier to effect.

Of the factors which contributed to the increase in the size of estates in the eighteenth century, marriage was the most important. Of these marriages, those with heiresses attracted most contemporary comment. Such marriages have at all times been an important source of accumulation of property; Sir Simon D'Ewes, in the early seventeenth century, took it for granted that "it was the greatest honour that can betide a family, to be often linked into the female inheritrices of ancient stocks." From the later seventeenth century, however, they were sought more systematically. It is not a question of a family marrying one or two heiresses but, in many families, of a continuous succession of such marriages. This was clearly due, in part, to the new legal forms, which made it easier to conduct a long-term policy of estate accumulation in this way, because they allowed greater weight to be given, when a marriage was being considered, to the family's long-term views on the interests of the estate, as compared with the personal inclinations of any particular eldest son. They made it easier for landowning families to bargain with each other, to enter into long-term commitments about their estates and to honour them.

Marriage with heiresses, as a factor in estate accumulation, has, however, overshadowed marriage to brides who were not heiresses but had large portions. The fortunes of the greatest heiresses were larger than the largest portions, but there were fewer heiresses. Moreover, the estates of an heiress were sometimes settled, after the death of her husband and herself, away from her eldest son, and there was no permanent accession of land to her husband's family estate. Marriage with a daughter who was not an heiress but who had a large portion normally resulted, on the other hand, in an accession of land which descended to the eldest son and remained permanently in the family. For the portions were usually spent, by the family receiving them, on the purchase of land. Since they are almost invariably

124

raised, by the family paying them, by mortgage of the family estates, the landowning class as a whole was mortgaging to buy more land, in effect "raising itself by its own boot straps."

In this way the spread of the arrangements associated with the strict settlement positively promoted the accumulation of estates and did not merely negatively impede their dispersion. But did the arrangements tend to the advantage of any particular class of landowner, the great territorial aristocracy, for example, as opposed to the smaller squires?

Those landowners were likely to suffer, whether great or small, who had many children, especially daughters, to provide for. Family fortunes were at the mercy of the birth- and death-rates. Children, no doubt, have been an economic liability in many periods, and landowners are always liable to provide for their children more generously than is warranted by the long-term economic positon of the family estates. It is not difficult to recall families in the sixteenth century, for example, who became heavily indebted because they gave their children large portions. What made a large number of children more of a liability from the later seventeenth century, and parents more likely to make over-generous provision for them, was the fact that the provision was specified at the time of the marriage, before the size of the commitment and the circumstances at the relevant time could be known.

Those landowners were likely to gain who offered substantial jointures, since they could command the brides with the largest portions; these were usually the landowners with the largest gross, rentals. And the effect was cumulative; a wealthy marriage in one generation put a family in a stronger position to make another in the next generation. Marriages on this pattern, therefore, tended to accelerate the rate of growth of great estates. The principal reason, however, why in the first half-century of the strict settlement, owners of large estates bought at the expense of the gentry must be sought outside the operations of the new arrangements; primarily in the heavy taxation on income from land, which, in the case of the smaller landowners, was less frequently offset by the perquisites of office under the Crown.

There is a final question to which an answer must be attempted. Why did not the debts incurred to pay portions ultimately grow so great as to force landowners to seek the relief of a private Act authorizing the sale of their settled estates, thus, over landowners as a whole, offsetting the increase in estates due to the acquisition of portions? Had this happened, the eighteenth century would have seen, not a tendency for large estates to grow larger, but a continual process of expansion and contraction, in which an estate gained in one generation only to lose in a subsequent generation. On some estates, it is true, debts contracted to provide portions did, in fact, force sales; and, on other estates, sale was avoided only because the normal conventions were relaxed and the bride's portion used, not to buy land, but to pay her husband's debts. But, over landowners as a whole, the land sold to pay debts incurred to pay portions was substantially less than the land bought with portions.

This was probably a consequence of the fact that strict settlement was not widely adopted until the late seventeeth century. Only then, therefore, on many estates, did large debts begin to be regularly incurred in providing for children; and where these were the only important debts they might accumulate for three or four generations before becoming sufficiently onerous to compel sale where this involved the expense and publicity of a Private Act. Provision for children was far from being the only source of debt among eighteenth-century landed families, and was certainly not the cause of their most spectacular debts, which were due to personal extravagance, excessive building and election expenses. This should not, however, obscure the fact that such provision was a more typical and widely diffused cause of debt. Indeed, the strict settlement tended to reduce the likelihood of heavy debts being incurred on other accounts; a life-tenant could not mortgage his estate except for purposes specified in his settlement, that is, in most cases in the early eighteenth century, only to raise portions. Estates could stand mortgaging for this purpose precisely because they could not easily be mortgaged for other purposes.

Nevertheless, the debts on this account could not have continued to increase indefinitely. Already by the middle of the century they had brought some families to a precarious position. What in fact saved the great landowners from a substantial reduction of their estates was the spectacular increase in incomes from land later in the century, when war, industrial revolution and population increase came to their rescue.

## 5. The Age At Marriage in England and Its Implications
by J. D. Chambers

It has usually been assumed that obstacles to mobility such as limitations of transport and particularly the operation of the Settlement Laws must have imposed limitations upon the choice of partners and served to keep down the rate of marriage. While these factors cannot be dismissed altogether, they must be relegated to secondary importance in the light of the mounting evidence that neither the Settlement Laws nor the condition of transport constituted a serious barrier to the movement of single able-bodied young men and women—as distinct from heads of families—in search of a job, a house, or a partner in life.

A study of village names in the Subsidy Rolls of Nottinghamshire villages between 1606 and 1641 shows that although the population had not altered appreciably in size between the two dates, more than 37 per cent of the names vanished, and their place was taken by others. "Names continually disappear," the author writes, "while new names occur, themselves in turn vanishing, leaving finally perhaps one family running through the series for a parish." Whatever the cause, these figures indicate a greater change than any due to the ordinary chances of life. "It seems therefore permissible to infer that the rural population . . . was not permanently rooted in its native soil." These findings have been confirmed by more recent studies, and the picture of a mobile country population incessantly engaged in the process of moving for the purpose of improving their condition, above all seeking their fortune in the towns, is now firmly established.

An important recent contribution to our knowledge of this phenomenon is that provided by Dr. Tranter, who was fortunate enough to come across a detailed survey of Cardington in Bedfordshire for the year 1782. In the single year of the survey 5 out of 150 cottage families moved out of the village, which, if it is a representative figure, could mean that the entire cottage population would change in thirty years. Of those who reached the age of fifteen, 64 per cent of the boys and 57 per cent of the girls had left the parish to earn a living elsewhere, usually as domestic servants or in husbandry. Half the cottage migrants went to villages within an approximate distance of 6 miles; only 27 per cent went beyond the boundary of the country and most of these went to London. The inward flow into the village was on almost a similar scale: of the 109 families whose places of birth were given only 7 had both parents born in it: 51 had both parents from another parish; of the men 33 per cent and of the women 27 per cent were born in the village. There was a stable element of propertied families with roots in the village and it seems to have been from them that the tradition of a static rural society had its rise and justification.

From this, and many other inquiries which could be cited, it would appear that the limit of settlement was not the parish, but a larger area comprising several parishes covering a distance of about 7 miles across. Apparently the pre-industrial villager knew the neighbouring parishes as intimately as he knew his own; when a cottage became vacant it would be snapped up as readily by a man from the next village as by those in the village where it occurred. Boys and girls would not only leave home, but leave their native parishes for places in service, and also for their partners in marriage. Moreover the high death-rate and low expectation of life would provide opportunities which these humble seekers after self-advancement would not let slip. Perhaps the most striking and poignant example of the incessant movement of the labouring classes in search of a living comes from the parish of Wrangle in Lincolnshire, where the ravages of tuberculosis and ague arising from the proximity of undrained fenland were so severe that the average life-span of all children born there in 1654-1753 was merely fourteen. Yet in spite of this appalling wastage of life, the village maintained itself at a steady level of between 200 and 300 owing to the inward movement of migrants from neighbouring villages in search of a livelihood, a cottage, or a partner in marriage.

There were other obstacles to marriage to which more weight should be given. Professor Ashton has pointed out that "women in particular might remain single, not because of a shortage of men but because the candidates for matrimony were socially ineligible." Preston—'Proud Preston'— subsisted, it was said, "by many families of middling fortune . . . and it is remarkable for old maids, because their families will not ally with tradesmen, and have not sufficient fortunes for gentlemen." And below the class in which social conditions weighed heavily were labourers and domestic servants living in, for whom marriage meant a great disturbance of their way of life and possible loss of their livelihood. According to the philosopher Hume, all masters discouraged "the marrying of their male servants and admit not by any means the marriage of the female," an attitude deplored by Joseph Hanway, who asked why should these classes of people be prevented from marrying more than any other.

On the whole, however, the various restrictive influences that were brought to bear affected the age at, rather than the rate of, marriage. This was partly due to the imbalance in the age structure of the sexes. There was always an excess of male over female babies, probably in the ratio of 105: 100, but since more boys died under the age of twenty than girls there was usually an excess of females by that age. However, mortality among wives was high and most women had a chance to marry, so that the propensity to marry was high in both sexes.

If the low level of nuptiality seems to have been peculiar to the aristocracy the comparatively high age of marriage was common to all classes of the community. Evidence continues to multiply that in the seventeenth and eighteenth centuries the age of marriage of women in England was about 24, though it could rise, as Dr. Wrigley has shown in his study of Colyton, as high as 30 after the plague of 1546. The age of men was usually about two years higher. From a study of marriage allegations and certificates in Nottinghamshire and Gloucestershire between 1650 and 1750 it was found that farmers—yeomanry and husbandmen—married between 25 and 30; gentlemen about 26; and apprenticed workmen at almost the same age, except framework knitters among whom apprenticeship had largely lost its meaning, who married between 23 and 24 and chose slightly younger wives. Incidentally the lower age at marriage of the industrial workers may be especially significant, pointing to a tendency asserting itself with increasing strength as the advance of industrialization accelerated: the relative growth of the industrial population would impart some tendency for the mean age at marriage to fall, apart from any other influences that may have made for this result.

This, the relatively high age of marriage of women, is therefore the crux of the special characteristics of marriage in pre-industrial England and indeed in Western Europe as a whole, while it is agreed that the age of marriage is one of the most important variables bearing upon reproduction rates. A mean age at first marriage for women of 22 (that of aristocratic brides in the early seventeenth century) could give rise to twice as many births in completed families as a mean age of marriage of 30 (as in the village of Colyton), owing to the high proporion of children born in the early years of the seventeenth century and the early years of the nineteenth century is found to be typical of the country as a whole, we have a significant pointer to one of the main causes of population growth in the eighteenth century.

## SOCIAL AND ECONOMIC IMPLICATIONS

From what has been said, and it is only a brief outline of what could be said, it is clear that very significant changes had taken place in the marriage pattern of Western Europe in the thousand years that had elapsed since the fall of the Roman Empire. Marriage had become more stable, usually unbroken, except by the death of one of the partners, and was associated with a relatively low level of illegitimacy; celibacy for social reasons, both of men and women, was by no means uncommon; and most significantly of all, the age of marriage of girls appears to have almost doubled, that is from 12-15 in the late Roman Empire to 22-6 among the women of England and France in the eighteenth century.

The combination of high age at marriage, the existence of various social and institutional obstacles to high nuptiality, and at the same time a quite remarkable degree of geographical mobility laid the groundwork for a competitive and acquisitive society in which the ratio of resources to population was thereby kept in a favourable balance. It was the ideal instrument of self-aggrandizement for enterprising families and provided a hand-hold for those with means and opportunity to make their way to the top as well as a check to blind procreation of those at lower levels struggling for subsistence. While some rose, others fell, but the ineluctable circulation of the social elements went on. From the fifteenth century, the rise of substantial yeoman families, often at the expense of poorer families, laying field to field and farm to farm and pushing their way into the ranks of the gentry, provided a scaffolding of immense strength and energy to the English rural economy. Along with the more enterprising landlords they enclosed whole villages for sheep in the wool boom of the fifteenth century, and changed over to the production of meat and corn under the influence of the rising prices in the sixteenth and seventeenth centuries. They built a scatter of substantial houses and palatial halls over the length and breadth of England, providing thereby a market for the products of an industrial expansion which was once accorded the name of an Industrial Revolution. At the same time, the endless circulation of footloose labour brought a tide of hungry and active boys and girls to the towns, and above all to London, which, by the end of the seventeenth century, was providing the means for food and shelter for one-tenth of the entire nation. There was, it would seem, from the fifteenth century a surging onward and upward of the human hive and every social class was involved in it. Among the upper ranks of the social pyramid the struggle was all the keener as a result of the comparatively high fertility rate of the upper classes.

The new middle class provided a superstructure of skill and enterprise incomparably stronger than that of the underdeveloped countries of today and fully capable of grasping the opportunities that economic expansion offered.

Of course it is not possible to say how far the marriage pattern contributed to this, but the examination of particular cases certainly suggests that we should not ignore it. Thus the spiral of social mobility was mounted, sometimes by hard work, often by lucky marriages; and the pattern set by the landed classes gave the clue to the middle classes and the new industrialists. The part played by marriage in floating industrial enterprise would repay more attention than it has received. We can think of John Wilkinson and Matthew Boulton, both of whom made lucrative marriages twice in their lives, and we may be reminded of the latter's advice to young men about to embark on a commercial career: "Don't marry for money but marry where money is." This advice fell on willing ears.

We should not therefore be surprised that marriage played such an important part in the literature of the times. The plays of the Restoration, and the novels of the eighteenth century from Defoe to Jane Austen, are embroideries, more or less sedate and studied, on the theme of marriage. Amongst the gentry the ace of courtship was a highly sophisticated branch of social relations. From the time the young lady left her finishing school at seventeen or eighteen, she was in the market for a husband, and it was her father's business to find the best that his estate could afford. Negotiations went forward with the formality of an alliance between sovereign states, and correspondence was exchanged on the question of jointures and portions between the fat and eligible young men, sometimes for years before a final decision was taken. Even in the case of a small squire like Nicholas Blundell of Crosby in Lancashire, who could only dispose of an income of a few hundred a year, the marriage of his eldest daughter Molly occupied a period of six years, during which time two suitors favoured by the father were firmly rejected by the young lady, albeit with tears of distress at having to disappoint her father's wishes, and numerous others were considered and rejected for one reason or another. All this took place, of course, through the medium of a series of balls, soirees, and family celebrations, when the young people went through the stately motions of the quadrille and the gavotte, forms of the terpsichorean art that were specifically adapted to the requirements of courtship in an age when it was pursued not for passion but for property. The young people could take stock of one another in the course of this pattern of courtly advance and withdrawal, of genuflexions and pirouettings, while the elders could do their matrimonial arithmetic in the window-seats. And this would, of course, be both complex and prolonged. Nicholas Blundell had only a small income but he had two daughters, and he had to spend nearly £150 on dresses for them on their "coming out." They still looked "graceless country lasses," we are told, in spite of their finery; "but the squire knew that what they carried on their backs was more important in the marriage market than what peeped out from under their bonnets," and it is happy to be able to record that after this amiable charade had gone on for five or six years both daughters found husbands to their liking, and the squire was blessed with a little Blundell by blood though not by name to carry the family on.

If this was the pattern for the squirearchy and the ranks above them, how far did it go down in the social scale? The artisans, the skilled workmen, the yeomen, and the husbandmen had a similar period of waiting before they could enter the marriage state. How was it occupied? No one can tell us. We get gobbets of facts and figures, items of a measurable magnitude as Professor Clapham described them; but the pangs of flesh and blood which the young people must have experienced escape us. Jacob, we are told, waited seven years for Rachael; but our country swains waited hardly less for their Annes and Abigails and Marthas. We have to go to the novelists, especially Defoe and Richardson, for a hint of this unknown country of the heart.

But for a glimpse into the depths where the labourer and his lass settled their affairs we must go to the ploughboy poet, Robert Burns. "Ay fond kiss and then we sever," sang the poet, usually leaving behind a more substantial token of his successful pursuit. In fact, out of his thirteen children, eight are known to have been illegitimate. Perhaps Bobby Burns was more irresistible than other men, especially Englishmen, where the bastardly rate was comparatively low, anyway this was Scotland, where whisky and bad weather may have breached barriers more readily than in England, which has a record for moderation in all things.

But the marriage institution I have been describing is a European, not a specifically English, phenomenon. If, as I have suggested, it exercised a favourable influence on the process of capital accumulation and the development of entrepreneurial attitudes, how do we account for the difference in the rate of progress in capitalist development in England compared with the rest of Western Europe?

The answer seems to lie in two fields of development which distinguished English practice and English social behaviour from most of her neighbours; first, the greater productivity of English agriculture which raised the effective demand of the English farming community for non-agricultural goods, particularly houses, clothes, fuel, implements, etc,; secondly, to the greater emphasis on commercial and industrial objectives which characterized English social ambitions compared with the more feudal outlook that prevailed, for instance, among the French bourgeoisie.

I think we can now return to the question posed by Professor Hajnal that sparked off this discussion: "Could the uniquely European marriage pattern," he asks, "help to explain how the groundwork was laid for the uniquely European take-off to modern growth?" In the light of the evidence submitted I think we must concede it provides at least a part of the explanation. Its contribution lies not exclusively in providing a differential level of fertility leading to a slower growth of population and higher resources *per capita*, although that was certainly important; it led also to the building up of a social system that was based on the autonomy of the individual family unit, free from dependence of kin, and accustomed to accept the sole responsibility for the bearing and nurture of children. This belonged to the parents alone. In this way was laid the groundwork of a society which learned not only the economic but also the demographic techniques that made continuous economic growth possible. To this extent Hajnal's thesis appears to be valid and important.

I think, however, it is necessary to add that by the middle of the eighteenth century the role of marriage in the gathering tempo of economic advance was changing. The factors of restraint which constituted its essential character were being weakened with important results on fertility and the birth-rate. Two circumstances combined to effect this important change; first, the disproportionate growth of the industrial sector of the population would impart a general trend towards a lower age of marriage as a statistical characteristic of the community as a whole. If we are to find evidence of the falling age of marriage we must look in the first place to the towns and the industrial villages; but by the early nineteenth century, if not before, it seems to have also reached the rural population, now more generally living in cottages rather than in the houses of their masters. The second was the erosion of ecclesiastical influences on the relations of the sexes, reflected in a rise in the proportion of bastardy and pre-martial conception. In the course of the century, the incidence of the latter probably doubled, but the evidence suggests that recorded bastardy may have risen four or five times in the same period. These two factors mark the end of an epoch in the history of European marriage which began in the last centuries of the Roman Empire and inaugurated a new phase in its evolution, the unfolding of which continues to influence our society down to the present day.

## 6. Quaker Marriage Patterns In A Colonial Perspective
by Robert V. Wells

Despite the obvious importance of marriage patterns for an understanding of the colonial family, and so of colonial society, the subject has only recently begun to receive close attention from students of the period. In the last few years, the studies of various Massachusetts towns done by John Demos, Philip Greven, and Kenneth Lockridge have led the way in exploring the relationships between marriage and other aspects of colonial society. Because of the focus on New England to date, a study of marriage patterns among colonists from a different region has an obvious interest. Therefore, the first part of this paper will examine some patterns of marriage of a particular group of 276 Quaker families from the middle colonies. The remainder of the essay will consider the possible existence of distinct patterns of marriage in the colonies and will explore the effect that such patterns may have had on family size in 17th- and 18th-century America.

As defined here, a family consisted of a husband and wife, plus any children born to that particular union. Because of an interest in change over time, the date of birth of the wife was used to divide the 276 Quaker families into three chronological groups. A desire to identify any demographic patterns that might be associated with the American Revolution and a concern to avoid groups with very small numbers were the principal determinants of the division. The first grouping of families included 80 couples in which the wife was born no later than 1730. The second group of families, numbering 65 in all, was defined by wives who were born between 1731 and 1755. A final group, which included the remaining 125 families, was determined by wives born between 1756 and 1785. Although most of the members of these families lived during the 18th century, a few unions were formed in the late 17th century and children occasionally were born to the couples under study as late as the 1820s. The records of their births, marriages, and deaths are to be found in the registers of the monthly meetings of the Society of Friends of New York City, Flushing, Jericho, and Westbury in New York; Plainfield and Rahway, Salem, and Burlington in New Jersey; and Falls and Philadelphia in Pennsylvania. From these records it has been possible to reconstitute the 276 families. As might be expected, the proportion of families from each geographic area did not remain constant in each of the chronological groups, but this does not seem to have caused the changes over time which will be described later. In fact, it is rather surprising to discover that, in this instance at least, regional variations (including rural-urban differences) in demographic patterns could not be readily identified.

The age at which persons, especially women, first marry is a subject of considerable interest, since a woman seldom is able to bear children for more than the thirty years between ages fifteen and forty-five. The age at which she marries plays, then, an obvious role in determining how many children she can bear and therefore directly affects family size and the growth rate of the population. Women who married at the age of fifteen (and a few of these Quakers did) would have had approximately twice as many years to bear children as women who remained single until thirty.

Furthermore, since the ability to bear children tends to decline as age increases, the women who married at a later age could expect to have their childbearing potential reduced still further.

Among the Quakers included in this study the average age at first marriage was 22.8 for women and 26.5 for men. The median age for first marriages among the women was 20.5 years, while the corresponding figure for the men showed half of them marrying before age 24.0 and half marrying after that age. These figures indicate that marriage tended to be concentrated in the younger ages. Of the men who married, 81.7 percent did so before the age of thirty, while only 10.4 percent of the women who married remained single that long. As might be expected, few of either sex married for the first time at an age of forty or more. One of the most striking differences between the marriage patterns of the men and women is in the proportions marrying for the first time under the age of twenty, since over a third of the women married before they were twenty, but only 2.4 percent of the men married before that age. In fact, 93.9 percent of all men waited to marry until they were over twenty years old, but once they attained the age of twenty-one, more men married at that age than any other. In the case of women, more were married at nineteen than at any other age. While women were younger than men on the average when they married for the first time, there were few child brides. The youngest women to marry did so at the age of fifteen, but only 1.5 percent of the brides were that young, and 87.0 percent were eighteen or older before they married.

Custom may have played an important part in determining when a young Quaker might marry, for most of the marriages of both the men and women were concentrated in just a few years. Between the ages of eighteen and twenty-two, 50.6 percent of the women got married, while in a similar five-year span, 53.1 percent of the men were married between the ages of twenty-one and twenty-five. Equally impressive is the fact that fully 75.5 percent of the brides married for the first time between the ages of sixteen and twenty-five; four out of every five men (79.3 percent) marrying for the first time did so between the ages of twenty and twenty-nine. It is difficult to believe that anything but a customary association of marriage with certain ages could produce such concentrations. The fact that marriages were concentrated in much the same way in Andover and Plymouth, Massachusetts, (and elsewhere, as well) lends further support to the conclusion that the age at first marriage was, to some extent, determined by custom in seventeenth- and eighteenth-century America.

When a Quaker man of this study married, his bride was often his age or slightly younger. In all, there was a difference of less than one year in the age of the husband and wife 16.1 percent of the time, when the marriage was the first for both partners; there was less than five years' difference in 62.0 percent of the marriages; and 85.1 percent of these couples were separated by less than ten years of age. Interestingly, in 10.3 percent of the marriages the wife was older than the husband, though only 8.2 percent of the wives exceeded their husband's age by a year or more. There seem to have been very few instances of an old man marrying a young girl, for only in 5.1 percent of the marriages was the husband over fifteen years older than his wife, but in no case was the difference in age between husband and wife as much as thirty years.

A similar study of marriages in which at least one of the partners had been previously married produced the same results. The ages of the husband and wife were much the same, as men chose wives who were younger but not far different in age. Only twice in twenty-two known cases involving remarriage was the difference in age between husband and wife twenty years or more, and in neither of these did the difference reach thirty years.

The average age at first marriage of both men and women was examined for each of the three chronological groups described above to see if there was any change in this particular aspect of marriage over time.

In the case of the men, the age at first marriage remained fairly stable. Although the men of the middle group married at an average age which was lower than for the other two groups, there was less than a third of a year's difference between the first and last group. The women, on the other hand, experienced a steady rise in their average age at first marriage. The women who were born after 1755 married at an average age of 23.4 years, an increase of 1.4 years over those women born by 1730, who married at 22.0 on the average. These changes in the average age at first marriage suggest a number of significant developments in colonial society that will be discussed later.

Studies which deal primarily with age at marriage emphasize the formation of families and the age at which women begin to bear children. But just as important in determining the size of the family is the duration of marriage, and for obvious reasons. Among the Quakers of this study, marriages lasted until one spouse died, for divorce among the Friends was rare in the 18th century.

The final aspect of marriage which concerns us here is the proportion of adults who never wed. The amount of celibacy, together with the age at first marriage and the patterns of remarriage, may reflect the extent of need and opportunity to marry in colonial society. At the same time, the proportion of adults who never marry is obviously pertinent to questions related to the growth of population. If fewer women marry, fewer will have children, unless illegitimacy is widespread. Thus, a decline in the number of women marrying can lead to a decline in the birth rate, even though each wife still has the same number of children on the average.

The proportion never marrying is one of the more difficult of the marriage patterns with which to deal. Since the available information is most complete for the families associated with the Plainfield and Rahway meeting, the study of this question has been limited to the evidence drawn from that particular group.

First of all, only 52.0 percent of the daughters and 52.2 percent of the sons born to the Quakers of the Plainfield and Rahway meeting are known to have married. Many who did not marry undoubtedly died before they had an opportunity to marry. But the fact that nearly half the children born never were known to have married has tremendous implications for the rate of growth from one generation to the next.

Since the proportion of adults who never marry is to some extent indicative of the need and opportunity to marry, it is useful to know how many of the celibates were adults who were either unwilling or unable to marry and how many represent children who died young. If a person lives to the age of fifty without marrying, it is generally safe to assume that he will remain single for the rest of his life, since virtually all first marriages involve persons under fifty. Therefore, by studying the deaths of all persons aged fifty or more to see what proportion of them were of single persons, it is possible to estimate the proportion of adults who never married. Among both the sons and daughters of the Plainfield and Rahway Quakers a surprisingly large proportion of those who lived until fifty died unmarried. 15.9 percent of the women who lived to fifty never married, while 12.1 percent of the men remained single at that age. Since populations rarely have a numerical balance between sexes at any one age, the fact that the two proportions are not equal is no cause for concern. The fact that men married on the average at a later age than the women may have made the difference in the numbers and the proportions never married greater than if the average ages at marriage of the men and women were equal.

By the end of the 18th century and in the early 19th century there was a noticeable increase among the women in the proportion never marrying. Fully 57.3 percent of the daughters of Plainfield and Rahway Quaker families born before 1786 lived to marry, but only 45.5 percent of the daughters born in 1786 or later married. Among the same two groups the proportion who lived to fifty but never married rose from 9.8 percent to 23 percent. Some marriages of women of advanced ages may have been missed by the Quaker registrars after the Hicksite separation split the Friends in 1827, but not enough to explain the shift of this magnitude. Clearly there was a marked rise in the proportion of women who never married among those born after the Revolution.

Many of the marriage patterns of these Quakers were similar to those of other colonists. Furthermore, the available evidence suggests that distinct patterns of marriage existed in 17th- and 18th-century America that were unlike those found elsewhere at the same time. By the late 18th century, however, marriage patterns in the colonies started to move into line with those found in Europe throughout the period under consideration. Recently, J. Hajnal has suggested that a new pattern of marriage emerged in western Europe about the time that colonization was just getting started in the Americas. This new pattern of marriage which Hajnal has called "European" has lasted until today, and its identifying features include late marriage (average age of first marriage for women of at least 23) and a high proportion of people who never married at all (at least 10 percent). Such patterns were quite distinct from the rest of the world at the time, or from those found in western Europe in earlier periods. Marriage patterns which contrasted with the European patterns, and hence were called "non-European" by Hajnal, have a low average age of first marriage (under 21 for women) and a low rate of celibacy (less than 4 percent of the adults never marry).

As the data in Table I indicates, women living in America before 1800 may have had "colonial" marriage patterns that were neither European nor non-European. The average age at first marriage for the Quaker women of this study was above that of the non-European pattern of marriage, but below the European pattern. The evidence for Plymouth and Andover in Massachusetts, Bristol in Rhode Island, and French Canada suggests that the Quakers were not unique in this regard. Actually, the earliest group of women listed for Plymouth, Bristol and Andover had an average age at first marriage which would put them in the non-European category. But none of the colonial women, except for those Quakers born from 1756 to 1785, and the last two groups of Andover wives, had an average age at first marriage which could be classified as European. The information presented in Table I is representative of a much larger body of evidence. From New England to the southern colonies, and in the French West Indies as well, the figures show that colonial women had a unique pattern of age at first marriage which does not fit either of Hajnal's categories.

By way of comparison it is worth noting that all of the French and English populations listed in Table I met the requirements for the European pattern of marriage with regard to the age at first marriage of the woman. These groups appear typical of the larger populations of which they were a part. A more detailed examination of the table reveals that colonial women were from two to six years younger when they married than any of the contemporary European women included here, with the exception of British noblewomen. As shall be seen later, this earlier age at marriage for the women combined with longer marriages to produce families in the colonies which were larger than those found in Europe in the period under consideration.

## TABLE I

### AVERAGE AGE AT FIRST MARRIAGE
### (COMPARISONS)

| AMERICA | MEN | WOMEN |
|---|---|---|
| Quaker Families | | |
| All Wives | 26.5 | 22.8 |
| Wives Born | | |
| By 1730 | 26.5 | 22.0 |
| 1756-1785 | 26.8 | 23.4 |
| Plymouth, Massachusetts | | |
| Wives Born | | |
| 1624-1650 | 26.1 | 20.2 |
| 1675-1700 | 24.6 | 22.3 |
| Bristol, Rhode Island | | |
| Before 1750 | 23.9 | 20.5 |
| After 1750 | 24.3 | 21.1 |
| Andover, Massachusetts | | |
| a. 1630-1790 | | |
| First Generation | 26.8 | 19.0 |
| Second Generation | 26.7 | 22.3 |
| Third Generation | 27.1 | 24.5 |
| Fourth Generation | 25.3 | 23.2 |
| Canada | | |
| 1700-1730 | 26.9 | 22.4 |
| | | |
| EUROPE | | |
| Crulai | | |
| 1674-1742 | 27.2 | 24.6 |
| Ile-de-France | | |
| 1740-1800 | 26.2 | 25.5 |
| Bas-Quercy | | |
| 1767-1792 | 27.1 | 26.3 |
| British Peers | | |
| 1750-1774 | 29.6 | 23.9 |
| Colyton | | |
| 1720-1769 | 25.7 | 26.8 |
| | | |
| HAJNAL | | |
| "European" | ---- | 23.0 or over |
| "non-European" | ---- | under 21.0 |

However, the distinct pattern of marriage observed among colonial wives was only temporary. In every case studied here, with the exception of the fourth generation of Andover brides, the average age at which women married for the first time rose steadily with time. The average age at first marriage of the Quaker women of this study increased from 22.0 in the first group to 23.4 in the last, as is shown in Table I. A similar shift seems to have occurred among other colonial populations as well. Both in Plymouth and in Bristol the age at marriage for women showed a marked tendency to rise. The Plymouth women who married for the first time at the start of the 18th century did so at an average age of 22.3, over two years older than had been the case in the middle of the 17th century. The change among Bristol women was not as great, but it was in the same direction. In Andover, the third generation women were five and a half years older on average than the first generation wives when they married for the first time. Although the fourth generation wives were slightly younger than their immediate predecessors when they married, they were still clearly above the lower limit of the European marriage pattern. Evidence from studies of family genealogies supports the conclusion that the age of marriage among colonial women was rising toward the limits of the European pattern, and in a few instances surpassed it, in the 18th century.

In contrast to their wives, colonial men seem to have followed European marriage patterns throughout the 17th and 18th centuries. As is evident in Table I, most colonial men married for the first time at an average age of between twenty-five and twenty-seven, much the same as their contemporaries in England and France. The relative stability of this aspect of marriage among the men is quite surprising in view of the steady increase in the average age at first marriage of the women throughout the colonial period.

The information available on the proportions never marrying is limited, but what there is of it also indicates the existence of distinct colonial patterns of marriage. Two separate studies have concluded that no more than 2 percent of 18th-century Yale graduates remained unwed after the age of fifty, a figure which stands in sharp contrast to the minimum of 10 percent never marrying which defines the European marriage pattern; in regard to taking wives, Harvard men of the 17th century were much like the later Yale graduates. Likewise, in Andover, Massachusetts, the available figures show a higher proportion ultimately married than in Europe, as only 7.4 percent of the third generation women who lived to the age of twenty-six were known to have been spinsters, while only 3.6 percent of the fourth generation men who lived to twenty-five never married. Only the Quakers studied above remained single in proportions which approached the European standard. 12.1 percent of the sons who lived to fifty never married, while among the daughters born before 1786 the corresponding figure was 9.8 percent, just below the minimum for the European pattern of marriage described by Hajnal. It is of interest to note, however, that the marital status of every spinster included in this study who died after the age of fifty was carefully recorded in the meeting registers, suggesting that the Friends considered such persons remarkable in the context of colonial society. Indeed, they may have been, for evidence from Canada in 1681 shows only about 5 percent of the women who had reached the age of thirty were still single, while in Mexico in 1793 only 9.6 percent of the women were unmarried once they reached the age of forty. Apparently, the tendency for most women to marry was not limited to the English-speaking colonies.

Only in the case of the Quakers is there readily available information regarding changes in the proportion of women who never married. But this evidence, too, indicates that a shift in marriage patterns occurred from a colonial to a more European pattern of marriage during the 18th century. Among women born before 1786, 9.8 percent of those who lived to fifty never married. But by the time the women who were born in 1786 or later were marrying, European marriage pattern apparently had become common, at least among these Quakers, for over 20 percent of those who lived to fifty remained unwed. The change in marriage patterns among the Quaker women was consistent for both the age of first marriage and the proportion never marrying.

Any interpretation of the marriage patterns of the Quakers of this study, and of other colonists as well, must explain why there was little apparent change in the marriage patterns of the men, at the same time that among the women the age at first marriage and the proportion never marrying were shifting from distinctive colonial patterns into line with those found in western Europe.

The best explanation which may be offered for this shift involves the opportunity to marry, which was related to the numerical balance between sexes. Over the course of the 18th century certain fundamental demographic changes occurred in the colonies which may explain why the pattern of marriage changed more for women than for men. Migration into a particular colony, whether from Europe or from another colony, tended to be predominantly male. As long as immigrants were an important part of the population, men were likely to be more numerous with the result that at any given age there were far more possible husbands than wives. In order for all the men to marry who wished to do so, it was necessary for them to take wives of a different, and generally younger, age, once most of the eligible women of their own age had married. However, by the end of the 18th century immigration was accounting for a smaller proportion of the total population than it had earlier. In some regions it had ceased altogether, or perhaps even reversed. The result was a more equal ratio between men and women by the time of the Revolution. Once men no longer found it necessary to seek younger brides, the age of marriage of the women tended to rise toward that of their prospective husbands. At the same time an increasing proportion of adult women may never have had the opportunity to marry at all. Widows may have found it harder to remarry in such a situation, as most of their possible suitors could find wives who had never been married before. All of these changes in the marriage patterns of the women could occur even though the men experienced no major change in their marriage patterns.

The changes observed above in the marriage patterns of the Quakers of this study were accompanied by precisely this kind of alteration in the ratio between men and women. In the middle colonies and especially Pennsylvania, immigration into the colony continued on an impressive scale to the time of the Revolution, but after 1775 movement into those colonies slowed and was, perhaps, even reversed. It is impossible to know how much the Quakers would have been influenced by the general decline in immigration; but it is clear that after the Revolution a sharp rise in migration to the frontier among Quaker men began. Although precise figures are not available, the records indicate that a surprising number of Quaker families had one or more sons leave the middle colony area for new settlements from Canada to Ohio and Indiana and south to Alabama. An occasional young man who had left the region returned to marry a girl he had probably known from childhood, but many did not. Thus, at the very time that fewer young men were moving into the middle colonies, many of the Quaker youths were leaving the area, thereby reducing the supply of possible husbands. The numerical balance between the sexes was clearly subject to alteration, and that in turn may have had an effect on the marriage patterns of the women. The men married much as they always had, but the women were forced to change as their opportunities to marry declined.

Much the same type of situation seems to have occurred in parts of New England. In Plymouth, for example, a steady increase in the age at first marriage among women (see Table I) corresponded in time with a decline in the number of men available for marriage. Andover experienced a similar change, as the average age at first marriage among the women rose from 19.0 in the first generation to 24.5 among their granddaughters. Although the increase began in the decade before large numbers of young men left Andover, it was accompanied by a sharp decrease in the number of women whose husbands came from outside the community. A changing sex ratio seems to have altered marriage patterns in New England as it apparently did among the Quakers.

In view of all this, it is of special interest to find that the status of women and the values placed on marriage seem to have changed considerably in the course of the 18th century, and especially at the time of the Revolution. Such changes may well have fostered the alterations in marriage patterns which were resulting from a more balanced sex ratio.

For much of the colonial period the prevailing values clearly encouraged marriage. No colony ever deliberately persecuted persons who were single in order to encourage marriages, although various 17th-century statutes make it clear that single persons were considered to require special supervision. For example, New England viewed single men with suspicion if they were not under the shelter and scrutiny of a larger family unit. Their movements were often limited; they were subject to special fines and duties; and they might even be prevented from receiving land grants until after they were married. Undoubtedly part of this effort to supervise single persons came from a desire to protect the community from strangers. At the same time, the Puritans encouraged marriage for the simple reason that it provided an acceptable outlet for normal human desires. In Pennsylvania, the Quakers on occasion actually taxed single men on a separate basis. Their purpose seems to have been to include such men within the overall scheme of taxation rather than to encourage marriage. However, at least one foreign observer noted the fact that single persons received special attention in the tax laws. Furthermore, many of Pennsylvania's laws regulating marriage specifically encouraged adults to marry, although none went as far as the suggestions made in 1683 that young men ought to be fined every year they remained unmarried after reaching twenty-one. Nevertheless, to remain single was to reject accepted social patterns.

After the Revolution these values may have changed. At least two scholars have found that the necessity to marry was reduced a little as social and economic values shifted. Men began to accept women as their equals in some matters. A woman's ability to own property improved, for example. As conditions altered the need to find a husband may have been reduced, since adult females could find alternatives other than marrying and raising a family. Those women who married after the Revolution apparently showed an increasing concern with love and happiness in their unions; and they may have expected a greater say in family matters. Of importance here is the fact that the Quakers were among the first people to give formal recognition to the rights of women. Changing values may have made it possible for unmarried men and women to find a satisfying role in post-Revolutionary America. If so, the need to marry no longer would be as great as in the colonial period. Those who wed may have taken longer to consider the implications of such action and the alternatives. Thus, the opinions which emerged at the close of the colonial period regarding the status of women and the importance of marriage were consistent with, and hence may have helped to bring about, changes in the patterns of marriage.

# 7. Marital Choice Among Quakers

by J. William Frost

Quaker epistles and tracts offering advice on selecting a wife or husband rarely mentioned love before marriage. Was love assumed to be present, or was it not deemed necessary until after the wedding? Edmund S. Morgan has argued that for the Puritans love did not become essential until after the marriage, and even then it was a rational love, although this did not in the least dampen its affectionate nature. So long as spiritual concerns predominated, a Quaker could decide to marry and even select a partner on a rational basis, since his financial situation and her character should be considered. Friends did expect a religious love before marriage, however. Such love was described by Thomas Ellwood—perhaps in imitation of Adam's relationship with Eve before the fall—as "chaste desire" that came from God, had no connection with anything earthly such as sex or self-gratification, and was closely akin to sympathy. This godly love bore no relationship to the emotions, and one can find nothing in official statements that would permit a blind romantic love to sweep aside all impediments to matrimony. In 1696 Joseph Sleigh advised his sons to make sure from "what ground your Love springs" and told his daughters not to accept the first "that may proffer Love to you, as in relation to marriage" but to wait for the Lord's counsel. William Penn wrote: "Never marry but for Love; but see that thou Lov'st what is lovely." His sons were told to marry "your Inclination rather than your Interest: I mean what you Love, rather than what is Rich . . . and be sure you are belov'd again." The love that Penn wanted never sprang from lust; Christian affection was based upon a *"Union of Souls"* rather than a *"Union of Sense."* But Penn did demand genuine feeling between two people before marriage, and his letters to and about both his intended wives were permeated with affection. Samuel Morris, after warning his nephew Samuel Powell about beauty or fortune, asked rhetorically, "Must we marry without Love? No, but let consideration and judgment precede it." A relationship religiously arrived at could become romantic, and the few surviving letters of Quaker courtship shift easily between pious phrases and terms of endearment. Meetings recognized that romantic love did exist, for parents were warned that contracts should be decided before the boy and girl became very attached. Symons Creek Meeting in North Carolina allowed a couple after one appearance before the meeting to drop the affair "for want of Love" but demanded an acknowledgment of fault. In 1726 Rhode Island Monthly Meeting found a couple who were too near kin to marry but permitted the wedding because "their affections were Drawn toward Each other before they knew the order of Friends in that Respect." Friends recognized that romantic love could not be turned off and on at will.

While Friends continued to discuss courtship and marriage officially in

143

religious terms until the 19th century, the actual narratives of courting show considerable interest in romance. Other concerns, such as those for property and religion were present, but love seems to have been the primary requisite. Since the course of romance has rarely been cut and dried, Quaker courting had its share of hectic and traumatic moments. The story of Israel Pemberton, Jr.'s, first marriage in 1737 reads like fiction. Before going to England on business in 1735, Israel had shown interest in Sarah Kirkbride, but he made no formal overtures before leaving. During his absence Anthony Morris, Jr., frequently visited the Kirkbrides and proposed marriage to Sarah, who neither accepted nor refused. Upon Israel's return he did nothing for three weeks but then informed his father that he had intended to propose to Sarah, for he believed she had an affectionate regard for him. Israel, Sr., tried to discourage his son, but Israel, Jr., visited the young lady—in the presence of Anthony—and informed her of his intentions. The Morris affair continued and his family blamed the Pembertons for intervening. After parental coercion, Israel, Jr., paid no more calls for six weeks and agreed to do nothing until Sarah either accepted or rejected young Morris. Finally Anthony demanded a decision; Sarah said no. Morris retorted that Sarah had been so free with her favors that she would have to become his bride. Her father announced that his daughter would never marry him even if she were in dire disgrace. For all practical purposes, this outburst ended the Morris-Kirkbride courtship, and Anthony soon wed another. Israel then married Sarah.

While neither piety nor wealth was absent from the courtship of John Smith and Hannah Logan, the romantic attitude predominated. Smith was a prosperous young merchant whose habit of listing in his diary only the names of females who went on outings with him around Philadelphia would incline one to believe that he had looked for a wife for a prolonged period. The first concrete sign of romance was Smith's recording in his diary that he had spent an evening at William Logan's in the company of "that dear Creature H.L., the Charm of whose Conversation Excells, if possible, those of her person. . . . Oh, could I be Blest with the favour of Retiring to it upon every occasion." For several months his courtship was confined to seeking Hannah's company as often as possible and writhing in agony when he thought the girl was displeased with him. He also informed his father that he wanted to marry Miss Logan. Eight months after confessing his love to his diary, John attempted to find an opportunity to see Hannah alone to ask permission to court. At the home of Anthony Benezet he broached the subject and stammered out his proposal "in a good deal of Confusion"; the maiden, who neither encouraged nor discouraged him, agreed to receive a letter. The epistle was most eloquent; Smith praised the girl's beauty, intelligence, and virtue and also mentioned that a Friends' minister had recommended her to him. She consented to receive him. Smith's state of mind during this time of good fortune was revealed in one of his entries in February 1747: "Drank tea at I. Pemberton's of Hannah Logan's making—Nectar and Ambrosia."

The next stage was to visit the home and ask James Logan's permission. William Logan, the brother of Hannah, had delivered John's first love letter and now brought him to the Logan home. The way had been smoothed by Sally Morris, a minister and friend of the Logans, who wrote a letter to the father recommending the young man. Perhaps because he recognized a kindred intellect, and also because he wanted Hannah to marry so that he could settle his estate, James Logan heartily welcomed John Smith and rebuked William for not bringing him more often. The father took great pains to entertain his daughter's suitor in the library, but Hannah became ill and Smith was so unnerved that he failed to ask the father's consent. On the next visit Smith asked both parents for permission and they agreed that if Hannah preferred him, she could marry him. Logan, in later visits, informed Smith that he had said a few words to his daughter on his behalf and advised "how to Court, to have perseverance." The sole problem was Hannah's consent, and Smith made frequent visits, went fishing with the family, and accompanied them to meetings and funerals. At one point Smith had to convince the maiden that her religious life would not be hindered by setting "affections upon any man." John Smith's father helped the courtship by sending Hannah a four-wheeled chaise. In June 1748 Hannah determined to call the whole affair off, and though Smith obtained permission to visit again, "she told me she could not give me the least hope by putting it off to a future time." Smith did not call again for slightly over a month, but then in a meeting:

> I waited in it for a sense whether it would be suitable for me to renew my visits to dear Hannah Logan; and in my waiting my mind was filled with sweetness, and enlarged in pure Love and a particular openness and freedom, so that I determined in the affirmative.

Absence softened this fair lady's heart for that evening Hannah confessed to John Smith that she loved him. On December 7, 1748, they were married.

The diaries of Elizabeth Drinker for the 1760s, Sally Wister during the Revolutionary War, and John Elliot Cresson during the 1790s show that the romantic, sentimental view of courtship predominated in the middle and upper classes. Elizabeth Sandwich's diary, which reveals a long romance, interrupted by Henry Drinker's visit to London, proved that a man and woman had ample opportunity to know each other intimately. Courtship in colonial days was not always carried on in parlors with young ladies being carefully chaperoned at all times; it often involved walks in the garden, short trips for recreation, parties, ice skating, and sleigh rides. John Cresson, when admonished by his father for sitting up with his "precious

Molly" until 1:00 A.M., complained, "Alas, if Age is imprudent and unwise, ought there not to be some Allowance, and more than is commonly made, for the Ardour of Youthful Affection."

The social historian faces formidable obstacles in determining the antecedents of Friends' practices and beliefs about marriage. Difficulties in the nature of the source materials and ambiguity in terminology make difficult any precision in locating the sources of Quaker ideas of love. While 17th-century Puritans denied the Quaker claim that the Holy Spirit gave personal direction in matters of courtship, the Puritans did stress the spiritual unity between a man and wife and saw marriage as requiring physical and religious love. There were also precedents for Quaker beliefs about marriages to people outside the faith. Early English Baptists had adopted stringent regulations about marriages to nonbelievers—regulations similar to those used by Friends. Before 1660 those Puritans who believed in reforming the Church of England from within were not faced with the problem of mixed marriages, except those to Roman Catholics. After the Glorious Revolution, the Nonconformists desired to promote marriage within their faith. Daniel Defoe designed his *Religious Courtship* (ten editions between 1722 and 1762) as a guide to marriage for all pious Englishmen. Defoe described at length the inconveniences of a mixed marriage when one party was an Anglican and the other a dissenter. The moralists of Georgian England saw in the ideal courtship and marriage a combination of *Sense and Sensibility*. Addison in the *Spectator* and Dr. Johnson in *The Rambler* savagely ridiculed marriages based only on love as well as those based solely on wealth. Such writers instructed their audience, composed of men and women, to select their mates on the basis of affection, virtue, equality of station, and compatibility of temper and intellect.

Throughout the colonial period the meeting continued to insist upon spiritual unity as a foundation for a God-inspired love between a man and a woman. Such a love was supposed to be completely divorced from physical attraction, wealth or romance. Affection between the parties was a needed, but by no means sufficient, reason for marriage. While data on early Quaker marriages are sketchy, the theory and the practice were in harmony. Even in the 19th century, a few Friends described their courtship and marriage in terms that followed the meetings' standards. The information presented in this chapter suggests that in the 18th century middle- and upper-class Quakers, without repudiating the meetings' counsel, used the same trinity in courtship as other wealthy Englishmen did—religion, wealth, and love. The increasing number of disownments plus the narratives of those who married within the faith show that nonreligious factors gained the adherence of many young Friends. Since few admitted that they had married for money, most courtship stories revolved around love. The love was different from the union of souls wanted by Penn or the rational but affectionate love desired by the Puritans. Perhaps it can be most aptly described as courtly love linked to marriage.

The increase in Quaker marriages to outsiders may be one index to the rise of the dogma of romantic love in America. Similarly, the concept of romantic love might offer an explanation for the rapid increase in marriages to nonbelievers. The supplanting of spiritual love by romance also helps to account for a trend that historians have often asserted but have had difficulty pinpointing: why was there an increasing secularization of life in an age when people continued to profess religious values? Choosing a wife after falling in love is far different from having God point out your helpmate. While we still know very little about colonial patterns of marriage, it seems reasonable to assume that Friends were not unique in succumbing to romantic love. What is still uncertain is whether or not what happened to the Friends was indicative of a general reorientation in English or American culture. Did Friends help to pioneer this change or did they lag behind? Did the religious caste of Pennsylvania Quakers (and New England Puritans) delay or foster a romantic view of marriage? Such questions, which are basic to the understanding of the family, cannot be answered until we have more understanding of the varieties of marriage customs in England and America. What is certain is that many 18th-century Quakers were forced to choose between religious purity and romantic love.

## 8. Parental Power In Massachusetts Marriage Patterns.

by Daniel Scott Smith

Perhaps the central conceptual issue in the sociology of the family is the relationship of modernization to family structure. Paradoxically the theoretical significance of this problem has not engendered an empirical preoccupation with the details of the transition from "traditional" to "modern" family structure. For sociologists, as Abrams puts it, "the point after all was not to know the past but to establish an idea of the past which could be used as a comparative base for the understanding of the present." While historians often implicitly use a conception of the modern family as a baseline for their researches into the past, formally at least they attempt to relate the family to the culture and other institutions of an historical period. Only rarely have either group of scholars actually measured the dimensions of change by analyzing data over a long time interval. Thus the element of change in family structure has been more usually assumed or inferred from casual comparisons of past and present than consciously measured and analyzed. A great chasm persists between the theoretical perspective on the family and modernization and a limited body of empirical evidence more often qualifying or denying these relationships than supporting or extending them.

The problem of the connections between modernization and family structure may be conveniently divided into three analytically distinct areas —the relevance of the family for the structuring of other institutions, the role of the family in shaping individual lives, and finally the significance to the individual of the family he is born into (family of orientation) for the one he creates by marriage (family of procreation). Since the historical trends in the first two areas have presumably seemed so obvious, systematic empirical data have not been collected and analyzed to establish the precise dimensions and timing of change. In the first instance the modern family is not as quantitatively important for the organization of other structures— economic, political, and social. What influence the modern family exerts in these areas is indirect, exerted either through early socialization and personality formation or mediated by intervening institutions. Male occupational status in modern America, for example, is related to the family of orientation mainly through the provision of education, not by direct parental placement. Few families today control jobs which can be given to their children. Having less of an instrumental role, the family is now a specialized institution providing nurture and affection for both children and adults. Perhaps the best historical study of the transformation in this second area is the impressionistic classic of Ariès which delineates the social separation of the family from the community and the emergence of the psychological centrality of the child in the conjugal family. Since this interpretation now rests on changes in ideals and lacks adequate behavioral support, more historical analysis is required to determine the extent of this shift. It is possible, for example, that emotional or expressive ties between parents and children have been essentially invariant over the course of American history. These affective relationships may appear to have increased historically only because of the separation of instrumental activities from the family.

Although not necessarily more significant than the changes in the first two areas, the relationship between the family of orientation and the family of procreation has often been considered to be the central issue in the modernization of the family. Davis, in fact, has argued that this distinction is the most adequate key to understanding other variations in family structure. If the family newly created by marriage is dominated by pre-existing families of birth, then households are more likely to be extended in structure, marriages are more likely to be arranged and will take place at earlier ages, intrafamilial relationships will tend to be authoritarian, etc. Despite Parsons' later disclaimer that his well-known analysis was mainly concerned with the isolation of the family from other social structures and his acceptance of the Litwack-Seeman critique as complementary not contradictory, he was not deterred from elaborating his earlier argument. The substance of the debate on extended kinship in modern American society continues precisely on the quantity and nature of interaction between married couples and their parents. Historians as well have concentrated on this question, usually employing the classic extended-nuclear dichotomy to summarize their findings. Greven has argued that by withholding land fathers in 17th-century Andover, Massachusetts, were able to exercise considerable power over their adult sons. Once land had become relatively scarce in the early 18th century, they found it more difficult or less desirable to do so. More recently an entire volume of papers has been devoted to crushing the proposition that extended *households* ever were a significant element in western society, at least since the middle ages.

## THE HISTORICAL PROBLEM

In a decade review of research on modern American kinship, Adams has suggested that the most recent work is moving beyond debate and description to the more significant tasks of specification, interrelation, and comparison. This change of emphasis is as important for historical as for contemporary studies, even though an adequate, empirically based, systematic description of the historical evolution of the relationship between the family of orientation and the family of procreation does not presently exist. Despite the fact that it is always easier to decry than to remedy scholarly failures, this absence should be a challenge rather than an obstacle for historians. Much of the critical evidence regarding the extent and kind of interaction between parents and adult children is, of course, unwritten. Despite their interest in the same substantive issues, historians inevitably are forced to employ different methods than sociologists. Yet there are serious problems in the interpretation of historical evidence on the family. While a body of literary comment on ideal family relationships does exist, it becomes progressively more biased toward higher social strata as one moves farther back into the past. Furthermore, the relating of historical information about ideals to actual behavior is not easily accomplished. Since literary sources are available, relatively inexpensive to exploit, and suggestive concerning the more subtle aspects of family interaction, it would be foolish to dismiss them as biased and unreliable. It would be equally risky to base the entire history of the American family on these sources. What appears to be crucial at this point for a reliable descriptive history of the American family is the development of series of quantitative indicators for various aspects of family behavior.

On both theoretical and historical grounds the idea that a shift from the centrality of the family of orientation to the family of procreation has occurred within the time span of American history may be questioned. American history, it is often argued, lacks a "traditional" or "premodern" period. If modernization and the transformation of the family from extended to nuclear are related, one would not expect to find evidence for it within the three and one-half centuries of American history. The classic polarities of sociological theory are often used by historians to contrast America with England or as a literary device to highlight rather small shifts over time. Still, the dominant theme in American historiography is "uniqueness" and this peculiar quality of the American experience is linked to the various characteristics of modernity. Ideal types, of course, describe no particular empirical realities. Since these classic dichotomies emerged from the attempt to understand the transformation of western society in the 19th century, their empirical relevance surely ought to be as much in the analysis of the history of western development as in the explanation of cross-cultural differences. If the discussion of historical change in the family is to progress, the selection of terms is less important than the precise specification of the extent of change along the theoretical continuum.

Some important aspects of the nuclear, conjugal, or family-of-procreation-dominant family system such as neolocal residence, undoubtedly have been dominant since the earliest American settlement in the 17th century. Other significant historical continuities such as the priority given to nuclear as against extended kin may also be present. If change is to be detected in an area of known continuity, a specific, well-defined problem and subtle and discriminating measures of change are required. The relative centrality of the family of orientation versus the family of procreation can be examined from various angles. Marriage formation, however, is probably the most crucial since it is the point of transition for the individual. Transitions involving decisions are inevitably problematic. Furthermore, marriages produce records for nearly the entire population, not just for atypical elites. Thus a substantial data base exists for historical analysis. If the American family has undergone substantial historical change, it should be reflected in the conditions of marriage formation. Were, in fact, the marriages of a significant segment of the American population ever controlled by parents at any point in our history? Parents today are, of course, not irrelevant in the courtship and marriage formation process. The earlier, "traditional," pattern of control should be direct rather than indirect, involve material rather than psychological relationships, and involve power exercised by parents in their own interest at the expense of the children.

A shift in the control of marriage formation is clearly to be expected by the sociological theory of family modernization. Confident, if vague, statements exist describing the emergence of a non-parentally controlled, participant-run courtship system within the time span encompassed by American history. Yet Reiss presumably relies on literary evidence in his broad summary and Stone on the decidedly atypical experience of the English aristocracy. Furthermore, the shift specifed is subtle—from a parental choice, child veto system in the 17th century to its converse by the late 19th or early 20th century. Given the particularistic relationship between parents and children, choosing and vetoing choices may not be a constitutional system but instead an ongoing process of action and reaction.

## METHOD AND SAMPLE

The dead, of course, cannot be subjected to surveys. The extent of parental power in courtship and marriage formation cannot be directly measured. Inherently, the concept has a certain diffuseness and multidimensionality. Parents, for example, could determine the actual choice of spouse, they could determine the age at marriage but not name the partner, or they could merely structure indirectly the range of acceptable spouses. The actual process of decision making and bargaining is forever lost to the historian of ordinary people. If the dead cannot be interviewed, they can be made to answer questions if various consequences of the larger issue of parental control over marriage can be explicitly formulated. This is possible through the construction of long-term series of indices which are logically associated with the operational existence of parental control. Unlike the possibilities available in direct interaction with respondents, these indices inevitably lack meaning in an absolute, substantive sense. Conclusions must rest not just on one measure but on the conformity of various indicators to some pattern. Quantitative measures, whatever their limitations, have the great advantage of providing consistent information about change over time—the great question in the sociological history of the family and the most severe limitation of literary source materials.

Since the expected transition to a participant-run courtship system allegedly occurred between the 17th and late 19th century, either comparable data sets separated by more than a century or a long continuous series seem appropriate. For sociological purposes the former would be sufficient since a test of the change is all that is required. For historical analysis the time-series approach is better suited since the timing and pace of the transition are equally interesting. If the change did occur, was it gradual or concentrated in a few decades as a result, say, of the American revolution or the inception of rapid economic growth.

The larger study from which the ensuing data derive covers the social and demographic experience of the population of one Massachusetts town over a quarter-millenium. Economically, this period—1635 to 1880—encompasses the shift, mainly after 1800, from agriculture to commerce and industry. Demographically, it includes the transition from a fertility level which was high by west European standards to the below replacement reproduction rates of the mid-19th century. The basic methodological technique of the larger study was family reconstitution—essentially statistical genealogy. Records of births, deaths, intentions to marry, marriages, and wealth data from tax lists were combined into family units for analysis. Various series of comparable data extending over the two centuries were

151

constructed to measure change in demographic, familial, and social behavior. By examining differences in the timing of changes in these indicators, the history of the evolution of the population and social structure can be interpreted. Every decision about research design necessarily involves a price. Although long-term trends and change can be studied by this approach, the conclusions strictly must be limited to the population of the town of Hingham. Furthermore, primarily because of migration, nearly one-half of the families could not be fully reconstituted. Although wealth is inversely related to outmigration after marriage, this distortion only marginally affects most indicators. Since the wealth-bias is fairly consistent over time, trends are affected to a lesser degree than levels for any particular cohort.

## EVIDENCE

In early New England, as in the pre-industrial West generally, marriage was intimately linked to economic independence. As a result, age at marriage and proportions never-marrying were higher in western Europe than in other cultural areas. Since the late marriage pattern tended to reduce fertility, European societies had less of a dependency burden from nonproductive children; the easy mobility of the young, unmarried adult population may also have facilitated the transition to modern economic growth. Arguing in theoretical terms, one historical demographer has suggested that mortality level was also an important mechanism in the determination of marriage age. Higher mortality would open up opportunities for sons who then could marry earlier than if their fathers survived longer. The growth of population was thus controlled by the countervailing forces of mortality and marriage age.

These central demographic characteristics of west European societies can be used to formulate a test of the extent of paternal economic power. Since newly married sons were not incorporated into the paternal economic or living unit, marriage meant a definite transfer of power intergenerationally. The transfer might be eased by custom, limited by paternal retention of formal title to land, and moderated by continuing relations along non-instrumental lines. However, fathers inevitably had something to lose—either economic resources or unpaid labor services—by the early marriages of their sons. One might expect, therefore, that sons of men who die early would be able to marry before sons of men who survive into old age. By law male orphans inherited at age twenty-one and were thus economically free to marry. On the other hand, if fathers either could not or would not exercise such control, no differential in marriage age should exist between these two groups of sons.

Over two centuries of the study 60 years was the approximate mean age of fathers at the time of marriage of their sons. For the three cohorts of sons born to marriages up to 1740, Table I shows a differential of 1.6, 1.6, and 2.0 years in the predicted direction between sons whose fathers died before age 60 and sons whose fathers survived that age. For sons born to marriages formed after 1740 and especially after 1780, the "paternal power" effect is greatly diminished. While one and one-half to two years may appear to be a small difference, this gap is wider than that between the marriage ages of first and younger sons or between sons of wealthy and less wealthy parents. Nor should an extreme differential be expected. Fathers had a cultural obligation to see their children married although it was not in their short-run self-interest. The most meaningful interpretation of the magnitude of the differential depends on comparison with results obtained from reconstitution studies of English population samples.

TABLE 1. DIFFERENTIAL IN MARRIAGE AGE OF SONS BY AGE
AT DEATH OF FATHERS

| Period of Fathers' Marriage Cohort | Age at marriage of sons by age at death of fathers: | | Difference |
|---|---|---|---|
| | Under 60 | 60 and over | |
| 1641-1700 | 26.8 ( 64) | 28.4 (142) | + 1.6 |
| 1701-1720 | 24.3 ( 30) | 25.9 (130) | + 1.6 |
| 1721-1740 | 24.7 ( 38) | 26.7 (104) | + 2.0 |
| 1741-1760 | 26.1 ( 43) | 26.5 (145) | + 0.4 |
| 1761-1780 | 25.7 ( 42) | 26.8 (143) | + 1.1 |
| 1781-1800 | 26.0 ( 71) | 25.8 (150) | − 0.2 |
| 1801-1820 | 25.7 ( 93) | 26.5 (190) | + 0.8 |
| 1821-1840 | 26.0 ( 42) | 25.9 (126) | − 0.1 |
| 1641-1780 | 25.73 (217) | 26.89 (664) | +1.16 |
| 1781-1840 | 25.86 (206) | 26.11 (466) | + 0.25 |

Note: Sample size of sons whose marriage ages are known in parentheses.

Since the meaning of this differential is inferential, this index cannot by itself confirm the argument that parents significantly controlled the marriage of their sons. An additional aspect of the relative centrality of the family of orientation in a society is a concern for the preservation of the line at the expense of a coexistent desire to provide for all children in the family. Inasmuch as the number and sex composition of surviving children are not completely certain and economic circumstances are not perfectly forecast, this tension is essentially insoluble for individual families. By favoring only one son, families could help to maintain the social continuity of the family line. Although strict primogeniture did not obtain in Massachusetts, the eldest son was granted a double share in intestacy cases before the egalitarian modification of the law in 1789. Fathers, however, were not legally required to favor the eldest son. They had a free choice between an emphasis on the lineage or giving each child an equal start in life. If common, this limited form of primogeniture should have an influence on the social origins of the spouses of first and younger sons. Having more resources eldest sons should be able, on the average, to marry daughters of wealthier men. In 17th-century marriage contracts the wife's parents provided half as much as the husband's for launching the couple into marriage. In order to test the influence of birth order on marriage chances, Table 2 compares the quintile wealth status of fathers and fathers-in-law who were living in Hingham at the earlier date to men who were taxed by the town at the later date. While these nonmigratory requirements limit and perhaps bias the sample, the differences are quite dramatic. First sons taxed on the 1680, 1779, and 1810 property lists were roughly twice as likely as younger sons to have a father-in-law who was in a higher wealth quintile than their own father. They were similarly only half as likely as younger sons to have a father-in-law who was poorer than their own father. Birth order was thus an important determinant of the economic status of the future spouse and influential in determining the life chances of men during the colonial period.

TABLE 2. RELATIONSHIP OF WEALTH STATUS OF FATHERS AND FATHERS-IN-LAW OF FIRST AND YOUNGER SONS

| Tax list date for: | | Percentage of men whose fathers-in-law were in: | | | | | | |
| --- | --- | --- | --- | --- | --- | --- | --- | --- |
| | | Same quintile | | Higher quintile | | Lower quintile | | |
| Fathers and | | as father | | than father | | than father | | |
| fathers-in-law | Sons | 1st | younger | 1st | younger | 1st | younger | |
| | | % | % | % | % | % | % | N |
| 1647--1680 | | 25 | 29 | 58 | 29 | 17 | 43 | 26 |
| 1749--1779 | | 30 | 33 | 44 | 26 | 25 | 41 | 94 |
| 1779--1810 | | 26 | 30 | 55 | 27 | 18 | 43 | 117 |
| 1810--1830 | | 36 | 27 | 30 | 36 | 34 | 37 | 139 |
| 1830--1860 | | 34 | 35 | 34 | 30 | 32 | 34 | 138 |

A radical change is apparent for men on the town tax lists of 1830 and 1860. Birth order in the 19th century exerted no significant effect on the relationship between the relative wealth of father and father-in-law. Instead of a gradual diminution in paternal power, as was apparent in the effect of father's survival on the marriage age of sons, a decisive break is apparent.

While the measure in Table 1 involves the operation of paternal power on the individual level, primogeniture reflected in Table 2 is more a social constraint on the "freeness" of marriage choice. Apparently it was easier for all fathers to discriminate automatically against younger sons than it was for individual fathers, after the middle of the 18th century, to postpone the age at marriage of their own sons. The change evident in both indicators relating to the marriage process of sons is consistent with the larger hypothesis of a shift away from the dominance of the family of orientation in the family system.

The distinction between individual and social aspects of parental control is also apparent for daughters as well as sons. Traditionally in western society women have been more subject than men to parental control, particularly in the area of sexual behavior. Although penalties for premarital fornication were assessed equally against both parties, colonial New England did not escape this patriarchal bias. As a symbolic example geographically-mixed marriages usually occurred in the hometown of the bride, suggesting that the husband had to receive his wife from her father. Post-marital residence in these cases, however, was more often in the husband's town. Although the Puritan conception of marriage as a free act allowed women veto power over the parental choice of husband, marriages in the upper social strata were arranged through extensive negotiations by the parents. In short the existing evidence points to a pattern intermediate between total control of young women by their parents and substantive premarital autonomy for women. The historical question, once again, is not either-or but how much? Were women, in fact, "married off," and was there any change over time in the incidence of this practice? Direct evidence does not exist to chart a trend, but a hypothetical pattern may be suggested. If parents did decide when their daughters could and should marry, one might expect them to proceed on the basis of the eldest first and so on. Passing over a daughter to allow a younger sister to marry first might advertise some deficiency in the elder and consequently make it more difficult for the parents to find a suitable husband for her. If, on the other hand, women decided on the basis of personal considerations when (and perhaps who) they should marry, more irregularity in the sequence of sisters' marriages should be expected.

Table 3 demonstrates a marked increase in the proportions of daughters who fail to marry in order of sibling position after the middle of the 18th century. Because of the age difference among sisters most will marry in order of birth. Since women may remain single for reasons independent of parental choice, e.g., the unfavorable sex ratio in eastern Massachusetts in the second half of the 18th century, the measure which omits these cases (left column of Table 3) is a more precise indicator of the trend. However, the increasing tendency in the 18th and particularly the 19th century for women to remain permanently single is certainly consistent with an increas-

TABLE 3. PERCENTAGE OF DAUGHTERS NOT MARRYING IN
BIRTH ORDER IN RELATIONSHIP TO THOSE AT RISK

| Periods when daughters are marriageable | Spinsters excluded | | Spinsters included | |
|---|---|---|---|---|
| | % | N | % | N |
| 1651-1650 to 1691-1710 | 8.1 | 86 | 11.2 | 89 |
| 1701-1720 to 1731-1750 | 11.6 | 138 | 18.4 | 147 |
| 1741-1760 to 1771-1790 | 18.2 | 176 | 25.1 | 191 |
| 1781-1800 to 1811-1830 | 14.9 | 214 | 24.9 | 245 |
| 1821-1840 to 1861-1880 | 18.4 | 298 | 24.7 | 320 |

ing absence of strong parental involvement in the marriage process of their children. More and more women in the late 18th and early 19th century were obviously not being "married off," suggesting the obvious point that their marriages were controlled more indirectly through the power fathers had over economic resources; a similar index of sons marrying out of birth order shows no secular trend.

Just as primogeniture relates to the intergenerational transmission of economic resources, so too does the relationship of parental wealth to the marriage age of daughters. If wealth transmission by marriage were important in the society, then parents obviously would have greater direct control over their daughters than if women were expected to provide no resources to their future husbands. If daughters brought economic resources to the marriage, then one would expect that daughters of wealthier men would naturally be sought after by other families as being the more desirable marriage partners for their sons. The higher level of demand should mean that daughters of the wealthier would marry at a younger age than daughters of the less wealthy. If, on the contrary, property transfer and marriage were not intimately connected, then the class pattern of female marriage age would conform to male class career patterns. Market conditions rather than the behavior of individual actors can be assessed by examining the differential by wealth in the female age at first marriage. For daughters born to marriages formed in Hingham between 1721 and 1780 there is a perfect inverse relationship between paternal wealth and marriage age. Once more there is evidence for a significant role of the family of orientation in structuring marriage patterns. This wealth pattern is dramatically reversed for daughters born to marriages between 1781 and 1840. The stability in the mean marriage age (bottom row of Table 4) masks the divergent class trends. Daughters of the wealthy married later in the 19th century, while daughters of the less wealthy married at a younger age than before. The slight positive relationship between wealth and male marriage age becomes much stronger during the 19th century as well. Nothing could be more sug-

Table 4. AGE AT MARRIAGE OF DAUGHTERS BY WEALTH
QUINTILE OF FATHERS

| Wealth quantile class of father | Daughters born to marriages of | | | | |
| | 1721-1780 | | 1781-1840 | | |
| | Age | N | Age | N | Change in mean age |
|---|---|---|---|---|---|
| Richest 20 per cent | 23.3 | 99 | 24.5 | 114 | + 1.31 |
| Upper-middle 20 per cent | 23.5 | 98 | 24.4 | 179 | + 0.96 |
| Middle 20 per cent | 23.6 | 110 | 22.1 | 172 | − 1.47 |
| Lower-middle 20 per cent | 24.5 | 92 | 23.1 | 159 | − 1.37 |
| Poorest 20 per cent | 24.5 | 57 | 22.9 | 135 | − 1.63 |
| Fathers not present on extant tax list | 22.7 | 37 | 23.0 | 96 | + 0.30 |
| Totals | 23.7 | 493 | 23.3 | 855 | − 0.37 |

gestive of the severing of direct property considerations from marriage.

During the 19th century, then, daughters were not property exchanged between families. Nineteenth-century marriage, in contrast to the preceding two centuries, was between individuals rather than families. Parents, of course, continue to play an important role in structuring the premarital environment of their children. Their role today is presumably more indirect and their influence is more psychological than instrumental. What may be conceded in principle may be denied in practice. The extent of parental resources and the age of the children are key determinants of the efficacy of parental power. One could argue that the historical shift has been not the disappearance of parental power but its limitation to the earlier phases of the life cycle of the child. On the symbolic-ideological level the shift, albeit incomplete, toward the recognition of the child's independence from his family of orientation is apparent in child-naming patterns.

The decline of parental involvement in marriage formation is also suggested by the decrease in the proportion of marriages involving couples who were both residents of the town. One may presume that parents were more knowledgeable about, and hence more influential in, marriages to children of other families in the town. Between 59.6 percent and 71.8 percent of all marriages in decades between 1701-1710 and 1791-1800 involved two residents of Hingham; by 1850-1853, only 48.2 percent of all marriages; by 1900-1902 only 32.0 percent and finally by 1950-1954, a mere 25.8 percent were both residents of the town. Improved transportation and communication in the 19th and 20th centuries, of course, modify the magnitude of this trend. Once again, the shift is in the predicted direction and it occurs at the time—the first half of the 19th century—consistent with changes in other indices.

## CONCLUSIONS

At least in the area of parental control over marriage, significant, documentable historical change has occurred in American family behavior. There are difficulties, of course, in extending the findings of a local study to the entire American population. The trend in the family parameter which has been best-documented on the national level, fertility, is consistent with the more detailed evidence on the families of Hingham. From the early 19th century onward American marital fertility has been declining. With a level of fertility lower than the national average in 1800, New England was the leader in the American fertility transition. What the sequence of change in the Hingham indicators suggests is an erosion and collapse of traditional family patterns in the middle and late 18th century *before* the sharp decline in marital fertility began. In the 17th and early 18th century there existed a stable, parental-run marriage system, in the 19th century a stable, participant-run system. Separating these two eras of stability was a period of change and crisis manifested most notably in the American Revolution itself—a political upheaval not unconnected to the family.

Articles which begin with a capsule or caricature of a theoretical perspective and then proceed to a narrow body of empirical evidence typically conclude that the theory fails to explain the data adequately. Only criticism and revisionism represent *real* scholarly contributions. Only covertly does this study follow that format. Substantively, the empirical measures presented above for the population of Hingham, Massachusetts, confirm, if more precisely define and elaborate, the conclusions and interpretations of Smelser, Goode, Reiss, and Stone. It is perhaps revisionist in the sense that the current state of the field is confused because of the great gap separating a bold and sweeping theory of change and the evidence which would support it. A systematic history of the American family can be reconstructed if sociological theory, long-run series of quantitative data, and historical imagination in devising subtle measures of change are combined. The vulgar notion of a drastic shift from "extended" to "nuclear" families had to be exposed and rejected in order to generate historical research. The equally simple-minded opposite extreme of the historical continuity of the conjugal family is just as fallacious both on historical as well as the better-known sociological grounds. American *households* may always have been overwhelmingly nuclear in structure, but household composition is a measure of family structure—not the structure of the family itself. Historians love complexity—the tension between change and continuity over time. Unravelling this complexity is the particularly challenging task for scholars working in the history of the family.

# 2
# Preparenthood

## 1. Introduction

Preparenthood as a phase of the family life cycle is a modern conception. People living during the early modern period did not identify a time period after marriage and before the birth of their first child as having special meaning or qualities that were different from the rest of their years of marriage. For our purposes, therefore, the imposition of a modern construct of preparenthood is a heuristic device, used in the attempt to take cognizance of a stage of family life during the 16-18th centuries, previously never examined. It would be useful, therefore, to suggest some generalizations about the preparenthood period as it is conceived in our present day and then to compare it to that of the past in order to identify differences and similarities.

In modern times preparenthood has usually involved the following steps: (1) the general custom of newlyweds to remove themselves from their normal routine of work on a honeymoon trip; (2) the resumption after the trip of their respective occupations apart from one another; (3) the cooperative decision in planning for the enlargement of their family; and (4) the pregnancy period itself which, upon the birth of the baby, would end this phase of the cycle. The salient features are intimacy, acquired during the honeymoon and resumed only during non-work times; long stretches of time away from one another during the day; and in general a concurrence on the appropriate time for pregnancy.

Thus, it might be asked, did a preparenthood period exist in the early modern period that bears some resemblance to our modern conception? If not, did a phase of preparenthood exist which had different features from those associated with the stage today? Or, finally, is the imposition of this phase of the family cycle on the past anachronistic?

Historians often use a wide variety of sources to develop an understanding of the past. In this chapter we have included the writings of some historians who utilize quantitative, descriptive and prescriptive types of data. The selection by Lu Emily Pearson analyzes prescriptive sources, particularly marriage sermons and advice books published during the 16th and 17th centuries, in order to determine the possible attitudes and expectations of English brides and bridegrooms when they entered the state of matrimony. Prescriptive literature, however, does not directly describe actual behavior. Yet it can be used as an important indication of how some people thought the young married couple should behave, and may, in fact, reflect how they did act.

Included also in this chapter are writings of Lawrence Stone, who discusses the English aristocratic class, and Julia Spruill, who describes marriage in the American Colonial South. Both historians examine journals, diaries, newspapers, wills and marriage settlements. These sources allow the historian to observe how some people in fact did behave and feel. Finally, the articles by P.E. Hair and Daniel Scott Smith-Michael S. Hindus are quantitative in their approach. These researchers examined marriage, birth and baptism records from particular geographic areas in England and America to uncover the amount of brides who were pregnant when they married. The question of how widespread premarital conceptions were is important to our understanding of preparenthood because we assume the quality of the relationship between a couple already anticipating parenthood, in comparison to those who had yet to experience a pregnancy phase, would be appreciably different.

The authors included in this chapter were not thinking of a preparenthood stage when they wrote their selections. Thus a considerable amount of extrapolation from their writings has been necessary in order to glean insights for a description of a preparenthood stage.

Most couples who married in the early modern era began their marriage differently from modern newlyweds. According to Pearson and Spruill, the young couple, right after their marriage celebration, established their household and immediately began to cope with the tasks that would involve maintenance of their new home. Thus the initial step identified with preparenthood in the modern era was absent. No honeymoon trip was planned and no time was scheduled apart from their daily routine of work. It can be assumed that the immediacy of involvement with daily sustenance would vary in proportion to the economic well-being of the couple. Lawrence Stone, for example, states that some aristocratic newlyweds stayed with the groom's family for about a year, or until a newly constructed home would be complete. The few that this involved were the exceptions; for the majority attention to the necessities of the household required immediate supervision and participation.

The occupancy of a new household brought the couple into continuous contact with one another. How they assumed their new responsibilities and performed their tasks would undoubtedly reflect each of their talents. Moreover, being in close proximity in and around the household subjected them to a more intense mutual observation than exists between modern newlyweds who work outside the home. The couple in the early modern era, therefore, had greater contact with one another during the day than does their modern counterpart, as well as a greater opportunity to evaluate each other's performance. This initial phase of their marriage could lead to feelings of respect or disdain, depending upon the capabilities they had continuous occasion to observe.

It would be easy to dismiss these first months or years in marriage as being essentially similar to the pattern followed even after a child arrived. There is much to be said for this perception because of the couple's immediate involvement with their household duties. Yet, not to distinguish the initial stage of matrimony from later stages, where children and additional responsibilities were undertaken and which were built upon the sentiments established during a preparenthood phase, would be to slight the adjustments involved in establishing this significant new relationship.

The significance of marriage to early moderns is demonstrated by Pearson who examines marriage sermons and advice books on marriage. The question continuously reflected upon was, how to make a marriage successful. Indeed, there is every reason to believe that this injunction to make the marriage work from its outset reflected the actual sentiments of the couple. Circumstances combined to enhance the value of marriage. For example, women had few other recognized career options apart from marriage. Although greater career choice was available for men, most males needed a female helpmate to maintain a home and most communities conferred additional civic privileges on the master of a household. Moreover, the seriousness of marriage can also be demonstrated by the general assumption that once the marriage vows were taken the relationship was to last for the lifetime of the husband and his wife. How to make this new enterprise successful, therefore, was a concern not only of the married pair themselves, but also of the moral and social agencies of the society. Thus, great attention was directed toward the newly married couple to help them launch their new relationship. It was believed that the path to a successful marriage initiated during this preparenthood stage would require the following conditions: (a) that the husbands and wives understand their respective roles in their home and in society, (b) that they treat each other in a kindly and tolerant manner so that love could flourish, and (c) that their marriage would prove fertile.

The roles of husbands and wives related not only to the different household tasks they were obliged to undertake but also to the prevailing concepts of hierarchy which contributed to a definition of the relationship between the two. Husbands were assumed to be masters of the household and in this regard responsible for the actions and behavior of wives. The law recognized and reflected this dominant-subservient feature of marriage. It declared that in most legal situations husband and wife were to be considered one. But the law assumed the "one" was the husband. Thus, for example, the husband was held accountable for any debts incurred by his wife.

The presumption of male responsibility led many concerned with successful marriage to ask such a question as, in what manner should a husband admonish a wife requiring discipline? The answers ranged from the infliction of corporal punishment to mild chastisement. Women, on the other hand, were advised to be tolerant, helpful and docile. Except for Puritans who rejected the sexual double standard, this tolerance might be expected to extend to the adulterous behavior of husbands. The aristocratic classes in England and the American South accepted a male's extramarital relationships as natural, but Puritans were certain that such a double standard was immoral and put great strain on marriage. It is, therefore, interesting to note that Lawrence Stone and Julia Spruill, who examine these two classes, attest to the marital difficulties of some of its members. Yet, an aristocratic marriage might be successful if the wife accepted her subservient role by tolerating her husband's infidelities.

This final ingredient for a successful marriage related to the fecundity of the married couple. Most people in the early modern era identified marriage with having children. Although it has been suggested that some birth control may have been practiced, a topic to be discussed in the next chapter, the mores of the time reflected the high value placed on having offspring. The importance of marital fecundity has been illustrated by Pearson. She suggests, for example, that the English monarchy demonstrated concern that a highly placed marriage be consummated. Other indications of the importance placed on fecundity may be seen in premarital sex practiced by a betrothed couple.

The desire of newlyweds for children appears to have been more immediate for newlyweds during the 16-18th centuries than it is today. In early modern times the first child was born from about 11 months to 15 months after the marriage, while during the last 80 years the average interval between marriage and birth has been 20 months.

Since pregnancy in the 16th-18th centuries was regarded as a significant ingredient to the success of marriage, it is important to ascertain how many brides were already pregnant when they married and to draw some inferences as to whether there might have been a different preparenthood experience for the couple who already knew they were to have a child. Women who were pregnant at the time the household was established might, for example, require and possibly receive more solicitude from their husbands in the organization of their household tasks, a subject further explored in the next chapter. Since parenthood was a desirable goal, those couples who were less fecund might have had more overt manifestations of marital strains, stresses and conflicts in the absence of the solicitude induced by pregnancy. Numerical quantifications of premarital conceptions, therefore, can help us to determine how often the preparenthood years were directed towards the impending parenthood rather than exclusively with establishing a household. Both the articles by Hair and Smith-Hindus provide us with these numerical indices.


## 2. Founding And Maintaining An English Home
### by Lu Emily Pearson

Concern for possessions, spiritual and material, gave more and more emphasis to the need for continuity of the family and for whatever might ensure harmony in the home through cooperation of its members—husband and wife, parents and children, masters and servants. This emphasis naturally stimulated the general interest in any marriage that might occur, till John Selden's *Table Talk* complained: "Of all actions of a man's life his marriage does least concern other people; yet of all actions of our life 'tis most meddled with by other people." But this "meddling" seemed necessary to Elizabethan social groups trying to adapt themselves to the strangely new life about them shaken by upheavals in intellectual thought, emotion, and religious belief. In the process of its adaptation social life naturally became very self-conscious, especially when opportunities for sudden wealth and its accompanying innovations in decorum added to the confusion. Consequently, the domestic books dealing with proper conduct as affected by marriage and family relations and duties became so necessary that no home could afford to be without at least one volume of such advice.

Each of these books stressed the importance of good manners for ensuring domestic peace and harmony, and each set down rules of etiquette for practically every member of the household. Like Coverdale's translation in 1546 of Bullinger's *The Christian State of Matrimony,* they followed a more or less set form: they gave some space to a discussion of conditions that might cause disruption in the family, such as divorce or separation, but they were mostly concerned with whatever might dignify marriage and the family relations. All recognized that the husband's government of the household must be "without tryanny," like Christ's care for the Church, and all set down carefully the duties of husband and wife and parents and children. They also discussed problems of housekeeping, proper dress, the education of children, and the directing of servants. Some of the authors, like Erasmus, Snawsell, and Tilney, preferred a semifictional form for their instruction; others attempted a book of organized rules, others published their sermons dealing with such matter, embellished by practical experience, and most of the Puritans supported their statements by biblical references, as in the case of William Gouge's *Of Domesticall Duties* (1622).

If there is any truth in the statement by André Maurois (*The Miracle of*

*England*) that the strength of England today "springs from the kindly, disciplined, trusting, and tenacious character" of its people, then one must give the home credit for achieving this miracle. And the home which still affects modern English life was the very foundation of the Elizabethan commonwealth. Without doubt the closest tie between England and America today is due to this same influence of the home upon American character, much of which is inherited from our English ancestors of the sixteenth and early seventeenth centuries.

Elizabethan domestic or conduct books, like all literature dealing with social etiquette, did not portray life as it actually was but as the authors believed it should be lived. Such material, therefore, measures standards rather than life. The creative literature, then as now, provided serious or satirical or sentimental or romantic sketches of character that sometimes skillfully employed details from life to give the effort some verisimilitude. In all this literature husbands and wives and their complicated relationship in founding and maintaining the home were the subject of many analyses, but in all Elizabethan literature of advice, perhaps the marriage sermon was expected to give most pertinent information on domestic matters. Discounting the personal bias that might distort these homilies, one can gather from them what was expected to appeal to serious members in Elizabethan society. Like Paul's Epistles, written to teach beginners in the Christian faith how to live the Christian life, these Elizabethan sermons also tried to set before the people instruction that would enable them to live like Christians in the sixteenth century home. The fact that these sermons were so well attended voluntarily is significant, especially when one remembers how long they were, and how very repetitious was their subject matter. For a check on these sermons, possibly personal letters are best if they are divorced from the formalities peculiar to the age. However, one must always keep in mind the difference between practice and moral ideas to which the preacher, the literary artist, and even the man in the street may give lip service only.

The preacher usually began his discussion of duties in the home with insistence on the wife's obedience of her husband, and followed this closely with a warning against the husband's abuse of his power through spurning or scorning his wife, whom he should love like his own body. She must love her husband so fully as never to forsake him. A live thing, love could not stand still; if it did not increase daily, it would surely die. Their first common duty to each other, therefore, was to cause love to grow from day to day. Like Bullinger, they agreed that daily prayer and reading of the Bible were necessary to the cultivation of a healthy love. Also, like Bullinger, they declared all property distinctions must be leveled between married people if they would live in harmony: what one owned, the other owned also, regardless of how much more one of them possessed before marriage.

Husbands and wives were told to bear with each other's moods, to answer impatient words kindly, gently, and with loving consideration for each other and for mutual friends and relatives. They should try to adapt themselves courteously to each other by an exchange of confidence with confidence and by refusing to hold resentment. They must never let the sun set on their wrath: nothing could be more dangerous to future happiness. They must avoid even the suspicion of evil in associations with others and in their recreations, and they must avoid all pleasures taking them from home. When children came, they must be the kind of parents they wished their children to become, and they must abide in a harmony that would knit together the entire family. Finally, husbands and wives must minister to each other in a cleanly, truthful, and friendly way, never withholding themselves lest they fail in their love for each other and the home.

After a century of sermons on these themes, the old, old material could still be turned into sermons by Jeremy Taylor that held his listeners spellbound. To marry for beauty, he said, was to marry for fancy and to love elsewhere in time. Husband and wife must take great care in avoiding offenses in conversation, particularly while becoming adjusted to each other. In the beginning, he said, both were likely to be observant, jealous, suspicious, easily alarmed; later, they would not need to exercise so much caution. "After the hearts of the man and wife are endeared . . . by mutual confidence," he explained, "and an experience longer than artifice and patience can last, there are a great many remembrances, and some things present, that dash all little unkindnesses in pieces." Nevertheless, husband and wife even long married should stifle little things as soon as they jar. "In the frequent little accidents of a family, a man's reason cannot always be awake; and when his discourses are imperfect, and a trifling trouble makes him yet more restless, he is soon betrayed to the violence of passion" unless he substracts fuel from the sudden flame. It is important, therefore, ever to remember that "discontents proceeding from daily little things do breed a secret undiscernible disease which is more dangerous than a fever proceeding from a discerned notorious surfeit." For example, the old Roman practice of forbidding donations between husband and wife was good in that it taught married people to take great care to avoid the distinction between "mine and thine." As they had "but one person, so should they have but one interest between them."

William Gouge stressed the need of husband and wife governing the family as partners. The husband, he said, added much to a wife's authority by aiding her in it, thereby preventing her from being lightly esteemed or even despised. Among the things in which the husband should take the lead he named the following: conducting the family worship, appointing and settling the ordering of goods, providing convenient house room and other necessities for the family, keeping the children "in awe," and ruling the servants. But the wife should be his partner even here, for she must nourish and instruct the young, adorn the house, order provisions as they were needed, and rule the women servants. Should her husband be sick or away from home, she must conduct the family worship. At other times she must merely gather the family for the worship, and if necessary remind her husband when to read the Bible and when to conduct the catechising of children and servants. By her own respect for her husband's instructions, she would impress upon the children and servants a proper regard for the master's teaching. In charitable work or in giving alms to the poor, husband and wife must always act together. By being abroad so frequently, the husband should be able to determine *whom* to aid; by spending so much time in the house, the wife should know *how* to aid. Always they should give mercifully of clothing and food to the deserving.

In a thousand and one ways Elizabethans were told how to maintain domestic harmony. Henry Smith's sermon, *A Preparation to Mariage* (1591), stressed the "division of offices and affairs." Like "two oars in a boat," the husband and wife should have equal rights and responsibilities. The wife should be "feared and reverenced, and obeyed of her children and servants" as entirely as her husband. Though the preacher insisted she must share her lord's privileges and honors, he called her the "underofficer" in their home. Unless the husband was duly considerate of her, the wife became an underofficer indeed in the household economy. Here was the rock on which the household peace might well be shattered, and much was said to avert such misery.

William Perkins described the dangers as well as the means to harmony. A wife might retain certain things as her very own; these things she might lawfully give, even without her husband's knowledge. Such things were hers because "either they were reserved upon the match between them, or else were peculiar unto her by their mutual consent." Such property was usually settled upon the wife at the father's or guardian's demands when the marriage contract was drawn up by lawyers. The goods common to both husband and wife she could not touch, of course, unless her husband was party to the deed. All other property brought by the wife in marriage became the husband's, and descended to the eldest son or, if there were no sons, to the daughters. If there were no children, the property returned to the wife's family by right of succession. If the wife had no property settled on her at her marriage, she was entirely dependent on the bounty of her husband. All the wife's movable property, said Perkins, such as plate, money, cattle, etc., belonged to her husband at her death. However, mutual consent about this movable property could prevent much discord if the wife wished to will any of it to relatives or friends, for such gifts were entirely out of order if the husband did not wish them made. If the husband died first, the wife could enjoy one-third of his estate while she lived, and no more unless it was willed to her. Harmonious relations between husband and wife, therefore, could ease the lot of the widow, for then the husband would have her welfare in mind when he made out his will. Otherwise there might be trouble and downright disaster. Under such a system, if the husband refused to share his goods with a wife who had none of her very own, she was indeed a helpless victim in circumstances controlled by financial arrangements.

Sometimes, however, God gave in wrath—to give trial, cure, correction, or punishment. Since no marriage on earth could be blessed except by divine mercy, the affections could not be forced at the matching of two people, though there might be such a thing as love at first sight. There was also such a thing as "strange alienation of affections" after matching even when parents had tried to link their children through careful consideration of "all inducements of person, estate, and years." Gataker believed that although a happy marriage was due to God's mercy, a man so blessed was not necessarily deserving but possibly an object of the inscrutable design of the Lord. In such a marriage the woman must remember that she was given to her husband "as to her owner," to live with him, to be guided by him, and never to forsake him. But as each was necessary to the other, the man should not forget that he too was an instrument of God. Acceptance of this type of reasoning, of course, depended entirely upon whether husband and wife were at least conventionally religious.

Naturally, the husband's place in the household was presented in most moral literature as weighed down with responsibilities. His first duty, love of his wife, was discussed in all its important aspects. Many writers, especially Puritans, would have this love first concerned for the wife's spiritual well-being; that is, the husband would seek to train her "in faith, fear, and love of God from the very beginning of their marriage." By gentleness, courtesy, and kindly persuasion he would lead her to respond to him with devotion, lovingly "obeying the ordinance that God hath made between her and her husband." If trouble came to such a union, the husband must look upon it as a means of bringing him and his wife to the joy derived from surviving a severe test of their faith. Becon urged the husband as his wife's spiritual keeper to help and comfort and cherish her, quietly bearing with all her weaknesses, never rigorously dealing with her, but gently and lovingly admonishing her to better amendment and more diligence.

Though he must protect his wife from needing any things necessary for the household, the husband must above all, said Becon, protect her good name. Unto the uttermost of his power he must not suffer her to be "injured, wronged, displeasured, or trodden under foot by her adversaries." This care for a wife's reputation was emphasized again and again by all writers of didactic literature, for Elizabethans knew that no woman could ever be a match for slanderous tongues. As Thomas Fuller was to write later, a woman's good name was like a tree in Mexico, "which is so exceedingly tender, that a man cannot touch any of its branches, but it withers . . . "

The contempt of a worldly-wise Elizabethan woman for a husband who failed to defend his wife's honor was very great. In a time when political intrigue was likely to involve all important families, women relied especially on their husbands for protecting their good name. One plot concerned with the support of Arabella Stuart instead of James as successor to Queen Elizabeth implicated two families in which the husbands were requested to sound out their wives by fair means or foul. One loosed his wife's tongue by "unwonted amiability," and when she discovered his purpose he could not be reconciled to her till after a long period of servile effort toward winning her good favor. The other wife discovered her husband's intent at the start, and so great was her anger that she refused ever again to have anything to do with him. And she kept her word even though her husband was imprisoned and died in poverty twenty years later.

Some writers urged husbands for their own sake to bear with their wives as the weaker vessels lest in their impatience the wives resort to spite of some kind. Certainly no man should ever expect to win a dispute with his wife, and it would be best for him to admit occasionally he had been vanquished. He should also, for his own sake, permit his wife some merrymaking before his eyes; otherwise, she would be likely to resort to it in secret. In *The Golden Grove* of William Vaughan the author advises the husband to be as generous as his means will allow and never to cause his wife to become jealous or suspicious. At the same time, he must never permit her a second bed, even as a temporary arrangement for ragged nerves, lest she seek to make it a permanent practice. Vaughan looked upon women as a somewhat necessary evil with which husbands were honor-bound to live in harmony though the effort would tax the patience of a saint.

Of course the perfect husband to whom writers referred most frequently was Sir Thomas More. They saw in his household discipline all that they idealized in a home, yet he himself declared that he did not think it possible to live with "even the best of wives without some discomfort." A man must expect cares when entering the state of matrimony, he explained, though he hastened to add that men usually made their wives worse by their own fault. All More's biographers praise his tolerant attitude toward his second wife, emphasizing her sharp tongue even as they admit she was an excellent housekeeper. "When any woman in his house or neighborhood was laboring in childbirth," writes Stapleton, Sir Thomas More "would always give himself to prayer and continue until he received tidings of a safe delivery." Yet More himself would be quick to admit that while his hands were folded in supplication his wife's were working busily and efficiently to aid the woman in her distress.

So generally was the husband's duty of providing food, clothing, and shelter accorded his responsibility, and his only, that there is little discussion of the matter. Instead, his other duties of leadership in the household were emphasized and critically analyzed. In matters of discipline he was to be supreme in command unless a capital crime should be committed within his doors. In that case he was responsible for taking the offender to the civil magistrate. In all minor offences, however, he was to punish and admonish according to the character of the offending deed and the condition and state of the person at fault. Should admonitions and corrections fail, he must take the culprit to the proper authorities of Church or State.

Because of the husband's position of authority in the home, his power over his wife became a subject of much discussion during this age. Possibly the husband's authority was partly responsible for Queen Elizabeth's choice of a lonely life as a people's sovereign rather than the married life she was urged to enter. She must have looked with dismay at the humiliating dependence of her sister Mary when she became subject to the will and mood of her husband from Spain. In all seriousness the heads of the Church and State discussed the right of husbands to discipline their wives even to the point of downright beating. Many divines deplored the practice of such chastisement, however, declaring that a man should never use "stripes or strokes" to one who was of his own flesh, but instead should give reproof by word of mouth. Others, not so mild, chanted with a right good will

A spaniel, a woman, and a walnut tree,
The more they are beaten, the better they be.

Some objected to the beating of wives because the Scriptures did not approve of such treatment except for children and servants. Jeremy Taylor declared the government of the whole family was disordered if the husband laid hands on the shoulder "which together with the other ought to bear nothing but the cares and the issues of a prudent government." Henry Smith proclaimed from the pulpit that for a man to beat his wife was the "greatest shame" that could be, not so much to her who was beaten as to him who performed the deed. "Every man," he said, "must be ashamed to lay hands on a woman because she cannot match him." Perkins felt that a man with a peevish wife must be pitied, but not excused for becoming impatient with her. A good husband, he said, should cover his wife's infirmities of anger and waywardness by his wisdom and patience. Gouge insisted that a man's love for his wife should enable him to bear with any weakness she might have, and he reminded the husband that since love begets love, he must set the right example to his wife by holding respect for her and by showing a proper regard for her place and person. Thus he must not be too strict in commanding obedience of her; indeed, his command should be as mild as his reproof was rare.

Yet some men of culture and learning did approve of wife beating. In a speech at St. Mary's Church of Oxford a scholarly and witty jurist and poet stated in all sincerity that husbands were granted the right by ancient law and sacred authority to beat their wives, and that when it was necessary they should administer such discipline. William Heale, a member of Exeter College, countered with his *An Apologie for Women*, in which he made the old statement that one mind and one flesh could not be fittingly used in this manner; rather, he urged some cordial should be sought to heal them, not a corrosive to afflict them. The law, he said, permitted a woman to leave her husband if he beat her and to receive from him sufficient maintenance, and she need not return to him till he provided good security not to beat her. He called wife beating inhuman and servile, and concluded with the statement: "God's law supported civil law against it, for man and wife should live together to honor marriage by the unity of their souls."

The wisest minds sought to find the cause of wife beating, and many of them agreed the most common provocation was the wife's shrewishness or the husband's disapproval of his wife's companions. Then they set about advising the husband on how to supplant his wife's friends by being so attentive and confiding that the wife would invariably turn to him instead. Gouge felt that such sympathy was particularly necessary to a woman when she was with child, and declared that "during travail and child-bed" the husband should make every effort to satisfy her "longings," and to provide the necessary companionship and other things required for the ordeal. He also warned the husband against failing to protect his wife at such a time, especially against slanderous tongues or from any danger that might arise, such as the irritation from "children-in-law."

Guazzo believed a husband should judge his wife only after examining his own love, for distrust of wives, he said, came from a weakness of affection. Once suspicion enters, love leaves, but a husband who loves his wife as the other half of himself will not tolerate suspicion. It is foolish, he chided, to watch over a woman "with diligence," for anyone should know a dishonest woman cannot be kept in, and an honest one does not deserve such treatment. Relations between husband and wife must be kept delicate lest the beauty of their association be blunted. For this reason he objected to wife beating. Since a wife was truly flesh of her husband's flesh; no man should torment an erring wife, but seek rather to comfort her. How could a husband embrace a body his hands had bruised? How could a woman love a man who had beaten her?

Other important duties in the husband's leadership were concerned with directing the family worship, for in spite of the Reformation and all its attendant countermovements, religion continued to influence every phase of public and private life even though it did not always dominate the heart. It not only affected all the daily habits, but was especially influential in dress and speech and even the choice of friends. All writing of the period shows these influences: in public announcements and moral literature, in private correspondence, and in the very broadsheets hawked about the streets. It is amazing that religion's hold was so strong when the form of religious service was so frequently altered and debated, and when the shrines were defaced, the priests outlawed, and the clergy that remained far too often lacking in the necessary training for their place in religious life. Even the very language underwent changes in the services. In Henry VIII's time religious faith caused well-known and respected public men to be accused of high treason for refusing to take the Oath of Supremacy, and in Mary's time it caused many people to be burned at the stake for not acknowledging the pope. Still religion retained its hold on life.

Family prayers, therefore, were customary in most homes. The loved story of Sir Thomas More's devotion to this family duty was often repeated. Once, while in the midst of the family service, he was summoned to the king, "even two or three times," but refused to leave till the morning worship had been concluded. When urged to come away and attend the king, he answered he must "finish his act of homage to a higher King," and Henry VIII himself would be first to acknowledge the rightness of that response. In great houses chaplains led the exercises. They lectured the households upon their duties, conducted the morning and evening prayers during the week, and preached twice on Sundays. In summer the services occurred at five in the morning, but in winter an hour later. In homes that had no chaplain, the father supervised the worship, kneeling with his family and servants in the great hall or some like suitable place, which might be perfumed at the command of his wife with rosemary or juniper or even frankincense, or freshened with rosewater or just plain vinegar. In the father's absence, the mother took his place at this worship, reciting short prayers or collects, and instructing the children and servants in the family faith.

Edmund Tilney, who must have learned a great deal about the disrupting influences in the lives of important people even before he became Master of the Revels at court, wrote *The Flower of Friendshippe* (1568) to give advice in domestic affairs. He felt the early days and weeks of adjustment were so difficult that the husband in particular should make every effort to build on them a firm foundation for a happy marriage. This he could do only if he made his wife "wholly his" by cultivating flowers instead of weeds. Among the noxious plants in married life were the man's addiction to gambling, excess banqueting, and rioting. The flowers of marriage the husband should cultivate were courteous speech, wise counseling, trustworthiness when confided in, careful provision for the house, diligence in caring for his possessions, patience with his wife's importunities, circumspection in honesty, and when children came, zeal in educating them. For one sharp command he should use a hundred loving exhortations. Should he and his wife differ about some trivial thing like the servants' apparel, he should turn the whole thing into sport. If his temper got the best of him, he should "walk it out." Since wise counsel came from hearing and seeing much, he approved of the tour for all young men before they settled down to the founding of a home. By this means the husband would avoid such pitfalls as spoiling his wife with too much indulgence or bringing home for entertainment the wrong kind of guests.

One of the first things the wife must do, said Vives, was to prevent her relationship with her mother-in-law from becoming that of a resented stepparent and child. He believed that the mother's natural jealous love of her son and the wife's natural objection to her husband's love for any woman but herself could be turned into a real attachment. He could not see why this relationship would be difficult for a wife who felt she and her husband were one through marriage. If she found it so, she must take tender care of her mother-in-law, especially in time of illness, and if by such care she did win the older woman's confidence, her own mother would surely rejoice with her.

In theory, the Elizabethan woman was subservient to husband, father, or brother in a way that present-day women cannot understand. In actual practice, her subservience depended upon the kind of husband and relatives she had and also upon her own temperament and dependence upon others. Shakespeare plays a game with these ideas in *The Taming of the Shrew*. Where does Katharina actually stand in this play? She has puzzled many critics by her speech after she has been subdued by her husband's rigorous training. Does she present a serious description in a rollicking comedy to please Elizabethans who liked that kind of juxtaposition? Or was she providing a comically fantastic application of Elizabethan psychology to the shrew for the intellectual members of the audience? Or was her speech merely a tongue-in-cheek romanticizing on the perfect wife? Or, finally, is the whole play merely a battle of wits to delight those demanding satire?

In real life the wives of tradesmen enjoyed an independence that was often shocking to the pious. Middle-class women were frequently admitted to guilds on an equal footing with men, and were permitted to engage themselves as shop managers and assistants. Often, too, they were valuable to their husbands in small business ventures, and after the death of a husband, the widow might carry on the business alone. Records of women printers and booksellers preserved in the Stationers Company books prove this fact. Nevertheless, even these women gave more than lip service to the idea of subjection of their sex when father, husband, or brother chose to be master. They had to bow to the fact that man's authority was supported by the Scriptures: "Even as Sarah obeyed Abraham, calling him lord . . . " (I Pet. 3:6), "And the Lord God said, 'It is not good for man to be alone: I will make him an help-meet . . . ' " (Gen. 2:18), "For a man ought to cover his head, forasmuch as he is the image and glory of God: but the woman is the glory of man . . . ' " (I Cor. 11:7). Some writers pointed out the disadvantage of this subjection, but said it was not in any way commensurate with the woman's danger of losing her good name, which obedience to the man having authority over her would avert. Plagued by these two fears, losing favor with her lord or protector and suffering the grief of scandal, an Elizabethan woman would find obedience far less onerous than the risk of losing her good name.

Women themselves wrote their approval of such abject humility expected of obedient wives. For example, Dorothy Leigh's *The Mothers Blessing* (1618) was written for this pious purpose when she wished to give advice to her children lest she, like their father, should die suddenly and leave them adrift in the world. In her apology for her authorship, she said that only her children's welfare caused her to sacrifice her womanly modesty and risk the censure of the world in making public her "scroll." Supported by her belief that her own husband would approve if he but knew, she made this effort to ensure the family reunion in heaven. She urged her sex to be ever willing to give men first place, for sin had entered the world through women. They must, therefore, be constantly on guard against all evil and see that their children frequently called on Christ for aid to cast out sin in themselves. In time she hoped her children would follow her example by writing down for their little ones what they had learned would show them the way to "true happiness."

A good wife must be humbly faithful in her obedient regard for a philandering husband, but in real life she might have him restored to her quite as dramatically as in the popular plays of the time. For example, it is not known just why Essex reformed so suddenly after the Cadiz voyage in 1596, but from this time on, he was a changed man. Was his wife's loyalty partly responsible? He became "sober, religious, and devoted" to her, "regularly attending prayers and preachings, and using language so replete with moral sentiments, with humility and self-distrust, as greatly to edify the astonished courtiers." Nor did he lapse again, according to his biographer, for "he no longer entered into such intrigues with Court ladies as he had enjoyed before, and which had inflamed the Queen's anger and scandalized his moral friends." So unaccountable was his alteration it has even been questioned as sincere, but for all that, Essex was never again wanting in affection for his wife whom he now acknowledged as of mind and attainments truly suited to him for companionship. Her first attractions had been her great beauty and sweet humility.

Any Elizabethan housewife too long away from home was likely to stir the curiosity of gossips or to suffer deeply from the abuse of critics in her own social circle. Often fiery-tongued preachers referred to such women as examples of evil. To be absent from home when the husband was well might be dangerous to a wife's reputation, but to be away during his illness made her guilty of an unforgivable evil. Henry Smith urged women ever to abide at home as if it were a paradise rather than a prison. Thomas Carter believed women went from home chiefly to display their fine clothes, and called them "street wives." No good women, he said, would ever "spin street thread." Such wives forced their husbands to lay more on their backs than they could put in a purse for a long time after; then the wives would gad from place to place, showing their pride and their husband's folly. Bullinger had insisted that no wife ever cross her doorstep without her husband's permission, and even then not go far from home. Most moralists agreed that a woman exposed herself to unspeakable dangers or illness. The countess, therefore, had good cause to bemoan her lot when she was separated from her home and husband as the Earl of Essex lay on his death bed. Indeed, she might well comtemplate the sacrificing of her very life.

Of course husbands did not wish their wives to leave home in their absence lest they be indiscreet, even innocently so, for men believed they knew the perils of scandal better than their wives did. Many wives were also tormented by just such fears about their absent husbands, and both preachers and writers of conduct books had much to say on the subject. Should a wife hear evil reports of her husband, she must stop her ears against them, and if on his return she should learn he had been with a mistress, she must remember that to leave a dishonest husband would only please the mistress. A wise wife, therefore, would seek to marry the mistress off to some honest servant. They quoted Vives about a husband not ceasing to love his wife while with his mistress, and even argued that a wife's displeasure might drive the husband to the mistress. Therefore, the wife had but to be patient, and her husband would return to her.

The moralists were right, however, when they said a good Elizabethan housewife, particularly among the upper classes, had little time for "walking abroad." She was indeed kept too busy supervising her servants even though she herself did not perform many actual tasks. True, the chief steward was supposed to take most of the responsibilities off the shoulders of the great lady, but many such women took pride in their housewifery, and did not care to delegate their duties to even the best of stewards. The training and directing of wards as well as maids took much of their time; even among good servants there was danger of undue extravagance unless all the offices were carefully controlled. Possibly the trait of orderliness was more strongly developed at this time, for preachers and writers continued to quote from Gentian Hervet's translation of Xenophon, *Treatise of the Household* (1537). Again and again they admonished the good housewife to see that there was a place for everything and everything was kept in that place. The husband had to go abroad instead of "slugging at home," and therefore the wife must not leave home "to walk about" when she was responsible for maintaining all things well in her household.

Most wives felt the need of economy in household management because of the expense involved in keeping up appearances. This was especially true of the ambitious middle class. Bullinger had advised the saving housewife to demand no more than necessary for her household simply because all unnecessary things were always dear, and "it was easier to save than to get." He had also urged performing all things in their season without delay, leaving to others nothing she could do herself and dispensing with nothing she might be able to use later. Such wives, he had argued, not only enabled their husbands to amass riches honestly, but were rich themselvs in their good works and in their giving of their substance to the poor.

Economy for its own sake and for its rewards was drilled into Puritans as a necessity in maintaining a home, but need frequently drove great Anglican or Catholic ladies to display this virtue. The thrifty housewife, if she relied on food from the markets, closely supervised the purchases made for the household, and the middle-class women journeyed to the shops and made the purchases themselves for the accompanying servant or apprentice to carry home. Then the cooking and baking and sewing and mending kept their own hands, besides those of their maids, busy from dawn to dark.

Since Elizabethan housewives looked upon their duties as a vocation or even a career, they took pride in their domestic achievements. It is doubtful whether many of them ever objected to their destiny; it is more than likely that most of them experienced great satisfaction from useful accomplishment. Besides having the daily preparation of food and its special preserving and curing for future needs, the fine and course needlework, the spinning of wool and flax, and the embroidery of linens, furnishings, and apparel, the good housewife, with her distilling of perfumes and medicines, was also doctor and nurse to neighbors and friends as well as her own household. Moreover, if her husband was a farmer, she might have to care for sick animals, and if her husband was a county squire, she might have to act for him in any lawsuits that arose. Only the weaklings in such a whirlpool of activities had time or inclination to become enmeshed in corroding distractions of mind or emotions.

The country wife in a large establishment was often called upon to perform heavy labor as well as to assume heavy responsibilities, and was usually the first up in the morning and the last to bed at night. Besides overseeing her maids and engaging in some of the preparation of fruits, herbs, and root vegetable for storage, she must be sure of enough lard for her household needs and enough seeds for the next plantings. She must be responsible for the kitchen garden and the honey bees, she must buy the household necessities or see that they were bought, she must have charge of oven and cellar and see that all supplies were stored under lock and key, she must keep hens, and perhaps geese, pigeons, pheasants and possibly peacocks, and she must know how her servants should handle hemp and sheer the sheep and keep the fleeces or supervise their transformation through spinning, combing, and weaving till they became cloth and then clothing for her family and servants. She might have to supervise the feeding of cattle, calves, hogs and other animals, and the milking of cows morning and evening.

If her husband owned much land and she had to take charge of it, she frequently saw to the leasing of farms, secured markets for the crops harvested under her supervision, and wrote or dictated to her husband long letters about details of management. Sometimes she even wrote business letters as well as the recipes for her book of domestic information she was to hand down to her eldest daughter. If she could not read or write, she might have to delay her letters till the arrival of the "coney-man" who came once or twice a month to buy her rabbits for market, for many a common man's wife depended on such people to write important letters for her. Some yeomen's wives, however, could read and write as well as their husbands, and their daughters at village schools sometimes got a smattering of reading and writing that enabled them later to manage business details in the absence of their husbands. Among the religious wives who could read, time must be found for reading long sermons to their household during the master's absence. In all the multitudinous tasks there was time for the woman's touch when such housewives named their cows and horses and ordered their names entered in the inventories of their wills.

The details in all this Elizabethan advice concerning the happiness or unhappiness in store for individuals are notable for the moral intensity with which they were regarded. For to Elizabethans, marriage and its ceremonious founding and maintaining of the home were essential acts of dignity and social importance. The husband and wife had common and separate duties they must perform if their lives, always more or less carefully scrutinized by members of their own social group, were to be approved. Responsibility to family or society could not be ignored, and those husbands and wives who would live with honor or with the approbation of their fellow men could never forget or deny their obligations to home, Church, and State.

This is why man's position as head of the household was maintained by a carefully planned moral and economic policy. Woman's subjection and obedience to the requirements of this policy were a matter of necessity if not of choice, though many a woman's wisdom enabled her to reconcile these two factors by weighing nicely, thoughtfully, or piously the advantages and disadvantages of the plan. If marriage was to be a partnership, there must be delegated to one of them the final authority; if it was to be a divine institution, it must have a divinely appointed lord and master; if it was to be a social necessity, both husband and wife must adapt themselves harmoniously to the demands of public and private living; and finally, if the relationship was to be used for preserving their individual selves, they must learn how to function as a unit and without friction in the irksome as well as pleasant details of life bounded by the household. The best minds and hearts, therefore, sought to fuse these elements into an adequate way of life that in spite of its complexity deserves the careful attention of those interested in the stability of home or of a nation founded on homes.

True, the head of the household was entitled to many privileges, but he also carried grave responsibilities. Concern for the welfare of his wife and children was not to be recognized one day and ignored the next. He must help to bring a continual harmony out of the "daily little things" that otherwise might become "more dangerous than a fever." He must always remember that morally he was responsible for the good name of his wife and children, and his responsibility could be carried lightly or only with great labor according to the way he chose a wife, or, if the wife was chosen for him, according to the way he instructed her in preparation for her duties as mistress of his household and mother of his children. Though the law permitted him to beat his wife if she was not responsive to his instruction, still he was liable for the consequences of such treatment as they manifested themselves in his home and in the society he frequented outside his home.

Woman's subjection to her lord and master might be easy or difficult, but her religion or intelligence as much as the mores of the times enabled her to adjust herself to the bonds of the marriage relationship. The protection afforded her by marriage and the respectful attitude of society toward a good or discreet wife were rewards sufficient in themselves to make her hesitate to abandon such security for the precarious delight of a personal liberty that might jeopardize both her economic and her social status.

## 3. The Stability Of Marriage

by Lawrence Stone

Marriage took place very early, the partners were often virtually strangers to each other and were chosen by their parents, the first years of their married life were usually spent in the house of the parents, consummating tended to occur in a blaze of publicity or else some years after the marriage ceremony itself, and was followed more often than not either by total sterility or by an infinitely repetitive cycle of child-bearing. Despite the physical and psychological strains imposed by these arrangements, the majority of marriages survived without open and serious breakdown, and in many cases there developed genuine affection and trust. Some turned out well after the most unpromising beginnings.

In view of the tremendous religious, social, legal, and economic pressures directed at holding the family unit together, it is none the less remarkable how many marriages publicly and completely broke up. Since full divorce was almost impossible to obtain, the only escape was a formal separation *a mensa et thoro* which condemned the wife to lonely isolation on a modest allowance, and left the husband free to do anything but marry again. The fact that release from the marriage bond could only be achieved by death was the reason for the spread of ugly rumours that two Elizabethan peers—Leicester and Howard of Bindon— had murdered their wives, and that one wife—Douglas Lady Sheffield—had been an accomplice in the murder of her husband. Our knowledge of less sensational marital discord among the peerage is necessarily very far from complete and has to be gleaned mostly from the reports of gossip-writers and from correspondence preserved among the public records. The explanation of the richness of this last source is that the King frequently—even normally—acted as arbiter in matrimonial disputes among the aristocracy. By doing so he was fulfilling the function of the chieftain of the tribe, a practice which must have had a remote pre-Christian ancestry but which survived as a bizarre anomaly in the law-ridden world of the seventeenth century.

If we disregard entirely the evidence of illegitimate children, in the ninety years between 1570 and 1659 we find forty-nine known cases of notorious marital quarrels, separations *a mensa et thoro*, or annulments among the peerage, which is about 10 per cent of all marriages. The worst period seems to have been between 1595 and 1620, when something like one-third of the older peers were estranged from or actually separated from their wives.

Why this generation should have been so exceptionally restless is hard to explain. It may be that it was the first reaction by women to the novel doctrine of greater equality between the sexes which was being put about by some puritan pamphleteers. Moreover the legal position of women was improving, and with it their ability to obtain satisfactory terms for a separation—a new situation which may have gone to the heads of some discontented wives. It was between 1580 and 1640 that successive Lord Chancellors gave judgements which substantially altered the law concerning married women's property by creating the doctrine of the Wife's Separate Estate. By the early seventeenth century the economic penalties of a separation for a woman had been substantially diminished.

It is possible that thereafter friction was reduced by the growing reluctance of parents to press children too hard to marry against their inclinations; it may be that the further spread of the puritan conscience damped down these public displays of temper; but it is unlikely to be an illusory product of imperfect evidence, though this may be the explanation of the more modest level recorded in the early Elizabethan period. The great majority of these separations occur in well-established families which had held a title for at least three generations, presumably because only the socially secure felt themselves at liberty to indulge in this unorthodox behaviour. There was also something of a tendency for marital quarrels to run in families. The 2nd and 3rd Earls of Sussex, the 13th and 15th Earls of Derby, the 2nd and 3rd Earls of Dorset, the 2nd and 3rd Viscounts Bindon, the 17th and 18th Lords Berkeley all ran into serious difficulties with their wives. It is noticeable that trouble very often arose in cases of marriages deliberately designed to capture an heiress or to cement a political alliance, when the compulsion used may be supposed to have been particularly severe. One of the heiresses of the 3rd Lord Chandos and both the heiresses of Sir Michael Stanhope came to grief, and the marriages of the Cavendish family were as disastrous personally as they were successful financially.

In practice, if not in theory, the early sixteenth-century nobility was a polygamous society, and some contrived to live with a succession of women despite the official prohibition on divorce. Take, for example, the career of Ralph Rishton of Ponthalgh, Lancs. In 1530 at the age of 9 he was married to the 10-year-old Helen Towneley. He was sent to be trained in arms at the house of Sir Ralph Assheton of Middleton, but began to cohabit with Helen about three years later, on occasional visits to her father's house. In the 1540's he went off to the Scottish wars, during which time Helen went mad. On his return he seduced Elizabeth Parker, bribed an ecclesiastical official to annul the marriage with Helen, and married Elizabeth. He lived with his second wife for eight years until the legal decision was reversed and the annulment of the first marriage declared invalid. He then deserted Elizabeth and took up with the half-sister of his military commander, Anne Stanley. When she was three months pregnant her mother forced her into a marriage with John Rishton of Dunkenhalgh, but Anne refused cohabitation and got an annulment. At this point Helen at last died, Elizabeth's attempts to assert her conjugal rights were defeated, and Ralph finally married Anne Stanley. It is an illuminating but not a very edifying story of life among the upper squirearchy of mid-Tudor Lancashire.

Presumably in deference to puritan criticism of the double standard, this casual approach to extra-marital relationships disappeared between 1560 and 1660, and in consequence we have mostly to look elsewhere than in wills for information about the illegitimate children of Elizabethan and Early Stuart noblemen. Between 1560 and 1610 one marquis, eight earls, one viscount, and six barons are known to have fathered children by women other than their wives.

Between 1610 and 1660 evidence for the maintenance of regular, semi-official mistresses becomes rare, apart from notorious cases like the 1st Earl of Sunderland, the 5th Earl of Sussex, and the 5th Lord Dudley. There is no very obvious explanation of this fact, though the following hypothetical model at any rate provides a possible solution. In the Middle Ages and the early sixteenth century, the arranged marriage was often accompanied and made tolerable by the mistress and the illegitimate children. This was a situation accepted by the wife and openly admitted by the husband, and as a result marriages held together as working business arrangements. But impressed by Calvinist criticisms of the double standard, in the late sixteenth century public opinion began to object to the open maintenance of a mistress, which would explain the increasing number of breakdowns of marriages, and the reluctance to mention bastards in wills. The arranged marriage was unable to stand the strain of the shutting down of this safety-valve and the scale of separations became so alarming that parents began relaxing the pressure and giving their children some limited rights of veto over the choice of marriage partners. As a result the number of open breakdowns of marriage and the number of illegitimate children declined after the first decade of the seventeenth century (though there may well have been an increase in both after the Restoration).

At the same time as there was a tightening up of the sexual *mores* of the nobility and gentry as a whole in the early seventeenth century, a small minority was moving swiftly in exactly the opposite direction. One of the most striking features of Early Stuart society was the growing cleavage in outlook and behaviour between Court and Country. An aspect of this development which attracted much contemporary attention and criticism was the sexual license at the Jacobean Court, which may well have rivalled or excelled the more notorious conditions at the Court of Charles II. Although court behaviour under Henry VIII appears to have been fairly lax, in the middle and late sixteenth century peers had taken lower-class mistresses but had jealously guarded the honour of their wives. It was only after about 1590 that there developed general promiscuity among both sexes at Court. Accustomed to the exercise of power, with little training in self-control, and with all the time in the world on their hands, noblemen have probably always been substantially more free in their sexual behaviour than gentry, yeomen, or merchants. When the general atmosphere of the day is tolerant, however, no harm is done to the prestige of the class and it is only in times like the early seventeenth or the mid-nineteenth centuries that trouble is likely to arise. It was an unfortuante coincidence that the behaviour of a minority—but a spectacular and much publicized minority—of the aristocracy was declining after 1590 as fast as general disapprobation of loose conduct was rising. Before 1590 peers were more prone to crimes of violence than to scandalous living, if we exclude lower-class mistresses as a source of scandal, although there was a flicker of excitement in 1557 when Lord Latimer was arrested for trying to rape his landlady—"to grete a vellany for a noble man, my thought." Despite all Elizabeth's efforts, however, moral standards at Court deteriorated during her later years. The 2nd Earl of Essex was notoriously "grateful to ladies," and certainly seduced Elizabeth Southwell and perhaps the Countess of Derby, and the 3rd Earl of Southampton, the 3rd Earl of Pembroke, and Sir Walter Raleigh got Maids of Honour with child.

The real break-through into promiscuity at Court only occurred under James. The popular reaction was that of Simonds D'Ewes, who spoke of "the holy state of matrimony perifidiously broken and amongst many made but a May-game . . . and even great personages prostituting their bodies to the intent to satisfy and consume their substance in lascivious appetites of all sorts." As early as 1603 Lady Anne Clifford said that "all the ladies about the Court had gotten such ill names that it was grown a scandalous place." The Countess of Nottingham found it necessary to rebut the accusation of the King of Denmark that she was a whore, and the 1st Earl of Salisbury was accused of "unparalleled lust and hunting after strange flesh," notably that of Lady Walsingham and Catherine Countess of Suffolk. The 5th Earl of Sussex was notoriously pox-ridden, the 3rd Earl of Dorset was said to be "much given to women," and the 3rd Earl of Pembroke "immoderately given up" to them, while James Earl of Cambridge died "more subjecte to his pleasours and the companye of wemen then to priests." The Earls of Holland and Newport, Lord Goring, and both the royal favourites were notorious pursuers of women. "I know those," wrote Lord Thomas Howard in 1611, "who would not quietly reste, were Carr to leer upon their wives as some do perceive, yea, and like it well too they should be so noticed." Buckingham was actively encouraged by King James in his amatory exploits and Mrs. Dorothy Gawdy is said to have saved herself from his advances only by climbing out of a window.

More unusual, perhaps, was the dubious reputation enjoyed by so many wives of noblemen about the Court. The playwrights were only voicing a widely held belief when they pointed to the different sexual *mores* of Court and Country. "That is right court-fashion: men, women, and all woo; catch that catch may." "A close friend or private mistress is court rhetorick; a wife, mere rustick solecism." "Do your husbands lie with ye?" asked Marston. "That were country fashion, i' faith." The Country was convinced, with mingled fascination and distaste, that at night the Court was the regular scene of "most strange surquedries."

It is clear that between the early sixteenth and the late seventeenth century family patterns and marriage customs underwent profound changes. The most striking feature is the emergence of a sense of family responsibility for personal harmony and moral virtue. In the Middle Ages the marriage state had been second best to a life of chastity, and it was the ethical exaltation of marriage by Protestant divines that began the transformation. The household shrank in size as the number of superfluous servants was pruned away and as the keeping of open house to all comers gave way to the issue of invitations to personal friends. In conformity with this emphasis on privacy and intimacy, the family withdrew from the hall to the great chamber and the private dining-room; by the end of the seventeenth century corridors were being built to avoid the necessity of tramping through rooms to get from place to place, the promiscuous habit of putting up truckle beds here, there, and everywhere was giving way to the establishment of private bedrooms. The concept of an inward-turned, isolated, conjugal family, already familiar to the *bourgeoisie,* was well on the way to acceptance among the aristocracy.

The most remarkable change inside the family was the shift away from paternal authority, a shift made possible by the extension of the power of the central government. As the state and the law courts came to provide greater protection to wives and children, so the need for subordination to husband and father declined. The fact that these movements are inversely linked was not appreciated by contemporaries, who were content to extend their anti-despotic notions to all levels of social organization. Owing partly to the growth of puritan opposition to the double standard and of puritan emphasis on contented Christian partnership in marriage, partly to the development of ideas about economic and political liberty, it was slowly recognized that limits should be set not merely to the powers of King or Church, but also to those of parents and husbands. Supporters of kingship had constantly compared the authority of the monarch over his subjects with that of a father over his children. Any weakening in the position of the one thus led to a questioning of that of the other. As Mary Astell pointed out, "if absolute sovereignty be not necessary in a state, how comes it to be so in a family? Or if in a family, why not in a state?"

## 4. Marital Duties And Relations In The South

by Julia C. Spruill

The home was the only field in which superior southern women might distinguish themselves. It was by no means a narrow sphere, but one wherein individual initiative and executive ability as well as many other talents might be put to use. But the fact that the care of a family was the only career open to them and that it furnished an opportunity for the expression of broad and varied abilities scarcely justifies a general assumption that all colonial women lived up to or even realized the possibilities of their calling. Their domestic activities, like those of women today, varied in accordance with their personal inclinations and capacities as well as their social and economic position. Wives of large planters and slaveholders, ladies in town mansions, women in frontier cabins, and the poorer sort in town, country, and backwoods naturally had very different employments, and all women of the same class by no means had the same interest, training, and skill in household affairs.

More is known of the life of the mistress on a large plantation than of other classes. She usually had a variety of interesting employments, sufficient help to save her from drudgery, and opportunities to express many-sided abilities. Her chief duties had to do with providing food for her large family and the innumerable guests enjoying her ever-ready hospitality. She had not merely to see to the cooking and serving of food but also to arrange for her supplies, many of which came from her own garden, smokehouse, poultry yard, and dairy. Some idea of the enormous quantity of provisions used in great houses is indicated in Fithian's report of a conversation with the mistress of "Nomini." She informed him that her family consumed annually 27,000 pounds of pork and twenty beeves, 550 bushels of wheat, four hogsheads of rum and 150 gallons of brandy. One hundred pounds of flour were used weekly by the immediate household; white laborers and

Negroes ate corn meal.

A feature of social life increasing the responsibilities of the mistress was the custom of inviting into her home all persons needing shelter and refreshment, strangers as well as friends. Beverley wrote that a traveler in Virginia needed no better recommendation to the generosity of the people than that he was to inquire the way to the nearest gentleman's seat. The other southern colonies had the same reputation for hospitality. Eddis observed that the Maryland mansions were "as well known to the weary, indigent traveller as to the affluent guest." Brickell found the North Carolinians as hospitable as any people in the world and was of the opinion that they gave away more provisions to guests than were consumed by their own families. A visitor in South Carolina in 1751 wrote that the inhabitants kept Negroes at their gates near the public roads to invite travelers in for refreshments.

The mistress had not only to be Lady Bountiful to these strangers within her gates, but had also to be prepared for unexpected visits from friends and relatives. Though they sometimes dined out by special invitation, the colonists considered such formality unnecessary. Whole coach loads of young and old with retinues of servants felt no hesitation in descending without warning upon an unsuspecting matron, and she was supposed to lodge and feed them however great their number might be. It is true, however, that she was not expected to furnish a great deal in the way of comforts. A place at the table and a half or even a third share in a bed was all that any guest expected. A bed to oneself was a rare luxury and a private room unthought of.

In the preparation and serving of food, the colonial mistress had for her guidance not only the verbal instructions handed down from her mother and the manuscript directions exchanged with friends, but also a number of printed treatises. *The Compleat Housewife, The British Housewife, Mrs. Glasse's Art of Cookery,* and other "Bookes of cookery" were mentioned in wills and inventories and frequently advertised in newspapers. Some of these manuals have been preserved, and throw light upon the culinary art and the etiquette of serving at the time. The recipes show that dishes were rich, highly seasoned, and often complicated. Meats were usually boiled, roasted, stewed, fried, fricasseed, or made into a ragout or pie, and were invariably served with rich stuffings, sauces, and gravies. A mushroom sauce highly recommended for fowl was made as follows: "Pick a Pint of Mushrooms very clean, wash them, put them into a Saucepan, and put to them one Blade of Mace, a little Nutmeg, and a small Pinch of Bay Salt; add a Pint of Cream and a good Piece of Butter rolled in Flour; set them on a gentle Fire and let broil some little Time, keeping frequently stirring them; when they are enough lay the Fowl in the Dish, pour this Sauce in, and garnish with Lemon." A gravy for veal cutlets was made of white wine, butter, oysters, and sweet breads. The numerous recipes for cakes, puddings, creams, syllabubs, and tarts, required lavish use of butter, cream, eggs, and spices. "Common Pancakes" were made with eight "new-laid eggs," "a piece of butter as big as a walnut," a quart of milk, and a glass of brandy. "Rich Pancakes" required a dozen and a half eggs, half a pint each of sack and cream, and several spices; and a "Quaking Pudding" called for a quart of cream and twelve eggs.

The mistress presided over the table and carved and served. Carving was one of the accomplishments in which the English lady took great pride. She was instructed in this just as she was taught to dance and play upon the harpsichord. The variety of terms and the complicated directions for carving lead us to wonder if this were not the most difficult of the arts she had to master. We read of Lady Mary Wortley Montagu, who as a girl presided over her father's table, that she not only had to "persuade and provoke his guests to eat voraciously," but had also to carve every dish with her own hands, carefully choosing the right morsel for every man according to his rank. She was instructed by a carving master three times a week, and on days when there was to be company she ate her dinner beforehand.

Wealthy colonial ladies in the eighteenth century were supplied with the equipment necessary for serving meals in the best English manner. Rich mahogany tables, costly damask tablecloths and napkins, handsome silver plate and china adorned their tables. Yet, there were features unattractive to a twentieth-century diner. Food, prepared in an outdoor kitchen by a Negro cook and a retinue of slave helpers, was carried by slave waiters through all kinds of weather into the mansion house. Despite the use of covered dishes, it must often have been tepid and limp by the time it reached the diners.

The colonial mistress was troubled by no concern for a balanced diet. Abundance and variety were the criteria by which her efforts were judged, and the recurrent bilious complaints of her family were not laid at her door but accepted as afflictions from above. Yet, one of her duties was the practice of "Family Physic." She not only doctored and nursed her patients, but sometimes prepared her own medicines, rivaling the apothecaries in the concoction of salves, balms, ointments, potions, and cordials. Receipts for various nostrums were handed down from mother to daughter and exchanged among gentlewomen like recipes for favorite dishes and were usually given an important place in handbooks on domestic economy. The *British Housewife* gave considerable attention to treatment of "the panes of the gout," cholic, agues, and fevers, the "spleen," the "vapour," the "evil," "hysteric fits," and "hypochondriac complaints," which were among the chief ailments in vogue. "Aqua Mirabilis," one of the cordials doubtless often in demand, was alleged to "be excellent in the Cholick, and against the Sickness and Uneasiness that often follow a full Meal." The mere thought of some of its potions must have been sufficient to frighten the most greedy gourmand into temperance. One highly recommended "Stomachick" was made by boiling garlic in sack. Another was of snails, worms, hartshorn shavings, and wood sorrel stewed in brandy and seasoned with spices and herbs.

Unlike northern and frontier housewives, the southern mistress in the settled counties did not generally spin and weave the clothing of her family. The southern planters had a staple agricultural product, which, while it fluctuated in price, always had a direct market, and, living on navigable streams or harbors, they conveniently exchanged their tobacco for English manufactured goods. Many had even their plainer garments made in England. Others imported large quantities of materials at one time, which, as the need arose, were made up by tailors and seamstresses among their indentured servants. It is true that in many houses there were spinning wheels; Negresses were trained as spinners; and, when the price of tobacco sank below the cost of production or foreign wars obstructed trade, cloth was made for domestic use; but ordinarily clothing, blankets, quilts, and such articles were imported.

Well-to-do housewives were not only generally relieved of the necessity of making the clothing and household linen for their families, but they also had considerable assistance in the procuring of food supplies and the performance of other duties. Unmarried women relatives, who commonly made their homes with their married kin, were expected to aid the mistress. They frequently took over the direction of one or more branches of housewifery, like the diary or poultry yard, and sometimes assumed the entire responsibility of housekeeper. The extract from a letter of Charles Calvert in Maryland to his father in 1663 suggests the situation of many unmarried gentlewomen: "My Coz Wms sister arrived here & is now att my house, & has the care of my household affaires, as yett noe good Match does present, but I hope in a short time she may fine one to her own content & yr Lopps desire, and I shall further what I can towards it."

Drudgery was done by white indentured servants and Negro slaves, the most intelligent of whom were used as house servants. In the early part of the seventeenth century most of the domestics were white, probably because the newly imported Africans were unfit for housework, but toward the latter part of the century Negro domestics became common. At the time of the Revolution wealthy families had an extraordinarily large number of house servants. Chastellux wrote that the luxury of being served by slaves augmented the natural indolence of the Virginia women, who were always surrounded by a great number of Negroes for their own and their children's service.

The colonial planter also had a share in the responsibilities pertaining to domestic economy. A number of women, during the absence or at the death of their husbands, supervised all the plantation business as well as their household affairs. But generally the mistress had few cares beyond her immediate household, and the master took responsibility for many domestic matters unthought of by most husbands today. The colonial gentleman, whose office was in the precincts of his home, had opportunity to attend to the education of his children, the entertaining of guests, and the ordering of many household affairs. Though his wife probably informed him of the need of provisions and expressed her preferences in the matter of clothing and furnishings, he commonly kept all household accounts and did the buying, giving careful attention to the selection of furniture, draperies, rugs, china, and silverware, as well as to the details of the whole family's wearing apparel. Furthermore, because perhaps of the inadequacy of his wife's education as well as his own sense of domestic responsibility, he took care of the social as well as the business correspondence of the family, writing the notes of invitation, acceptance, and regret, and the usual letters to absent friends and relatives.

Many letters of Washington illustrate the surprising amount of attention which men, occupied with extensive public and private business, gave to the minutiae of household economy. He ordered the clothing of his wife and stepchildren from Europe, and it appears that he and not Mrs. Washington ordinarily bought most of the provisions and selected the furniture, carpets, wall paper, and other furnishings for "Mount Vernon." Even after he became president, when confronted with the various duties of setting a new government to work, he still found time to give minute directions for the remodeling of the Morris house, engaged for his Philadelphia residence, and to attend to the distribution of the rooms among his family, the selection of new furniture, the employment of additional servants, and other housekeeping arrangements that one might expect to have been left to his wife's supervision. His letters to Tobias Lear, his secretary, are filled with such details as the placing of furniture and ornaments, the color scheme of the curtains, the exchange of laundry equipment with Mrs. Morris, the choice of housekeeper and steward, the making of servants' uniforms and caps, which washerwomen to bring from "Mount Vernon," and whether the cook should or should not make the desserts and have a hand in planning the meals.

Not much is known of the life of the less well-to-do. The wives of smaller farmers in the settled sections, like the matrons on larger plantations, doubtless were concerned largely with procuring supplies and serving food to their families. But, while they often had indentured servants and slaves, they did not have efficient housekeepers, skilled gardeners, and other paid white helpers to relieve them of the supervision of the various branches of housewifery. They did, however, often have the help of one or more kinswomen living in the home and of their daughters, whose few weeks of school each year interfered little with their household tasks. With the aid of these women in her family and of her servants, the farmer's wife cared for her dairy, poultry yard, and garden, cured meats, pickled and preserved, cleaned house and prepared meals for the household.

Some of the more industrious of this class spun and wove materials, of which they made clothing for their children and servants and furnishings for their homes, and sometimes earned pin money selling their cloths. Brickell found that the North Carolina girls were "bred to the Needle and Spinning" as well as to the dairy and other domestic affairs, which, he declared, they managed with a great deal of prudence. Many of the women, he observed, made a great deal of cloth of their own flax, wool, and cotton, and some were so ingenious that they made up all the wearing apparel for husbands, sons, and daughters. Governor Fauquier wrote in 1766 that the Virginia women made the cotton of the country into a strong cloth, of which they made gowns for themselves and children and coverlets for beds, and that sometimes they offered some of their cloths for sale in Williamsburg.

The wives of tradesmen in the towns helped in their husbands' shops, which were usually in the home, and, with the aid of a few servants, cared for their children and housekeeping. Unlike the country housewives, they did not produce their food supplies but bought them in local stores or on the streets. Newspaper advertisements show that grocery shops carried many provisions. Fresh vegetables raised on nearby plantations or in local gardens were sold by slaves, who strode up and down the streets crying out their wares. Butter, eggs, chickens, vegetables, and sometimes jellies, pickles, and preserves were bought from farmers' wives. In the larger towns there were confectionery shops, where pastries, jellies, cakes, tarts, potted meats, and other delicacies were on sale or made to order. For housewives who could afford these services, there were Negro laundresses, cooks, nurses, and chambermaids to be hired by the day, month, or year; tradeswomen to clean and mend their laces, fine linen, and silk hose, quilt their petticoats, stiffen and glaze their chintzes; seamstresses, who would come into the home and sew by the day; and milliners and mantuamakers, who designed and made their best clothes.

It was the housewife of the back settlements who had to depend most upon her own labor and ingenuity. The frontiersman's remoteness from waterways and highways and his lack of a marketable staple crop prevented his trading much with the outside world and made it necessary for him and his wife to produce almost everything consumed in their household. With broadaxe and jackknife, he made his cabin, furniture, and many of the farming implements and kitchen utensils; and with spinning wheel, loom, and dye-pots, she made all the clothing of the family, the household linen, blankets, quilts, coverlets, curtains, rugs, and other furnishings. She made her own soap and candles, and, to a greater extent than the plantation mistress, had to be doctor and apothecary to her family. From the woods she gathered herbs and roots, from which she made various purges, emetics, syrups, cordials, and poultices. She needed also to understand the use of firearms that she might protect her home from wild beasts and Indians, and kill wild animals for food. William Byrd wrote in 1710 of a well-to-do frontier woman who had entertained him and the other dividing-line commissioners: "She is a very civil woman and shews nothing of ruggedness, or Immodesty in her carriage, yett she will carry a gunn in the woods and kill dear, turkeys, &c., shoot down wild cattle, catch and tye hoggs, knock down beeves with an ax and perform the most manfull Exercises as well as most men in those parts."

The food, clothing, and household comforts of frontier people varied greatly according to the wealth, energy, and skill of the master and mistress of the household. But generally houses were much smaller, furniture and clothing more scanty and crude, and food less varied than in the more populous regions. The backwoods housewife, who had no skilled gardener and no greenhouse where she could raise vegetables out of season and who found it impossible to get the imported delicacies available to the housewives near the coast, supplied her family with a diet which seemed plain and monotonous to refined visitors from older sections. Food in the back country consisted of pork, wild fowl, game, and Indian corn, supplemented in the more industrious families by beef, milk, butter, eggs, domestic fowl, and a few fruits and vegetables. The prevalence of pork was due to the case with which it was produced. In many sections, hogs roamed about through the woods, feeding on acorns and roots and requiring no attention. Corn, which was raised in little patches near the cabins, was beaten in a hand mortar into course hominy or into meal, which was sometimes boiled into a mush and sometimes baked on the hearth as a hoecake. Homemade beer, cider and brandy were the drinks. William Eddis, who visited the western settlements in Maryland shortly before the Revolution, wrote that Indian corn beaten in a mortar and baked or boiled was the principal subsistence of the poorer inhabitants. When salt beef or bacon was added, he declared, no complaints were made respecting their fare. Another visitor in the backwoods wrote: "The meaner Sort you find little else but Water amongst them, when their Cyder is spent, *Mush* and Milk, or Molasses, *Homine,* Wild Fowl, and Fish are their principal Diet."

The backwoods women had the reputation of being more given to labor than their husbands. Lawson found them the "most industrious sex" in North Carolina. Byrd, writing of the outlying settlements in Virginia and Carolina, declared that the men, like the Indians, imposed all the work upon the women and were themselves "Sloathfull in everything but getting Children." The women, he observed, "all Spin, weave, and knit, whereby they make good Shift to cloath the whole Family; and to their credit be it recorded, many of them do it very completely." Oldmixon wrote of the Carolina women: "The ordinary Women take care of Cows, Hogs, and other small cattle, make Butter and Cheese, spin Cotton and Flax, help to sow and reap Corn, wind Silk from the Worms, gather Fruit, and look after the House." Brickell also found the wives of the poorer farmers "ready to assist their husbands in any Servile Work, as planting when the Season of the Year requires expedition.''

The colonial housewife of tradition was a person of superhuman attainments, a composite of all the virtues and talents of women of every class and type. Actually, there were different kinds of housewives in colonial days as today, and women's occupations and achievements varied greatly according to their individual abilities and the circumstance of their lives. Superior women in frontier settlements were strong, daring, and self-reliant, as well as skillful and industrious. With practically no help from the outside world, they fed, clothed, and physicked their large families, made the household furnishings, and on occasion even defended their homes. But they were not supposed to possess drawing-room accomplishments or to maintain the refined standards of living expected of matrons in town mansions and on large plantations. If they had few servants and no markets where they could buy their household necessaries, at the same time they did little entertaining and were expected to supply their families with only the simplest kinds of foods and clothes. Their houses were small, and they had no costly china, furniture, and silver to keep. Housewives in settled communities, on the other hand, were not expected to possess the physical courage and strength necessary to protect their families from Indians and wild beasts or to suffer hardships common to pioneers; and when they had the care of large and luxurious establishments they had a great deal of assistance in the performance of their duties. The plantation mistress of the class to which Martha Washington and Eliza Pinckney belonged was often a person of easy and hospitable manners, industry, and housewifery skill. She directed a large household and entertained numerous guests. Without the aid of canned goods, refrigerator, or near-by markets, she loaded her table with a variety of foods prepared and served in the best taste of the time. She often doctored the sick of her household, sometimes making the medicines she administered, and occasionally, when trade with England was obstructed, she helped to direct the making of clothing for her household. But she did not do all this single-handed. The cooperation of her husband, the efforts of women relatives living in the home, the skill of experienced hired housekeepers and expert gardeners, and the labor of many servants and slaves went into the accomplishments with which she alone has generally been credited.

Keeping in mind the prosaic, businesslike manner in which marriages were often made in colonial days, and considering the immature age of many persons undertaking marital responsibilities, the haste with which a deceased mate was frequently replaced by another, and the numerous ventures often made by the same person, one wonders what was the sequel to this kind of marriage-making. Unfortunately the matrimonial histories of individual couples have not been preserved. But abundant materials at hand reflect the prevailing conception of proper conjugal conduct and throw light upon the general state of marriage.

The subject treated in most detail by seventeenth-century family books was the mutual duties of husbands and wives. Generally it was stated that the husband should guide, defend, and provide for the wife, while she was to serve him in subjection, be modest in speech and dress, and be a good housewife. "A wise husband," declared *A Godly Form of Household Government*, "and one that seeketh to live in quiet with his wife, must observe three rules. Often to admonish: Seldom to reprove: and never to smite her." The commonly accepted idea of the proper treatment of a husband was described by a "well-spoken" wife in *A Looking Glasse for Maried Folks:* "When he lookt at any time very sad, & there was not fit time to speak to him, I would not the laugh & daily with him, and play the tom-boy . . . but I put upon me a sad countenance, and lookt heavily . . . So it beseemes an honest wife to frame herselfe to her husbands affections . . . And if at any time he were stired, I would either pacify him, with a gentle speech, or give way to his wrath . . . This course also I tooke: if he came drunken home, I would not then for anything have him a foule word, but I would cause his bed to be made very soft and easie, that he might sleepe the better, and by faire speeches get him to it."

These views somewhat elaborated were embodied in ladies' books and treatises on marriage throughout the next century, though later writings usually gave more attention to the wife's duties and less to the husband's. She was supposed to exist for her husband, be an agreeable and obedient companion to him, a tender mother of his children, a capable and industrious manager of his house, and a gracious and attractive hostess to his guests. This feeling expressed by an exemplary matron in *The Spectator* was that of the true wife: "I am married, and I have no other concern but to please the man I love; he is the end of every care I have; if I dress, it is for him; if I read a poem, or a play, it is to qualify myself for a conversation agreeable to his taste; he is almost the end of my devotions; half my prayers are for his happiness."

The *Virginia Gazette* offered the "fair sex" these "Rules for the Advancement of Matrimonial Felicity": "Never dispute with him [your husband] whatever be the Occasion . . . And if any Altercations or Jars happen, don't separate the bed, whereby the Animosity will cease . . . by no Means disclose his imperfections, or let the most intimate Friend know your Grievances; otherways you expose yourself to be laugh'd at . . . Read often the Matrimonial Service, and overlook not the important word OBEY." One "Receipt for the Ladies to retain the Affections of their Husbands" emphasized good humor and discretion as most desirable wifely qualities, and another described the "Good Wife" as one "humble and modest from Reason and Conviction, submissive from Choice, and obedient from Inclination." A North Carolina paper urging upon wives the importance of neatness in dress and a sweet temper, concluded with this advice:

> . . . her Wit must never be display'd,
> Where it the husband's province might invade:
> Be she content sole *Mistress* to remain,
> Nor poorly strive for the *Mastership* t' obtain.
> This would occasion Jars, intestine Strife,
> Imbitter all the sweets of nuptial Life:
> Then let her not for Government contend,
> But use this policy to gain her end—
> Make him *believe* he holds the Sov'reign Sway,
> And she may *rule,* by seeming to *obey.*

To what extent colonial wives subscribed to these rules and attempted to put them into practice does not appear. Nor is it known whether husbands generally took advantage of their position as "lords of creation." The records show on the one hand a great deal of conjugal affection, loyalty, and happiness, and on the other discord and discontent. As evidence of mutual confidence and devotion, one might point to many wills in which the testator made careful provision for his "beloved wife," to affectionate letters, and to occasional glimpses of happy married life in private papers. Governor William Berkeley of Virginia left his "deare and most virtuous wife" all his estate with this declaration, "if God had blest me with a far greater estate, I would have given it all to my most Dearly beloved wife." Likewise John Smithson of Maryland, in a nuncupative will, declared of his wife, "All I have I leave her, and if I had more she should enjoy it." Some wills included a verbal tribute besides a generous bequest as did that of Benjamin Harrison, who gave his wife handsome legacies besides her thirds and added this explanation, "she hath at all times behaved in a most dutiful and affectionate manner to me and all-ways been assisting through my whole affairs." John Rutledge explained that because of his wife's "good understanding" and tenderness to his seven young children, he was leaving her his entire estate with the right to use or dispose of it according to her discretion. John Randolph made a large provision in different kinds of property, jewelry, and money for his "dear and most beloved wife," stating that it was for "her ffaithfulness affection and prudence."

Scattered through the records are many declarations of tender sympathy and expressions of anxiety at the suffering or grief at the decease of a beloved mate. In 1716 Mann Page of "Roswell" in Virginia wrote in his Bible: "On the 12th day of December (the most unfortunate day that ever befell me) about 7 of the clock in the morning, the better half of me, my dearest wife, was taken from me." At about the same time, grief-stricken William Byrd informed a relative of his "dear Lucy's" death, exclaiming: "Alas!

how proud was I of her and how severely I am punished for it." Louis Henry de Rosset of North Carolina declared of his "dear best friend" that her many virtues had so endeared her to him that he "fully enjoyed every conjugal felicity for thirty years." William Stephens of Georgia mourned for a wife with whom he had lived for nearly forty-four years, during the whole time, he declared, "a mutual tender affection" had remained between them. Henry Laurens was overwhelmed at the passing of his "bosom friend," whom he praised as "ever loving, cherishing and ready to obey—who never once,—no, not once during the course of twenty years' most intimate connection threw the stumbling block of opposition" in his way.

Mutual confidence, loyalty, and devotion were doubtless enjoyed by many other couples. But there were also unhappy marriages. Those who point to the colonial period as a golden age of family relations can hardly be acquainted with the eighteenth-century discussions lamenting the decadence of the domestic virtues, with the suspicion and distrust reflected in private papers, with the large number of public notices of absconding wives and voluntary separations, and with the many complaints by husbands and wives in court records.

"Reflections on unhappy marriages" was a favorite subject of journalists. Among the reasons usually given for the "degeneration of the Married state" were "female extravagance," excessive fondness for dress and display, and neglect of domestic duties. A correspondent, to the *Virginia Gazette*, declaring one of the greatest "unhappinesses" of the time was that matrimony was so much discountenanced, suggested as causes of the "interruption of domestic peace" the fact that ladies gave themselves up too generally to an idle and expensive life, and that men, for the sake of beauty or wealth, ran the "desparate hazard" of taking to their bosoms a "fury" or an "ideot." A note familiar to every generation was sounded by a contributor to the *Lady's Magazine*: "If women would recover that empire which they seem in a great measure to have lost . . . they must change their present fashionable method of living, and do what their grandmothers did before them, go often to church, and be well acquainted with their own houses."

Misunderstanding and dissension were reflected now and then in colonial wills, as in this provision made by Willie Jones, prominent North Carolina patriot: "Now, as it is possible and indeed probable that my wife will not be satisfied with the provisions which I have hereinbefore made for her, and consequently could refuse to be bound by this very will . . . I leave to my wife to do better for herself if she can."

A cause of much wretchedness of wives must have been the unfaithfulness of husbands, which, though not considered serious by courts or society in general, could hardly have been borne with the equanimity advised in ladies' morality books. These writings usually upheld a different morality for men and women and advised the wife to conceal from everyone her knowledge of her husband's infidelities. A husband might have a practical motive in verifying his suspicion, it was explained, namely, that he might cast off an unfaithful wife. But as a wife could not cast off an offending husband or get any redress, she should not desire to find proof of her suspicions. The inquisitive matron who attempted to pry into her mate's lefthanded connections was held far more contemptible than her philandering husband, so long as he kept his amours private.

Freedom in sex relations was not just a fashionable vice of the well-to-do, but was also found among other classes. Disagreement as to who was entitled to perform the marriage ceremony, the lack of churches in which banns could be published, and often the long distances to be traveled to reach a minister or justice, as well as the excessive freedom of frontier society and the presence of servile women, encouraged the formation of loose unions. Brickell wrote that the "generality" of the Carolinians lived "after a loose and lascivious Manner." An Anglican missionary declared that in North Carolina polygamy was very common, bastardy no disrepute, and concubinage general. A similar situation was described in a complaint before the South Carolina Assembly in 1767 by a group of inhabitants of the upper part of the province. Through the want of churches and ministers, they declared, many persons had been married by itinerant preachers of various denominations, and supposing these unions only temporary had separated and formed new ones whenever they desired, " . . . Swapping away their Wives and Children, as they would Horses or Cattle."

More evidence of lax morality is found in court records, which abound with grand jury presentments of both men and women for adultery and with bastardy cases. These offenders were usually not persons of high social standing, but those without sufficient pride or wealth to make private compensation for their lapses. The justices, who were concerned more with saving the community from charges of dependent mothers and children than with the suppression of immorality, apparently did not trouble themselves with apprehending and punishing the person who voluntarily undertook the responsibility of providing for his reputed child or its mother.

# 5. Bridal Pregnancy In Rural England

by P. E. H. Hair

This paper describes a method of investigating the incidence of pregnancy among brides in rural England in earlier centuries, and reports the result of a sample investigation. The marriage and baptism registers of a single rural parish are examined: the date of marriage of each bride is compared with the date of birth, or, if that is not available, the date of baptism of the first child registered as being born to her after marriage, and the interval is calculated. "Eight and a half months interval between marriage and maternity may be taken as the dividing line for statistical purposes between the maternities resulting from pre-marital conceptions and those resulting from marital conceptions." So wrote the Registar General in his 1938 report, the first to discuss bridal pregnancy. We shall accept this dividing line.

A sample of 3,786 marriages has been investigated. All printed registers of English rural (or semi-rural) parishes were inspected, and a large proportion of those which contained entries in the marriage and baptism registers in sufficient detail were used in the formation of the sample, the entries being drawn from 77 parishes in 24 counties. The marriages investigated took place at dates ranging from the late sixteenth century to the early nineteenth century. But few individual registers are available or suitable for more than a small part of this range, and it is seldom possible to trace the experience of a single parish throughout the centuries. However, the available and suitable sections of the registers together contain more entries than we were able to handle: samples were therefore taken from these sections, a sample consisting of all the entries in a period of time, usually extending from four to ten years. On the average, each parish in the national sample contributed the marriage entries of eight years: thus the sample represents about 3% of all the marriages in these parishes between 1550 and 1820.

Birth dates are more reliable indicators of bridal pregnancy than baptism dates, since baptism can be delayed to "legitimize" a birth in the record. Unfortunately registers giving birth dates are largely confined to Northern England in the later centuries, and any national investigation covering all the centuries of parochial registration must also make use of registers which provide only baptism dates. We discuss the effect of this below. Apart from the categories of birth dates and baptism dates, the national sample has been divided in the tables into two chronological and three regional divisions, i.e., marriages before or after 1700, marriages in Northern, Central, and Southern England.

Of the 3,786 brides investigated, only 1,855 or 49% could be traced from the entry in the marriage register to an entry in the baptism register of the same parish. The proportion of traced brides varied from parish to parish in the same period, and from sample period to sample period in the same parish, but almost never fell below 30% or rose above 70%. No very marked chronological or regional pattern is apparent, and it would seem that the variation arose almost wholly from local parochial factors. The most likely general explanation for the failure to trace roughly half the brides is that, on marriage or before the birth of their first child, many brides moved away from the parish of marriage, for reasons unrelated to their condition at marriage. An investigation of a sample of 900 untraced brides has shown that they were much less likely to appear subsequently in the burial register of the parish of marriage than were traced brides, and this tends to confirm the out-movement of untraced brides. We believe that a majority of the missing brides were untraced for this reason only (and when it becomes practicable to carry out such an investigation, they will be traced in the registers of other, mainly neighbouring, parishes); but certainly a proportion of the untraced were lost sight of for other reasons, a few of which are directly relevant to the interpretation of the results of our count in the registers and which therefore must be discussed at some length later.

Of the 1,855 brides who were traced to a maternity, roughly one-third had their maternity recorded in the parish register within eight and a half months of their marriage (and roughly one-fifth within six months of marriage), and must thus have been pregnant at marriage. The remaining two-thirds had a maternity recorded after eight and a half months, but a proportion of them were also pregnant at marriage, for the following reasons. The first pregnancy of many brides (perhaps well over 10% in past centuries) terminates in a spontaneous abortion or still-birth: the first recorded maternity is therefore not always the first pregnancy. A second and probably more important reason is that the parish registers recorded baptisms only in many cases. We must inquire how long after birth baptism took place, to discover how many pre-maritally conceived maternities were "legitimized" in the register, accidentally or deliberately, by the interval between birth and baptism.

An investigation of 1,111 baptisms, in 14 parishes in 7 counties, all between 1700 and 1850, in registers which happen to record birth dates as well as baptism dates, gave the following result: in four parishes less than 10% of the children, but in five parishes more than 50%, were still unbaptized six weeks after birth. No regional or chronological pattern emerges from this considerable variation, and since there is reason to believe that in the end almost all children were baptized, it looks as if the main factor was the relative activity of individual clergy. However, it is clear that in most parishes at all dates a large proportion of children were not baptized till several weeks after birth, and a varying proportion not till several months after birth. Obviously a count using baptism dates will underestimate bridal pregnancy, and for this reason we have preferred registers showing birth dates when available; unfortunately, as has already been explained, these are not generally available for earlier centuries. Later, the figures from the national sample show the proportion of traced maternities by eight and a half months to be some 6-8% higher for registers giving birth dates than for those giving baptism dates. Whether the difference was as large in the earlier centuries cannot be inferred from the figures available (because the pre-1700 birth date sample was a very small one): a judgment must rely on a consideration of general issues, such as the relative rigour of the clergy in this period and the contemporary social attitudes of the laity, and this must be left to specialists in the period. However, if we allow that an adjustment from baptism dates to birth dates of 5% in the earlier centuries is sufficient, and take this together with the rate for birth dates only for the later centuries, then the proportion of traced maternities by eight and a half months in the whole sample is raised from roughly one-third to roughly two-fifths.

If we now make allowance for the proportion of brides whose pre-maritally conceived pregnancy terminated in an abortion or stillbirth and hence was not recorded in the register—and the proportion was most probably not less than 4%—the figure for pregnancy among trace brides begins to approach half of the sample.

As Table I shows, the national sample reflects population growth in that the sample for later centuries is much larger than that for earlier ones. This means, however, that the general proportion given conceals an important variation: the rate for earlier centuries is significantly lower than that for later centuries, being only about one-half. Unless it can be shown that baptism was much more frequently delayed in earlier centuries, which is unlikely (we pass over the negative evidence of the rate from birth dates, since the sample is too small to be completely trustworthy), it would seem that bridal pregnancy increased after 1700, perhaps fairly considerably.

In one aspect the last conclusion is ahead of our argument. Strictly, we have not so far been discussing rates of pregnancy among all brides, but only rates among brides traced to maternities in the parish of marriage, i.e., 49% of the original sample. To discover the overall rates, we must investigate the experience of the missing brides. Since this is not shown in the

TABLE I. *Traced maternities by interval since marriage*

| | Percentage of traced maternities registered by | | | | | | |
|---|---|---|---|---|---|---|---|
| | 3 mths. | 6 mths. | 8 mths. | 8½ mths. | 9 mths. | 12 mths. | 24 mths. |
| 685 traced to *births* | 12 | 26 | 36 | 39 | 41 | 62 | 85 |
| 1,170 traced to *baptisms* | 7 | 18 | 26 | 28 | 31 | 58 | 82 |
| *pre-1700:* 85 births | 9 | 15 | 20 | 22 | 27 | 48 | 76 |
| 358 baptisms | 4 | 10 | 16 | 17 | 20 | 49 | 78 |
| *post-1700:* 600 births | 12 | 28 | 38 | 41 | 43 | 64 | 86 |
| 812 baptisms | 8 | 21 | 31 | 33 | 36 | 62 | 84 |
| *pre-1700: South:* 84 baptisms | 2 | 8 | 13 | 13 | 15 | 46 | 77 |
| *pre-1700: Central:* 158 baptisms | 3 | 6 | 10 | 13 | 16 | 46 | 76 |
| *pre-1700: North:* 116 baptisms | 6 | 18 | 26 | 27 | 30 | 57 | 81 |
| *post-1700: South:* 176 births | 16 | 31 | 39 | 43 | 47 | 70 | 90 |
| 141 baptisms | 9 | 25 | 35 | 35 | 38 | 62 | 83 |
| *post-1700: Central:* 135 births | 8 | 24 | 36 | 36 | 37 | 58 | 80 |
| | 6 | 18 | 27 | 29 | 32 | 59 | 81 |
| *post-1700: North:* 289 births | 11 | 27 | 38 | 42 | 44 | 64 | 88 |
| 372 baptisms | 10 | 22 | 33 | 36 | 38 | 63 | 86 |

registers (that is the register of the parish of marriage of each; and the investigation of the whole national contemporary set of registers is impracticable as yet), we are limited to speculation and the weighing of possibilities. However, some of the possibilities approach moral certainty. For instance, among the missing brides were those who avoided the baptismal register by remaining childless. Since re-marriage by aging widows and widowers is known to have been fairly common in past centuries, and since among potent younger couples the proportion of infertile marriages was probably between 6% and 8% (as today), it is not inconceivable that as many as one-third of the missing brides were missing because they were not pregnant. The remaining missing brides were not childless, though their maternity was not recorded in the parish of marriage. Among minor reasons for this (and we believe that even their total effect was slight) was the failure of some parents to have their child baptized and registered because they were Nonconformists: close inquiry suggests that the effect of this has often been exaggerated and that most Nonconformist maternities were registered (even when the child was not actually baptized). The major reason for the missing brides is, we are reasonably confident, a simple and direct one, the movement of brides away from the parish of marriage.

It was (and is) customary for marriage to be celebrated in the bride's parish. We have investigated 1,048 marriage entries in registers which record the parish in which each partner was living before marriage, and find that 23% of the grooms were from another parish (as compared with only 8% of the brides). It is reasonable to suppose that a large proportion of the "foreign" husbands carried off their bride to a home in their own parish in which their first child was eventually born. In fact, 66% of the brides who married foreigners cannot be traced, against 46% of the brides who married men of the parish. Thus, in this sample, about 15% of the brides had married foreign husbands and were untraced, and it is likely that most of these had removed from the parish of marriage at marriage.

To those brides who moved away at marriage must be added the possibly greater number who moved after marriage but before their first maternity. Territorial mobility in the English countryside has never been thoroughly investigated, but there is evidence that, at least in districts where workers were engaged on an annual contract, regular migration of households was common. Movement away from the parish of marriage would therefore seem to offer a perfectly reasonable explanation of almost all the untraced, but not childless, brides.

What then was the experience of the untraced brides as regards bridal pregnancy? Putting on one side those brides, perhaps a third of those untraced, who remained childless, we believe that the experience of the remainder is likely to have been the same as the experience of the traced brides. That is, between one-third and one-half, and probably nearer half, were pregnant at marriage. Hence this same proportion of all brides—other than brides in childless marriages—were, we suggest, pregnant at marriage. Including the childless brides, rather over a third of all brides were pregnant. The proportion in earlier centuries may not have been more than a fifth: later it was probably around two-fifths.

These last estimates derive from our conclusion that the experience of about two-thirds of the untraced brides was no different from that of the traced brides, and this conclusion was drawn from general considerations and not from direct evidence in the registers. In will be wise, therefore, to note the limit of alternative estimates if this conclusion were not accepted. The count in the register gives conclusive proof that roughly one-sixth of all brides in the national sample were pregnant—roughly one-tenth in the earlier centuries, one-fifth in the later. The brides can be named and listed, and these figures represent the lowest possible estimate of bridal pregnancy based on our sample. However, to accept this estimate without allowing for upward modification is to ignore the effect of the delay between birth and baptism, an effect which can be demonstrated from the registers giving both birth and baptism dates; and also to hold that while one-third of the traced brides were certainly pregnant, none of the missing brides were, which is surely inconceivable. The lowest reasonable estimate is therefore that more than one-sixth (but how many more cannot be directly calculated from the registers) of all brides in the national sample were pregnant at marriage.

But if it be argued that the experience of the missing brides were essentially different from that of the traced brides, it is logically possible that it was different in that more, and not fewer, of the untraced were pregnant. It might be reasonably argued that the failure of some of the brides to record maternities in the register of the parish of marriage was due to their obviously pregnant condition at or soon after marriage, so that shame drove them to another parish where their recent date of marriage was unknown. The speculative part of this argument is the assumption that bridal pregnancy was shameful. In view of the high proportion of brides who were pregnant, including many who were obviously so at marriage, it is difficult to believe that this assumed shame was widespread, or indeed markedly existent. Had shame been a major factor in movement away from the parish of marriage, then a very large proportion of the untraced (but not childless) brides might have been pregnant at marriage; and hence, the proportion of all brides pregnant at marriage might have been even higher than the highest estimate already suggested, with an extreme limit of just over one-half (i.e., all brides other than childless and trace non-pregnant). But we are not convinced that a significant number of brides moved for this reason.

We are now in a position to present our conclusions. The make-up of the national sample was described earlier. We believe that the sample is sufficiently representative of the whole population of brides at risk throughout the period, to enable us to apply our conclusions about the sample experience to the national experience. We conclude that it can be deduced from our investigation in the parish registers of a sample of marriages and baptisms, that certainly more than one-sixth of all brides in English rural and semi-rural parishes between the late sixteenth and the early nineteenth century were pregnant at marriage: that it is conceivable but not likely that more than one-half were pregnant: and that is very likely, though it cannot be proved from direct statistical evidence, that in fact about one-third were pregnant. Putting aside those brides subsequently childless, it is very likely that of the brides capable of being impregnated before marriage between one-third and one-half had been.

But the proportion of brides pregnant in earlier centuries appears to have been only about half of that in the later centuries. This means that it is very likely that in the earlier centuries about one-fifth were pregnant, and in the later centuries about two-fifths.

Regional variations appear to have been limited. In the later centuries, the experience of the South and that of the North were almost exactly the same, while the experience of the Central region was not greatly different, the rates at eight and a half months being 43%, 42% and 36%. If the sample (by birth dates) for each region were again divided into two sub-regions (South-East, South-West; East Anglia, Midlands; Yorkshire-Lancashire, Northern four counties), the lowest rate at eight and a half months was 32% for the Midlands, and the highest 57% for the Northern four counties, with the remaining rates between 35% and 45%. In the earlier centuries, there was more variation between regions: South and Central were very similar, but at eight and a half months the North rate was double that of the others. The sample is too small to examine sub-regions, but it is worth noting that most of the parishes in the North sample were in the Northern four counties. It thus appears as if, in both periods, the Northern four counties had the highest sub-regional rate in England. Elsewhere rates varied chronologically more than they did regionally, and chronologically other parts moved towards the experience of the Northern four counties.

In 1938, the first year for which the Registrar General published statistics of the modern experience, 18% of brides aged between 15 and 45 in England and Wales were pregnant at marriage. In the 1960s the figure has risen to over 20%. A group of almost one thousand English women married between 1900 and 1924 included 22% who had been, on their own testimony, pregnant brides. But in the agricultural parish of Gosforth, Cumberland, 40% of all brides between 1920 and 1951 were pregnant. We have come across no statistics of later Nineteenth-century experience but it is a reasonable hypothesis that the national bridal pregnancy rate has fallen steeply in the last 80 years or so, thanks to the introduction of efficient contraceptive methods practiced in all but the most backward districts.

The social interpretation of the figures we have presented is outside the scope of this paper, although many questions are suggested. Were the pregnant brides the result of a system of peasant or trial courtship? Or of a system of betrothal licence? What amount of pre-marital sexual experience on the part of the brides do they in fact indicate? What conclusions can be drawn about communal and ecclesiastical discipline? We round off this paper, however, with one further thought-provoking estimate. The parish registers of Scotland are in general in a form not suitable for this method of investigation, but we have discovered a handful of registers to which the method could be applied; and in these Scottish rural parishes the bridal pregnancy rate was roughly one-third of that in contemporary rural England.

## 6. Premarital Pregnancy In America 1640-1971
by Daniel Scott Smith and Michael S. Hindus

Sexual expression is a basic human drive and its control, a ubiquitous feature of all societies. Although all cultures prescribe sexual intercourse within marriage, in Western and especially American society sex has been proscribed without. Since behavior obviously does not always conform to norms, essential to uncovering the history of sex is some objective measure of the extent of non-marital intercourse. As Schumpeter once put it, "we need statistics not only for explaining things but also in order to know precisely what there is to explain." Since children are a measurable, if not inevitable, result of intercourse, premarital pregnancy—operationally defined as the conception, before marriage, of the first post-maritally born child—provides an index of change in sexual behavior. This measure has the advantages of coverage (since nearly all adults marry), reliability (since the births are legitimate and more likely to be recorded than illegitimate births), objectivity (since its measurement depends on the matching of records collected for other purposes), and sensitivity to change in the underlying phenomenon (since premarital pregnancy is a relatively minor violation of the prevailing ban on non-marital intercourse).

What has to be explained in the white American premarital pregnancy record is the cyclical pattern of troughs in the seventeenth century (under 10 percent of first births) and mid-nineteenth century (about 10 percent) and peaks in the second half of the eighteenth century (about 30 percent) and in contemporary America (between 20 and 25 percent). This cycle cannot be explained away by changes in the variables intermediate between premarital coitus and post-marital birth—fecundability and pregnancy wastage, contraceptive usage, induced abortion, and illegitimacy. Although these variables influence the level, we are concerned with the direction of the trend. It is unlikely that the underlying biological bases of American reproduction has varied enough to account for the magnitude and timing of the fluctuations in the premarital pregnancy ratio. Although contraceptive use obviously lowers fertility, since World War II both illegitimacy and premarital pregnancy have increased. Historically the trend in premarital pregnancy has paralleled that in illegitimacy. Although the proportion of bridal pregnancies in all non-maritally conceived births is not constant over time and space, it appears to be a rule that when the overall level of non-marital conception increases, the proportion of non-marital pregnancies born outside of wedlock also rises. To explain the major swings in premarital pregnancy, primary emphasis must rest on an analysis of the variation in the proportion of women who have engaged in premarital coitus. A similar long cycle also exists in West European illegitimacy and premarital pregnancy data. Superficially at least the cyclical variation in premarital pregnancy is a striking regularity of early modern and modern social history.

The basic strategy of this analysis is to distinguish between the periods with high ratios by comparing differentials in premarital pregnancy between groups, and then to assess eras with lower ratios by focusing on differences in the social control of sexuality. The social relationships underlying similar premarital pregnancy levels are strikingly dissimilar. The analysis of the transitions thus concentrates on the changing relationships between sexual behavior and the social mechanisms controlling it. Throughout we will be concerned with individual behavior, the role of the family as the principal regulator of sexual expression, and the larger societal context.

PERIODS WITH HIGH RATIOS   The families of orientation (family of birth) played a much more direct role in the high premarital pregnancy level of the late eighteenth century than it does in the modern peak. This contrast is apparent in the incidence of premarital pregnancy by age; the incidence by class; the relative incidence among interclass unions; and the transmission and support of the tendency toward premarital pregnancy.

*Age*   In contrast to the relatively constant age-specific pattern among pre-industrial women, modern premarital pregnancy is increasingly concentrated among teen-agers (Table I). Although the low teen-age rates for seventeenth-century Hingham, Massachusetts and pre-industrial West European samples may be attributed to adolescent subfecundity, the relative stability after age 20 can be best explained by the absence of a clear demarcation between youth and maturity in preindustrial society. Couples in their late 20s entered into marriage in the same social context as those marrying at an earlier age. In contemporary populations, by contrast, teen-agers do not employ contraceptives as often and as effectively as women in their 20s. Aging in modern society from 15 to 25 involves qualitative changes in the context of behavior which did not occur two centuries earlier.

*Economic strata*  Although family income had little impact on the incidence of premarital coitus of white 15-19 year-old unmarried females surveyed in 1971, parental economic status was inversely related to the frequency of premarital pregnancy in the eighteenth-century case. Based on a Detroit sample of 1960, parental status also has relatively little effect on the frequency of premarital pregnancy. Higher economic status no longer provides parents with leverage over the sexual behavior of their children.

*Heterogamy*  In the Detroit sample, premarital pregnancy ratios were markedly higher when the wife's father was of higher status than the husband's father; pregnancies in which the male's family had higher status presumably ended in illegitimate births. Interclass marriages in Hingham show the same lower pattern of premarital pregnancy exhibited by marriages within the wealthier 40 percent of the population. Since behavior followed the pattern of the higher status partner, parental control is more evident. The absence of a differential in interclass marriages suggests that community coercion overcame the more serious consequences of pregnancy for women. Further suggestive detail on the roles of parental and community authority is available for the reconstituted Hingham families established between 1761 and 1780. Men who married daughters of wealthier parents were penalized most by premarital pregnancy, implying that there was no necessity for the girl's father to contribute economically to a marriage that had been made inevitable by pregnancy. For the children of poorer parents, premarital pregnancy seemed to have involved no economic setback. Lacking economic resources, less wealthy fathers could not restrain the sexual activity of their unmarried children.

*Sexually Restrictive and Permissive Groups*  Continuity is apparent in the institutional basis of the sexually more restrictive subculture. In both eras, religious involvement is associated with lower levels of premarital sexual activty. On the Hingham first parish tax list of 1767, only 18.4 percent of the cases where the property holder or his spouse were church members volved premarital conceptions; in 30.3 percent of the cases where neither spouse was identified as a church member, there was a premarital pregnancy. This relationship holds, however, only for the wealthier stratum. In the 1971 survey of teen-age sexual experience, females who attended church on less than three occasions in the previous month were, depending on denomination, two to three times more likely to be non-virgins than those who attended four or more times. Active religious participation is also closely related to restrictive sexual attitudes.

The association of religiosity and premarital sexual restrictiveness does not automatically imply a casual relationship. In more than 80 percent of the Hingham cases from the 1767 list, church membership followed marriage, often by five or more years. Arguing from chronology, premarital pregnancy deterred religious affiliation among the wealthier rather than vice versa. Although the children of Hingham church members were less likely to be pregnant at marriage, this minor effect disappears when one controls for wealth. Since beginning sexual intercourse and abandoning church attendance are part of a general change in life style of maturing teen-agers, the association of religiosity and premarital sexual restrictiveness in cross-sectional surveys may be largely spurious. Religion can be said to have an impact on the overall incidence of premarital sex only when it is an encompassing and controlling force in the lives of the young and not merely an option.

The more impressive relationship is the consistent difference between the daughters whose mothers were pregnant at marriage and those whose mothers were not. Inasmuch as there existed a sexually permissive sub-culture in eighteenth-century Hingham, its continuity depended on the female line and on the less wealthy section of the population. The former relationship did not pass unnoticed by contemporaries, as is evidenced by the subtitle and following lines of an anonymous poem published around 1785:

> Some maidens say, if through the nation,
> Bundling should quite go out of fashion,
> Courtship would lose its sweets; and they
> Could have no fun til wedding day.
> It shant be so, they rage and storm,
> And country girls in clusters swarm,
> And fly and buz like angry bees,
> And vow they'll bundle when they please.
> Some mothers too, will plead their cause,
> And give their daughters great applause,
> And tell them 'tis no sin nor shame,
> For we, your mothers did the same.

In summary, intergenerational family relationships are deeply involved in the great boom of premarital pregnancy in the eighteenth century.

Premarital sexual activity in modern society is structured through the peer group and more broadly through a youth subculture, which is rein-forced by age-stratified institutions such as schools and promoted by other forces such as marketing and the mass media. Although objective family background characteristics such as income, education, or religious preference have little impact on the incidence of teen-age intercourse, higher familiar status, especially parental education, is associated with the more frequent use of contraception by sexually active teen-agers. Modern parents generally lack the power to be oppressive in an effective way. This absence of parental control and influence is strikingly demonstrated by the low correspondence between the political opinions of parents and children. If teenagers are not controlled by their parents, neither are they autonomous. The adolescent way station between dependent childhood and independent adulthood is characterized by an alienation but not a separation from parental values and culture. Survey research suggests that premarital coitus is directly related to the extent of this estrangement. Although the modern family fails to restrict successfully the sexual activity of children, it and the other institutions involving youth limit the possibilities of a rational separation of sex and procreation.

PERIODS WITH LOW RATIOS   Just as the peaks in premarital pregnancy when examined in detail reflect quite different underlying patterns, so the troughs of the seventeenth and nineteenth centuries result from different systems of control. Although a sexually repressive ideology characterized both centuries, the emphasis in the Puritan seventeenth century was on external controls, while internal control or self-repression was the central feature of Victorian morality. Premartial sexual restraint was possible both in the seventeenth-century community and in nineteenth-century society, but not during the transition. Maintenance of morality, however, shifted from direct to indirect, from being based primarily on social control to resting principally on socialization.

The importance of external controls in the seventeenth century may be readily demonstrated. Premarital pregnancy ratios were low not just in North America but in England and France as well. English premarital pregnancy, for example, was 26 percent below the sixteenth-century figure, and illegitimacy ratios between 1651 and 1720 were less than half of those prevailing between 1581 and 1630 and from 1741 to 1820. English North America shared the organized religious intensity that pervaded Western Europe during the seventeenth century. With a premarital pregnancy level less than half that of England, mid-seventeenth-century New England, as Governor Bradford of Plymouth was "verily persuaded," was a society "with not more evils in this kind [sexual deviation], nor nothing near so many by proportion as in other places; but they are here more discovered and seen and made public by due search, inquisition and due punishment; for the churches look narrowly to their members, and the magistrates over all, more strictly than in other places." Instead of the Puritans becoming "inured to sexual offenses, because there were so many," as Morgan puts it, they prosecuted their comparatively few sexual offenders vigorously. Morgan was right in his now classic reading of the court records, however, when he emphasized the calm, matter-of-fact approach of the Puritans toward even the most extreme manifestations of sexual deviance. Although this composure had its roots in the theological belief in original sin, the elaborate structure of social repression maintained by the Puritans suggests that they did not expect the population at large to have internalized sexual control. Broadly speaking, Puritanism may be characterized as a communal response to the strains accompanying the disintegration of the bases of medieval society.

Nineteenth-century morality was forged in a new social matrix and constructed with different materials. The reappearance of premarital sexual restraint in the nineteenth century was based on the autonomy of the young adult and the incorporation of the groups tending toward premarital pregnancy into a new social order. By the early nineteenth century, people were generally independent in life at a younger age than ever before. Although there were objective changes, such as the economic shift from the apprentice to the wage system and the substitution of boarding for service as the transitional living arrangement for young people, most significiant was the social acceptance of youthful autonomy.

The new independence of nineteenth-century youth was recognized in various ways. The practical impact of the introduction of universal male suffrage was not so much the enfranchisement of a permanent proletariat as the granting of political rights to young adults. Proponents of manhood suffrage presented their arguments in terms of the reality of allowing young men the political autonomy commensurate with their social and economic status. During and after the Second Great Awakening, religious conversion became a common experience for teen-agers. Not unrelated to early religious involvement is the fact that youths began to play important roles in reform movements.

The early nineteenth century also witnessed the social incorporation of the groups previously prone to premarital pregnancy. The erosion of the social base of the sexually permissive segment of the population was partly the result of a dramatic expansion of religious participation. Estimated formal church membership in America tripled from 7 to 23 percent between 1800 and 1860. With younger conversion, religion could have a more effective impact on premarital sexual choices. The concomitant splintering of American Protestantism meant that each stratum had one or more denominations tailored to its particular condition and needs. Although denominations differed in social base and religious style, the regulation of individual morality was a central concern of nineteenth-century Protestantism. Although seventeenth-century Puritanism stressed external controls, antebellum religious enthusiasm rejected Calvinist determinism in favor of free will doctrines. The basic social support of nineteenth-century sexual restraint—religion—rested on the centrality of autonomy and individual choice. Finally, nineteenth-century Protestantism incorporated women, the apparent source of the intergenerational transmission of premarital pregnancy in the eighteenth century, into the social order. If women did not entirely dominate religion symbolically and organizationally in the nineteenth century, the churches did provide an important outlet for a wide range of female needs. A more active part of the churches, nineteenth-century women absorbed the message of sexual restraint more completely.

Since the supporting social restraints involved voluntary action, the new anti-sexual ideology of the nineteenth century was necessarily more total than the Puritan hostility to non-marital sexual expression. Intellectually intertwined with the entire system of liberal bourgeois ideology, Victorian morality was more than a functional system for the control of premarital sexual behavior. The exaggerated aversion to masturbation, for example, is inexplicable if the system were merely designed to prevent premarital pregnancy. Victorian morality was relevant to the immediate needs and social position of both young men and women. Tocqueville emphasized the free marriage market at the structural determinant of the high degree of sexual restraint among young American women. "No girl," observed the aristocratic visitor, "then believes that she cannot become the wife of the man who loves her, and this renders all breaches of morality before marriage very uncommon." Since women were on their own in the marriage market but lacked economic resources therafter, Victorian morality raised the price of sex and thus substantially increased the bargaining power of both single and married women.

Because sexual restraint was compatible with the norms of thrift and abstinence required of the upwardly striving young capitalist, the morality advantageous to women also appealed to the rationality, if not the passion, of males. The early age of independence from the family of orientation prepared young middle-class men not for early marriage but for a period of capital accumulation and entry into a career, the two prerequisites to marriage. Having internalized the mechanism of deferred gratification in terms of his economic life, the nineteenth-century American male would not risk the consequences of a marriage precipitated by a premarital pregnancy. Although not every man was making it in nineteenth-century America, more and more were caught up in the competition. Most importantly, the obstacles to advancement in society were seen as within the capacity of the individual to overcome.

THE TRANSITIONS AND THEIR IMPLICATIONS   Have basic American institutions changed gradually and easily? Have the external forms of control been painlessly modified to conform to new or more freely expressed desires of individuals? Or did "crises" arise in the older social arrangements before new patterns of behavior appeared? With more than three centuries of data on the key aspect of human behavior which is under examination here, some insights are possible concerning this fundamental problem in American history. Since two thirds of white women were not pregnant at marriage throughout the course of American history, continuity in the efficacy of control is obviously apparent. Yet, since premarital pregnancy is at least a mild form of deviancy, the magnitude of the cyclical fluctuation is impressive. Our contention is that rising premarital pregnancy is a manifestation of a collision between an unchanging and increasingly antiquated family structure and a pattern of individual behavior which is more a part of the past than a harbinger of the future. The downturn in premarital pregnancy follows as a necessary but not sufficient consequence of a transformation in the family's role as a regulator of the sexual behavior of the young. Neither the old institutional pattern of control nor the rebellion against it can predict the subsequent sexual behavior of the young. The sexual revolutionaries of the eighteenth century, if the premarital procreators may be so labeled, were obviously not the vanguard of a sexually liberated nineteenth century.

The increase in premarital pregnancy in late seventeenth-century New England provides empirical evidence for the notion of the declension of Puritanism from a "golden age." At first the authorities attempted to maintain their vigilance in the face of increased sexual deviance. As late as the 1670s, at least by a rough estimate of the number of premarital pregnancies in Essex County, well over half of the guilty couples were being convicted. Before any marked socioeconomic change occurred in New England, cracks surfaced in the sexually repressive order. During the last third of the century punishment declined from corporal to monetary, and individuals were given the choice between fines or whippings. Although illegitimacy prosecutions continued after 1700, civil punishment for premarital pregnancy gradually disappeared. Although the churches then picked up the burden of repression by requiring confessions for baptism and admission, individuals, typically, were ready to join only after their premarital experience had passed. As premarital pregnancy continued to increase during the eighteenth century, the churches dropped or diluted the confession requirement. In short, the severity of active social repression is inversely related over time to the level of premarital pregnancy.

The removal of the communal controls of Puritanism left exposed a set of traditional relationships. Although pressures in the direction of the substantive autonomy of youth may have been inherent in the American wilderness from the beginning, environmental forces were more than blunted by traditional familial, social and ideological arrangements. Nearly a century passed before the customary high male age of marriage was lowered. Other indices of traditionalism in family patterns persisted well past the middle of the eighteenth century. Even the modernity of the influential *Some Thoughts Concerning Education* may be questioned. Although Locke stressed affection between mature sons and their fathers (who handily reserved the right to disinherit), the psychological basis for this rational relationship developed in the context of a severe, but not total, crushing of the son's will as an infant. "Fear and awe," proclaimed Locke to fathers, "ought to give you the first power over their minds," and thus compliance "will seem natural to them."

Alternative explanations do not account adequately for the transition to higher premarital pregnancy levels in the eighteenth century. Premarital sex was never normatively approved, even during enagement. Most premaritally pregnant couples (from two thirds to three fourths of those marrying in Hingham between 1741 and 1780) were also pregnant at the time of legal engagement—the filing of the intention to marry. On the other hand, over 40 percent of women not pregnant at marriage had been legally engaged for three months or longer. If betrothal license is an unsatisfactory explanation, the custom of bundling is even less adequate. Although an environmental explanation (cold weather and poorly heated houses) has been seriously advanced, the low seventeenth-century incidence of premarital pregnancy and its seasonal pattern contradict this argument. Premarital conceptions occurred year-round with a slight bulge during the warmer months. Bundling was an eighteenth-century compromise between persistent parental control and the pressures of the young to subvert traditional familial authority.

As a system with contradictory elements, eighteenth-century courtship was not dominated by the newer theme of romantic love. If interpersonal affection and attraction—resulting in premarital pregnancy—had been replacing the old criteria of property and status in mate selection, then one would expect that "love matches" would be more heterogamous than "property matches." To the contrary, however, premaritally pregnant couples were as similar in wealth origins as non-pregnant couples. The eighteenth-century surge in premarital pregnancy did involve a revolt of the young, but it was constrained within the framework of traditional motivation. The generational interpretation is not, of course, new. Eilert Sundt, the most astute observer of courtship practices in nineteenth-century rural Europe, saw the phenomenon as "a form of protest against inordinate parental authority: its decline was in part explained by the moderating of familial controls which young people sought to subvert." And an Anglican polemicist in 1763 anticipated Sundt's conclusion. "Among dissenters, when a married pair happen to have a child born too soon after marriage," he noted, "they do not repent but if they were again in the same circumstances, they would do the same again, because otherwise they could not obtain their parent's consent to marry."

The transference of this generational conflict to the political domain during the pre-Revolutionary crisis with Great Britain was not, as two scholars have recently maintained, because the contractual, Lockean, and republican nature of the family was a settled issue in everyday experience. Rather, power relationships within the family were being challenged, and the very ambiguity of the relationship between parents and children heightened the salience of the familial analogy for the parallel struggle that was developing between the colonies and the mother country. Nor did the leaders of the resistance to England wish to incite a revolution in the family.

For example, among the other evils which Jefferson cited in the preamble to the Virginia bill to abolish entail was that this custom "sometimes does injury to the morals of youth, by rendering them independent of, and disobedient to their parents." The Revolution did signal, however, a general shift from passive to active consent on the part of the people; although an analogy is necessarily vague, it is not unreasonable to assume that a similar shift occurred in intergenerational relations. By the 1830s this new republican consensus on the family was firmly established. The father, according to Tocqueville, "exercised no other power than that which is granted to the affection and experience of age . . . The master and the constituted ruler have vanished, the father remains." The sexual expression underlying the eighteenth-century peak in premarital pregnancy was a product of a situation of profound social disequilibrium, not an end in itself. Once the familial and social context had altered, sexual restrictiveness reappeared.

The crisis in traditional family structure was resolved by a republican solution—the acceptance of the maturity of young adults. Men and women in the nineteenth century responded to the risks of premarital freedom by constraining their sexual drives. Yet, the ideology of the participant-run courtship system emphasized romantic affection and love. Although elaborate dichotomies between pure love and evil sex were developed, the potential for premarital sexual intimacy was built into the Victorian system of courtship. As the Victorian cultural synthesis collapsed in the late nineteenth and twentieth centuries, the dominant themes in premarital sexuality continued to be commitment, love, and marriage. For the young adults who had become autonomous as a result of the transformation in age roles in the family a century earlier, higher rates of sexual intercourse did not produce proportional increases in premarital pregnancy. Contraception made possible the temporary separation of sex and procreation. Teenagers, on the other hand, remained psychologically enmeshed in but not controlled by their families of orientation. With the extension of schooling in the twentieth century, the trend toward youthful autonomy perhaps has been reversed.

The dependence-independence ambivalence is crucial in the explanation of the high premarital pregnancy ratios of contemporary teen-agers. With an estimated decline in the age of menarche of 2.5 to 3.3 years during the twentieth century, American females are biologically mature earlier but socially immature as long or longer than in the nineteenth century. Not independent in society (and therefore not responsible for the consequences of their actions), teen-aged girls accept the risk of pregnancy rather than consciously separate sexual intercourse from procreation. The rational use of contraception requires a teen-aged girl to adopt a self-definition inconsistent with her own assumptions. The "problem," then, is not an absence of "morality" among teen-agers, but rather the persistence of a morality based on the sexual restraint of women presumed to be independent and responsible. In modern America, teen-age sexual behavior is guided neither by the old standard of prohibition nor by a new one of rational expressiveness.

SUMMARY   The historical variation is premarital pregnancy in America suggests a notable absence of a Malthusian constancy of passion. Sexual restraint before marriage typified eras in which intergenerational relationships were well defined, in which extrafamilial institutions reinforced familial controls, and in which the population was relatively well integrated into the central structure of values. Conversely, premarital sexual activity has been more prevalent when there was more ambiguity and uncertainty in the parent-child relationship, when the social supports of morality were weakened or not appropriate to the current realities of coming of age, and when there emerged a segment of the population outside the mainstream of the culture. Discontinuity is the central fact of the premarital pregnancy record. In this important area of behavior, American history has not been a "seamless web." The transitions, furthermore, have not involved the simple triumph of new behavioral patterns over outmoded institutions of control. During the crisis periods the actions of the "rebels" appear, ironically, to be well integrated into the old regime of sexuality and its control.

Perhaps the cycle in premarital pregnancy should not surprise social historians. It fits two well-known models of the discontinuities of modern history—the cultural and the structural stages. The first perspective is the familiar Puritan-Enlightenment-Victorian-Post-modern organization of the four centuries of American cultural history. The latter and more interesting model involves a sequence of equilibrium-shock-adjustment-new equilibrium. In this perspective, the eighteenth-century surge in premarital pregnancy is related to the disintegration of the traditional, well-integrated rural community and to the beginnings of economic and social modernization. Once the crisis of transition to modern society had passed, premarital pregnancy began to decrease. Expectations among individuals and groups were once again predictable, and the various parts of the social system meshed together. Contemporary Western societies also appear to be in a similar transitional phase. The proliferation of transitional terms, e.g., post-industrial, post-modern, post-Protestant, suggests an awareness that a social order is dead but a new one is not yet definable.

What, then, of the future of premarital pregnancy and sexuality? If sexuality and procreation do become separated in the future through the universal acceptance and use of contraception and abortion in premarital relations, and if teen-agers emerge as an autonomous age group in society, then premarital pregnancy will obviously decline. Whether sexuality will continue within the romantic boundaries of love and relatively permanent commitment between individuals or jump to the utopian sexuality envisioned by Herbert Marcuse and Wilhelm Reich is more problematic. Alterations in the social control of sexuality historically have had unanticipated consequences for sexual behavior. Thus the future qualitative meaning of sexuality cannot be categorized as either romantic or utopian. Evidence exists that the structural basis for such an option is being constructed at present. The eighteen-year-olds' vote, for example, is a symbolic recognition of a younger age at maturity. Less symbolic but more to the point at issue here is the sharp drop from 68 percent of Americans in 1969 to only 48 percent in 1973 who think that "it is wrong for people to have sex relations before marriage." If the analysis in this essay has validity, such a redefinition of the family and age groups in society has a clear historical precedent.

# 3
# Childbearing

## 1. Introduction

### THE TIME DIMENSION OF CHILDBEARING

In our own time childbearing has been segregated generally into a distinct period of marriage. Until very recently couples had reserved the first years of marriage for bearing children. Women normally had borne their last child by the age of twenty-six. Lately a new pattern has emerged in which many parents postpone parenthood until their late twenties or early thirties, when they are more certain of their ability to cope with the material and psychological demands of parenting. This newer pattern, like the older one, segments childbearing into a distinct and limited time frame.

This is not the case in the early modern era. Then a married woman could expect to be regularly pregnant through her fecund years, which usually meant until her late thirties, if she lived that long. Rather than being a single, compartmentalized aspect of a married woman's life, as it is today, childbearing was an ongoing and probably dominant facet of the married woman's life. As such, it must be seen as a continuing part of the early modern family cycle.

In their roles as mothers and wives, then, women were regularly pregnant, although the older they became the greater the intervals between conceptions. The greater spacing of births among older women appears to have been a matter of biological capability rather than planning, for with age conception becomes more difficult. Still, as Robert Wells concludes below, the average interval between births for European and colonial American mothers was 24 months. Thus English and colonial married women were normally pregnant every couple of years from their date of marriage in their early or mid-twenties at least until their late thirties, if not into their forties.

A pattern in which the average intergenesic interval was 24 months is possible in a population that does not practice birth control, as long as the mothers nurse their babies for upwards of the first year. Nursing appears to impede conception for two reasons. The first is biological. Although it is possible for a nursing mother to conceive, the likelihood is not high. Secondly, in some traditional societies, the couples are enjoined from having sex while the woman is nursing. In any case, historians of the early modern era have interpreted a 24-month intergenesic pattern to indicate the absence of birth control.

Yet birth control appears to have been an option for people even in early modern England and America. The method may have been no more sophisticated than *coitus interruptus,* although some writers equated that method with the sin of Onan. But the findings of demographers point to a conclusion that where there was a will there was a way, and that some groups did in fact deliberately limit the size of their families. The availability of birth control, albeit unreliable, must lead us to conclude that couples who had children regularly probably wanted them.

In New England, which appears to have had either the highest fecundity rate or the lowest perinatal mortality rate in the Euro-American world during the 17th century, the typical completed family (one where the mother reached the age of 45) had 7 to 8 surviving children, each of whom was about two years older or younger than his nearest sibling.

Research subsequent to Robert Wells's article has shown that all of colonial America did not share in the high birth rate experienced by New Englanders and groups like the Quakers. The average mother in 17th-century Maryland and Virginia bore less than half as many children as her northern counterpart. The Chesapeake mother's experience was closer to that of the typical Englishwoman's in this respect. And native Chesapeake women did not marry later than New England women. On the contrary, the pressure in the plantation colonies was on females to marry early because of the severely imbalanced sex ratio. What appears to have been consequential for the lower fertility rate there was the extraordinarily high adult mortality level. The average Chesapeake mother in the 17th century died well before the age of 45. High parental mortality in the Chesapeake, we will see in subsequent chapters, has important implications for the quality of family life there.

Chesapeake and English married women may have experienced a much higher pregnancy to birth ratio than did New England women. That is, they may have been pregnant with the same degree of regularity but may have suffered through a higher fetal mortality rate. This would be important to ascertain because the treatment of and attitude towards pregnant women by their family members, especially their husbands, may have been significantly different from those accorded nonpregnant wives.

PREGNANCY

A modern parent can find remarkably familiar themes running through early modern writings about pregnancy. Most striking is the concern for what we call prenatal care. Michael Eshleman's review of the advice literature regarding pregnancy reveals 17th-century writers working from the modern premise that childbearing is substantially controllable by man. The birth process was not considered wholly a mystery to be left resignedly by people to the will of providence, as is the attitude in some traditional, pre-industrial societies. Pregnant women themselves were charged with the primary responsibility for prenatal care, according to R.V. Schnucker's findings. The prescriptive writings focused on three components that made for good prenatal care: (1) a proper diet, (2) proper exercise, and (3) a helpful husband. In fact, the advantages a pregnant woman stood to gain from a solicitous husband may have mitigated the very real dangers and fears associated with childbirth, and even encouraged women to welcome it. Moreover, the frequency and regularity of childbearing suggests that for much of the early modern family cycle husbands were at least expected to be especially tender and accommodating to their wives, which maybe partially compensated them for the constant risk that childbirth involved.

The marital advantages that might accrue to a pregnant woman may explain the pride with which she carried that condition. Leastwise there appears to have been none of the prudery and even shame that attended "the condition" in the 19th and early 20th centuries. Julia C. Spruill finds 18th-century Southern women announcing in the newspapers that they were "in the increasing way." Children were valued, and the bearers of children were not constrained from publicizing their good fortune.

Puritan New Englanders had more children than any other Anglo-American population. And they would seem to have been among the least likely to be ignorant of birth control methods, for they were one of the most highly educated groups in the Atlantic world at that time. Can their failure to limit their family size be attributed to a sense of fatalism about their lives, a suggestion that Robert Wells has offered elsewhere? We think not. For although predestination was the central tenet of their theology, the Puritans did not adopt a passive attitude toward the challenges of earthly life. On the contrary, they engaged in an energetic effort to master and control themselves and their environment. No group of 17th-century Europeans were driven by a more intense need to manage and even re-shape the world they had inherited than did the utopian reformers who settled early Massachusetts and Plymouth. They had many children, it would seem, because they wanted them.

The reason why people wanted children is less easily established than the fact that they wanted them. Spruill concludes that children were valued for what they could contribute to their parents. Certainly, she says, more was said about children's duties than about parental responsibilities. In particular, children may have been desired as insurance against a neglected old age or infirmity. Although the early modern state had begun to intervene unprecedentedly into the economic and social affairs of their populations, the family still had to assume the principal responsibility for its dependents. Grown-up children were expected to take care of their disabled parents, as we shall see in the last chapter. Thus, childbearing may well have been viewed as a wise investment in one's old age security.

For most couples, the actual birth process was an exclusively female affair. In England by the beginning of the 17th century, male physicians, to be sure, had made some inroads into this female province. And there appears to have been a slow but steady erosion of the monopoly by women of the delivery process. But it was not until the 19th century that the male physician began to replace the midwife as the person in charge. Earlier, in most instances, a midwife and neighborhood women and girls attended the birth, which usually took place in the couple's home. The presence of these neighborhood females was an educational device for disseminating information about delivery. Moreover, it served to provide eyewitnesses who could later testify to the child's legitimacy, in the absence of reliable written records. Whatever the reason for the exclusion of men, and modesty may have been a motive, it must have underlined for the husband his inferiority vis à vis his wife in this facet of their marriage. Exclusion meant that the birth process would necessarily remain something of a mystery for him, and ignorance was perhaps a useful way of keeping him in his place.


## 2. Family Limitation In England

by J.D. Chambers

The difficulties in the way of calculating the rate of births to which the marriages gave rise is great. The Church authorities could bring some degree of pressure through the Court of the Ordinary upon parents to bring their offspring to the font. A charge in the Archdeacon's Court might be preferred against them if they delayed more than a fortnight; but it was backed by no penalty, only a reprimand. At the worst, and very rarely, it might amount to excommunication, i.e. the refusal of the cup at Communion for the persistently recalcitrant. In the elongated parishes of Lincolnshire, for instance, where marshland farmers might be 5 miles away from the church on the edge of the higher land, the bringing of the babies to the font was a less pressing problem than the disposal of a corpse in the graveyard; and to overcome this difficulty, the family might be baptized *en masse* at a suitable time.

There were other possible loopholes through which unrecorded births could slip. It is unlikely that all bastard children were entered as such in the registers, though most investigators think that the record is realistic at least until the last decades of the eighteenth century. Still-births would usually not be recorded at all; infants who lived a few hours might be entered as 'chrisom child' though the numbers are suspiciously few; and what can be said of abortions and infanticide, of which there is no record at all? The number of entries, therefore, in the baptism register represents only a proportion of the actual births and a still smaller proportion of the conceptions.

What can we learn from the various methods of parish-register analysis about patterns of fertility in pre-industrial England and the factors that accounted for them?

Let us begin with some examples based on the aggregative method of analysis, that is, by simply summing baptisms, marriages, and burials and comparing their incidence over time. Dr. Eversley has analysed the remarkable response of a number of Worcestershire villages to the onslaught of mortality in the notorious epidemic years of 1725-9. It was a period of wet summers, hard winters, food shortages, and fevers, and in twelve parishes roughly within a radius of 5 miles of Bromsgrove, there was a huge excess of burials over baptisms; at the height of the epidemic baptisms declined owing to mortality among actual and potential mothers; but as soon as the epidemic was over there was an upsurge of marriages and a rise of the crude birth-rate to 42 per thousand or more. Eversley calculates that the turn-over of jobs and tenancies would have risen from 4 to 8.8 percent per annum, providing opportunities for advancement and for living accommodation which would be reflected in this stampede to the altar. An observed increase of the marriage rate from 10.35 to 14.34 per 1,000 in 1730-4 would, he thinks, represent two extra marriages, or re-marriages, and two 'anticipated' marriages; and by 1735-44 the rate had fallen to 8.46. This example represents the kind of response the population made in a rapidly expanding area in the neighbourhood of Birmingham in a period of prosperity. The recovery was astonishing; nevertheless, he says, it took more than 25 years for the population to recover the position of 1725. But it would be a younger population than would otherwise have been the case. This fact, together with the improved conditions making for greater expectation of life, must be taken into account in explaining the expansion of the 1740s and '50s.

The period of 25 years mentioned by Eversley required to recover the position of 1725 calls for further comment. It coincides remarkably with the findings of Dr. Tranter for thirty villages of Bedfordshire, though in this case the long-term effect was attributable not only to the set-back of 1727-30 but also to bad epidemic years in 1740-2 and 1747-8. Had it not been for these, the earlier losses, he thinks, would have been made up in 10 years; but as a result of the combined effect of these various set-backs, the population total did not reach its pre-epidemic level until 1752, a period of 26 years. In the case of a number of Nottinghamshire villages the loss was made up in about 10 years, but the town of Nottingham did not make up its arrears by its own natural increase for over 30 years. If, then, we may postulate a period of 25 years during which urban-population growth and in some cases rural-population growth was catching up on the losses of the epidemic years, we are faced with a situation in which in the second quarter of the century the remarkable resilience of fertility was scarcely able to hold its own against repeated crises of mortality. At least, this appears to hold true for the regions mentioned; it is not known whether the same could be said of other areas (e.g. Lancashire or Yorkshire), where conditions may have been more favorable.

We may now turn to the second important result of the aggregative study of the registers. This relates to the differential fertility rate of industrial and agricultural parishes as illustrated by the Nottinghamshire study, which shows the consistently higher fertility of the partially industrialized villages, compared with those that were wholly agricultural. By dividing marriages into baptisms, their comparative fertility following the disastrous years 1727-9 is shown in Table I:

## Table I

*Differential Fertility in Eighteenth-century Nottinghamshire*

|  | 1730-9 | 1740-9 | 1750-9 | 1760-9 |
|---|---|---|---|---|
| Agricultural villages | 3.3 | 3.3 | 3.4 | 3.7 |
| Industrial villages | 3.9 | 4.4 | 4.8 | 4.5 |

|  | 1770-9 | 1780-9 | 1790-9 |
|---|---|---|---|
| Agricultural villages | 3.6 | 3.7 | 3.7 |
| Industrial villages | 4.8 | 4.7 | 4.8 |

On the basis of these figures, the fertility of industrial parishes appears to have been between 20 and 30 percent higher than that of agricultural parishes. As was shown in the last chapter, there is some evidence that the industrial population married a little earlier—two years in the case of the men—one year in the case of the women—but in addition to this explanation, we should also consider the factors within marriage that could contribute to this result: for example, shorter intervals between births and greater expectation of life of the mother when living conditions, in terms of wages and prices, and cottage accommodation were good, although the necessary research for this (which would require family reconstitution) has not yet been done. It is also possible that migration played its part in accounting for these results: newly married couples may have moved into industrial villages before their families had arrived, with the result that bonus baptisms were added to the registers of the industrial villages without a correspondng addition to the marriage registers. To that extent the differential fertility of the industrial villages may be illusory, and we must keep this in mind when we meet the same situation in the Lancashire and West Riding parishes which were similarly drawing recruits from neighbouring rural areas. But even with this important qualification I think one must allow that the evidence points to a higher level of fertility among the industrial population at the time and to a confirmation of the view that the industrial population grew not only as a result of transference of population by migration but also by a higher rate of self-recruitment.

Thirdly, existing parish studies based on aggregative methods of analysis have been re-examined from a somewhat original point of view by Professor Pentland of Manitoba University in a paper to which I should like to refer briefly here. His first important comment is that the several series of absolute totals of baptisms exhibit a marked volatility, i.e. short-term movements upward and downward, which tends to be obscured when attention is confined to the national figures collected at the time of the first census by John Rickman and used as the basis of calculations by Talbot Griffith and others in their studies of population in the eighteenth century. Furthermore, following through the behaviour of the series over time reveals a still more significant characteristic; he observes a "lack of relationship at any reasonable interval between baptisms and the apparent availability of parents [which is] so pronounced that a social rather than a biological explanation for the fluctuation of baptisms is needed." These findings imply the existence of a population able to recognize economic opportunities when it saw them, and ready to adjust marriage and child-bearing propensities more quickly, and to a greater extent, than is commonly allowed by those who assume that in the pre-industrial world birth-rates were more or less constant at the limit of biological potential.

Professor Pentland is raising the question of controlled fertility in response to economic conditions and there is no doubt some measure of truth in this view. However a qualification needs to be made at this point; the society in which this responsiveness is supposed to have operated was still essentially agrarian in character. Three-fifths of the labouring population still derived a livelihood from the soil, and a very large proportion of these would be servants living in. Another large proportion of the labour force was domestic servants as well as apprenticed workmen forbidden to marry within the period of their indentures. This being the case, pre-industrial nuptiality, and as a consequence fertility, was probably at least as much determined by social institutions and habits as by conscious calculations of economic advantage, at least until the obvious advance of industrialization and rapid growth of cottage labour at the expense of indoor agricultural labour in the later eighteenth century reduced traditional barriers to marriage and opened the door to a more rapid expansion of the labour force. In some areas of course, these conditions obtained at an earlier date, notably in districts of equal partition of holdings, which permitted the proliferation of families on small holdings; and in the industrialized villages of the Midlands and the north-west, particularly Lancashire and the West Riding. For such areas, as will be shown later, there is indeed some evidence to suggest that the barriers to expansion had already been lowered long before the period traditionally allotted to the demographic revolution of the last quarter of the eighteenth century.

On the basis of the aggregative studies so far discussed, three important suggestions seem to emerge:

1. As a result of high mortality in the epidemic years, especially 1725-9, urban and in some cases rural populations spent up to twenty-five years recovering the position of 1725. In the areas discussed, fertility was hardly able to hold its own against repeated crises of mortality, although it is not known, at present, whether the same sort of check to population growth was also operative elsewhere in the same period.
2. There existed a differential fertility pattern between industrial and agricultural populations (on the basis of the Nottinghamshire figures), and the industrial population tended to have a higher rate of self-recruitment.
3. Economic and social conditions affected nuptiality and fertility, although there is likely to have been an element of inertia arising out of social structure, institutions, and habits. These factors are, however, likely to have been eroded over time, as industrialism offered wider and on the whole more secure opportunities of earning a living.

Before we arrive at firm conclusions, however, especially in the matter of the responsiveness of the population as a whole to complex and changing circumstances, we need to look more closely at the behaviour of the fertility variable as far as present research permits. At some points, we can take the inquiry rather further than the above-mentioned aggregative studies permit. Recent studies of marriage and, in particular, fertility patterns have enriched our knowledge considerably, although it cannot yet be said that anything like a clear picture has emerged. In particular, I should like to take this opportunity to review recent evidence on class or status differences in fertility, on the conscious control of births within marriage together with the apparent importance of psychological factors in this process, and on changes in the incidence of illegitimacy and pre-martial conceptions.

## STATUS DIFFERENCES IN FERTILITY AND FAMILY SIZE

If we take the child-bearing period as the 24 years lying between 15 and 49 and the average number of years of married life as 15 or 16, we should expect about 7 or 8 births per family at least. But the evidence points to lower average fertility; including childless and broken as well as fertile and complete marriages, perhaps no more than 4 or 5 children on the average, at least until the last quarter of the eighteenth century.

Moreover, family size varied between different socio-economic groups. For instance, an Elizabethan survey of 450 poor families of Norwich shows that households consisted usually of parents and 2 or 3 children, at the time of the count; whereas the well-to-do merchants of Norwich and Exeter had 4.25 and 4.7 children respectively. No doubt differential infant mortality played its part in accounting for this discrepancy, as did the fact that poor men and their wives could not expect to live long enough to have as many children as their richer neighbours. Indeed, contemporary surveys often reveal a large number of second marriages. In Clayworth 35.5 per cent of all children had lost one parent, whilst in Manchester in the 1650s a quarter of the marriages were between widows and widowers and half of the brides and bridegrooms marrying for the first time were reported as fatherless.

How far the Norwich finding may also be taken to reflect a genuine fertility difference is, of course, problematic; but the evidence for the peerage is distinctly less ambiguous. Both in regard to age at marriage and conditions of life, aristocrats had an advantage over the lower social classes that was reflected in a considerable disparity in fertility. Between 1550 and 1625 the sons and grandsons of peers married at 25 or 26, the daughters at 20 or 21, probably two or even three years younger than those of husbandmen and labourers. This might be expected to make a difference of one or possibly two births per marriage, since fertility was particularly high in the first years of marriage. Moreover it is reasonable to suppose that there would be relatively fewer marriages broken by death and therefore a higher average period for child-bearing among the peerage. Whatever the reason, the fertility of the peerage after the period 1680-1729 was remarkably high until well into the nineteenth century.

Table 2

*Ducal Families: Female Fertility, 20-49, Births per Married Woman*

| Cohort Born | |
|---|---|
| 1680-1729 | 4.98 |
| 1730-79 | 7.29 |
| 1780-1829 | 7.91 |
| 1830-79 | 5.67 |
| 1880-1939 | 4.81 |

With the aid of Dr. Tranter's researches into the villages of Bedfordshire, we can go a little further in this inquiry. There, the average number of baptisms per marriage hovered about 3½-4, and the figure for completed marriages exhibited a slight rise from 5.1 and 5.16 baptisms between 1690-1720 and 1750-75, although one parish, Cardington, attained 6.17. The mean age at first marriage for completed unions of the second period was for men 27, for women 24, and the proportion of childless marriages was 10 percent. Even including the exceptional case of Cardington these fertility levels are considerably lower than those of the aristocracy, and it will be noticed that there is no evidence here of a similar sudden jump in fertility in the post-1750 period.

Additionally, there is some reason to think that differential fertility may be found *within* the village population itself. In a personal communication, Tranter indicates that 13 marriages of farmers in Cardington for 1782 produced 92 children, giving an average of 7.08 baptisms per marriage. He has shown earlier that 51 completed cottagers' marriages in Cardington produced an average of only 5.41, and this was higher than in any other Bedfordshire village examined. This meant that the average size of cottage households at the time of the local listing of 1782 was only 4.18, and the mean number of children residing at home was 2.27. One-third of their children, he suggests, would normally die before reaching the age of twenty-one, and one child would have left home.

Are we to infer from the smaller size of the completed family of the cottage labourer that either a large number of pregnancies ended negatively or that birth control was practised? Tranter himself is not inclined to accept the latter alternative. The reason for the difference, he thinks, was that the farmers' wives had a somewhat longer child-bearing period (i.e. the interval between the last and first birth which he finds was 10.77 years) and, more significantly, shorter intervals between births, possibly due to the longer period of lactation that was customary among labourers' wives. We are back again, therefore, with the fact of poverty and hard conditions of life making for lower fertility. Even so, the possibility of deliberate regulation of fertility according to circumstances deserves further consideration in the light of recent work.

## EVIDENCE OF FAMILY LIMITATION

G. C. Coulton long ago reminded us of the indictment brought against the peasantry by the Franciscan Alvarus Pelagius is in the early fourteenth century; that "they often abstain from knowing their own wives lest children should be born, fearing that they could not bring up so many, under pretext of poverty". For eighteenth-century France M. Goubert has discovered that the mean interval between births was only twenty months in a Breton parish as against thirty observed in South-West France, "a difference that cannot be due to chance" and which he attributes to the greater powers of the confessional in Britanny. It is therefore not improbable that family limitation could occur in Protestant England when special circumstances seemed to demand it. Some evidence has been unearthed recently by Dr. Wrigley for the Devonshire village of Colyton.

As one might expect, Wrigley finds that an important regulator of fertility was the age at marriage, which appears to have fluctuated over time. From 1560 to 1646 the mean age of women at first marriage was between 26 and 27; in the period 1647-59 it rose to 30 and remained so, with little change, until 1719. During this period the female marriage age was actually two years higher than that of the men. From 1720 the female age at marriage tended to go down, and by 1825 it had fallen to 23.3. Whereas in 1647-1719 only 4 percent of the brides were in their teens and 40 percent were over 30, by the first quarter of the nineteenth century 25 percent of the brides were in their teens and only 7 percent were over 30. There had obviously been a marked shift towards earlier marriage. Such a change in the mean age of marriage, Wrigley thinks, provided scope for a very wide range of rates of increase or decrease of population. "In marriages not prematurely interrupted by death, an average age at first marriage for women of, say, 24 might well produce two more children than marriages contracted at an average of, say 29". Between the two extremes of 23.3 in 1825-37 and 30.7 in 1700-1 a difference in the size of family by 2 could easily follow.

The importance of these statements scarcely needs emphasizing, but even more significant in this context is the evidence suggesting the regulation of fertility within marriage. In Wrigley's words, "any changes on the fertility side of population history of Colyton which arose from changes in the mean age of first marriage were considerably amplified by changes within marriage". Between 1560 and 1629 age-specific marital fertility rates were high, pointing to a mean completed family size of 7.3 for brides married by the age of 24, and 5.7 for those married by 29. There was a marked decline from about 1630, a decline that became more pronounced after the renewal of the plague in 1646. "The change from a high to a low level of fertility within these families was abrupt and complete"; a fall, in fact, to 5.0 and 3.3 respectively for the two age groups mentioned. Notably, there occurred a marked rise in the interval between the penultimate and the last birth which "is typical of a community beginning to practice family limitation."

It has sometimes been supposed that the intuitive reaction of the population after a heavy loss of life is to increase fertility and to fill the gaps created by death, but this does not appear to have been the case at Colyton. The numbers are, of course, small, but the picture is none the less suggestive. Fertility rates apparently dropped sharply and immediately to the levels which were to be characteristic of Colyton for the next two generations, although the women in question had displayed a fertility well above the average in the period before the swingeing losses of 1646. In fact only 18 percent of women marrying under 30 between 1647 and 1719 and living right through the fertile period had families of 6 children or more, compared with 55 percent in the period 1560-1625, 48 percent in 1720-69, and 60 percent between 1770 and 1837.

As a warning against a too easy acceptance of deliberate family limitation we should not omit to mention the footnote in which Wrigley draws attention to Creighton's invocation of the tradition that plague was associated with sterility in the surviving female population. Nevertheless, after a consideration of all other possibilities he leaves little room for doubt that not only was there restriction of births within marriage, but that, in view of the rise in age of women at first marriage, a catastrophe such as a sharp attack of plague may have had an adverse effect upon the *propensity* to marry and have children. This important suggestion is worth pursuing further.

It is possible that the same factor may help to account for the failure of population to recover from the setbacks of the plagues of the fourteenth century. The Black Death of 1349 is generally believed to have been followed by further virulent outbreaks in 1361, 1369, and 1375, but it has recently been argued by Dr. Bean that these subsequent sporadic attacks were too localized and scattered to account for the strange phenomenon of a hundred years of population stagnation, when economic conditions might have been expected to have the opposite effect. Land was not plentiful and prices were low. In terms of the ratio between population and subsistence, the peasantry were enjoying a golden age; but the population refused to rise. In a recent contribution of great interest Professor Thrupp has hinted at a psychological factor that should not be overlooked; after referring to the spread of disease as a result of the movement of the peasantry and traders from village to village and market town to market town, she says "to the extent that migrations were aimless, or motivated by moods of fear, despair, desire to enter the Church or *otherwise to evade family responsibilities*" (my italics), we have a cultural interpretation of the phenomenon of demographic stagnation.

Professor Chevalier, the distinguished French demographer, would go further. Speaking of the puzzling phenomenon of demographic stagnation in France in the nineteenth century he writes: "During the years following the wars of the Revolution and Empire the birth-rate declined, and some years, fell below the death-rate." Demographers and economists who first became aware of it about 1856 found it hard to believe, and when asked to explain it had to confess their ignorance. "And we have to repeat this confession of ignorance," he says. De Tocqueville attributed it to the political instability following the French Revolution, which he saw as "the cause of the lasting social and demographic disturbances in France." He goes on, "and the social and demographic repercussions of revolutions like those of 1830 and 1848 have been incomparably greater than their political consequences; their extent cannot fail to surprise one." Between 1815 and 1848 fertility diminished, increased again to about 1861 (a period of political stability), and only began to fall again in 1865. "This is, indeed, one of the more curious problems of the demographic evolution of nineteenth-century France.''

If psychological factors could thus serve to depress the rate of population growth either by delaying marriage or through the conscious control of births, we may assume that the converse was also possible. We may be sure that psychological factors were at work in the acceleration of growth in England in the last quarter of the eighteenth century. It was a period of impetuous economic development on all sides, of fresh opportunities for employment, with new facilities for housing and for the provision of domestic equipment. The propensity to marry would be at a maximum, and that there was a rise in the birth-rate, at least in towns, seems indisputable. In Nottingham the crude birth-rate, which had risen to 40.32 per thousand in 1770, reached the unprecedented height of 46.29 in 1790, but then fell back to 41.07 by 1800. Coupled with high fertility was a marriage rate of 12 per thousand. Houses by the hundred were being built to serve the needs of a bourgeoning population and the double lure of living accommodation and high pay was irresistible. The birth-rate rose primarily as a reflection of the new age structure which a massive immigration of young country labour brought about, although it may be presumed that high marital fertility would also be in evidence in these propitious circumstances.

In view of its losses by migrations, it is all the more surprising that the eighteenth-century rural population showed such remarkable buoyancy. Birth-rates in the Nottinghamshire agricultural villages remained at over 30 per thousand while in the industrialized villages they rose to more than 35 per thousand. In the towns, the death-rate tended to rise to the level, and if anything above the level, that it reached in the early part of the century, so that those who looked to the birth-rate as the most important urban variable in the explosive period from 1790 have some foundation for this view. Whether the same can be said of the rural population is doubtful. The evidence points to a fall in the death-rate as being the most important factor, at least in the agricultural villages, and since they were by far the more numerous, their influence would be paramount at that time; but there is no doubt that fertility was well maintained, owing perhaps to the greater use of cottage labour and the relative decline of the numbers living in. The largest inquiry that has yet been attempted in this area of investigation is that of Dr. Tranter who made a comparative examination of marital fertility for eight Bedfordshire parishes in the two periods of the last quarter of the seventeenth century and the third quarter of the eighteenth. He found only a slight tendency for the age of marriage to fall, perhaps only by one year, and for fertility rate of completed families to advance only by a fraction. For Colyton, Dr. Wrigley found evidence of a marked fall in the age of marriage in the early nineteenth century, so that we may tentatively conclude that, if there was any substantial change in rural family size, it took place very late in the eighteenth century and more probably at the beginning of the nineteenth.

It is difficult to escape the conclusion that by the second half of the eighteenth century, among the factors that influenced fertility we must include the phenomenon of a changed moral attitude.

We are left with the general conclusion that the history of fertility in pre-industrial England went through a series of changes reflecting both the physical circumstances and the moral attitudes of the time. The onslaught of plague in the fourteenth century and again in the case of Colyton in 1646 was followed by a fall in fertility of considerable duration reflecting, it would seem, psychological as well as biological factors. Each instance was followed by a period of recovery, but the long-term sequel in the two cases was very different. Whereas the recovery of the sixteenth century was followed by a further setback in the seventeenth, that of the eighteenth century was the prelude to an acceleration amounting to a veritable population explosion in the last decade of the century. Evidently new factors were at work. One was the factor of greater confidence in the opportunities now being offered, and another a relaxation in the traditonal moral code, finding a reflection in rising fertility especially in the last decade of the century. Yet, more important than either was the factor of the death-rate, which in the two earlier periods of recovery had reasserted itself; in the eighteenth century the death-rate failed to catch up with the birth-rate. The gap between them was never closed; instead it widened, and in falling, the death-rate brought a new age structure into being.

## 3. Diet During Pregnancy In The Sixteenth And Seventeeth Centuries

By Michael K. Eshleman

Today a woman's diet during pregnancy occupies an important position in what we consider to be good prenatal management. Discussion of the amounts and kinds of foods to insure adequate protein, vitamin, and mineral intake generally takes up a good part of one of the early prenatal visits with her obstetrician. The well-being of the pregnant woman, which includes preventing anemia and decreasing the likelihood of toxemia, and considerations of normal fetal growth and development underlie current dietary advice. These considerations include the weight of the fetus at term, which influences neonatal survival as well as growth and performance in the first year of life, and the long-term effects of fetal malnutrition on the central nervous system.

The obstetrician's advice, however, is founded on information that has emerged only in the last 100 to 150 years with discoveries of the caloric basis of nutrition, the metabolism of protein, vitamins, and minerals, and some of the effects produced by deficiencies of these substances. Before this time, was diet during pregnancy an important consideration? If so, what were the goals of prenatal diet and how were they accomplished?

In seeking answers to these questions, I have selected the sixteenth and seventeenth centuries as a suitable period for investigation. Before this time little on obstetrics was published; during this time, however, there emerged several books on midwifery and obstetrics that included discussions on prenatal diet. This period also represented a time of little change in the notions of the role of diet in health, medical treatment, and pregnancy. Most of these ideas had come nearly unchanged from Hippocrates, Aristotle, and Galen.

Traditionally diet, or regimen, encompassed a person's way of life. This included the six non-naturals, external factors that affected the functioning of the body: air, or climatic conditions, meat and drink, sleeping and waking, exercise and rest, fullness and emptiness, and passions of the mind. Most authors, however, felt that meat and drink exerted the most influence on the state of the body; they tended to limit the meaning of diet to include only meat and drink. This restricted meaning is used in this paper.

Three kinds of diet were employed during this period: full, moderate, and thin or sparing. A full diet increased the strength, flesh, and humors and was appropriate for young, growing, active, and strong individuals. A moderate diet preserved the strength and was for those who had attained full growth and were in good health. A thin diet diminished the strength and was employed only in time of a febrile illness.

Temperance or moderation in diet represented the key concept that related diet to one's state of health. A temperate diet provided only that amount of food and drink that the stomach could digest and assimilate completely for the nourishment of the body. This amount of food would disturb neither the balance nor quantities of the humors in the body; consequently, the individual would remain in good health. However,

> . . . temperance is not to be understood as if there were a set proportion for all alike, for it is according to every one's *Constitution:* what is too much for one Man or Woman, may be too little for another; it is then *such a quantity of Meat or Drink, that the Stomach can well master and digest, for the feeding of the Body.*

The other five non-naturals as well as a person's age, sex, occupation, and temperament were the principal factors that affected the amounts and kinds of food one might eat for a temperate diet. Exercise, for instance, increased the natural heat, which aided digestion, and allowed the ingestion of more food.

An excess of food and drink resulted in a state of surfeit or repletion. Surfeiting could lead to an overabundance of humors as well as to an imbalance of the humors. These conditions produced in the body a disequilibrium of temperature and moisture which was manifested as sickness. Since each humor exhibited specific characteristics, a diagnosis of the offending humor(s) was possible. Appropriate therapy usually included a diet rich in foods of qualities contrary to the aberrant humor(s): "That when any Man is sick or distemper'd, his Meats should be of contrary Qualities to his Disease; for Health itself is but a kind of Temper gotten and preserv'd by a convenient Mixture of Contrarieties." Alternatively, since most disease followed from excess humors, ridding the body of these humors also represented a logical treatment. This could be accomplished by evacuation, "which is nothing else but an expulsion of the humor out of the body," and included phlebotomy, vomiting, diarrhea, and sweating. Special characteristics of certain foods could be used to induce vomiting, diarrhea, or sweating to purge the offending humor(s). In many cases both expulsion and diet of contrary qualities were used together.

Additionally, it was felt that food during a febrile illness not only nourished the body but also nourished the disease:

In healthy people the strength of nature is to be preserved or increased with nourishment, not to be broken; which cannot be in sick persons, because a moderate diet preserving the health in healthy people, diminisheth it in those that are sick, by increasing the disease; because by how much the more you feed it, by so much the more you hurt the body of the patient.

In examining the application of these principles of diet and nutrition to pregnancy, only their role in carrying the pregnancy to a successful parturition will be considered. Consideration of this goal of preventing abortion allows us to view dietary manipulations during pregnancy as rational therapy for achieving a term pregnancy and a healthy child and mother.

Diet, through its role in nourishing the embryo and fetus, related directly to the prevention of abortion. The 'navel-vein' conveyed blood from the mother to the fetus. It is obvious that the nutritive quality of this blood depended not only upon the amount of food ingested by the mother, but also upon the kinds of food and their effects upon her humoral balance.

The inability of the maternal circulation to provide adequate nourishment to the fetus initiated parturition: "When the naturral prefixed and prescribed time of childbirth is come, the childe being then growne greater, requires a greater quantity of food: which when he cannot receive in sufficient measure by his navell, with great labour and striving hee endeavoureth to get fourth . . . " Or put more simply, when the fetus could not obtain sufficient nutriment in the womb, it came out to seek sustenance. Thus, in giving general dietary advice most treatises on midwifery counseled that "when the child is bigger, let her diet be more, for it is better for women with child to eat too much than too little, lest the Child should want nourishment." Provided the woman was otherwise in good health, she could rely upon her appetite to regulate the proper amount of food to nourish her and her fetus.

The idea that insufficient fetal nourishment initiated labor figured prominently in explanations of abortion. Diminished nutriment in the maternal blood for whatever reason and at any time during gestation could result in a weakened, sickly fetus or abortion: ·

Defect of Humors fitting to Nourish, springs from such Causes, which are able to draw the Nourishment from the Child, as fasting, whether voluntary or forced; as when women with Child loath all kind of Meat, or vomit it up again; a thin diet in acute diseases, immoderate bleeding by the Nose, Haemorrhoides, Womb, or by immoderate Phlebotomy . . . If a woman with Child go very much to stool, it is to be feared that she wil Miscarry. Hereunto may be referred extream leanness of the whol body, wherein there is not Blood enough to nourish the Infant.

Paradoxically surfeiting could also lead to fetal demise and abortion. The plethora of humors suffocated, strangled, or choked the fetus. Revière in *The Practice of Physick* briefly explained the mechanism for this and considered other mechanisms of abortion that resulted from overeating:

But badness of Humors, is either chollerick and sharp, so as to open the Orifices of the Veins, or by provoking Nature, to stir up the expulsive faculty, whereby the child comes to be expelled with those evil Humors; or by reason of plenty of Excrements heaped together in the First Region, and distending the belly, it suffocates the Child, or it vitiates the blood in the whol habit of the Body, rendring it unfit to nourish the child, or it fils the Vessels of the Womb which retain the child, ful of slime and snot.

Finally, too much nutriment might cause the fetus to outgrow the womb, "which constraines him either to come forth, or else makes him sickly seeing that those meates are corrupted wherewith hee is nourished and fed."

These extremes of diet, fasting and surfeiting, fell in the province of moderation or temperance in diet. Temperance and other dietary means of preventing abortion usually appeared in midwifery manuals in a section outlining general dietary advice for the pregnant woman. *The Compleat Midwife's Practice Enlarged,* a representative seventeenth-century midwifery manual, contains this counsel:

For her Diet, she ought to choose meat that breeds good and wholsome nourishment, and which breeds good juice; such are meats that are moderately dry . . .

All meats too cold, too hot, and too moist, are to be avoided, as also the use of Salads and Spiced meats, and the too much use of salt meats are also forbidden, which will make the child to be born without nails, a sign of short life. Her bread ought to be good wheat, well baked and levened. Her meats ought to be Pigions, Turtles, Pheasants, Larks, Partridge, Veal, and Mutton. For herbs, she may use Lettice, Endive, Bugloss, and Burrage, abstaining from raw Salads: for her last course, she may be permitted to eat Pears, Marmalade, as also Cherries and Damsins; she must avoid all meats that provoke urine, or the terms; and such meats as are windy, as Pease, and Beans . . .

The concern for adequate nourishment for the fetus is prominent, as is the counsel of moderation. Moderation, it will be remembered, constituted the best means of avoiding maternal illness, which always carried the dangers of abortion and maternal demise. Avoiding extremes of temperature, moisture, and seasoning as well as foods of difficult digestion, such as poorly leavened bread and raw salads, contributed to achieving a moderate diet.

Not only did the quality of the blood affect the pregnant woman's ability to nourish the conceptus, but it also affected the quality of the seed, or germ cells, of both sexes. The quality of the seed in turn contributed to the quality of the conceptus and child; in other words, defects in the seed could cause congenital anomalies. In general, other explanations of congenital defects, such as hereditary factors, divine retribution for intercourse during the menstrual period, intercourse with animals, the woman's imagination during pregnancy, and events occurring during pregnancy, gained much more notoriety than a defect in the seed. Rueff, however, suggested that "the corruption and fault of the seed is to bee acknowledged, to wit, which was either too much, or too little, or corrupted, from whence those monsters are ingendred," and proposed that "the immoderate desire of lust" caused these defects in the seed. "Likewise we allege the immoderate desire of lust to be a cause, whereby it commeth to be very feeble and imperfect, wherby of necessity a feeble and imperfect Feature must ensue. For the defect of seede going before, the consequence is, that a defect of the Feature doth follow . . . "

Attempts were made to explain the etiology of these defects in the seed by reference to the quality of the blood. An intemperate diet, as one might expect, degraded the quality of the blood. The defect in the seed caused by dietary excess manifested itself not only by obvious congenital malformations but by subtle aberrations that resulted in death during infancy. The pathophysiology and the prevention of this defect come directly from the principles examined earlier:

This *intemperance of parents,* is the cause that *many Children die before their time*; for what is *too much,* can never be well *concocted* [digested], but turns to ill and raw Humours, and if the Stomach turn the Food into *crude Juice, or Chyle,* the *Liver that makes the second concoction can never mend it, to make good blood;* nor can the *third concoction* of the Stones to turn that *Blood into Seed, make good Seed of ill Blood . . .*

Along with the poorly explained effect of too much salt during pregnancy mentioned earlier, these examples stand out as the only obvious attempts to relate diet to congenital anomalies. They also represent attempts to end credence to the doctrines of moderation in diet by invoking consequences of transgression, the high perinatal and childhood mortality rates, that were obvious but impossible to verify.

Before looking at the role of diet in specific disorders that could occur during pregnancy, it will be helpful to examine the medical implications of pregnancy in the sixteenth and seventeeth centuries. Pregnancy at that time was regarded as a more fragile condition that it is today, for at that time pregnancy represented a kind of sickness:

A Woman with Child, in respect of her present Disposition, altho' in good Health, yet ought to be reputed as tho' she were sick, during the neuter Estate (for to be with Child, is also vulgarly called a Sickness of nine Months) because she is then in daily Expectation of many Inconveniences, which Pregnancy causes to those that are not well governed.

Although pregnancy was seen popularly as a time of sickness, physicians did, in fact, consider pregnancy a manifestation of the "neuter Estate." As the terms implies, it represents a state between health and sickness:" . . . But the Physicians term that unhealthy, or morbous state, when some actions of the body are manifestly out of tune; healthy when they persist in a symmetry; but neutral, when they are neither manifestly vitiated, nor altogether whole; such a disposition is evidently apparent in those which are in a tendency to, or in a recovery from a Disease . . . " To use a modern analogy, the neutral condition seems to represent the prodromal state of a viral illness or the period during a bacterial pneumonia just after antibiotic therapy has assisted the patient in overcoming the infection but when he might be particularly vulnerable to reinfection by a resistant organism or virus.

The concept appears, then, that the pregnant woman existed in a condition that balanced precariously between health and sickness that could, if not prevented by good prenatal management, change rapidly into a state of disease with potentially grave consequences for both mother and fetus. Mauriceau provides a clear illustration of how proper prenatal management considered this precarious balance:

She should in this Case resemble a good Pilot, who being imbarked on a rough Sea, and full of Rocks, shuns the Danger, if she steers with Prudence; if not 'tis by Chance if she excapes Shipwreck: So a Woman with Child is often in Danger of her Life, if she doth not her best Endeavor shun and prevent many Accidents to which she is then subject: All which Time Care must be taken of two, to wit, herself and the Child she goes with . . . .

A temperate diet that provided adequate nourishment for the mother and fetus while minimizing digestive difficulties and avoiding foods that might bring on dangerous situations, such as constipation, vomiting, terms and fluxes, served as the foundation of prenatal care. Adequate care also included proper treatment of these potentially dangerous conditions, some of which appeared to be inherent to pregnancy.

Pica, or a depraved appetite, afflicted many pregnant women and seemingly resulted directly from their being pregnant. The most popular hypothesis for its etiology proposed that cessation of the menses in pregnancy engendered evil humors which normally were expelled but now flowed into the stomach. This resulted in a condition in which "the sides and tunicles of the stomacke, and orifice thereof, are infected, and stuffed with divers excrements, and ill humours." It could begin during the first week or as late as the fortieth day after conception, and brought on cravings for vinegar, salty foods, coals, ashes, plaster, sand, chalk, and more. The condition generally lasted until the fourth month of gestation when it ceased for the following reason: " . . . the child is [sic] growne bigger, and having need for mor Nourishment, draws to him a greater quantity of blood the which he consumes: and so by consequent, it turnes backe no more into the stomacke."

Further explanation will make the pathophysiology of this condition clearer. Once the male and female seeds had commingled in the womb in the act of conception, the blood otherwise lost in the menses began nourishing the conceptus in the following manner:

Now this *blood,* presently after conception, is distinguished into three parts: the purest of it drawn by the Child for the nourishment of itself; the second, which is less pure and thin, the *Womb* forces upwards to the breast, where it is turned into milk. The third and most impure part of the *blood* remains in the *Matrix,* and comes away with the *Secondines,* both in the Birth, and after the Birth.

Initially the amount of blood required by the embryo and placenta was less than that normally lost in the menses; the excess blood settled in the stomach, which caused pica. Generally by four months of gestation the fetus and placenta consumed the surplus blood.

Careful selection of diet based on a few general principles comprised the treatment of choice in pica. Above all the diet must be flexible and able to accommodate to the unusual desires that characterize the affliction: "Meat and Drink, tho' not so wholesome, if more acceptable, is to be preferred before that which is wholesome, and not so pleasant: Which in my Opinion is the rule thay ought to observe, provided what they long for, is commonly used for Diet, and not strange and extraordinary Things; and that they have a care of Excess." If allowed to eat coals and the other unusual foods listed above, the pregnant woman subjected herself and her fetus to malnourishment, which could result in abortion. She should include broths made with sorrel, lettuce, succory, borrage, and new-laid eggs, all of which purified the blood "because big-bellied Women have never good Blood . . . She must avoid hot-seasoned Pies and baked Meats, and especially Crust, being hard on Digestion, extremely overchargeth the Stomach." In addition she should augment her meals with a bit of wine diluted with water to enhance digestion and "comfort the stomach, always weak during Pregnancy."

The abundance of humors afflicting the stomach early in pregnancy could also cause vomiting. In addition, vomiting in pregnancy might result from "the ill meats they eat, and that in great quantity, as also because they fill themselves too much with good meat, which doth putrifie and corrupt, (the naturrall heat being weak) and requires rather to bee cast forth, than kept in the body." Both Guillemeau and Mauriceau agreed that this vomiting could and did ensue soon after conception. Because of the short time between conception with cessation of the terms and the onset of vomiting, Mauriceau rejected the above, popular hypothesis that excess humors from the stopped menses caused vomiting. Instead, he attempted to explain the origin of this early vomiting by a nervous connection between the uterus and stomach: " . . . these first Vomitings proceed from the Sympathy between the Stomach and the Womb, because of the Similitude of their Substance, and by means of the Nerves inserted in the upper Orifice of the Stomach, which have Communication by Continuity with those that pass to the Womb, being Portions of the sixth Pair of those of the

Brain . . . ." The irritation of the womb caused by the events of conception produced the stimulus to the stomach responsible for inducing this early vomiting.

Such vomiting, if not too violent, frequent, nor lasting beyond the third or fourth month, benefitted the gravida by casting out those evil humors that induced it and, if applicable, pica. However, continuing longer than four months, vomiting could have the following dangerous effects on the mother and fetus: " . . . The Aliment being daily vomited up, the Mother and the Child having Need of much Blood for their Nourishment, will thereby grow extremely weak, besides the continual Subversion of the Stomach, causing great agitation and Compression of the Mother's Belly, will force the Child before its Time, . . . "

Although the vomiting could not be abolished, its severity and frequency could be reduced by altering the diet. The pregnant woman was to follow the general dietary advice set forth earlier, but to eat smaller amounts more often, since the stomach in pregnancy was thought to be less able to digest larger amounts. Smaller portions of food would also allow the stomach to "contain it without Pain, and not be constrained to vomit it up, as it must when they take too much, because the big Belly hinders the free Extension of it." Juice of citrus fruits with the meal or marmalade of quinces eaten after the meal served to strengthen the stomach. She was to abstain from foods too fat or too sweet, which tended to induce vomiting and soften the membranes of the stomach, already weakened from vomiting. If these measures failed to alleviate excessive vomiting, the evil humors would then have to be dissolved from the lining of the stomach and purged in the stool by drugs.

Some of the other rocks in the rough sea of pregnancy, capable of endangering the pregnant woman and her fetus, included constipation, tenesmus, fluxes, disorders of the womb, and febrile illness during pregnancy. These conditions did not accompany pregnancy seemingly as a natural consequence, as did pica and vomiting, but could develop if she were careless with her diet.

Every midwifery manual consulted agreed that constipation and tenesmus, disorders of different natures, could lead to abortion by the same mechanism of excessive straining at stool. The usual explanation of the etiology of constipation emphasized the effects of the uterus pressing against the large bowel, as in this example: " . . . the guts are pressed by the unevennes of the wombe, which is too full, and being placed upon them, (and chiefly upon the great gut) crushes and thrusts them against another, in such sort, that they have no means to enlarge and dilate themselves, therby to void the excrements contained with them." Other hypotheses included an improper diet that contained frequent use of "meate or fruits which doe exircate or drye, and constraine or binde' and 'all such things as doe harden, restraine, and constipate, as meats broyled or rosted, and Rice, hard egges, beefe, chestnuts, and all sowre fruits, and such like.'' And still another explanation proposed that in pregnancy the heat in the intestines increased and made their contents unusually hard and dry and unable to move easily. The tendency to become more sedentary during pregnancy added to these other effects.

Tenesmus, an ulceration of the rectum, posed an imminent threat of abortion:

... *Tenesmus* [that is perpetual going to the stool and voiding nothing but a little slime] which above all other Diseases is wont to cause Abortion, because by that frequent and almost continual endeavor of going to stool, which perpetually attends this disease, the Muscles of the Belly are perpetually contracted, and do more compress the Womb than the streight Gut upon which the Womb rests; which continual compression or squeezing of the Womb, doth at last cause Abortion.

The preferred treatment for constipation resided in the diet. The pregnant woman was to avoid those constipating foods listed above and eat foods that tended to loosen the bowels, ''which must be done with great discretion: for too much moisture may at length over-much relax the ligaments of the womb, and of the child, and therby hasten the delivery.'' In addition, she was to avoid using strong suppositories, clysters, or drugs to induce an evacuation, for ''if a big-bellied Woman have a violent looseness, she will be in danger of miscarrying.'' The following foods were recommended for her diet: ''Notwithstanding, a woman with child being too costive, may use tender meats, as Veale, wherewith they may make Broths, with Lettuce, Purslane, Sorrell, Spinach, Beets, Buglosse, Violet leaves, and sometimes a little of the herbe called Mercury. Let them use Prunes, and Baked Apples.''

Fear of inducing a flux or looseness of the belly led to the above caution against use of strong suppositories, clysters, or drugs when constipated during pregnancy. Our concept of diarrhea corresponds to a flux of the belly. Depending upon the severity, a flux could be either a lientery, diarrhea, or dysentery:

There are ordinarily reckon'd three sorts of Loosenesses, which in general is a frequent Dejection of what is contained in the Guts, by Stool: The first is called *Lienteria,* by which the Stomach and the Guts, not having digested the Nourishment received, lets is [it] pass almost quite raw. The second is called *Diarrhoea,* by which they simply discharge the Humours and Excrements which they contain. And the third, which is the worst, is *Dysenteria,* by which the Patient, together with the Humours and Excrements, voids Blood with violent Pains, caused by the Ulceration of the Guts.

Tenesmus represented a special case of dysenteria where the ulceration existed only in the rectum.

If any of these fluxes continued for very long, or if violent, the result was the same; the mother's body was unable to absorb adequate nutriment from her food for herself and her fetus. This led to malnutrition of both and eventually to abortion. The added effect of the pregnant woman's straining down to go to stool, which was particularly severe in dysenteria because of the painful ulcerations, further hastened an early delivery.

The bad diet ingested by those unfortunate women afflicted with pica led to the flux of the belly:

Women with great bellies are commonly subject thereto, because of the meats they eat, which are of ill juyce: whereby the stomack being weakned, and not able to concoct them, the expulsive faculty is compel'd to thrust them downward, halfe concocted and indigested: otherwise they are corrupted, and turned into some maligne, sharpe, and biting humors: as into fretting choller, rotten flegme, or melancholy, which doe corrode and stir up the bowels, and cause the flux of the belly.

Initially the flux began as a lientery but could progress to a diarrhea and to a dysentery if not treated adequately.

If the flux were still a lientery caused by a weakened stomach, she was to "abstain from all those irregular Appetites, and accustom herself to good Food of easy Digestion, and a little at a time, that so her strength may be able the easier to concoct and digest it." As in the pica and vomitings, she was encouraged to drink wine diluted with water to comfort her stomach.

If the flux developed into a stubborn diarrhea that was not self-limited with the above diet, she was to purge the evil humors from her intestines by purging medicines. If a dysentery developed, in addition to purging, she was to adopt the following measures designed to breed as few bad humors as possible:

. . . the which may bee easily done by a good dyet, which shall breed as little choller, or other bad humours, as may be: using broths made with Purcelane, Sorrell, Buglosse, and the cold seeds, addition thereto a little Rise, or French Barly. The use of new laid Egges is much commended, which must be epoched in water: Her meat must be rather rost than boiled: All spices are to bee eschewed.

Rivière's *The Universal Body of Physick* explains the qualities of these foods that made them appropriate therapy in this condition. Sorrel, for instance, "helps the hot distemper of the bowels . . . [and] tempers the acrimony of choler." The qualities of rice also demonstrate the rationale of this diet: " . . . and the frequent use thereof by reason of the thicknesse of the substance [rice] begets obstructions, because of the thickning, and binding faculty which it hath; it is very good for such as are subject to bloudy Flixes, Lasks [diarrhea], and other affections proceeding from a defluxion of thin humours."

Uterine disorders could affect the conceptus in two general ways: (1) distempers of the womb could make it inhospitable for gestation, and (2) the persistence of menses could deprive the fetus of needed nourishment which often led to abortion.

A phlegmatic distemper of the womb appeared to have the greatest propensity for abortion by making the uterus so slippery that the conceptus and placenta could not adhere to it: "Or slimie, flegmaticke, and other waterish humors, that the cauitie or hollownes is therby made so slippery, that the feature conceived cannot there remaine, but slippeth and slideth forth againe." Obesity, some felt, also made the uterus too slippery to retain the conceptus. Or, in trying to expel these corrupt humors, the womb would expel the fetus along with them.

Another humoral disorder supposedly affected the cotyledons of the uterus, which were "the vaynes by which the conception and feature is tyed and fastened in the Matrix (thorow the which also the feature receiveth nourishment and food . . .)." These vessels became occluded by corrupt humors and the fetus died from lack of nourishment:" . . . [the cotyledons] be stopped with viscous and ill humours, or else swollen by inflation so that they breake, by the which means the feature, destitute of its wonted nourishment, perisheth and dyeth, and that most commonly in the second or third moneth after conception." None of the authors citing this example offered any evidence to support this mechanism of abortion during the second or third month. The explanation was apparently advanced by Hippocrates to give some understanding to abortions occurring at this time in gestation in young women who were neither overly fat nor thin.

The menses often occurred during the first two or three months after conception in normal pregnancies since the embryo required so little blood at that time. In instances when the pregnant woman had an abundance of blood, the loss of menstrual blood served a beneficial purpose:

If they proceed from the sole Abundance, being more than the Fruit can consume for its Nourishment, it is so far from hurting either Mother or Child, that being moderate, it is very profitable to them; because if the Womb were not discharged of this superfluous Blood, the Fruit, which is as yet but little, would be drowned by it, or, as it were, suffocated. . . .

However, in cases when the woman was weak and thin , or if the menses continued beyond three months or flowed heavily, the blood loss could be great enough that the conceptus would abort for want of adequate nourishment. To prevent this the woman was to rest in bed and eat the following diet:

. . . a strengthening and cooling Diet, feeding on Meat that breeds good Blood, and thickens it; as are good Broths made with Poultry; Necks of Mutton, Knuckles of Veal, in which may be boiled cooling Pot-herbs; new lay'd Eggs, Gellies, Rice-Milk, Barly-broths, which are proper for her: Let her drink the Water in which Iron is quenched, with a little Syrup of Quince. . . .

Diet played a critical role in the treatment of any febrile illness; in that instance a thin diet was felt to diminish the fever. In pregnancy, if the fetus was not killed by the illness, the thin diet might well accomplish the same end. The diet must represent a compromise between adequate treatment of the illness (a thin diet) and adequate nourishment of the fetus (a full diet). During the third trimester this dilemma became most pronounced. The following represents the course pursued in such a situation:

As for Matter of Diet, it is not to women with Child in Acute diseases to be enjoyned to spare, lest the little Infant be famished; neither is it to be allowed so liberal, that the Feaver should be thereby strengthened; but we must steer a middle course, with this Caution, That in the first months of their Belly-burden, a thin Diet be enjoyned, and in the latter somwhat more solid and plentiful, because the Child doth then stand in need of more nourishment. Yet if there must needs be some error in Diet, it is better to err in keeping too ful, than too slender diet; for recovery is chiefly to be expected from the strength of the Mother, and the Child.

In considering the role played by diet in the prenatal care of the sixteenth and seventeenth centuries, certain aspects stand out. Probably the most important of these is the objective of sustaining the pregnancy to produce a healthy baby and mother. According to the current edition of *Williams Obstetrics* the goal remains: "The objective of prenatal care is to insure as far as possible that every pregnancy culminates in a healthy mother and a healthy baby." Our concept of a healthy baby includes the potential for maximal growth and central nervous system development. By focusing on results that can only be realized and evaluated years after birth, these goals imply an assumption that the threat of abortion, in most cases, is minimal. This was not the case three and four centuries ago when the possibility of miscarriage appeared to influence nearly every facet of prenatal care.

A comparison of the understanding in each period of the physiologic state of pregnancy illustrates the nature of this difference. The neutral state, or sickness of nine months, implied a condition highly susceptible to a variety of situations dangerous to the mother and fetus. Today, although there still exist remnants of the earlier view in popular conceptions of pregnancy, obstetricians feel that "*a priori* pregnancy should be considered normal . . . [even though] the myriad changes in the maternal organism during pregnancy sometimes make demarcation between health and disease less distinct." Constipation reflects this fundamental difference in the conception of pregnancy in the two periods. Today we view constipation as a common, uncomfortable accompaniment to pregnancy that can lead to painful hemorrhoids at worst. During the sixteenth and seventeenth centuries, however, constipation represented a dangerous situation believed capable of causing abortion.

The concern with the omnipresent threat of abortion was undoubtedly justified by experience. Although there exist no statistics comparable to our figures of abortion and perinatal mortality in the sixteenth and seventeenth centuries, some records of fetal death were kept. Forbes has determined the rate of "still-born" infants in London during this time by collating this information from the records of the Parish of St. Botolph. He speculates that "still-born" included "fetuses dying at any time during pregnancy as well as at term." From 1584 through 1598 there were 124.2 stillbirths for every 1,000 christenings; from 1609 through 1623 the rate was 44.6. The higher death rate in the earlier period probably reflects the effects of the plague in 1592-93. In the United States in 1963 there were 23.0 fetal deaths regardless of gestational age per 1,000 live births.

This justified regard for miscarriage tended to produce a strong emphasis on diet as a preventive measure. It seems clear that sixteenth and seventeenth century authors believed that fluxes, constipation, and many instances of vomiting and uterine disorders, all of which resulted from humoral imbalances, could be prevented by following the proper diet. Strong association between fetal nutrition, the stimulus for labor, and abortion certainly strengthened this prophylactic role for diet.

Diet was also essential in managing specific disorders during pregnancy. Several of these disorders, including vomiting, fluxes of the belly, and uterine distempers, could arise from dietary indiscretions. Others, such as pica and some cases of vomiting, seemed to result from humoral disorders brought on by pregnancy itself. Dietary treatment in all of these disorders included attempts to restore the humoral balance and to exploit the characteristics of specific foods to alleviate a dangerous condition, as with the use of rice in treating a dysentery.

Seen within the rigid confines of the humoral theory of disease, the use of diet in prenatal management in the sixteenth and seventeenth centuries reflected a rational use of food in preventing and treating dangerous situations in pregnancy. Within this system diet represented the primary means to maintain humoral balance and to rectify states of imbalance. Given the conception of pregnancy as a finely balanced condition in a system that not only saw disease as the manifestation of humoral imbalance, but also saw insufficient fetal nourishment as the stimulus to initiate labor, diet assumed the central role in prenatal care. The obstetrical literature of the time reflected this role by emphasizing the preventative nature of a proper prenatal diet in avoiding these situations that could lead to abortion. In addition it showed the important role diet assumed in treating those medical disorders that could lead to abortion.

## 4. Childbearing Among English Puritans

by R.V. Schnucker

The breeding, bearing, and bringing up of children was of such a serious matter for Puritans that one of their ministers, Thomas Gataker, who lost two of his four wives as a result of complicated childbirths, warned the unmarried woman in his book *A Wife Indeed* to recognize the requirements and consequences of being a wife and mother. The soundness of his warning is revealed in a letter of autumn 1626, in which Mary Proud wrote of Anne Faversham who had given birth to a daughter and almost died from hemorrhaging. Another example of the sensitivity to the dangers of childbirth was expressed by Elizabeth Jocelin. After her marriage when she was twenty-seven and pregnant, having never suffered a sick day in her life, and after having felt the first movement of the foetus, she secretly bought a new winding sheet. Elizabeth died as her child was born. The fate of

Elizabeth brings our attention to pre- and post-natal knowledge and attitudes among English Puritans, specifically pregnancy, delivery, and breast feeding. The first part to be discussed in this paper is their knowledge concerning conception and their attitude toward pregnancy.

The Puritans did not understand the process of conception. For example, it was taught that the male child was conceived on the right side of the womb as the result of plentiful sperm issuing forth from the right testicle of the man. Female children came from the left testicle of the man and were conceived on the left side of the womb. The Puritans reasoned that the male was hot and the liver, the source of the hot moist blood and on the right side, provided the proper environment and position for the conception of male children. Females who were cold would be conceived on the left cooler side of the womb. It was believed that the age of the parents and the quality of their "seed" affected the ultimate character of the child. For example, the children of old men seldom had a good temperament for ". . . old men beget most part wayward, peevish, sad, melancholy sons, and seldom merry." Those men who engaged in coitus when the stomach was full, would father children who would be either sick or crazy; a drunken man causing conception would father a brainless child; ". . . foolish, drunken, or haire-brain women, most part bring forth children like unto themselves . . . " Those men who ate great quantities of garlic or onions or who fasted inordinately, or studied too hard would make their children subject to madness and melancholy for ". . . if the spirits of the brain be fusted . . . at such time, their children will be fusted in the brain: they will be dull, heavy, discontented all their lives." If a woman at the time of her conception thought of another man, the child to be born would be like him; similarly during pregnancy, by desiring something intensely or by being scared, the mother could cause moles, warts, hare-lips, monsters, and scars on the unborn child.

Signs of pregnancy given by one medical writer included the following: if a woman drank cold water and her breasts became cold, she was apparently pregnant. If the woman's urine was poured over barley seed and it sprouted after ten days, she had conceived. If a man felt a sucking at the end of this penis during coitus, the woman was pregnant. A woman had conceived if she took great sexual delight in her husband; if her stomach became flat; if she suffered from morning sickness; if her menstrual period stopped; if her breasts swelled; if she felt movement of the foetus.

William Gouge, a famous Puritan clergyman, charged the mother with the major responsibility for pre-natal care. The first age of a child was its infancy, he wrote, and the first part of the infancy was while the child was in the mother's womb. As soon as a woman realized she was pregnant, she ought to have special care about herself so that the child would go full term and be safely delivered. His reason for this was " . . . the child being lodged in her, and receiving nourishment from her (as plants from the

earth) her well-being tends much to the good and safety of the child . . . ''
If the suggestions made by Gouge and many of the medical manuals were
followed, then the pre-natal care was basically sound by modern standards.
The suggestions consisted of a good diet, moderate exercise, and a helpful
husband.

The diet was to be substantial but minus spicy and salty foods. The diet
was to include bread made of good wheat well baked; meat consisting of
chicken, capon, young pidgeons, turtle, pheasant, veal, mutton; any kind
of fruit preferably at the end of the meal; starchy foods such as peas and
beans were to be avoided. Exercise was to be moderate and the woman was
to avoid running, leaping, dancing, and riding long distances in wagons and
coaches. Rueff told the pregnant woman to be cheerful and to get sufficient
rest. During pregnancy, there was often a desire for strange foods; this was
called the "longing for Pica" and various causes were assigned to this desire
such as the growth of the child's hair, or the time of the new moon, or the
vomit of a newly pregnant woman. The pregnant woman's dress was to be
light and comfortable and she was to avoid lacing herself tightly to match
the fashions. Under no circumstances was blood letting to occur, particularly if the foetus had grown large because it had more need of good
nourishment than it had required earlier. In the event the pregnancy became
burdensome for the woman due to the size of the edema, it was recommended that a sling be devised that would keep her from having too much
pain and would keep the skin from stretching too much.

The husband was advised to treat his pregnant wife kindly, to use his utmost to ease her pain, discomfort, and needs with sweet and loving words.
Gouge told his male readers to be very tender with their wives and helpful to
them for they owed such help and tenderness to their wives and children.

Today when the practice of midwifery in America has practically become
a lost art, how many wives could go next door to help their neighbor in
delivery as Richard Oxinden's wife did for her neighbor Mrs. Francis
Tilghman in the early seventeenth century? In the world of the English
Puritans there were no sterile hospitals into which mothers could enter for
delivery; there were no medically trained obstetricians surrounded by
various modern devices that would make delivery easier and safer. Delivery
in the Puritan's world would usually take place in the bed in which the conception also had occurred; those in attendance were neighbor women or
relatives knowledgeable in the art of midwifery; and no anaesthetics were
available to assuage the pains of labor and birth. If complications
developed and a caesarian delivery was necessary, it was performed only
upon dead women or those sure to die. The more experienced midwives
were licensed by bishops since they had the authority to baptize a newly
born infant if its chances for survival were not good. The bishop's license
apparently meant the midwife knew the proper formula for the sacrament
of baptism and that her character was generally good.

The custom of the time was to send for the midwife and a few responsible women of the neighborhood to aid the pregnant woman when time for delivery was imminent. There were two reasons for more than one or two women to be present; first they functioned as witnesses for the birth of the child; second, they would learn about delivery and could thus disseminate this information among other women for any of them might be called upon in an emergency to help deliver a child.

The skill of the midwife depended a great deal upon her experience and ability to glean helpful information from some of the works available to her that dealt with childbirth. Not a great deal was available in written form in England until the early seventeenth century when some French works were translated into English. This paucity of written information was partly due to the attitude that childbirth was a mystery reserved for the observation of women only; thus male physicians were excluded from the delivery room. It was not until the Chamberlains, the innovators of the forceps, came to England that much of an effort was made in England by male physicians to enter the area of obstetrics. As late as 1658, Dr. Willoghby, called to advise a midwife about a difficult delivery had to creep into the delivery room on hands and knees and then had to examine the laboring woman while she was covered in a semi-lighted room. Upon finishing the examination, he had to crawl out of the room and consult the midwife in the hallway. When difficuilties in delivery occurred, the outcome was not pleasant to contemplate. Boaistuau made this painfully clear in his description of what might happen:

> But that which is more cruel, and that we cannot apprehend with out horror, is, that sometimes they be forced to call Chirurgians, Mediciners, and Barbars, instead of wise Matrons and mid-wives, to dismember the children and pull them out by pieces, and sometime it behoveth to open the poor innocent mother alive, and put iron tools in her body, yea to murder her, for to have her fruit.

By 1637 at least two French works were available in English that could have served as valuable guides for the midwives. *The Expert Midwife* by Jacob Rueff was published in 1736 while a quarter of a century earlier, *Childbirth* by Jacques Guillimeau had been published. Both translators of these works apologized to the female reader for intruding into her sanctuary. Yet they were concerned about the lack of information among the midwives. The translator of Guillimeau's work asked, was it better for millions to perish through want of help and information or that " . . . such means which though lawful in themselves, yet may by some be abused, should be had and used?"

The above books said that a midwife should possess certain qualities. She was to be beyond the age of child-bearing, but neither too young nor too old. She was to be healthy and have no diseases nor be deformed in any part. She was to be neat in her dress and in her person. Her hands were to be small with nails pared and very clean and even. She was not to wear rings when she was about her business. She was to have a pleasant and merry disposition and accustomed to hard work so that if necessary she could stay awake two or three nights. She was not to be gossipy nor report anything she might hear or see in the privacy of the childbirth room.

There were three ways in which childbirth took place: squatting, supine, or sitting. Rueff recommended the birth stool while Guillimeau preferred the supine position in a bed. The Puritans and their Anglican colleagues had nothing to say about which position was better or worse, or which had more theological signification or was an archetype of this or that in the Scripture.

The birth stool was similar to a very sturdy chair with a strong back and the most of the seat cut away so that the remaining part was in the form of a new moon. Around the bottom was draped black cloth and the seat covered with cloths so that the woman would not be bruised and neither would the child as the two of them moved about in the process of labor. As the labor pains became more frequent and birth was imminent, the woman was placed on the stool, the midwife stationed another woman behind the back of the stool to better hold down the laboring woman. Two other women were stationed at either side of the stool to hold her arms as the pains became greater and more rapid. Then the midwife knelt before the laboring woman and after having greased her hands with a concoction of the oil of lilies, sweet almonds, and hens grease or some other ointment, she reached into the vagina to determine the opening of the cervix and the closeness of the birth as well as the position of the child. If necessary, the midwife gently stretched open the mouth of the womb and helped to direct the child's entry into the world being careful not to let the child drop to the floor. As soon as the child had emerged, the midwife cut the umbilical cord and bound it and wrapped the child to keep it warm. The midwife then returned to the new mother and helped with the afterbirth. The midwives were very much aware of the necessity of the expulsion of the afterbirth and had various prescriptions to aid in this process such as seven pills of ungentum bascilicum.

The same basic process was followed if the woman was in the supine position, a woman at each side, the midwife standing at the foot of the bed ready to aid in receiving the child. Both men suggested a kind of breath control that would aid in labor but only to be used as the mouth of the womb was opened. Guillimeau gave his instructions concerning this to the midwife this way:

> when her throws come upon her making them double and increase, by
> holding in her breath and stopping her mouth and forming herself, as
> though she would go to the stool, which is much fitter for her to do

then to lie crying and lamenting.

The clearest explanation of a normal birth and the more detailed instructions were found in Guillimeau's work. Rueff's work went into more detail with illustrations of how to handle abnormal births. He even included drawings of various tools, such as the forceps, that could be used in aiding the birth of the child. Many of these techniques with modern refinements are still used in hospitals today.

Although the Puritans said nothing theological about the technique of delivery, they did have a good deal to say about the labor pains that accompanied birth. Bullinger, often the precursor of many Puritan attitudes on human sexuality, stated the woman must put her trust in God and gladly suffer labor pain because it was a cross placed upon her by God as the result of Eve's sin. He quoted I Timothy 2.15 where it stated that woman brought sin into the world but her honor could be recovered by the bearing of children; thus " . . . should Christian wives remember in all their cross and to be glad willing and of a good courage therein." In his *New Catechism,* Becon took the same stance; labor pain was due to the first sin and was a means for women to redeem themselves. This idea was not unique to England. In 1574 John Alday translated and had published Boaistuau's *The Theatre or Rule of the World* and in this work, Boaistuau declared that if a man would consider carefully all the misery and pain of birth, he would find in it the truth of an old proverb: ". . . we are conceived in filth and uncleanness, born in sin and care, and nourished with pain and labor." He went on to state that man's entrance into the world was bathed with blood and pain ". . . which is nothing else but the image and figure of sin . . . " The curse of the woman turned into a double blessing said Smith, when she suffered the pangs of childbirth. First she brought forth a child, the first blessing in Scripture, and second she had salvation through the labor process. This redemptive quality of labor pain appeared also in a prayer written by Samuel Hieron. The prayer was to be used when the labor was about to begin or while it was in progress.

> O Lord, I now find my experience the truth and certainty of thy word, and the smart of the punishment which thou layest upon me being in the loins of my Grandmother Eve, for my disobedience towards thee. Thou hast greatly increased the sorrows of our sex, and our bearing of children is full of pain . . . Make me still to lift up my Soul unto thee in my greatest anguish knowing that thou alone must give a blessing to the ordinary means for my safe delivery.

While men were seldom allowed into the room where birth was taking place, they had a healthy respect for what was going on. Gouge for example instructed the husband to provide for his wife during the time of her delivery for she could not provide for herself in her pain. Gouge envisioned labor pain to be the greatest that ordinarily was endured by any. The pain was manifested by screeches, outcries which came not only from weak and faint-hearted women but also ". . . are forced from the strongest, the stoutest woman that be, and that though before hand they resolve to the contrary." Perhaps this reflected Gouge's own experience while he paced the floor outside the room where his wife was giving birth; his wife gave birth to thirteen children, the last one in 1624, two years after the publication of *Domestical Duties,* and she died as the result of this complicated pregnancy and childbirth. Richard Rogers during the painful labor of his wife's first delivery, reflected upon what was happening and what he would do if she died as a consequence of the birth; he paused again during her next childbirth. Perhaps he had in mind a situation similar to that described by Lucy Hutchinson. She recalled that a relative of her husband had given birth to twins but the birth was so difficult that the young mother went insane. Although the Puritans thought of childbirth with labor pain as justifiable, it was still a time of fear and trembling for both husband and wife. Research concerning the aristocracy has born this out; mortality among aristocratic women was high, with 45% dying before fifty years of age and one-fourth of them from the complications of childbirth.

One of the reasons for numerous women in the birth room was to serve as witness. Some mothers, having given birth alone, abandoned their newly born baby in a convenient place so that it would become a ward of a parish, or killed the child and disposed of it. It was commonly believed that a woman would not tell a lie while in the midst of labor. The witnesses would note if the father was proclaimed to be someone other than the husband, or in the instance of an unmarried mother, the man named was then to care for the child's support. The consequences of bastardy were serious in a land where inheritance laws were followed strictly and only legitimate children could inherit. As Agrippa said in 1534: "For he is base born, and is the son of the people, yea rather the son of no man, which is the child of a woman not lawfully married." Even in cases of bastardy when the parents were prosecuted with the punishment involving public repentance and whippings, it still was hard to control. In Wiltshire in 1578, there were eighty-four cases of bastardy that came before the court. Perhaps this was why Barnaby Rych wrote this sarcastic comment: "She that hath born a bastard to a man of note, she thinks it to be no blemish at all to her reputation; nay, she thinks the better of herself."

## 5. Comparative Family Sizes

by Robert V. Wells

Many of the effects that the colonial marriage patterns had on American society in the seventeenth and eighteenth centuries are of considerable interest. But none is of greater concern than the relationship between the patterns of marriage and the size of colonial families. On average, the size of families in the colonies tended to be larger than those found in contemporary European populations, as the information in Table I shows. In this

TABLE I

FAMILY SIZE
(COMPARISONS)

| Study by | Before 1700 | 1700-1749 | 1750-1799 |
|---|---|---|---|
| | | AMERICA | |
| Completed Families | | | |
| Demos -- Plymouth | 8.6 | --- | --- |
| Greven -- Andover | 8.7 | 7.5 | --- |
| Freeman | --- | 7.2 | 6.8 |
| Henripin -- Canada | --- | 8.4 | --- |
| Wells -- Quakers | --- | 7.5 | 6.2 |
| Children per Wife | | | |
| Wells -- Quakers | --- | 6.7 | 5.7 |
| Henripin -- Canada | --- | 5.7 | --- |
| Crum | 7.4 | 6.8 | 6.4 |
| Engelmann | 6.4 | 6.6 | 6.1 |
| Jones | 5.8 | 5.9 | 6.1 |
| Sage | 5.9 | 6.9 | 6.0 |
| | | EUROPE | |
| Children per Wife | | | |
| Gautier and Henry -- Crulai | --- | 4.0 | --- |
| Ganiage -- Ile-de-France | --- | --- | 5.2 |
| Hollingsworth -- British Peers | 4.6 | 4.2 | 4.9 |
| Knodel -- Bavaria | --- | 5.0 | 5.0 |

table, family size refers to the total number of children born to a particular couple. In the case of completed families, in which the marriage remained intact until the wife had reached the age of forty-five, and hence had normally completed her childbearing, the average number of children born to a couple ranged from a high of 8.7 in Andover, Massachusetts, in the seventeenth century, to a low of 6.2 among the Quakers of this study whose childbearing occurred at the end of the eighteenth century. Apparently, couples who lived together until the wife was at least forty-five could expect an average of between 7 and 9 children, though the number may have fallen slightly by the end of the period under consideration. The figures for the average number of children born per wife, including those families in which childbearing was curtailed by the death of one spouse before the wife was forty-five, naturally are somewhat smaller. Nevertheless, most colonial couples apparently could expect an average of 6 to 7 children in the course of their marriage. As was the case with the marriage patterns, family size in Canada was much the same as in the English colonies.

In contrast, European families appear to have been considerably smaller. The largest average family size listed in Table I was 5.2 children among the French of the Ile-de-France in the late eighteenth century; the smallest families were those found in Crulai, in France, in the early eighteenth century, where a couple might expect only 4.0 children on average. These figures are in agreement with the standard recently suggested for France in the eighteenth century of between 4 and 5 children per family. A study of families in a Bavarian village indicates an average of 5 children per couple throughout the eighteenth century. In England, the situation was much the same. The average family size of the British peerage was well below the number of children born to colonial couples. A study using a different definition of family size points to the same conclusion regarding the population of England as a whole, namely, that English families were smaller than American families before 1800. By dividing the total number of persons listed in various censuses by the number of households mentioned in the same documents, Peter Laslett has found that English families averaged about 4.75 persons in the seventeenth and eighteenth centuries. This figure is considerably below corresponding average "family sizes" for various American populations. In Bristol, Rhode Island, the average family size as calculated from a census taken in 1689 was 5.99; Massachusetts families in 1764 and Rhode Island families in 1774 both averaged 5.8 persons; and the first United States census counted 5.7 persons for every family in 1790. Clearly colonial couples had more children on average than did their European counterparts.*

---

*(Ed. note) Subsequent studies of the Chesapeake colonies show a much lower childbearing rate there, about half the New England average.

In seeking to explain the larger colonial families, one thinks first of the possibility that American women had children more often than did wives on the other side of the Atlantic. But the evidence in Table II indicates that childbearing in America occurred at much the same rate as it did in Europe in the period under study. Wives who lived in the seventeenth and eighteenth centuries could expect to have a child every 24 to 30 months on average, regardless of whether they lived in America or Europe. The French

TABLE II

BIRTH INTERVALS
(COMPARISONS)

| Study by | Length of Interval Between Births in Months |
|---|---|
| **AMERICA** | |
| Demos -- Plymouth (Before 1700) | 24. |
| Greven -- Andover (1705-1724) | 26.5 |
| Lockridge -- Dedham (1636-1736) | 29. |
| Jones (1651-1800) | 30. |
| Wells -- Quakers (a. 1650-1830) | 27.7 |
| Henripin -- Canada (1700-1730) | 23.3 |
| **EUROPE** | |
| Wrigley -- Colyton (1720-1769) | 29.1 |
| Ganiage -- Ile-de-France (1740-1800) | 25.2 |
| Gautier and Henry -- Crulai (1674-1742) | 27.3 |
| Goubert -- Beauvais (1600-1730) | 29. |

wives of the Ile-de-France and Crulai actually had a shorter interval between births *and smaller families* than did the Quakers studied above. Although the data are not strictly comparable, it is clear that in at least one part of Bavaria families were smaller than those found in America in spite of a birth interval of under 24 months. Apparently, the difference in size between European and American families was not the result of more rapid childbearing in the colonies.

By marrying younger and remaining married longer than was common in Europe, wives in the colonies were able to have more children than their English and French contemporaries. Since a higher proportion of women married in the colonies than in Europe, the effects of the larger colonial family size on the birth rate was enhanced. For this reason then, and for others which remain to be explored, the distinct patterns of marriage which seem to have existed in America before 1800 were of considerable importance in determining the character of colonial society.

## 6. In The Increasing Way In The South

by Julia C. Spruill

The pregnancies of great ladies were sometimes announced in colonial newspapers and the "delicate situation," lying-in, and delivery of ladies were among the most frequently mentioned topics in social correspondence. We find Margaret Calvert, sister-in-law of the fifth Lord Baltimore, writing her niece in Maryland: "I am Extreamly glad to hear ye Ladys are all brought safe to bed but here you are most of you in the way again I am sure I sincerely wish you all a happy minute"; and Rebecca Dinwiddie, wife of the governor of Virginia, addressing the wife of the Reverend Thomas Dawson, president of William and Mary: "I do assure you will give me pleasure to hear . . . Mrs. Harrison is well recovered from her lying in: tho by the time you gett this she may be in the way again, if so I sincerely wish her health . . . " A letter of Andrew Miller to his friend Thomas Burke of Halifax, North Carolina, declares his wife "is now confirmed of her Pregnancy," and another hopes that by the time Mr. and Mrs. Burke can visit him "Mrs. Miller will be in the Straw and restored to her former Temper, which is what she Seldom has during the months of Pregnancy." Among the news related by a Carolina gentlewoman to a gentleman friend and neighbor then in England was this: "Mrs. Thos. Hooper bro't to bed, and her child dead. . . . Mrs. George—of the name—(Enceinte) again." The lively letters of Molly Tilghman contain many allusions to Maryland ladies with "a blessed prospect" or "in that way," and the many confinements of the Charles Town ladies are recorded faithfully in Mrs. Manigault's journal.

Among well-to-do ladies, lying-in appears to have been treated as somewhat of a ceremony expected to take place at more or less regular intervals. Every wife had her "child-bed linen," which was usually as handsome as her circumstances would afford. Shopkeepers advertised "suits of Childbed Linen" and "quilted Satin Childbed Baskets and Pincushions" along with their "elegant" jewelry and millinery. So valuable was this equipment that it was quite often bequeathed in wills and sometimes presented as a gift. Frederick Jones of North Carolina, for example, bequeathed his eldest daughter "all her Mothers Child bede Linnen with white silk Damask Gown," and Mary Atkins of Charles Town in South Carolina left a kinswoman her "best Gowne and petticoate" and all her "childbed linen and all other Cloaths belongeing to a Child." In a seventeenth-century Maryland letter, we find a gentlewoman writing of having presented as a wedding present to her cousin "a suett of laced child bed linnen."

Among the superstitions of the period was the notion that a pregnant woman was likely to miscarry if denied what she "longed for." In the minutes of the General Court of Virginia for 1625 is a case involving a complaint by Elizabeth Hamer against Dr. Pott for denying her a piece of hog flesh, thus causing her miscarriage. The judges' opinion was that the doctor's action was not criminal since he had no way of knowing "she had A longing to it." Whether this belief was widespread we do not know, but that some women continued to take advantage of it years later appears in a letter in *The Spectator,* March 14, 1711/12, in which the writer complains of the extravagant "longings" of his wife. "To trouble you only with a few of them," he writes, "when she was with child of Tom, my eldest son, she came home one day just fainting, and told me she had been visiting a relation, whose husband had made her a present of a chariot and a stately pair of horses; and that she was positive she could not breathe a week longer, unless she took the air in the fellow to it of her own within that time. This, rather than lose an heir, I readily complied with. Then the furniture of her best room must be instantly changed, or she should mark the child with some of the frightful figures in the old-fashioned tapestry. Well, the upholsterer was called, and her longing saved that bout. When she went with Molly she had fixed her mind upon a new set of plate, and as much china as would have furnished an Indian shop: these also I cheerfully granted, for fear of being father to an Indian pagod. . . . What her next sally will be I cannot guess. . . . This exceeds the grievance of pin-money; and I think in every settlement there ought to be a clause inserted, that the father should be answerable for the longings of his daughter."

The wives of the well-to-do as well as of the poorer sort customarily "lay in" at their own homes attended by the neighborhood midwife. Toward the close of the period physicians came more and more to be called in, but many persons still considered the employment of a man-midwife a breach of female modesty. Others felt that while the experienced but unlearned midwife was capable of taking care of the great majority of cases, scientific assistance should be available in case of unusual developments. Thomas Jefferson's advice to his depressed and fearful young daughter illustrates the attitude of the most progressive. "Take care of yourself, my dearest Maria, have good spirits, and know that courage is as essential to triumph in your case as in that of a soldier," he wrote at one time, and a few weeks later advised: "Some female friend of your mamma's (I forgot whom) used to say it was no more than a jog of the elbow. The material thing is to have scientific aid in readiness, that if any thing uncommon takes place it may be redressed on the spot, and not be made serious by delay. It is a case which least of all will wait for doctors to be sent for; therefore with this single precaution nothing is ever to be feared." Despite his reassurance, however, Jefferson was afraid. Well he might be. Not many years before he had been in "perpetual solicitude" about Maria's mother, who, after bearing six children in ten years, had died shortly after the birth of the last. For Maria, too, childbirth was more than a "jog of the elbow," for she never recovered from the ordeal which she had feared so pathetically.

Among rich and poor, mother frequently died in childbed. Many notices like the following appear in the newspapers:

> On the 22d of January, Died in Child-Birth, in the 33rd Year of her Age, Mrs. Sarah Carlyle, Wife of Col. John Carlyle, Merchant in *Alexandria,* and Daughter of the late Honourable William Fairfax, Esq: President of Virginia. . . .

> Of a Miscarriage of Twins, on the 10th Instant, died here, in the 24th Year of her age, one of the most pious and accomplished young Women in these Parts, in the Person of Mrs.Calhoun, the Wife of Patrick Calhoun, Esq: and Daughter of the Rev. Mr. Alexander Craighead.

Women married young, often suffered continuous ill health thereafter, and all too frequently, before reaching middle age, succumbed to the strain of incessant childbearing. Tombstone inscriptions like the following witness the cruel and fatal strain placed upon the womanhood of the time:

> Underneath / lies what was mortal of / Mrs. Margaret Edwards / Wife of Mr. John Edwards, Merchant of this place / Daughter of Mr. Alexander Peronneau, Gent / She died / in Travail with her tenth Child / Age 34 years and about 4 months / a Sincere, modest and humble Christian / . . . She committed her Soul to Him whom she ardently loved / and died without fear or a groan / Augt 27th, 1772.

The colonial wife and her husband asked not if these tragedies might be prevented, but accepted them as part of the divine plan to which they must bow uncomplainingly. This attitude is illustrated in the private papers of Henry Laurens, in which he writes of the protracted illness, frequent confinements, and finally the death in childbed of his sincerely beloved wife. Mrs. Laurens' life was not unlike that of many gentlewomen. She married in 1750 at nineteen and during the next twenty years bore twelve children, seven of whom were buried before her. In November, 1764, her husband was writing that it had been a "year of sorrows; a dead eldest daughter, a sick and dying wife." She continued in a "precarious state," but continued to bear babies for the grave, "suffering extremely," according to one of her husband's letters, "notwithstanding her exemplary patience and meekness." In October, 1768, he wrote that Mrs. Laurens was "confined to her chamber (as usual once in the round of a twelve-month) under the mortifying reflections which arise from the loss of a fine girl." Laurens' biographer suggests that Mr. Laurens ought himself to have felt some mortification at being in a position to write a parenthesis like that. But Laurens, like colonial husbands, felt no responsibility in such matters. When another eighteen months rolled around, he was writing of the birth of a little girl, adding, "but I have been too deeply affected by the mother's deep distress to take any notice of it." A few weeks later his weary wife finally closed her life, leaving the baby girl who was herself to die in childbed twenty-two years later. Laurens suffered real anguish, but in the spirit of the age submitted to this "stroke of Providence."

Many mothers, like Mrs. Laurens, laid down their lives to bring forth children only for the grave. The rate of infant mortality was shockingly great. Wills of the period show surprisingly few large families, yet other records give evidence of many births. Many small graves in churchyards and burying grounds explain the difference. This tombstone inscription tells a story often repeated:

In memory of

HELEN daughter of EBENEZER and ELIZABETH STOTT, who departed this life . . . aged one year and three weeks. Of another daughter . . . who died three days after her birth, and of five others of their infants still born. . . . "

In the Friends' Burying Ground at Charleston, South Carolina, lie seven children of Thomas and Isabella Sikes, all buried between 1751 and 1765, and in the Congregational Churchyard are inscriptions marking the graves of five children of William and Sabina Ellis, all born and buried between 1753 and 1765.

Even among the most intelligent and well-to-do, the loss of a large number of children was expected, and like the death of mothers was accepted as the will of Providence. William Fitzhugh wrote his brother in 1686: "God Almighty hath been pleased to bless me with a very good wife and five pledges of our conjugal affection, three of which he has been pleased to call into the Arms of his Mercy, and lent me two, a hopefull boy and girle, and one other that . . . is preparing to come into the world." Thomas Chalkley, the famous Quaker preacher, after burying nine of his children, wrote soon after the death of his tenth: "It was some exercise to me thus to bury my children one after another; but this did a little mitigate my sorrow, that I knew . . . it was safer and better for them, and they more out of danger, being taken away in their infancy and innocency. . . . "

Six of Major Lewis Burwell's fifteen children preceded him to the grave, and eight of Colonel James Gordon's fourteen died in infancy. Only two of Jefferson's six children reached maturity, and only one of these survived him. All four children of Lawrence Washington, older brother of George Washington, died as infants; Charles Carroll of Carrollton lost four of his seven children; Nathaniel Barnwell of South Carolina lost six of his fourteen in infancy; and Henry Laurens survived all but three of his twelve or fourteen. The family Bible of the Grimballs of South Carolina tells a story of the distressing waste of womanhood not very uncommon in all the colonies. Isaac Grimball married in 1734 and had six children, three of whom died in infancy. His wife died and he married again in 1747 and had three children, only one of whom survived him. His son John married six wives, three of whom died in childbirth. Of his nine children, five were stillborn, two died as infants, and of the remaining two it is not known whether they survived their father.

Considerably more appears in the records concerning childbearing than child rearing. A rather general notion seems to have been that she was the best mother who bore the greatest number of children. Ladies' books and magazines contained volumes of advice on how to make a pudding or how to treat a husband, but were usually silent on the subject of child training.

# 4

# Childrearing

## A. INFANCY

## 1. Introduction

Infancy is the first stage of the life cycle. The human life cycle is a concept of the stages of human development describing the changes which occur in life from birth to death. Implicit to this concept is the belief that each stage of life carries its own unique characteristics, including also the potential for change into the next stage. Thus, after infancy comes childhood, then youth, and so on. The term infancy can be found in a variety of sources from ancient and European history. During the early modern era, writers, including pedagogues, religious leaders and physicians, were well acquainted with the stage of infancy. Indeed, even the parish records in England dating from at least the 15th century separately recorded deaths of infants.

The concept of infancy during the early modern era, however, did not include a precise age for termination. The writers mentioned above appeared more preoccupied with the characteristics of the infant stage and took one of its traits as the clue or crisis point for the transition into the next stage, that of childhood. Either weaning, teething, or talking would be the one variable which would signal the arrival of childhood and the end of infancy. Thus, there appears to have been a variety of conceptions about the exact duration of the infancy period, although no controversy about its beginning point, that of birth.

At birth the infant came under the control of his patients, who were legally responsible for its well-being. The law recognized this obligation by making infanticide a crime as well as requiring an investigation if infant death appeared to stem from other than natural causes, as in cases of smothering. It was also a common law misdemeanor to neglect or expose a young child in one's care so as to cause it serious harm. The protection of infants included the requirement that local parishes provide parental surrogates if the parents of an abandoned infant could not be found. Moreover, religious authorities involved themselves with the welfare of infants and exerted pressure on parents to have their newborn babies baptized. This was considered a prerequisite for their entering the church and heaven.

There are other historical sources which demonstrate that there existed an interest in infant well-being. The prescriptive literature of the 16th-18th centuries, for example, urged mothers to nurse their own infants in order to enhance their physical and moral development. These prescriptions were responses to the perceived needs and vulnerabilities of infancy and serve to provide an insight into the contemporary attitude towards infants.

The articles included in this infancy section are primarily concerned with the particular characteristics and needs of infants from the perspective of the early modern period. The topics discussed are the manner in which an infant should derive nourishment, the plasticity of the newborn and the problems related to infant mortality. It should be noted that infant care in the early modern period was not devoid of controversy. Despite the broad agreement that there were distinguishable infant characteristics, advice literature reflected a variety of opinions about what kind of adult response was necessary to enhance the infant's proper development.

Death was a constant feature of the early modern world. Infants were particularly vulnerable because they had not yet built up an immunity to illnesses, to diseases, to infection or to the periodic plagues. Their vulnerability was especially acute during times of extreme food shortages, when their death rates rose very sharply. Selections by Peter Laslett and J.D. Chambers are included in this chapter in order to introduce the demography of infant mortality. Laslett estimates the rate of infant mortality while Chambers explores some of its causes. They include the purposeful killing of infants and death by parent neglect, as reflected in the shipping of infants to nursing farms whereby the travel itself or the inadequate wet-nursing would often result in death. Although Chambers claims the number of deaths in these areas were probably insignificant in comparison to death due to natural causes, his conclusions seem unprovable since the numbers are difficult to establish with certainty.

Infant death due to parental neglect or murder, however, draws our attention to the helplessness of the newborn and to the harsh world that awaited him if he survived. The question of why mothers neglected their infants so that they died, or whether some even committed infanticide has stirred conflicting opinions among historians. Some have suggested each was a form of birth control practiced by those who could not afford an increase of their families, while others have pointed to a more general lack of parental concern, since such deaths occurred among classes who could well care for their infants.

From at least the 12th century in England, the ideal, however, was for the mother to nurse her baby rather than to relegate this necessity to a stranger, the wet nurse. As the article by Schnucker demonstrates, 17th-century English Puritans took up this cause to convince mothers of the significance of nursing their own infants. Puritans believed in the generally prevailing idea that human milk transmitted character traits to the infants, and that nursing generated a close feeling of love between the mother and child. Since most people writing on the subject of infant feeding seemed to have accepted the belief that good milk was necessary for proper character development, it was urged that if a wet nurse were to be chosen, careful selection was necessary. Such a belief carried the corresponding view that infants were pliable and required the correct ingredients in order to mature along the desirable path.

The pliability of the newborn is one of the most ancient and pervasive notions about the infancy stage. Although various writers had different views as to whether infants were inherently good, evil or born with a *tabula rasa* (blank mind), all agreed with the proposition that the way an infant was cared for and socialized would bear great weight on the way it would develop in the subsequent stages of life. The literature on proper infant care and education is not a modern invention. Greeks like Plato, Aristotle, and Hippocrates; medieval Europeans such as St. Augustine and St. Thomas Aquinas and early modern Europeans, as for example, Erasmus, Vives, Thomas More, and John Locke, all contributed their views on the significance of infancy as the stage in which education should be initiated.

Despite these prescriptive values, however, it is generally assumed by Schnucker that women who could afford to hire a wet nurse did so. It is impossible to reconstruct why women hired or sent their infants to wet nurses. Schnucker, however, suggests some influencing factors such as the attitude of husbands, who might have induced their wives not to breast-feed, and the general responsibilities of wives to their household, which required much time and effort. Both these explanations point to a different set of priorities of the wife and mother during the early modern period from what is generally associated with maternity in the modern time. Although many new mothers in the modern era might not nurse their own children, in general they would not consider sending their infants away from the house to feed. They viewed the nurturing of the newborn as their prime responsibility. During the 16th to the 18th centuries, however, nurturance was regarded only as one among many obligations of the new mother. She had to balance her maternal role against other familial demands. Only when wet nurses were financially out of reach did women nurse their own children. But the question must be raised, were women unaware of the dangers associated with sending their infants away to be nursed? There is evidence that some mothers may have been, although the concern and questioning may have been psychologically suppressed or rationalized by their own perceptions of their role as female head of the household. On the other hand, there are no figures on how many English women did in fact nurse their infants. Since it has been estimated that most babies were born every 24 months, it is possible to suggest that most mothers did nurse for at least a year. If lactation does prevent conception, as it has been generally assumed, then the two-year birth interval can be explained because mothers breast-fed their children.

American historians, as indicated in the selection by Walzer, seem to believe that most colonial mothers nursed their own children during the 17th century. Walzer contends, however, that maternal nursing was on the decrease during the 18th century despite the defense of breast-feeding by American reformers. In the south, however, it has been generally accepted that by the 18th century black women nursed infants of white parents who could afford slaves.

The long-held European belief in swaddling infants as a way of insuring correct growth of limbs can be taken as an indication that Europeans long realized that the period of infancy required nurturing. Paintings and child care books from England during this period illustrate and discuss the manner in which a child should be swaddled. Yet it is impossible to determine how widespread a practice it was. In America, however, some historians have contended that there was no evidence that infants were swaddled at all. It is a difficult assumption, however, to accept that colonial Americans varied so greatly from this European practice or from their English heritage because no significant evidence has yet been unearthed.

Care of infants also included rubbing their limbs with oil, keeping them warm, changing soiled cloth, and bathing. Babies kept at home were picked up when they cried, fed when hungry and generally nursed until they were between one and two years of age. Nothing, however, has yet been uncovered about systematic toilet training. John Locke in the 17th century appears to be the first English educator concerned about the manner in which infants were to be toilet trained. Much of the above information about how infants were treated, it should be noted, is taken from advice literature and may not necessarily reflect how infants were treated in reality.

In 18th century England reformers began to develop an increasing concern about infant mortality and a greater preoccupation with child abandonment. In both England and America the prescriptive literature about infancy increased and parents' attention was still directed to the importance of breast-feeding. Yet, as John Walzer illustrates, the ambivalence of some parents persisted towards their infants. Infanticide was still practiced in England, though it was possibly on the decrease, while an increasing amount of American mothers stopped nursing their own children.

The stage of infancy was and still is recognized as the time when humans are most helpless, requiring nurture and attention from the adult world. The preponderance of parents must have given some attention to their newborn babies; otherwise most infants would not have survived the infancy stage. The quality of care of newborns, however, more than likely varied depending upon the economic conditions, the social status and the psychological disposition of individual parents.

## 2. The Chances Of Life

By J.D. Chambers

Wrigley has reminded us that

> the parish register. . . carries no clues as to the methods of family limitation used. These may never be known with certainty, but it is likely that there was scope for the quiet disposal outside the ecclesiastical purview of abortions, and, indeed, of the victims of infanticide . . . The early hours of a child's life provide many occasions when it is easy to follow the maxim that "thou shalt not kill but needst not strive officiously to keep alive."

It is with this in mind that Professor Krause has written, "the usually cited infant death-rates greatly exaggerate pre-industrial infant mortality, especially among infants born to families which wanted to keep them alive." To what extent recorded burials were inflated by names that should or need not have been there is impossible to say, but if we could add to that those who had no name at all and passed out of the world as surreptitiously as they came in, the proportion would be substantial. Something is known of this aspect of infant mortality from the grim records of London. Rickman calculated the London death-rate on the assumption that one-third of the deaths escaped registration, and of this a considerable proportion must be regarded as the direct or indirect result of human agency. Exposure in the streets, desertion by parents, and a deliberate destruction of infant life by parish authorities were everyday occurrences in London, perhaps especially in the first half of the eighteenth century. Dr. J.C. Cox in his classic study of parish registers shows that the practice of sending out children from London and other large towns to nurseries in the country goes back to Elizabethan times, and from the large incidence of burials among them he concludes this must be regarded as a form of baby-farming. Again, alongside the 240 foundlings whose names are found in the register of the Temple in the eighteenth century there are 170 burials. It is interesting to note that to nearly all of them the surname Temple or Templer is assigned. Many other examples of surnames derived from the place in which a foundling was taken up could be given, but none quite so remarkable as that recorded in the register for St. Helen's, Bishopsgage, in 1612—"Job Rakt-out-of the Asshes, being borne the last day of August in the lane going to Sir John Spencer's back gate and there laide in a heape of old cold asshes, was baptized the first daye of September following, and dyed the next day after." It is known, too, that in 1715, when the House of

Commons set up a committee on the care of the poor in the parish of St. Martin in the Fields, they found that 900 of the 1,200 babies born every year in the parish died, many of them being exposed or over-laid by women described as nurses. The evidence of Thomas Coram is quite explicit on the point. "No expedient has yet been found out," he wrote in 1739,

> for preventing the murder of poor miserable infants at their birth, or suppressing the inhuman custom of exposing newly-born infants to perish in the streets; or the putting of such unhappy foundlings to wicked and barbarous nurses, who undertake to bring them up for a small and trifling sum of money [and] do often suffer them to starve for want of due sustenance and care.

Appalled at the sight of children exposed and dead in the streets of London, he worked for seventeen years to establish the Foundling Hospital and by 1745 one wing of the building was in use. In 1756 it received government help on condition that its doors were open to all who might apply. Its gates were thereupon besieged by parents not only from London but from the country outside. The children were entrusted to carriers and wagoners, even vagrants. Untold numbers, it is said, died on the way, and the site of the hospital was turned into a burial ground. During a short-lived period of three years and ten months of wholesale admissions, 14,000 children were taken in of whom only 4,500 lived to be apprenticed. Under the influence of an enlightened body of governors of whom Josiah Hanway was one, the death-rate was reduced after 1760 to 1 in 4 and by the end of the century it was less than 1 in 6. At the same time, steps were taken to check the appalling waste of life in workhouses; out of 291 children taken in by 11 workhouses in 1763, Hanway reported that 256—94 per cent—were dead by the end of 1765. It says something for the changing attitudes of the age that this remarkable man was able within two years to steer an Act through Parliament which put a stop to this terrible scandal. By the Act of 1767, all parish children under six were to be sent out of London to be nursed, and nurses were to have a reward of 10 shillings for every child sent to them under nine months whom they successfully reared. For the first time in our history, the State was beginning to spend money on the saving of life, and though in numerical terms the saving was no doubt marginal, it is a sign of the times that must not be overlooked. It also had the effect of providing a source of child labour to the cotton mills in the second half of the century and to that extent made a direct contribution to the recruitment of the labour force for the Industrial Revolution.

How large a factor private and institutional infanticide was, we shall never know: but we can be sure that, compared to the natural causes which hovered over them from the moment of birth, death by direct or indirect human agency was of minor significance, a mere eddy on the tide of mortality that swept away the generations, sometimes, and in some places, with such speed that they were scarcely given time to replace themselves.

## 3. Infant Mortality

By Peter Laslett

Infantile morality is a very well-known and much used index of welfare, and certainly varies with adequacy of nourishment. The French crisis of subsistence was marked by very sharp increases of deaths amongst the new born, and in abortions too, though abortions are very difficult to reckon even from French parish registers. It so happens that Ashton-under-Lyne is one of the very few places where burial of abortions are registered in our parish books at the relevant time, and they were higher in the early 1620's than at any other time when the clerk recorded them, reaching nearly 7 percent of births in 1623. But even at this level they did not much exceed the rate of nearly 6 per cent which can be derived from John Graunt's extracts from the London bills of mortality for the early 1630's, and neither figure is as high as the estimated rate for our own day.

More marked at Ashton during the years of crisis was the peak in the total of "nuncupative" babies, or "chrissoms" as they were called, who had to be buried. Chrissoms were those who died before there was time to baptize them; they were put into a grave wrapped in the christening cloth which had been prepared for the ceremony at the font. Our ancestors had other curious and to our generation rather ghoulish customs. In some places when a mother died in childbed the baby was christened on her coffin. Chrissom children buried numbered nine in the crisis year 1623-4 at Ashton, when fifty-eight was the total of those conceived. They were even more numerous in 1621, the first of the two years of high mortality, when they reached nearly a fifth of all conceptions. The increase in babies buried in the first year of life can also be seen at Greystoke at the same time, at its worst when persons were actually dying of starvation.

Infantile mortality has a wider significance than its relationship with periods of want and starvation in the traditional world. It enters into our general attitude in the twentieth century towards the world we have lost, because of the widespread belief that industrialization in its early stages had a disastrous effect on the health of the newly born. It seems to be supposed that only recently and in only the most advanced industrial countries has the mass of the population been able to go back to anything like healthy, natural conditions under which the peasant woman had her babies, and therefore only recently has the tragic waste of infant life which comes from industrial conditions begun to be stemmed. Historians have sometimes referred in an ominous way to some isolated index for the mortality of babies in an early industrial suburb, and the national proportion of 153 per thousand dying in the first year of life in the decade 1841-50 has occasionally been cited as an indication of a general deterioration. What evidence we now have on the issue points to a somewhat different conclusion.

The French historical demographers, in fact, tend to suppose that a figure much greater than 150 per thousand, a figure nearer to 200 per thousand and probably even higher, was typical of rural villages in preindustrial France in normal times.

In England we have found it difficult to confirm an infantile mortality as high as 200 per thousand. Our best figures so far come from Wrigley's reconstitution at Colyton, and give an infantile mortality rate of 120 to 140 in the second half of the sixteenth century, 126 to 158 in the first half of the seventeenth, 118 to 147 in the second half, 162 to 203 in the first half of the eighteenth century and 122 to 153 between 1750 and 1837. Cruder methods provide a rate of almost 300 in the 1660's for the parish of Wem in Shropshire, and at Ashton-under-Lyne the minimal rate certainly rose above 200 in the years of crisis in the early 1620's to which we have already referred. Though it was 176 for the six years 1629-34, it never reached 200 for any prolonged period in the seventeenth century.

The largest sample available known for any European country for so early a date is contained in Graunt's study of the bills of mortality in London. His tables can be made to yield a rate of infantile mortality of over 200, but only on the assumption that all those he records as "Chrissomes and Infants" at their burial were in fact less than twelve months old. Between 1629 and 1632, for example, there were 9,277 such burials out of a total of 36,024 baptisms, which would mean a rate of 257 per thousand. Even this estimate leaves open the question of whether any of those he classifies as dying of "Convulsions" or "Teeth and Worms" were in fact under one year of age. We can reckon infantile mortality fairly accurately and with interesting additional details at Clayworth during the pastorate of William Sampson. It is interesting to find that in his village over the whole period the rate was on average 215, not so very different from that at Crulai. Since such information is still rare it might be as well to present it in full, together with some rough indication of the prices the villagers were paying for the wheat, rye or barley they made into bread, those of them, that is to say, who had to buy their food rather than living off their own crops.

If it had not been for the very unfavourable years in the 1680's, it will be seen, registered infantile mortality even here would have been on a somewhat lower level than it seems ordinarily to have been in France at the same time. Nothing can be made of the vague tendency of the level of local cereal prices to vary with the numbers of babies dying. But it is not without interest, that the number of baptisms, marriages and burials as a whole shows that there was something of a demographic crisis in the years 1678-81 with its peak of thirty-one burials in 1679, whilst the average during Sampson's time was under five overall. He never mentioned hunger during the twenty-eight years he lived in Clayworth, but he does record November and December, 1679, as "sickly months," when, after "a very wet time about autumn . . . the quartan ague was almost in every house and none in some escaped it.''

Mortality at Clayworth interests for other reasons, but it would be difficult to use it even as a token demonstration that the liability of infants to die in their first year of life was increased by the coming of industry in England. The truth seems to be that infantile mortality was unlikely to have been higher under Queen Victoria than it was under the Stuarts, and the first rough indications are that it was lower.

## 4. Maternal Nursing And Wet-Nursing Among English Puritans

By R.V. Schnucker

After the child was born, it had to be nursed. Baby-bottles were generally unknown although in some instances a cow's horn was used to serve the purpose of nursing and in some wealthier homes, a silver papboat was used; but these devices were rare. The normal procedure was for the mother to nurse the infant or for a wet nurse to be employed for that purpose. In some instances the nurse came into the home or the infant was sent to a village to be nursed. Many protested against wet nursing but the women of the wealthier families still tended to give this reponsibility to other women.

The Puritan ideal, overwhelmingly affirming the necessity of the mother to nurse her infant, was based upon the Scripture, and grudgingly allowed the use of wet nurses when the life of either mother or infant was endangered. Henry Smith wrote that as the fountains of the earth gave forth water for drinking, so were the breasts of women made to nurse their infants. Drawing further from nature, Smith observed that every beast and bird was bred and nourished by its mother except the human female who allowed someone else, the wet nurse, to feed her young. He likened this to the cuckoo who laid eggs in a sparrow's nest to be hatched and fed by the sparrow. When some acted as if the female breast was only for show and ostentation, the staunch Puritans Robert Cleaver and William Perkins argued that God had given the female two breasts to nourish infants. Even the bachelor Dillingham gave his affirmation to the practice of the mother nursing her infant. ''I refer the duty that the mother is to perform to her child: namely, the duty of nursing the same . . . why has nature given women breasts full of milk, but that they should nurse their own children.''

The Puritans turned to the Scripture to support their position that the nursing of an infant by its mother was not only the way of nature but was also God's will. Gouge for example was convinced that God's word implied in some passages that nursing was a duty; in other places God expressly commanded it through the example of holy women; and in still other places it was taken for granted by God that it would not be denied a newly born infant. The passages most frequently cited involved Sara, Mary, and the injunction of 1 Timothy 5.10-14. After having given the samples of Sara and Mary, Cleaver said that it was a commendation for any woman to have nursed her own children and those who had not done so ". . . make themselves but halfmothers. . . " This was the attitude of Elizabeth Clinton and of Gouge. In his gloss on Titus 2.4 where the mother is encouraged to love her children, Gouge declared that the best way for a mother to do this was ". . . . by letting it suck her own breasts. . . for daily experience sheweth that mothers love those children best to whom they themselves give suck." These biblical examples could be aimed at any class of society; Sara was considered a wealthy princess and she nursed Isaac; Mary was considered to be poor and she nursed Jesus. The justification given by non-nursing mothers for shirking their duty was also based upon scriptural precedent. Some pointed to Rebecca, Deborah, and Naomi who hired nurses, but the Puritans explained this away with the declaration that these hired nurses were dry and not wet nurses.

According to the Puritans two important advantages occurred to the infant nursed by its mother, advantages not available to the infant given to a wet nurse. The first advantage was physical and the second psychological. Basic to both advantages was the belief that the best milk for the infant was that of its mother. Concerning the physical advantage, Cleaver wrote ". . . the mothers milk should be much more natural for the child, than the milk of a stranger," and Guillimeau and Gouge concurred in this belief. It was their position that the best way to keep an infant physically healthy was to have it nursed by its mother. The experience of Elizabeth Clinton tended to confirm their position. She wrote that she was convinced that those of her children she nursed were physically healthier than those given to wet nurses; in fact she feared that deaths of some of her children were due to the default of wet nurses.

The second or psychological advantage was two-fold. First, the mother passed on to her infant through her milk certain qualities that shaped the infant's future character and behavior. This belief was expressed by Becon: "For children by drinking in strange milk, drink in also strange manners and another nature. . ." The same idea found in an old saying was cited by Smith: "*He sukt evil from the dug:* that is, as the nurse is affected in her body or in her mind, commonly the child draweth the life infirmities from her. . ." When the mother gave her child to a wet nurse, there was no guarantee as to what would happen to the child physically or psychologically; but if she nursed the child, then she would determine what the child would be like. The second part of the psychological advantage given to an infant nursed by its mother was that the child learned of his mother's love and in turn would love her. It was the opinion of Gouge that children who loved their mothers most were nursed by their mother. This was the opinion of Elizabeth Clinton who admitted that at one time she did not believe that it was possible to have such advantages from nursing, but she had repented when she had seen the fine results in nursing her own children.

The Puritans warned that by refusing to nurse their children, mothers were offending God. It was declared that those who said they could not nurse because they were dry, ought to call the words in Hosea 9 where dry breasts were called a curse. To those who could nurse their infant and did not, their actions declared their refusal to be thankful to God and the rejection of the fruit of their own womb. The most common caveat was that a mother should not be surprised if her child denied her later in life since she had denied it her breasts early in life. A husband who hindered or forbade his wife's nursing or complained about the inconveniences of it, or refused to buy what she needed to better nurse the infant, or who did not actively encourage her and suggested a wet nurse, was warned he was an accessory to sin. The husband was not to forget that he was for the most part responsible for his wife's pregnancy and certainly he could not abuse his child by denying it its mother's milk. If husbands would only take a positive attitude toward nursing wrote Gouge, " . . . where one mother now nurseth her child, twenty would do it."

Although the Puritans recommended nursing, those who practiced what others preached, knew that there were disadvantages and complaints connected with breast feeding. For example when Mrs. Josselin attempted to nurse her first born, her difficulty was of such a nature that her husband recorded in his diary ". . . it pleased God my wives breasts were sore which was a grievance and sad cut to her, but with the use of means in some distance of time they healed up. . ." Sore nipples and sore breasts were a common complaint, but they did not stop the dedicated from nursing. Mothers were told that the best way to cure a sore breast was to give the child suck. Further, if a woman suffered from sore nipples, she ought to endure a little more pain and continue to nurse. "Many mothers have given their children suck when blood hath run by the mouth of the child by reason of sore nipples, and yet both mother and child done very well." This comment from Gouge was probably the result of his wife's experiences in nursing their children. Gouge also dealt with a question which concerned some Puritans; was it wise to engage in coitus while the wife was lactating? His answer was that since nursing was the duty of the wife, the husband ought to do what he could to contain himself.

Two common complaints heard today and heard in the past were: "I can't nurse because I can't produce milk" and "I can't nurse because my breasts are underdeveloped." To the latter complaint the knowledgeable Gouge declared the flat-breasted should use the known means to raise the nipples so nursing could be done. To the former complaint, Cleaver summed up the Puritan attitude to the inability for lactation. "But whose breasts have this perpetual drought? Forsooth, it is like the gout; no beggars may have it, but Citizens or gentlewomen." In other words, only the wealthy who could employ wet nurses seemed to be afflicted with the inability to lactate. Although Robert Burton suggested witches might be responsible for dry breasts, Gouge correctly diagnosed the cause for many not lactating. "Some are themselves the cause of wanting milk because they will not let it be drawn down: or because they will not use means (for means there are) to get and increase milk."

Some complained they didn't know how to nurse and the Puritan reply was as one would expect: "Let them learn seeing it is their duty." Still others complained they could not endure the pain of nursing. Gouge made a biting reply that if such was their attitude, then if they could, they probably ought to try to hire someone to endure the pain of nine months of gestation and the labor pains as well. Since they were willing to accept gestation and labor pains, they might as well nurse their own infants. It was partly a matter of mental attitude. "If women would with cheerfulness set themselves to perform this duty, much of the supposed pain and pains would be lessened."

Some of the middle class who worked with their husbands at a trade objected to nursing because it caused them to be absent from work; thus it was cheaper to hire a wet nurse. The Puritan answer to this was that no business in the world was more acceptable to God than the mother nursing her child. Another rather common complaint was that nursing was inconvenient and troublesome. It disturbed the sleep of both parents and disrupted their ease and quiet during the day. "Seeing children come from the loins of the father as well as out of the womb of the mother," said Gouge, "they must be content to endure some disturbances. . ." Nursing was messy, was another objection. It soiled one's clothes and meant that the mother must open her breasts to the public. "Ask. . . any modest loving mother," wrote the Countess of Lincoln, "what trouble they accounted it to give their little ones suck: behold most nursing mothers and they be as clean and sweet in their clothes. . . as well as that suck not."

A major objection to nursing was the belief that a mother who nursed would suffer impaired beauty. The young mother by nursing would look older faster and her breasts would sag. The reply given to such an objection was that the reverse was true. Did women lose their beauty because of nursing? " . . . it hath been observed in some women that they grew more beautiful, better favoured, by very nursing their own children . . . " was the reply of Elizabeth Clinton. The woman who dried up her breasts was the one who lost her beauty, for nursing was a means to better health and to greater strength. "The drawing forth of a womans milk by her child is a means to get and preserve a good stomach, which is a great preservative of good health." Still others complained about nursing for it did not given them the freedom they wanted for gossiping. This was self-love declared Gouge, and those who thought this way possessed very little love for their child, little respect for God and were half-mothers.

With all the insistence that mothers nurse, yet the Puritans recognized that there were some instances when this could not occur. As great an example as Mrs. Gouge only nursed seven of her thirteen children. Thus exceptions to this God-given duty were made. For example, Becon wrote that the mother should do the nursing "except very necessity compel her . . . " to to otherwise. Perkins allowed these conditions for the use of a wet nurse: the mother's health was poor; the mother lacked the ability for some reason; or any just impediment. After listing the usual objections as to why it was difficult for a mother to nurse, Gouge said: ". . .if therefore in truth it be so that the mothers giving suck to the child will be dangerous to her self or to the child, she may and ought to forebear. . ." The overwhelming spirit however was that such exceptions demanding a wet nurse were rare and most mothers ought to and were capable of nursing their own infants.

Let us turn now to the often maligned wet nurse. Apparently many of the wet nurses came from the country where they had lived active lives working in the fields and continued to do so after marriage. They normally would have had a good appetite because of their strong vigorous existence. They were the ones usually used by the gentry and the aristocracy for wet nursing. Those who lived in the country were aware of this and to meet the need, there is some evidence that human cows gathered into certain locales and flourished in their trade of selling their milk as wet nurses. Hints that such a practice had developed were given by Gouge for example. He claimed that such a practice had been observed in many country villages that on the most part the children who died there were nurse children, and the number who died every year was very great. In the anonymous tract *The Pilgrimage of Man,* the author commented upon how often women brought forth their children and would not take time to nurse them; so the children were sent ". . . to sorry villages to be nursed of strange and unknown nurses. . ." In the parish registers of Saints Peter and Paul, Mitcham, there was more evidence of the sorry villages with their high death rate of nurse-children. The registers contained the records of the burial of many such children who had been sent there, apparently by their parents for wet nursing.

The problems involved in wet nursing were known then, and seem incredible to us today. The wet nurses in some villages would get the infants confused and returned them to the wrong parents. Others would claim to have sufficient milk, only to starve the infant because they were at the end of their lactation. Others who promised to be faithful in taking care of the infants were careless and interested only in the small pay they received. As has been stated previously, Elizabeth Clinton suspected that the slothfulness of some of the wet nurses she had used was responsible for the death some of her little babies.

There was one continuous objection to wet nurses shared by the Puritans that has been mentioned before and needs now to be reiterated: the character of the wet nurse, her illnesses, almost her very being was thought to transfer via her milk into the infant being nursed. The statement of Ferrand was typical of the sentiment of the time: ". . . the milk of the nurse. . . is of the very great force, either in correcting, or corrupting as well as the manners of the mind; as the Constitution of the Body." The physician Anniballe in Guazzo's *Civile Conversation,* made the same observation except that he took an analogy from nature and applied it to the human sphere. He claimed that if a lamb was nursed with the milk of a goat and a kid was nursed with the milk of a yew, the kid would have very soft hair and the lamb very rough wool. Therefore,

> it is to be thought, that as a child, by reason of the milk, taketh after the complexion of the Nurse, so the disposition of the mind, followeth the complexion of the body; and therof also it commeth, that the daughters of honest women, prove altogether unlike them, both in body and mind, so that to deliver children from their mothers to Nurses, cannot be said to be other than a corrupting of nature.

It was the opinion of Boaistuau that cheap, corrupt, and deformed nurses were so apt to create future human misery, that it would have been better for the children to have been nursed by ". . . some brute beast in the wilderness, than to be put into the mercy of such nurses . . ." If the nurse was a drunkard or forward, these evils would pass to the infant; he even suspected that syphilis and leprosy could be passed by a wet nurse to her charge. Sir Hugh Cholmley claimed that his weak and stunted body as a child was the result of having a wet nurse who was pregnant at the time he was nursed by her.

"Every one knows how hard a thing it is," wrote Guillimeau concerning wet nurses, "to find a good one because they have been so often beguiled and deceived therein." He then gave the qualities and characteristics of the ideal wet nurse. He was but one of many who attempted to aid in the selection of a wet nurse. He described a young woman of good stock between twenty-five to thirty-five years of age who was neither too large nor to small. She was not to be fat nor skinny but she should have strong solid arms and legs. She was to have normal vision, neither lame, nor hump shouldered, she was to be healthy and with no disease. Her complexion and the general color tone of her body was to be lively and rosy. In particular she should not be blotched nor have red hair. Her chest was to be broad and garnished with two breasts of reasonable bigness neither limber nor hanging down, neither hard nor soft, full of Zaure veins and arteries. The breasts were not to be knotty nor swollen bigger than they ought to be. The nipples were to be pronounced and the color of a strawberry and of reasonable bigness and thickness so the child could get a hold of them in order to secure an easy draught of milk. She was to be chaste and not pregnant nor desiring coitus with her husband for ". . . carnal copulation . . . troubleth the blood, and so by consequence the milk; also it diminisheth the quantity thereof, by provoking the natural purgations . . ." She was to have a good quality of milk and it would be better if she had too much of it rather than not enough. The milk must be white, have as sweet a taste as possible, and a pleasant odor. The nurse ought not to breast feed her charge until two months after her own delivery. The Scottish physician Makluire also suggested many of the above qualifications for the wet nurse but added some equally important considerations—namely the attitudes of the wet nurse. He wanted the wet nurse to be diligent, lusty, merry, sober, chaste, meek, not sluggish nor sad, not a glutton, nor delicate in her eating, but gentle and courteous. For Burton, it was the latter considerations of Makluire that were of the utmost importance for ". . . passions corrupt the milk and after the temperature of the child . . . "

We might wonder after reading about the ideal wet nurse if anyone took it seriously. In a letter from Richard Leveson to Anne Newdigate, Leveson commented that Queen Anne was pregnant and the royal physicians were looking for a wet nurse. They were going to ". . . examine and give their opinions of their aptness for that charge as by tasting of their Milk, etc." He was of the opinion the royal physicians were going to ask his wife to submit to the examination and the "etc." and so Leveson remarked in the letter, "I'll walk on foot to Arbury to keep her at home."

What can we conclude from this; The Puritans were not insensitive to the condition and needs of pregnant women and they suggested special care to be taken to secure a good diet and have moderate exercise. The Puritans were aware of the danger connected with delivery and saw revealed in the labor pains a punishment for Eve's sin as well as a redemptive element. The Puritans shared their society's fear of bastardy. Using Scripture precedents and proofs, they strongly favored the ideal of the infant being breast fed by its mother since such a practice was of great physical and psychological benefit to the child and the mother, and was in accord with God's design. But the careful reading of Puritan comments on breast feeding reveals considerable evidence that the ideal was not always realized partly because psychological problems that hindered nursing were present then as now. Comments such as: the milk won't draw down; my breasts are underdeveloped; my breasts become too painful and sore in nursing; be cheerful while breast feeding; the father's complaints against his wife nursing; the fear of sagging breasts which would impair physical attractiveness; present a picture of an environment in which some mothers found it difficult to nurse and even if they started to nurse might have found it difficult to sustain lactation.

Concomitant with this was the necessity to use a wet nurse which in turn presented other problems. If the wet nurse was in a village, would the infant be physically healthy in the hands of the wet nurse; was there a chance for babies to be confused and their proper identity lost; would the milk of the nurse corrupt the infant? There are also the haunting problem of the mother's possible guilt of having rejected the fruit of her own womb and subsequently in the future being rejected by the child and also by God. Elizabeth Clinton summed it up by writing:

> We have followed *Eve* in transgression, let us follow her in obedience. When God laid the sorrows of conception, of breeding, of bringing forth, and of bringing up her children upon her, and so upon us in her loins, did she reply any word against (it)? Not a word: so I pray you . . . reply not against the duty of suckling them, when God hath sent you them.

## 5. Ambivalent Infant Care In Eighteenth-Century America
### By John F. Walzer

While we today accept the idea of an initial ambivalence toward children as normal, we ordinarily attribute the more extreme manifestations of continued ambivalence to the realm of the abnormal, the unhealthy, and the bizarre. Good and proper parents love their children, if not for every waking minute, then at least in a basic way. They could not really want to kill or abandon them, much less badly harm them. And yet such behaviour was neither wholly fantastic nor unusual in the past. Quite normal parents harbored unconscious wishes of such an extreme nature that they could not be admitted to the conscious mind. In colonial America, the attitudes of parents toward their children were shaped by the basic ambivalent wishes to retain and to reject their offspring, to hold on to them forever, and to be rid of the noisome creatures, at one and the same time. When these contradictory wishes were restrained and balanced, they can be said to have disappeared. When not so well integrated, the results were less happy.

By the eighteenth century, the practice of abandoning new-born children where they were likely to be found, so common in London as to be institutionalized, was almost non-existent in America. In 1775, Dixon and Hunter reported in the *Virginia Gazette* that a post rider carrying the mail between Newcastle and Richmond found "a young child" in the road, "carefully placed in a box, with £10 cash," together with a letter saying that there would be more money forthcoming should the finder take care of the child; whereupon the post-rider carrying the mail promptly took it up and became the foster father. Other such incidents, if they took place, were not frequently mentioned in the press.

Cases of infanticide were more commonly recorded, though they can hardly be said to have been frequent. The murderers were usually though not exclusively the mothers of the victims, and the murdered children illegitimate, although again, not always. The willful act often took place immediately after birth, a kind of late abortion.

Unconscious infanticide is even more difficult for the historian to evaluate. Who can say whether or not Esther Burr, wife of the president of Princeton College, was entirely free from destructive motives when she took her little baby, Aaron, age about 11 months, on a long and dangerous trip to Stockbridge, Massachusetts, from which he nearly died? Certainly she knew there was a good possibility he would be exposed to inclement weather. Esther's stated reason for taking Aaron along on a visit to her parents was that she could not bear to leave him at home. But for all her declared adoration, she does not say one word about how the baby fared in the drubbing rain she caused them both to endure by insisting that the wagon-master drive on as they neared the end of their journey, and this despite the fact that she saw the bad weather coming up. Admittedly, it was an exceedingly dangerous time to be near Stockbridge, for the woods were so full of Indians that Esther told her diary again and again she could not sleep for fear "they will get me." But if this helps explain the urge to drive on, it also causes one to wonder how a young mother could take a tiny baby into such a dangerous situation. She does not appear to have been troubled for the babe, however, or at least she never makes note of the danger he was in. She sincerely feared for his life only when he became very sick as a result of all the exposure. Parents often dangled their children before the maw of death in the eighteenth century. Numerous accidents occurred in which children were killed while "playing alone near a Cyder Tubb," or when their clothes caught fire when left alone.

If cases of outright infanticide were rare in colonial America, the reverse was true of "putting out." Eighteenth-century American infants and small children were readily and frequently "put to" a nurse, a school, or a relative, and, as older children, to a master. The situation might be said to have been closer to that which exists in a primitive tribe where the child is seen as a child of the tribe as much as a child of a particular couple. It is impossible to determine what percentage of children were put out of their natural parents' home, either temporarily or permanently. Of those women who have left some record of themselves (almost always from the upper classes) many used outside nurses in the eighteenth century. Esther Burr nursed her own two babes, but Mrs. Robert Carter, of Nomini Hall, relied on outside wet-nurses for at least some of her numerous progeny. "Your sister Fanny lies in with a daughter," Anne Tucker of Bermuda wrote to her son, St. George Tucker, of Virginia, in 1780: "she is too weakly to suckle her little girl, and is obliged to put it out to nurse." Similarly, Gabriel Ludlow recorded the birth of his little girl on April 3, 1700, who "was put to nurse the 19th Instant in New York at 12 per annum and 12 weight of sugar, and dyed at 6 weeks old, buried in Trinity Church Yard."

The *New York Mercury* featured in an article in 1754 on "the inconvenience of Hired Nurses" (first printed in an English newspaper) without any indication that this was some evil English practice from which the Americans were mercifully free. The common argument that infants sucked in the physical disorders and crude passions of the far-from-tender nurses was often aired in the press, with examples drawn from ancient history. Later in the century, the nurse often came to the baby rather than the baby being taken completely away from the mother. In 1786, for example, Philadelphia merchant Thomas Leaming, Jr., wrote to a relative that one Abagail Williams, a widow, could come down to keep house. "She is recommended as a good nurse and if she don't go to keep house for you expects to go out a Nursing in Philadelphia at much higher wages, but in that case can't take her child with her."

Perhaps we can learn something about the matter from an examination of the putting to nurse of Henry Drinker, Jr. In July, 1771, his mother, Elizabeth, complained in her diary of ill-health, and said of her four-month-old son, "Dr. D_____ says I must wean my little Henry or get a nurse for him. Either seems hard," she added, "but I must submit." If this were all that the historian had to go on, one might be tempted to mistrust Elizabeth. "If a woman knows her husband can spare three to six shillings per week," a newspaper reported in 1754, "she . . . will persuade the good man to get a nurse, by pretending indisposition." But Elizabeth Drinker truly seems to have agonized over the problem. A few days after receiving the doctor's advice she recorded that her side and breast were "painful," and that she went to one Sally Oates' house and "agreed with her to take my sweet, little Henry to nurse." She stayed for an hour or two and then went back again in the afternoon to see her child. "I seem lost without my little dear," she confided to her diary that evening. The next morning, before breakfast, she was off with her husband to see "our little dear." In the evening that was "no going out," but she sent one Johnny Foulk to see how her son was. Johnny brought back "pleasing accounts." The next day she was off to Sally's house bright and early again.

On Sunday, the whole family went to Oates', not once but twice. In fact, from July 22, when she gave up the babe, to August 22, the only time she does not record a trip to Oates was when she made no entry whatsoever, one rainy day excepted. Occasionally she took the baby for a little ride while visiting. During the next three months, the impression one gets from the fewer entries is that she and her husband continued to visit the child, if not so regularly. On February 1, 1772, Elizabeth ordered Sally Oates to begin to wean Henry. On March 8, Sally brought the baby back to Drinkers to stay. She had had him approximately seven and one-half months, and he was just over a year old when she brought him back to his natural mother.

It is evident that Elizabeth harbored some genuine reservations about putting her baby out to nurse. It also seems that she got used to the situation. She undoubtedly could have hired a wet-nurse to live in. The powerful possessiveness toward tiny babies that we sometimes take for granted has not always existed undiluted. It was not the standard attitude in the world of Elizabeth Drinker; but neither did she abandon it, or send it to a baby farm, as some still did in 1771. Clearly Elizabeth cared a lot, and did not get rid of the baby casually. At the same time she was able to go off for a month, enjoy herself, and dismiss the infant from her mind, or at least not lament his absence in her diary.

One way "to be rid of them at home" after they were back from the wet-nurse was to send children away to school at an early age. Where there were public-subsidized nursery schools, parents sometimes sent their children soon after they were weaned. In Georgia, "a great many poor people that could not maintain their children . . . [sent] their little ones for a month or two, or more, as they could spare them. . . . " In Philadelphia, the Swedish traveler Per Kalm alleged that children a little over three were sent to school both morning and afternoon although it was realized that they would not be able to read much. In Virginia, there were instances of quite young children sent far from home to school. Indeed, distance was considered by some as essential. "I hope it will be for the boys' advantage to be placed at school at a distance from home," Mary Norris wrote to her daughter.

Parents sometimes openly expressed their ambivalent feelings. Richard Smith of Pennsylvania sent his young son away to school, but put him under the care of his grown son, with instructions that the older boy should take a fatherly care of the young one. "He seems to affectionate to me that it goes a little hard to me to part with him. . . ," he added, "but I apprehend it is for his good to get a little more schooling. . . ." Similarly, Thomas Frame wrote to John Penn: "You seem to think my fondness for my child will be his ruin. I hope not, for I do assure you I had rather see him dead than to have him when he is grown up, a blockhead."

# B. CHILDHOOD

## 1. Introduction

Four questions have preoccupied the new historiography on childhood: (1) What was the adult conception of childhood in the past? (2) How did adults, particularly parents, treat children? (3) How did the conception and treatment of children change over time? (4) What explains changes in the history of childhood? Each of the readings in this chapter tries to answer one or more of these questions. In this introduction we shall encapsulate the answers historians have offered and will indicate our own conclusions with regard to the years 1500 to 1800.

The first question on the conception of childhood owes its formulation to the pathbreaking *Centuries of Childhood* by Philippe Ariès (1962). Drawing on iconographic and literary sources mainly from continental Europe, he concluded that until the 1600's adults were, for the most part, insensitive to the special character of childhood and that they considered children to be miniature adults. Whereas today we think of childhood as a distinct stage in the individual's life history, with its own emotional inclinations and cognitive capacities, Ariès inferred that late medieval and Renaissance adults thought of children from the age of five to be simply small scale versions of themselves. He found that family life in rural villages was played out in a largely public arena, where the boundary between the community and the household was thinly drawn, and where children mingled regularly with adults in the tasks and recreations of the community. Ariès in fact postulated a "discovery of childhood" after 1600 and a new withdrawal of the family from the community into the private domain of the household, both correlative developments of the early modern era.

The recent scholarship on childhood in colonial New England has been especially influenced by Aries' concept of minature adulthood. Beginning with Demos (1969), several students of 17th-century New England have suggested that when the New England child reached the latency years he was considered an adult and was initiated into adult patterns of dress, behavior and responsibility.

The applicability of Ariès' concept to New England may in fact be enhanced when we view it within the context of his overall model. He linked the conception of miniature adulthood to a social network in which the lines between private and public spheres of family life were nearly indistinguishable. This pre-modern pattern was more closely duplicated in early New England than elsewhere in the colonies and possibly more so than in most parts of England. For no group placed as much importance on the role of the community in reenforcing and supervising family life than did the Puritan immigrants. They even created a special class of officials who were charged solely with overseeing the domestic governance of families in their neighborhoods. If the connection Ariès drew between the family-community network and the conception of children as miniature adults was as interweaved as he implied, then the argument of historians who see Puritan New England children being treated as mini-adults would seem to be strengthened.

Yet, as Ross Beales (1975) has written elsewhere, there were numerous ways in which colonial New England parents demonstrated their realization that children in the latency years were still children who were distinguishable from adults. The Puritans were aware of several essential characteristics that separated childhood from youth, let alone from

271

adulthood. Some writers did not believe that the attainment of a particular chronological age necessarily marked the arrival of full mental understanding. Others were apt to demarcate the years 14 or 16 as automatically denoting the onset of full discretionary intelligence. In neither case did writers believe that children who passed the age of 7 to 8 normally achieved the cognitive capacities of an adult. Both English and New England law made special allowance for the misbehavior of children who were under 14 or 16. They were subjected to lesser penalties on the ground that they were not yet fully accountable for their actions.

Perhaps we can place the matter of miniature adulthood in a broader perspective by looking at the ways modern parents try to hasten the maturation of their children. Do not many parents even today, as Ebel (1976) has observed, describe childhood "in terms of levels not yet attained, as if the child were merely an incomplete adult"? Does he talk yet? Does he walk yet? Does he go to school yet? Does he date yet? These are the concerns of adult-oriented adults who are impatient with the childishness of their children. Indeed, in some ways we tend to rush the development of our children in comparison to early modern parents. Whereas we ship our children to school when they are four or five, they did not impose formal socializing demands on their youngsters until the age of seven or eight, although many may have attended dame schools at younger ages as Spufford (1979) has recently suggested. And what could be more projective of adult values than to attribute to infants sexual impulses that early moderns associated exclusively with the onset of puberty? The Freudian framework of child development is much more compatible with a notion of miniature adulthood than any aspect of the early modern conception of childhood.

Our feeling is that a different attitude towards childhood does divide early modern from modern adults, but that the difference cannot be gauged by the concept of miniature adulthood. It is not that early modern parents were obtusely insensitive to the developmental processes operating in their children. It is rather that they generally perceived those processes in a negative light, while we tend to view them more positively. Whereas we have celebrated childhood as a time of natural innocence, they considered adulthood to be a worthier stage. Adults were viewed as the products of a systematic socialization designed to offset the Lockean *tabula rasa* passivity or the anti-social inclinations innate to the newborn.

With this difference in mind, we can better understand the answer to the second question: how were children treated? The answer to this question is the easiest of the four to document. Accordingly, no matter how much historians disagree on the reasons for the treatment of children, they do concur that children in England and America well into the 18th century were disciplined by corporal punishment by their parents, their teachers, or their masters; were sent from their homes to schools or to other families at some point after the age of 7; were subjected during their latency years to one form of rigorous socialization or another; were expected to honor and obey their parents and others in positions of superior authority; were inculcated with the fear of God; were educated primarily by rote learning; and were instructed in the moral standards of their parents.

Less easily documented is the answer to the third question: how did the history of childhood change over time? Much of the interest and energy that this question has generated is owed to a seminal but controversial essay by Lloyd deMause. In his now famous opening sentences he wrote: "The history of childhood is a nightmare from which we have only recently begun to awaken. The further back in history one goes, the lower the level of child care, and the more likely children are to be killed, beaten, terrorized, and sexually abused." (deMause, 1974). DeMause postulated for the history of childhood in the West an evolutionary schema that stressed the pivotal nature of the early modern era (especially the 18th century) as the time in which a new sensibility towards children emerged. Like Ariès, deMause found that childrearing in this period marked a dramatic break with the past insofar as parents and adult society generally now sought to bring children under intensive systems of nurture both at home and at school.

The selections below measure changes in the conception and treatment of childhood over much narrower time frames than were assessed by Ariès and deMause. For the historians of early modern England and America have in effect accepted the thesis that something new occurred in childrearing between 1500 and 1800, and they have set out to delineate that development more closely than was the original purposes of the sweeping studies by Ariès and deMause.

When read in succession, Stone, Illick, and Plumb depict the image and treatment of children as changing in a progressive manner between 1500 and 1800 in England. Although they do not make explicit value judgments, they cannot (and perhaps should not) avoid completely the use of value-laden words. Thus Stone speaks of the "brutal and authoritarian" conditions facing children of the 16th and early 17th centuries in their homes and schools; while Plumb describes the attitude towards children in the 18th century as representing a change "from tyranny to benevolence." Illick's description is phrased in more neutral terms. If there is a trend to be gleaned from the advice literature Illick consults, it appears, at first glance, to be the obverse of what Stone and Plumb are charting. For Illick finds a "permissive" and "indulgent" attitude towards children in early 17th century prescriptions and an increasing emphasis on teaching children control and self-discipline later in the century.

Yet we should note that this restrictive emphasis coalesced with a plea to free children from swaddling bands and with a growing recognition of the cognitive and psychological value of play for children. Towards the end of the 17th century, then, there was a greater interest in and sensitivity to the special needs of childhood. Taken together, in sum, Stone, Illick, and

Plumb point to the linear improvement (in terms of our value system) in the treatment of English children between 1500 and 1800.

In tracing the conception and treatment of children in early America, colonial historians, with few exceptions, have tended to measure change cross-culturally more than chronologically. That is, they have compared childhood among different regions of America or between the colonies and England. Individually they have not measured change between the 17th and 18th centuries.

The issue that many of the historians of colonial childhood have focused upon is parental control vs. the autonomy of the child. If there is a general overview that we can extract, it would seem to be as follows. While some historians of early Massachusetts towns have argued for greater community cohesiveness and trans-generational control than existed in England, some recent English scholars have emphasized the degree of comparative stability there as well. Whatever the case comparatively, such Massachusetts towns as Andover and Dedham do appear to have established communities of considerable stability in the 17th century when parents were able to impose their will upon their children. In the Chesapeake colonies, on the other hand, a high parental mortality rate, a semi-isolated pattern of settlement, and the absence of strong institutional supports, provided children with greater independence from parental authority than their peers in the north. In the 18th century, American parents continued to try to maintain control over their children, but Walzer "is struck by the repeated assertion that children in eighteenth-century America were unusually recalcitrant." This conclusion is in consonance with the findings of Greven (1970), who followed the patterns of familial relationships for four generations in Andover, Massachusetts. He found children achieving greater autonomy after 1700.

Although Walzer may be right when he suggests "that the American mother of the eighteenth century was in closer and more constant contact with her children, and interacted more often and more deeply than her counterpart in Europe," the selections by Stone and Plumb suggest that the trend towards greater intimacy in the relationships between parents and children also characterized English family life by the 18th century. A warmer, more affectionate tone in the overall quality of family relationships appears to have been added on both sides of the Atlantic by the 1700's; and the treatment and conception of childhood was not unaffected by this change.

While it is possible to synthesize the answers of childhood historians to the first three questions we have examined, we can do no more than summarize their respective approaches to the fourth question, which asks for the reasons behind the changes in the conception and treatment of children in the past. Answers to the first three could be synthesized because they are essentially matters of description that are derived from observation. The fourth question, however, calls for an explanation that proceeds from the historian's basic premises about causality. And nothing divides historians so profoundly as their different interpretative frameworks for explaining the causes of individual and collective behavior.

Stone and Plumb, for example, respectively take a socio-economic approach. Stone explicitly rejects the psychological analyses he is familiar with. A psychological interpretation of childrearing that stresses how successive generations of parents repeated the modes to which they had been subjected as children, Stone rightly notes, does not account for change. Accordingly Stone looks outside the interpersonal network of the family for his explanation of parental attitudes towards children. He finds the sources of parental values and behavior located in the social system, particularly in the relationship of people to property. He suggests that there was a direct correlation between the amount of property parents controlled and their effort to control their children; the more property, the greater the attempt at control. Reenforcing this upper class inclination, writes Stone, was the negative view of human nature that the Protestant clergy articulated. They declared children to be born willful and proud and therefore needing to have their natural inclinations rigorously suppressed.

Although Plumb's model of causality is not boldly relieved, a theme throughout his essay is the link between attitudinal changes after 1700 and the expansion of economic opportunity and social mobility. The connection is not clearly drawn, but he seems to suggest that the opening of doors to occupational and status advancement made parents more alert to the value of their children and that this buttressed an emerging attitude which stressed the inherent goodness of human nature and therefore of children.

Illick adopts a psychohistorical approach, which insists that an explanation of parental attitudes and behavior must be anchored to an understanding of individual psychology. But while he describes the different psychologies of repressive and indulgent generations of parents, he does not account for the transformation of the one into the other. He does not resolve the problem that Stone has posed: what psychological process enabled children to mature into different kinds of parents from the ones they had been reared by?

No survey of childhood in the early modern era can ignore the important shift that now occurred in the educational experience of children. For the first time a comparatively large proportion of youngsters were sent to school away from their homes. The point when parents began to transfer the responsibility of educating their children from the household to the school would seem self-evidently to signal an important change in the history of both the family and of childhood. But what can we make of this change? By itself, it does not lead inexorably to one set of inferences. For example, does it mean that parents valued their children and were trying to provide them with whatever advantages they could? Or should we infer that parents found schools to be a convenient way of getting rid of their kids for prolonged periods? Or was some irretrievable admixture of these motives at play? Moreover, does the growth of schools necessarily mean that families were relinquishing their responsibilities for socializing their children? The opposite conclusion has in fact been suggested recently. Cremin (1970) has observed that the increase in schools did not reflect the diminution of familial responsibility for education. On the contrary, the increase in schools went hand in hand with the expansion of household education in England during the late Renaissance. Murrin (1972), moreover, has argued that in America only those areas marked by stable family structures in which parental control of children was successfully asserted also produced schools as well as other institutions, while colonies with a weak base of family life could not support viable educational, religious, or even political institutions. Thus the establishment of schools in New England was a result of its strong family life, while the scarcity of schools in the Chesapeake is a reflection of its unstable family system.

When juxtaposed, the selections by Jordan and Plumb may suggest a continuity in educational development between 1500 and 1800 that does not do full justice to Plumb's perception that something new was happening in the 18th century. Plumb is right in saying that the expansion of schooling after 1700 was new, if he is comparing it with the retreat from education that occurred in the second half of the 17th century in the wake of the English Cival War. But the educational fabric of the 1700s was not cut from whole cloth. As Jordan documents it, the proliferation of schooling began with the Tudors and continued into the 17th century. And it was supported for much the same reasons that Plumb finds underlying the educational expansion of the 18th century.

For New Englanders public schools occupied a significant place from the beginning in their overall attempt to socialize children into the service of God and the commonwealth. The famous Massachusetts law of 1647, which enjoined the erection of grammar schools in towns of 100 families, was passed by men who recently emigrated from a society where an educational revolution had just reached its highest point. Modeled after their English prototype, New England grammar schools at first were charged with inculcating piety and the classical curriculum in the boys who entered at the age of seven or eight in expectation that these children would be prepared to study at Harvard when they reached fourteen. By the 18th century this mission of these grammar schools was transformed. Around 1700 the schools became wholly tax supported and therefore more broadly available to poor and rich alike than they had been earlier. Girls were increasingly admitted after 1700. The curriculum was likewise broadened to deemphasize Latin and to respond more practically to the future vocational needs of the students. Yet two components of instruction appear to have remained fairly constant to the end of the 18th century, the reliance upon rote learning and corporal punishment. This suggests that in New England the view of children remained essentially negative, with the assumption being that a child's natural inclinations must be overpowered and channelled into an adult approved direction.

In the south, the striking absence of schools in the 17th century as well as the scarcity of towns and churches threw children virtually entirely into the adult dominated environment of their widely scattered rural households. The significantly smaller birth rate in Virginia and Maryland than what occurred in New England also meant that Chesapeake children had comparatively few peers with whom to interact. Combined with the extraordinarily high parental mortality rate in that region, these circumstances may well have imposed on southern children a premature assumption of adult responsibilities. It is not that their parents thought of them as miniature adults, but that circumstances forced these children to grow up faster than northern and even English youngsters had to.

Allowing for these exceptional circumstances in the American south, we conclude this summary of Anglo-American childhood by noting how impressed we are by the continuum we discern in the way children were treated during the early modern centuries on both sides of the Atlantic. Historians are no doubt picking up something significantly new when they tune in to the new language of benevolence, sentiment, affection, and companionship in the primary sources of 18th century family life. But we sense that while there was a new sensibility emerging, it was not translated immediately into dramatically new modes of behavior. School children continued to be beaten and taught by rote, for example, just as they had been a century earlier, when adults used language and imagery that was less expressive of benevolence and love.

In approaching these readings, the reader should be mindful of the methodological difficulties involved when historians try to assess changes in the attitudes of whole societies over time. Is it really possible to measure attitudinal changes sufficiently to suggest that the sensibility of the people of one century was qualitatively different from those of an earlier one? It is noteworthy that none of the selections in this section represents a quantitative approach. For none of the four questions that preoccupy childhood historians lend themselves to statistical analysis. They require evidence that is necessarily impressionistic and that must be used cautiously.

## 2. English Childrearing In The Seventeenth Century

By Joseph E. Illick

Assuming that the child survived infancy, his training after that point cannot be described with certainty. There is, for example, practically no notion of toilet training in the early seventeenth century. Guillemeau did note precautions to be taken against bed wetting, including getting children up during the night, as well as threatening and shaming them, but he warned against harsh treatment. Other writers assumed that infants would dirty their swaddling cloths, which must mean that bowel training did not begin until after the age of one—and perhaps much later, given the indulgent attitude toward crying and its association with soiled clothes. Indeed, the reader of *The Child-Bearer's Cabinet* would assume a long and protected infancy, followed by a permissive approach to early childhood.

From three years of age until the seventh, they are to be educated gently and kindly, not to be severely reprehended, chidden, or beaten, for by that means they may be made throughout their whole life after too timorous, or too much terrified, astonished, and sotted.

Being yet in their first years, they are not to be compelled to going [walking], for seeing all their bones are soft as Wax, and the body fall the heavier, they either become lame or universally resolved in their feet. . . .

In the sixth or seventh year of their age, they are to be sent to schoole, and committed to the breeding and introduction of courteous and temperate Schoolmasters, who may not terrifie them.

Before these yeares they are not to be compelled or forced to harder labours; otherwise they will not thrive well, but stand at a stay, and keep little, or become Dwarfes.

Yet, despite this timely advice, it is clear that children were being beaten in the early seventeenth century; frequently by their mothers and seemingly without regard to sex. (Indeed, there were apparently few exceptions, at least in the upper class, to John Aubrey's observation that "in those dayes, fathers were not acquainted with their children.") In schools, beating was the generally accepted way of maintaining order and ensuring learning, "spare the rod and spoil the child" having Biblical sanction—though there were dissenters from this strict regimen.

Far from discouraging a child from early walking, domestic scenes painted in the seventeenth century give testimony to the use of contraptions with wheels which accommodate toddlers learning the rudiments of ambulation. Leading strings were attached to clothing, the purpose also being to steady youngsters attempting to walk. The portrait of a nine-month-old child standing up must testify to an adult's aspiration if not to a child's competence. Precocity was of concern to the parent in physical development as well as in the mental realm.

The diarist John Evelyn, writing in mid-century, certainly pushed his child to "harder labours." He taught his son to pray as soon as he could speak. At age three the boy was reading and, soon afterward, writing.

Before he was five he could recognize Greek and Latin words; simultaneously his mother was teaching him French. Evelyn's motives were clear enough. He thought the mind of the child was vulnerable, making it imperative that he be guarded from bad thoughts, that learning serve as a bulwark against the world as well as a determinant of future growth. To strengthen the child's resistance, manliness must be nurtured: his locks should be sheared in the cradle and, thereafter, a Spartan regime followed, though physical punishment was to be more a threat than a reality. Only occasionally was the child to be soothed and flattered, a concession which would not have been granted by Evelyn's contemporary, Ezekias Woodward, who asserted: "Indulgence is the very *engine* of the Devill . . . "

Evelyn might well have emphasized the vulnerability of children and, consequently, the need for discipline. His personal tragedy was the death of this cherished son at the age of five. The ubiquity of illness, the not unlikely possibility of death—for the life expectancy of children (ages 1-14) declined from 42.5 to 34 in England in the seventeenth century—was a constant source of anxiety to parents. Children, though infrequently mentioned in personal correspondence, were most commonly depicted in the setting of a sick room. Thus, Sarah Meade kept her mother informed about her son for two years after his delivery.

> He has been a little froward [peevish] this day and last night, but I hope it is but wind. . . . We are well and the child thrives. . . . I hope the child has not taken cold. . . . Nathaniel had a looseness for above 2 weeks, which wee thought did him good, & carried of his flegme & stoppage at his stomacke; & I was in hope, when hee came into the country, it might have abated, but it yett continues upon him; having 4: or 5: stooles in a day & night, which keeps him pretty weake and low; & his stomacke is weake; we are fearfull to give him things to stopp it least he should be worse; for we suppose he is A breeding some more great teeth; and several have told mee that many children breeds their teeth with A Looseness, which many Reckons best:—I am a little fearful of him about it. . . . our little boy is fine & well & his looseness is much abated, & I think has noe more now fine than doth him good, goeinge to stoole but about 3 or 4 times in a day & a night; his teeth troubled him much; & wee gott James Wass to come & cutt his gumms in 2 places, since which he has been much better.

In addition to the explicitness and the constant overtones of worry evident in these letters, it is notable that Sarah was aware of information to be found in books on child care. Mrs. Sharp pointed to loose bowels as a consequence of the "breeding of teeth," while Robert Pemell was the first English physician to advocate gum-lancing during teething. It seems probable that child care manuals were reaching more people in the later seventeenth century, and that children were receiving more attention.

Sarah Meade's concern with teething might be the least of a parent's worries. Lady Hatton wrote her husband: "my daughter Nancy presents her duty to you she is very well Susana is not very well she has another tooth just ready to cut little Betty has had the chiking pox but they are now beginning to dry away & I hope the worst is past with her never any poor child has been so ill that lived. . . . " To comfort Lord Hatton at the time of his wife's miscarriage, Lady Manchester pointed to the misfortune of "Sir Robert Cotton [who] lost this year 5 daughters which was all the children he had in three days time," while Lady Hatton heard from her brother that "upon my telling [Lady Northumberland] some remedies for her child's convulsions, we all wish it well in heaven, to be no more a disturbance to us here . . . for once a week we are all troubled with it, either loosing balls or some other diverting appointments through it. . . . " There are three reactions to disease involved here, in addition to the earlier one of concern: identifying it and, presumably, attempting to control it; affecting a callous or disinterested attitude toward it; declaring it out of human hands and, thus, a religious matter.

Insofar as identification and control of disease were concerned, the claim has been made that the "middle period of the seventeenth century witnessed the awakening of medicine from its age-long sleep of well-nigh 2,000 years." At the end of the Tudor period, the study of children's disease was a combination of "crude theories and meager observations" based on classic and contemporary writings, hardly separate from pedagogical considerations. During the Stuart era, the names of William Harvey, Francis Glisson, Thomas Sydenham and many lesser but important pioneers appeared, not to mention such luminaries as Bacon and Locke. Yet despite efforts to raise the level of medical therapy (most obviously in the areas of pharmacology and epidemiology) and the attention paid to preventative medicine (especially regarding the plague), effective techniques were slow in coming. "The change which occurred in the seventeenth century was thus not so much technological as mental. In many different spheres of life the period saw the emergence of a new faith in the potentialities of human initiative."

But what good was medicine if divine intervention was purposeful? Lady Warwick's first child was a girl, "whom God was pleased to take from me by death." During her second confinement, with a son, her father died— "but I, being young and inconsiderate, grief did not long stick with me." She learned to grieve, and to accept. She felt she sought too much comfort in the world, and claimed to have had

> some inward persuasion that God would, in some way or other, punish me for my doing so. And, at last, it pleased God to send a sudden sickness on my only son, which I then doated on with great fond-

ness. I was beyond expression struck at it; not only because of my kindness of him, but because my conscience told me it was for my back-sliding. Upon this conviction I presently retired to God; and by earnest prayer begged Him to restore my child; and did then solemnly promise to God, if he would hear my prayer I would become a new creature. This prayer of mine God was so gracious as to grant; and of a sudden began to restore my child; which made the doctor himself wonder at the sudden amendment he saw in him.

At the time of her husband's unexpected inheritance of his title, due to the deaths of his elder brothers, Lady Warwick feared she might be drawn "to love the glory of the world too well." Her only surviving son contracted small pox and died. She was prepared but her spouse was not.

I did endeavour to comfort my sad and afflicted husband, who, at the news of his death . . . cried out so terribly that his cry was heard a great way; and he was the saddest afflicted person could possibly be. I confess that I loved him at a rate, that if my heart do not deceive me, I would, with all the willingness in the world, had died either for him or with him, if God had only seen it fit; yet I was dumb and held my peace, because God did it.

This incident was not isolated and discreet. The reaction of Lady Warwick, like that of Alice Thornton, suggests that girls were taught to sublimate anger or aggression through religion. A recent literary study claims that reading between the lines of seventeenth-century women's prayer books, one finds a concern with childbirth and sickness, just as the readers of these books were admonished to be silent, chaste and obedient. Repression and religion were complementary.

Significantly, the men who invoked the Almighty at times of illness or death were usually ministers. Many fathers, as already noted, chose not to know their children. Most men, unlike Lord Warwick, chose silence, aloofness, a cold civility rather than showing emotion outwardly. The Dutchess of Newcastle's encomium for her husband—"My Lord always being a great master of his passions"—was a common term of praise, at least to the upper class.

The Dutchess also noted that "both My Lord's parents, and his aunt and uncle in law, shewed always a great and fond love to My Lord, endeavouring, when he was but a child, to please him with what he most delighted in." But such indulgence was probably as unusual as Clarendon's companionship with his father. Moralists inveighed against it. John Donne observed with pride: "Children Kneel to ask blessing of parents in England, and where else." Thomas Cobbett, a mid-century Puritan writer, warned children to "Present your Parents so to your minds, as bearing the image of

God's Father-hood, and that also will help your filiall awe and Reverence to them.'' Parents were cautioned against undermining their authority ''by being too fond of your children and too familiar with them at sometimes at least, and not keeping constantly your due distance: such fondness and familiarity breed contempt and irreverency in children.'' Even child-rearing books warned against ''cockering'' children.

Yet it seems clear that the drive to love children was strong, and Roger North demonstrated how the tendency to be lenient could serve the ends of authority:

> great use may be made of that fondness which disposeth parents to gratifie children's litle craving appetites, by doing it with an adjunct of precept, as a reward of obedience and vertue, such as they are capable of, and at the same time being kind, and tender in Gratifiing them. This makes yong Creatures thinck that their will is not enough, without other means, to obtein their desires, and knowing that, they will Conforme, which breeds an habit of order in them and lasts to the end. The Contrary is seen, when fondness makes parents Indulg all things to children.

In this manner, parents could succumb to children without feeling guilty at having totally sacrificed personal restraint. Emotional display would be disciplined.

Self-control appears to have been the crucial issue of this situation. Projected onto the child, the obverse of self-control was seen in willfullness, a quality which North clearly opposed. His attitude was hardly novel; it could be seen in depictions of the child dating at least to the beginning of the century. In *A Godly Form of Household Government* (1621) the Puritans Robert Cleaver and John Dod wrote:

> The young child which lieth in the cradle is both wayward and full of affections; and though his body be but small, yet he hath a reat [wrong-doing) heart, and is altogether inclined to evil. . . If this sparkle be suffered to increase, it will rage over and burn down the whole house. For we are changed and become good not by birth but by education. . . . Therefore parents must be wary and circumspect . . .they must correct and sharply reprove their children for saying or doing ill.

Education, then, was necessary to protect a child against his own self-destruction. The attitude to be fostered in a child would have to be one of constantly questioning himself, making himself feel inadequate, engendering self-doubt.

There was a quite opposite view on the nature of the child, that of total innocence, which was succinctly announced by John Earle in *Micro-cosmography* (1628):

> A child is a man in a small letter, yet the best copy of Adam before he tasted of Eve or the apple. . . . His soul is yet a white paper unscribbled with observations of the world. . . . he knows no evil. . . .

Again, the antidote to the world's corrupting influence was education, as John Evelyn's regimen for his son made clear. A child nurtured on languages and the classics might not be so prone to self doubt as one whose diet was the Scriptures. But in either case precocity was at least a denial of self-expression, the forcing of adult values on the defenseless child.

This aggressive response to infant vulnerability may seem ironic until it is recognized that concepts of childhood innocence or depravity were themselves parental projections, either of helplessness or of rage, in the face of death that could not be controlled. The child learned his lesson, coming to understand his own mortality, as did women and clergymen, through religion. Alice Thornton recalled the passing of her daughter, Elizabeth.

> That deare, sweet angell grew worse, and indured it with infinitt patience, and when Mr. Thornton and I came to pray for her, she held up those sweete eyes and hands to her deare Father in heaven, looked up, and cryed in her language, 'Dad, dad, dad' with such vehemency as if inspired by her holy Father in heaven to deliver her sweet soule into her heavenly Father's hands, and at which time we allso did with great zeale deliver up my deare infant's soule into the hand of my heavenly Father, and then she sweetly fell asleepe and went out of this miserable world like a lamb.

Indeed, a children's literature concerned with impending death emerged in the seventeenth century: sermons preached at the passings of young people, memorials, warnings, tokens, looking-glasses, messages, confessions, exhortations, testimonies, admonitions.

Probably the most well read of these many books was James Janeway's *A Token for Children* (1671), a compendium of case histories of youngsters who experienced dramatic conversions and, in the course of dying shortly thereafter, exhorted sinful adults to lead virtuous lives. The death-bed admonitions to parents—"Oh Mother," said he, "did you but know what joy I feel, you would not weep but rejoice"—allowed adults to absolve themselves of guilt felt for bringing vulnerable children into the world. Youngsters themselves might be called upon to shoulder the burden of mortality, as demonstrated in John Norris' *Spiritual Counsel: A Father's Advice to his Children.*

be much in the Contemplation of the last four thyngs, Heaven, Hell, Death, and Judgment. Place yourselves frequently on your death beds, in your Coffins, and in your Graves. Act over frequently in your Minds, the Solemnity of your own Funerals; and entertain your Imaginations with all the lively scenes of Mortality; Meditate much upon the places, and upon the Days of Darkness, and upon the fewness of those that shall be saved; and be always with your Hourglass in your hands, measuring out your own little Span and comparing it with the endless Circle of Eternity.

However, the development of this sort of religious precocity was extreme, while the aristocratic ideal of the seventeenth century was moderation, which hinged on self-control. No man better articulated this goal than John Locke, whose stream of ideas on child rearing carried some sediment from the earlier part of the century as well as the distillate of his observations as scholar and physician. In the latter category may be placed his thoughts on pregnancy and early child care. When confronted with an expectant mother who was breathless following a fright, he raised questions meant to determine whether the woman suffered from cardiac failure, toxaemia of pregnancy or hysterical overbreathing. During childbirth, if the infant could not be put into a natural position, "surgery must be at once applied to bring forth the foetus while the mother still has strength." He did not approve of swaddling, noting that Spartan nurses had brought up children "admirably" without it. He also observed that infants of the Gold Coast at seven or eight months were left "on the ground so that you see them dragging themselves like kittens on four paws; this is also the reason why they walk earlier than European infants." Unlike some of his predecessors, Locke was unworried that thought and care be given to raising children, believing that "little, or almost insensible impressions of our tender infancies, have very important or lasting consequences." He stood somewhere between advocates of infant innocence and infant depravity, arguing that few of "Adam's children" were born without "some byass in their natural temper." No childhood determinist, he believed that "Men's happiness or misery is most part of their own making," and his advice was generally aimed at strengthening character toward the end of self-sufficiency.

If the parent were to accomplish this task, he must from the cradle not give into the child's will but, rather, "distinguish between the wants of fancy and the wants of nature." Locke recognized "cockering and tenderness," indulgent and corrupting practices, as an upper class phenomenon and exhorted gentlemen to imitate the discipline of "honest farmers and substantial yeomen." To harden the children, for example, their feet should be accustomed to cold water (poor people's children went barefoot, after all). Open air and minimum of clothing, always loose-fitting, were essential to good health. Locke claimed that "the body may be made to bear almost anything."

A simple diet, without permissive feeding, was recommended. Crying was not to be indulged. Long hours of sleep were to be tolerated, but on a hard bed. "The great thing to be minded in education," Locke observed, was "what habits you settle." Most striking among these was "going to stool regularly," to be accomplished by enforced sitting. No previous commentator had ever mentioned toilet training. The purpose of this regimen was to cultivate the strength and vigor of the body "so that it may be able to obey and execute the orders of the *mind.*"

It follows logically that the virtue of the mind would be "that a man is able to *deny himself* his own desires . . . and purely follow what reason directs as best." Locke called for a change in current disciplinary practices: "What vice can be nam'd, which parents, and those about children, do not season them with . . . violence, revenge and cruelty. *Give me a blow that I may beat him,* is a lesson that most children hear every day." As parents should not be too tender, neither should they be too hard. The rod should be avoided, as well as rewards. Shame should be the instrument used to motivate children.

> *Esteem* and *disgrace* are, of all others, the most powerful incentives to the mind, when once it is brought to relish them. If you can get into children a love of credit, and an apprehension of shame and disgrace you have to put into 'em the true principle.

Praise and commendation for accomplishment were to be counterbalanced by a "cold and neglectful countenance" for failure.

Locke recognized the limits of rules (and, especially, of rote learning), saw the possibilities of play ("nothing appears to me to give children so much becoming confidence and behaviour. . . as *dancing*") and emphasized the importance of parental example and a growing friendship between father and son as the boy gradually became a man ("The only fence against the world is, a thorough knowledge of it, into which a young gentleman should be entered by degrees. . . . ") Not only would children be watching their parents for the proper examples of behavior, but to carry out Locke's plan parents (or tutors) would have to spend a good deal of time surveilling their children.

Nor would supervision account of all the time spent, since the stricture that all children be dealt with as rational creatures could only lead to hours of explanation and persuasion. But the energy might be better used than formerly, since Locke took an honest (and refreshingly realistic) view of educational approaches to children. He realized that reading first had to be encouraged for its entertainment value, strongly recommending *Aesop's Fables* but remaining traditional enough to advocate learning the Lord's

Prayer, the Creeds and the Ten Commandments. A chapter-by-chapter approach to the Bible, he noted, could only convey "an odd jumble of thoughts." He approved learning foreign languages (*"Latin* I look upon as absolutely necessary to a gentleman") but was not convinced of the worth of studying English grammar ("persons of the softer sex . . . without the least study or knowledge of *grammar,* can carry them to a great degree of elegancy and politeness in their language").

Locke disclaimed having made a comprehensive and definitive statement on child rearing, and he made it clear that each parent must finally consult his own reason for the proper education of his child. Locke himself deviated from conventional wisdom in child-rearing by changing the conditions of infancy: swaddling clothes would be discarded, crawling might be tolerated and, though crying would not be indulged nor feeding be so much a matter of demand, the mother would probably be present (how else would the nurse be surveilled?). The early years of childhood would witness the introduction of toilet training and the discarding of corporal punishment for the inducement of shame. (Engendering doubt, of course.) More attention would be paid to children and to the nature of their education.

Interest in school learning, notably in the middle class, had been strikingly evident since the middle of the sixteenth century. It has been claimed that the "English in 1640 were infinitely better educated than they had been before," as they moved through the educational complex of petty schools (basic literacy), free schools (mathematics, English composition and rhetoric), grammer schools (free school curriculum plus classical linguistics and English grammar), universities and Inns of Court. The expansion of education owed to the impetus of the bourgeoisie, who were moved to mimic the bookishness of the gentry; humanists, who viewed schooling as the road to universal moral improvement (which might render unnecessary the protection of the innocent child against the corrupt world); and Puritans, who viewed ignorance as the root of evil (and, as a corollary, infant depravity as remediable). Another way of viewing this transformation would be from a changing perspective on childhood: in art, costume, leisure activities and literature, it can be seen that a separate world was being created for children in the seventeenth century.

Perhaps the most interesting change in this regard had to do with the English practice of sending children out of the home at six or seven years to a school or an apprenticeship. By the middle of the seventeenth century, parents were hanging onto their children a few years longer. The Reverend Ralph Josselin's children, born in the mid-seventeenth century, left home to be educated or become servants and apprentices between the ages of ten and fifteen. Nor was this a middle class pattern only. The gentry on one end of the social scale, the yeomen and poor on the other, kept adolescent children at home more often, but it still was exceptional to do so.

A foreign observer in the early sixteenth century had attributed the putting out of children to the "want of affection in the English," while more recently an American historian of the Puritan movement has suggested that parents "did not trust themselves with their own children, that they were afraid of spoiling them by too great affection." The many strictures against overfondness, against cockering and tenderness, suggest that affection was a crucial issue—Ralph Josselin valued his children "above gold and jewels." Possibly it was *the* crucial issue, despite the fact that financial burdens and educational aims motivated parents to send older children out of the home.

In the middle of the seventeenth century there were only two counties in England where there was not a grammar school (offering a possibility of free tuition) within twelve miles of any family, a fact which suggests that other than pedagogical motives were involved in pushing children out to learn. The educator John Brinsley wrote: "If any are sent to school so early, they are rather sent to the school from troubling the house at home, and from danger, and shrewd turns, than from any great hope and desire that their friends should learn anything in effect."

The troubles, dangers and shrewd turns must have included the unwholesome influence of servants, seemingly inevitable confrontations with step-parents (the likelihood of both natural parents surviving until a child reached his majority was not high), and a matter that involved servants, house guests and parents—the intimacy of sleeping arrangements. Sexual attractions and rivalries in the family were, at most, alluded to and disguised. Thus, Lord Halifax addressed his daughter:

> *You* are at present the chief Object of my *care,* as well as my *kindness,* which sometimes throweth me into *Visions* of your being happy in the World, that are better suited to my partial *Wishes*, than my reasonable *Hopes* for you. At other times, when my *Fears* prevail, I shrink as if I were struck, at the Prospect of *Danger,* to which a young Woman must be expos'd. . . . Your *Husband's* Kindness will have so much advantage of ours, that we shall yield upon all *Competition,* and as well as we love you, be very well contented to surrender to such a *Rival.*

Halifax tried, not obtrusively, perhaps not consciously—to develop a conspiracy between himself and his daughter toward other women, which must have undermined the authority of Lady Halifax. Moralists encouraged mothers to establish close relationships with their daughters, while they recommended modesty, chastity and piety in young girls.

Conflict of authority in domestic relations was usually between father and son (unless it involved step-parents, when the matter of inheritance often took precedence over sex). The fact that these conflicts were frequently religious in nature (almost any journal kept by a male Quaker gives testimony to this observation) is significant when it is recalled that the typical seventeenth-century father was apt to be a secularist while his wife was inclined to religiosity and inculcated these values in her children. Note the testimony of Reverend Oliver Heywood:

> But tho my parents were godly [it later appears the father did not attend church] yet my birth and my nativity was in sin, and so was my conception, for they were instruments to bring me into the world not as saints but as man and woman . . . of Adam by natural generation. . . . I am by nature a child of wrath, a limb of satan . . . and that not too fruitful root began to sprout in infancy. . . .
>
> I have observed from my childhood and youth my natural constitution exceedingly inclined to lust, which hath discovered itselfe betimes, and many times assaulted me both waking and sleeping. . . . tho I may take much paines in mortifying dutys to crucify the flesh and beat down my body. . . .
>
> I doe with thankfulness to god remember, that many a time my dear mother did zealously and famililarly presse upon me truths of the greatest concernment . . . I confesse I took much delight in waiting upon her abroad, but what my ends were I cannot tel, yet this I beleeve, that god disposed of it for much good to my poore soul, yea I am sometimes thinking it may be god that made that time a time of love. . . .

It could not be expected, however, that sexual attraction could always be sublimated since this would not prepare most males for their careers. The alternative was a strict discipline, the control of sexuality through a different sort of religious sublimation—preparation for the "Calling." Certainly the school provided discipline. John Brinsley, the Puritan divine and educator, put forth the regimen. School would begin at six, with punishment for tardiness (virtually every picture of the classroom showed the master with a birch in one hand). Homework in Latin was presented and other studies pursued until nine, when there was a quarter-hour break. The work resumed until eleven, when there was a two-hour hiatus. From one to five-thirty students were again at their desks, with a quarter-hour break at three thirty. The purpose of education was divine, "God having ordained schools of learning to be a principall means to reduce a barbarous people to civilitie" and Christianity. The challange was to gain "the verie savage amongst them unto Jesus Christ, whether Irish or Indian. . . . " Or, Brinsley might have added, "Child."

The punctuality demanded of the student, the restraint needed to remain sitting almost all day at a desk would foster the self-discipline which was the object that the guilds attempted "to instil self-discipline and respect for the social code into those for whose industrial training they were responsible.'' The Shoemakers of Carlisle forbid apprentices and journeymen to play football without the consent of their masters; the Merchant Adventurers of Newcastle forbid "daunce dice cards mum or use any musick" and inveighed against extravagant dress and long hair, even establishing a prison to jail offenders against these rules. There are instances of masters imposing fines for missing prayer, "toying with the maids," teaching children "bawdy words" or even wearing "a foul shirt on Sunday." Working conditions were apparently as exacting as school situations, though in the seventeenth century apprentices were protected by law.

There is no denying that parents in seventeenth-century England were interested in their children, but that interest took the form of controlling youngsters—just as adults restrained themselves—rather than allowing autonomous development.

## 3. Corporal Punishment, 1500-1660

by Lawrence Stone

During the period of 1500 to 1660 there is overwhelming evidence of a fierce determination to break the will of the child, and to enforce his utter subjection to the authority of his elders and superiors, and most noticeably of his parents. The first pastor of Plymouth, Massachusetts, was only reflecting current ideas when he observed that "there is in all children . . . a stubbornness and stoutness of mind, arising from natural pride, which must in the first place be broken and beaten down." "Children should not know, if it could be kept from them, that they have a will of their own." In other words, in the seventeenth century the early training of children was directly equated with the breaking in of young horses or hunting dogs.

In the Middle Ages, schools had used physical punishment to enforce discipline, and the characteristic equipment of a schoolmaster was not so much a book as a rod or a bundle of birch twigs. The emblem of *Grammar* on Chartres cathedral porch is a master threatening two children with a scourge; at Oxford University the conferral of the degree of Master of Grammar was accompanied by presentation of a birch as symbol of office and by the ceremonial flogging of a whipping boy by the new Master. But only an infinitesimal minority was subjected to such discipline in the Middle Ages, since so few undertook the study of Latin grammar, and those who did were presumably highly motivated to learn. Moreover, even in the schools, at any rate in France, there is a good deal of evidence to show that many punishments took the form of fines. It was only in the fifteenth century that flogging began normally to be substituted for fines, and then it was confined to the poor who could not pay the fines (and who were thought socially suitable for physical punishment) and to the very young boys.

In the early sixteenth century, three things happened. The first is that flogging became the standard routine method of punishment for all schoolchildren, regardless of rank or age; the second was that a far larger proportion of the population began to go to school, and therefore became liable to this discipline; thirdly, since education became more widespread, many were now poorly motivated to learn, and therefore more liable to be beaten to force them to do it. Moreover, in the sixteenth century severe physical punishment was practiced in the home, the school, and even the University as a matter of principle and practice. To what extent the greater evidence of this brutality in the sixteenth century school is a reflection of a harsher reality, or merely of a larger and more revealing body of written records, is very hard to say. For the moment the evidence suggests that both played their part, that conditions were certainly extremely brutal and authoritarian in the sixteenth and seventeenth century home and school, but that the deterioration from the late medieval period may be exaggerated by the differences in the amount and nature of the evidence. All that can be said is that whipping was now so normal as part of a child's experience that when a later seventeenth century moral theologian wished to convey to children some idea of Hell, the best way he could think of describing it was as "a terrible place, that is worse a thousand times than whipping. God's anger is worse than your father's anger."

Scholastic punishments normally took two forms. The first and most common was to lay the child over a bench, or alternatively to horse him on the back of a companion, and to flog his naked buttocks with a bundle of birches until the blood flowed. The second was to strike his hand with a ferule, a flat piece of wood which expanded at the end into a pear shape with a hole in the middle. One blow with this instrument was enough to raise a most painful blister.

There can be no doubt whatever that severe flogging was a normal and daily occurrence in the sixteenth and seventeenth century grammar school, and some of the most famous headmasters of their day, like Dr. Busby of Westminster School or Dr. Gill of St. Paul's were notorious for their savagery. Indeed, some of them seem to have been pathological sadists, and John Aubrey's account of Dr. Gill's "whipping-fits" suggests a man who had become the slave to an irrational obsession. But what is significant is that society was willing to give him a free hand without censure or restaint, since flogging was then regarded as the only reliable method of controlling both children and adults.

It seems likely that institutionalized brutality was standard in public schools and grammar schools, but varied from master to master in the countless small private schools run by clergymen for a handful of local children and boarders in the seventeenth century. Some were virtual prison camps run by sadists, while others were models of compassion and understanding. But these latter cases, when they are mentioned in the records, are always described as exceptions to the rule. Thus Simonds D'Ewes records that he was never flogged by his London schoolmaster Henry Reynolds, explaining that,

> *he had a pleasing way of teaching, contrary to all others of that kind. For the rod and the ferula stood in his school rather as ensigns of his power than as instruments of his anger, and were rarely made use of for the punishment of delinquents. For he usually rewarded those who deserved well. . . . and he accounted the primitive punishment of not rewarding the remiss and negligent equipolent to the severest correction.*

Despite the kindly treatment, D'Ewes asked to be removed to Bury Grammar School, since he did not think that Reynolds' learning was sufficiently deep for him. But D'Ewes was an exceptionally diligent and able student, always one of the best in the class, and as such was presumably normally free of the ferocious punishments meted out to his more dim-witted or idle companions.

The extension of flogging even reached into university education. During the late sixteenth century the colleges of Oxford and Cambridge had received for the first time a huge influx of sons of the wealthy laity, for whom the accommodations had been greatly enlarged. The key feature of the sixteenth century college was the application to lay children of the strict, prison-like conditions previously applied to regular clergy in monasteries and colleges. This was the time when the college assumed its now familiar function of acting *in loco parentis,* with all the aids of high walls, gates closed at 9 p.m., and strict internal surveillance by the tutors. This was also the time, between 1450 and 1660, when colleges freely used physical punishments on their younger students, normally, but not always, under the age of eighteen, either by public whippings in the hall or over a barrel in the buttery, or else by putting them in stocks in the hall. By the medieval statutes of Balliol and Lincoln colleges, the college head had powers of physical punishment, but in the sixteenth century this authority was greatly extended, and delegated to deans and even tutors. Aubrey, who entered Oxford in 1642, noted that there "the rod was frequently used by the tutors and deans on his pupils, till Bachelors of Arts."

It should be emphasized that this widespread and constant use of flogging as the prime method of spreading a knowledge of the classics was the last thing that the Humanist educational reformers had in mind when they pressed for a classical training of the European elite. From Guarino to Vives to Erasmus they were, without exceptions, opposed to the use of severe physical punishments. They believed that children could and should be enticed into the classics, not driven like cattle. But what happened in practice was that hard-pressed schoolmasters continued and extended the medieval tradition of flogging on an ever increasing scale as classical education spread, since it was the easiest and least troublesome means of drilling Latin grammar into thick or resistant skulls. Renaissance school practice thus bore no relation whatever to Renaissance educational theory: the subject matter was identical, but the method of instruction was in substantial contradiction.

This extension of the use of physical punishment throughout the whole educational system merely reflected a growing use of this method of social control throughout the society. A late sixteenth century Dutchman—appropriately enough called Batty—who was rapidly translated into English, developed the theory that the providence and wisdom of God had especially formed the human buttocks so that they could be severely beaten without incurring serious bodily injury. The late sixteenth and early seventeenth centuries was for England the great flogging age: every town and every village had its whipping post, which was in constant use as a means of preserving social order.

Children were particularly singled out for harsh treatment, and John Aubrey in the late seventeenth century could reflect that in his youth, parents "were as severe to their children as their schoolmasters; and their schoolmasters as masters of the House of Correction. . . . Fathers and mothers slashed their daughters in time of their besom discipline when they were perfect women." As a result, "the child perfectly loathed the sight of his parents as the slave his torturer." Aubrey was clearly exaggerating, but his remarks are significant since he is contrasting this period in the past to the more amiable relations that he thought prevailed when he was writing in the late seventeenth century. In France, Pierre Charron also spoke of the "almost universal" custom of "beating, whipping, abusing and scolding children, and holding them in great fear and subjection."

One case in which this disciplinary process in the home can be followed in great detail is that of the young son and heir of King Henri IV of France, the future Louis XIII. The child was first whipped at the age of two, and the punishments continued (usually for obstinacy) after he became king at the age of nine. He was whipped on the buttocks with a birch or a switch, administered first by his nurse immediately upon waking on the morning after the transgression. The whippings increased in frequency when he was three, and on one occasion his father whipped him himself when in a rage with his son. As he grew older, his nurse could not control him, and the child was held down by soldiers while she beat him. At the age of ten he still had nightmares of being whipped, and the threats to whip him only stopped in 1614, not long before his marriage. If this was the treatment meted out to a future and even reigning king in the early seventeenth century, on the instructions of his father, it is clear that Aubrey and Charron were describing a harsh reality about late sixteenth and early seventeenth century domestic relations between parents and children in the home.

This stress on domestic discipline and the utter subordination of the child found expression in extraordinary outward marks of deference which English children were expected to pay to their parents. They had to kneel before their parents to ask their blessing, perhaps one or two times a day, a practice John Donne believed to be unique in Europe. The children of the widowed Lady Alice Wandesford in the 1640s knelt daily to ask her blessing, and in 1651 her twenty-eight-year-old eldest son knelt for her blessing before leaving on a journey. Even as adults, children were expected to keep their hats off in their parents' presence, while daughters were expected to remain standing in their mother's presence. "Gentlemen of thirty and forty years old," recalled Aubrey, "were to stand like mutes and fools bareheaded before their parents; and the daughters (grown women) were to stand at the cupboard-side during the whole time of their proud mother's visit, unless (as the fashion was) leave was desired, forsooth, that a cushion should be given to them to kneel upon, . . . after they had done sufficient penance by standing." Well into his middle age Sir Dudley North "would never put on his hat or sit down before his father unless enjoined to it." Elizabeth Countess of Falkland always knelt in her mother's presence, despite the fact that she had married above her parents into the peerage. In the early seventeenth century, a son, even when grown up, would commonly address his father in a letter as "sir," and sign himself "your humble obedient son," "your son in continuance of all obedience" or "your most obedient and loving son." As late as the 1680s, Edmund Verney as an undergraduate at Oxford cautiously began his letters home with "Most honoured Father . . . " while those he received began with the peremptory word "Child."

Parents were advised that the only way for them to enforce their authority was to avoid any hint of friendliness towards the child. "Bow down his neck while he is young," recommended Thomas Becon in his catechism of 1560, "and beat him on his sides while he is a child, lest he wax stubborn and be disobedient unto thee, and so bring sorrow to thy heart." In the newly sanctified conjugal marriage, the duty of the wife and mother was to assist her husband in the task of the repression of their children. She "holds not his hand from due strokes, but bares their skins with delight to his fatherly stripes." One theory has it that this obsession with childish "stubbornness" or "obstinacy" was caused by the personal insecurity of the parents in a hierarchical society; that there existed in all pre-modern societies a constant tension between the insubordination of the will of the individual and the pressing need for social order. According to this theory, parents were determined to break the wills of their children since their own wills were constantly being subordinated to those of others. It is perfectly true that in the hierarchical, deferential society of early modern Europe, men and women were constantly obliged to emphasize their subordination to superiors by overt marks of respect, particularly the removing of their hats in their presence. Conversely, they constantly asserted their superiority over inferiors by insisting on identical marks of respect and obedience from those below them. It was indeed an authoritarian society in which the free expression of the will was not to be tolerated. Since all authoritarian societies depend on authoritarian child-rearing practices, early modern England was no exception to the rule.

The cause of this passion for crushing the will of the child went deeper than this, however, since it was applied with particular emphasis to the social elite, including kings. It was at the most elite public schools like Eton and Westminster that flogging was at its most ferocious—and where it has lasted longest, even into our own day. The instructions given by Henri IV about the treatment of his son and heir were clear and explicit:

*I wish and command you to whip him every time that he is obstinate or misbehaves, knowing well for myself that there is nothing in the world which will be better for him than that. I know it from experience, having myself profited, for when I was his age I was often whipped. That is why I want you to whip him and to make him understand why.*

The motivation in whipping a future king was clearly not to teach deference in a deferential society, since he was destined to become the apex of the pyramid.

Another theory has it that the process was a cyclical one related to individual psychology. "Fathers whipped their sons for their own good because they themselves were whipped as children. These fathers had been thwarted in their own infantile efforts to be autonomous," leaving them with "a pervasive sense of shame and doubt." But there is absolutely no evidence that Henri IV himself suffered from any such feelings; he seems to have been the very epitome of the well-adjusted, dynamic and commanding extrovert personality. Moreover, such an explanation blocks off any possibility of change, since each successive generation is automatically obliged, by the very fact of its own childhood experience, to impose the same experience on its children. And yet there were to be very significant changes over time in the eighteenth century in this very area of the enforcement of the young child of obedience to superiors.

There is undoubtedly some little truth in these explanations of highly repressive child-rearing practices, based on modern theories of ego-psychology, but it is essential for a fuller understanding to dig deeper into the particular values of the specific historical culture. The first of these was the firm belief in the innate sinfulness of children, which has already been discussed; and the second was the particular need for filial obedience dictated by the social aspirations of the propertied classes in the early modern period. The whole story of the dauphin's relations with Henri IV show that what the latter was particularly determined to enforce was obedience to the will of himself, the father. It was this that he was so anxious should be forcibly impressed upon his son. It was an obedience which began in little things, but was planned to lead to obedience in big ones. In the case of Louis, this obedience concerned one critical decision only, but in the cases of most children who were not heirs to great titles and estates, it concerned not one but two.

The principal justification of these extraordinary measures taken to break the child's will at an early stage was that he would accept with passive resignation later on the decisions of his parents in the two most important choices of any man's life, that of an occupation and more especially that of a marriage partner. It was the parents who decided, with the interest of the family primarily in mind, whom a child was to marry and whether he was to be trained for the church, the law, trade, or some other occupation. When Sir Peter Legh forced his younger son Thomas to adopt a clerical career in 1619-22, against repeated objections and declarations of a total lack of vocational interest, all the young man could do was to write acidly to his father that "I. . . trust you have begged to God, together with my consent unto your will, his acceptance of my weak endeavors and performances."

This was not an exceptional case, for in upper-class circles it was the father who decided while they were still children which of the younger sons should be educated at the university to enter the church, which should learn Latin and go on to the Inns of Court to become a lawyer, and which should be apprenticed to London to become a merchant. Each case involved long planning ahead and a heavy financial investment, and once begun there was no turning back. The only children of this class who were free were those who were trained for nothing in particular, and were left to make their own way in the world as best they could.

The choice of marriage partner was even more critical than the choice of a career, especially in a society where divorce was unknown. In the early sixteenth century, marriages among the landed classes were normally strictly controlled by the parents, with little or no freedom of choice allowed to the children, especially the daughters. Noblemen and gentlemen made arrangements for the marriages of their children in their wills, and contracts by which children were bartered like cattle were still being made by squires in the more backward North right up to the end of the sixteenth century. Thus in 1558 Michael Wentworth specified in his will that "if any of my daughters will not be advised by my executors, but of their own fantastical brain bestow themselves lightly upon a light person," then that daughter was to have only sixty-six pounds instead of the one hundred pounds which was promised to the obedient. This was powerful posthumous economic blackmail. Further down the social scale, even more dictatorial terms were being set at an even later date. In his will of 1599, William Shaftoe curtly decreed: "To my daughter Margery, 60 sheep, and I bestow her in marriage upon Edward, son of Reynold Shaftoe of Thockerington." When high politics were at stake, extreme measures were sometimes resorted to; and it is alleged that in the early seventeenth century, Sir Edward Coke, the ex-Chief Justice, not only abducted his daughter by force from her mother, but also had her "tied to a bed-post and severely whipped," in order to force her consent to marriage with the mentally unstable brother of the Duke of Buckingham, a maneuver that was designed to restore her father's lost favor at Court.

Filial obedience in the sixteenth and seventeenth centuries was not limited to the choice of career and marriage partner, but extended into all spheres of life, including education. In 1685 Edmund Verney wrote furiously to his nineteen-year-old eldest son Ralph: "I hear you hate learning and your mind hankers after travelling. I will not be taught by my cradle how to breed it up; it is insolence and impudence in any child to presume so much as to offer it." The memory of this mild act of insubordination still rankled some months later, when young Ralph died suddenly of a fever. His father saw the hand of God in the tragedy and hastened to press the moral home to his second, and now only, son: "I . . . exhort you to be wholly ruled and guided by me, and to be perfectly obedient to me in all things according to your bounden duty. . . . For should you do likewise and contrary in the least, . . . I am afraid that you will be in that evil circumstances snatched away by death in your youth, as your poor brother was last week.

Because the key to the system of controlled marriage was the exchange of property, it theoretically follows that children lower down the economic scale would be left with greater freedom of choice. Whether this is so or not is not at present known for certain. Harrington thought that the arranged marriage system did not press "so heavy on the lower sort, being better able to shift for themselves, as upon the nobility and gentry." On the other hand, a large proportion of the population owned some property, and there is plenty of evidence for arranged marriages among the yeomanry in the sixteenth century. Napier's casebooks suggest that the choice of marriage partner was the principal issue which divided parents and children at all social levels above that of the poor in the early seventeenth century.

Among the bottom third of society, however, conditions were probably very much freer, as they certainly were in the eighteenth-century. In the first place, their parents had little economic leverage over their children since they had little or nothing to give or bequeath them. In the second place, most of their children left home at the age of ten to fourteen in order to become an apprentice, a domestic servant, or a live-in laborer in other people's houses. This very large floating population of adolescents living away from home were thus free from parental supervision and could, therefore, make their own choice of marriage partners. The only thing that held them back was the need to accumulate sufficient capital to set up house and to start a shop or trade, which was the principal cause for the long delay in marriage into the middle twenties.

Apart from the need to break the child's will, a secondary cause of the widespread brutality towards children was the enormous extension of elementary and secondary education, much of it still conducted in the home. This fundamental shift in the upbringing of children forced them to do such unnatural things as to sit still and to concentrate their minds on rote book learning. When the subject was as boring and irrelevant as Latin grammar, this could only be achieved by relentless physical punishment. Renaissance education, because of its insufferably tedious content, demanded effective repression of the will. In part, at least, the increased use of physical punishment was a natural accompaniment of the spread of the Classics as a subject of study in school and home. This connection was clearly seen by Locke, who asked, "Why. . . . does the learning of Latin and Greek need the rod, when French and Italian needs it not? Children learn to dance and fence without whipping; nay arithmetic, drawing, etc. they apply themselves well enough to without beating."

## 4. The Schooling Of English Children 1480-1660
By W.K. Jordan

The aspirations of the London burghers and their incredible generosity are perhaps best exemplified in the steady and massive support which they lent to education during the whole course of our period. Moreover, their determined effort to found and endow an educational system held in view the whole realm and its needs, for only a relatively small proportion of the immense endowments vested was for the necessarily limited needs of London itself. These merchants believed in the virtues of education with an almost fanatical intensity, for a variety of reasons to which they gave eloquent testimony in the phrasing of their great bequests. In many cases they had themselves been handicapped by the imperfect education of their own youth. They believed that an increasingly elevated standard of education was required for the ever more complex necessities of trade and finance in the modern world. They held to a man the view that affording a competent education to aspiring youth was the surest and most fruitful way open to their society for the prevention of poverty by the destruction of the ignorance in which it was spawned. And they believed, and said so, that only a literate citizenry could create a truly godly community able to understand and defend God's truth against the enemies with which it was beset.

During the whole span of our period London donors were to contribute the vast total of £510,890 17s towards the strengthening—one can perhaps more accurately say, the foundation—of the educational resources of the realm. This great capital aggregate amounted to 27.04 per cent of all the charitable wealth accumulated by London in these years. The vastness of this wealth can perhaps be suggested when we say that it somewhat exceeded the total provided for all charitable uses during our whole period in the two great counties of Kent and Yorkshire.

The devotion of London to the cause of education, never particularly strong during the Middle Ages, was impressive even in the decades prior to the Reformation when the influence of Christian humanism began to be felt under the leadership of men who were in several instances themselves sons of London merchants. During these years, the large total of £76,581 9s was given for various educational uses, slightly more than twice as much as was provided for the poor and, remarkably enough, not incomparably less than the £111,997 1s given for religious needs in this same long generation. In the brief interval of the Reformation, the relatively large total of £32,586 5s was bestowed on educational foundations, this being rather more than twice as much as was given in these years for the whole range of religious needs. The £83,319 12s provided for educational uses during the Elizabethan era represented almost a third (32.00 per cent) of all charitable wealth given during the interval and, it will be noted, was something like five times as much as was bestowed for religious uses in this intensely secular era. The great outpouring came during the early Stuart years when the huge total of £246,492 3s was given to secure an almost revolutionary extension of the educational facilities of the realm, though it should be said that these outlays amounted to little more than a quarter (25.70 per cent) of the whole of the charitable wealth vested in this incredibly generous age. The needs of education were by no means neglected during the two decades of political disturbance with which our period ends, the large total of £71,911 8s given for these uses amounting to 26.94 per cent of all the charitable contributions of these unsettled years.

The predominant interest of London benefactors during most of our period was in the founding or the strengthening of schools across the length and breadth of England. From 1480 to 1660, there was poured into these foundations the immense sum of £259,263 2s, this representing 13.72 per cent of all charitable wealth and somewhat exceeding in amount any other single charitable head save for the £331,502 4s provided for the household relief of the poor. This great sum, moreover, was almost wholly (99.67 per cent) in the form of endowments designed to build and perpetually to maintain the institutions with which this age sought forever to destroy ignorance and illiteracy. Firmly supporting these foundations, and frequently vested in them, was also a huge accumulation of scholarship and fellowship endowments, which were by the close of our period to total £92,465 8s and which were to link tightly the fabric of secondary education with that of the universities.

The accumulation of grammar-school endowments began modestly enough in the years prior to the Reformation, no more than £320 of these funds having been given during the first two decades of the period. But from 1500 onward the flow of gifts for this use never really faltered. Thus during the two generations before the Reformation the impressive total of £14,559 was given by a considerable number of donors for school foundations, though this was far less than the £57,814 19s settled on the universities by London donors. What one can perhaps describe as the velocity of these contributions was approximately trebled during the Reformation period proper, the large total of £15,274 17s being provided for the further enlargement of the school resources of the city and of the realm. There were many and there were notable school foundations in the Elizabethan age, when the total vested for these institutions was £32,530, supplemented, it may well be noted, by additions totalling £18,269 5s to the scholarship and fellowship resources of the nation. But the great period stretches from 1591 to 1630, when not less than £11,093 7s was contributed in any single decade, and with the climax of generosity being attained in the second decade of the seventeenth century when the generous total of £78,386 was provided. During the early Stuart period proper, the huge sum of £148,263 17s was given for schools, this constituting slightly more than 57 per cent of the great sum given for these foundations during the whole of our long period. This incredible achievement was made despite the fact that gifts for school foundations fell away most drastically during the decade just prior to the outbreak of the Civil War, an era of profound unsettlement and uncertainty in which men could not clearly discern the outlines of the future. But there was an immediate revival of interest in bringing to completion this age of foundation of the grammar-school system of England during the period of Puritan warfare and victory, for the great sum of £48,635 8s was given by men and women who, having witnessed, as they believed, the triumph of the elect, were now determined to rout finally the forces of ignorance.

# 5. The New World Of Children In Eighteenth-Century England

By J.H. Plumb

In the late seventeenth century a new social attitude towards children began to strengthen, and it was this attitude which John Locke gave literary force and substance in what was to prove as influential as any work that he produced, his *Some Thoughts Concerning Education,* published in 1693. The dominant attitude towards children in the seventeenth century had been autocratic, indeed ferocious. "The new borne babe," wrote Richard

Allestree in 1658, "is full of the stains and pollutions of sin which it inherits from our first parents though our loins." From birth English children were constrained. They spent their first months, sometimes a year, bound tightly in swaddling bands. Their common lot was fierce parental discipline, even a man of a warm and kindly nature such as Samuel Pepys thought nothing of beating his fifteen-year-old maid with a broomstick, and locking her up for the night in his cellar, or whipping his boy-servant, or even boxing his clerk's ears. Samuel Byrd, of Virginia, who rebuked his wife for severity towards a servant, could make a young dependent of his, Eugene, drink, according to Byrd's diary, "a pint of piss" as a punishment for bed-wetting. A fortnight later the same punishment was inflicted, apparently with success, because some weeks later Eugene, according to the diary, was flogged just "for nothing." Lloyd de Mause reports that "earliest lives I have found of children who may not have been beaten at all date from 1690." And of two hundred counsels of advice on child-rearing prior to 1700, only three, Plutarch, Palmieri and Sadoleto, failed to recommend that fathers beat their children.

Subservience was expected from children, and sometimes the autocratic power of the father was enforced by law. It was a crime in New England, punishable by death, for a child of sixteen to curse or strike a parent. Harsh discipline was the child's lot, and they were often terrorized deliberately and, not infrequently, sexually abused. Their toys were few, often home-made, and, except for the very rich, their pets were usually purposeful—a pony for riding, a dog for shooting and hunting. Much of their education was devoted to religion and to the catechism. Naturally, there were many exceptions to this dark picture—parents who doted on their child, and who played with them; they were a minority, for most of the upper and middle classes rarely had their children at home. If they had children in the house, they were more often than not other people's, and therefore more likely to be ill-treated. The typical childhood of an upper-class English boy of the late seventeenth century was Sir Robert Walpole's, who was born in 1676. Almost immediately after birth he was sent out to a wet-nurse at the nearby village of Syderstone, where he remained until he was weaned, at about eighteen months. At six he was dispatched to a school of Great Dunham kept by the rector, Richard Ransome, where he remained, enjoying only very brief holidays, until he went to Eton; nor did he go home for all of his holidays. Often he stayed with Townshend relations nearby. Indeed, until he was summoned home from King's College, Cambridge, in 1698, after the death of his elder brother, Walpole had rarely spent more than a few weeks at his Norfolk home in any year since he was six. Not all families, however, sent their children away from home so early, or for so long. The Ishams were kept at home by Sir Justinian, their father, and taught by a tutor who lived at Lamport. Some others, however, like the earl of Sandwich, sent their sons in the first instance to the local grammar school.

We need a far more systematic study of the education of the gentry and aristocracy than we have, but the impression is that the Ishams and Sandwiches were a minority, and most gentry families acted like the Walpoles. This meant that children and parents shared few pursuits together, and the art of the seventeenth century would seem to bear this out. Up to about 1730 portraits are formally posed groups; increasingly, however, after 1730 children are shown playing or reading or sketching or fishing or picnicking with their parents—family scenes of mutual pleasure and enjoyment, and ones which the parents wanted recorded. One has only to compare Michael Wright's "Sir Robert Vyner and Family" (1673) with David Allan's "Family of Sir J. Hunter Blair, Bt.," or Wheatley's entrancing "Browne Family." Also, portraits of individual children are far more common in the eighteenth century than in the seventeenth, again arguing both for a change in fashionable attitudes, and also, may be, for a greater emotional investment in children by parents.

There had been, however, towards the end of the seventeenth century, a perceptible new attitude—John Evelyn, long before Locke, had practised many of the Lockeian ideas on education on his own son, preferring a system of rewards, provocations, emulation and self-discipline to physical punishment or verbal chastisement. His whimsical friend, Aubrey, was also strongly against corporal punishment, although he allowed the use of thumbscrews as a last resort! Indeed, Locke's book encapsulates what was clearly a new and growing attitude towards child-rearing and education which was to improve the lot of the child in the eighteenth century.

Locke, although not opposed to corporal punishment as a final sanction, nor indeed for very young children of an age too tender to be reasoned with, in order to instill the necessary fear and awe that a child should have for an adult, strongly disapproved of beating once formal education had begun, just as he was equally opposed to bribing the child to work through material rewards.

> The *Rewards* and *Punishments* then, whereby we should keep children in order, are quite of another kind; and of that force, that when we can get them once to work, the Business, I think, is done, and the Difficulty is over. *Esteem* and *Disgrace* are, of all others, the most powerful Incentives to the Mind, when once it is brought to relish them. If you can once get into Children a Love of Credit, and an Apprehension of Shame and Disgrace, you have put into them the true principle . . .

As well as arguing for a more liberal attitude towards the child, Locke also pleased for a broader curriculum. He believed education should fit man for society, as well as equipping him with learning, hence he pressed not only for lessons in drawing, but also in French. Indeed, he opposed rigid grounding in English grammar and urged that Latin be taught by the direct method, as it would have been had it been a living language.

only for lessons in drawing, but also in French. Indeed, he opposed rigid grounding in English grammar and urged that Latin be taught by the direct method, as it would have been had it been a living language.

Locke's attitude to child-rearing was as modern as his view of education. In his letters he encouraged breast-feeding by the mother, and was concerned with early toilet-training—indeed, his attitude towards the child was ahead of his time, but in no way original. There had been a current of antipathy to the strict Calvinist view of the child throughout the seventeenth century; and the concept that, given the right environment and the proper course of education, compassion and benevolence, the essential goodness of the child would triumph over its propensity for evil, already had a longish history.

John Earle, as early as 1628, likens the child to Adam before the Fall—all innocence which time destroys, for experience corrupts; yet the original nature of the child is pure. However, this thin stream that stems from earlier generations becomes a broad river in the generations that follow Locke.

After Locke the education of the child increasingly becomes social rather than religious. Morality is still uppermost, but it is a social morality with which parents and teachers are concerned, not the repression of old Adam, the suppression of evil, or the breaking of the will, and, in consequence, the view that a proper submissiveness in the child can only be achieved by harsh discipline weakens, at least for a time. The birch existed, particuarly in the older public and grammar schools, nor was it absent from some of the newer schools, if the denunciations of some publicists are to be believed. Nevertheless, no one can read through the hundreds of advertisements in the provincial press for private schools, or the numerous handbooks on the care and education of children, or the occasional prospectuses of academies that have survived, without realizing that the emphasis on education had changed. Its aim was social, to equip the child with accomplishments that would secure for it gainful employment, and this, doubtless, was a major inducement for parents to spend money; but every advertisement boasts that the school will instill those virtues—sobriety, obedience, industry, thrift, benevolence and compassion—that educationalists regarded as the virtues of a successful social man. And the best way of achieving these ends was through developing the child's sense of emulation and shame. The true aim of education, according to the author of the *Dialogues on the Passions, Habits, Appetites and Affections, etc., Peculiar to Children,* was not to teach bad Latin, harsh French, as if the children were "a parcel of Parrots or Magpies," but "to teach them the Government of themselves, their Passions and Appetites." Better an increase of virtue than "their abounding in human literature." And teaching should be quite natural and the pupils free to speak as they wished before their masters. Indeed, the author was against all restrictions. Children should never realize that they are on a curb or under its direction. They must be taught through benevolence and sympathy; when the necessity arises shame may be used, but fear only in the last extremity, and then "with such delicacy that if possible the habit may not gather strength by the use you are constrained to make of it." This, indeed, is a far cry from Sam Byrd's "pint of piss" or beating his boy Eugene "for nothing." The attitude to children had radically changed. True, there were still plenty of pockets of sadism where the whip and the birch were freely used. Not all fathers, or mothers were converted so easily from tyranny to benevolence, but, by the 1740s, a new attitude to children was spreading steadily among the middle and upper classes. By 1780 John Browne could make one of the principal virtues of the expensive academy for gentlemen's sons that he proposed to set up a total absence of corporal punishment. This gentle and more sensitive approach to children was but a part of a wider change in social attitudes; a part of that belief that nature was inherently good, not evil, and what evil there was derived from man and his institutions; an attitude which was also reflected among a growing elite in a greater sensitivity towards women, slaves and animals.

Not only did this new attitude towards children begin to emerge among educationalists in the middle decades of the eighteenth century, but we can deduce also from the success of small private academies, from the development of a new kind of children's literature, and from the vastly increased expenditure on the amusements and pleasures of children, that parents, too, were no longer regarding their children as sprigs of old Adam whose wills had to be broken. Many had come to look upon their children as vehicles of social emulation; hence they began to project their own social attitudes as the moral imperatives of childhood. And so education for society became paramount. Owing to the growth of economic opportunity and social mobility, it was now less necessary to make a child accept its calling as a dictate of God. Locke's attitudes were replacing those of the catechism.

The repercussions on the world of children were very great. Society required accomplishment, and accomplishment required expenditure. The children's new world became a market that could be exploited. Few desires will empty a pocket quicker than social aspiration—and the main route was, then as now, through education, which combined social adornment with the opportunity of a more financially rewarding career for children.

From 1700 to 1770 there was a steady growth in England of educational facilities, especially for the commercial classes, and probably for the skilled artisan; after 1770 this growth became very rapid indeed. About provision for the poor, except for charity schools, we know very little. Many villages had dame schools, and in most major towns evening classes could be very cheap. Some aristocrats, such as the marquis of Rockingham, provided a school on their estates, supporting the schoolmaster and buying the books.

Sunday schools were more concerned with religious indoctrination and social conformity than education, and only a few encouraged reading. Many of the patriarchally minded founding fathers of the Industrial Revolution ran schools, as Robert Owen did at New Lanark, or provided a craft teaching, as did Josiah Wedgwood, or supported schools, as did Jedediah Strutt and Richard Arkwright. The variety of educational opportunity increased considerably after 1750, whatever may have been happening at the universities and the more ancient grammar and so-called public schools.

The greatest surge in education took place in the small private schools and academies, most of which provided an education that was modern in outlook and socially orientated. The lifetime of these schools was often short, no longer than the working life of the schoolmaster or mistress who started them. Indeed, frequently less, for many rapidly failed. The competition was intense and almost anyone with a little education felt that the teaching profession was an open road to financial security. Sometimes, however, the school rooted itself in a house and was sold, and so remained a school sometimes for decades, like Mrs. Barbauld's famous school at Palgrave, or the even more famous school at Cheam which still exists, as fashionable today as it was when it first started in 1752.

The only source which gives an idea of the range of these small schools are advertisements in local newspapers which can be supplemented by town and country directories of the late eighteenth century, and occasionally by trade cards and handbills. Almost no county or district has yet been studied with the thoroughness which the subject deserves. The size of these schools varied considerably, and so did the age of the pupils. Most were single-sex schools, but not all, and one ingenious schoolmaster took both sexes, but segregated them for teaching by placing his usher in a booth in the middle of the partition which kept them apart. The subjects varied from the three R's for infants to navigation, fortification, trigonometry, surveying, merchants' accounts, and almost every European language. Music, art, dancing and fencing were the common extras. The emphasis, however, was overwhelmingly on commercial subjects for boys and social deportment for girls.

What, perhaps, is most surprising, is that these schools were to be found more frequently in the old county towns, and the surrounding districts, than in the new manufacturing towns. The *Leeds Mercury* advertises surprisingly few schools, whereas the newspapers of Northampton, York, Norwich, Ipswich and similar towns are full of them. G. A. Cranfield counted one hundred schools advertised in the *Northampton Mercury* between 1720 and 1760, and sixty-three in the *Norwich Mercury* between 1749 and 1759. Ipswich, however, provides a fascinating example, for the *Ipswich Journal* throughout the eighteenth century carried more advertisements than most provincial newspapers. Between 1743 and 1747 the

*Ipswich Journal* carried thirty-five advertisements for schools, of which ten were situated in Norfolk (one at North Walsham, seven at Norwich and two at Great Yarmouth), and three in Essex (Colchester, Much Baddow and Dedham). Between 1783 and 1787 ninety-one schools advertised, and a further ten are mentioned through the individual advertisements of dancing masters. The geographical range is somewhat wider, for there are single advertisements for a school in Yorkshire, at Catterick, another in London, and one in Cambridgeshire, but the overwhelming majority are situated in west Suffolk—only two Norwich schools advertised in this period, and one of these is for a new headmaster, and not to solicit pupils. From this list it is clear that every town in Suffolk, no matter how small—for example Debenham, Needham Market, Boxford, Woodbridge, Lavenham or Long Melford—had their schools. But so did many villages, villages as small as Wyverstone, Walsham-le-Willows, Fornham St. Martin or Stonham Aspal. Ipswich, apart of course from its Grammar and Charity schools, schools which did not advertise, had eight such schools and four more were in villages in the immediate vicinity, two at Tuddenham, one at Claydon, and one at Hintelsham.

As many of these schools were located in villages, one might expect that the overwhelming majority of schoolmasters would be clergymen. Not so. Only fourteen schools were run by the clergy; of the rest seventeen were run by women, one by a man and wife, and the remainder by men. This should, perhaps, not be surprising, as the subjects taught were largely those for which clergymen had not been trained—for the education offered was more frequently commercial and social, and less frequently classical and mathematical. The curriculum of most schools was very varied, and although all schools do not advertise their wares, many do, either in the newspapers, or by prospectuses and handbills, or by both. In the 1780s only five schools advertised the teaching of reading, which would imply that almost all schools expected that the child would have been taught to read at home, even though schools offered to take boys of six. The availability of attractive primers for small children had made the teaching of reading in the home much easier. The most popular subjects were writing, which almost certainly implies the hands required by clerks, either legal or mercantile (thirty-four advertisements), arithmetic (twenty-nine), English (twenty-two), drawing (nineteen), dancing (sixteen), and music (twelve). Other subjects offered were French, Latin, mathematics, mensuration, accounts, navigation, surveying, needlework, and one school taught experimental philosophy.

Children had become counters in the parents' social aspirations; their son's or daughter's education reflected status. And the image of the child which the schools, as well as children's literature projected was the image of an ideal parent's child—industrious, obedient, constantly respectful; and indeed a pet, never too spoilt, but occasionally indulged as a reward for virtue. Reality was, of course, harsher, but you do not sell much except through hope and illusion—at least educationally.

Parents were commercial targets through their children—they could, through the best of motives, be made to spend money on schools which they could scarcely afford, but there were other ways to the parents' pocketbooks, educational games and industrial toys, which became increasingly available as the century progressed.

Books by which children could be taught had existed from the first days of printing—alphabets, grammars, and the like, but few, if any, were designed specifically for children. Authors and publishers made very little attempt to entice the young mind. Fairy stories, ballads, riddles and fables were intended as much for adults as for children. Indeed, Aesop was not specifically adapted for children until 1692, when Roger L'Estrange produced his edition.

As with so many cultural developments, the late seventeenth and early eighteenth centuries saw the beginnings of a changed attitude towards children's literature and methods of learning to read. In 1694 "J.G." published "A Play-book for children to allure them to read as soon as possible. Composed of small pages on purpose not to tire children and printed with a fair and pleasant letter. The matter and method plain and easier than any yet extant," which was, for once, a true statement in a blurb. The book has wide margins, large type; its language simple and concrete and mostly within the compass of a child's experience. The author states in his preface that he wished "to decoy Children in to reading." It did well enough to be reprinted in 1703, by which time a few other authors—notably William Ronksley—were attempting to find methods and materials more suitable for very young children. He believed in teaching by verse according to the metre of the Psalms—first week, words of one syllable, the next week words of two syllables, and so on. And he used jokes, riddles and proverbs to sugar his pills. Even so, his and other innovative children's books of Queen Anne's reign were designed, quite obviously, to be chanted, to be learnt by the ear, rather than by the eye. They were more for teachers and parents to teach with than books meant for a child's own enjoyment. Similar books were slow to appear and it is not until the 1740s that the change in style of children's literature becomes very marked. The entrepreneurial noses of Thomas Boreman and John Newbery twitched and scented a market for books that would be simple in production, enticing to the eye, and written specifically for children. Of course, it was not quite as simple as that. Children do not buy books, adults do.

So the new children's literature was designed to attract adults, to project an image of those virtues which parents wished to inculcate in their offspring, as well as to beguile the child. These alphabet and reading books, by their simplicity, also strengthened the confidence of parents in their ability to teach their children to read in the home. The new children's literature was aimed at the young, but only through the refraction of the parental eye.

The contrast of, say, 1780 and 1680 in the range of what was available for children is vivid. By 1780 there was no subject, scientific or literary, that had not its specialized literature designed for children—often beautifully and realistically illustrated. The simpler textbooks—for reading, arithmetic and writing—were carefully designed, with large lettering, appropriate illustration with a small amount of print on a large page; that is as well as books for children there were books for very young children. Novels specifically written about children for children began with *Sandford and Merton,* by Thomas Day. And the arts, as well as letters, were catered for—Master Michael Angelo's *The Drawing School of Little Masters and Misses* appeared in 1773, and there were books designed to teach children the first steps in music. And, as with adult books, less prosperous children could buy their books a part at a time. Nor was it necessary to buy the books, they could be borrowed. By 1810 there was a well-established juvenile library at 157 New Bond Street, run by Tabart. Some owners of circulating libraries kept a special juvenile section.

And children's books, as well as becoming far more plentiful, also became cheaper. John Newbery had used every type of gimmick to extend his market. With the *Pretty Little Pocket Book* he had offered—for an extra twopence—a ball for the son or a pincushion for the daughter. He had used new types of binding that did not stain, and he had even tried giving a book away so lng as the purchaser bought the binding. He advertised his books in every possible way—rarely did a parent finish one of his books without finding in the text a recommendation of others. He sensed that there was a huge market ready for exploitation. He was right. Within twenty years, children's books were a thriving part of the Newcastle printer's trade; indeed, educational books attracted a very large number of provincial printers in the late eighteenth century, for they were well aware of the hunger of shopkeepers, tradesmen and artisans, such as weavers, for education, not only for themselves, but also, and most emphatically, for their children. By 1800, children's books at 1d. were plentiful and this was a time when books in general, because of inflation, had increased in price by 25 per cent. Nevertheless, Oliver and Boyd of Edinburgh turned them out by the score, under the title of *Jack Dandy's Delight.* They published forty at sixpence, twenty-six at twopence, forty at one penny, and ninety at a halfpenny. The penny books were well printed and delightfully illustrated. Only the very poorest families of unskilled labourers could not afford a halfpenny. Like Tom Paine's *Right of Man,* children's literature was within the range of the industrious working class, and particularly of those families where social ambition had been stirred by the growing opportunities of a new industrializing society—more and more clerical jobs were available, and more and more parents were willing to make sacrifices to secure them for their children.

Education was public as well as private. and there was far more entertainment designed both to amuse and instruct, to which parents were encouraged to take their children by sharply reduced prices for them. Children were expected to be companions of their parents in ways which would have been impossible in the seventeenth century, because the attractions did not then exist. Exhibitions of curiosities; museums; zoos; puppet shows; circuses; lectures on science; panoramas of European cities; automata; horseless carriages; even human and animal monstrosities were available in provincial cities as well as in London. Sir Ashton Levers's Museum of Natural History at Leicester House, a typical eighteenth-century hotchpotch, advertised family tickets. A yearly season ticket for the entire family was quite expensive at five guineas, but it included both the tutor and the governess, and so was aimed at the rich. In April 1773 families of Leeds were regaled by Mr. Manuel of Turin with his display of automata which, as well as having an Indian lady in her chariot moving around the table at ten miles an hour, also contained the "Grand Turk, in the Seraglio dress, who walks about the table smoking his pipe in a surprising manner." All, of course, to the accompaniment of mechanical musical instruments. The prices were cheap enough, 1s. front seats, 6d. back, and servants at 4d. Mr. Manuel also sold fireworks as a sideline. After Mr. Manuel, Mr. Pitt arrived with his principal marvel, a self-moving phaeton which travelled at six miles an hour, climbed hills, and started and stopped with the touch of a finger. He also brought along his electrifying machine, his camera obscura, his miraculous door which opened inside, outside, left or right by the turn of a key. All for one shilling. The phaeton either wore out, broke down, or at five hundredweight proved too expensive to move, for it was dropped by Pitt, who continued for some years to travel the Midland circuit, Nottingham, Coventry, and so on, but only with his scientific apparatus. Quite obviously he made a tolerable living.

The emphasis was on marvels, curiosities that were new and remarkable, and usually mechanical or optical; hence many children were given a keen sense of a new and developing and changing world in which mechanical ingenuity, electricity and science in general played an active part—a totally different cultural atmosphere to that in which their grandfathers had lived. Their cultural horizons, too, were widened by the availability of music to listen to in festivals and concerts, the cheapness of musical instruments, and the plentiful supply of music teachers; the same is true of art. Art materials were to be found in every provincial town, and so were drawing masters, who taught in the home as well in the school. Prints of old masters and modern artists were a commonplace of provincial as well as London life. Visually it was a far more exciting age for children than ever before. And they could travel. By the end of the century middle-class families were on the move, visiting country houses and ancient ruins, viewing the industrial

308

wonders of Boulton and Watt, Wedgwood, Arkwright, and braving the dangers and dirt of coal-mines, sailing in splendid barges along the new canals, going off to the sea—to take the water externally and internally—an outburst of travel that is recorded in hundreds of illustrated books which depict children with their parents, enjoying, as they themselves enjoyed, the wonders of their world. The intellectual and cultural horizons of the middle-class child, and indeed of the lower middle-class child, had broadened vastly between 1680 and 1780, and this change was gathering momentum. Parents, more often than not, wanted their children with them, not only in the home but on holidays.

However, through most of the amusements ran the theme of self-improvement and self-education. The same is true of indoor games, as well as outdoor excursions. Playing cards had long been used to inculcate knowledge—largely geographical, historical or classical. One of the earliest packs of about 1700 taught carving lessons—hearts for joints of meat, diamonds for poultry, clubs for fish and spades for meat pies. But more often than not these were importations, usually from France. The eighteenth century witnessed a rapid increase in English educational playing cards, so that almost every variety of knowledge or educational entertainment could be found imprinted on their faces. The majority of booksellers, provincial as well as metropolitan, stocked them. Some cards were designed for the education of adults, or at least adolescents, but there were packs, very simply designed, for young children to play with and learn at the same time. One pack taught the first steps in music.

Children, in a sense, had become luxury objects upon which their mothers and fathers were willing to spend larger and larger sums of money, not only for their education, but also for their entertainment and amusement. In a sense they had become superior pets—sometimes spoilt excessively like Charles James Fox, sometimes treated with indifference or even brutality, but usually, as with pets, betwixt and between. Whatever the attitude of parents, children had become a trade, a field of commercial enterprise for the sharp-eyed entrepreneur. Nor was education and amusement the only field in which children had become a market. The eighteenth century was exceptionally dress- and fashion-conscious; indeed, fashions in textiles had begun to change every year. And naturally parents who were sufficiently affluent began to spend more and more money on the clothes of their children and they were increasingly induced to do so by tailors and milliners who specialized in making clothes for children. And not only children, but also babies; infant materials which the seventeenth century had produced in the home were now sold wholesale in London—diapers, cradles, cradle blankets, Moses blankets, satin coverlets, baby clothes of all kinds were being produced for bulk sale. Athough children were still dressed as miniature adults, towards the end of the century it became fashionable to dress children up as soldiers, sailors, highlanders, milkmaids or gardners. Dress for children became lighter and freer, and it was quite customary for boys to wear open-necked shirts. A number of tailors and haberdashers found it profitable to specialize entirely in children's clothing. Clothes-consciousness, also, among children and adolescents became quite strong, particularly among adolescents, and working-class adolescents at that. Sheffield, in spite of its dark satanic mills of the Industrial Revolution, possessed plenty of working-class gaiety. There were dress shops where the young cutlers' apprentices and their shop-assistant girl-friends, could hire their finery for Saturday night—dresses for the girls, suits for the boys, so that they could go decked out like the middle-class to their penny and threepenny dances or "hops" as they were known, then, as now.

A hundred years had brought about a remarkable change in the lives of middle- and lower middle-class children, and indeed of the aristocracy as well. From Locke onwards there had been a greater preoccupation with educational ideas; indeed, in the second half of the eighteenth century, stimulated by Rousseau, the advanced radicals—the Burghs, the Days, the Edgeworths, and the rest—had been deeply concerned. Many, particularly the Edgeworths, disapproved of the growing indulgence of parents towards their children, particularly the waste of money on useless toys. Maria Edgeworth denounced dolls and dolls' houses, had no use for rocking-horses, and strongly disapproved of baa-lambs, squeaky pigs and cuckoos, and all simple action toys. She was for a pencil and plain paper, toys which led to physical exercise—hoops, tops, battledores and a pair of scissors and paper for a girl to cut out her fancies; later boys should by given models of instruments used by manufacturers—spinning-wheels, looms, paper-mills, water-mills which, as I have said, were readily available. Marie Edgeworth resonates with modernity, but the interest in her long discussion of toys lies in the huge variety which obviously abounded in the 1790s—a variety not as extensive, of course, as today, but reflecting our world rather than that of seventeenth-century England. Indeed, wherever we turn in the world of children—clothes, pets, toys, education, sport, music and art, their world was richer, more varied, more intellectually and emotionally exciting than it had been in earlier generations.

And yet all was not gain. One must not paint too radiant a picture, too exciting a world. Mrs. Timmer was there, so was Hannah More. One must remember the Fairchild family trooping off to view the corpse decomposing on the gibbet, the frightful treatment of William Cowper at Westminster, the horrors of Harrow and Eton and Winchester that drew boys into violent rebellion. Nor should we forget the dangers to children in the growing sentimentality about the innocence of the child which needed to be protected at all costs, nor the dangerous intellectual concept that regards each human life as recapitulating that of the human race, which firmly placed the child in Eden, but surrounded by serpents and cluttered with apples.

As a richer life in material objects became available to children, so did their private lives, in some aspects, become more rigidly disciplined. The world of sex was to become, in the eighteenth century, a world of terror for children, and one which was to create appalling guilt and anxiety. We know little about the history of sexual attitudes. In eighteenth-century children's literature, adultery is mentioned, not approvingly, of course, but as a fact of life. In some tales for children men and women were discovered in bed together. This certainly would not have been allowed in Victorian literature for children. And such references were few, and vanish after the 1780s. In another respect, at least, there had been a disastrous development. In the sixteenth century Fallopius had encouraged masturbation in boys as a method of enlarging the penis, and Pepys, who had considerable guilt and shame about his fumbling of women, took masturbation in his stride, and indeed mentions with considerable pride that he had managed it without using his hand and with his eyes wide open. He did, it is true, wish it had not happed at midnight mass in the Chapel Royal, but that was his sole reaction. The early eighteenth century witnesses a total change of attitude, if Pepys and Fallopius are at all typical. The publication, probably around 1710, of *Onania: Or, The Heinous Sin of Self Pollution, and all its frightful Consequences in both Sexes considered with spiritual and Physical Advice to those who have already injur'd themselves by this abominable Practise,* unleashed a deluge of denunciation about masturbation. By 1727, this book had reached twelve editions, with fatter and fatter supplements of horrifying and lurid letters of saved sinners. This book was advertised extremely extensively in the provincial as well as the London press, and it proved a best-seller for decades, and gradually accumulated about it a horrific literature that attributed every disease and inadequacy to self-abuse. The medical quacks rapidly got on to the bang-wagon, and many pamphlets were merely puffs for curative medicines or restrictive machines. And by 1800 crimes of unbelievable cruelty were being practised on young boys in order to cure them, such as circumcision without, of course, anaesthetic. This development was not an English phenomenon. Dr. Tissot produced an equally alarming and equally popular book in Switzerland and France in 1760. And Kant denounces the practice with intense moral fervour in his *Über Pädagogik* (1803).

Chastity and abstinence, however, were imposed with an increasing verbal and, at times, physical, violence on the growing boy and girl. The practical results of this campaign were probably minimal, but the psychological danger to the sensitive was considerable, as we may see from the diaries of men so different in temperament as Samuel Johnson and William Ewart Gladstone. Childhood had become more radiant, but there were dark and lowering clouds. Children, in fact, had become objects: violence and noise, natural to children, were deplored, so was greed for food as well as lust. Obedience, sweetness, honesty, self-control were the qualities desired and inculcated. They were to stay firmly in Eden with their hands off the apples and deaf to the serpents. Fortunately the images that society creates for children rarely reflect the truth of actual life. If we turn from theory, from projected literary images, to the artefacts of childhood, then we can rest assured that children, both girls and boys, had, so long as they were middle-class, entered a far richer world. They had more to stimulate the eye, the ear and the mind, and that was pure gain.

## 6. Cotton Mather And His Children

By Elizabeth Bancroft Schlesinger

History too frequently emphasizes the public life of great figures, neglecting intimate family relations. Glimpses of the home life of Cotton Mather, for example, mellow the austere and pompous image of the great Puritan priest and bring into focus the characteristics of a loving father, deeply concerned with the upbringing of his family.

The comfortable Mather home was not as luxurious as those of the wealthy merchants, but it was large enough to accommodate visitors on occasion and also to give the children rooms of their own, "well fitted up, in which they may read and write and pray" and ponder on "that Question, *What should I wish to have done if I were now adying.*" Servants were at hand to help in the housework, although Mather frequently complains of the dearth of good ones. A study gave the father privacy; there he could retire to write and pray. "Be Short," the injunction above the door, warned only the caller, for sessions of prayer with his family sometimes lasted many hours. Affection glowed in this home as brightly as the fire upon the hearth, its gentle light softening the grim, religious pattern of life. It penetrated to the heart of the old Puritan, quickening the love of a father who playfully called his "little birds" by pet names.

Cotton Mather had profited from the lessons he had learned at his own father's fireside. There the wrath of a fearful God had been placated by daily rites and the power of His punishments kept constantly in mind; but it was also a loving home. Increase Mather had once said of his children that they were "so many parts of myself and dearer to me than all the things which I enjoy in this world." These two conceptions of a parent's role, deeply implanted in his youth, became the pattern the son followed with his own offspring.

Three wives wandered, at intervals, through the household; two of them bore his family. They are scarcely mentioned in the Diary, and it may be assumed that their contributions to the education and training of their little ones was slight. Out of fifteen sons and daughters, only six—Increase, Samuel, Elizabeth, Abigail, Katharine and Hannah—survived the rigors of a Puritan childhood. Many pages of the Diary record the father's anxiety and hopes for his children. In his *Essays to Do Good,* he states clearly the responsibilities which he believed every parent should assume:

> Parents! how much ought you to be devising for the good of your *children!* Often consider, how to make them "wise children;" how to carry on a desirable education, an education that may render them desirable; how to render them lovely and polite and serviceable to their generation. Often consider how to enrich their minds with valuable knowledge; how to instill into their minds generous, gracious and heavenly principles; how to restrain and rescue them from the "paths of the destroyer," and fortify them against their peculiar temptations. There is a world of good that you have to do for them. You are without the natural feelings of humanity, if you are not in continual agony to do for them all the good that lies in your power.

Thoughtful parents in any age might subscribe to this philosophy.
He believed that a wise parent should cultivate self-discipline.

> If any little Occasion for my Anger, do occur by any Neglect, or by something amiss, in my family, I would with all possible Decency govern my Passion. My Anger shall not break out, into any froward, peevish, indecent Expressions. I will only let them see, that I don't like what I take notice of.

A child should never be punished, he wrote, "in passion and fury." Pastoral duties took him away from home many hours, and he frequently scolds himself for spending so much time with his neighbors rather than with his family, where it could be turned "to much better Account." He taught his children to be generous, not only by his own example, but also by giving them "a piece of money, that with their own hands they may dispense something to the poor." He helped to establish charity schools for white, Indian, and Negro youth, in the belief that all children should learn to read and write.

His thoughts hovered often about his "little ones." "Every Monday morning," he writes, *"what to be done* in my family." Each night, after prayers and a song together, he questions them on what they have been doing and whether they have *"sought the Face of God, and read His word, this Day."* Their late hours worried him, since a "more early rising in the morning for every one in my Family, would be of unspeakable Advantage unto us all." Such a reform was not easily effected, however, and he repeatedly refers to this shortcoming.

At meals, the whole family sat at the table, where the father tried to make the "Table-Talk facetious as well as instructive." In many colonial homes, the children had to stand behind their elders, eating what was handed them.

Mather also endeavored to instill attitudes which he thought would help his children in later life.

> Betimes I try to form in the Children a Temper of *Benignity.* I putt them up doing of Services and Kindnesses for one another and for other children. I applaud them when I see them delight in it. I upbraid all Aversion to it. I caution them exquisitely against all Revenges of Injuries. Instruct them, to return Good Offices for Evil Ones.

He carefully observed individual dispositions and "would warn them against the peculiar Indiscretions and Temptations, whereto they may be exposed in their Tempers. Then I would see whether I can't suit their Tempers with motives that may encourage and animate their Piety."

Mather agreed with his contemporaries that the authority of the father should be implanted early in the minds of children, a belief supported by colonial law. He knew he was "better able to judge what is good for them," and that they should understand that "tis a Folly for them to pretend unto any Wit and Will of their own." While he "would bring them to believe that it is best for them to be and to do as I would have them," it is interesting to observe that Katy and Nibby did not join the church until they were grown, and it is doubtful whether Cresy ever was a member in good standing. Actually, persuasion seemed to be the only force he used to bring them to his way of thinking.

He searched for the golden mean of discipline in wishing "to avoid that fierce, harsh, crabbed usage of the children, that would make them dislike and tremble to come in my presence. I would treat them so that they shall fear to offend me, and yet heartily love to see me." He disapproved of corporal punishment "except it be for an atrocious crime, or for a smaller fault obstinately persisted in." He reprimanded the child "perhaps by exacting some moderate sacrifice (such as staying in the house for some hours) for the purpose of preventing the mind's too soon exchanging salutary impressions for youthful levity." "To be chased for a while out of *my Presence,* I would make to be look'd upon, as the sorest punishment in the Family." He was discriminating about companions for his children, especially for Cresy, "lest some vicious and wicked Lads do corrupt him and ensnare him."

The children, despite the somber, religious atmosphere, had many normal experiences. Once Sammy, cross with his little sister Lizzy, was scolded by his father, who then gave her "a piece of Pomecitron," but, as a penalty, none to him. "I had no sooner turn'd my back," he wrote, "but the good-conditioned Creature fell into Tears, at this Punishment of her little Brother, and gave him a Part of what I had bestowed upon her." They amused themselves, even though the father complained of Sammy's "inordinate Love of Play" and often sought "to insinuate the Maxims and

Lessons of Piety" into their games.

Medical knowledge, limited in colonial days, tended to neglect the ills of children. The large Mather family had the usual "Feavours," "Convulsions," and "malignant colds." The desolating epidemics of smallpox and measles entered their home as freely as any other. While Mather knew more about medicine than the ordinary person, his first thought in illness was not of the body, but of the spirit. Sickness was a chastisement from Heaven and the direct result of his own shortcomings. He spent long hours praying for forgiveness and the recovery of his loved ones. *"Truth is not a Fancy,"* he writes. "My little Daughter *Nanny* is wonderfully recovered. The Lord Show'd us how to encounter the Malady." Once he called small Katy into his study to tell her that "some dreadful Afflictions might befal her" unless she gave herself to the Lord.

Smallpox flared up at intervals. In 1702, his study became a hospital, and though his children "came alive out of the *Fiery Furnace,"* his wife and servant succumbed. The disease, brought to Boston by sailors in 1721, flew swiftly from house to house. Mather had read in the *Journal* of the Royal Society of London about a "new method of inoculation," which had proved successful with "the Africans and Asiaticks," so he prepared an address on the subject to the physicians of Boston. Dr. Zabdiel Boylston, the only one of them with enough courage, tried it on a member of his own family. Many people were violently opposed to the treatment. "They talk not only like Idiots but also like Franticks, And not only the Physician who began the Experiment, but I also am an object of their Fury," wrote Mather. An attempt was even made upon his life.

When Sammy came home from Cambridge, where the smallpox was raging in the college, his father had to decide whether to subject him to "transplantation," as the treatment was called. "If he should miscarry, besides the loss of so hopeful a Son, I should also suffer a prodigious Clamor and Hatred from an infuriated Mob, whom the Devil has inspired with a most hellish Rage, on this Occasion." Cotton, encouraged by his own father, performed the operation, which had the desired effect. His boldness and that of Dr. Boylston, both of whom braved public opinion, helped to lay the foundation for the control of this pestilence.

Measles crept through the household in 1713, depriving it of the mother who had nursed the sick and the twins born during the siege. "Lovely little Jerusha," only two and a half became ill. The father's anxiety regarding her is very touching: "My pretty little Daughter *Jerusha,* on whom we have been so fond, as to make me fear whether we should not lose her, now lies very sick of a Fever." His grief at her death is as poignant now as when he wrote: "I begg'd, that such a bitter Cup as the Death of that lovely child might pass from me." The epidemic was so serious that Mather published directions for the better care of the sick.

Open fires and candles were hazardous, and the Mathers were constantly being "scorched." Little Nanny fell into the fire in the study and was severely burned about the face and arms. "Alas, for *my sin,*" the father bewails, "the just God throwes *my Child* into the Fire!" When Katy went to the cellar with a candle, "her *Musslin* Ornaments about her Shoulders took Fire from it and so blazed up to sett her *Head-gear* likewise on Fire." Fortunately she was saved. Cresy and Lizzy, in their turn, were "scorched" with gunpowder and underwent a "smart that is considerable." Such incidents inspired the father to preach a sermon on "What Use ought Parents to make of Disasters befalling their Children" and brought home to the children dramatically "their Danger of Eternal Burnings" if they failed to follow the word of God.

It is in the field of secular education that Cotton Mather's wisdom gleams most brightly. He educated his daughters, as well as his sons, at a period when girls were usually neglected. All his children, he maintained, should be trained in "some profitable Avocation (whether it be painting or the law, or medicine or any other employment to which their own inclinations may the most lead them)." This would provide a "comfortable subsistence," in case they were "brought into destitute circumstances." In this spirit, he writes, "it is time for me to fix my three Elder Daughters in the opificial and beneficial mysteries, wherein they should be well instructed; that they may do good unto others. . . . For *Katy,* I determine Knowledge in Physics, and the Preparation and the Dispensation of Noble Medicines. For *Nibby* and *Nancy* I will consult their Inclinations." He would have them be "very good Mistresses of their Pens" and "have them well instructed in *Shorthand.*" Nor should their training neglect the household arts, for, "to accomplish my little Daughters for House-keeping, I would have them at least once a week, to prepare some new Thing, either for Diet or Medicine; which I may show them described in some such Treatist as the *Family Dictionary.*" Cresy should be "accomplished in certain Mathematical Sciences (as well as those of the fencing and Music Schole) namely Geometry, Trigonometry, Navigation."

He put his ideas on the education and training of children into a chapter for parents in his *Bonifacius or Essays to Do Good,* published in 1710. John Locke's *Some Thoughts Concerning Education* had appeared in England seventeen years before, and there can be no doubt of its influence on Cotton Mather. The views of the two men on education and training are similar, sometimes almost word for word. Mather's book addressed various groups in the community and was highly recommended as an "invaluable treasure" of directions for the good life. Perhaps Benjamin Franklin is the best known person to have benefited from it. In a letter written to Samuel after his father's death, Franklin says "If I have been as you think a useful citizen, the public owes the advantage of it to this book."

Mather desired that his children be "expert, not only at reading with propriety, but also writing a fair hand." He liked to assign books to them and have them write an account of what they had read in a notebook, "neatly kept," so as to impress their minds with the contents. He endeavored to "keep a strict eyes," however, to see that they did not "poison themselves with foolish romances, novels, plays, songs or jests." He wanted them to consider it a privilege to learn, hence he thought ill of education "carried on with raving and kicking and scourging (in *Schools* as well as *Families*)." He casually remarks that his concern with the training of his children "spends me no little *Time.*"

The young Mathers were sent to school, but this instruction was always supplemented by the father and the grandfather, as well as by private tutors. Since Cresy seemed destined for "secular business," Cotton decided "to alter diverse Points of his Education, especially to have his Writing and Cyphring perfected." He encouraged the two younger ones when he discovered that they "of their own Accord, incline to learning the French Tongue." He conferred with Sammy's teacher about some work for him, since his "ingenuity" enabled him to finish his tasks ahead of other pupils. When he was not satisfied with the school, he removed his children. As to one such instance, he remarked, "the Condition of the Schole, will now require me to take in a Manner, the whole care, of my dear Sammy's Erudition."

As the family grew older, his concern assumed a different character. "The Consideration of bringing my eldest Daughter into the married State," he writes, "is a Thing, that will now engage my more than ordinary Supplications to the Lord." Nibby was sought after "by a hopeful young Gentlemen," whom she later married, and he writes that Lizzy is "on the point of being disposed of." Since Nancy did not get on happily with her stepmother, the father was forced to find a place for her to live outside his home. Katy's fatal illness of consumption and the deaths of other children caused him deep sorrow. But his greatest grief was the straying from the fold of Cresy, his favorite child. Mather tried to steer him into a useful business, but Cresy never succeeded in establishing the pattern for a happy and useful life.

Seldom out of his father's thoughts, his name appears more frequently in the Diary than that of any other child. According to his brother Samuel, Increase was "a young man, *well beloved* by all who know him, for his *Superior Good Nature* and *Manners,* his elegant Wit and ready Expressions." Nonetheless, he was always in trouble. He took part in a "night-Riot with some detestable Rakes in the Town," and when he was sixteen, he was accused by "a Harlot big with a Bastard." Even though "the most sensible Judges upon the strict Enquiry believe the youth to be Innocent," it is clear that the father did not agree with them. His anguish as he writes, "I considered the Sins of my Son, as being my own; and as also calling to Remembrance the Sins of my former Years," repeats the agony of all parents in similar circumstances. After being driven to despair by Cresy's actions, he questions whether he should not tell him "that I never will own him or do for him or look on him" until he is reformed.

But his profound love for this wayward child caused him to relent and permit him to return home again. Cresy's conduct showed little improvement, however, for the father complains that "a vile Sloth, accompanied with the Powers of Satan, still reigning over him, ruins him, destroyes him." At last, a place was found for the youth on a ship, and he set forth with his father's good wishes. The news of Cresy's death when the ship foundered brought torment to the devoted parent. He prayed long hours, blaming himself for all the shortcomings of his beloved son. "I exceedingly loathed and judge myself before the Lord, for the Sins of that Child, as being on some accounts my own; and for all my other Sins which have procured such astonishing Rebukes of Heaven upon me."

Sammy, however, fulfilled the hopes which Cotton had failed to realize in his eldest son. He caused his father no sleepless nights or long vigils of prayer. At Harvard he was good at his studies, and there was no need for his parent to assign, as he did, "some superior students" to "keep a strict Inspection of Him, and oblige him to observe certain Points of Good Conduct." In 1723, at the age of seventeen, he graduated and later traveled to New Haven, where he had "the uncommon Respects of the Degree of M.A. conferred on him at Commencement there." Samuel was invited to speak in his father's church, and Cotton's account is quite restrained. "This Day," he wrote, "my son Samuel (while yett short of eighteen) appeared in the Pulpit where his Father and Grandfather before him, have served our glorious Lord." When the youth decided to go to England, the father was greatly worried. "If I cross his Inclinations, I know not what grievous Temptations I may throw him into." Fate intervened, however, and the plans were changed, thus relieving his terror of an ocean voyage for another son. Samuel and his sister Hannah were the only ones to survive the father.

Little is known of what the children thought of their father, but it is evident that they loved him. Both sons publicly defended his name against his enemies. Samuel's devotion and pride shine through the dull and respectful life he wrote of the *"Best of Fathers."* Mather himself said that *"The Affection* which my *Children* have and show to me, causes me to delight in them." This we may well believe. It fully repaid him for the occasional worries and sorrows they caused. Possibly these few pages may show that this old Puritan, who daily walked and talked with his God, took time to love his children to give them the best education and training he could devise, and to offer unceasing prayer for God's "Favour to my Children; that they may be pious, useful, happy Children."

# 7. Ambivalent Childrearing In Eighteenth-Century America
By John F. Walzer.

The institution of the children's birthday celebration did not exist in eighteenth-century America. The birth of a child was mentioned only briefly; the anniversary of the birth was seldom noted, and when it was, it was done in a morbid way: "this day being my brother Hugh's birthday, who if alive enters [sic] the 28th year of his age." Upper or middle class parents did sometimes give their children presents, however. Father's return after a long absence sometimes provided the occasion, significantly. If a father could not come home, he sometimes wrote to his children. The letters of St. George Tucker to his stepsons, although they contain the standard stilted expressions of love and duty, illustrate that these children were not just incidental waifs who happened to be standing around in the wings of a busy man's life. Indeed, he scolded his wife for forgetting to mention one of his several children specifically. Mrs. Tucker made amends in her next letter with a multitude of details about the children. "I have not been guilty of the omission in any other" letter, she pointed out. The mention of children in letters, while frequent, was often a formality, or an after-thought. One is often struck by how infrequent, brief, casual, and sometimes hard-hearted are the references made to children by eighteenth-century Americans. Yet they did take a definite interest in what those children were up to, and, above all, in what they would become.

The evidence suggests that the American mother of the eighteenth century was in closer and more constant contact with her children, and interacted more often and more deeply than her counterpart in Europe. Servants were certainly less available. It is true that in *Virginians at Home,* Edmund S. Morgan could characterize the relationship between parent and child in Virginia as "pleasant," because the tutor or governess often had the unpleasant task of punishing the children. But Mdmes. Drinker, Burr, Sedgwick, and Tucker had a regular, close contact with their little ones. Mrs. Burr's only servant was a twelve-year-old girl, whom the good woman attempted to educate, and nursed when she fell ill.

Fathers, when they were home and available, on occasion played with the kiddies. "I suppose you twert yourself very often in play with your little sons when you are able," Anne Tucker wrote to her son, St. George in 1780. Pamela Sedgwick told her husband that the children missed him and wished for his company, "that they may hang around [your] neck. . . " On one occasion, Samuel Shoemaker was made physically ill by nine-year-old Edward's return to school. The Virginia planter William Byrd was a similarly intense father.

Just as there were sometimes genuine if brief expressions of "a great deal of joy" at the birth of son or daughter, so occasionally one finds heart-felt sorrow at the death of an infant, toddler, or older child. One Mrs. Brown, an Englishwoman considering emigration to America, and on visit here, did not return to England at the death of her child, Charlotte, but she definitely felt a sharp and lasting sorrow, sense of loss, and depression when she heard of Charlotte's death. For a week or so she lamented to her diary that she could not go on. Esther Burr likewise spoke of real anxiety when Aaron almost died. Other parents recorded genuine grief and despair in their letters and diaries, although such records also contain passages that may be paraphrased, "he died, God's will be done, did the pickles get there without spoiling?" Mrs. James Burd wrote to her husband in 1764 with a casualness hard to believe that no doubt he had already heard of the death of one of their children.

On May 12, 1710, William Byrd recorded in the secret diary he kept, in code, that his son, Parke, age about twenty-two months, was very sick of a fever. The child continued unwell, and on the 17th Byrd sent "an express" for a Mr. Anderson. Anderson was not a doctor, but a person with some medical skill. On the next day the boy was a bit better, "thank God," but on the 21st, Evie, Byrd's two-year-old daughter, came down with the fever. Byrd therefore sent excuses to Colonel Harrison, with whom he was scheduled to dine. On the 24th Byrd and his wife stayed up until midnight with the children, and then turned the job over to an apprentice to the secretary at Westover plantation, who was followed in turn by the overseer.

On June 3, Byrd "rose at 6 o'clock, and as soon as I came out news was brought that the child was very ill. We went out and found him just ready to die and he died about 8 o'clock in the morning. God gives and God takes away; blessed be the name of God." The most charitable way to read this evidence is that Parke suddenly became a lot sicker than he had been; yet these parents do seem different from those who might have taken turns sitting up each night with the child, or given orders to wake them if the child took a turn for the worse.

The entry for June 3 continues:

Mrs. Harrison and Mr. Anderson and his wife and some other company came to see us in our affliction. My wife was much afflicted but I submitted to his Judgment better, notwithstanding I was very sensible to my loss, but God's will be done. Mr. Anderson and his wife with Mrs. B-K-r dined here. I ate roast mutton. In the afternoon I was griped in my belly very much but it grew better toward the night. In the afternoon it rained.

Byrd is "very sensible of his loss," but he does not spend the space and energy remaining for the diary entry on enlarging upon it. Rather, he recorded what he ate, as he usually did. Also, on this day and several of the following days, he has a stomach ache, and does not know why, or says he does not. Twice he says he is suffering "for no thing." It did not occur to him that it might be because the death of his infant son had upset him. On the contrary, it is as if it was especially important to him to consciously deny this. Although he never again refers to the boy, it seems evident that his death upset him more than he wanted to admit.

Mrs. Byrd, by Mr. Byrd's account, was not as stoical. It may be that Mr. Byrd dealt with the grief which, according to the accepted attitudes of his day, he was supposed to minimize, by attributing it to Mrs. Byrd. "My wife had several fits of tears for our dear son," Byrd recorded in his entry for the next day, but "kept within the bounds of submission. I ate hashed mutton for dinner." The next day "my wife continued very melancholy, notwithstanding I comforted her as well as I could." This probably was the first child that Mrs. Byrd had lost. After the funeral, Byrd wrote, "my wife continued to be exceedingly afflicted for the loss of her child, notwithstanding I comforted her as well as I could. I ate calf's head for dinner." He did not note that his wife was melancholy for a week or two thereafter. Then he appears to forget why she should be depressed, for in subsequent entries he mentions her headaches, and melancholy, and wonders what could be troubling her.

When the Puritan experiment began to fail in New England in the 1660's and '70s, owing to the lack of zeal of the new generation, the saints occasionally lapsed into the familiar lament of frustrated parents: "but we did it all for you!" In saying this they were momentarily being a little dishonest about the means and ends. Usually, Puritans admitted rather openly that their children were a means to an end: namely, the perpetuation of the parent's life-style, or ideology. Indeed, when they published anything on the subject of children, it usually dealt with this particular aspect of the subject. Of course they did not stress their selfish interest; perhaps they did not even see it. They brought up their children, they said, for "the honor and interest of God." For "how should the interest of God be promoted" if they were not careful to "hand religion down in the truth and purity of it, to their posterity?" Children were "a Holy Seed" to serve God when the present generation of saints was rotting and consumed by worms. They would be replaced by a "rising generation" which was again and again referred to as a godly or visible seed, "the seed of the blessed of the lord." As such they were superior to "a new ingrafting," whereby the true way might also be preserved.

The character of the child was seen to reflect on the "credit and reputation" of the parent. "Verily, we may often guess at the parent from the manners of his children," New England parents were warned, as they no doubt point out to their children to this day. But what was involved in the "seed of the blessed" idea was something more serious than credit and reputation. Puritan parents were not supposed to think themselves to be in a position to decide whether they cared or not what people thought of them because of their children's behavior. For if God's charge "perish at last through your default," parents were threatened, God would not be merciful. "Unnatural wretch, you neglectful parent, how will it sting you to hear your children roar out against you from the place of eternal torment?"

Parents who did not give their children the wherewithal to perpetuate the true word of God, who did not shape their children so that they would *not* reshape the word (or the world), were worse than cruel sea monsters. That "a perfect subordination" or "a hearty submission," at least in ideological matters, was wanted, is very clear, although the Puritans were actually ambivalent on this crucial matter. The oft-quoted text, "know ye Solomon, the God of thy Fathers, and follow him with a perfect heart," best sums up the attitude and purpose. God, it seems, knows one's thoughts so absolutely no deviation is allowed. "God's eye is *ever* upon them," parents were admonished to remind their children. "He sees and inspects them day and night in all their youthful prophaneness and dissolute courses." What was in store for those children who forgot about the omniscient eye of the omnipotent parental figure, and who forsook the way of the Lord in any thing? The eighteenth-century parent was not yet merciful, or at least not supposed to be, when it came to ideological soundness. "If indeed there should happen to be any Shimei, or Rabshekah in the family, one that reproaches the living God, and mocks and reviles you, and your offerings, it were better that you should turn such an one out of your doors, than that you should shut God out of your house."

Such complete submission, such an effort to subdue the individuality of the child, to hold on so completely, when actually accomplished, could manifest itself in a way that the opposite form which rejection sometimes took: infanticide by smothering. James Janeway, a Puritan Mrs. Hennyfalcon, who "dearly loved children," delighted in reciting the strange cases of children who succumbed to heavy doses of "omniscient eye," and wasted away at an early age. Of one four-year-old he wrote, she was often in "one Hole or another," in tears upon her knees. Another "sweet" five-year-old "buried himself" in praying, reading the Bible, and saying his catechism. Both were actually buried soon enough. In other words, many parents in colonial America wished to hold on to their children completely, wherein they saw their own interests bound up. While parents were doubtless sensitive to the notion that "the sooner they are made acquainted with the world the better," they were at one and the same time eager to establish their children "in the knowledge and [perfect] service of the true God." These two quotations could stand as symbols for two opposing conditions which parents wished to impose on their children: independence and dependence.

Having children also involved a more immediate compensation which was frankly admitted and even stressed. Proper upbringing "makes your children an honor and a comfort to you," was the promise. "A wise son maketh a glad father." Conversely, "a foolish son is the heaviness of his mother." Children properly tied to their parents would care for them in their old age, in unfavorable comparison to "some of the old pagans," whose "children [were] under no obligation to do anything for . . . parents when a needy old age might overtake them." The self-interest and manipulative quality of parental love for children was further revealed by an occasional unveiled threat that it would be withheld if undeserved. "I send Edward my love," Rebecca Shoemaker wrote to her husband in 1784, "which he may always be assured of while he continues so worthy of it." "I . . . send my love and a kiss to Mopsey," wrote another parent at approximately the same time. "If she ceases crying in the night you may do her that courtesy, but otherwise I hardly think her entitled to it."

It is abundantly clear that parents did not always succeed in imposing a hearty submission, a perfect subordination. Even when one takes with a large dose of salt the eternal complaint of parents that their children are not behaving as they should, one is struck by the repeated assertion that children in eighteenth-century America were unusually recalcitrant. In New York, at the beginning of the eighteenth century, Dutch children were blamed for having "played at their unusual games" outside the doors of the churches on the sabbath. Moreover, the children even of rich Dutch parents were "usually without shoes or stockings," a sure sign that they were not under proper, civilized restraints. Lists of "don'ts" for children gave us some idea of a few of the omissions of the time, and what was feared from "the wild asses." "Don't gnaw on bones," one New Yorker admonished, don't dip your sleeves in sauces when you reach for them, don't run about wildly on the streets, don't go on the ice, don't snowball, don't go sledding with disorderly boys, don't join hands with other children, and, as a general rule, "learn to curb thy affections."

But for all the failure, the written evidence left to us suggests there was a large measure of success in the efforts of colonial parents to "hold on" to their children. One way in which this success might be measured is by the salutations and closings employed in such correspondence. "Honored Sir," "I am your dutiful son," "your ever dutiful son," "Honored Parent," "I am in all respects your dutiful son," "I am, dear Sir, your Humble Dutiful [sic] Son," "My duty to Papa," "My love and duty to Papa"—these are what one finds, with far fewer "My dear Sir," "Dear Father," or similar, more modern salutations. Further, the obligation that "gratitude to your parents demands," was often mentioned by children writing to their parents. "I am very sensible of the many obligations I am under to you," John R. Coombe wrote to his grandparents who had brought him up. "I hope I shall . . . in some measure, dear Papa, repay the obligation that I am under by paying constant and diligent attention to my studies," Theodore Sedgwick, Jr. wrote to his father.

The assiduousness by which adults urged proper attention to their aging parents is further testimony to the degree to which parents succeeded in obtaining a sense of duty from their children. In fact the impression one gets from the sources is that the concern of such adults for their aging parents was greater than that exhibited by parents for their young children. Pamela Sedgwick wrote to Boston after her mother's death to ask for a lock of her mother's hair, just as in our time a young mother often preserves a lock of her baby's golden tresses. Mrs. Sedgwick, who could not go to Boston when her mother died, spoke glowingly of her stand-in sister-in-law's behavior. She "could not have possibly attended one of her natural parents with more tenderness and unwearied kindness than she has my mother," Pamela told her husband. But the clearest re-kindling of the dependence relationship, which has the added interesting feature of a reversal of roles, can be found in Mrs. Morris' letter to her son, penned on November 28, 1793. "May heaven preserve thee," she tells him in closing, "to 'rock the cradle of reposing age.' This is the fervent and affectionate prayer of thy tender mother." The child, held on to properly, becomes the parent, and the aging parent can return to the comfortable encapsulation of childish dependency, and be "draw[n] towards her long desired home," and "gathered into the fold of rest."

Child-care was even more demanding on such well-to-do, middle class mothers as Mrs. Sedgwick, Mrs. Burr, and Mrs. Tucker, when one or more of their children was sick, which was frequently the case. "Last night up almost the whole night," Esther Burr complained in January, 1757, and the next night, "very little sleep." The third night she was "up the whole night" again. When Sally was a little better her mother found her "extremely cross, crying all day, *Mam, Mam* If I hav't her in my arms." She was "more troublesome than when she was sicker." "I begin to feel almost worried out, for she will go to nobody but me," a tired Mrs. Burr complained after Sally had been ill for six months. "I am afraid this illness will cause another whipping spell," she admitted.

In all likelihood, not all mothers were as attentive as Esther Burr, although few houses in America were spacious enough to allow the parents much distance to separate themselves from sick or squalling infants. Even the wealthy planter, William Byrd, got up quite late on one occasion "because the child had disturbed me in the night." And a review of eighteenth-century parental correspondence leaves one with the very strong impression that there was always at least one child ill in the colonial home.

Some of the pressure of a parental duties spilled over on to American fathers, and there is some evidence that it was not entirely unwanted. Although Fanny Tucker and Pamela Sedgwick complained that their politically active husbands were too often gone from home, the implication of their complaints, and of the apologies offered by their husbands in return, was that they were fond parents when at home. The busy William Byrd and the merchant Henry Drinker took time to involve themselves in the problems relating to their small children, and Byrd seems to have been especially fond of their little three-year-old daughter. Children were taught to stand in awe of their fathers, but the distance appears to have broken down in some cases. The example of David, who would himself be a teacher of his child, was held up to colonial fathers to emulate. Robert Carter, in contrast, clearly turned over his duties as father to tutor Philip Vickers Fithian. When Fithian could not cope with the rambunctious second son, Ben, he handed the duty of chastisement by the rod back to the great man in the big house. Ben was duly frightened and behaved himself, for a few days.

The symbol of the government of children was the book. Children must be always "kept at their book." The book symbolized civilized refinement. Book-learning might be conveyed at home by a parent with time and ability. "The schools here are not such as I choose so that I have not sent either of my girls to them," Isaac Morris confessed in 1748. A few parents could afford a tutor. But the emphasis on books, reading, and especially on "a good hand," certainly encouraged the spread of schooling. Fathers had little leisure to look after such matters, and few mothers felt much confidence, especially in spelling and penmanship.

It has already been seen that early "putting their children . . . to school" was a form of abandonment. But schools were also a means of holding on, an important part of inculcating the proper attitudes and ideals, and at the same time a place of confinement and protection. Protection, "by removing the hindrances of an unfavorable environment," dovetailed nicely with confinement and restraint. What children in school were protected from was a world which offered too much freedom. Upon examining the home for orphans in Georgia (which was also open to children with parents), George Whitefield remarked, "Here are none of the temptations to debauch their tender minds." An early advocate of compulsory, public-supported schools in New Jersey and Pennsylvania pointed out that at such schools "our children will be hindered of running into that excess of riot and wickedness that youth is incident to. . . ."

Protection from the wickedness of the world could not be complete, naturally. When the child was led astray it was essential that he be speedily corrected. As of old, the rod was the great symbol of such correction. We have already seen that bodily chastisement could be applied early. Even little Sally Burr's serious illness did not grant her immunity. One mother, whose youngster was temporarily out of reach, summed up the position concisely: "tell Tommy I will have him whipped for I will have him very good," she wrote.

At school as well as at home, direct action was often the course taken. Catching a boy in a lie, a school teacher recorded, "I took my ruler," which was "a large, round ruler, made of cherry wood," and "repeated the operation of the ruler against his hand till I made him confess the crime." The boy's hand turned black and swelled up a good deal, whereupon an irate father threatened court action. Schoolmaster Felton therefore sought the support of the selectmen. "Colonel Barnes told me the law was very favorable to schoolmasters," he reassured himself. Robert G. Livingston recorded in his diary that he had flogged James Powers and given him a black eye. William Byrd never took a stick to his "little Evie," but he did flog his niece Sue Brayne, and on one occasion used a different and unusual physical punishment on a dependent. "Made Eugene drink a pint of piss," he recorded in his diary entry for December 3, 1709. But Eugene did not stop wetting his bed, so Byrd gave him another dosage a week later. That may have stopped the lad, for on the 16th Byrd noted that he whipped Eugene "for nothing." Such irresponsibility in his wife, however, the well-to-do Virginian could not tolerate, and he questioned her closely when she caused her maid to be burned for some small mis-step which Byrd did not think warranted corporal punishment. If one were to broaden the definition of children to all wholly dependent persons, which should in truth be done, then it is clear that the rod and the whip found widespread application, indeed, in the eighteenth century.

We delicate people of today may cringe at the idea of drinking urine, but many colonial medicines forced down the throat of infants and small children were not much lovelier. Without giving it too much emphasis, it is worth considering that foul-tasting medicines are sometimes a form of physical punishment. Of course, other painful forms of healing, such as bleeding, and "the blisters," were regularly imposed on children.

On the more subtle side, parents increasingly employed shame in order to keep their children on the straight and narrow path. "My dearest sweet child," Theodore Sedgwick wrote to his first son, Theodore, Jr., in 1790, "do you love to have me write to you? I know you do. How much more am I pleased when my children write to me? . . . Besides, my dear fellow, by writing to me you will learn and will be ashamed to write in a slovenly manner." The relatively enlightened Puritan ministers Josiah Smith and John Barnard joined with their much more old-fashioned colleagues to suggest that shaming children was a legitimate and effective way to obtain desirable behavior in them. Even the still more liberal *Advice on Children,* published by Pennsylvania Quakers, called the inculcation of "a sense of shame" a "benevolent art in instruction."

In addition to shaming, parents resorted to playing on a child's greatest fears as an effective way to force him to behave properly. The dark closet, together with "tying to the bedposts," rough-handling, and the rod were begun to be banned from the nursery in the more sensitive days of the early nineteenth century, so one may guess that they were earlier techniques. The closet was a favorite place to send children to pray. There is some unusual direct evidence that at least one child in eighteenth-century America had the sort of fears associated with dark places. In 1780, St. George Tucker wrote to his wife that he hoped his stepson Theodore had "overcome his dread of the double-backed monster."

It is significant that while early nineteenth-century how-to-do-it manuals for parents warned against the dangers of "telling frightening stories to children," the eighteenth-century guidebooks read in America did not. The old-fashioned frightening techniques of the morbid James Janeway were repeated by such later preachers as Samuel Phillips. Phillips warned naughty children who "had rather spend their time in play than to learn their book" that God knew where all such children lived and what their names were. Even Josiah Smith, generally very "enlightened" compared to other would-be advisers to parents, reminded children of their closeness to death. The technique of scaring children by waving the scepter of death at them seems all but unforgivable in our times, but parents found it impossible to deal with their own anxieties without this technique. As late as 1790, the good Mrs. Sedgwick sent her fourteen-year-old daughter to attend the funeral of a girl who was soon to be married but had died instead. "I hope this afflicting providence will make a good and lasting impression on her tender mind," the mother wrote without conscious cruelty. "There is surely something. . . uncommonly striking in the death of a young person cut off in the bloom of youth. . . . " Warnings to children issued early in the century were the most extreme in delighting to threaten children with their imminent demise in order that they might mind. James Janeway's little Mary A. went as joyfully to death as to school, happy that she was dying for her mother's "reproofs and corrections, too." But it was Benjamin Bass, writing in the 1740's, who pointed out the further danger of going to "a dark place" forever. Janeway offered instead the comfort that if they were good, children who died suddenly would go to a place where "they shall never be beat anymore."

As early as 1727, the advocation of a careful and considered "prudent government," attuned to the needs of individual children, could be detected in Massachusetts Bay, in Pennsylvania, and in South Carolina. Moreover, there were signs that parents were listening. Certainly there were those who felt that children were "running away with their parents."

"Be not over-rigorous in your Government," "temper. . . your family government with a suitable degree of mildness," "be very careful to uphold a prudent government of. . . children"—these were the phrases used by John Barnard, minister at Marblehead, in Massachusetts in 1737. They characterize what was perhaps a new attitude toward children beginning to be held about this time. Children should be "managed mildly, in love, without brow-beating, or striking terror," Pennsylvanians were advised in 1732. "Ye Father, provoke not your children to wrath," Josiah Smith told his Carolina audience in 1727. "With patience, curb your passions." Be not too hasty to discover your resentments. Wait patiently upon their weakness. Teach by example, they have eyes to see as well as ears to hear, and are very much governed by the life and behaviour of their parents.

A prudent government was more demanding of parents than a more severe government. It was also less tolerant of their "using" their children. Especially, the rod must be used discreetly. Where a gentle reproof and admonition will answer, use that, "for a reproof entereth more into a wise man than a hundred stripes into a fool." Some children are stubborn, and must be used with severity. Some "discover a temper more soft and generous, and a word to these is more than a rod to the other." They should be encouraged rather than reproved. Parents should use discretion with regard to age, capacity, and temper of their individual children. They were not all exactly the same, after all, like the offspring of brutes.

Moreover, all must be done "with calmness." The great error of parents was in "giving correction rather from their own passion than the importance or consequence of the fault." Very few things in children required bodily correction. Even the more old-fashioned Samuel Phillips agreed in 1739 that "it is hazardous for any to be abusive toward them. . . . Children . . . are tender and we must lead them as they are able to endure."

"Gentleness" was the recommendation of Thomas Coombe to his son, when the latter received his little Johnny back in 1781. The boy had "a mild and gentle disposition," the grandfather explained, and "severity of discipline" would be a great mistake. "Suffer me to remind you that tenderness in every shape must be attended to" in the management of the little boy. Esther Burr, after she had disciplined Sally, confessed to her friend, "none but a parent can conceive how hard it is to chastise your most tender self. I confess I never had a right idea of the mother's heart at such a time before." The gleeful schoolteacher, Silas Felton, who "caught" a boy in a lie, "examined witnesses carefully," and "made him confess," himself confessed "I took a wrong way to punish him." William Byrd showed strong signs of doubt and ambivalence about whipping.

If punishment was to be adjusted to the child, so also was education, particularly reading material. In 1727, Josiah Smith advised parents to use language which children could understand when instructing them, language that was "free and easy," but not "mean." Throughout the second half of the eighteenth century, books adjusted to children in size, language, and format began to pour from American presses. This adjustment was relatively new to both England and America. 1744 is said by one historian to be a watershed year. One of the earliest such works, *A Child's New Plaything,* was "intended to make the learning to read a diversion instead of a task." "Young people will have language, pathos, and picturesque images, or they will not read," one author rationalized. "Some little condescension is due to their weakness."

328

Books adjusted to the supposed "capacity of children," such as *The Protestant Tutor for Children,* although simplified in language, did not show much real understanding of children. A heavy dose of sugar sweetness was no substitute for real empathy. In contrast, one child-advocate associated with early Pennsylvania history did succeed in putting himself "in the place of the child." Count Zinzendorf, who underwrote the Moravian experiment at Bethlehem, believed in free development where "rules are for the most part unnecessary." A less empathetic European visitor to the colonies complained that it was whispered of him "that I cannot talk to children." Such a remark at least suggests that this was considered undesirable. The Englishman in question, for his part, was not eager to be "pestered with the petulances of ludicrous prattle," and was quite sure that Americans had no more sense than his hostess, who assumed that others "can be as interested in her own children as herself." He warned: "early licentiousness will, at last, mock that paternal affection from whose mistaken indulgence it arose."

There is further evidence that a new indulgence toward children was already well underway in America in the eighteenth century. The various pamphlets offering *Advice and Caution* to parents all spoke of a "growing degeneracy" among the young, noted also by Peter the Hermit in 1274. One man warned against "too great remissness in parents and governors of families," and concluded that "most of the evils that abound among us proceed from the defects [of] family government." Little Edward Shoemaker, temporarily in England with his Loyalist father, was indulged with "thy favorite Lobsters, sweet oranges, etc." The willfulness of small children in Virginia was attested to by Morgan in his *Virginians at Home.* Edward Shippen, Jr., of Lancaster and Philadelphia, Pennsylvania, was unable to follow the advice to "accustom them to submission" offered by most experts. "I sometime ago gave my little Betsy a half promise to take her to Lancaster," he admitted to his father in 1748. "She now so strenuously presses me to keep my word that if the weather should be fitting I have thoughts of setting off with her. . . ." Henry Tucker, Jr. admitted to his brother that Nan, "the saucy Baggage, runs some risque of being spoilt." In 1774, Phillip Vickers Fithian observed that his charges were all "in remarkable subjection to their parents," which was a gross exaggeration, perhaps the result of a comparison with his own failure to keep the Carter children until control.

We turn now to one final aspect of eighteenth-century childhood: play. A detailed description of the games and sports of colonial children can be found in Jane Carson's book on the subject. In the eighteenth century, play was still extremely suspect. "Of idleness comes no good, but in all labor there is some profit," the liberal John Barnard told his congregation in 1737. "Keep them within doors at their book, at some little service," rather than allowing them to go out to play. Play, which it was admitted children delighted in, was connected with sin, and the demands of the flesh. Especially was play wicked when it took place while children should be listening, or on Sunday. At the same time, the eighteenth century in America saw a definite recognition of the idea that "there is a time for all things under the sun, and that children have their times of instruction, which parents and teachers must be cautious not to exceed. Time must be allowed for recreation and innocent diversions, to unbend the mind and preserve the health," according to Josiah Smith. Sam Moody said good children "play sometimes, a little, and there is no hurt in it, but they are often thinking of Christ, while they are at their play.

## CONCLUSIONS

This chapter has been built around the premise that parents entertain a basic ambivalence toward their offspring. It is now time to argue that children are motivated by a basic ambivalence which is complementary to their parents' ambivalence toward them: namely, to be rejected and be retained. Or, to put it more precisely, children, as they are raised by their parents and become adults, want both to become independent and to remain dependent. Perhaps the latter wish exists first, and remains the stronger of the two. But it does seem as if, beginning in the eighteenth century Western men and women have been less ready to accept a continued dependent state and more eager to assert independence and mastery.

This shift in attitudes toward independence was probably caused by a shift in parental attitudes toward children, and at the same time caused a significant change in these. A great deal of unnecessary disagreement sometimes arises over the question of which of such inter-related phenomena brought about the other. In this case, one may have proceeded the other in a significant way, but very quickly the two developments became what might be characterized as "casually reciprocal." By the eighteenth century it would seem that the shift in parents' attitudes toward their children and the shift in children's attitudes toward dependence and independence had surfaced and probably had a great deal to do with the Atlantic revolutions which occurred at the end of the century. Both were also clearly related to two of the most central developments of modern Western history: the growth in the importance of the individual as an increasingly independent and responsible entity who was no longer primarily a member of a corporate body and the replacement of hierarchical relationships by egalitarian relationships as an ideal.

What could possibly have affected early modern men and women so, altering the forms of their basic wishes relating to rejection and retention of his children and leaving the fabric of eighteenth-century American society wrenched by these adjustments? Any attempt to answer this basic question at this time must be highly tentative and hypothetical. And yet, one is tempted to put forward a grand theory, if only because it is in the character of this study: that is, psychological and sweeping. Melanie Klein once supposed that in pre-Hellenic times there was no super-ego. Although this assertion may or may not have merit, it gives rise to the speculation that this faculty, however defined, is something that at some time or another must have evolved in the human species. This, in turn, suggests the idea of psychological evolution. If man has evolved biologically, does it not follow that he must have evolved psychologically? And is it not possible that this evolution has been slow?

A sense of the past and a linear view of history involve an anticipation of the future. Any scheme of psychological evolution places us now in a period where an especially possessive attitude toward our natural offspring, coupled with the seemingly opposite wish for their independence, continues to be predominant. But it may well give way to a new state characterized by inter-dependence, or the recognition of the mature dependence of equal and fully developed individuals on one another. It is to be recognized, however, that this scheme is itself predicated upon some of the ideas which affected eighteenth-century American attitudes of parents toward their children. That is to say it is itself shaped by a linear sense of time and history.

# C. YOUTH

## 1. Introduction

Youth is the last of the three stages identified with child development. During the early modern period the term was generally applied to the years between puberty and adulthood.

In the following selections, Smith and Hiner note that English and American society attached great significance to this particular stage of the life cycle. Sermon and advice literature written in England during the 16-18th centuries and in America during the 18th century discussed the great potentialities of youth. For both males and females youth was considered the appropriate stage to leave home, either to begin training in apprenticeship or to work in service. This skill-acquiring phase was considered necessary prior to the assumption of adult role and responsibilities. Since most of this training was accomplished under the auspices of families, youths had ample opportunity to observe the organization and management of households. This household experience was considered good preparation for marriage.

In England most females prepared for marriage during their youth by working as servants in wealthier households. The more affluent girls were educated often at other wealthy homes in such skills as weaving, dancing, writing and the proper etiquette that would prepare them to be managers of households of their own. For the small percentage of wealthy Englishmen in the 16-18th century the time of youth was regarded primarily as the appropriate occasion to acquire an education in a university or college or in one of the Inns of Court. After their formal education English youths who could afford it would travel on the continent. The grand tour increasingly crowned the education of young gentlemen in the 18th century. While Southern youth often studied in England, New England youth attended college in the colonies, mainly at Harvard and Yale. A great wave of college building after 1745 increased the opportunities for youth to prolong their education in the colonies.

Some historians have suggested an important biological difference between youth in the early modern era and contemporary youth. Pubescence may have occurred about four years later during the 16-18th centuries than it does today, although some historians such as Keith Thomas (1976) take exception to this view. Furthermore, full physical maturity, in both height and weight, may not have been achieved until the late twenties during the early modern period. Historians have attributed the lower age of puberty in recent times largely to improved diet and better health conditions.

Although the word adolescence as a concept did not gain widespread currency until the 19th century, adolescence as a term and concept was nevertheless part of a conceptual model of the life cycle delineated by the ancient Greeks. The term and concept were incorporated into a European literary tradition and were used by pedagogues and religious reformers involved with the intellectual and religious education of youth.

Several historians, such as Demos (1969) and Kett (1977), contend that in the 19th century a unique set of social conditions developed which created a unique adolescent experience for youth. They identify the following social features as instrumental in effecting this experience: increased years at school where youths were both graded according to age and separated from the adult world; longer dependence on parents for financial support, which deprived youth of independence; greater use of contraception by the middle class, leading to family limitation and greater involvement with their smaller families; a more complex society as a result of industrialization and urbanization which made for greater confusion in the choice of adult roles; and finally, improved diet and health conditions which lowered the age of sexual maturity. As a result of these conditions, it is believed, new behavioral and psychological theorists produced a new literature on adolescence. In particular, G. Stanley Hall's works on *Adolescence* has been hailed as the first full conceptualization of this stage.

What were the characteristics identified as typical of adolescence? Although writers about adolescence stress different salient qualities, there emerges a core of descriptions which both historians and psychologists have come to accept as generally illustrative of this stage. Adolescents in modern times are viewed as pre-adults who often experience inner turmoil, or who feel alienated from parents or society. During this period of "storm and stress" they become involved with peer approval and conscious of their sexual changes. They are also affected by spurts of energy or periods of laziness. This energy, moreover, could involve them with sports or, if misdirected, into such antisocial activity as crime. Adolescents, furthermore, are youth seeking an identity and in this search there could be great attachment to peer groups and ideological reforms.

Although the above description is accepted as characteristic of the modern adolescent, there are some historians who contend that the phenomenon of adolescence is not unique to modern times. Fox (1977) traces the concept and word usage to the ancient Greeks and reviews its development in European literature. Smith and Hiner find adolescence in early modern England and America, as is seen in the selections below.

John Demos (1970) explores the Plymouth colony of the 17th century to see if Plymouth youth experienced the "storm and stress" or the uncertainty or the rebelliousness that is associated with modern adolescence. His investigation convinces him that adolescence as we know it today did not exist in 17th-century Plymouth, because there is no evidence that youth behaved in the manner that we currently associate with the stage of adolescence.

Smith, who writes about English youth in the 17th century, and Hiner, who investigates the matter in early 18th-century New England, contend that adolescence, as we know it, *did* exist during their periods and places. Both find evidence in the religious literature of the times which suggests a heightened awareness to and an identification of the characteristics we consider adolescent. Youth in this literature is described as sensual, proud, susceptible to peer pressure, fickle, unsettled and unreasonable. In England and America youth was viewed as a distinct stage that was pre-adult and a time of uncertainty. Indeed, Smith includes autobiographical material which illustrates the conflict youth experienced between their new sexual urges and their Christian morality of pre-marital continence.

Both Smith and Hiner maintain that the religious leaders attempted to influence and direct youth into early religious conversion, as a means of restraining their sexual desire, and as a mechanism for channeling the instability and waywardness of their youth. Religious conversion, it was believed, would also mitigate the influences of adolescent peers who were also experiencing similar crises and uncertainties. In short, Hiner and Smith find sufficient evidence to conclude that adolescence as we define and know it existed well before the 19th century.

How is it possible for Demos to find no evidence of adolescence while Hiner and Smith found an abundance of examples?

We can suggest that during historical periods that were more complex, youths' potentials were greatly stressed by their contemporaries, while their vulnerabilities also became apparent to them. Seventeenth-century England and eighteenth-century America may have been such times: of greater change with more educational opportunities; of increased urbanization where youth could congregate and be greatly influenced by their peers. In contrast, seventeenth-century Plymouth may have been a simpler community which did not focus on or record youthful characteristics. In 17th-century Virginia an extraordinarily high parental mortality rate forced or enabled children to assume the responsibilities of adulthood at an earlier age than their New England or old England counterparts. This situation combined with the absence of schools and towns where children could form peer group associations, has led Quitt (1976) to suggest that youth passed from childhood to adulthood without the identity crisis characteristic of the adolescent stage. However, youth in the more complex societies *did* attract the attention of people who were involved with their education and their spiritual well-being. These educators and religious reformers were "youth watchers," concerned with stretching youths' potential and minimizing the dangers they perceived and associated with this stage. In much of these writings youth was described in a strikingly similar manner to adolescence, as it has been described in the modern era. However, even in the absence of complex social conditions and even without men educated in the literary tradition of Europe, all youths shared the common experience of puberty and all youth in the early modern age had been regarded as pre-adults.

## 2. Religion And The Conception Of Youth In Seventeenth-Century England

By Steven R. Smith

This article examines sermons and guidebooks for young people to determine how preachers and writers perceived youth and then looks at some autobiographical materials to see whether or not youth saw themselves in the same way. Much of the material dealt with here could be termed "puritan," but this should be understood as referring to certain underlying attitudes and convictions which were shared by men of various political persuasions and theological views. As John E. Mason found in his survey of English conduct books, there is little difference between "royalist" and "puritan" writers on the topics of ethics and religious training. Similarly, there is no reason to think that there would be any difference between the conception of youth held by an archbishop of Canterbury and that of the most outspoken nonconformist.

In a century in which religion was a pervasive and all-powerful force, any conception of youth certainly would have been expressed in religious experience and thought. Kett and other historians who have written about the emergence of the conception of adolescence have pointed out the importance of the religious conversion experience, and Ariès, in his examination of youth in seventeenth-century France, found that the Jansenists, who were the theological equivalents of the English Puritans, emphasized the importance of religious training. The Demos generalization about the importance of urbanization has merit: the seventeenth-century Puritans were concentrated in the urban centers of England and were what Christopher Hill has called "the industrious sort." Certainly not everyone passed through a special stage of life known as youth: the great silent majority in the countryside probably did not, and the sons and daughters of the nobility may well have escaped it, but for the young people in the towns and especially in London, there was a phase of life distinct from both childhood and adulthood.

The seventeenth century did not share the twentieth century's concern for precision, and then, as now, "youth" as well as "children" was often used metaphorically to refer to attitudes rather than ages, as in "children of God" or "young at heart." The definition of youth is not easy, even in the twentieth century with its emphasis on age-grading and its obsession with classifying people and ideas. Kenneth Keniston has argued that there is today a new type of youth, but his definition is somewhat imprecise and refers to only a small minority of American young people. If twentieth-century social scientists are fuzzy on their conception of youth, seventeenth-century writers, who, for better or worse, were not social scientists, can be excused for some inexactitude. Yet there were attempts in the seventeenth century to set age boundaries for youth. *The Office of Christian Parents* divided life into six stages: infancy (from birth to age seven), childhood (ages 7-14), youth (ages 14-28), manhood (28-50), gravity (50-70), and old age (over seventy), acknowledging that these stages would vary with the individual. The stage of youth, in which "the child is most sensible, full of strength, courage, and activeness," was ended by marriage or by an unmarried person establishing a separate household, rather than by a particular age. The author used six of the commonly accepted "seven ages of man" established in sixth century B.C. and disseminated by a thirteenth-century Latin compilation which enjoyed a revival in the early modern period. Other seventeenth-century writers combined some of these stages but preserved the distinction between childhood and youth and between youth and adulthood.

The notion of a period of life beginning in the mid-teens and continuing into the twenties would have made sense to seventeenth-century Englishmen, especially those who lived in urban centers. The institution of apprenticeship through which many passed on the way to adulthood spanned some of those years. According to the 1563 Statute of Artificers and to the customs and regulations of the City of London, a proper apprenticeship should end at age twenty-four and therefore ordinarily would have begun at age seventeen. This rule was ignored by many, but its existence indicated an awareness of the relationship between the mid-twenties and maturity. The association of the concept of youth and apprenticeship was common: Nathaniel Crouch's *The Apprentice's Companion* consisted in large part of a revision of Samuel Crossman's *The Young Man's Calling,* and, during the civil war era, the London apprentices often associated themselves with the "young men" of the city in political petitions, the young men being journeymen who recently had finished their apprenticeships but who continued to live in the homes of their former masters. The conception of youth contained sections on choosing wives and establishing households. They also contained advice on vocational choice and emphasized the doctrine of Calling, which would not have been of interest to either children or adults. Marriage, commonly acknowledged as one of the rites of passage, was the end of a stage of life and the mean age at marriage for seventeenth-century men was close to twenty-seven.

Youth, as well as children, were expected to attend church services with their families or households, so that preachers were always addressing themselves in part to young people. Some sermons contained special sections for youth when the preacher wanted to make a special application of his text. But many sermons were preached especially for young people. It is impossible to estimate the number of such sermons, but some of them were printed and since only a small portion of ordinary sermons (as opposed to sermons preached before some official body or some prominent person) were printed, the custom of preaching to youth must have been fairly common. There were also religious manuals and books of devotions for young people and many of the more general or "how-to-be-a-gentleman" guidebooks included sections on religion. Two prominent Puritans felt that whatever attention was being directed to youth was insufficient or poorly conceived. Richard Baxter, in his *Compassionate Counsel to all Young Men,* urged ministers to give more attention to youth in order to make them holy and then keep them holy. He pointed out the importance of youth to society since one generation could undo whatever good the previous generation had done, a timely warning in the post-Restoration era. John Bunyan, in the preface to *A Book for Boys and Girls,* expressed his opinion that improper attention had been given youth.

Our ministers, long time by word and pen,
Dealt with them, counting them not boys but men:
Thunderbolts they shot at them, and their toys:
But hit them not, 'cause they were girls and boys.

Special sermons for youth meant that special services for young people were held in addition to the catechism classes held in many churches. William Kiffin, later a Baptist preacher and London businessman, reported that after his conversion to Puritanism in 1631 while a London apprentice, he and other apprentices went together to lectures at 6 a.m. and met an hour earlier "to spend it in prayer, and in communicating to each other what experiences we had received from the Lord; or else to repeat some sermon which he had heard before." Oliver Heywood, later a Presbyterian minister, noted that he had joined with about twenty other young men in a Christian study group which met every fortnight while he was a student. Another example occured in May of 1641; while many Londoners attended services of "humiliation and fasting and prayer" to celebrate the execution of the Earl of Strafford, a special service for apprentices was held at Dyers' Hall. About five hundred young men gathered there to listen to six ministers for several hours. Some of the sermons discussed below were preached to special audiences of young people and others at the funerals of youth where a large portion of the mourners would have been young. In addition to these more formal occasions, there were religious societies for apprentices and young journeymen; these associations offered opportunities for young people "to excite and stir up one another." All of these occasions would have reinforced the feeling of youth as a separate group. They served the same purpose as twentieth-century youth organizations, both religious and secular, and met the need of adolescents for peer approval.

Those who preached to the young on such occasions and those who wrote for them were concerned with impressing their listeners and readers with the desirability of early conversion and holy living. What they said *to* youth reveals how they perceived youth and an examination of these sermons and books should contribute to an understanding of the seventeenth century's conception of youth. Youth was depicted as fickle, unsettled, unreasonable, and unconcerned about the "big questions of life." Samuel Crossman described youth as a time of doubting and wondering, with "the mind for a long time like the wavering scales, rising and falling, going and coming ere it can settle." Furthermore, he felt that youth did not give enough attention to man's purpose in life or to the difficulty of conversion. Henry Hesketh, in a funeral sermon for a young man, compared youth to "a new ship launching out into the main ocean without helm and ballast or pilot to steer her." For Robert Abbot, who preached at the funeral of William Rogers, a young apothecary, youth was "a most unsettled age." Thomas Brooks' *Apples of Gold for Young Men and Women* characterized youth as rash; "they many times know little and fear less;" and he condemned this rashness as "ungodlike," "effeminate," and "below manhood." After saying that youth is concerned more with the present than with the future and unconcerned about "what we are! and why we were made! or what is our business in the world!" John Shower, in a funeral sermon, suggested that the reason the devil works more on youth than on either children or adults is because children are "not capable of making a choice" while adults are "fixed and resolved in their ways." Richard Brathwait compared youth to "the horse or mule which hath no understanding," and said that they are "as ready to consent as the devil is to tempt." A similar comparison was William Guild's statement in *A Young Man's Inquisition* that "youth, like an untamed or wild colt, can hardly hear or will obey the strait bridle that restraineth liberty."

Though it was an age characterized by fickleness, youth was also an age full of strength and vigor. Brooks, who had criticized the rashness of youth, also said, "Now your parts are lively, senses fresh, memory strong, and nature vigorous." Francis Fuller, in *Words to Give to the Young Man Knowledge and Discretion,* said that youth is the best time in life "for action, both as to the natural and moral frame of the body and mind," because of its strength and vigor, a purer conscience, and a softer heart than an old man. Other writers also contrasted the vitality of youth to the dullness of old age and demonstrated a preference for the former condition.

The most prominent characteristic of youth was sinfulness. Of course, preachers also constantly reminded adults of the universality of sin, yet most of the men who directed their attention to youth felt that young people were especially sinful and were subject to greater temptations than adults. Contrary to Pinchbeck's and Hewitt's conclusion that no concessions were made to the young, preachers were well aware of the exuberance and immaturity of youth. Such awareness did not lead to the conclusion that Christianity and morality were impossible for youth, but to the more optimistic conclusion that youth would have to exercise more diligence and care. It is also difficult to agree with Fleming's assertion that Puritans thought that the same means could be used for youth as for adults; Puritans began with the assumption that youth were subject to greater temptation than adults. The Puritan writer, Guild, pointed out that man is sinful in all ages, but youth, he said, "is carried with more headlong force unto vice, lust and vain pleasures of the flesh." Henry Jessey's *A Looking-Glass for Children,* despite the misleading title, was written "chiefly from consideration of my daily observation of youth's great need of all endeavors to prompt them to that which is good, they being naturally addicted to be drawn away through their own inclinations, and the powerful prevalency of Satan to sin and disobedience." Abbot told his youthful audience that "ye are now subject to the horriblest sins," because sin "hath in your age more instruments to bring it to outward appearance, as flourishing wit to invent and dexterity in other members to put in execution." William Cowper, in a sermon, held that Satan "works most busily and prevails most mightily" on young people, whom he compared to "wild she-asses" and said that of all the ages of man, youth "are nearest and most ready to fall."

Not only were youth more likely than children or adults to fall into sin, but there were special types of sins which were characteristic of youth. A great many sins were mentioned and almost all of them fall into the two categories of sensuality and pride. Brathwait found two causes of youthful sensuality: "that natural heat or vigor, which is most predominant in youth," and "want of employment, which begets this distemperature." He warned would-be gentlemen that lust would be increased by rich food, strong drink and evocative literature. Shower issued a similar warning, saying that lust depends on the "temper of the body, heightened by drinks" and condemned it as more animal than human. He pointed out that the sensual pleasures are often insincere or affected and lead to serious feelings of guilt: "look upon the young sinner swelling in pride, or burning in lust, or drowning in sensuality: consider him racked with impatient desires and burdened with avoidable fears, lest his attempt be unsuccessful, or lest he be disappointed in the secrecy of the enjoyment and his shame and folly published to the world, and yet this is the merry life of the sensual Epicure." This concern for the lust and sensuality of youth demonstrated an awareness of youth's newly discovered sexuality. This is a clear indication of a conception of youth as warnings about sexuality would have been inappropriate both for children who had not reached puberty and for married men and women who had found a disciplined and socially approved method of handling their sexuality.

The sins of sensuality included not only those of sexual lust, but, depending on the writer, extended to such as attending the theater, drinking, gambling, and a variety of other activities. What was most reprehensible about these was that they seemed to be more animal than human and resulted from the failure of self-discipline. The sensuality of youth could be attributed to man's basic animal instincts. The great danger was the failure to see that this was only one aspect of man's nature. Too often, youth saw this animal nature as the sole characteristic of man and one which would last forever; thus the moralists frequently used the analogy of youth and spring to show that neither was permanent. Benjamin Keach's *War with the Devil* and Thomas Sherman's *Youth's Tragedy,* both of which dealt with the necessity of early conversion, featured conversations of Youth with such figures as Conscience, Truth, Wisdom, Death, the Devil, etc. Both books begin with Youth comparing himself to spring and proclaiming his intension of fully enjoying the pleasure of life. The ministers' task was to persuade young people that sensuality was but one part of human nature.

The second major category of youthful sin was vanity. Brathwait identified vanity in four areas: demeanor, appearance, speech, and clothing. He said that young men walk and strut with excessive pride, especially when they are with girls, which is completely contrary to God's command to walk "in holiness and integrity." Secondly, youth "is ever noted to show a kind of contempt, expressing by his eye what he conceives in his heart." This appearance of contempt violates God's commands for a good Christian who ought to spend his time in contemplation of God. The third area in which youth express vanity is speech: often they speak without thinking. It is not only a matter of "rashness in resolving:" youth also has a "hastiness in proceeding," rejecting and ignoring advice and remaining "nailed to their own opinion." Finally, Brathwait questioned how any man could be proud of "rags" when all men are such great sinners and clothes ought to be reminders of Adam's sin. Certainly, vanity was not confined to youth; it was the principle sin of adults also. But Brathwait specifically tied his examples to other characteristics of youthfulness such as "hastiness in proceeding" and budding sexuality (walking with girls).

Another characteristic of youth was susceptibility to peer pressure. One of the most common injunctions in the sermons and guidebooks was to avoid bad company. Since youth were fickle and unsettled, it was advisable to avoid compromising situations and associates, but this also indicates the importance of the peer group and the adolescent desire for peer approval. After urging youthful conversions, Brooks raised and answered several objections that youth might have. One of the objections was the young man's fear that he might lose his friends if he gave up the ways of the world and tried to lead a godly life. To this objection, Brooks had four responses: first, it would be an exchange of old friends for new ones; "bad ones for good ones." Secondly, a person would be better off having no friends if those friends cost him his salvation. Thirdly, "the favor and friendship of such carnal persons is very fickle and inconstant." Fourthly, it makes no sense to reject Christ for the friendship of any man. The next objection of the young man was "I shall meet with many reproaches;" to which Brooks replied that many have suffered such reproaches and that anything a young man might suffer would add "pearls to thy crown." He also said that the reproachers would be punished at the final judgement. The next objection was that "we observe that most men mind not these things, but rather give liberty to themselves to walk in ways that are most pleasing to the flesh." Brooks answered that, while there are many bad examples for youth to follow, there were also good examples. Besides "you must not live by example, but by precepts." Finally, Brooks said that the many examples of evil in the world do not justify sin. Earlier in the book, he had said that "young men are very apt to compare themselves with those that are worse than themselves," and warned against this because it could lead to overconfidence and consequently the letting down of one's guard against sin.

Crossman answered similar objections by telling his readers not to shift responsibility for sin to anyone else; the individual must bear the burden of his sins. He suggested that any friend who urged sin was not a true friend and that a young man's true friends (which would include his pastor) and his parents would want him to live a godly life. To the objections that no young person follows religion very strictly, Crossman replied that the objector ought to become an example for them. In Sherman's *Youth's Comedy,* which like his *Youth's Tragedy* was written in dialog form, the recently converted Youth was tempted by his old companions to return to his old ways and lack of belief. They offered him wine and good fellowship, but Youth was saved when his Soul convinced him that his friends were "slaves to lust, captives to Satan's will." A similar experience happened to Youth in

Keach's *War with the Devil* except that death intervened before Youth was restored to righteousness. Abbot devoted part of his funeral sermon to a description of the life of the deceased youth and told how Rogers had been taught religion during his childhood but then fell in with bad company. Abbot had tried to convert Rogers and had warned him of the consequences of his action but the young man was too firmly tied to his evil friends. Later in the sermon, Abbot returned to this theme and told how easily many young people fall into sin because of social pressures since they "are loath to offend their wicked companions." He asked his audience to weigh the importance of worldly friends against the importance of God and to consider how much help those friends would be at the time of death. This same theme was part of the sermon preached in 1642 by Samuel Burrowes at the request of "divers young men and apprentices." Burrowes also appealed to the adolescent desire for adult approval, telling the apprentices that one of the chief advantages of early conversion was that the example of young people leading godly lives was a great encouragement to older people, and, near the end of his sermon, urging them to live righteously so that people might "say you have been the better since you came among these Puritans." Baxter also found youthful Christians useful in converting adults; "many children did God work upon at fourteen or fifteen or sixteen years of age; and this did marvelously reconcile the minds of their parents and elder sort to godliness; they that would not hear me would hear their own children."

Finally, most writers thought that youth had special favor with God. Daniel Rogers, in *Matrimonial Honour,* a book of advice on marriage, said that youth "is your golden time; each period following will prove worse downward, even brass, iron, and clay;" youth had a "golden opportunity" to learn before taking on the responsibilities of adulthood and marriage. Burrowes told his youthful congregation that they must begin early to serve God because God had a special appreciation of first fruits, because "the time of youth is the fittest and most choicest time for to give God your hearts," and because God realizes the great sacrifice that youth must make "if we consider how all manner of pleasure doth invite them." These same points were made frequently by others. John Gore, in a sermon on the text: "I have been young and now am old," urged his listeners to follow the example of the Old Testament David who had used wisely "that time which other young folk waste and melt away in folly and vanity, or in the pleasures of sin." In an appropriate metaphor, he asked them "to bind themselves apprentices to God in their youth," because God "makes more account of a little goodness in a young body than of a great deal more in one that is of a greater age." Fuller urged early conversion because religion and good living come more easily for young people who are strong and vigorous, and also because God is especially pleased with young converts. Brooks' *Apples of Gold* provided a detailed explanation of why youth should live righteously and seek God, and among the reasons was that youth's vitality would enable them to better serve God, who took delight in them: "It is no small honor to you, who are in the spring and morning of your days, that the Lord hath left upon record several instances of his love and delight in young men." He warned that it would be "just" for God "to reserve the dregs of wrath for them who reserve the dregs of their days for him." He went on to say that "the Lord is very much affected and taken with your seeking of him and following him," because as children want fruit as soon as it is ripe, God wants youth and waits impatiently. These examples suggest that seventeenth-century preachers had some notion of what later and more secular centuries turned into the idea of youthful innocence. Surely if God gave special approval to youth, man could do no less.

To help God get his first fruits, religious training should begin early in life. The need for this early start was recognized by Puritan ministers ranging from Anglican bishops to radical Quakers. John Tillotson, archbishop of Canterbury, in a sermon on family relations, told parents that they should begin religious training early not only out of a sense of obligation to the children, but out of self-interest since religion was "the best and surest foundation of the duties of all relations and the best caution and security for the true discharge and performance of them." Thomas Horn, in a sermon to the scholars of Eton, gave five reasons for early religious training: (1) it is the "great foundation of wisdom;" (2) it makes a person less liable to error in later life; (3) it is a preventive of sin and the best means of enabling a person to overcome temptation; (4) it makes a man more obedient and socially useful; and (5) children dedicated to God receive his blessings and protection. Humphrey Smith, a Quaker, not only urged standard religious training with prayer sessions and Bible study, but felt that if parents instilled the principles of true Christianity in children, the religious problems and struggles of young people would be eased. He described his own childhood and the difficulty he had had in overcoming sinfulness; had he been taught "to do no evil, nor waste the creatures" of God, his childhood would have been more godly and therefore his conversion easier. Much of the domestic literature of the century dealt with the religious training of children and youth and stressed the importance of regular family worship with prayers and Bible reading. Significantly, religious writers frequently made a distinction between the religious training of children and the religious training of youth, showing that these were considered as separate stages of life. Bishop Gilbert Burnet thought that early training was essential, but he emphasized fourteen as the beginning of a new period of life; "now is the time wherein the governor should with all diligence infuse in the youth's mind, the true and solid principles of the Christian religion," because it is after fourteen that "piety is chiefly to be looked to."

Parents and teachers were not the only ones to be told of the significance of early religious training. Young people were reminded that what they did would affect the rest of their lives. Richard Baxter urged young men to reject sinfulness and to accept God so that they would come to adult life "with a clear conscience not clogged, terrified, and shamed with the sin of your youth." The characteristics of youthfulness could be used to support the desirability of early conversion. If it were a time of fickleness and uncertainty, religion would provide assurance and security. The strength and vitality of youth could be used in God's service and would therefore be especially pleasing to God. The great sinfulness of youth supposedly was so obvious that young people would recognize the need for divine mercy and grace. And the notion that youth was somehow a time of special favor with God served as a further inducement to conversion.

One of the most common arguments for early conversion was the ever-present possibility of death. Much of what the sermons and guidebooks had to say about youth and to youth emphasized that youth does not last forever and that early death is always possible. This view was often contrasted with the typical youthful interpretation of itself as far removed from death which was associated with old age. John Hynd, in his description of youth, said that youth has a false sense of security, while it was constantly threatened by death; there could be "nothing more fleeting than youth, nothing more movable, for the time of it is unstable, it flieth away little and little without any noise." Baxter urged young men not to expect long life and to act as if death were imminent. He admitted that many young people doubt life-after-death, but suggested that even the slightest possiblity should be sufficient to bring about early conversion. Brooks reminded his readers that death could occur at any time and pleaded with them to consider eternity rather than life on earth. Funeral sermons offered excellent opportunities to hit hard at the possibility of early death; Abbot warned his listeners: "Now is the accepted time, now is the hour of salvation. God hath fired a warning shot from heaven." Of course youth's view of itself and the temptations of pleasure might prevail once the power of oratory was forgotten or illness passed, but the reminders from pulpit and page were frequent and vivid.

The emphasis on death should not be taken as evidence of morbidness nor dismissed merely as an appeal to youthful emotions. In a broadside reporting a dialog between the devil and a young man, the devil suggested that "some nice preacher hath raised those needless fears" of death in youth, but such fears were hardly "needless." One of the inescapable facts of seventeenth-century life was the high mortality rate; a young person would have been much more familiar with death than a young person in the twentieth century. By his mid-teens, he probably would have experienced at least one death in his family and perhaps the death of a friend his own age. The ministers and writers were concerned that he not interpret youthful vitality as a guarantee of long life, as indeed it was not. Having survived infancy, the young person had escaped the years of greatest danger, but death during the teens and early twenties was a very real possibility. Historians should keep in mind seventeenth-century mortality rates when interpreting warnings about the dangers of early death.

Fear of death combined with youth's special qualities and special favor with God, as well as the commands of God, all required early commitment to Christianity and the godly life. But with youth's propensity to sin, how was sin to be avoided and conversion effected? Both the sermons and the guidebooks suggested that meditation was one of the principal means and presses turned out a number of devotional books for young people. Many of the general collections of prayers included sections for youth. For example, Thomas Dekker's *Four Birds in Noah's Ark* had a section entitled "Dove," which consisted of twenty prayers for the young and "simple sort;" of these twenty, one was for students and one for apprentices. One of the country's most popular religious books, Lewis Bayly's *The Practice of Piety* was dedicated to the young Prince of Wales and urged early commitment to God. *The Prentice's Practice in Godliness,* a similar work specifically designed for youth, was written by an apprentice who wanted to tell his fellow apprentices about the joys of Christianity. Another apprentice wrote a pamphlet describing how he had succumbed to the devil's entreaties until his master brought a minister to him; he hoped other masters would do the same for their apprentices. Francis Cockin, author of *Divine Blossoms,* also asserted his youthfulness and his confidence that young people would not resent a fellow youth telling them how to behave and how to pray, while they might resent the same advice from an older person. Such devotional books as these contained in addition to model prayers and devotional suggestions, lists of moral injunctions. Nathaniel Crouch's *The Apprentice's Companion* had brief chapters on such topics as evil company, drunkenness, whoredom, profanity, lying, gambling, etc. The rules were sometimes very detailed and repetitious as in Fuller's book, when, under the heading of lying, he urged: "Do not lie at any time." "Do not lie upon any account." "Do not lie for anything." "Do not lie to anyone." "Do not lie for anyone." To help young Christians, many of the books provided models in the form of examples of religious youth in history. Crossman's examples included Isaac, Joseph, two Roman martyrs, Edward VI, Jane Grey, and Henry, Prince of Wales, among others. Brooks used several from Greek and Roman history as well as Biblical characters and figures from English history.

There was also advice on how to deal with sensuality and how to achieve grace. To the objections of youth that they ought to be allowed to indulge themselves in pleasure and that religion was too serious and grave for them, the ministers replied that worldly pleasures were not as satisfying as the true joys of Christianity. Shower admitted that many young people thought of Christians as "sad and unsociable, melancholy and dejected . . . [who] lead a life of continual complaints and sorrows." He answered by arguing that Christianity is full of pleasure because it gives assurance of future life and peace of mind, and that communion with God could give a man pleasure despite any adversity. He also said that sensual pleasures "hath but the appearance of joy" because they are short-lived and leave "a sting in the conscience." Guild outlined a program for achieving salvation in which the young man would first "enter into a diligent examination and inquisition of his ways . . . with and before God alone." After accepting his sinful nature, he must strive to know the way of righteousness and to live a truly godly life. One of the ways he could avoid sin was to avoid idleness; "Idleness is the door to let in sin and the devil even in the godliest." Brooks provided a fifteen point program leading to salvation. In addition to warning against the ensnarements of sensuality, his suggestions pointed to the insecurity of youth, warning them against flattery, rationalization ("carnal reason"), and comparison with others. He advised young people to model themselves after Christ and to choose only godly people as human examples. Though much that he said might also have applied to adults in need of conversion, he was particularly appealing to youth who were passing through a stage of life full of doubts and concerned about self-image.

It seems clear that preachers were interested in the salvation of young people and that they saw youth as possessing distinctive characteristics. But literary evidence, while answering some questions, raises others. It is not easy to determine the appropriateness or the effectiveness of what was being said to and about young people. One test of both the appropriateness and effectiveness is autobiographical materials. These can show whether or not the dialogues featured in several guidebooks were realistic, and whether the moralists were concerned with the problems experienced by young people.

Though they were usually remembering their youth from the vantage point of adulthood or old age, many autobiographers agreed with the general characterizations of youth. Of his own experience, Oliver Heywood wrote, "I may say that childhood and youth are vanity, yea and next akin to brutish stupidity and atheistical blasphemy." He also acknowledged the importance of peer pressure; when he joined a group of young friends for regular religious study, he was afraid of the reaction of his schoolmates, thinking he would "be derided for it." Sydnam Poyntz wrote that while serving an apprenticeship, he realized "how near youth and rashness are of affinity." Walter Pringle recorded that when he left home for school at the age of fourteen, "then did youthful lusts and corruptions begin to prevail over me, being stronger in me than the grace of God." Thomas Raymond, who became an apprentice in London at the age of fifteen, recalled "the great danger young lads do undergo at their first coming to London through bad company, counsels, and indiscrete masters." Ralph Josselin, the diarist, claimed that he had been virtuous as a young man because God had preserved him "from many untowardnesses that young boys fall into."

More significantly, the limited autobiographical materials reveal that many young persons did experience serious religious crises. In his study of the autobiographical writings of the century, Paul Delany found that there was a "falling-off in intensity from youth to maturity" in the religious fervor of the writers of diaries and autobiographies:

> The crisis of religious belief and anxiety over election usually comes between the ages of ten to twenty-five, after which the soul endures less torment and uncertainty; the excitement of the early crisis cannot be maintained indefinitely, external events gradually take on more importance, the presence of both God and the Devil makes itself felt less vividly.

The conversions experienced by youth usually followed the pattern described by Keach in *War with the Devil*. In the beginning of this book, Youth, contemplating the enjoyment of life, refused to listen to and self-confidently denounced Conscience:

> Speak not another word, don't you perceive
> There's scarce a man or woman will believe
> What do you say, you're grown so out of date?

But faced with Conscience's persistence, Youth agreed to talk with Truth, hoping that Truth would agree that Youth might enjoy the pleasures of the world without any danger. Truth, however, said that God requires the prime of life and commanded Youth to give up worldly pleasures. Youth tried to silence Truth by saying that such "heavy stuff" was unsuitable for youth, but by this time, Youth realized that the conversations had so unsettled him that he could never enjoy life with the reckless abandon of the past. Conscience and Truth each spoke at length to convince Youth of his sinfulness and of the necessity of sincere repentance. Youth agreed and promised that he would give up his sinful pleasures and rely on the advice of Conscience. The Devil then appeared and asked Youth to reconsider what he was about to give up. The Devil enlisted the assistance of Old Companions who argued with Youth, telling him that it was foolish to give up his fun. To avoid their reproaches, Youth gave in and went back to his old ways until he became ill and feared death. Again he repented and promised Conscience and Truth that he would now make a serious reformation. This reformation, though it amazed his old friends, was only outward; in his heart Youth remained unconverted. Conscience and Truth tried to tell him this, but Youth insisted on his sincerity. Conscience confronted him again and again, arguing that lust remained in his heart:

> Thy secret lust and what is done i' th' night

Which thou ashamed art should come to light.

After much argument, Youth confessed that he was not yet truly converted and asked for Jesus' help. He admitted his baseness and corruption and prayed for grace and a new birth. Finally Jesus accepted him, and Conscience proclaimed that Youth was fully converted. In one final attempt, the Devil returned and tried to tempt Youth, but Youth resisted and the "war" ended with Youth lifting his voice in hymns of praise.

One of the most detailed autobiographical descriptions of youthful conversion is that of Richard Norwood, who described himself as outwardly religious during childhood, but not truly converted. He sinned frequently, often in company with his school companions. At the age of fifteen, he was apprenticed in London first to a fishmonger and later to a shipmaster. It was during his years as an apprentice that "the corruption of my heart showed itself abundantly in lust" with several maids and with his master's daughter, and he sinned further by reading "vain and corrupt books." Norwood left his apprenticeship and served for a time as a soldier in the Netherlands before beginning several years' travel on the continent. He faked conversion to Roman Catholicism and made a journey to Rome, to see that city and to learn more about the religion. During the trip to Rome he began to suffer anxiety about his sinfulness:

> . . . after my entering into Italy, I began first to be troubled with that nightly disease which we call the mare, which afterwards increased upon me very grievously that I was scarce any night free from it, and seldom it left me without nocturnal pollutions; besides, whilst it was upon me I had horrible dreams and visions. Oft-times I verily thought that I descended into Hell and there felt the pains of the damned, with many hideous things. Usually in my dreams me thought I saw my father always grievously angry with me. . . . And sometimes I seemed to see a thing on my breast or belly like a hare or cat, etc.; whereupon I have sometimes taken a naked knife in my hand when I went to sleep, thinking therewith to strike at it, and it was God's mercy that I had not by this means slain myself.

These experiences began during his late teens and continued until his conversion which took place when he was twenty-six. Norwood returned to London when he was twenty and had thought himself converted shortly thereafter when he fell under the influence of powerful preaching, but this proved to be his outward reformation. True conversion eluded him and his sins continued for several years while he was at sea. Not until after he had gone to live in Bermuda did Norwood experience the final phase of conversion, complete with "heavenly raptures."

Norwood's nightmares were clearly sexual in nature. Such nightmares

347

were apparently a common feature of seventeenth-century youthfulness. William Lilly, later a well-known astrologer, recorded in his autobiography that "in the sixteenth year of my age, I was exceedingly troubled in my dreams . . .; in the nights I frequently wept, prayed and mourned for fear my sins might offend God." Norwood, Lilly and other young men probably suffered deep feelings of guilt stemming from masturbation and sexual desires. Masturbation usually was referred to in an oblique manner; one of the autobiographers to be explicit was George Trosse who reported that while he was an apprentice, "a lewd fellow servant led me to practice a sin which too many young men are guilty of and look upon it as harmless; though God struck Onan dead in the place for it." Christian moralists considered masturbation to be a serious sin, but it was not until the early eighteenth century that explicit printed warnings became common. During the seventeenth century, it was subsumed under the more general and euphemistic rubric of youthful lust.

Gervase Disney did not detail any youthful nightmares, but his conversion followed the standard pattern. Apprenticed to a London merchant at the age of nineteen, he fell into a life of sins which he catalogued in his autobiography: wasting his master's time, neglecting his duties, lying, occasionally stealing money from his master, missing church services, wasting time at an alehouse during working hours, leading a fellow apprentice into sin, and visiting bawdy houses (on the pretense of increasing his abhorrence of sin). Yet though often tempted, he was able to avoid fornication. During a serious illness Disney resolved that if he recovered he "would (through grace) mind religion as my business and follow the Lord fully." This was the start of his outward reformation, but sin continued until at age twenty-five, "the Lord was pleased again to check and stop me in my career of sin, to awaken my drowsy conscience." Still he could not free himself from sin, especially the youthful sin of vanity, manifested in fancy clothes. On a visit to his hometown, he was led back into a life of revelry by some of his former companions. Not until "after some reproofs and advice from parents and serious friends," did Disney once more mend his ways and achieve conversion.

Another years-long process was described by William Kiffin, who, while serving an apprenticeship in London, was bothered by his great sinfulness and therefore began attending "the most powerful preaching" he could find. This marked the start of his outward reformation, which he once mistook for true conversion until he realized that his "heart was so carnal so that it was a burden to me." He concluded that he did not have grace and was deeply disturbed until he heard a sermon which made him think that perhaps he did have a little grace. From this small beginning, by diligent reading of the Bible and attendance at sermons, he gradually increased grace and eventually arrived at a state of true conversion.

John Bunyan described his conversion in his spiritual autobiography,

*Grace Abounding to the Chief of Sinners.* His "natural life" before conversion was given over to sin to such an extent that God "did scare and affright me with fearful dreams and did terrify me with dreadful visions." He recorded that when he was about ten years old, "I did still let loose the reins to my lust and delighted in all transgressions against the law of God; so that until I came to the state of marriage, I was the very ringleader of all the youth that kept me company, into all manner of vice and ungodliness." Since Bunyan married when he was about twenty years old, he used the term "youth" to refer to the years from ten to twenty, which means that he displayed youthful characteristics rather early. After his marriage, he became outwardly religious and finally experienced full conversion. His outward reformation began after his period of youth, but it was during his youth that he experienced the anxiety connected with conversion and which characterized youth.

Samuel Clarke's *Lives of Sundry Eminent Persons,* which described the lives and works of nineteen English divines, several Scottish divines and fifteen prominent laymen, including nine women, provided several accounts of youthful conversion. Sir Nathaniel Barnardiston was reported as having been converted in his youth; during "the very time when others of his rank and quality gave up themselves to the greatest degrees of licencious wantonness and immoderate excesses, pretending that the heat of nature and strength of the lusts of youth produce a sufficient apology and discharge for the same," Barnardiston was leading a godly life, which led Clarke to praise all young gentlemen who converted in youth despite their greater sensuality and their "brisker nature." In describing the conversion of Edmund Staunton, who later became a Puritan divine, Clarke quoted from a letter which Staunton had written when he was twenty: he reported "many sad and serious thoughts" about religion, until he read a religious book which explained man's sinful nature. He then began a period of self-examination and recognized his own sinfulness. For about two months, Staunton was "under a spirit of bondage, being full of fears and inward trouble," until God answered his prayers and gave him grace. A third youthful conversion recorded by Clarke was that of his wife, Katherine, who found "the seeds of grace in her heart" at the age of fifteen, but this marked the beginning only of her outward reformation, for the "heavenly sparks" were soon cooled by vanity. At the age of seventeen, she was sent as a servant to the home of a gentleman in another county. While there, "so far from my near and dear relations, and meeting with some other discouragements in the family . . . I grew very melancholy," which was the beginning of her true conversion. She realized her great sinfulness and, after her return home, suffered spiritual anguish until, under the tutelage of her parents, she grew in grace.

The experiences of Katherine Clarke must have been typical of many young men and women since the practice of sending young people out of the home as apprentices or servants was widespread. This practice in itself played an important role in the lives of adolescents. Especially in the case of apprenticeships, many young people were exposed for the first time in their lives to the opportunities and temptations of life in the city. Those whose horizons had previously been limited to their own families and their own home towns were given the opportunity of broader experience and contacts. Alan Macfarlane has suggested that this was one of the chief advantages of the whole system. Another advantage was the one "source of tension, the changes in patterns of authority as the children approached adulthood, would also be diminished." Another of Macfarlane's suggestions touches on the sexuality of adolescence: any incestuous temptations would be removed. Joseph Illick has suggested that one of the motivations was the prevention of parents developing an "overfondness" for their children. Whatever the reasons for the system, it seems likely that the removal of young people from the family and community might have caused them to seek the security of religious conversion.

Another possible cause of the religious anxieties and struggles of youth may have been the dominant theology of the period. The sermons and guidebooks for youth were certainly capable of inducing such experiences. There was no special theology for the young; the pattern of conversion was the same regardless of age. Where the eternal decrees of God were concerned, there was no distinction between youth and adults. But the question is not whether there was a different theology for youth, but whether the society even had a conception of youth which was revealed through and in religious training and experiences. The question is not whether religion heightened or even created anxieties in young people, but whether religion did anything to help youth with their special problems.

Efforts at conversion began in childhood rather than in youth and continued as long as a person lived. In an era of precocity, a "fully" converted child of six or seven years was a possibility, but the general pattern was for the conversion experience to begin in youth. Since it was such an important stage of life, society needed to have a fairly concrete conception of youth. It would be anachronistic to think that seventeenth-century men would express that conception in statistics or in terms of twentieth-century psychology. They did not romanticize youth as later centuries did, but they saw youth as a special period of life and one which somehow found favor with God despite the great sinfulness of youth. Youth was characterized as a time of strength and vigor; this was hardly a condemnation. It was characterized as fickle and uncertain and whatever security youth might claim, Puritans dealt with by warning of death and the eternal fires of hell; this was realistic, given the theology and mortality of the era. Youth was characterized as more animal than human; this was simply another way of saying that youth lacked self-discipline. Self-discipline was a virtue much admired by Puritans and they were determined that it should begin in youth. The domestic literature of the time as well as law and custom allowed parents and masters of apprentices to punish young people in the same way they punished children, or, in other words, to respond to their animal or undisciplined natures. On the other hand, a high degree of self-discipline, with only occasional correction by church or state, characterized adulthood. Youth were admonished to substitute human, rational behavior for animal, irrational behavior, and, in this sense, youth was perceived as a time of transition from childhood to adulthood.

Proper moral behavior was stressed during this time of transition. While the morality taught to young people was the same morality taught to children, the autobiographical writings show that many who had extensive religious and moral training in childhood experienced sinful periods of youth; there was a need for continued training and the characteristics of youth gave special significance to moral training, and the conversion experiences of youth created a need for more intensive religious training. Many of the young people would have been away from home as apprentices or servants and thus experiencing a new and different environment. In some cases this might mean greater freedom, and, for a young person from a rural community, an urban setting, especially London, would offer opportunities for testing childhood moral precepts. Much of what the moralists had to say to young people was directed at these situations, just as much of it was appropriate for the budding sexuality of youth. Keach's warning against "secret lusts . . . i' th' night" would have been meaningful to those young people who fought to reconcile the accepted moral code with their newly discovered sexuality, but would have had less meaning to children who had not reached puberty. Stern warnings against youthful sexual activities may have added to the problems of youth, and are certainly at odds with twentieth-century psychology, but they were consistent with the prevailing religious thinking in the seventeenth century.

Despite important differences, the seventeenth century's conception of youth has some remarkable parallels with that of the twentieth century. Psychologists today associate youth with an "identity crisis," which is similar to what religious writers had in mind when they wrote of youth's uncertainty. A major part of a seventeenth-century man's identity was his religion and the religious crises experienced by seventeenth-century youth were an important part of establishing their identities. These religious crises were not unlike those teenage conversions during the Second Awakening in the United States, which Joseph Kett has acknowledged as important in forming the conception of adolescence. Nor were these youthful religious crises unlike the vocational crises experienced by many twentieth-century youth. Of course, seventeenth-century young people had to make decisions about their life's work and the ministers gave some attention to this, emphasizing the doctrine of "calling" and the desirability of useful work as a deterrent to sin. But the crisis of identity was primarily religious. There were plenty of models on which the young person could base his life; the Puritans insisted on godly models or on no models at all, but the precept of God. They tried to show youth that they must find their identity as sinners and as persons with a moral and rational nature as well as an animal nature. The Youth in *War with the Devil,* compared himself to spring, without care and free to enjoy life; this was his perception of his identity. The author's response was to point out another aspect of Youth's identity; he was also loathsome sinner.

The seventeenth century's response to the problems of young people was quite different from the response of the twentieth century, but it was in keeping with the religious attitudes of the seventeenth century. This approach forced young people to go through a period of rigorous self-examination in order to achieve salvation, self-discipline and identity. Perhaps it created some anxieties, but it also helped young people come to grips with their emerging sexuality. It might have caused some nightmarish fears of torture in hell, but it helped youth deal with the very present danger of death, which they might otherwise have ignored.

The seventeenth century's conception of youth, expressed in religious terms and having as its object the development of Christian adults was useful both to young people and to those who were concerned with religious training. The early modern conception of youth seems to have some similarity with the modern conception in that both recognize some sort of "identity crisis." Furthermore, there is in the early modern conception some foreshadowing of the modern romanticization of youth. Acceptance of these similarities does not violate Kenneth Keniston's warning against applying twentieth-century psychological experiences and conceptions to history, for the differences between the conditions and problems of early modern youth and the conditions and problems of twentieth-century youth cannot be overlooked. These differences were not only in religion, but also in economic arrangements, educational theory and practice, family relationships, and political socialization. Keniston has also suggested that "in societies where adolescence does not occur many of the psychological characteristic which we consider the results of an adolescent experience should be extremely rare." This is certainly true in the case of seventeenth-century English youth; they did after all become seventeenth-century English adults. The fact that they did not turn out to be twentieth-century adults should not obscure the fact that there was a conception of youth. Those historians who have failed to see this may have heeded Keniston's warning, but have gone too far in stressing the differences. They have stumbled on the religious ideas which seem harsh, but were, in fact, realistic for that time. Building on the basis of this conception of youth, it should be possible to develop an even clearer picture of what it meant to be young in the seventeenth-century by correlating the conception with the economic relationships (primarily apprenticeship), educational policy (especially educational reform), family relationships (for which Alan Macfarlane's study of Ralph Josselin's family life provides an excellent model) and the process of political socialization.

## 3. Adolescence in Eighteenth-Century America
By N. Ray Hiner

Children should be seen and not heard—at least according to the traditional maxim. Unfortunately, in the work of most American historians children and youth are not only silent, they are rarely even seen. Children and youth have been granted little more than cameo roles in the drama of American history. Although a scarcity of sources has contributed to this lack of attention, American historians have too often failed to take children and youth seriously, and this failure has had lamentable consequences. Historians have been unable to grasp the full significance of generational factors in American history; and social and behavioral scientists have thereby been denied an indispensable historical perspective from which to assess the validity and universality of their theories of personality development. Only recently, when, as Leon and Marion Bressler remind us, many young people have made themselves increasingly visible and highly audible, have American historians begun to give more careful attention to this neglected group.

The new history of childhood and youth will no doubt develop in several directions, but one especially promising topic which deserves more attention from historians is adolescence. In their studies of adolescence, psychologists have generally concentrated on biological and maturational factors and thus tend to stress its near universality as a stage of life. Anthropologists and sociologists, on the other hand, usually argue that the cultural and social conditions of premodern or traditional societies precluded the appearance of adolescence as we know it until very recent times. On the rare occasions when historians have treated this question, they tend to agree with the social scientists and emphasize the historicity and culture-bound nature of adolescence. John Demos probably expressed the prevailing opinion among American historians when in a recent article he (and his wife) declared, "the concept of adolescence, as generally understood and applied, did not exist before the last two decades of the nineteenth century." This statement by Demos, a specialist in seventeenth-century family history, has been echoed somewhat by Joseph Kett, who writes primarily on the nineteenth century. According to Kett, "a class of books aimed specifically at youth" did not appear until the nineteenth century. He notes that Cotton Mather published several sermons on the rising generation in the early eighteenth century, but Kett says he was "left with a feeling that

Puritans used 'youth' more as a noun than as a concept." The Puritans, declared Kett, "hardly believed that individuals moved through stages of life." Kett doubts that teenagers became *"truly conspicuous"* in America before the teenage conversions of the Second Great Awakening led to "the emergence of a conviction among evangelicals that adolescence was the ideal time to induce religious conversion."

The importance of the nineteenth century in the development of the modern concept of adolescence cannot be disputed, but do we know enough about the history of childhood and youth to justify such sweeping statements? Can we say with such certainty that nothing like modern adolescence existed before the nineteenth century? Lloyd deMause has pointed out that the notion of youth as a part of the "Ages of Man" concept has existed for centuries, and recent studies such as those by Steven Smith of seventeenth-century England and Natalie Davis' work on sixteenth-century France directly challenge the standard view that adolescence evolved rather late in European history. My own analysis of essays on youth published in New England during the first three decades of the eighteenth century also raises serious questions about the validity of the views expressed by Demos, Kett, and others. Young people were very much on the minds of the adults of New England during this period. Scarcely a year passed that did not bring forth a large number of sermons and essays concerning youth, their behavior, their social and psychological characteristics, and their spiritual needs. The unprecedented quantity and remarkable sophistication of this body of literature requires a fundamental revision of the belief that adolescence either did not exist or was little noticed or understood in America before the late nineteenth century. Modern adolescence and colonial "youth" are certainly not synonymous, but, as Ross Beales has suggested, their similarities are at least as striking as their differences. If adolescence in the social-psychological sense is "the experience of passing through the unstructured and ill-defined phase that lies between childhood and adulthood," if it is a period in which a young person struggles to acquire psychological autonomy and self control, and seeks to create a sense of identity within a context of prolonged economic and social dependence, then it existed in early eighteenth-century New England, and it occupied a central place in the thought of those leaders who sought to maintain the efficacy of traditional values in a society undergoing profound social and cultural stress.

When the spiritual leaders of New England surveyed the social and cultural landscape at the beginning of the eighteenth century, they saw an increasingly complex, fluid, heterogeneous, and secular society. By 1700, Boston, the primary mercantile center of New England, possessed the beginnings of what Richard Brown has called the basic characteristics of an urban society: "communication, heterogeneity, cosmopolitanism, and choice." After 1700 Boston's urban character became more pronounced, and during the 1720s a striking increase in crime, violence, economic distress, epidemics, bitter disputes in the press, and defiance of authority forced even Boston's most optimistic citizens to fear for the continued health and stability of their community. Noting the great tension and unrest in Boston during this period, Gerald B. Warden declared that it was "something of a miracle" that no revolution occurred.

Not even the rural communities of New England were able to escape the pressures of social change. By 1700, the stable hierarchical and patriarchical character of the towns of the first two generations was being undermined by the dynamic vicissitudes of an expanding society. The primary culprits in this historical drama seem to have been population growth and migration, the development of a commercialized economy, ecclesiastical disputes, and political factionalism. For whatever reason, by the 1720s life in rural New England was profoundly unsettled and shared to some degree with Boston the effects, if not the characteristics, of a society in the early stages of modernization. Puritan culture was fast becoming Yankee culture.

For anyone seriously concerned with preserving Puritan values, there was real cause for alarm. Many Puritan leaders sensed that they were losing control of their collective spiritual destiny and failing in their traditional mission to maintain a holy commonwealth in New England. How could New England be protected from the ravages of secularization? How could these trends be stopped or reversed? Like many others in times of social and cultural stress, Puritan leaders looked to their children and youth as both a source of many of their problems as well as the key to their solution. Writing in 1705, Solomon Stoddard explained that although "the example of other neighboring nations, the temptations of wealth," and "the evil opinions" of others had no doubt contributed to the spiritual decline of New England, he was convinced that "the main reason of the degeneracy" was the lack of conversion of a new generation. Increase Mather agreed: nothing would contribute more to the reformation of society than a revival of piety in the rising generation. William Williams concluded that if the people of New England feared the Lord, if they hoped to preserve their society from spiritual destruction, then their faith had to be "transmitted carefully to posterity, and be upheld from generation to generation."

Puritan writers on youth during this period were sensitive to the complex and delicate nature of their situation. They knew the conversion of young people was problematical, and they realized they had to gain a deeper understanding of their youth. Hence, they undertook a comprehensive and systematic analysis of the physical, psychological, social, and spiritual characteristics of youth by (1) searching the scriptures, (2) examining their own experience, and (3) studying the lives of individual young persons. The insights produced by this inquiry were woven into the basic fabric of their essays and sermons on youth. Often addressed to young people, these essays had both didactic and analytic purposes, but the promotion of the spiritual growth and conversion of youth was paramount.

Concern for the conversion of the rising generation was of course not new in New England; for decades Puritan ministers had made it a fundamental theme of their Jeremiads. Yet the statements by Stoddard, Mather, and Williams, and many others were earnest and contained an element of urgency which should not be ignored. As Stoddard pointed out, they could have turned to other equally logical means of explaining and solving their problems. However, by concentrating on the conversion of the rising generation during this critical, transitional stage in New England's development when a wider range of life choices was becoming available to young people, Puritan leaders had perhaps unknowingly placed an enormous amount of psychological power in the hands of their youth. Only young people, it seemed, had the ability to save their communities from corruption; their parents or ministers could not do it; the decision and the power was theirs! Thus by simply refusing to act, by choosing not to enter into the difficult, intense, and often painful quest for psychic transformation, the young could assert their independence from adult authority. There is in fact some evidence that many Puritan children in the seventeenth century had found it difficult if not impossible to experience conversion until after their fathers had died or unless they left home and settled in new communities. As John Murrin has put it, "a son who did not love his father could not easily persuade himself that he loved God." And "dead fathers," he concludes "were easier to love than live ones." In a hierarchical society where even a hint of overt resistance to parental or adult control had often been suppressed, this more subtle, less direct, perhaps unconscious, but quite profound form of resistance must have continued to be very attractive to those young people who harbored conscious or unconscious resentments toward their parents or elders.

If Puritan young people possessed a significant amount of psychological leverage, they also carried an enormous psychological burden. They were reminded incessantly, and in very clear language, that they had not only the power but, more importantly, the responsibility to save their communities from corruption. Benjamin Colman, speaking in 1720, asked a group of young people to remember that

> We have spoken to you in your own languages, to your capacity when babes, and to your ability to receive words in your childhood. And since that you have been charged by parents, by ministers, by guardians, and friends, that you remember and keep in mind what you have learnt of God and your souls. . . . Yea it may be your dying as well as living parents have charged you. . . . They have prayed over you many a time, and you have heard them; they have wept for you and over you, and begged of you, yea entreated you—about your souls

and your duty to God, and that you might be blessed of him.

"Will you not obey their voice?," asked Colman. If they did not obey, if they remained unconverted, Colman assured his young audience that they stood condemned as a corrupt, perverse, and ungrateful generation. Better, he warned, if they had been born heathen and never known God. Young people had to realize that they faced a basic choice in their lives: they could become "children of God" or "children of the Devil." No young person could escape this fundamental decision.

It would be easy to assume that the young people of the early eighteenth century did not take this responsibility seriously. But it is possible, even likely, that many unconverted youth experienced a strong sense of conscious or unconscious guilt for their failure. By remaining unconverted they damned themselves to eternal punishment and threatened the spiritual health and safety of their communities. At the very least the intense social and psychological pressure applied to Puritan youth by their parents and ministers must have reinforced a deep ambivalence within them between the urge to submit to adult authority and internalize the traditional values and norms of Puritan culture, and an equally strong temptation to resist this pressure, assert their personal autonomy, and thereby gain a degree of power over those who exercised authority over them.

So ambivalence and choice lay at the very heart of the relationship between Puritan adults and their youth. The writers on youth sensed this, and this awareness permeated their descriptions of the essential character of youth as a stage of life. "The time of youth," wrote Israel Loring in 1718, "is the time of a man's choice." In a more comprehensive but no less representative statement, Benjamin Colman emphasized the same theme when he spoke to young people in 1720:

> Now O young people is your chusing time, and commonly your fixing time; and as you fix now, it is like to last. Now you commonly chuse your trade; betake yourself to your business for life, show what you incline to, and how you intend to be employ'd all your days. Now you chuse your master and your education or occupation. And now you dispose of yourself in marriage ordinarily, place your affections, give away your hearts, look out for some companion of life, whose to be as long as you live. And is this indeed the work of your youth.

Colman and his fellow ministers realized that the character of youth as a stage of life was defined in part by the social and cultural context in which it existed. The economic system, the family system, and the educational system converged to force young people to make several very significant decisions regarding their futures. Choice and youth seemed almost synonymous.

357

In Boston, and by the 1720s even in the towns of New England, the educational and occupational choices available to youth had increased, but the capacity of families or kinship units to guarantee a secure economic and social status for their children had weakened considerably. In 1715, Josiah Franklin found that he could not afford to keep Benjamin, his tenth and youngest son, in the Boston Grammar School, so he enrolled him in George Brownell's school for writing and arithmetic. A year later, at the age of ten, Benjamin's formal education ended, and he was put to work making candles for his father. Benjamin tells us in his autobiography that he was dissatisfied with this arrangement and wanted to go to sea instead. Benjamin notes that his father, fearing that if he did not put him to a "more agreeable" trade that "I should break loose and go to sea, as my brother Josiah had done, . . . sometimes took me to walk with him and see joiners, bricklayers, turners, braziers, etc., at their work that he might observe my inclination and endeavour to fix it on some trade would keep me on land." Josiah later placed Benjamin with a cutler for a short time, but decided the fee for the apprenticeship too high. Benjamin was finally "persuaded" at the age of twelve to sign an indenture with his brother to serve as an apprentice printer until he was twenty-one. Five years later, in 1723, he ran away to Philadelphia, and after an adventure in London eventually returned to Philadelphia where he married and settled down to become a successful printer. The experiences of the precocious, venturesome Franklin were certainly not typical, but they do illustrate dramatically the range of vocational and educational choices becoming available to New England young people and the tensions and problems these new alternatives could create in the relationship between parents and children. Basic life choices were becoming more contingent and problematical for the individual, and youth as a stage of life was coming to be characterized by a unique tentative quality.

Furthermore, youth as a stage of life was increasing in length; all of the major indices of maturity during this period show that New England youth entailed a long period of dependence and marginality. Throughout the first half of the eighteenth century, New England's young people were generally converted after marriage, and most delayed their marriage until their middle twenties. Adult legal and political status also came late, and the attainment of complete economic independence occurred even later. J. M. Bumstead's observation concerning youth in Norton, Massachusetts seems applicable to New England as a whole: "The problem was not that upward progress and the achievement of full recognition as an adult member of the community did not come, but rather that a number of interrelated steps were involved in the process. A man was usually in his thirties before everything had fallen into place." Growing up was a slow and difficult process. But contrary to the pattern in most traditional societies, recent studies show that New England young people also experienced expanded vocational choice, greater privacy, increasing rates of literacy, and a widening range of formal educational alternatives. Thus, biologically and intellectually mature young people were expected to accept several years of social and economic dependence even though their awareness of the possibilities for autonomous behavior was growing. Youth was beginning to take on the character of a moratorium with its opportunities for intellectual and psychological growth, and its potential for tension, ambiguity, and uncertainty.

The tentativeness and uncertainty of youth both frightened and encouraged Puritan leaders. If youth was a stage of life when the individual was forced to concentrate on making educational, vocational, and marital choices, it threatened to divert the attention of the young person from his spiritual development. Yet, it also gave the young person more time to work on this problem. So Benjamin Colman asked young people to consider if youth was not above all else the

time for you to fix too in your general calling, your heavenly calling? Your Father's business and the working out of your salvation? . . . . You are to chuse for life, and to dispose of yourself for eternity! Whose and where and what you will be! How dreadful is the thot! Dispise heaven and eternal glory? And cast away thyself into the arms of the world, the flesh, and the Devil! And into the flames of Hell forever! God forbid it! Wherefore now in thy chusing time remember thy creator and chuse the ways of God the things that please him.

Colman and his colleagues hoped to persuade young people to place spiritual matters at center stage during this critical period of their lives when they were making many irreversible decisions concerning their identities. Only if they kept their spiritual calling uppermost in their minds could they resist the seductive enticements of a worldly life, realize their full potential as children of God, and protect their community from moral corruption and decay.

Important as they were, the external pressures of vocation, education, and marriage were not the only threats to the spiritual welfare of youth. A far greater danger, the ministers believed, lay deeply embedded in the hearts and souls of the youths themselves. Every person, young and old, bore the mark of original sin, so even "the very best of young people," warned Cotton Mather, "have a corrupt nature in them." Although persons of every age were thought to be naturally corrupt and therefore vulnerable to all the temptations of a sinful life, the writers of this period also believed that each stage of life was characterized more by some sins than others. "The different ages of men," declared Thomas Foxcroft in 1719, "have their divers lusts and various corruptions. The impure streams run in distinct channels agreeing to the differing complexions of men in the several stages of life." Thus "stubborness" and "falsness" were often identified as the special sins of childhood; "ambition" was called "the predominant vice of middle age"; and "covetousness" was described as "the more peculiar lust of old age." The two sins that seemed to "hang upon youth and dogg that season of life more than any other" were "pride" and "sensuality."

Neither pride nor sensuality could claim unanimous support as the most characteristic or dangerous sin of youth. Each offense was thought to be deeply rooted in the basic nature of young people: youthful pride was seen as a fresh reassertion of man's original rebellion against God's authority, and the sensuality of youth was viewed as an outgrowth of man's natural lust for things of the flesh reinforced by the strength and vigor of the young person's maturing faculties. Both sins created major, almost insurmountable barriers to the conversion of youth, for each was the parent of many other sins. Thus, out of pride grew disobedience, apostasy, rebellion against family government, anger, self-conceit, boasting, sabbath breaking, swaggering and vaporing, scoffing at religion, vain and profane mirth, and extravagant attire, to name a few. According to Thomas Foxcroft, pride caused many youth to become "impatient of family government, and by an affection of lawless liberty, bro't them into snare and ruin." Pride, echoed Daniel Lewes, too often made young people "impatient under restraint, disrespectful to their superiors, and apt to slight the grave and wholesome advice that is given to them by those that will them well. . . ." Joseph Sewall agreed that young persons were "apt to be conceited, and to magnify themselves, to be desirous of vain glory and ambitious of more honor and respect than they deserve." Many young people, he charged, demonstrated this ambition in their "looks, gestures, and carriage," and therefore resembled "the Daughters of Zion," who "were haughty and walked with stretched forth necks." In short, youth were often so "puffed up with pride" that they were unwilling to submit to the will of their earthly or heavenly fathers and therefore unable to begin the painful and humiliating quest for their own regeneration.

Sensuality, the second major sin of youth, spawned its own dangerous offspring: immodest dress, night revels, filthy songs, chambering, tipling, frolicking, wanton dalliances, masturbation, fornication and adultery, among others. Joseph Sewall cautioned a young audience in 1721 that they were likely to have "the highest quest and relish for and the most exquisite sense of carnal pleasure." Daniel Lewes also warned that during youth "sensual pleasures relish well, and the gaities of the world are apt to charm persons in this age, and to make them forget God and the duty which they have unto him. Furthermore, Satan knew of youth's natural sensuality and used it as a snare and trap for their souls.

Sometimes the danger was very close at hand. Cotton Mather was troubled by an apparently increasing auto-eroticism among Puritan youth, and, in 1723, he published one of the first essays on the subject of masturbation. Writing anonymously to "My Son," Mather condemned the "libidinous practices" of those "who do evil with both hands" and "have the cursed way of procuring a discharge, which the God of nature has ordered only to be made in a way which a lawful marriage leads unto." Onanism, warned Mather, could have dreadful consequences: impotence, sterility, or "offspring that shall prove a grief of mind." Mather prescribed several specific antidotes for the young person who had fallen into such a lewd and dangerous habit. Since "Christ and sin will never dwell together," Mather reasoned that one of the most effective things a young person could do to resist such "libidinous tendencies" was to

> Think on a Christ. His glorious person, His natures, His offices, His benefits, His maxims, His patterns, what He has done for His people, and what He will do for them. And if these thoughts are in an ejaculatory way darted up to the heavens, they may stil be more effectual to quench the fiery darts of the wicked one, which are fastening upon you.

If the young person nevertheless found himself on "the brink of a precipice, and upon the point of doing what is done by none but the fools of Israel," then Mather advised him to stop and ask himself: "Is not the eye of glorious God upon me!"; "Am I not a spectacle to angels who may be near unto me!" And even if the young person was weak and finally succumbed to his sinful urges, Mather implored him not to despair, but realize that he could with God's help be "finally victorious."

Some Puritan youth were apparently more interested in the genitals of the opposite sex than their own. In 1717, Solomon Stoddard expressed his concern that young men and women were too often in the evenings "in company together, toying and dallying," and "stirring up corruption with one another." There were, he lamented, many "awful instances" where "whoredom" was the result of these "wanton dalliances." Some young people even had the audacity to cite Holy Scripture in support of premarital sexual intercourse. In response to these heretical arguments, Samuel Phillips commented publicly on the meaning of a passage from Paul's First Letter to the Corinthians:

> But if any man think that he behaveth himself uncomely toward his virgin, if she pass the flower of her age, and need so require, let him to what he will, he sinneth not: let them marry.

Phillips insisted that it was absurd and perhaps malicious to suggest, as did some young people, that Paul had granted young couples the liberty "to come together as man and wife before marriage." This interpretation was based on an obvious "misunderstanding of that text." Phillips assured youth that Paul's words were "directed to the father of the virgin, and not

361

to the young man who makes suit of her." Joseph Sewall also warned young people that "for persons that contract an intimate acquaintance with a purpose of marriage to come together before it is consumated" is "not to be accounted a small sin: No! It is a dishonour to God, a scandal to religion. . . ." And it was dangerous! All fornicators and adulterers were well advised to heed the admonition offered by Cotton Mather when he described a machine constructed "in the shape of a beautiful woman, and contrived with such exquisite art that it would rise up and embrace the person that approached unto it, and at the same time stab them with a multitude of mortal wounds, when it grasped them in its iron arms." Such a fate, concluded Mather, was the inevitable product of all forms of unchastity.

Thus the Puritan writers considered vigorous sexual drives to be a natural but dangerous feature of their young people's developing personalities which, if uncontrolled, could interrupt or even terminate their spiritual development and undermine the social stability and spiritual health of their communities. Hence they were frightened and appalled by what they believed was a shocking increase in promiscuous behavior among their youth. Their fears were not entirely unfounded. Recent studies by Daniel Smith and Michael Hindus reveal that there was a striking increase in premarital pregnancy in New England during this period. Beginning in the late seventeenth century, premarital pregnancies rose from under ten percent of first births to around thirty percent by the end of the next century. (By the mid-nineteenth century they fell to close to ten percent, only to rise again to around twenty to twenty-five percent by the mid-twentieth century.) This phenomenon may have been the American version of what Edward Shorter has described as a change among the lower classes of Europe from manipulative to expressive sexuality, but Smith prefers to explain it as one product of the special transitional character of eighteenth-century New England. According to Smith, the surge in premarital pregnancies was part of a larger shift from the traditional, well-integrated rural society of the seventeenth century which emphasized external controls, to the dynamic, expanding society of the nineteenth century which depended more on voluntary, internal means to regulate the behavior of its young people. By the eighteenth century, Smith suggests, social and demographic change had weakened parental or communal controls over young people, but the voluntary, internal controls we associate with Victorian morality were not yet effective. Traditional family patterns and relationships were therefore left exposed, and young couples, when faced with parental restraints and the custom of late age for marriages, may have resorted to premarital conception as a weapon to force their parents to consent to the marriage and provide economic support. In this context, then, the sexuality of Puritan youth was not only viewed as a threat to their spiritual development, but had also become an implicit factor in the struggle of the rising generation for greater social and economic autonomy.

In addition to pride, sensuality, and the external pressures of vocation, education, and marriage, the ministers believed that there remained one important obstacle to the spiritual growth of their young people. Sociability, a distinctive though not inherently sinful characteristic of youth, when found in concert with pride or sensuality, was thought to make young people highly vulnerable to Satan's effort to gain control over their souls. Warnings against bad company were therefore ubiquitous, and concern about this problem prompted Josiah Smith to urge parents to keep their children and youth at home because, as he said, "the times are so degenerate that 'tis hardly safe to trust them anywhere, from your own inspection and care without danger to their morals." In 1717, Soloman Stoddard decried the tendency of the young to gather together in "the evenings, on wet days, and on public days" to engage in "a great deal of vain worldly, proud discourse, and corrupt communication." Israel Loring was even more adamant. Writing in 1718, he declared,

> When children and young people are suffered to haunt the taverns, get into vile company, rabble up and down in the evening, when they should be at home to attend family worship; in the dark and silent night, when they should be in their beds, when they are let alone to take other sinful courses without check or restraint, they are then on the high road to ruin.

Cotton Mather summed up the feelings of his colleagues on the problem when he wrote: "Man is both a sociable and an imitable creature. Experience of all sorts hath made it a proverb among us: one scabbed sheep will infect a flock." "What then," he asked, "would become of one sheep in a scabbed flock?"

What indeed! Mather's own son Increase succumbed to the dangerous infection of evil company. From the beginning, Mather labored diligently to instruct his son in the faith and sought good companions for him, but as early as 1711, when Increase was twelve years of age, Cotton wrote in his diary that he was "full of distress concerning my little son Increase; lest some vicious and wicked lads do corrupt and ensnare him." This fear was apparently justified, for six years later, in 1717, Mather confided to his diary that the evil he had feared had come to pass: "an harlot big with bastard, accuses my poor son Cressy, and layes her belly to him. . . ." Mather confessed he was at a loss to know what to do for "the foolish youth." Cressy continued to disappoint his father and in 1721, Mather exclaimed in sorrow: "My miserable, miserable, miserable son Increase! The wretch has brought himself under public trouble and infamy by bearing a part in a night-riot, with some detestable rakes in the town." Finally in 1724, after continued troubled relations with his son, Mather learned that a ship on which Cressy was returning from a trip to England had sunk and that he had drowned. Perhaps to work through his grief, Mather composed some sermons in Cressy's memory. In one he included what were supposed to be excerpts from Cressy's private notes concerning the dangers of evil company.

There is more than a little irony in Increase Mather's delinquency, for his father was one of the first New England ministers who sought to use young people's natural sociability as a constructive educational tool. As early as 1694, five years before Increase was born, he gave enthusiastic support to those young people who met "every week, to seek the face, and sing the praise, and repeat the word of God. . . ." He campaigned for the formal establishment of young men's associations for this purpose and published a model charter which could be used as a guide for such groups. This proved to be a popular idea: the number of young men's associations grew rapidly and became an important feature of the religious education of New England youth. Unfortunately, in his son's case, Mather's labors seem to have borne little fruit except to provide evidence for the validity of his own warnings against the serious consequences of misdirected sociability among even the "best" Puritan youth.

Cotton Mather's didactic use of his own son's misfortunes was not so unusual. In fact, the writers on youth during this period rarely missed an opportunity to demonstrate in concrete terms how the special sins and characteristics of youth could endanger their souls. Thus, they often encouraged young people who had been convicted of serious crimes to provide a detailed account of how and why they had arrived at their shameful condition. These accounts were sometimes published and no doubt offered powerful object lessons for those youth who heard or read them. One of the most dramatic—one might even say sensational—accounts was that of Esther Rogers, a twenty-one year old woman who was executed in 1701 for murdering her two illegitimate children at birth. In her autobiographical confession she recalled that she had been apprenticed at thirteen, taught to read, and had learned Cotton's catechism. But she admitted that she was "a careless hearer of sermons," and had failed to keep up her secret prayers. "At about the age of seventeen," she confessed, "I was left to fall into the foul sin of uncleaness, suffering myself to be defiled by a Negro lad living in the same house." After learning she was pregnant, she decided to kill the infant if it were born alive. "Being delivered of a living child," she continued, "I used means presently to stop the breath of it, and kept it hid in an upper room till the darkness of night gave advantage for a private burial in the garden."

Esther claimed this was all accomplished in secret and that no one, not even the father, knew she had the child. However, in her next sexual adventure she was not so fortunate. After moving to another house, she began to practice her "old trade of running out at nights," and "entertaining" her "sinful companions in the back part of the house." And, she lamented, she fell once more "into the horrible pit . . . of carnal pollution with the Negro man belonging to that house." Again she became pregnant and when the time for the birth arrived, she explained: "I went forth to be delivered in the field, and dropping my child by the side of a little pond (whether alive or still born I cannot tell) I covered it with dirt and snow and speedily returned home again." This time, however, she was suspected and questioned about her absence, and the following morning the child was discovered by some neighbors and brought before her to her "terrible shame and terror." This tragic story ended on the steps of the ladder to the gallows where Esther turned to the multitude around her, admonished young people to take warning from her example, and urged them to be obedient to their parents, to stay in at nights, and avoid bad company.

Approximately three decades later (1733), another unfortunate young woman, twenty-seven year old Rebekah Chamblit, was executed at Boston for "concealing the birth of her spurious male infant, of which she was delivered when alone . . ., and was afterwards found dead." Although she may have given birth prematurely, Rebekah confessed that she threw the newly born infant into a vault "about two or three minutes after it was born," not knowing whether it was dead or alive. Her autobiographical statement, published as a broadside, also included a brief description of her childhood and youth. She said she had been "very tenderly brought up, and well instructed" in her father's house until she was twelve years old. When about sixteen, she was baptized, but within two years she confessed she was "led away into the sin of uncleaness, from which time I think I may date my ruin for this world." Rebekah also felt obligated to offer some "dying advice" to young people. She said she regretted the lies she had told, the sabbaths she did not keep, the prayers she did not offer, and the religious instructions she did not utilize. She also admonished young people not to be complacent, for hardly a year before, she had felt as "secure" as many of them, but, alas, "lust when it has conceived bringeth forth sin, and sin when it is finished bringeth forth death, it exposes the soul not only to temporal, but to eternal death." If young people were wise, advised Rebekah, they would heed her warnings, immediately, "foresake the foolish and live."

The message to be drawn from the lives and deaths of Increase Mather, Esther Rogers, and Rebekah Chamblit was clear: if young people ignored the instruction and authority of their elders and abandoned themselves to a life of pride, sensuality, and evil company, they would face physical or spiritual death, or both. The wages of sin, even for youth, were certain.

Although Puritan ministers spent a great deal of time and energy describing the sins of youth, they by no means ignored their positive qualities or denied their potential for spiritual growth. These writers certainly cannot be accused of ascribing to the modern cult of youth, but they did find many of the characteristics of youth quite attractive and promising. If youth was depicted as a "chusing time" which could lead a person into rebellion, profligacy, and dissoluteness, it was also described as "the choice time," "the flourishing time," "the flower of our time," "the time of pleasures," the time in which "health and strength, and complexion" was "in its verdue," when a person's "faculties and powers" were "lively and vigorous," and when his "capacity to learn" was "in its blooming." In the words of Thomas Foxcroft, youth was the age

> most capable of instruction, most flexible to convictions, most susceptible of impressions. Now the understanding is ordinarily most ready and perceptive, the will most obsequious, the affections and passions most governable, the memory most deeply retentive, and all the faculties of life most apt and able for service and employment. For youth is the age of business (as well as tractableness), the morning of our day, the excellency of our strength, the spring of life, most free and vigorous for labour, dispos'd to action, and admirable at dispatch. Now the faculties of soul and body are in their prime, most capable of bearing the difficulties and doing the duties that attend the work of sanctification. . . .

Samuel Moody agreed with Foxcroft that youth was "the very best season" that a person "can ever have" to begin to come to Christ. Then, he declared, the heart was "most tender, the affections most lively and flowing; the conscience most wakeful and the will most pliable to the motions of the Holy Spirit; which are now most frequent and powerful." In short, the characteristics of youth which if uncontrolled could lead to a life of sin, could if properly directed lead in precisely the opposite direction—to salvation. If young people nurtured the "motions of the Holy Spirit," if they turned their developing, invigorated senses toward God and waited carefully for his instruction and guidance, they would find their quest for spiritual transformation much easier during youth than later in life when they had become hardened sinners. Young people obviously possessed great spiritual potential.

This attitude represented a significant change from the opinion commonly expressed in the seventeenth century that middle age, not youth, was the best time for conversion. By the eighteenth century, ministers had become convinced that if a young person were not converted before he chose his vocation, education, and mate, then he was far more susceptible to the temptations of the secular world. In the words of William Cooper, a young person who delayed his decision about his spiritual identity had "put that last which should be first." Once spiritual identity was established, however, one could rest assured that a young person would make other decisions wisely and develop his full potential as a person.

CHILDREARING

So for every Esther Rogers, Rebekah Chamblit, or Increase Mather who failed to realize this great potential there were many others who were converted, who made the right choices, and who made God the guide of their youth. When one of these saintly young people died, it was customary to publish a eulogy which occasionally included extensive excerpts from the diary or spiritual autobiography of the deceased youth. One such youth was John Coney, "a very hopeful and pious young man," who after a brief illness died in 1726 at the age of twenty-five. According to William Cooper, who preached his eulogy, Coney began very early to seek God. Apprenticed at thirteen, by sixteen he had become "deeply convinced that if he did not leave his sins and turn to God, he should not be saved." Then, after a period of unproductive praying and attending to religious duties, he read Mr. Shepard's *Sincere Convert* which brought him to understand that he had been trusting too much in his own works and not enough in Christ. Thereafter religion "became his business"; he chose good companions and he joined a religious society of young men who met "every Lord's Day evening for the exercise of religion." When John was eighteen he made a "solemn profession of religion" and was admitted to Cooper's church. Cooper reported that Coney was a very faithful member: he loved sermons about Christ, and he enjoyed religious conferences, "not only with those of his own age, but with some elder christians that knew and valu'd him." John was also very concerned about the salvation of others, but as Cooper explained, his piety was "unaffected," and he was "not showery in any of this."

Coney was indeed a remarkable young man. During the last five years of his life (beginning during the last of his apprenticeship), he kept a spiritual diary and also recorded his thoughts on a variety of religious topics. Cooper reprinted long excerpts from these documents in an appendix to his eulogy, and they reveal a young man driven by an intense desire for spiritual growth and a gritty determination to keep his natural but corrupt tendencies under control. At one point John resolved to keep his heart "in an affectionate frame," because he found it "easiest to keep the heart with God, when the natural affections being sanctified are carried out toward God." Yet John knew that these "natural affections" could also turn his attention away from God if not carefully controlled. For that reason he often engaged in private fasting and prayer, and in his diary he recorded his struggle to suppress the anger that rose in his heart against "a person that spoke against me." He also reminded himself to control his eyes lest they lead him astray, for, as he confessed, "The world is wooing and enticing my heart to draw it from God, and I am sometimes almost overcome." John eventually decided that it was better to stay at home than "to wander abroad at night." After he completed his apprenticeship, and began to think about "the marriage state," John convinced himself that "in all probability it will be considerable time before I shall be settled in a way of business, it may be several

367

years, and for me to keep company with a person so long may have great inconveniences attending it." In any event, he concluded, "I do not look upon myself capable as yet, of making judicious choices; being biased more by fancy than judgement." Coney's remarkable self-discipline contrasted sharply with the sensual abandon of Esther Rogers.

Even so, Coney's struggle for spiritual meaning was not easy. At times he reached heights of religious ecstasy. On January 16, 1722 he recorded in his diary that in his morning prayer he was "serious and affectionate." "O how sweet is such a frame," he exclaimed. But little more than a month later, on February 25, he was depressed, and in "a dull frame." "I fear," he wrote, that "I am losing my first love, and that God's spirit is withdrawing from me, but I desire to return to God as the rest of my soul, in whom alone I find by experience, true solid comfort, delight and satisfaction are to be found." Yet Coney never abandoned his quest for his first love. The last words in his diary were: "But O my God, do thou quicken me!" And according to Cooper, Coney testified on his deathbed that his hope was still built "upon Christ, the Rock of Ages." Cooper doubted it was possible to find a better example of "an improved experienced Christian." Coney's life, declared Cooper, should be "a little glass in which to distinguish between the vital power of religion, and the dead image of it. . . ." To Cooper at least, Coney's life proved that "strict religion" was "possible and pleasant" for young people.

Hardly less inspiring was the life and testimony of Mercy Wheeler. Born in 1706, the fourth of ten children, Mercy was in good health until her twentieth year when she "was taken sick of the burning augue. . . ." By 1727 she was confined to her bed, eventually subsisting almost entirely on a liquid diet. After almost five years, in April 1732 she regained her lost power of speech and began to praise God and offer advice and counsel to young people. Some of her comments were taken down by Samuel Stearns and printed in 1733 as a pamphlet for youth. Mercy implored those of her generation to remember that "tho' youth be indeed the flower of the age, yet it is the most dangerous season of the mind." She asked them to think of her condition as an example of what could happen to their strength and vigor. Finally, she urged every young person to "run to Christ" and save their souls. Christ was so "lovely" that Mercy could not find words adequate to describe the great blessings that he could bring to young people.

When Puritan ministers reflected upon the lives of saintly young people such as John Coney and Mercy Wheeler, they became effusively optimistic about the spiritual capabilities of youth. "Lovely, lovely the young people," exclaimed Cotton Mather, "who so love God, and seek him early." Young people did not have to surrender to their naturally corrupt urges; they could with the guidance of the Holy Spirit use their abundant energy to do God's will and thereby become the beautiful persons God had intended. To be sure, the writers of this period were often fearful and ambivalent in their attitudes toward young people—they spent more time describing the sins of youth than listing their virtues, and when they saw the pride, sensuality, and misguided sociability of their youth, they feared for their souls and the fate of their communities. This is hardly surprising, given the unstable social conditions, the didactic purpose of their essays, and the nature of their theology. Youth in their "natural" state were viewed as sinful beings because without Christ they were unfinished, incomplete beings. Young people could never reach their potential unless they confronted their own incompleteness. By forcing youth to look at their sins and reflect on the direction of their lives, the ministers hoped to start young people on this spiritual odyssey. So what appears at first glance to be a pessimistic and morbid preoccupation with the depravity of youth can also be viewed as an important element in an optimistic program to promote their spiritual development. Puritan writers on youth remained hopeful, perhaps unrealistically so.

As we look back to the 1730s, the secularization of New England society and culture appears inevitable, but it did not seem so to these leaders who lived at the time. They continued to hope, and some even believed, that their young people would turn to God, affirm their commitment to the faith of their fathers, and thereby restore the health of their communities. When that happy event occurred, promised Daniel Baker, "then shall our peace be as a river; and then, may we hope that the Lord will return in mercy, and not only grant us a little reviving, but establish us a quiet habitation. . . ." Very soon, many New England young people would indeed embrace their father's religion, and for a brief time during the Great Awakening peace did flow as a river across New England. The spiritual leaders rejoiced; God had blessed their efforts; their young people had come home.

However, contrary to the millennial expectations of the New England clerics, it is doubtful that the Great Awakening wrought any fundamental or long-lasting change in character of youth as a stage of life in New England. We have little if any reason to believe that it caused any permanent alterations in the social, demographic, economic, or political conditions which might have reduced the period of dependence for young people or made the transition from childhood to adulthood any less difficult. Although the average age of conversion did drop noticeably during the Awakening, it apparently soon reverted to its pre-awakening levels. We also know that although the average age of marriage declined somewhat, it remained relatively high and that both the rate of literacy and premarital pregnancies continued to rise until the end of the century. In other words, the young people of New England were forced to continue to accept a social and economic position which was to some extent inconsistent with their intellectual and sexual maturity. When a New England child reached puberty, he still faced an extended period of marginality and dependence before he would be allowed to assume the role of an adult. And even if he were converted before he chose his vocation or mate, the experience of John Coney suggests that these years were not necessarily free of uncertainty, ambivalence, or even conflict. Early eighteenth-century New England was clearly not an adolescent-free society in which the "coming of age" coincided with an individual's assumption of work and family responsibilities.

On the other hand, there are important differences between New England youth and modern adolescence. If choice was characteristic of New England youth, the enormous scope and complexity of industrialized society has made it an omnipresent feature of modern life; what must have been a challenging task for New England youth, has become a confusing burden for modern adolescents who must find their way through a bewildering maze of educational and vocational alternatives before they attain adulthood. And if New England youth were able on occasion to band together and escape the immediate supervision of their elders, the adolescent peer group of today has become a subculture which both insulates young people from the intrusion of adults and at times protects them from an awareness of their own marginality and redundancy. In addition, New England young people, unlike modern youth, never developed an articulated self-consciousness; nor did they ever become so alienated from traditional values that they became openly rebellious, although in at least one instance, they may have come close.

In 1715 John Tufts, a young Harvard graduate, published a pamphlet calling for the reform of the method of singing in New England churches. Unlike the ordered psalmody of the first generations, by the eighteenth century it had deteriorated to the point that after a tune was "lined out" by an appointed deacon, each person proceeded according to his own time and pitch. The result was a cacophony which could have brought pleasure and spiritual sustenance only to those who were musically deaf or whose aesthetic sense had been dulled by the effects of years of repetition. Tufts's proposal was simple but revolutionary: congregations should sing together according to the tune provided for each psalm. Other ministers, especially younger ones, joined Tufts in his campaign and young people, who were attracted by its novelty, flocked to special classes established to teach "regular singing." Many older people in New England congregations were extremely reluctant to give up their traditional style of singing and they expressed their deep resentment at "being turned out of their old way" just "to gratify the younger generation." Nathaniel Chauncy, a supporter of the new way, reminded these elders that "as old men are not always wise, so young men are not always fools." The bitter dispute over this matter did not end until late 1720s. The importance of this controversy can be exaggerated, but as Ola Winslow has pointed out, it was "a battle of generations" in which parental authority could be defied. Normally, however, the rebellion of New England youth tended to be less direct, more subtle and individualistic, and therefore at times even more difficult for adults to comprehend than the open defiance of modern adolescents.

Still, the essential characteristics of youth as described by the writers of the early eighteenth century have a familiar ring to students of modern adolescence. Pride, sensuality, sociability, and spiritual promise are nicely paralleled by modern portrayals of youth as defiant, sexually active, peer-oriented, and idealistic; and the delay of consummation of genital maturity may have produced the regressive revival of autoeroticism, grandiosity, and playfulness among New England youth in much the same way that Erik Erikson claims it does in today's young people. Moreover, the basic developmental tasks of adolescence as described by modern psychologists would have been acceptable at least in part to the Puritan analysts: (1) self control (sublimation and neutralization of libidinal and aggressive drives); (2) independence (detachment from infantile object ties); and (3) identity (consolidation and integration of personality, and the organization of behavior into available social roles). The Puritans were no doubt more concerned with the development of self control in their youth than independence, but they would have heartily agreed with Erikson's emphasis on the importance of identity formation, the concomitant danger of identity diffusion, and his contention that the formation of identity and ideology are two indispensable parts of the same process. Finally, the ambivalence which is so characteristic of adult-youth relations today was clearly present in the eighteenth century. Fear and hostility, optimism and love—these are perennial feelings which reverberated between young and old in the eighteenth century as they do today.

But it is not only in their broad outlines that New England youth and contemporary adolescence are similar. They also resemble each other in many of their more precise features, in the kind of adjustments that specific young people made to this stage of life. The unrestrained impulsivity and poor reality testing of Esther Rogers and Rebekah Chamblit; the delinquency of Increase Mather, the minister's son; the inhibited, perhaps neurotic religiosity of Mercy Wheeler, the ascetic intellectualism and idealism of John Coney, and even the egocentric rationalism of the runaway Benjamin Franklin—all have their counterparts in the adjustment repertoires of modern youth. New England young people masturbated; they engaged in fantasy; they became withdrawn and depressed; they loved and hated their parents; they sought out each other's company as an escape from parental authority and control; they acted out sexually and socially; they employed the full range of classical defenses to control their impulses and prevent regression; but in the end most of them persevered and made the difficult transition from childhood to adulthood with relatively intact, healthy personalities which, like those of young adults today, were neither the exact replicas nor the complete opposites of their parents'.

Thus the standard view that nothing like modern adolescence emerged before the late nineteenth century must be revised. In the unstable social conditions they faced, in their prolonged dependence and marginality, in their psychological characteristics, in their relations with their elders, and in the specific adjustments they made as individuals, the youth of early eighteenth-century New England had a great deal in common with today's adolescents. Did this similarity continue after the Great Awakening through the Revolution and beyond, or was it only the temporary product of the special transitional character of New England between 1700 and 1730? Was the strikingly modern character of youth in early eighteenth-century New England only an aberration which soon disappeared, or did it remain to shape the character of life in revolutionary America? The answer to these questions must await a more comprehensive investigation—an investigation informed by the insights of modern psychology and the new social history and guided by the empathetic conviction that the youth of the past can be heard if we learn how to listen. Only then will youth find their proper place in the history of the eighteenth century.

# 5

# Post-Childrearing

## 1. Introduction

The end of childbearing as a stage in the family cycle is doubtlessly easier to demarcate for contemporaries than it was for early modern Englishmen and Americans. For just as parents today compartmentalize their childbearing stage into a definite but limited segment of their married life, they also are able to anticipate the day when all of their children will have left their home to start their own families or to live independently. Few parents in the early modern era could realistically expect to reach a point together when all of their children were out on their own. Even in 17th-century New England, where an exceptionally high longevity rate resulted in many couples living together into their fifties or even sixties, few were likely to reach an unambiguously post-childrearing stage in which no child shared their home. For the high proportion of unmarried adults that characterized the Anglo-American pattern meant that parents who raised seven or eight children the way New Englanders did were likely to have at least a bachelor son or spinster daughter living with them. This was especially true in a society that discouraged single people from setting up quarters for themselves but instead pressed bachelors and spinsters to remain attached to a family unit governed by a married head.

Although childrearing occupied a much greater proportion of the years that married couples spent together then than it does today, many early modern parents reached the point where their childrearing responsibilities were sharply reduced. This reduction occurred progressively with each child who got married, or attained the legal age of majority, or left home permanently, or became economically independent of his parents. But rare was the family in which all of the surviving children achieved at least one of these conditions while both parents were still alive. Thus to speak of post childbearing in the early modern family cycle is to refer to that stage when both parents had to establish relationships with adult children and when they had more time to relate to each other because of the diminishing intrusion of dependent children.

Historians who have analyzed the relationship between early modern parents and their grown-up children have focused almost exclusively on two specific events, two significant moments, in that relationship: marriage and the transfer of property. Both events have been treated as dual facets of one central issue in the relationship between the generations: the older generation wanted to maximize their control over the younger, while the younger wanted to achieve complete autonomy. Their relationship has been cast by family historians into adversary terms, with the two generations treated as if they were engaged in a contest, divided from each other by antagonistic interests, with the advantage of one coming necessarily at the expense of the other. Not surprisingly this dialectical approach has been taken by scholars who believe that materialistic considerations were the overriding matters at stake. Thus they assume that the child wanted to marry for love while his parents wanted him to consider property and status; and that the married child wanted to live in his own home on property that had been transferred to him outright, while his parents preferred to keep him bound to them on property they continued to control. Accordingly, if a son marries a girl who is from a lower social class and the two of them set up house on land that he has received outright from his father, the situation is treated as a victory for the son, for love, for modernization and, conversely, a setback for parental influence, for prudence, and for traditional society.

The starkness of the issue of parental control vs. adult child autonomy in some of the recent historiography concerns us. We do not deny that parents in the 16th and 17th centuries, especially those with substantial property or status to protect, were anxious to bring pressure to bear on their children to marry spouses at least of comparable wealth and position. Nor do we deny the evidence that much of this pressure was effective. What we question are the assumptions that parents and children were necessarily at odds and that parental influence in that period can be described solely in material terms. While early modern parents may in fact have been more willing to employ material sanctions to influence the behavior of their children than their more psychologically oriented successors, we cannot ignore the psychological dimension to intergenerational relationships at that time. Thus, if we find a married son living as a tenant on land his father continues to own, we cannot necessarily infer that his economic dependence renders him more likely to honor his father, to carry out paternal values, or even to feel more controlled by his father than does a son who has been provided by his father with material independence. The former may in fact feel more rebellious towards his father, less desirous and less likely to transmit the father's value system, than the latter, who may have been trusted by his father to fulfill his filial obligations without the need to be coerced by the threat of economic sanctions. In either case, the relationship between father and son cannot be adequately understood only in terms of property exchange during adulthood.

Nevertheless, we have learned a great deal from recent research about the residential and property arrangements that early modern parents made for their grown-up children, and the research provides us with a more accurate view of the material arena in which their relationships were played out. Of particular importance is what we now know about the structure of the household in which both generations lived. Indeed the post-childrearing stage is the point in the family cycle when the household structure is determined. For the way historians categorize household structure depends on the residential pattern adopted when children marry. While households may vary in size, the essential component of structure, suggests Robert Wheaton, is the number of married couples living under the same roof (Wheaton, 1975). Thus he recognizes three basic types of household structures: a nuclear household in which one married couple presides; a stem household where parents and one married son share the same dwelling; and a joint household in which separately married siblings live together. Each of these models can operate in various degrees of extension, with servants, unmarried children, and kinfolk dwelling together. But by differentiating household types on the basis of married couples rather than the number of individuals, we have a more consistent standard of comparison. Moreover, to the extent that the issue of intrahousehold power concerns historians, the differences related to married couples would seem to be more significiant than those derived from size itself. For if authority in the household was normatively vested in the married heads, the number of married couples and the number of generations they represented would be critical to the distribution of power among household members.

Until recently, historians believed that the early modern family was generally extended in size with households occupied by at least two generations of married couples. The basis for this belief was contemporary utopian and prescriptive writings that described multigenerational households in optimum terms. The nuclear household with which we are so familiar in the present was considered to be a modern phenomenon, produced by industrialization and urbanization. This overview has been set in shadows by the discovery of demographers that since 1600 most dwelling units in England and America have been occupied by no more than one married couple. This finding, summarized in the monumental *Household and Family in Past Time* (Laslett, 1972) was based primarily on the examination of census lists. It has led to some conclusions that the evidence of census lists does not by itself sustain. The most important of these inferences have been (1) that households have been uniformly small in size for the past 400 years, (2) that young people have immediately moved into their own quarters following their marriage, and (3) that most households have consisted of two generations, parents and their pre-adult or at least unmarried children.

While these conclusions remain descriptive of the modal experience, important variations should be kept in mind. Edward Shorter (1975) has reminded us that in the early modern period richer folk tended to have larger numbers of people living in their homes than did poorer families, even though both may have had nuclear structures. For the richer could afford servants as well as dependent relatives. Moreover, New England families, as we have seen, were larger in proportion to their household living space than families in the south or the English countryside because of their higher fertility rate. Thus the degree of extension varied considerably on the basis of social class or geographic location.

The second inference also requires some modification. Although most households were nuclear in structure most of the time, the census taker may not have called while many families were at the point in their respective cycles in which stem arrangements obtained. Stone (1965) observes, for example, that English upper-class parents often had their newly married children live with them for upwards of a year until the couple could afford to set up appropriate quarters for them. For these parents the post-childrearing stage included co-residence temporarily with another married couple, a situation that must have produced unique stresses. And Greven notes that while the first two generations of Andover newlyweds moved into their own places after their wedding, they usually lived in close proximity to the groom's parents on property the older generation continued to own.

There were also variations from the two-generation household. Widowed men and women sometimes lived with married children and their issue in three-generation households. The presence of grandparents was more common in New England than elsewhere because of the exceptional longevity rate there. And while it was extremely rare for surviving couples to live with married children and grandchildren, Margaret Spufford (1976) has found in England some couples who "retired" by transferring property to married children and then moving in with them. Most of the time when such arrangements were made a legal document would specify the rights and privileges of the widowed parent.

In some ways the transfer of property across the generations was a more critical issue to early moderns than it is today. Well into the 18th century, Anglo-American thinkers had posited the control over one's property as a central and indispensable condition of liberty. A man's property was essential to his security and that of his family while he was alive and provided testimony to the value of his life after he died. Control may not have been exactly synonymous with ownership, especially for the upper classes. The heads of such families might control their property but they often viewed themselves as its trustee, especially with the introduction of strict settlement. But English fathers were not legally barred from disinheriting their children, in contrast to the situation in France. Even within the limitations of fee tail, English courts of law, at least, from the 15th century allowed

376

fathers to alienate their freehold estate.

Thus from medieval times heads of families came to regard their property as theirs to dispense with: they could sell it or pass it on to their heirs. Current research indicates that both options were chosen. The point to be stressed, however, is that English fathers did have considerable material and legal leverage over their would-be heirs. Our impression, however, is that early modern parents rarely disinherited. Disinheritance during that time period would leave the child more vulnerable perhaps than would be the case today. For the early modern state did not provide people with the kind of services that could effectively substitute for the security derived from private property. Nor did early modern society offer too many opportunities that would enable the younger generation to become "self-made" without material support from parentally transferred property. In agricultural societies the security of parents and the economic independence of their children depended largely on their respective positions to the land. Thus for many parents with any kind of property it remained a critical question as to when and how they should devolve their property upon their grown-up children. Fathers, who normally possessed control over the land, had five choices. They could transfer all of their property until they died; they could transfer ownership to part of it while they were alive and pass on the remainder as a posthumous bequest; they could share titular rights over the property with adult sons; or they could sell all or part of their land during their lifetimes. The first option appears to have been the least common. But it was practiced in Cambridgeshire and the Midlands where the parental couple "handed over their property by pre-mortem transfer, frequently creating a kind of 'stem-household,' with effective control in the hands of the junior generation" (Goody, 1976, p.6). The second option has been documented more fully for 17th-century Andover, Massachusetts by Greven than it has for any other area. There elderly parents retained ownership over the land that their married sons moved onto as tenants. Not until the 18th century did third generation Andover parents increasingly turn over the property outright to their sons upon marriage. The 18th-century pattern in Andover, whereby parents conferred some of their property on their married sons while keeping the land they themselves lived on, appears to have been the typical practice in the colonies. Moreover, where land was plentiful, especially in the south, each married son could expect to receive his own parcel upon which he could set up house with his bride. Primogeniture in the south usually meant that the eldest son would inherit the home plantation, not that younger brothers would be deprived of sizable tracts.

In Tudor and early Stuart England eldest sons of large landowners normally received a portion of the family estate as part of their marriage settlement, with the bulk of the family property coming to them upon their fathers' decease. Younger sons might receive smaller parcels of land or, when money came into increasing circulation, capital to prepare for a profession or to emigrate. Small landowners from the 13th century, however, appear to have engaged in the sale of part or all of their lands as has recently been documented by Macfarlane (1978). After the Restoration, a significant innovation, the strict settlement, was more and more adopted. By the 18th century it has been estimated that over half the land in England was under strict settlement (Mingay, 1963). Its provisions have been discussed in Habbakuk's essay in Chapter I. What should be noted here is that it reduced the control that either a father or son could exercise over the part of their property which was passed to the son at marriage. Both were now in the position of life tenants on their land, and both would have to cooperate in the management which was equally shared. This increasingly widespread English practice had no parallel in the colonies, where outright control to the younger generation upon marriage became the norm in the 18th century. Strict settlement also appears to have provided for younger sons and daughters better than the earlier patterns had. Can we therefore infer that in the 18th century property arrangements in England allowed for closer, more harmonious relationships between parents and their adult children than did those in America? Conversely, should we not ask what kind of intrafamilial relationships made English parents adopt the strict settlement while American parents conferred outright control upon their children? Both questions are raised to suggest lines of further research. An aspect of post-childrearing that has not yet received much attention from historians of the early modern era is the relationships between husbands and wives whose children married or otherwise entered adulthood. Outside of colonial New England, where longevity rates in the 17th century were comparable to modern figures, couples who lived long enough to experience an empty nest at home were in the minority. The quality of the relationship between these surviving couples has not yet been explored. Determining the number of couples who lived into their late forties and fifties with all of their children having reached adulthood remains an important task for demographic historians. We suspect that the adjustment such couples had to make to their post-childrearing stage was probably more difficult than it has been for modern couples because childbearing and childrearing had been ongoing facets of their lives. One must wonder to what extent the capacity of the couple for mutual companionship now became a crucial issue. If tasks, property, status, and even spiritual considerations had been uppermost criteria for their marriage, and if childbearing were now completed, what bound them together during this penultimate stage of their marriage? What tasks remained for them? Did they jointly discuss and decide how to devolve their testamentary estate on their adult issue? Did they develop a new intimacy after years of busy parental responsibilities? Did they discover they had little to bind them after the children were grown up? In the 18th century did older men stray more? That is, was the apparent upsurge in sexuality exclusively confined to youth or was it reflected in the behavior of older husbands as well? There was an increasing incidence of divorce in 18th-century Massachusetts. Were post-childrearing couples more apt to separate than those still actively involved in parenting?

Like Preparenthood, Post-childrearing is a stage in the early modern family cycle that holds rich possibilities for future work.

## 2. Patriarchalism And The English Family
By Lawrence Stone

Between 1500 and 1750 it is clear that there was a decline in the role played in society by the kin. This was a relative and not an absolute change, for society always includes both the kin system and the nuclear family, which together share the tasks of reproduction, consumption, socialization, placement and welfare, while the state itself always has some part to play in these matters. There is rarely a clear-cut alternative between the kin, the conjugal unit, and the state. What happened in Early Modern England was a slow readjustment of the previous distribution of emphasis, both in the articulation of the conjugal family to the larger kin-based structure, and in the relationship of both to the impersonal institutions of the state.

The evidence for change can be traced in a number of areas. One indication is that claims to cousinhood ties in the subscription of letters occur far less frequently in the late seventeenth and eighteenth centuries than in the sixteenth or early seventeenth, presumably because it was no longer so useful in creating a favorable predisposition in the recipient. It would, for example, be hard to parallel in the eighteenth century the claim to cousinhood advanced in the early seventeenth century by Thomas Wentworth in a letter to Sir Henry Slingsby. The connection was indeed there, but there were no fewer than seven links in the genealogical chain which joined the two, three of them by marriage through the female line.

More concrete is the very clear decline in the concept of kin responsibility for individual crimes and actions. In the sixteenth century, at any rate in the Highland Zone of the north and west, the royal writ and the royal law-courts were less important as law enforcement agencies than the blood feud and the vendetta. Under the vendetta there is collective kin responsibility for individual action, as opposed to the legal theory of individual responsibility: the law will punish the criminal but no one else; the vendetta is perfectly satisfied by the punishment of the criminal's brother, father, uncle, or nephew. By the end of the sixteenth century, this custom had virtually died out in England. Henry VIII was the last English king to punish whole families, such as the De La Poles, for the treason of one member.

This erosion of the penal solidarity of the clan, by which the kin or immediate family of a fallen politician suffered punishment with him, first occurred among the patriciate of Florence as in the fifteenth century, a century before it happened in England. In France the custom lived on into the eighteenth century. In the late seventeenth century, Louis XIV exiled the family of Fouquet, and imprisoned that of Cartouche. Moreover, the penal solidarity of the family in the payment of taxes remained a part of French law until it was abolished in 1775 by Maupou, who denounced it as "This odious law which, from the fault of a single man, incriminates a whole family." In Russia the practice only died out in the mid-twentieth century, marking the final triumph in the West of the principle of individual responsibility, first affecting the kin and later the nuclear family itself.

In national politics, there took place a slow decline in the role of kinship as the central organizing principle of political groupings. In the fifteenth century, the Wars of the Roses were almost entirely a struggle of aristocratic kinship factions and alliances for control of royal authority and patronage. In the sixteenth century, kin groupings remained powerful in politics, but slowly gave way to religious conviction and personal ambition as the state strengthened its grip on society and began to attract loyalties to itself. Even so, much of the political infighting of the century revolved around certain kinship rivalries, in particular that between the Howards and the Dudleys, until the last, illegitimate Dudley finally went into exile at the end of the century, and the Howards hitched themselves on to the court of James I. But the degree to which kinship loyalties had become subordinated to political and religious ideology became clear during the English revolution of the 1640s, when one aristocratic family in seven was divided father against child or brother against brother. If the divisions within the conjugal group were so frequent, it is obvious that the cousinhood was even more hopelessly fragmented. Other loyalties now took precedence among the English political nation at the top, although how far this change penetrated down the society is at present unknown. No one knows, for example, whether yeoman or merchant families divided father against son, brother against brother in the Civil War.

At the end of the seventeenth century, the English political nation was bitterly divided into two parties going under the labels of Whigs and Tories. In binding together these political groupings, there were four main elements: dependence on a political patron, professional clientage, personal friendship and kinship. Kinship was certainly a help, and was used by politicians to increase their influence. Thus Harley carefully cultivated the remotest of cousins, and found it advantageous to find ways of signing his letters "your most faithful and humble servant and kinsman." But for every family connection which carried clear political associations, there were three or four about which nothing is known. There may have been no connection, or the kin may in fact have been split down the middle. Thus of the ten M. P.'s and candidates of the Bertie family in the reign of Queen Anne, seven were Tories, two Whigs, and one a Whiggish waverer. Kinship often remained useful in the formation of the Whig factions in the eighteenth century, such as the Pelham Whigs or Rockingham Whigs, but it was no more than one element among several, and not necessarily the most important or the most durable one. The impermanence and unreliability of these connections in English eighteenth century politics, as compared with those of the early sixteenth century, suggest that in the early modern period kinship was replaced by "bastard kinship," just as in the late Middle Ages the ties of feudalism had been replaced by those of "bastard feudalism."

In local affairs, kin ties undoubtedly continued to be important well into the eighteenth century. As the English elite fissured down religious lines in the sixteenth and seventeenth centuries, religious endogamy developed among Catholics and Puritans, but in this case the lines of kinship followed and reinforced the ties of religion, not *vice versa*. (For example, Catholic priests acted as marriage brokers for Recusant families.) After the middle of the seventeenth century, the amount of social mobility among the squirearchy shrank to a trickle, so that little new blood was coming in to keep the system fluid. Meanwhile in each county, for century after century, the squires were intermarrying with one another, until the web of cross-cousinhood became so dense and so universal that it lost its meaning. If everybody is everybody else's cousin, the connection does not matter any more, and the recent discovery that Charles I was a remote cousin of John Hampden does nothing to advance our understanding of the English Revolution of the seventeenth century.

Another test of the declining role of kinship is the respect paid to nepotism in recruitment to state and private offices. There is also some evidence that nepotism generally was meeting increasing competition from two alternative sets of values. In the first place, many offices, especially in the law and the army, were obtained by purchase from the incumbent or his superior, and here money was usually more important than kinship. To the extent that saleable offices increased in the seventeenth century, as they did, this undermined the importance of kinship. Secondly, here and there in the two sectors of administration where efficiency was absolutely essential for the life of the nation (the Treasury to supply and handle public funds and the Navy to protect England's shores and to blast open the sea lanes of the world for English goods and English merchants) there are signs, beginning with Samuel Pepys in the late seventeenth century, of the development of a new, impersonal, meritocratic, professional spirit.

Another area in which the principle of kinship can be shown to have been on the decline in the seventeenth century is that of aid and welfare. In traditional societies these problems are handled by the conjugal family and by the kin, but in modern societies they are managed primarily by the state and various impersonal institutions, only secondarily by the conjugal family, and hardly at all by the kin. In sixteenth century England, the prevailing demographic conditions meant that support was needed for large numbers of orphans, many widows, many cripples and sick, some able unemployed, and relatively few old people. During the sixteenth century, these welfare functions were progressively taken over by public bodies. In the early sixteenth century, some towns began to organize their own poor relief system, paid out of taxes, and in the second half of the century the practice spread to the countryside, on a voluntary and emergency basis. In about 1600 a nationwide system based on local compulsory taxation and expenditure was instituted, and during the seventeenth century it became a fully functioning organization which effectively relieved the kin, and also the conjugal family, of much of its responsibility for relief of the poor and sick. In addition to these public arrangements, private charity built and endowed a significant number of orphanages, hospitals, and almshouses for the old, and set up supplementary funds for poor relief in a fair number of villages.

In the socialization of the child, his training for life responsibilities, the seventeenth century also saw a partial transfer of function from the kin and the family to impersonal institutions of dame schools, grammar schools, and colleges, providing literacy and piety for the many, and classics and piety for the few. While much borrowing from kin relatives continued to take place throughout the eighteenth century, the growth of country banks and joint stock companies provided increasingly important alternatives. An examination of Midland wills between 1676 and 1775 shows over half of the testators making bequests to the nuclear family, and a quarter to kin relatives. This suggests that by the eighteenth century kinship affiliations were weakened, but that they were still far from extinct.

This slow decline of kinship occurs both in the realm of function and that of values. As society became more dense, more complex and more organized, there developed a series of semi-public bodies, town authorities, parish overseers of the poor, schools, banks, etc., which took over many of the functions previously performed by the kin and by the family. This was a very slow and very relative process, however, and far more important at this stage were changes in the levels of social mobility, and a shift in values away from the kin towards the state.

Among the poor and the artisan classes, the extraordinary geographical mobility of English society in the seventeenth century, which has now been established beyond a reasonable doubt, made it almost impossible for kinship associations to retain their old strength. Muster rolls of male adults liable to military service and detailed census returns of two villages both suggest a population turnover in the village as high as 50 percent or more in ten years. Even if removal by death accounted for some 20 percent of those who disappeared, there are still some 30 percent or more who moved on elsewhere in a given ten-year span, which indicates that the seventeenth century English village was far from being a static or isolated unit. In one Worchestershire village, 80 percent of the seventy-five surnames disappeared from the parish records between 1666 and 1750. Village continuity was preserved by a mere five large and enduring families, which inevitably inter-married a great deal among each other. Similarly, a study of witnesses in rural court cases between 1580 and 1640, who were all men well above the poverty line, show that two-thirds had moved to a different parish during their lives, even if about half of them had only moved five miles. A 1782 census of a Bedfordshire village showed that only a third of the heads of households, of either sex, had been born in the village, although most of them came from less than ten miles away. Thus among the lower, lower-middle and middle class groups, horizontal mobility was remarkably high.

These changes cannot be accounted for merely by youths and young girls going out into service or apprenticeship and moving on from master to master. What is involved is both the emigration of youth away from the parental home, and also the migration of whole nuclear families from place to place, thus breaking the bonds of kinship. Some of this flow was short-range migration for marriage or work as a servant. But a good deal of it was longer range; from the more densely populated rural areas into the forests and the underpopulated Highland Zone, and even more from the coun-tryside into the towns. Between 1580 and 1640, three-quarters of Canter-bury residents who served as witnesses in court cases were immigrants into the city from elsewhere. But the truly massive influx was into London. The population of London and its suburbs increased from about 60,000 in 1500 to about 550,000 in 1700, despite the fact that the urban death rate was so high that the city was far from reproducing itself. This staggering growth was, therefore, caused by a constant and massive flow of immigrants from the countryside. Once entered into the anonymity of the city, these im-migrants often tended to remain transients without deep roots. A London parson in the days of Elizabeth remarked that every twelve years or so "the most part of the parish changeth, . . . some going and some coming." A sample of deponents in lawsuits in Stepney between 1580 and 1639 shows that less than 8 percent had been born in that parish or neighboring Whitechapel. Moreover, the evidence of apprenticeship records suggest that artisan immigration in the sixteenth century was of a very long-range variety, with nearly half the immigrants coming from the North of England. Only at the end of the seventeenth century did immigrants begin to come predominantly from the surrounding areas.

This very high rate of mobility from place to place, much of it over long distances and sustained for over a century, must have done more than anything else to weaken the ties of kinship among the lower levels of so-ciety. Travel was both slow and expensive, and correspondence among il-literates difficult if not impossible. Many of these movements must have permanently detached the nuclear family from its parents and kin in the village, and permanently detached the adolescent children from their parents. For these large numbers who were mobile, the web of kin relations that enveloped them in the home village was now cut, which necessarily

383

threw them back on the isolated conjugal family type. Some migrants no doubt found temporary shelter with a kin relative, but before long, the nuclear pair, or the lonely adolescent, were on their own in alien corn, and only a minority could hope to marry into a wider kin which could offer support in the new surroundings.

Parallel to, and part consequence of, this enhancement of the importance of the conjugal family and the household, was an increase in authoritarianism in internal power relationships: an increase, that is to say, in patriarchy. Before discussing this development, it should be noted that patriarchy in its ideal type, which flourished on the southern and eastern shores of the Mediterranean, was never present in England in more than a much attenuated form. If one defines patriarchy as a Weberian ideal type, it has the following characteristics. In terms of power relationships, the man rides to work on a donkey or mule—if he goes to work at all—while the wife follows behind on foot with the heavy tools. The husband is legally and morally free to beat his wife, although not to the point of maiming or murder. A wife has no right whatever to dispose of her own property, and all she owns passes to her husband on marriage. A wife serves the husband and eldest son at the table, but rarely sits down with them. In terms of sex, male adultery is a venial sin, female adultery an unpardonable crime. Female premarital chastity is a matter of family honor, unmarried girls are always chaperoned, and seducers are killed. Marriages are arranged by the fathers without consulting the wishes of the bride or groom. A wife provides the sexual services demanded by her husband, but is not herself expected to achieve orgasm in sexual intercourse. In religion, the Virgin Mary is the most venerable symbol of worship, and women create a female church culture of their own, being the main supporters of and attenders at church. Priests are celibate and visit the homes by day.

It is obvious from this description that at no time, so far as we know, did England conform fully to this ideal, which was present only in a very modified form. In the sixteenth century, however, there are clear signs of a strengthening of paternal authority in the family. For a time, the powers of fathers over children and of husbands over wives were both strengthened.

A legal change, which probably had little to do with this trend, nonetheless powerfully reinforced it. During the Middle Ages control over landed property through entail meant that the head of the family was no more than a life tenant of the estates, with little freedom to dispose of them at his pleasure. In the late fifteenth century, the lawyers found a way to break entails without too much difficulty, and some confusing legislation of the 1530s had the result of still further widening the breach. This greatly strengthened the ability of the current head of the family to dispose of the property as he chose, although it also greatly weakened his capacity to prevent his heir from doing the same thing. He could now quite easily either sell land to meet current needs or split it up amongst his children as he thought fit. The increase in this freedom of action of the current owner meant an increase in his capacity to punish or reward his children or siblings. Thus it meant the further subordination of the children, including the heir, to the father, and of younger sons and daughters to their elder brother if he inherited the estate before they were married.

It would be wrong to assume that this major transformation in the disposal of property within the family flowed from specific feats of ingenuity performed by certain lawyers. After all, lawyers strive to please their clients, and the root cause of the changes must therefore lie in changing attitudes towards family responsibility held by different generations of landed proprietors. To account for these changes, one is compelled to enter into the realm of speculation. There can be little doubt that the landed classes of the late fifteenth and early sixteenth centuries underwent a severe crisis of confidence: their medieval military functions were eroded, but nothing else was available to take the place of these functions as a justification for the landowners' enormous wealth and power. They first threw themselves into a romantic revival of the ancient chivalric ideal, but that was too brittle to sustain the weight placed upon it, and it soon collapsed.

The reckless alienation of property by the great old families at this period can be explained in part as a reaction to the takeover of many of their functions by state-appointed lesser men, and to the frustration and sense of despair this loss of power engendered. Many other late sixteenth century landowners were new men, recently risen upon the ruins of church property, who had not had time to develop a mystique about the sanctity of the family estates, and who therefore felt free to alienate them, either to provide for their younger children or to support current consumption. There can be no doubt that these generations faced severe problems about the disposition of younger sons, since so few job openings were available. The military career was very insecure, since there were long intervals of peace and no standing army. The law was mostly occupied by elder sons, positions in the post-Reformation church were now despised, and the state bureaucracy was very small with hardly any local offices at all. Since openings in the professions were so scarce, the best—indeed in many cases the only—way to provide for surplus sons seemed to be to settle upon them a portion of the family estates, so that they could continue to support the life style of minor gentry. All these explanations are plausible, but all that we know is the fact that the more flexible legal arrangements considerably increased the power of the head of the household over his children, and to a lesser extent over his wife. He could now not only bribe them with promises of more; he could threaten them with total exclusion from the inheritance.

## 3. Patriarchalism And The American Family

By Philip J. Greven, Jr.

Most of the first-generation settlers had immigrated to Massachusetts either alone or in the company of their own immediate families. Some came with other relatives; none, however, brought an extensive group of kindred with them from England to America. The common experience of migration evidently limited the degree to which families were likely to be extended in structure during their early years in the New World. After their arrival, though, some men began to form kinship connections with other immigrants through their marriages, and many of the settlers established either personal or familial connections with each other before or soon after settlement in Andover began. Kinship often served as an influential factor in bringing additional settlers to Andover as well. From the outset, there were several embryonic kinship groups settled together in Andover.

It is evident that the structures of families were being extended rapidly by the time the second generation began to reach adulthood, and that the character of families was being reshaped by the circumstances of life in the new community. The combination of relatively abundant land, large families, a proclivity to remain permanently settled in Andover, and long delays in the actual transmission of land from the first to the second generation fostered the development of families which were extended in their structures, patriarchal in character, and rooted to this one community.

The intimate relationship between paternal authority over children and the possession of land is revealed with some clarity in the marriage negotiations of the sons and daughters of New England families. Marriage in the seventeenth century was often as much an economic as an emotional affair, involving the transference of property from one generation to another and from one family to another. Although relatively few records of such marriage negotiations have survived, either for Andover or for other communities, enough do exist to serve as models for actions which almost certainly were commonplace at most levels of society during the seventeenth century. The implications of such negotiations over the disposition of properties to children are far more significant than is sometimes realized, revealing vividly the expected and the fulfilled roles of fathers in the marriages of their children. The marriages themselves depended not only upon obtaining parental consent but, equally importantly, upon obtaining parental support in the form of a marriage portion, customary and necessary throughout this period.

The marriage of sons, in particular, depended upon parental, especially paternal, consent and support. Until a son had been given the means to support a wife, or had acquired them on his own, marriage was virtually impossible. In effect, marriages of second-generation sons in seventeenth-century Andover depended upon the willingness of fathers to permit sons to

386

leave the parental homestead and to establish themselves as married adults, usually in houses of their own built on family land designated as the married son's responsibility. The late age at which so many second-generation sons married during this period indicates both the difficulties experienced in acquiring sufficient means to support separate families and also the reluctance of many parents to allow their sons to set up households of their own. The examples of several families suggest the reasons.

The Allens probably were typical of the majority of the families in Andover with estates of more than 100 acres in the town. The negotiations in 1681 for the marriage of Andrew Allen's oldest son, Andrew, Jr., to Elizabeth Richardson, of nearby Chelmsford, indicate the role of parental settlements in making marriages of sons possible. Andrew Allen, Sr., then about sixty-five years old, had been among the first settlers of Andover, receiving a five-acre house lot and appropriate accommodation lands from the town. His eldest son was twenty-four years old when he sought to marry, but the negotiations for his marriage were conducted on his behalf by his father. Two of his prospective bride's kinsmen, Major Thomas Hinckman and Captain Josiah Richardson, from Chelmsford, came to Andover to inquire about the marriage settlement which Andrew's father proposed to give the couple. Meeting at William Chandler's inn, they asked the senior Allen "what he would give his son for incouradgement for a Livelyhood," a question which vividly reveals the customary expectations regarding marriage portions and the father's role in determining their son's ability to support a wife and family. Allen promised that upon the the contract of marriage "he would give his son Andrew at present if he married w$^{th}$ Elizabeth Richardson his house & Land laying ab$^t$ 3 miles from y$^e$ town & y$^e$ meadows belonging to it, & half his orchard at home," thus providing his son not only with a house but also with land to farm for himself out of the original family estate in Andover. In addition, Allen also promised to give his son "all his house & land at Town & y$^e$ home meadow that belonged to it" after both he and his wife were dead. The couple married January 1, 1682, and resided in the house promised to them by their paternal family and given as an inheritance after Andrew's father's death.

In the case of sons whose occupation as husbandmen made them totally dependent upon the land for their livelihood, the possession of land by their families clearly was a factor shaping their relationships to their parents and influencing their decisions to marry. In the case of sons whose occupations were not essentially dependent upon the land, parental influence continued to be exerted and felt despite their relative economic independence. Fathers evidently continued to play a significant role in the lives of sons who became craftsmen as well as those who became farmers. A trade did not necessarily indicate independence from family ties or family influence.

That fathers often continued to influence the marriage decisions of sons long after they had come of age and no matter what their occupation was is indicated by the experience of Henry Ingalls, Jr. A carpenter and the second of seven sons, he did not marry until 1688, at the age of thirty-two. Ten years later, his father, a husbandman, gave him a deed of gift to ten acres of upland and swamp and a few other small pieces of land for the love which he felt for his son and "in Consideracon of a Marriage with my allowance approbation & good liking Contracted & Consummated" between his son and Abigail Emery of Newbury. What is significant is not so much the land itself, for the acreage was comparatively small, but the reasonably explicit assumption that this marriage settlement and inheritance was given to this son as a result of his father's approval of his marriage. The fact that a middle-aged craftsman would feel the need to seek and to obtain the consent of his aged father before proceeding in marriage is a suggestive indication of the persistence of paternal authority.

Paternal consent, marriage, settlements, and inheritances were all closely interrelated in the actions of most families in seventeenth-century Andover. It could scarcely be otherwise considering the fact that marriage of sons generally brought about a division of a family's land. Since in most instances it was the father's own estate which was to be settled, in part or in its entirety, upon the couple, the father necessarily had a major role in deciding what was to be done with it. And the actions taken by most first-generation fathers indicates their unwillingness to give up legal control of their property to their children at the time of their marriages.

The reluctance of most first-generation fathers to hand over the control of their property to their second-generation sons is evident in their actions recorded in deeds and their last testaments. Only two first-generation fathers divided their land among all of their sons before their deaths and gave them deeds of gift for their portions of the paternal estate, although both waited until late in life before giving the sons legal titles to their portions. Seven first-generation fathers settled their sons upon their family estates in Andover but gave a deed of gift for the land to only one of their sons; the rest of their sons had to await their father's death before inheriting the land which they had been settled upon. Two men gave deeds to more than one son. Fourteen of the settlers retained the title to all of their land until their deaths, handing over control to their sons or daughters only by means of their last wills and testaments. The actions of four are uncertain. For the great majority of the second generation, inheritances constituted the principal means of transferring the ownership of land from one generation to the next.

The general use of partible inheritances in Andover is evident in the division of the estates of the first-generation families. Twenty-two out of twenty-three first-generation families that had two or more sons divided all of their land among their surviving sons. Out of a total of eighty-five sons whose inheritances can be determined, eighty-two or 96.5 per cent received land from their fathers' estates. Often the land bequeathed to them by will was already in their possession, but without legal conveyances having been provided. Thus although the great majority of second-generation sons were settled upon their fathers' lands while fathers were still alive, only about one-quarter of them actually owned the land which they lived upon until after their fathers' deaths. With their inheritances came ownership; and with ownership came independence. Many waited a long time, as the experiences of members of several illustrative families reveal.

The majority of households established by second-generation sons after their marriages were nuclear in the sense that such families resided apart from the paternal house; occasionally, however, in those instances in which one son inherited the paternal homestead, three generations did reside together in a single house. Because of the proximity of their residences to those of their parents and siblings, the majority of the first- and second-generation families were extended in structure. The basis was laid for the creation of elaborate kinship networks which continued to expand, in greater and lesser degrees, for generations to come.

Equally important, and a fundamental characteristic of most first-generation families, was the prolonged exercise of paternal authority and influence over sons. Long after the ostensible achievement of maturity, indicated by marriages which often were delayed until men were in their late twenties, sons remained economically dependent upon their fathers, who usually continued to own and to control the land upon which their sons had settled. This, above all, was of the utmost importance in creating, and in maintaining, the extended, partriarchal families characteristic of the first and second generations in Andover. In this seventeenth-century American community, at least, patriarchalism was a reality, based firmly upon the possession and control of the land.

The growing complexity of family life and of family structure was reflected clearly in the increasingly complex methods of transference of estates from the second to the third generations. The second generation, like the first, usually preferred to divide their land and to give it to more than one of their sons, thus maintaining the earlier pattern of partible inheritances (three-quarters of them did so); but they transferred the control of the land to their sons prior to their deaths more frequently than the first generation did. This is revealed by the fact that out of 58 second-generation fathers whose actions concerning their estates can be determined by surviving records, only 11 used their wills exclusively as their method of distributing their entire landed estate among their sons, and an additional 18 left at least some of their land to some of their sons by means of their will alone. Out of a total of 160 third-generation sons whose inheritances are known, only 30 (about 19 per cent) got land from their fathers by will alone, although an additional 17 sons got land from the intestate estates of their fathers, distributed to them by order of the probate courts. This meant that a total of 47 sons, or approximately 30 per cent, inherited land *after* the deaths of their fathers.

Significantly, 47 of these 58 estates had been transferred at least in part by deeds given to sons *before* their fathers' deaths. At least 57 third-generation sons were given their portions of paternal estates by deeds of gift from their fathers, and at least 35 sons purchased their portions of the paternal estate and received their land by deeds of sale. More than half of the sons whose portions are known thus received their land by deeds.

In the case of one-quarter of the families with more than two sons (13 out of 52), only one son was given the paternal land, indicative of an increased use of impartible inheritance as well. Out of a total of 214 third-generation sons, 139 are known to have received land from their fathers' estates (65 per cent) and 75 apparently did not (35 per cent). Those sons who did not receive land from their fathers usually received money, trades, or a liberal education, or a combination of these. The distribution of the estates of the second generation thus indicates that about three out of every four fathers still preferred to divide their land among as many of their sons as they could without doing harm to the productivity and value of their estates. Even so, only about two-thirds of their sons were able to inherit any land at all.

Unlike the first generation of settlers, the second generation generally lacked sufficient quantities of land to provide portions for all of their sons. This, undoubtedly, was to be a factor of the utmost importance in reshaping the characteristics of the family and modifying the attitudes of fathers toward their land and toward at least some of their sons. The control of the land by the older generation could have little meaning for sons who were destined to be landless. But it did have meaning to the majority who eventually inherited it.

The transference of paternal property to sons by means of deeds rather than as inheritances after death indicates a certain willingness to enable sons to establish their independence and to obtain some control over their inherited property prior to the deaths of the older generation. Prolonged control of the land, which the first generation had sustained, was often relinquished sooner by the second, judging by the increased use of deeds of gift conveying land from fathers to sons. Yet nearly 60 per cent of the third-generation sons were at least 30 years old when they received deeds of gift for their portions of the paternal estate from their fathers: the average age of fifty-four sons at the time of the deeds of gift was about thirty-one years. Twenty-eight per cent of the sons received deeds either before or within one year after their marriages; 54 per cent received deeds from their fathers between two and nine years following their marriages; and 18 per cent waited more than nine years for deeds to their land. For 72 per cent of the third-generation sons, then, there was some delay between marriage and full control of their portions of the paternal land.

Since deeds of gift often contained restrictive clauses or specific conditions which had to be fulfilled before the deeds became valid, the transference of part of an estate in this manner did not necessarily assure a son his full independence when he received his portion. Some fathers continued to exert some control over their property even after formally transferring it. The continuation of paternal control over the land remained a factor of the utmost importance in shaping the relationships within many Andover families during the lifetimes of the second and third generations. Patriarchalism was still the rule, however difficult it might be to maintain in practice. Whenever they could, fathers continued to exercise their influence over their sons by means of their control of the land which their sons needed. The delayed marriages and the delayed transferences of land from fathers to sons combined to demonstrate the continued power which many fathers could exert over the lives of at least some of their sons.

It is clear, however, that such control over sons was often either altogether impossible (particularly when sons took up a trade, followed a profession, or moved away) or very difficult. Also, even for those sons who settled in Andover upon paternal land, usually following the livelihood of husbandry, an increasing desire for, and an ability to achieve, complete economic autonomy during the lifetimes of the second generation was evident.

The most pointed indication of the desire for autonomy was the significant innovation of purchasing inheritances. This involved the payment of substantial sums of money to fathers by sons in return for their portions of the paternal estate. Although this had been done occasionally prior to 1720, the practice of transferring land from one generation to the next by means of deeds of sale increased appreciably thereafter, since 82 per cent of the deeds of sale to the third generation were written after 1720. Nearly three-quarters of the third-generation sons who purchased their portions from their fathers were either eldest or second sons. The average age at marriage of twenty-nine sons who purchased their portions was 28.4 years, and the average age of thirty-nine sons at the time of the purchase of their lands from their fathers was 33 years, with their fathers being, on the average, about 67 years old. Forty-two per cent of the sons purchased their portions either before their marriages or within only one year after their marriages; four purchased their portions between two and four years after marriage, seven between five and nine years afterwards, and eight after ten or more years of marriage.

More often than not, the sons who purchased their shares of the paternal estate were mature men rather than youths just out of adolescence or in their early twenties. This is scarcely surprising since the prices they paid were often substantial, and many sons thus undoubtedly had to wait a considerable period of time before either acquiring cash of their own or being in a position to obtain a bond or mortgage to cover their debts to their fathers. What is impressive, though, is the willingness on the part of so many third-generation sons to pay for their own inheritances, thereby acquiring lands which otherwise undoubtedly would be theirs to inherit without cost eventually.

The acquisition of paternal land by deeds of sale reflects a fundamentally different attitude toward inheritances and toward father-son relationships than inheritances either by deeds of gift or by last testaments. More than anything else, it reflects the assumption that sons ought to become fully independent of their fathers while their fathers remained alive, even if this took a long time. What it does not usually reflect, however, is the willingness of fathers to see their sons fully independent upon land which they themselves once inherited and owned, often after considerable delays. It was still unusual to find fathers eager to establish their husbandmen sons independently as youths. But whatever the wishes of fathers in this matter, many sons discovered a way, however expensive it might prove to be, to establish their complete economic independence from their fathers. Even for some farmers, life was no longer the same as it had been before.

From another point of view, though, deeds of sale not only established sons who were independent of fathers, but also ensured that fathers, in their old age, would be independent of their sons. Hitherto, the prolongation of paternal control of the land and the restrictive clauses written into so many deeds of gift reflected, at least in part, the fears of the older generation that they might not be taken care of in their later years. In view of the longevity of men and women during these years, such worries were fully justifiable—quite apart from any attitudes toward the proper authority of fathers and parents over their children. Since the problem of the aged continued to be largely in the hands of the family, the control over the land often was one of the most potent means available to parents to sustain their authority over their sons. It would be a mistake, however, to overemphasize the coercive element in paternal control of the land, since the language of the wills and deeds of the period convey affection and love and remarkably little overt worry about undutiful, disrespectful, or callous children. Yet, one way or another, the problem of maintenance and care in old age presented itself to more families than not. Most families still assured the care of the older generation by means of wills and deeds of gift, and most sons accepted their responsibilities as mature sons to care for, and often to live with, their aged parents. But some, at least, preferred not to do this; their purchasing of their portions guaranteed that their filial obligations to their parents were fulfilled by the payment of a sum of money instead of years of service and care.

Often, though, sons who received the parental homestead as their portion of their fathers' estates also received part of their parents' houses and lived in them while their parents were still alive, thus forming households which effectively consisted of three generations under a single roof. A widow nearly always was specifically bequeathed a room or rooms in her husband's house and provisions to be given to her annually by one or more of her sons. Sometimes both parents lived in the house with their sons, as in the case of John Farnum, a husbandman who died at eighty-three in 1723, having left his wife "y^e use of that Part of my House that I now Dwell in." Generally, of course, married sons lived separately in houses of their own, but aged parents usually expected to share a house with one of their children. Extended households, for the most part, were the product of old age and the necessities for care and attention which elderly men and women obviously required. This was a duty which most third-generation sons, especially those who inherited their parents' own homesteads, accepted and fulfilled.

The permanent settlement of two-thirds of the third-generation sons in Andover augmented and solidified the kinship networks which had been established during the seventeenth century. The extended families established by the first generation were thus continued into the eighteenth century by the marriages and the residences of the majority of sons of most early families. For many, settlement upon paternal land in Andover sustained their close relationships with their parents, both in terms of the control and the use of the land, and in terms of the proximity of their residences to their parents and often to other siblings. Even sons who became fully independent of their parents economically—whether by virture of trades or by their acquisition of complete control over their land—still continued to live in a community in which their parents, siblings, grandparents, uncles and aunts, and cousins also lived, thereby involving them constantly with people who were related to them by birth and marriage. As the second and third generations acquired their inheritances through the successive divisions of family land, members of families often lived upon adjacent parcels, their boundaries cutting across land which their fathers or grandfathers once had held undivided. Farming land often was bounded on one or more sides by the lands owned by brothers, cousins, or other kindred.

Many members of families lived within reasonably short distances of each other, with family groups often concentrated together in particular areas of the town. The Abbots, Ballards, Blanchards, Chandlers, Holts, and Lovejoys, for instance, were largely concentrated in the South Parish, whereas the Barker, Farnum, Foster, Frye, Ingalls, Osgood, and Stevens families were concentrated in the North Parish. Some families obviously had been more prolific than others, with the result that more of them lived together in Andover. In 1705, for example, there were sixteen Abbot men taxed in Andover, mostly in the South Parish, and there were nineteen in 1715 and twenty-three in 1720 and in 1730. There were large groups of Chandlers, Farnums, Fosters, Holts, Johnsons, Osgoods, and Stevenses. Other families usually had between four and ten men residing in the town and paying taxes, and often they were connected by marriage and kinship to many other families in the town as well. A few families failed to flourish and died out, including the Bradstreets and Aslebees (or Aslets), or barely maintained the family name in the town, like the Russes, Allens, and Tylers.

With the maturing of the third generation, it was evident that Andover had come to resemble many Old World communities in which families had lived for several generations and formed complex extended family networks. These networks were based upon the continued residence of a family in the town in which they had been born, their marriages among other families within the town, and the extensive kinship ties which they had with many of the people and families living in their community. In large measure, the stability of Andover throughout the eighteenth century rested upon the intricate pattern of family ties and kinship connections, which wove the old established settler families into a complex and familiar social world and often served as the means of integrating outsiders who married into these families.

Since in many families some sons were apprenticed to trades and some were prepared to take over the farming of paternal land, the relationships between fathers and sons must have varied considerably. As a general rule, however, sons with trades were more likely to establish their personal autonomy more readily than sons who became farmers, although many sons with trades also waited a long time to marry and even craftsmen sometimes built houses upon paternal land and waited for considerable periods before receiving titles. And as long as they remained in Andover they continued to live in close proximity to parents and siblings as well as other kindred. Their independence from paternal oversight and control was probably more often a matter of degree than of kind in comparison to their brothers who farmed. Although their ties to their families might have been looser than those of some of their siblings, these family ties undoubtedly remained an ever-present factor in their lives. Residence in Andover assured that.

The most drastic changes in the character of family life and in the nature of the relationships between the generations were experienced not by those who remained in Andover but by those who left. For all of the innovations in behavior and attitudes evident in the lives and actions of families in Andover during this period, and for all the complexities in the shapes and characteristics of their families, it is clear nevertheless that the most radically different experiences were those encountered by men and women who emigrated and resettled in other towns. The many third-generation sons who chose to migrate—leaving behind parents and kindred, leaving the community in which they had been born and raised and which had grown familiar by long experience, voluntarily moving to places where most of the people they would encounter were strangers, often living in new towns and upon new lands—these sons achieved a degree of autonomy that was impossible for those who remained in Andover. By their actions, they added yet another dimension to many Andover families.

Underlying the uprooting of so many third-generation Andover men were both economic factors and the more elusive psychological factors which traditionally have complicated the decisions of men to move. The economic motives are the most readily discernible, owing to the nature of the evidence which has survived. The limitations upon the estates possessed by most second-generation fathers, their inability to provide land for all of their sons, the less obvious but very important fact that sons could not expect to make a decent living by working as laborers and therefore were dependent upon either land or trades for livelihoods: all these factors served to limit the prospects of many of the third-generation sons who were raised to maturity in Andover.

At the time they were reaching maturity, however, many new towns and new areas began to be opened up in Massachusetts, Connecticut, and New Hampshire, thereby providing them with both land and opportunities if they were willing to move away to gain them. At the time that land values in Andover were beginning to rise steeply, land was available for very little money elsewhere. In New Hampshire, for instance, land values during the 1720s and 1730s were low, adding the attraction of low cost to ready availability for those willing to undertake the risks and hardships of pioneering and beginning farms of their own, just as their grandfathers had done earlier. The economic inducements of new towns—cheap and abundant land—were sufficiently powerful to attract many third-generation Andover men who emigrated to Connecticut, to western Massachusetts, and later to New Hampshire.

But decisions to move were not the result solely of economic considerations, important though they undoubtedly were. Other, more personal, considerations and motivations must also have played a role. Families no doubt differed in their feelings for each other, with some fathers and sons remaining on closer terms than others, with some sons willing to accept their fathers' control over the land in return for the land itself. Many men obviously preferred to remain in Andover despite a relative decline in their economic positions. A preference for family and for friends, a need for rootedness, perhaps inertia, too, were powerful forces maintaining the families of Andover. Often they could stay because others were willing to leave, and many families had sons who stayed and sons who went away. We can only surmise what personal feelings and choices entered into these very different decisions.

Families varied even in the way in which they emigrated: some evidently chose to isolate themselves altogether from kindred, settling in towns in which they were alone and without other members of their families to fall back upon for assistance or friendship; others clearly chose to settle in places where they had members of their families living also, maintaining some degree of family connection both in their new communities and with their families remaining in Andover. But whatever the circumstances of their emigration, those who departed invariably led lives and created families which differed markedly from those who stayed in Andover.

For the most part, households in Andover in the middle of the eighteenth century continued to be nuclear in structure as they had been in previous generations, with the majority of married couples residing in houses of their own apart from parents or other kindred. During the course of the middle decades of the century, though, it became increasingly common for households to be extended in their structures by the residence of married children in the houses of their aging parents, thus forming trigenerational households. The census of 1764, for instance, reveals that 438 families in Andover lived in only 360 houses, which suggests that 78 families must have shared houses with other families. Some of these probably were unrelated, boarding or renting their space in other households. Others, however, were clearly constituted of grandparents, children, and grandchildren, as evidence from wills and deeds confirms. Such extended households remained the exception, but they evidently were becoming more and more common in Andover during the lifetimes of the third and fourth generations.

In mid-eighteenth-century Andover it was almost impossible for the families of descendants of early settlers to be completely nuclear so long as they remained settled in the community. Whether their own particular households consisted of two or three generations—and thus were either nuclear or extended in their structures—they were nearly always parts of larger networks of kindred. Collectively, these households formed the extended families which remained a permanent part of the familial experiences of descendants of the settler families through the lifetimes of at least four generations. Even when men married wives from outside Andover but continued to live in Andover, their own kindred within the town—including their parents, some of their siblings, uncles, aunts, and cousins, both in their own particular family and in the families related to them by other marriages—provided them with a complex web of family relationships and connections.

What matters most, however, is not simply that so many of these families were extended in structure, but that the degree of extension varied so widely. Depending upon many factors—some demographic, some economic, some residential—these families could expand or contract in size. Nearly everyone was a part of a kinship group, to be sure, but the kinship world of an Abbot or a Holt was more extensive than that of a Chandler or a Frye, and far more extensive than that of a Ballard or an Allen. In this sense, the structures of their families were varied and variable, responsive to the changing circumstances of life and of actions governing individuals and families in the third and fourth generations. But—equally significantly— what did not change appreciably over time was the persistence of these extended families within this particular community. They provided a basic source of stability and continuity in the midst of many profound changes reshaping the lives of Andover's inhabitants in the mid-eighteenth century.

The changing circumstances underlying the patterns of experiences that shaped the lives of the maturing fourth generation were reflected most strikingly in changing relationships between generations. Although some fathers continued to act like patriarchs and to prolong their control over their maturing sons, many no longer did. In retrospect, it is apparent that this generation was increasingly independent.

A combination of circumstances probably fostered the relatively early autonomy of many fourth-generation sons and encouraged their fathers to assume that their sons ought to be on their own as soon as possible. The rapid expansion of new settlements and the emigration of many third-generation Andover men had amply demonstrated the opportunities which existed outside Andover for those willing and able to leave their families and begin life for themselves elsewhere. The diminished landholdings of many families and the constantly rising prices of land in Andover during the first half of the century also put great pressure upon sons who wished to remain as farmers in Andover and made it imperative that many sons take up trades instead of move elsewhere for the land they needed. Less obvious (but surely no less important) must have been the heightened sense of the impermanence of life itself, reflecting the diminished chances for survival in childhood and youth among the fourth generation. Perhaps this, too, might have encouraged fathers to let their offspring establish their own independence sooner than they themselves had generally done. By examining their actions in transmitting their estates to their sons and in settling their sons in livelihoods of their own, such elusive developments can be demonstrated. For the history of the family, the loosening of the ties binding the generations together was of the utmost importance, distinguishing the fourth from earlier generations.

For the fourth generation, as for earlier generations, the family provided the principal source of support in making the transition from youth to adulthood. Sons continued to need substantial assistance in the form of money or land in order to be able to assume responsibility for families of their own. Parents still played an indispensable role in the lives of their maturing children. The principal difference was that many had grown more willing to let go of the economic bonds tying their children to them. They now offered help without the strings binding earlier generations together. And this, more than any other single thing, is what distinguished their families from those of earlier generations.

Fourth-generation sons, like their fathers and grandfathers before them, often were dependent upon their fathers for the inheritances which constituted a substantial portion of their livelihoods and which would provide them with at least an initial start in life, whether in the form of land, money, education, or a trade. An even larger proportion of third-generation estates were transmitted intact to the fourth generation than had been the case in the previous generation, thus augmenting the trend toward impartible inheritances. Whereas 95.7 per cent of first-generation estates and 75.0 per cent of second-generation estates had been divided among all or most sons in families with at least two surviving sons, only 58.3 per cent of third-generation estates were divided among two or more sons. Out of 43 yeoman families, 24 chose to divide their land among several of their sons, giving some land to 67 out of 93 of their surviving sons (72 per cent), in contrast to 19 yeoman families having more than one son but preferring to bestow their entire landed estates upon one son only, with the result that only 19 out of their 68 sons received inheritances in Andover of their fathers' farms (27.9 per cent). Of the 8 gentlemen whose actions are known in dividing their estates among two or more sons, only 2 left their entire landed estates to one son and a total of 17 out of 25 fourth-generation sons of Andover gentlemen inherited a portion of their fathers' Andover farms (68 per cent). Out of a total of 74 third-generation fathers, 60 had to provide inheritances for two or more surviving sons, 13 had only one son surviving and one had no sons for whom to provide. Out of a total of 226 fourth-generation sons at least 152 were given land from their fathers' estates (67.3 per cent), with at least 46 receiving deeds of gift for their portions or by buying them with deeds of sale, and with 106 sons receiving their land either by wills or by the actions of probate courts in those cases in which their fathers died intestate. About two-thirds of the inheritances of paternal land by will alone involved the paternal homestead, the majority of inheritors being eldest sons.

The average age at marriage for sons inheriting their fathers' land by will was 25.2 years, and their average age at the time of inheritance was 30.4 years, indicative of frequent delays between marriage and inheritance of land in Andover. Slightly more than three-fifths of the fourth-generation sons waited less than ten years to receive their inheritances, having gotten their land before marriage in 38.9 per cent of the cases. On the other hand, an equal percentage waited more than ten years before becoming full owners of their share of the paternal land, a reflection of the longevity of many of their fathers, forty-seven of whom died at an average age of 69.5 years.

A larger percentage of sons receiving deeds of gift for their portions married before the age of thirty than had done so in the previous generation (60.9 per cent instead of 40.7 per cent). A somewhat smaller percentage (53.4 per cent) of those buying their portions by deeds of sale married before thirty, but this was considerably more than the 42.1 per cent in the third generation. A larger percentage of the fourth generation receiving deeds of gift for their portions received them either before marriage or within five years of their marriage than had been true for the third generation (85.7 per cent versus 54 per cent), although the percentage of fourth-generation sons buying their portions within five years of their marriages was similar to that for the previous generation (57.1 per cent versus 54.5 per cent). It evidently was still difficult for men to acquire the capital or to achieve a position from which to purchase their portions of the paternal estates. The large percentage of sons receiving deeds of gift to their lands so quickly after marriage, if not before, does suggest a tendency for fathers to establish some of their sons independently at earlier ages and with less delay than had been apparent during the previous generation.

The sharp drop in the average age of marriage, the rising proportion of impartible inheritances, and the tendency to convey land by deed to sons of younger ages and without undue delays all suggest the willingness on the part of third-generation fathers to permit and to encourage many of their sons to establish themselves economically on the land as independent farmers sooner than most second-generation fathers appear to have done. When these factors of inheritance are linked to the increased rate of mobility among fourth-generation sons, the evidence points toward the increasing independence of sons, the loosening of family ties binding the older and the younger generations together in Andover, and an increased awareness of, and willingness to take advantage of, economic opportunities outside of Andover itself. The changing patterns of inheritance thus suggest other changes within the families of the community as well.

The continued viability of family life in Andover during the mid-eighteenth century clearly demanded that many sons would have to leave and establish themselves elsewhere. The willingness of fathers to help sons settle outside of Andover testifies to their awareness of this necessity and to their concern for their offspring. In this sense, Andover, having grown old and crowded, served as a seedbed for the new communities being established elsewhere. They, in turn, would provide land and livelihoods for many people for several generations. The recurrent process of migration again served as a web of experience binding together many people otherwise separated by time and space. But though many left, many also stayed. Their lives, and their differing families and experiences, form two persistent poles in colonial American history. Neither the rooted nor the uprooted alone can tell the whole story of family life in colonial Andover.

# 6

# Spouse Loss

## 1. Introduction

The termination of a marriage partnership did not mean the termination of the family. The loss of a spouse through death, desertion, divorce or separation was both a terminal and a starting point in the family cycle. It represented a conclusion without an ending. The task of maintaining the family now shifted to those remaining members of the household who would continue or begin a new family cycle. This chapter will explore this important transitional stage in the family cycle by focusing on the effect of spouse loss on the surviving family.

During the 16-18th centuries, with the exception of the New England colonies, death was an omnipresent phenomenon at all stages of the life cycle and was the primary reason for spouse loss. All literature dealing with the theme of death gives testimony to its damage to the human psyche. To immediate family members the ending of life of a Mother-wife or Father-husband must have caused great hardship and, to many, suffering. If there were feelings of love and dependency no shield would be strong enough to insulate against such finality. Moreover, it is not convincing, as will be discussed at the end of this introduction, that widespread mortality in earlier times significantly muted the mourning of those left behind.

Perhaps almost as potent as the emotional trauma was the fear of material dislocation caused by the death of a valuable family contributor, especially the father, who was the head of the household. It is not surprising, therefore, that he attempted to insulate his family from the material privations that could result from his death. To this end he relied upon jointures, marriage settlements, antenuptual agreements and intricately drawn up wills.

Spouse loss due to divorce or separation no doubt evoked very different familial and individual emotions from those experienced when a death occurred. However, we are unable to describe precisely for the past the sentiments each type of loss evoked. But there is a plethora of valuable data which does help the family historian to reconstruct some of the circumstances affecting family members during the early modern period. These include demographic data on death, divorce laws, court decisions and the actions of public institutions, such as the Workhouse in England. The articles included in this section address themselves to the economic, legal and social effects of spouse loss rather than to its psychological consequences. This last dimension still requires investigation.

## THE DEMOGRAPHY OF DEATH

Since most spouse loss resulted from death, the first and perhaps most important question is how many families were affected? Peter Laslett's article attempts to answer this question by directing our attention to the plight of orphans who suffered parental deprivation. Depending upon the sample he examines, Laslett finds the numbers of English orphans varied from one third to one half. His analysis of parental deprivation due to death in the past is correlated to parental deprivation due to divorce in contemporary America, which he finds to be approximately similar.

In the Southern colonies parental death was probably higher. The Rutmans' study of a 17th-century Virginia county (1976) is highly revealing. Their demographic data demonstrates that by the age of five almost a quarter of the children lost one or both parents, by age thirteen over one half suffered parental loss, and by age twenty-one seventy percent did so. In a study of native burgesses in the same colony, Quitt found the median age at the death of their fathers to be nineteen (1976).

The picture changes remarkably in New England as well as in some of the Middle colonies where individual and marital longevity appears to have been typical. It was not unusual, therefore, for a Puritan or Quaker couple to have celebrated their twenty-fifth or thirty-fifth wedding anniversary when their last child had become independent. The demographic experience of these groups, however, was anomalous to the general pattern where at least one third to one half of the children mourned the death of at least one parent prior to their majority.

According to much recent work, spouse loss resulted more often from the death of husbands than of wives, and therefore, fatherless families were more common. Although childbearing exacted a significant toll from early modern women, statistically a wife had a much greater chance of becoming a widow than of dying during childbirth. Once she passed her childbearing years, she enjoyed a much greater life expectancy than all men her own age. The greater longevity of wives is at least a partial explanation for why fathers took care to provide for their daughters in the jointure settlement and why many husbands wrote wills detailing the way their wives should be cared for. Furthermore, it should be noted that the topic of widowhood is more extensively treated in historical literature than is widowerhood. This may reflect a tacit acknowledgement of the historical reality that most wives outlived their husbands, the dangers of childbearing notwithstanding.

## ORPHANAGE

Since records are incomplete for the early modern era and because of local demographic variation, it is impossible to generalize on the ages at which children lost their parents. Laslett in this chapter notes that in England it was rare for children to lose both parents, although a child was regarded as an orphan if one parent died. In contrast, the 17th-century Chesapeake offers a gloomy portrait. For there the risk was great for the loss of both parents.

The fate of orphans was affected by a number of considerations, not the least of which were the rules concerning guardianship. In England it was the father not the mother who was the legal guardian of the child. Even if the mother were specified as guardian in the father's will, the courts had the right to supervise her guardianship or to appoint another guardian. Thus if the minor male or female were heir to a particular kind of property (an estate held in military tenure, for example), the Crown could and often did exercise its feudal right to wardship as a means for advancing the Crown's economic interests. Until 1660 when the Court of the Wards was finally abolished, such a minor heir or heiress usually became the Crown's ward. The Crown, moreover, often sold its right of wardship to an interested party who would then take over the Crown's right and become the child's guardian. The result could range from benevolence, to behavior where the motivation was purely penurious and the orphan shabbily treated. To the orphaned child, therefore, treatment would depend upon the character of his new guardian.

The Court of the Wards was administered by a Master whose function was the protection of a ward's rights. How well a Master attended to these duties could well determine the future fate of the orphan. If a ward's education were neglected or his property dissipated his future prospects could be gloomy indeed. The frequency with which this occurred contributed to the poor reputation of the court. In the 17th century parents who were determined to control the destiny of their children and their estates joined forces with reformers who felt that orphans should not be in the hands of strangers. By 1660 the court had been put out of business by Parliament.

In addition to the Court of the Wards, the King extended his right of *parens patriae* through the Court of Chancery where a body of law known as equity was administered. The Court's function in the case of orphans was to supervise their appointed guardians, even the ones chosen by parents. This supervisory function acquired in the 17th century survived the dissolution of the Court of the Wards. Guardians had to adhere to a prescribed set of obligations developed by the Chancery Court in order to protect the orphan's rights. Unfortunately, the machinery of the court was slow, often not acting as expeditiously as some situations warranted. In these circumstances orphans' property might not have gotten the sufficient protection required.

Various English municipalities had their own orphan's courts which claimed jurisdiction over legitimate orphans of city freemen. The most famous of these was the Court of Orphans in London. The pronounced purpose of the court, according to Carlton, was to prevent exploitation of the estates of minors and to insure that all family members received their fair share. The Court's judgment on these matters occasionally superseded the directions in the parent's will. Accordingly, its general policy was to divide the estate into three parts: one third going to the widow, one third to the children and one third distributed according to the wishes of the deceased. The London Court of Orphans lasted until 1724 when the protest of fathers, that the disposition of their estates should be according to their wishes rather than the Court's, prevailed. Thus the abolition of the Court of the Wards during the 17th century and that of the Court of the Orphans during the 18th century resulted from strong objections by parents of different classes who collectively felt that the family rather than the institutions of government should control the destiny of their children and their property.

In England, minor orphans who were left destitute were a social problem to which the local parish and the Elizabethan poor laws addressed themselves. Parishes gave various kinds of support to poor one-parent families with small children. This was often in the form of money or goods which helped to keep the family intact, family integrity being a value important in Tudor and Stuart England. If, however, maintenance of all the children were impossible, the parish assisted in locating and supporting a surrogate family for some of the children. An Act of 1601 not only included outdoor relief but also directed the parish to find employment or apprenticeship for older minor children.

By the middle of the 17th century an institution known as the Workhouse emerged. One of its purposes was to provide shelter, food and some education, usually vocational, for impoverished orphans. In the 18th century more Workhouses were built as individual parishes became increasingly burdened or unwilling to support their own poor. Outdoor relief was reduced, as public sentiment placed greater stress on work and self-help than had previously existed. Thus the state of the destitute widow with small orphans was now more likely to evoke feelings of hostility rather than charity. And, although national poor law legislation had been enacted during our

403

time period, the protection it afforded survivors of spouse loss depended ultimately on the disposition of local authorities, who increasingly reflected an adversary attitude toward the poor.

Institutional policy toward orphans in Colonial America offered some variations from the English scene. There was not, for example, a Court of Wards or Chancery, but there were Orphan Courts. These, however, were not separate entities as in England but were special activities of courts with broad jurisdiction. In the southern colonies, the County Court usually had oversight over orphans. It discharged this responsibility by setting aside special days during the year to attend to matters pertaining to orphans, including the appointment of guardians.

The courts made special efforts to keep families together. For example, when both parents were deceased, courts attempted to place orphans in the homes of relatives or godparents and to keep siblings with one another. The authority and responsibilities of these courts were regulated by legislation passed by colonial assemblies, as Watson's article shows for the Edgecome County Court in North Carolina. The statutes of 1760, furthermore, attempted to deal with the economic burden of illegitimacy by requiring the father to pay for a mid-wife and for child maintenance.

In Virginia and North Carolina, Orphans' Courts were empowered to oversee the future of both wealthy and poor orphans whereas English Orphans' Courts only protected freemen's orphans who had inheritances. The interest of the poor orphan in the older world was attended to by national poor laws whose enforcement, as we have seen, was determined by the attitude of the local authorities of the parish. We cannot assume, however, that colonial statutes regarding the care of orphans were any more faithfully enforced at the local level. As Watson shows, for example, the Edgecome Court did not always meet its statutory commitment to hold sessions of the Orphans Court. And guardians did not always receive the necessary scrutiny which the policy of the court claimed as one of its significant functions.

Still, if an English or American orphan were left an inheritance, the courts did offer some real protection. They discouraged guardians from dissipating the child's legacy and required that the orphan be provided with proper care, education, and a suitable marriage. At the age of 14, moreover, the common law allowed the orphan to choose a new guardian if he desired, although there are few indications in England or America that children actually exercised this right. Guardians controlled the inheritance of children until they came of age. Such power could be lucrative, especially if abused. This too often common phenomenon led the courts to insist that guardians post a bond for the inheritance under their trust and undergo periodic checks on the way they were managing the orphan's estate.

In contrast to the generally acknowledged English inheritance custom of primogeniture, Orphans Courts adhered to a policy of partible inheritance, that is, of children sharing equally in the wealth of their father. Some deviation existed. The courts in 17th-century Virginia may have favored older sons, while the London Court of the Orphans attempted to take accounts of gifts fathers had already given to their children. Primogeniture seems to have been practiced more widely in 16th and 17th century England than in Europe or in 17th century Colonial America (Thirsk 1976). The practice of passing on the family estate to the oldest son, however, did not exclude other family members from inheriting some wealth, mostly in the form of personal property.

Thus fathers in their testamentary provision, courts in their supervision of guardians, and poor laws in their relief to destitute orphans reflected a broad recognition of the hazards that faced children who lost a father before they reached their majority.

## WIDOWS

Widows had to face a society that felt threatened by the seductive image of a sexually experienced but unmarried woman, particularly if her attractiveness was augmented by wealth. The article by Pearson deals with the manifestations of these anxieties, that the sinful or Eve part of woman's nature would emerge if she continued alone in her widowhood. The expectation of the upper classes was that widows would remarry, particularly if there were minor children. Many, in fact, did quite quickly after their husband's death, not only in England but also in the 17th-century Chesapeake, where the male death rate was high and where there was a severe shortage of women. Puritan widows were advised to remarry shortly so as not to idolize their departed spouses, while Quakers were expected to wait for upwards of a year. This prolonged period of grief is probably a consequence of the greater emphasis placed on love in Quaker marriages.

In Massachusetts, a widow in need might seek assistance from the General Court. If she were still able to work, some small task might be given to her, otherwise the community would provide some form of support. Old, deserted, poor widows, moreover, conjured up a different image than did the young wealthy ones. Macfarlane's book on witchcraft (1970) suggests that a substantial population of witches came from this older group of widows. During this witchprone age there was the belief that as one aged the quantity of sin might increase (Thomas, 1971). The indigent old widow who was turned away without bread, cursing as she left, may have been thought the cause of subsequent calamities that befell the uncharitable family. She might then be accused of being a witch.

## SEPARATIONS AND DIVORCE

Since the values of the Anglo-American world were weighted toward the inviolacy of marriage and family life, spouses who were separated or divorced were deviating from the "rules of the game." But it is difficult to assess who experienced the greater social ostracism, the one who initiated the separation or the party left behind; although clearly the abandoned spouse and young children would have experienced the greater emotional stress. The most difficult separation to document, except in New England, was when one spouse deserted another. Desertion probably occurred more in lower class families where there was little or no property at stake. Although there are no available statistics except for Massachusetts divorce cases, desertion is mentioned frequently in official documents.

More than likely the difficulties in tracking down the abandoning husbands or wives accounted for the existence of some of the one-parent families that were known to exist in such large cities as London. The general impression, moreover, is that it was the husbands who usually deserted rather than the wives. Women and children would then either work or perhaps receive some charitable assistance. The London Foundling Hospital established in the 18th century was filled with abandoned infants and children who may have been the product of such deserted households.

For the English upper classes the church granted legal separation, but it was not until the last decade of the 17th century that divorce was permitted. The divorce, however, could only be obtained after a legal separation had been granted, and then only through a private act of Parliament. This procedure took many years and was quite expensive; thus only the very wealthy had refuge to this privilege. Although women had earlier petitioned under this procedure with similar grounds as men, it was not until 1801 that the first woman obtained a divorce. Prior to that time favorable outcomes were only procured by men. It thus appears that a double standard ideology operated in the process of obtaining a divorce, especially in England.

Similar sexism appears in the matter of legal separation. Adultery was one of the acceptable grounds for legal separation, but the ecclesiastical courts granted it to a man more easily if his wife committed adultery than if the reverse were true. The only ameliorating feature for the woman was that during the separation proceedings she was entitled to alimony even if she had been the party who committed adultery.

The new world offered some interesting and important departures from the practice in England. The double standard was less rigidly adhered to, especially in Massachusetts. There divorce was accepted as a logical consequence of civil marriage, and wives as well as husbands could successfully sue for divorce in desertion and adultery, although adultery committed by women was treated more harshly than if committed by men. Another American innovation was that women might continue to be entitled to their dower rights even if they were the guilty party in the divorce. In England divorce on grounds of adultery extinguished dower rights.

In the 17th century, Virginia law accepted the English principle that divorce was not possible. Legal separations, however, were not scarce. Women as well as men could initiate the separation and the Virginia courts not only insured the financial security of the separated female, but also allowed her to make contracts. The absence of ecclesiastical courts in Virginia, it has been argued, made separations easier to obtain than in England once the parties agreed. Moreover, the Virginia courts assured the protection of the female, making separation an easier process for her than it was for her English counterpart. When it came to separation and divorce, then, the American colonies took a greater leap toward equality of women's rights than did mother England.

A final aspect to our discussion of spouse loss in the early modern world directs itself to those features of life which seemed to assuage the burden of death; for it was death, as stated earlier, which accounted for the greatest loss in marriage. The modern reader may not be able to appreciate how fortuitous life was in earlier times. There are the numbers to remind us, but they are merely past facts not present experiences. We can ask the question if the high divorce rate that pervades the modern world minimizes the distress and dislocation individuals undergo during the divorce proceedings. The evidence points to the contrary view. The large numbers of divorces do not seem to offset individual fears and stress. Can we then assume that the large loss of life in the past prevented or substantially reduced individual fear or grief if a loved spouse or parent died? Certainly it was far from ignored. Just as social scientists, lawyers and feminists of our day deal with the emotional currents related to divorce, so did the church and religious reformers tackle the questions and problems related to death.

Preached to be out of man's control, religious leaders saw death to be in the domain of God. In the attempt to minimize the amount of grief and personal anxiety always ancillary to death, they painted a *glorious* potential for the departed spouses and parents. Churches with paintings and statues were present to bring to life the reality of afterlife. Religious funerals offered the mourner the opportunity to expose his sorrow and in the process overcome it. Finally religion gave the community of believers a common experience with which to handle the vagaries of death. For many this may have cushioned the shock, but for how many people, especially young children, did it make up for the loss?

## 2. Changes Wrought By Death

By Lu Emily Pearson

Elizabethan widows, as a rule, were given little time to mourn, especially if they were young. Mother and father, son and daughter, brother and sister, and even a husband might find solace in friends or relatives at the time of bereavement, but as soon as a widow laid the body of her husband in the tomb, she was expected to bury her independence and her grief. Indeed, most widows, as soon as death left them alone, "modestly" put themselves into the hands of their nearest kin, who might proceed with or without haste to launch them into matrimony again. There were exceptions to this convention, however, as when wives of men very popular among the people of their own age married again hastily; then people criticized the lack of respect shown for the dead. If there had been a great attachment between the husband and wife or if the husband was a darling of the people, the widow's marriage would be criticized regardless of when it might occur or to whom she gave her hand. For example, though the widow of Essex waited two years before she married again, her act was frowned upon, and this in spite of the fact that she was left with three sons and two daughters to rear and educate. True, two of the sons died early, but she was still burdened with much responsibility, and needed a person to help her as only a husband could. When a widow's relatives chose to make a good bargain for themselves as well as for her by means of new marriage contract, the widow might have little to say in the matter, particularly if she voluntarily put herself into the hands of such relatives.

In any case, however, the rich widow must be quickly matched. Those closest to her and those who were responsible for her financial welfare governed as much as possible the expenditure on funeral and wake unless the will of the deceased placed such matters beyond their control. Then they bargained with suitors for her hand, and if the widow was very rich, she had many suitors of all ages. The old sought her in order to enhance their financial holdings or to increase their power; the young, to acquire the fortune denied them by their older brother's inheritance or to repair an inheritance wasted by their own extravagance or that of their forebears. Some, of course, were but clever fortune hunters. The widow's guardians, according to the deceased husband's will, were to arrange the remarriage, but they were not forbidden to drive a close bargain with the suitors and, for the sake of their own profit, give the prize to the highest bidder. Widows of less wealth, but for the difference in degree, shared a like fate unless, of course, the widow herself was a woman of an unusually strong, independent nature. For even the most unscrupulous guardians had to reckon with the fact that woman's consent to marriage was necessary to any matching, and the longer she was a widow, the less tractable she might become.

Just how much a widow's youth and beauty might count in the marriage mart depended a great deal upon the desires of her suitors; in the case of the rich widow, such charms were often extremely dangerous to her personal happiness. Aware of the hazards that surrounded them, harassed widows yielded more or less readily to the hasty marriages arranged for them by their "protectors." Meanwhile, to offset the charge of being "lusty," they had to conduct themselves with extreme modesty. Yet those who came through the ordeal with a clear reputation did so more through the grace of God than through their own wise or discreet behavior. It was to protect these widows from the human wolves that would rob them of their good name as well as their possessions that Elizabethan society condoned their early marriage. The only stipulation was that the widow must not receive any suitors till her husband's body was buried. For those whose husbands had died abroad, this period of retirement from the social whirl might be longer than one would suppose: two or more months might pass before the body could be transported to its final resting place.

In some instances, especially among the upper classes, the hazards of war and disease might widow a more or less sheltered woman three or four times. Yet for her, happiness in remarriage could be expected with almost as much certainty as for one whose marriage was not interrupted by her husband's untimely death.

Should the mother of a family die—and mortality from childbirth ran high in this age—the father was expected to find a new mother for his children as soon as possible. Such hasty marriages for men were common to all classes of society, though material possessions were important elements affecting new ties for men as well as for women. In fact, it was a common practice, even among Puritans who were likely to be sensitive to the charge of lustiness, for either man or woman to marry soon after losing a mate in death. The Dutch mother-in-law of Philip Stubbes, the Puritan, was a middle-class woman widowed on September 22, 1563, and she remarried on November 8 of the same year. When she was widowed again some twenty years later, she was licensed to marry within less than two months, yet the moral Stubbes always spoke of her as a woman of "singular good grace and modesty," declaring she was both discreet and wise and chiefly adorned by being "both religious and zealous."

A widow of the lower middle class, unless left with a small shop or estate by which to support herself and family, could do little to make an honorable living. The mother of the great scholar, John Cheke, was the wife of a beadle, but being left poor at her husband's death, she could maintain herself and children only by keeping a wine shop in the town of Cambridge. In spite of her humble position, however, she managed to do very well by her children. Her son John went to college, where he became famous for his knowledge of Greek, and where he formed some important friendships, among which were those with Cecil, later Lord Burghley, and Ascham, his distinguished pupil. One of the widow's daughters married Cecil, who frequented the wine shop during his college days. Though this wife died early, the marriage was not unhappy in spite of the fact that for a time it crushed the parents' high hopes concerning their son's brilliant alliance with an important family. The widow Cheke, however, was no doubt pleased with her disposal of her daughter to Cecil.

Among the upper middle class, a widow with much property needed her family's protection in contracting a new marriage, though at times a headstrong girl might flout such care. Lest she become the victim of a fortune hunter, her family usually took the precaution to see that the new husband offered security for the privilege of taking charge of the widow's property. At the same time the family might seek to profit from the arrangement as did some guardians of rich widows among the nobility. Even such a man as Sir Francis Walsingham, therefore, had been conventionally bound to prove that his intentions were honest when in 1565 he engaged to marry a widow.

In July of that year he promised to settle upon the widow Ursula lands to the yearly value of one hundred marks, for which he was bound to 2,000 marks. For Dame Ursula's "further advancement," he had to convey to her brother-in-law, John Worsley, "the manor and mansion house of Parkebury . . . to the like uses," and was bound on July 22, 1566, to 1,000 marks for this part of the transaction. At this time he was also required to give security "for £500 in plate to be bequeathed by him to his said wife, upon whom by a still later deed" he settled a manor valued at £100 a year. When a rich widow was protected by such bargaining, she might expect a happy marriage if her family was genuinely concerned about her welfare.

Abuse of such protection of widows might lead to their barter and sale regardless of their birth. If honest measures were not taken to protect rich widows from mere fortune seekers, such women might have good cause to bewail their lot. Besides the matter of money was that of religion, for Protestant and Catholic households alike frowned on intermarriage between members of two faiths. When a rich widow took into her own hands the making of an alliance with a new husband, seldom or never did she engage in such an act unless the barriers of wealth or religion lay between her and the object of her affections. Otherwise she trusted to the integrity and kindly interest of those who were duty-bound to look after her welfare.

A widow's children usually complicated her problem of remarriage a great deal, especially if a widower with children presented himself as an acceptable suitor. Writers of conduct books expressed themselves fully on this subject. Vives, whose opinions were borrowed as freely in this matter as in others, justified the marriage of a young widow on the grounds that she needed someone to care for her property and to control her servants and to keep her household in order. Of course he agreed with Paul that the new husband would serve as a means of keeping her from lustful living, but he objected to second marriages when two sets of children were involved. A widow would not have the liberty with the other children that she had with her own. Her love of her own children might make her second husband jealous of her first husband and cause the stepfather to regard her children indifferently or with dislike. But what troubled many a timid mind was that if one of the husband's children should sicken, the widow might be accused of being a witch, and if she forbade giving it food at such a time, she would be called cruel, or if she gave it food and it died, she would be called a poisoner. In spite of such fears and admonitions, however, families of two sets of children often lived together amicably, and the family structure was frequently as patriarchal as that in the Bible.

If the widow had children old enough to comprehend their mother's problems when she contemplated remarriage, they might help or hinder her in her plans. When, for example, the Countess of Southampton was first widowed, her only son and heir approved so heartily of her acceptance of the proposal of Sir Thomas Heneage that he was chief master of the ceremonies at the elaborate wedding which followed. When, however, after the death of this second husband she contemplated a third marriage, the son raised troublesome objections. There were probably several reasons for his disapproval. First, the rank of her choice, Sir William Harvey, was inferior to that of Sir Thomas Heneage. Second, she had entered into her plans without consulting her son, probably because he himself had just secretly married one of the Queen's maids in waiting, and thereby offended his mother and put himself in disgrace with the Queen. Finally, and possibly most important of all, there may have been financial arrangements necessary for the union that were embarrassing to the newly wedded youth. At any rate, so great was the feeling aroused between mother and son that outsiders had to come to their assistance before harmony was once more established between them.

Vives had given very explicit advice in regard to the widow and her servants. First, widows must not shut their doors to the world lest they be given an ill name with their servants. Next, they must not array any servant in "over gorgeous apparel" lest the servant suspect his mistress of liking his body or looking on him as "apt for pleasure." Special favors to a servant were likely to make him arrogant or "high minded" through knowing "he was loved of his mistress: which love, though it be well hid, yet many times it appeareth when he despiseth his fellows, as they were his bondsmen." Shakespeare's careful attention to all these details is shown in his portrayal of Malvolio's stupid vanity, the revenge taken on him by disgruntled servants, and Olivia's delicious amazement at her steward's conduct in the skylarking comedy of *Twelfth Night.*

Vives would also have the menservants in a widow's household diminished in number, and the widow's close companion some aged kinswoman upon whose virtue and wisdom she might rely. He considered it better still for her to dwell with her mother-in-law's kin, for this would make her seem to love her husband's blood better than her own, and add a further safeguard to her chastity. Though suspicion of a widow's virtue appears in all Elizabethan literature, and its classical models, it is the subject of close analysis in most moral writing of the sixteenth century. When, therefore, Becon exclaimed, "How light, vain, trifling, unhonest, unhousewifely young widows have been in all ages, are also at this present day, experience doth sufficiently declare,'' he did not preach to deaf ears. Indeed, the Pauline admonition that young widows should marry again soon to avoid the "danger of everlasting damnation" was on the tip of all tongues. Guazzo had also warned that widows were exposed to such harsh judgments they must be extremely circumspect in talk, countenance, apparel, and behavior, and he had strongly recommended that they live retired lives. "Even the wisest and honestest" widows "serve for mark for ill tongues to shoot at," his English translator had written, "and it seemeth the more they cover their face and their eyes with their masks, the more busily men labor to discover in them some faults.''

After her first grief is past, however, she should "begin to study for consolation," which should consist of the Christian belief in "immortality of the soul and in reunion after death of friend and friend.'' Death, said Vives, does not merely separate body and soul: when a husband dies he is not utterly dead, "but liveth both with life of his soul, which is the very life," and in his wife's remembrance. Just as her friends live with her, whether absent or dead, if she keeps a lively image of them imprinted on her heart by thinking of them daily, so her husband will wax fresh in her mind. But if she forgets him, he dies for her indeed. He would not have the image of the husband remembered with weeping, however, but with reverence. This she can do by taking "a solemn oath to swear by her husband's soul" whom she will seek to please from now on as "a spirit purified, and a divine thing." Thus a widow should take her husband for her "keeper and spy, not only of her deeds, but also of her conscience." Then she can manage her household to please him and bring up his children in the same manner, feeling that she is making him happy by leaving a wife so well able to carry her responsibilities. The husband's soul will never have cause to "be angry with her and to take vengeance on her ungraciousness" if she follows this pattern of living, but she must cease her weeping, lest she give the impression of believing her husband "clean dead, and not absent." It is a pity, says Vives, that widows are not properly instructed by their spiritual advisers at funeral feasts instead of being told to be of good cheer for they will not long lack a new husband. Such promises he accounts for by saying they come from those who "be well wet with drink.''

After the husband's death, the widow should not care for "trimming and arraying her body in order to make it beautiful" as in the past when she sought to please her husband. Such "trimming," said Vives, would make her seem to be "seeking a bargain." She should refuse at this time any offers of men for a second marriage, for "what body would not abhor her, that [soon] after her first husband's death, showeth herself to long for another . . . ?" Now she must go covered with a long black veil, accompanied always by her good, grave companion, and directing her steps to a quiet church where she will be seen by few people and where she will not be disturbed at prayer. If she feels the need of spiritual advice, she must avoid priest and friar and seek out a wise, aged man "past the lust of the world," and counting nothing dearer than truth and virtue. Such a man would possess no desires of the flesh and would covet no worldly wealth to be gained by flattery. Always the widow must avoid gatherings of men and people, remembering that no matter where she goes or what she does she must now guard her chastity even more carefully than when she was a wife.

To maintain this virtuous life, the widow must pray "more intensely and oftener, fast longer, and be much at mass and preaching, and read more effectually" as she devotes herself to spiritual things, says Vives. He believes the best marriage for a widow is Christ, whom she would do better to please than even her husband. This is especially true since now that she has her freedom, her real self, formerly inhibited by marriage, may seek to assert itself. Now as never before, therefore, she must walk most warily, even fearfully. Now the influence of her husband can no longer augment her virtues and minimize her weaknesses; now she alone is responsible for herself. Christ as her incorruptible champion would rejoice in an obedient, earnest widow seeking the spiritual life, and that is why she would do best of all to be married to her Savior. With such precepts in mind, Shakespeare has the Duchess of Gloucester in the play of *Richard II* ask John of Gaunt to whom she can complain about the death of her husband, whose murder has never been avenged. Quick as a flash the duke answers, "To God, the widow's champion and defence" (I:ii:43).

Up to this point in his advice, Vives has been concerned with young women. Now he turns to widows "well worn with age" and "past the pleasures of the body," and admonishes them to devote themselves to holiness. Before her husband's death such a woman should be unknown to the world, but after his death she should become famed for her virtue and acts of charity. He was more concerned about her health than were most writers of conduct books, saying he would have her labor more in mind than in body, praying more, thinking more of God, fasting less, and wearying herself less with long walks to church. Although she must give all possible aid to those needing her ministrations, she must also give her aged body proper care so that she may live long to give wise counsel and to set a good example. Later, Becon agreed to all this program, but with less consideration for old age. Instead, he emphasized the need of widows busying themselves by prayer, attending sermons, visiting the sick and needy, and even washing the feet of saints. It was such stress on the importance of good works that must be performed by widows which probably kept the mother of Essex making her morning pilgrimages to her poor neighbors till she was past ninety.

The pious, modest widow was presented as a model for all widows in one of the first books printed in England. In 1487, William Caxton translated and printed Le Grande's *Boke of Good Maners,* in which the author wrote much of widows, saying they must possess "great humility" and "great devotion" and spend their time in going on pilgrimages and performing "other good deeds." So much was the widow's humility or modesty stressed during the sixteenth century that widows sought to be known for this trait no matter what their station in life might be. Lady Russell, for example, in spite of all her independence and forthrightness of speech, was always careful of her modesty. When she besought her nephew, Sir Robert Cecil, to help the widowed Earl of Kent, she insisted that he keep her part in the matter secret because of her widowhood.

The virtuous widow, however, is like the palm tree that does not thrive by "the supplanting of her husband." Since she married "that she might have children," for their sake she marries no more. Like the purest gold used only for princes' medals, she receives but one man's impression. She cannot be sought by "large jointures or titles of honor," for she feels it would be a sin to change her name. She thinks she has "travel'd all the world in one man; the rest of her time therefore she directs to heaven." True, she is a bit superstitious, for she feels her husband's ghost will walk if she does not perform his will. "She gives much to pious uses, without any hope of merit by them," and as diamond dust polishes diamonds, so she is "wrought into works of charity with the dust or ashes of her husband." She lives out her long life only because she is "necessary for earth," and therefore "God calls her not to heaven till she be very aged." In the frailty of her last years she stands "like an ancient pyramid, which the less it grows to man's eye, the nearer it reaches to heaven." Her chastity in late life "is more grave and reverend" and serves as a mirror for young dames to dress themselves by. No calamity can touch her after the death of her husband; all else is but trifles. She buries her husband "in the worthiest monument that can be . . . in her own heart." Of all precious beings in this world, therefore, she is "most reverenced."

The later domestic books were seldom as kind to widows as Vives was; usually they tolerated them as a necessary evil. *A Discourse of marriage and wiving* (1615) by Alexander Niccholes, like Chapman's play, condemned all widows as a matter of principle. To marry a widow, he said, was to thank death if she was good and to upbraid death if she was evil. Marriage with a widow meant to take a woman half-worn, to become involved in trouble over her estate, to take one for whom marriage meant ease and lust more than affection and love, and to cause the dead husband to accuse by her tongue and be flattered by comparison with her next husband.

When the ballads took up the hue and cry against the widow, no doubt they gave many an Elizabethan a chuckle and left the widow to face the attack with whatever grace was at her command. The ballads were often written in two parts, and illustrated satirically a popular proverb or a catch phrase of the day. Such a ballad, based on the proverb, "Strike while the iron is hot," and sung to the popular tune of *Dulcina,* advised young men to marry widows "while there is store." Two of the stanzas indicate how the proverb was applied to marriage with wealthy widows:

> Wealthy widows now are plenty,
>   where you come in any place,
> For one man there's women twenty,
>   this time lasts for but a space:
>   She will be wrought,
>   though it be for naught,
> But wealth which their husbands first got,
>   Let Young-men poor
>   make haste therefore,
> 'Tis good to strike while the Iron's hot.
>
> Now is the wooing time or never,
>   Widows now will love Young-men,
> Death them from their mates did sever,
>   now they long to match again,
>   they will not stand
>   for House or Land,
> Although thou be'st not worth a groat,
>   set forth thyself,
>   thou shalt have Pelf,
> If thou wilt strike while the Iron's hot.

In the second part, sung to the same tune, the following stanzas show how the young man is urged to heed the command in the proverb:

> If a poor Young-man be matched
>   with a Widow stored with gold,
> And thereby be much enriched,
>   though he's young and she is old,
>   'Twill be no shame
>   unto his Name,
> If he have what his Friends have not,
>   but every Friend
>   will him commend
> For striking while the iron is hot.
>
> Young men all who hear this ditty,
>   in your memories keep it well,
> Chiefly you in London city,
>   where so many widows dwell,
>   the season now

415

doth well allow
Your practice, therefore lose it not,
fall to't apace,
while you have space,
And strike the iron while 'tis hot.

Because there was so much disparagement of the widow in plays, sermons, conduct books, character sketches, and ballads, one wonders how much of this literature reflects the actual attitude of the age and how much of it was merely designed to be entertaining or to propagandize moral beliefs. Just as we tend to judge our own age by pictures of society in sermons, the printed word, stage plays, and the films, possibly we preserve from the past similar sources of "information" largely because we attach importance to what they seem to tell us of life long ago. When private records bear out these sources, we feel still more confident that we know something about the lives of our ancestors. With due allowance for exaggeration in all these sources, we cannot help wondering why the Elizabethan widow was shown favor by society only as she won it by some Herculean effort from the unwilling regard of those about her. True, the age reflects the influence of Paul in regard to widows as well as the whole moral pattern his teaching set before readers of the Scriptures. But the feeling toward widows seemed to be an instinctive one more than an attitude implanted even by constant moral preachment. Gossip in official letters or in private letters about important personages, for example, shows general distrust of the widow. What, then, of the unprotected widow in private life? If she was so insignificant as to escape the morbidly speculative interest in her every word or speech, was she, nevertheless, aware of the unfriendly, suspicious, and abusive attitude she might arouse if she thoughtlessly deviated from the pattern of perfect decorum?

Or course, much of the upheaval in sixteenth-century thought and feeling about womanhood was caused by the Protestant tendency to discard everything connected with worship of the Virgin Mary. When, therefore, the old worship of virginity and the chivalric ideal of woman on a pedestal were so powerfully affected by decline in Mariolatry, widows naturally suffered far more than did maids or wives. The widow's supposed knowledge of married life's pleasures put men on the defensive in any relationship they might have with such women, and strangely enough, most men assumed that the knowledge they resisted was actually far greater than it was. Perhaps this was because society, though it no longer worshiped virginity itself, still held fast to the conventional attitude toward a maid's or a wife's chastity. In these women the preservation of chastity was more important than the preservation of life. The widow, not sheltered by this fetish, stood alone unless her family immured her against the dangers that threatened. Those without this family protection could survive only by the grace of their acquired experience or by sheer good fortune. If they escaped the dangers of slander, they presented a challenge to both their protected sisters and the protectors of their sisters. Their own sex disliked them for their supposed worldly wisdom, and the opposite sex distrusted them because of the supposed power in that worldly wisdom.

Widows, therefore, no matter how innocent their motives, were not given the benefit of the doubt in anything that invited suspicion regarding their conduct. The old war of the sexes, which from as far back as the memory of man had always revolved more or less about the widow, now made her more than ever the target at which to hurl the bitterest invectives against the "weaker" sex. Furthermore, when the people read in the Bible or in conduct books Paul's advice concerning the duties and position of the widow, they were strengthened in their antipathy to women who had lost husbands. And this strong admiration for Paul's Epistles was largely due to Colet's and More's interpretation of them, with the precepts they emphasized in regard to the government of the home by the man as head of the household.

True, long before Paul, the Old Testament had taken a definite stand against the widow. In the precepts for the priests as set forth in the book of Leviticus, the widow is classed with poor company when the law states: "A widow, or one divorced, or a profane woman, or a harlot, these he shall not take: but a virgin of his own people shall he take to wife" (21:14). Ezekiel's ordinances for priests find among women who had lost their husbands only the widows of priests worthy of marriage (44:22). With the Bible in their hands, the common people could have found many convenient quotations to support their contentions about the supposed unstable character of the widow. Perhaps they referred to Paul so frequently because he was more detailed than any other biblical authority in his instructions concerning the widow, but even more likely because his statements as to why widows should marry were so agreeable to the male sex and to women dominated by the male sex. In his words they found the quintessence of their prejudices, and pious widows as well as maids and wives quoted his words: "But I say to the unmarried and to widows, it is good if they abide even as I," which was quickly followed by: "But if they have not continency, let them marry: for it is better to marry than to burn" (I Cor. 7:8-9).

In an epistle to Timothy, Paul set forth specific rules of conduct for old and young widows, and as he gave the rules, he gave reasons for their stringency. Of course Elizabethans interpreted these rules with the idea of literal adaptation of them to their own time instead of considering them in relation to the time of Paul.

Now she that is a widow indeed, and desolate, trusteth in God, and continueth in supplications and prayers night and day. But she that liveth in pleasure is dead while she liveth. . . . Let not a widow be taken into the number [i.e., into the congregation] under three score years old, having been the wife of one man, well reported for good works; if she have brought up children, if she have lodged strangers, if she have washed the saints' feet, if she have relieved the afflicted, if she have diligently followed every good work. But the younger widows refuse: for when they have begun to wax wanton against Christ, they will marry; having damnation, because, they have cast off their first faith. And withal they learn to be idle, wandering about from house to house; and not only idle, but tattlers also and busybodies, speaking things which they ought not. I will therefore that the younger women marry, bear children, guide the house, give none occasion to speak reproachfully. For some are already turned aside after Satan. If any man or woman that believeth have widows, let them relieve them, and let not the church be charged; that it may relieve them that are widows indeed.

Here is shown the source for most of the rules for a widow's proper conduct as set up by Vives and his followers. And here also is shown the weak and foolish and even evil nature of the unstable widow as opposed to that of the saintly widow loaded down with years as well as with good works. It is significant that distrust overshadows the picture—that unless a widow be old indeed, she is to be married, or to be taken in charge by her own people.

But there are other factors involved in the distrust of widows. Enough has been said about the influence of women sovereigns during this age to make it unnecessary here to do more than refer to the effect of Elizabeth's reign upon women's status in the economic life. Never, perhaps, had woman been so close to her coveted position of economic freedom and equality with the male sex. But this economic freedom was enjoyed in general by widows only, for the rich maid was likely to have relatives that guarded her possessions carefully, and the dutiful wife gave into her husband's hands full control of her wealth when she exchanged vows with him at the marriage ceremony. The widow, especially when left with a fortune, was thereby possessed of a tangible independence, but only, of course, if she grasped the full significance of her freedom and had the strength of character to keep up the fight to maintain her freedom.

If a woman was sufficiently strong-minded, she might try to use her new freedom to her own advantage, even to the point of disregarding the wishes of her deceased husband not made binding by his will. Instead of being married off by parents or guardian to a suitor not to her liking, she might choose one more acceptable to her own tastes, even though she might endanger the interests thereby of her deceased husband's heir. Or she might refuse another marriage altogether. It took more than a strong will, however, for an Elizabethan widow to stand alone. Unless the widow could think for herself, she might be convinced that she was in an unenviable position, or if suspicion could be directed at her in such a manner as to leave her still marriageable but not too marriageable, her family's concern about her stubbornness might be dispelled, and a new alliance formed that would satisfy all those who had some interest in her holdings. The Pauline teaching could be a formidable weapon for those waging war against a redoubtable widow, but in the case of the pliant widow, it might be used persuasively, gently, to move her either way—to marry or not to marry.

A strong economic reason for the abusive attitude toward rich widows was the scarcity of men caused by wars and the inability of maids with small dowries to compete with the wealthy widow. As the whole inheritance system left most younger brothers with but two alternatives if they did not wish to go to war—a rich marriage or losing caste by entering trade—it was seldom indeed that such a youth failed to join the group of suitors about a rich widow. Maids in real life as well as in ballads might well complain that they had little chance in marriage when men were out to win their fortunes in the quickest and easiest way possible. Among middle-class widows in particular many a woman felt the barbs of both rejected suitors and disgruntled maids with small dowries. It took a great deal of hardihood on their part to be a target for arrows sharpened by wit or poisoned by ingeniously fabricated scandal. Women of such courage might well pause before they roused the ire of envious ones, weighing well in their minds the question of whether the prize was worth the price that must be paid for it.

When a widow did exercise her rights, she was so great a novelty that she was inevitably accused of taking undue advantage of every person within her power. The women themselves were as severe as the men in condemning her. Certainly no widow's abuse of her advantages could ever have justified the cruel slander which satirists directed against her in their plays, or which other writers accused her of in their bawdy stories and ballads. Yet among many Elizabethans, delight in the sensational and sensual made such literature popular and helped to strengthen the prejudice against the widow. The scorn or cynicism of these men and women who thoughtlessly criticized widows kept the prejudice alive in the undercurrent of thought. Most Elizabethan widows who married again (and perhaps again) asked that their bodies be buried by the side of the first husband, even though their married life with another husband may have been far happier. What was that called forth this earnest request? Convention was back of it, but what was back of convention? Perhaps it was the desire to unite in this way the founders of a broken household, to re-establish in the only way they knew how the order of things changed by death. Or perhaps the request was due to mere disillusionment—to a realization that life is hard no matter how one may look at it. The widow may have felt she would have done better to follow her first husband, not only to the grave, but into it. For the disease of melancholy had swept in with its brooding darkness, and the answers to life's riddle were no longer clear.

Unless a man's life was closely bound up in his home with few contacts outside—and that was unlikely, even in the rural districts and not at all in towns and cities—he might find the changes wrought by his wife's death not impossible to meet. Had he lived many years with his wife and had she become very dear to him, he might find it most difficult to face the stretch of loneliness before him, but in time he would gather his forces together and bury himself in his work. If he was still young, with most of his life before him, he would marry soon, especially if he had children to be mothered. A new wife to train to his way of life (if she could be so trained), some minor changes in housekeeping to please the new mistress, and then once more the home would swing into its daily round. For if he had used good judgment in his choice of a stepmother for his children or of a mother for his future children, and if his financial arrangements had been satisfactory and economic problems did not trouble him too much, then, in time home would be home again, with its duties and contentments, its responsibilities and cares, its pleasures and, perhaps, its rewards.

Among those who most feared the changes wrought by death was the young wife, who had cause to feel her soul caught and held in a grip of terror when her husband died. Her little world had indeed fallen about her. Children might console her, but they also weighed down her shoulders with the responsibility she felt for their future. When, after the interment of her husband's body she entered her home again, she might find the household of relatives and friends and servants willing and anxious to share her grief, but since human emotions are of necessity short, she knew she must soon take up her burden alone unless she could put herself trustingly into the hands of her nearest kin. When she could do this with full confidence, she might well expect changes in her life to follow swiftly. A new husband, a new household of servants to manage, possibly new children to mother and to adjust to her own children, new relatives to win by a careful graciousness on her part—all these she must be prepared for with what good will and Christian charity she could summon to her aid.

But if her love for her husband had been so great that the thought of another was repugnant? Then she would be told kindly or brutally of the future trials she would have to meet as a widow. If she was rich and intelligent, she would learn that men feared the power in a rich widow's hands, that some even envied that power, and that out of their envy grew hate. She would learn that men believed widows incapable of talking over financial matters impersonally, that one reason for their distrust was due to woman's tendency in a crisis to fall back upon her womanhood—even to trade upon it—and to refuse to meet an issue straight, like a man. If she was exceptionally intelligent, she would learn that man and woman could never meet as equals, but most widows would be only instinctively aware of this fact without knowing the cause for it. This was why so often they used the weapon of sex to fight their battles. But a wise widow did not, as a rule, try to fight her way against the current of opinion held by friends and family unless love for her husband gave her unusual strength of soul. That such a gentle creature as the wife of Essex could hold out two years against another marriage, urged by her family and frowned on by the wavering common people who had idolized her husband, speaks much for her devotion to him. In her place most widows would have followed the dictates of those who felt responsible for guiding them through the crisis of bereavement.

Now, if a widow thought of the perplexities she had faced as a young bride, how small and trifling were they likely to seem in comparison with those she must brace herself to meet presently. Changes wrought by death might try the souls of men, but they brought havoc into the lives of women born and reared to the belief that a wife's whole life was centered in the home. But life about her was geared to mutability. Stoically, if not heroically, she must bury the past, or seem to do so, and meet the present and its future with grace and ease and a smiling composure. To do this her whole life had been more or less conditioned: to meet each crisis as it came, sternly or gracefully. So she brings serenity to her features, she lifts her head and veils her eyes in an obedient smile, and once more she is ready to step into the new-old role demanded of her. She is ready to take the vows of love and obedience "till death do us part."

## 3. Widows In London

By W.K. Jordan

London was a vigorous and a forward-looking city not only in the immensity and the boldness of its charitability dispositions but likewise in the organization of the social system which created and disposed this wealth. It was accordingly a community in which the status of women was particularly advanced and in which their property rights enjoyed substantial respect. The merchant class tended to contract its marriages within a quite strictly defined fraternity of commerce, and the widow of a merchant, on whom the pressures for remarriage were very heavy indeed, normally married within the circle of her late husband's livery. In point of fact, in hundreds of wills of the period husbands all but prescribed the remarriage of their widows by careful property dispositions which made it at once difficult and unrewarding if the widow married outside the company of the late spouse. Within this tightly knit community, which respected property quite as much as sentiment, the position of the wife who had brought a marriage settlement to her husband's business or the widow who had been left with working control of a substantial trading firm was very secure indeed. In an age of heavy mortality among men in their early prime, substantial wealth found its way into the hands of women, much of which was disposable and most of which seems to have been managed with a prudence and success suggesting how fully women bred and married in this remarkable class had absorbed its *mores* and values. We shall likewise have occasion to comment on a considerable number of charities, often very large ones, which were evidently the creation of merchant couples, the survivors completing or augmenting the sometimes most elaborate design begun by the spouse who happened to die first. We are, then, dealing with a period in which the legal rights of women were improving slowly indeed, but in which the status of women and their actual rights were undergoing substantial amelioration in all urban communities, and particularly in London.

There were 1100 women donors in London, these numbering not quite 15 per cent (14.88 per cent) of all benefactors of the city. This proportion exceeds somewhat that noted in any other county, save, significantly, for Bristol. It should also be mentioned that the proportion of women donors in the successive decades of our whole period was relatively high in the last two decades of the fifteenth century and then remained quite stable until 1620, when a remarkably rapid gain set in which reached its climax in the period of the Civil Wars. In the years 1641-1650, somewhat more than 20 per cent of all charitable benefactors were women, reflecting in London, as in all other counties, the interesting tendency of women to make great social and economic gains during periods of profound political unsettlement. During these years men were away at war, were seeking to protect their estates by the prudent device of vesting at least part of their property in their wives, or were yielding to the new and radical social views regarding the status of women evoked by the reforming thought of a revolutionary era.

The women benefactors of London gave in all £172,635 5s to the various charitable causes, or an average of slightly more than £156 18s for each donor. The whole of their contribution to the charitable needs of their community represents 9.14 per cent of the vast total of London's charitable wealth, a proportion considerably less than that observed in the rural counties of Buckinghamshire and Yorkshire.

We have been able to gain reasonably full particulars regarding the estates of sixty-nine of these women donors who were members of the merchant class of the city, which would suggest that the wives and, of course, more particularly, the widows of the great merchants were in many cases very rich in their own right. Of this group, forty-two were widows and the remainder wives dying earlier than their spouses, the former group being in average terms slightly more than twice as rich as the latter. In all, these sixty-nine women left estates with a total worth of £85,611 2s, charities being included, which they disposed of their own right, or the very substantial average sum of £1240 15s for each member of the group. These estates ranged in total worth from the £50 12s of a goldsmith's widow in 1568 to £11,205 left in 1618 by a merchant's widow, certain lands of an unknown value not being included in this last huge estate. It is likewise interesting to note that eighteen of these women bequeathed lands held in their own names and subject to their own testamentary control, ranging from those who left London houses or small parcels of property, usually in Middlesex or Surrey, to six women testators who possessed at least one manor and including two who disposed real property worth upwards of £400 p.a. These women as a group left £8598 16s to various charitable uses, this amounting to 10.04 per cent of the whole of their disposable estates, which, though a generous proportion, suggests feminine prudence when compared with the extraordinary generosity of the merchant class as a whole, whether in London or elsewhere.

Taking in view the entire group of 1100 women donors, it should at once be remarked that the structure of their charitable interests differed rather sharply from that of the generality of benefactors of the city. They were particularly concerned with the plight of the poor, towards whose relief they disposed more than 41 per cent of all their gifts, as compared with just over 35 per cent for the city at large. Quite surprisingly, they were also relatively more interested in the various schemes for social rehabilitation than were their husbands, these uses commanding 14.81 per cent of all their benefactions as compared with somewhat more than 13 per cent for all donors. Their interest in the several forms of municipal improvement was scant (3.05 per cent), though not markedly less than that of the city as a whole. They were also less concerned with the improvement of the educational resources of the nation than were men, just under a fourth (24.78 per cent) of all their benefactions being devoted to this great need, while the proportion for the city at large came to 27.04 per cent. It may also be noted that their support of education was largely concentrated on the universities, to which women donors gave in all the substantial total of £25,053, this being 14.51 per cent of the whole, of which, however, the immense sum of £18,000 was the gift of one woman donor, the incomparable Margaret Beaufort. And, finally, London's women donors were more secular in their aspirations than were its benefactors as a whole, they having designated slightly less than 16 per cent for religious uses as compared with 19.50 per cent for the city at large. Moreover, it must be observed that nearly half the scanty total afforded by women donors for the various religious uses were represented in the large sum of £12,694 3s which with a quite persistent zeal formidably Puritan ladies vested in lectureships from 1583 onwards.

We might well comment on the difficulties involved in certainly determining the social status to which women donors of our period belonged, often even when they possessed considerable wealth. The decorous title of "widow" with which they so frequently clothed themselves in social anonymity is on occasion quite impossible to resolve unless there is additional and more informative evidence in the will, the inventory, or some other legal document. In London, rather surprisingly, we have had more difficulty in providing a social census of women donors than in the rural counties. Of the women in our donor group, a large total of 467, these being 42.45 per cent of the whole, simply cannot be positively identified as members of a particular social class, though incomplete evidence would suggest that at least twenty of this number were merchants' wives or widows and that well over half were of the shopkeeper or tradesman class, while the remainder (206) defy even the processes of conjecture. The largest single group of definitely identified women donors were merchants' wives, widows, or daughters, who numbered 260 in all, or slightly less than a fourth (23.64 per cent) of the whole. There were ninety-seven women certainly of the tradesman class, while forty-eight were of the somewhat amorphous group we have had to describe as "additional burghers", and twenty-seven were the wives or widows of professional men. There were twenty women donors drawn from the nobility, while there were nineteen who were widows of clergymen and four who described themselves as of yeoman status. Most surprisingly, there were in all eighty-nine women donors in London who were clearly of the upper gentry and sixty-one who were drawn from the lesser gentry, it evidently having been common for widows of men of these normally rural classes to take houses in London after the death of their husbands, one would suppose because of the greater comfort and security to be gained in the city.

The women of the merchant class constituted by far the largest, though, somewhat surprisingly, by no means the dominant, group of charitable donors of their sex. These 260 women gave in all £68,303 12s to various charitable uses, this amounting to slightly less than 40 per cent (39.60 per cent) of the whole given by women donors. Most of these benefactions were of course relatively modest, though there were considerable donors with charitable gifts amounting to £1000 or more. Widows and wives of the upper gentry, of whom there were eighty-nine, gave the impressively large total of £31,518 1s for charitable needs, five of these bequests amounting to £2000 or more, though it might well be noted that two of the largest charitable gifts made by members of this class disposed wealth only one generation removed from the trading halls and wharves of London. There were as well twenty members of the nobility who as a group gave the considerable total of £28,330 for various charitable uses, a large proportion of which was accounted for by the great benefactions of Margaret Beaufort, who left a charitable fortune quite large enough to excite the greed of her royal grandson. We have certainly identified ninety-seven of the women benefactors who were members of the tradesman class, their combined charities amounting to £11,065 3s. The large group of women of uncertain social class, numbering 467 in all, gave a total of £23,873, the average of their benefactions as well as more persuasive evidence making it probable that a considerable number of them were the widows of tradesmen. All the remaining social classes gave in total £9545 9s for charitable uses, women of the professional classes and of the lower gentry together accounting for well over half of the whole amount. But from whatever class they may have been drawn, the women donors of London were at once numerous and generous and shared with the urban society of which they were an increasingly significant part a mature understanding of the shape and direction of a new England just coming into being.

# 4. Widowhood In Eighteenth-Century Massachusetts

By Alexander Keyssar

In the society of colonial New England, where the family was the principal unit of social organization and economic production, the death of a married man was, potentially, an event of considerable consequence. In addition to the immediate emotional strains of grief and loss, such a death placed the surviving members of a household in a set of new relations to one another, to property, and to the law. The widow of the deceased, of course, lived at the center of the changes in family life. Although her precise situation depended upon factors such as age, wealth, and family size, a widow, no longer the dependent partner in a marriage, had to adjust to new needs and circumstances. The responsibility for her economic support was shifted to different shoulders. The total labor available to the household was reduced, and patterns of authority within the family were altered. As a woman, a widow possessed legal rights which, although expanding in the eighteenth century, were much more limiting than those possessed by men. Widowhood, clearly, was a possible source of social and economic problems for the members of a newly incomplete family.

According to traditional accounts of family life in the colonies, however, the problems actually generated by widowhood were very few. Potential dislocations were avoided by one simple and widespread phenomenon: widows remarried, rapidly and, if necessary, repeatedly. Widowhood was of short duration, and adult women spent little time living outside a complete household, needing independent rights as women. The traditional history offers a model of marriage in early New England that incorporates this view of widowhood. The colonists married early and married often. Many young women died due to childbirth and overwork; their husbands remarried as soon as they could locate a partner. A woman might become a widow by the premature death of her husband or, more likely, if, as a second or third wife, she were considerably younger than her spouse. According to this model, there would be many more widowers than widows. The Puritan emphasis on living in families, coupled with the preponderance of adult men in the society, created a high demand for all marriageable women.

Still another factor, historians have claimed, contributed to the rapid remarriage of widows. Puritan marriage was largely an economic affair, as any reader of Samuel Sewall's diary must know, and widows were at a premium because of their wealth, their "third" almost always being larger than any portion that a maiden daughter might inherit. Indeed, it seems that the judge's diary has been the principal source of information about marriage in eighteenth-century Massachusetts, and one can hardly find a discussion of widowhood which does not recount Sewall's financial haggling with the widows Denison and Winthrop. In the eighteenth century, when women were no longer numerically scarce in eastern New England, widows, due to their wealth, were presumably able to cope with the problems of their new status by rapidly exchanging it for another marriage.

In recent years, however, a few historians have begun to challenge the traditional version of family life and history in colonial New England. Using the methods of historical demography, their studies suggest that seventeenth- and eighteenth-century New Englanders married in their mid-twenties rather than in their teens, that individual households tended to be nuclear rather than extended, and that various aspects of family life were deeply influenced by the changing pressures of population upon the available land resources. Philip Greven, in his detailed study of Andover, Massachusetts, has found that marriages broken by an early death were the exception rather than the rule and that remarriage was not nearly as widespread a phenomenon as had been believed. If the conclusions which Greven and others have derived from local studies are applicable to larger areas of New England, then the outlines of the life and history of the Puritan family must be redrawn.

For instance, if widows did not commonly remarry, then the potential problems of a woman living outside a complete household may have been actual and sustained problems. Death, and thus widowhood, are natural crises, but the impact of and response to these crises vary with the demographic, social and economic environment. How did widows and their children survive? How did the family, the community, and the political authorities of the colony respond to the problems of widowhood? What was the legal status of widowhood? Beyond these questions lie others even more basic. Who, in fact, were the widows? How old were they? A widow of thirty poses different challenges to a family and a community than does a widow of sixty. What were the frequency and duration of widowhood?

These questions, as well as the different models of family history, may be tested by examining, in detail, one local situation and associating it with other, broader data in the economic and social history of early America. Woburn, Massachusetts, during the first half of the eighteenth century, was an agricultural community, typical of many eastern Massachusetts towns which had been settled in the seventeenth century. Its population can be studied through surviving vital records, genealogies, tax lists, and probate records. The problems of and responses to widowhood cast a revealing light upon the history of women and upon the interactions of the individual family with population patterns, economic pressures, and legal structures.

## II

The town of Woburn, in Middlesex County, is situated about twelve miles north and west of Boston. Incorporated in 1642, Woburn had 60 families and 74 church members within a decade. Growing steadily and dividing its common lands with some rapidity, the town, by the turn of the century, had 187 taxpayers (thus a total population of roughly 800) and had abandoned the open-field system in favor of more dispersed but easily workable farms. In the first decades of the eighteenth century, Woburn experienced the burst of population growth common to the area (by 1725, there were 305 taxpayers) and in 1730 spawned a second parish and the new township of Wilmington. Located inland, the economy of Woburn was little affected by the fishing and shipping trades along the coast: its inhabitants were farmers, and their daily activities were those of the great bulk of the colonial population.

By 1700, Woburn's third generation was beginning to marry, establish households, and confront the pressures of an increasing population upon a fixed amount of land. According to the vital records, a total of sixty marriages, each involving at least one resident of Woburn, took place between 1701 and 1710. The demographic data on the lives of these sixty couples challenge the traditional models of marriage and widowhood in eighteenth-century Massachusetts.

The average ages at marriage, for the men and women in the sample, agree closely with those found elsewhere, and affirm that images of youthful marriage in early Massachusetts have no statistical basis. The average age at first marriage was 26.5 years for men and 23.6 years for women. For marriages where either party had been married previously (a sample of only fourteen, twelve men and two women), the average ages at marriage were 42.6 for men and 28.9 for women. Men, of course, were almost always older than the women they married; as might be expected, the gap between the ages of husband and wife was greater in marriages that ended in widowhood than it was for marriages which terminated in the death of a wife.

It was possible to trace, with certainty, thirty-seven of the marriages until they were terminated by the death of one spouse. Twenty-two, or roughly 60 percent, ended with the death of the husband. Fifteen were broken by the wife's death. The average duration of these marriages was the remarkably high total of 23.9 years. For marriages which ended with the death of the husband, thus leaving a widow, the average duration was 25.8 years; in those marriages where the wife died first, the duration, on the average, was 20.6 years. Table I presents the distribution of the duration of these marriages.

## Table I

### DURATION OF MARRIAGES

| Length of Marriage | Number of Marriages Where Husband Died First | Number of Marriages Where Wife Died First | Total |
|---|---|---|---|
| 1–10 years | 2 | 3 | 5 |
| 11–20 years | 7 | 6 | 13 |
| 21–30 years | 5 | 2 | 7 |
| 31–40 years | 5 | 2 | 7 |
| 41–50 years | 2 | 1 | 3 |
| 51–  years | 1 | 1 | 2 |
| Total | 22 | 15 | 37 |

These figures are simply not compatible with the traditional account of colonial family life. There were more widows than widowers in the Woburn sample, a situation which would not arise if the primary threat to the endurance of a marriage were the death of a woman in childbirth. Only four women died before the age of forty, in illnesses associated with childbirth; indeed, as many men as women died in the first twenty years of marriage. More than half of the marriages lasted longer than twenty years; few were broken in less than ten. For better or worse, marriages in Woburn tended to be durable contracts.

In consequence, these Woburn residents tended to be advanced in years when their households were disrupted by death: overall, men had lived 60.1 and women 50.6 years before the death of either spouse. In marriages where the husband died first, thus leaving a widow, the men were, on the average, 63.0 years old at death and their wives were 55.4 years old when they became widows. Table II, for an unfortunately small sample, presents a profile of those Woburn women whose precise ages at widowhood were determinable.

## Table II

### AGE AT WIDOWHOOD

| Age | Number of Women |
|---|---|
| 25–40 years | 2 |
| 41–50 years | 5 |
| 51–60 years | 3 |
| 61–  years | 5 |
| Total | 15 |

SPOUSE LOSS

The Woburn data strongly suggest that relatively few young women, with young children, had to face the problems associated with the death of a husband. Most widows were mature in years: some, at least, of their children were adults. Widowhood, as a social issue, involved the accommodation of middle-aged or elderly women to a set of new roles in the family and society.

Remarriage, of course, was one possible accommodation: a widow who remarried would, at least, or be an appendage to a younger family. Yet the Woburn sample indicates that the remarriage of a widow was not a frequent event. Only four of the twenty-two widows are known to have remarried, and only two of the sixty women who married between 1701 and 1710 were widows at that time. Thus, only 10 percent of the women in the Woburn sample are known to have married more than once. Although there may be omissions from the vital records, if remarriage (especially rapid remarriage) were the *typical* pattern of behavior, one would expect to find a far greater number of recorded remarriages.

The data on remarriage of males lend support to these conclusions. Roughly between one-fourth and one-third of the men in the sample were known to have married more than once, and only one man more than twice. This proportion is only slightly lower than that found by Greven for third-generation Andover males and buttresses his conclusion that one marriage was the norm for early eighteenth-century colonists. Moreover, it is entirely consistent that men would remarry with greater frequency and ease in a society which contained more widows than widowers.

The extant tax lists of Woburn provide further information about the duration of widowhood and the remarriage of widows. These lists were examined for all of the even-numbered years between 1700 and 1750: the widows who appeared on the lists were then traced, through the vital records, until their remarriage or death. The data must be used with caution, but, nonetheless, this sample offers convincing evidence that widowhood, for most women, lasted for some years and was not terminated by remarriage.

The names of seventy-six widows appeared on the tax lists which were examined. Table III indicates the length of time during which these widows remained on the lists.

Table III

LENGTH OF TIME ON TAX LISTS

| Span of Years | Number of Widows |
|---|---|
| 1 | 24 |
| 2 | 12 |

429

| | |
|---|---|
| 4 | 4 |
| 6 | 6 |
| 8 | 5 |
| 10 | 7 |
| 12 | 6 |
| 14 | 1 |
| 16 | 5 |
| 18 | 2 |
| 20 | 1 |
| 22 | 2 |
| 24 | 1 |
| Total | 76 |

Widowhood, clearly, was a social situation which often endured for a significant period of time. Forty women were on the tax lists for at least four years; twenty-five women, or a third of the total sample, were on the lists for ten years or more. The fifty-two women whose names appeared on the lists more than once averaged 9.2 years on the rolls. And these figures understate the time that women spent as widows since the span of years on the tax lists must, on the average, be shorter than the duration of widowhood. For instance, the vital records reveal that even those women whose names are inscribed only once on the tax rolls spent an average of four years as widows. The exact dates of death were determinable for twenty-three women who died as widows: their deaths occurred, on the average, 12.3 years from the time of their first appearance on the tax lists as widows. (See Table IV.) Although no precise figure can be calculated, the average duration of widowhood in Woburn was, apparently, between seven and ten years; the median would be slightly lower. As Table IV indicates, some women, undoubtedly, would live large portions of their adult lives as widows.

### Table IV
#### Women Who Died As Widows

| Years after First Appearance on Tax Lists | Number of Widows |
|---|---|
| 0–5 | 7 |
| 6–10 | 5 |
| 11–15 | 2 |
| 16–20 | 4 |
| 21–25 | 1 |
| 26– | 4 |
| Total | 23 |

The evidence from the tax lists also indicates that remarriage was not the norm for the widows of Woburn. Only eight women from the sample are known to have remarried: all remarried within 5 years of their first appearance on the lists and after an average of 2.5 years. An additional seven women probably remarried, after a somewhat longer period of time. It is notable that many more women are known to have died as widows than are known to have remarried. Even with calculations to correct the bias in the sample, the total number of Woburn widows who remarried is extremely low.

In sum, the traditional view that colonial widows remarried easily and rapidly does not conform with any of the data. In Woburn, during the first half of the eighteenth century, probably not more than a fourth of the women whose husbands died found new spouses. Moreover, after the first few years of widowhood had passed, their chances of remarrying were extremely slim. This was certainly due, in part, to the advanced age at which women generally became widows. Once widowed, a woman was far more likely to die a widow than to enter into a second marriage.

The residents of Woburn, during this period, married relatively late, married once, and married for a long time. However great the social and economic pressures to live in complete households, many women, in Woburn, would expect to live some part of their mature lives without a husband. The odds were that a Sarah Richardson, married in Woburn in the early eighteenth century, would outlive her husband and would pass some years in a different economic and social situation. The community would re-dub her "widow Richardson," and she, her family, and the community would face a new complex of problems.

### III

A State of Widowhood is a state of Affliction: and very singularly so, if the widow is bereaved of the Main Support that after the Death of her Husband was left unto her . . . when her Widowhood was yet more darkened by the Death of her Only Son who was now doubtless the Main Support of her Family. And how much are her Sorrows Embittered, by New Anxieties and Encumbrances coming upon her; Debts to be paid, and Mouths to be fed.

—Cotton Mather, 1728

The central problem of widowhood was the need for new sources of economic support for the widow and any young children living in the household. The death of a husband signified the loss of the labor and guidance of the legally recognized head of the household. If he had been a merchant, shopkeeper, or even perhaps an artisan, his widow might possibly earn a living by continuing the family business. In towns like Woburn, however, the chances were great that the family occupation was

431

farming and that a widow alone or a widow with small children would find it impossible or, at best, very difficult to continue operating the farm. The data on age at widowhood, however, indicate that most widows did have adult children, and, since the family was the basic institution of social welfare, these children were the most likely bearers of the responsibility of providing for the widow. Yet the support of widows was not entirely a private matter. Widowhood was a problem that all families had to anticipate and many had to confront: the society had guidelines and rules for the care of widows. The laws pertaining to widowhood reveal some of the ways in which the government of the colony superintended the functioning of the family. Coupled with the probate records, they shed light on a variety of issues relating to widowhood, including the widespread failure of widows to remarry.

By the early eighteenth century the basic legal provisions for the care of widows in Massachusetts were firmly established. A detailed body of law referring to widowhood was legislated in 1647, and, after fifty years of minor vicissitudes, the principles of English common law dower were clearly expressed in colonial and provincial legislation. Laws governing the distribution of the estates of intestates determined the methods of widow support in the large number of cases where a man died without leaving a will; they also served as guidelines for more private arrangements.

In brief, Massachusetts law provided that the widow of an intestate would receive one-third of her husband's personal property forever and one-third of his real property, lands and houses, as a life estate or dower. If the real estate could not be divided, the widow would be endowed "in a special and certain manner, as of a third part of the rents, issues, or profits" of the estate. Although a widow could dispose, as she wished, of the personal property that she inherited, no such freedom attached to her rights in the lands and houses. The widow had full rights to the use, improvement, and profits of the real property, but she could not sell it, and, at her death, it reverted to the heirs of the estate. A widow, under common law, could not be an heir: unlike certain local English customs such as freebench, the common law gave to a widow no right of succession. The widow's thirds in real property were a kind of trust fund, designed to give her support while protecting the estate and the line of succession.

A number of details of the law protected the widow from any encroachment upon her property rights. Dower rights attached upon marriage and could not be waived without her consent: to transfer clear title to land required the signatures of both parties in a marriage. Furthermore, dower lands (but not personal property) were free from the claims of creditors. In the distribution of insolvent estates, the widow's portion was safeguarded: after her death, it would be distributed among her husband's creditors. A later act, in 1710, ordered that "bedding, utensils, and implements of household" which a widow found "necessary for the upholding of life" were also not subject to creditors' claims: indeed, the act also instructed judges of probate to distribute such items to widows if a will existed and had made no mention of them. Even the widow of a felon had her dower right reserved when her husband's crime resulted in the forfeiture of his estate. Finally, the widow's interests were safeguarded by elaborate procedures for the administration of the estates of intestates, including the right to bring suit if her portion were not speedily assigned.

Although these requirements, of course, did not technically apply to cases in which the husband had left a will, they were regarded as minimal standards for the support of widows. Early in the colony's history, the authorities of Massachusetts assumed the responsibility of insuring that families provide adequately for widows regardless of the precise stipulations contained in wills. The Body of Liberties of 1641 had two clauses entitled "Liberties of Women." One of them, Liberty 79, specified that "if any man at his death shall not leave his wife a competent portion of his estate, upon just complaint made to the Generall Court she shall be relieved." Although legislation in later periods made no specific reference to supplementing the portions that widows received from wills, it was apparently an accepted practice that a widow could always choose her common law dower in place of her legacy. Moreover, there is evidence that probate courts also exercised considerable discretion in determining the percentage of the estate allotted to widows. The seventeenth-century probate records from Essex County indicate that the size of the estate determined the proportion that a widow received: a widow from a poor household was likely to receive more than the thirds assigned to her by law. Protecting the "best interests of the widow" meant that the courts could not be bound by the "rigid precedents" of English law. The governmental authorities, by statute or by court action, could guarantee the use of family property for the satisfactory support of widows.

The laws of Massachusetts, thus, reflected a desire to protect both widows and landed estates. Implicitly, they recognized a social obligation to provide for widows, but, perhaps to limit the responsibility of the larger community, they sought to compel the family to fulfill that obligation. Closely following the English common law, the legal structure aimed at the sustenance, rather than the economic freedom, of widows. Women whose husbands had died could use but not dispose of the primary form of property and source of income that existed in Massachusetts. What this meant in practice for women in towns like Woburn is revealed by the probate records of Middlesex County.

The wills and administrations of the men in the Woburn marriage sample and some of their neighbors indicate that the problems of widow support were complex and were not entirely resolved by the statutory supervision of the family. Approximately two-thirds of the men whose probate records were examined left widows: their wills or administrations contain provisions for widow support. Although there were potentially important differences between the terms of wills and the terms of administrations, there were not discernible social distinctions separating the men who wrote wills from those who died intestate. Both forms of legal conveyance are rich in detail; indeed, the very fact that they are so detailed suggests some of the problems generated by the need for widow support in many colonial families.

The administrations of estates were fairly uniform in their provisions for widows: distributing the property, in general, among a widow and her children, the administrators (often the widow and the eldest son) closely followed the legal requirements. The widow received one-third of the lands and buildings for her natural life and a comparable portion of the personal property for ever. The most striking feature of the administrations is the detail of the real property provisions, the scrupulous reservation of the most minute rights. The administration of Joshua Sawyer, who died in Woburn in 1738, is typical. His widow was to receive, as her dower,

> the northwardly end of the new house with the whole of the cellar under the south end of said new house and the small chamber over the entry way with liberty of using the fore door and the entry way and the stairs up into the chambers and garrots, and of going out at the back door and liberty of using both the two wells belonging to said house.

Clearly the legal division of rights to different parts of a single farm and farmhouse created, at least in theory, awkward problems of domestic travel. Joseph Hartwell's administration divided his entire large estate between his widow and his only son: their mutual rights of passage, outside the house, were spelled out in detail.

> The said widow is to have liberty to pass and repass from the road through the two thirds to her part of the barn yard for driving carts and creatures as there shall be occasion. The barn floor is to be for the use of each. Joseph is to have liberty of passing and repassing from the road through the thirds to his part of the house the usual way for driving carts and creatures and other ways as there shall be occasion.

According to the administrations, a widow usually lived with at least one of her children who was the legal owner of part of the family real estate. They shared the same dwelling house, but a specific part of the house was formally reserved for the widow's use. Precise stipulations guaranteed the widow's rights against unfair treatment by one of her own children.

In wills, Woburn men and their neighbors had more latitude in the distribution of their property. They could freely select the size and duration of grants, and they could bind their heirs to the fulfillment of specific obligations. The wills too display a remarkable quantity of detail; the widow's portion of the real and personal property was carefully described and safeguarded. Freed from the restraints of the common law, a man, in a will, could express his own desires and address directly the concrete problems of widowhood in eighteenth-century Massachusetts.

Often, wills granted to widows portions of the real and personal property larger than what they would have received under the rules for intestacy. Several poor men, like John Richardson, Jr., who died in 1745, left to their wives "the use and improvement" of their entire estates even though they had children. Others, like Matthew Johnson, in 1740, who apparently had no living sons, left all of the personal property and the "use, profit, and improvement" of all real property to their widows. In this way, a will could prevent the immediate distribution of parts of the estate to more distant heirs. A widow might also receive control of an entire estate if her children were all minors. Thus, James Converse, Jr., left the use of his real property to his widow until his son, Josiah, reached the age of twenty-one; she would then enjoy one-half of the housing and lands. The precise configurations vary according to the size of the families and the estates, but many of the men in Woburn and surrounding areas clearly felt that a third of their real property would not satisfactorily support their widows. The widow's share was increased to prevent hardship or, in some cases, simply to provide more comfort.

Yet freedom from the laws governing intestacy also signified that a man could, in a will, regulate the length of time during which his widow would retain property rights. Moveable or personal property (generally of little value) was almost always granted "for ever," but a widow's portion of the real property, set out in a will, was not necessarily an estate for life. The writer of a will could lengthen or shorten that term, and this latitude did not generally redound to the widow's benefit. Only one man in the entire sample gave any significant amount of real property to his wife "for ever": in a document highlighted by what may be a revealing Freudian slip, Joseph Stevens, in 1721, left all of his lands (valued at £1000) "to dispose of and do with at her pleasure" to his "dearly beloved wife," Sarah. On the other hand, a large number of wills reduced the widow's rights in real property to the "term of her widowhood." James Converse, for instance (the father of the James Converse, Jr., mentioned above), left his wife one-half of his real estate only as long as she remained his widow. Daniel Reed, in lieu of a dower, gave to his wife all of his personal property forever and all of his real estate "during her continuing my widow." Apparently, men often concluded that a widow, if remarried, would have less need of real property than would the heirs to the estate. Whatever the motive behind limiting the duration of a grant, such restrictions could seriously influence the future prospects of a widow.

The wills also indicate that, in many cases, the legal right to the use of lands was not considered a sufficient source of support for widows. In part, no doubt, because a widow alone could not work a farm, men often demanded that their heirs and executors furnish the widow with annual supplies. These provisions, too, are remarkable for their detail; the will of John Lynde, who died in 1723, is representative.

> And further I give to my said wife two cows to be maintained by my executors summer and winter as they do their own and to hasard the cows and said cows to be good cows. And my executors shall provide her a horse suitable for her to ride on during her widowhood. And further I give to my said wife yearly and every year eight bushels of indian meal, two bushels of rye meal, three bushels of malt and eighty pound of beef and fifty pound of pork. And all these before mentioned to be brought to her house. And further I give to my wife five pounds of money to be paid the first year after my decease and five pounds the second year after my decease and after that three pounds a year yearly and every year of her life. And also ten cord of wood to be laid at her door every year for her own firing. . . . And further if my said wife Judith shall die my widow, she shall be decently buried by my executors out of my estate.

Certain patterns of economic support for widows emerge from these documents. A widow with adult children would generally be allotted a specific "end" or room of the dwelling house, water and barn rights, the use of certain lands and orchards, a cow or two to be kept by the son ("as well as he keeps his own cow, or as a cow ought to be kept," one will specified), and a variety of yearly provisions. The latter generally included significant quantities of meat, grains, and firewood and were to be supplied by the sons of the widow. The yearly portions were to be continued throughout the widow's natural life or widowhood. Moreover, a son could not afford to take his annual obligations lightly. Those sons responsible for the yearly supplies were, almost invariably, the executors of their fathers' estates. As such, they took out a bond to the judge of probate—a bond which generally was worth as much as the entire estate and which they would forfeit if they failed to carry out fully the terms of a will. John Lynde, Jr., stood to lose one thousand pounds if his mother did not receive her provisions.

Although the scrupulous legal regulation of intra-family affairs may seem surprising, the detailed clauses of the wills and administrations were not simply repetitions of legal formulae. Their appearance in agreements less burdened by precedents of language and law affirms that these details were a response to the actual needs of the colonists. For instance, a marriage contract between a widow and her new husband, late in the seventeenth century, specifically guaranteed to the woman, in case she should be

436

widowed again, "the new end of the dwelling house" and yearly supplies. And the agreement of the heirs of John Richardson of Woburn, in 1715, is extremely revealing. Eschewing the formality of an administration, the widow and her adult children made a private settlement of the estate. Timothy Richardson, the eldest son, was to inherit the largest portion of the homestead.

> Also he the said Timothy Richardson . . . is to provide and find for his honored mother, Susanna Richardson, widow of said deceased, in consideration of her right of dowry in the said estate, one good and convenient fire room in the said deceased's dwelling house and all other necessaries and conveniences . . . And further the said Timothy Richardson . . . is to provide for and keep two cows for his said mother both summer and winter free from charge to her from year to year, and to find and provide for her yearly, good convenient and sufficient firing wood. Also to allow and pay or cause to be well and truly paid five pounds money yearly. All which is to be paid, done and performed to and for her the said Susanna Richardson, widow, yearly and each year during the term of her widowhood.

A crucial clause was reserved until the end of the document.

> And the said Timothy Richardson to give, sign, and pass unto his mother, the widow of the said deceased, good and sufficient security for the faithful performance of his agreement and engagement to her during her widowhood.

In a private agreement, too, the "honored" mother and widow could not rely on familial bonds and affections: she demanded a security deposit to guarantee that she would not be forsaken in her widowhood.

These arrangements for the economic support of widows both reveal and explain some of the problems of widowhood in towns like Woburn. As noted earlier, for example, the infrequent incidence of widow remarriage cannot be attributed entirely to the demographic environment: if, as has been claimed, the wealth possessed by widows made them particularly attractive marriage partners, the disadvantages created by the surplus of adult women could have been at least partially overcome. But the probate records indicate that these women, quite simply, did not possess forms of property which would be an incentive to a potential new spouse. The bulk of a widow's wealth lay in land which she could not sell, and the chances of renting the land very profitably were extremely slim. Moreover, the westerly end of a small dwelling house, shared with another generation, would not necessarily be an alluring living arrangement for a new husband. On the other hand, if a widow moved to the homestead of her spouse and he did not happen to be a nearby neighbor, her land would not be accessible to be worked, and thus given the labor-scarce conditions of the economy, little or no income could be drawn from it. These facts, coupled with the restriction of many widows' estates to the terms of their widowhood, render untenable the theory that widows were in high demand for remarriage because of their wealth. Widow Denison may have held property that generated a considerable income, but most widows, in Woburn and similar towns, did not. In fact, the Woburn tax lists reveal only a slight correlation between wealth and remarriage. It is true that the poorest widows did not remarry, and the women who did remarry generally had average or better than average holdings, for a widow. Nonetheless, some of the widows with the largest estates lived for many years without remarrying. The limitations on a widow's property rights combined with the demographic environment to make the remarriage of an early eighteenth-century widow an unlikely event.

The juncture of the law with the peculiarities of the colonial economy enforced the dependence of widows on their children. Widows, in general, inherited little property which could be converted to their immediate support. Not only was a widow's estate usually far smaller than that of the average taxpayer, but most of what widows received, land and housing, was capital in an economy where such capital was abundant and where labor was scarce. A widow could not work a farm alone, and finding tenants or farm workers was likely to be difficult and expensive. When land could readily be possessed in western areas of the state, men were unlikely to rent land or hire themselves out as laborers in Middlesex County. Widows, thus, possessed property which, without family labor, was difficult to utilize and which, because of legal restraints, they could not sell. Whatever the effects of dower law in England, where land was scarce and labor relatively abundant and cheap, widows in Massachusetts could not simply sit back and reap a steady, even if small, income from their property. The provisions for yearly supplies in the wills were one result and resolution of this problem.

The economic dependence of widows, in turn, had significant effects on the lives of their children. The sharing of a house and the annual delivery of provisions resolved certain problems and generated others. In poorer families, no doubt, the care of a widow by a young household may have been an economic burden. More widespread, however, were the limits imposed on the mobility of the younger generation by the specifications for widow support. A widow possessed legal rights which could inhibit her children from selling the family estate and moving to a new area. In eastern Massachusetts, at a time when individual estates were growing smaller and the rate of mobility was high, these rights could have been of great consequence to many families.

Indeed, the presence of real or potential conflict between the dependence of a widow and the wishes of her children may explain some of the problematic features of the probate records. Why were the details of living arrangements for a family that had spent years together spelled out so precisely? Why could filial love or loyalty not be relied on as sufficient security for a widowed mother? Why was it not just assumed that a widow would be granted a room in the dwelling house? It appears that these details of the wills and administrations were explicitly designed to give the widow some control over the future actions and movements of her children. Unless a prospective purchaser were willing to live in a house whose "westerly end" was occupied by a widow (who also had claims to part of the lands and the barn), a son could not sell the family homestead against the wishes of his mother. Similarly, the legal obligation to deliver yearly supplies was an obstacle to emigration. Familial and generational tension were reflected in the probate records: crucial clauses suggest the presence of anxieties about old age, about the fragmentation of the family due to mobility, and about the prospect of a newly dependent relationship between a mother and her children. Faced with these fears, the older generation sought security, in part, by imposing restraints upon the younger.

Most widows, then, did have adult children who would see that they did not become destitute. Such support was forthcoming, as one would expect, without resort to legal action. Neither the probate records nor the records of the Inferior Court of Pleas offer much evidence of disputes about dower or other rights of widows. A widow, advanced in years and with a grown child, would expect to be cared for within the family; in case of difficulty or perhaps just to allay anxiety, she possessed a number of legal ways to fulfill that expectation. Relatively poor, dependent, and lacking in other options, she would at least be assured of a minimum level of sustenance until her death.

## IV

Yet not all widows had adult children who were able to support them. Although the evidence indicates that most widows did not face such a predicament, many women in the eighteenth century must have had to feed, clothe, and shelter themselves and perhaps their young children without the assistance of other adult members of the family. These widows probably possessed some real property, but they would find it difficult to convert that property into an annual income. Possibly it was these women, seeking employment in Boston, who provided that city with its disproportionate number of widows. Regardless, widows without families to support them became the concern of the larger community: the town records of Woburn and the private resolves of the General Court of Massachusetts offer some indication of the society's response to widows who could not fend for themselves.

The local community could subsidize the income of a widow in several different ways. The widows of Woburn's ministers, for instance, continued to receive their husbands' salaries during the first period of their widowhood. These grants, however, were in recognition of special, rather than typical, relationships between towns and widows. Others who possessed the requisite skills, like the widow Walker, could earn a small living by keeping school for the "lesser children." In addition, some widows could put their dwelling houses to use by taking in boarders—often at the town's request and expense. In 1745, for instance, the town's debts included four payments to widows "for keeping" a presumably poor or helpless person. The town, thus, could promote the welfare of a widow by engaging her to perform social welfare functions which the town required.

More direct methods could also be utilized. Tax exemptions recognized that widows might well possess property but have very little income. The town records of 1705 and 1749, for example, describe the town voting to pay a widow's rates out of the public treasury because she herself was unable to do so. In cases of extreme need, the town would even assume the burden of supporting an indigent widow.

> The Selectmen being informed that the widow Hensher was in want, they ordered the Constable Holding to pay her five shillings for a present supply, out of the town rate committed to him to collect.
>
> (September 9, 1700)

> There was a contribution made for the widow Hensher: there was then gathered 3 = 5 = 3 and the Selectmen provided a cow for her supply with milk, and the cow cost 59 shillings and the cow remains the town's, only the said widow hath the use of the cow free; and the Selectmen laid out 7$^s$ 6$^d$ for cloth to make her dumb child a coat, and 3$^s$ 6$^d$ for a pair of shoes; and the remainder of the said contribution, being 6$^s$ 3$^d$ it was delivered to the said widow by the Selectmen.
>
> (October 29, 1700)

Although such relief was clearly administered on an *ad hoc* basis and its frequency and extent cannot be determined, these examples do indicate that local communities considered widows without grown children as legitimate recipients of town aid.

The General Court of Massachusetts also became involved in the problem of widow support. In addition to general laws granting tax exemptions to the widows of ministers and the payment of wages due to the widows of deceased soldiers, the General Court passed a large number of private resolves designed to remedy the plights of individual widows. Many of these resolves concerned the payment of relief or expenses to the widows of soldiers, and they expressed the province's somewhat niggardly willingness to relieve out of public funds the widows of men who died in public service.

In 1708-1709, 1712-1713, and again in the 1720s, the General Court received bursts of requests for small sums of money to be paid to the widows of soldiers and mariners who were killed in action. Most of the widows argued that they ought to receive money not simply because they were needy but because wages were due to their husbands, guns and clothing were lost in military operations, funeral and sickness expenses had to be met, or their husbands had spent considerable amounts to raise other volunteers. In a few cases, the widow of a slain soldier would simply plead her "poor and distress'd condition." Such requests, for relatively small sums at least, were invariably granted although often the money was paid not directly to the widow but rather to a third party (such as the selectmen of her town) to be expended for her benefit. The General Court thus made clear that provincial funds were not to be utilized for widow support without specific and rather extreme cause. These authorities, however, seem to have been less miserly when dealing with people of their own social class: in 1732, they granted one thousand acres of land to the widow and children of the late "Honorable William Tailer, Esq. as a testimony of gratitude of the court for his services to the country."

The records of the General Court also contain numerous private resolves which aimed to alleviate a central economic problem of eighteenth-century widowhood. These were acts enabling widowed women to sell real property in order to support themselves. (A few additional resolves extended the right to sell dower lands to a son or son-in-law so that he could pay for widow support.) Dozens of these petitions, involving exceptions to dower law or comparable stipulations in wills, were granted by the General Court in the first half of the eighteenth century; they suggest the ways in which widows' rights had to be expanded in order to meet the requirements of the provincial economy.

The petitions from the widows follow one distinct pattern: the widow requested the right to sell land or housing because "the income or profit thereof" was "of very little value." One of the petitioners explained quite succinctly the economic reasoning behind the desire to sell land for cash. Abiel Metcalf, in 1725, argued that "Most of the personal estate is gone to pay the deceased's debts, and the real estate (though of considerable value if sold) will not support" by its rent the widow and her seven children. Many cases simply pleaded that the land had to be sold for the "necessary relief and subsistence" of a widow. These women possessed property, but the property did not yield a sufficient income, and only legal action could permit a widow to sell the estate.

This problem could affect the widows of Boston as well as those on farms in outlying districts: without the aid of adult children, elderly women often could not support themselves. The case of Katherine Nanny "alias Naylour" presented one extreme instance of need:

Setting forth that she has been blind for near fifteen Years past and labours under the Infirmities of Old Age, and has been at great Expense for her necessary Support, and must now perish without some better Relief than is provided for her by her said Husband's Will who thereby gave her the Rents and Income of his Real Estate only during her Life, which consists of an old Dwelling House in Ann Street in Boston, now become ruinous and run to despair, the Charge of Repairing the same amounts to near as much as the yearly Profits. Her said Husband's Children being all dead without Leaving any known Relations in these Parts Praying she may be allowed to Make Sale of the said House and Land or to mortgage the same for a certain Term of Years to provide for her Support and Comfort.

In this case, increased capital rather than labor could make the property profitable, and the court ordered the petitioner's nephew, who was willing to do so, to take possession of the estate, improve it, and use part of the income to support his widow aunt. The General Court was willing to suspend the law to enable people to help themselves.

The case of Abiel Metcalf also suggests that the expanding, diversifying economy of eastern Massachusetts offered new means of widow support. The court ordered widow Metcalf to sell her land and invest whatever she received: a third of the interest or profits could be used for her support, and the remaining two-thirds would go towards the maintenance and education of her children. There are numerous similar examples. Land values in the region increased substantially throughout the eighteenth century: in settled areas, a considerable cash price could be obtained for landed estates. Equally important was the rise of investment opportunities. A widow could become self-supporting by selling her real property and investing her capital in some enterprise which did not require her own intensive labor.

Although the family had primary responsibility for the care of widows and the law sought to insure that families fulfilled that responsibility, indigent widows were not simply left to "perish." The town was the secondary agency of social welfare and was expected to intervene when family support was not available. In rare cases, when a destitute widow did not belong to "any town from whom she can have support," the General Court paid for her relief. But outright poverty was not the only issue. Many widows possessed property but still found it difficult to live. The crucial economic need of an eighteenth-century widow was the possession of a form of property that could generate an adequate annual income without a great deal of labor. Thus, widows without adult children often confronted an economic problem caused by the bad fit between dower law and traditions and the labor-scarce conditions of the Massachusetts economy. The provincial authorities recognized that widows' lack of freedom to dispose of their real property could only increase the number of people who required public relief. The private resolves of the General Court implicitly acknowledge that stringent adherence to the law could undercut the ability of individuals to support themselves. Exceptions to the law could be made, and new economic opportunities rendered such exceptions quite promising. The private resolves, though affecting few people directly, were signals of the breakdown of an old system and harbingers of future changes in the modes of widow support.

Population patterns, economic conditions, laws, and customs combine to determine the effects of the death of a married man upon family and society. The problems of widowhood, thus, are variable, and, contrary to the evidence of some literary sources, the eighteenth-century American family did not circumvent these problems by the widespread and rapid remarriage of widows. During the first half of the eighteenth century, in eastern Massachusetts, the longevity, structure, and mobility of the population produced a large number of widows, relatively advanced in age, whose chances for remarriage were notably slim. The economic support of widowed women, consequently, was a problem frequently confronted by colonial families. The limitations on widow's property rights and the particular conditions of the Massachusetts economy restricted the ability of widows to be self-supporting and made them more dependent upon aid from their children or, less commonly, from the town in which they lived. The province itself supervised and enforced the fulfillment of the individual family's responsibility to care for widows.

The particular form of widowhood in Massachusetts had an impact on various aspects of eighteenth-century life. What continuity there was in the population of eastern Massachusetts, for instance, may well have been affected by the need to provide for widows. Even the eldest sons of many third- and fourth-generation families did not inherit very large or productive estates. These sons, generally, were in their late twenties, at least, when their fathers died. Not yet burdened by a large number of young children, they would have been free to move elsewhere—except for the responsibility of supporting a widowed mother who could prevent any sale of the homestead. Ten or fifteen years later, they would be less likely to migrate. To be sure, there were many reasons for remaining in a town like Woburn, but the problems of widowhood were certainly an obstacle to geographic mobility. In this way, widowhood was not only influenced by but also could have influenced the population patterns of provincial Massachusetts.

The structure of families, too, was affected by widowhood, in particular by the existence of a significant number of widows who did not remarry. In eighteenth-century Woburn, most families, most of the time, were completely nuclear: households consisted of one couple and their children. But categories of family structure should incorporate the different stages of development through which all families pass. Widows in eastern Massachusetts often lived in the households of their children, and consequently many families, perhaps a majority, lived for some period of time with three generations under the same roof. The frequency and duration of these somewhat "extended" households were, no doubt, increased by the prevailing pattern of widowhood. Family structure is not static, and widowhood is one of the determinants of its dynamic cycles.

Finally, the problems faced by widows reveal certain dimensions of the role and status of women in early Massachusetts: the solutions to these problems suggest ways in which widowhood affected the expansion of women's rights in the eighteenth century. Women were expected to marry, but women whose husbands had died occupied a legitimate station in society. Whether married or not, however, women were subjected to restrictions that men would have found unacceptable. A widow did not acquire the property rights of the male head of the household: she was to be cared for, protected, and dependent. According to the terms of most wills and administrations, a widow's needs were to be met and conveniences provided, but there was little room for a widow to choose the kind of life she wanted to lead after her husband's death. The society sought to guarantee the sustenance of widows, but the statutes were also designed to protect landed estates, and this aim was not compatible with the economic independence of widows. An adult woman, whose husband had died, was constrained as well as sheltered.

Still, the rights of women, both married and single, were being enlarged in the eighteenth century, more rapidly in America than in England. In particular, women acquired greater legal rights to possess property and to make contracts. This expansion of proprietary and contractual rights has been attributed both to the importance of women as controllers of land and to the increasing significance of different types of property. It appears, however, that the precise problems of widowhood in the colonies also contributed to this growth of women's rights. The frequency and duration of widowhood clearly augmented the number of women who had some control over real property. Moreover, Massachusetts society contained a significant percentage of adult women, without husbands, who lacked full proprietary and contractual rights to the property upon which they depended for a living. Since the traditional methods of satisfying a widow's economic needs—remarriage and dower lands—did not successfully apply to local conditions, widows, at times, had to seek new avenues of economic support. For some, this demanded taking over and running a husband's business. For others, it meant eliminating restrictions on their property rights. Women's rights in Massachusetts, thus, were expanded at a time when a large number of widowed women stood in need of greater rights. The private resolves of the General Court, admitting exceptions to dower law, are a concrete indication that the widespread problems of widowhood created pressures towards the increased independence and equality of women.

Nonetheless, the family remained the primary agency of social welfare in Massachusetts, and the history of activities such as care for the aged or the widowed is one dimension of the history of the family. Shifts in the population, the economy, and the law converged upon the individual family: the particular, detailed problems of eighteenth-century widowhood affected the daily and yearly living patterns of innumerable households. The ability or inability of the family to respond effectively to these problems influenced, in turn, the social development of the colony. As the fundamental unit of economic and social organization, the family was a crucial participant in and indicator of the changes in America in the eighteenth century.

# 5. Parental Deprivation In The Past

By Peter Laslett

Parental deprivation is a term typical of the social observation which goes forward in our day, perception of a body of facts diffused through a strong sympathy for the position of those to whom the facts relate. Illegitimte children are likely to be parentally deprived, because they are brought into the world without proper fathers: they arouse our interest because of that circumstance, for they appear as the helpless victims of a powerful social and familial convention. ...[T]he numbers of children born outside wedlock were sometimes quite large in the past, and the numbers so conceived considerably larger. In our day the proportion of children alive who were registered as illegitimate at birth must be substantial. But bastard children cannot be anything like a majority of the parentally deprived, now or at any time in history. Those who suffer the actual loss of the father—or of either parent—have always far outnumbered those who never had recognized fathers at all.

In spite of the fact that so many conceptions and births took place outside marriage in the past, few, or very few, of the children alive at any time were illegitimate. This is because bastards died so quickly and because some of them ceased effectively to be bastards by the marriage of their mothers, sometimes, though not always, to the men who had procreated the children in question. In England in the 1970s the marriage of parents of illegitimates has been fairly common, and so many of the remaining bastards are adopted by quite other parties that the concept of parental deprivation has to be modified for the whole body of children in this class. But the loss of the father, and to a lesser extent of the mother, through the breakup of the marriages of parents with children, has become substantial and is growing all the time. Parental deprivation has accordingly become a subject of considerable importance, and parentally deprived children a preoccupation of the concerned observer.

There is undoubtedly a great deal in the situation of these young people to be concerned about. The psychologists insist that parental loss has a significant effect on the development of the personality, and this is true whether it comes about by rejection, estrangement—as through divorce—or death. Rejection need not be accompanied by physical separation between parent and child, but there can be no doubt that such separation can be very widespread. In the United States at the present time something like a sixth or more of all children under the age of 18 may well have suffered departure of a parent from the home. It is probable that less than a quarter of these parentally deprived persons have actually lost father or mother because of death, for orphans so defined only make up something over 4% of all children of these ages. The rest, that is, some 12% to 15% of American children who are 17 or younger, have been cut off either from father or from mother because of divorce or because their parents are living apart as separated couples.

We can take this as the highest proportion of parentally deprived children we are likely to find in our time, since estrangement, divorce and remarriage are so much commoner in the United States than they are elsewhere. Nevertheless, there is growing concern in other highly industrialized countries, including our own, about the increase in the breakup of families, with its regrettable effects on children, especially young children. There seems, moreover, to be the same tendency here as the historical sociologist has observed for other issues: to look on our own generation as burdened by the problem to an extent never paralleled in the past. Arguments in support of such self-sympathetic views are seldom advanced, and I am not aware that any previous work has ever been done of a properly historical kind on the breakup of vertical family links. The only exception is an interesting set of numerical calculations about grandparenthood, great-grandparenthood and orphanage in France in the 1970s as compared with three villages in the Paris basin in the eighteenth century published by the French demographer Le Bras in 1973.

I want to try to give a provisional answer to the following question: are there more parentally deprived children today than there were in traditional, pre-industrial England? The answer cannot of course be very definite at this stage, since estimates of the proportion of children in such a position two or three hundred years ago are subject to so much error. But the evidence we do have for England, when prompted by the French figures I have referred to, seems to me to suggest that we may not be justified in believing that parental deprivation is commoner now than it has ever been before. There were so many orphans present in the seventeenth- and eighteenth-century English communities that they must have equalled or surpassed the proportion of children who have lost a parent by death, divorce or separation in England at the present time. Indeed, there are indications that the number of orphans in pre-industrial English society—children who had lost either father or mother or both—was very likely to have been of the same order as the maximal figures I have quoted from the United States, or even larger. This certainly seems to be true for individual communities at particular points in time, although, as must be expected, orphanage levels varied very widely from place to place.

Such a circumstance need not surprise us, because the demography of pre-industrial times required that high proportions of all children should have lost one or other of their parents by the age at which they ceased to be children, which in the traditional social order means the time when they got married. With the expectation of life varying between the late 20s and the late 40s—with perhaps a tendency to fluctuate about the early and middle 30s at ordinary times—anything from about two-fifths or perhaps as much as two-thirds of girls, for example, could be expected to have lost their

447

fathers by the time of marriage. When losses of mothers are added to these proportions, it can be seen how few young women were likely to have had both parents alive when they themselves became wives. Boys married a year or two later, of course, so being orphaned whilst "children" was even more likely for them.

The proportion orphaned at a particular age is considerably greater than the proportion of all persons of that age and younger who are orphaned. The two statistics are related in a rather complicated way, not all that easy to estimate with the vital statistics so far available to us for pre-industrial populations. For this reason it is of considerable interest to see how many orphaned *children*, defined as those orphaned at the age of which they got married or of younger age, are actually described as such in our usable sources. These sources are lists of inhabitants which provide such descriptive detail, and provide it accurately enough to inspire credibility.

It has to be admitted that children are rather uncomfortably defined by taking them in this way to all unmarried persons, and this makes the proportionate or comparative statistics of this essay somewhat ambiguous. The difficulty arises because it is essential to be able to reckon for the most part without ages in years, since numerical details of age are so rare in the evidence we have about the past persons who concern us, in England at least. But it is also due to a fundamental difference, as we shall see, as to who counted as a child in traditional society in contrast to who counts as a child today.

This issue is at its sharpest when it comes to the servants. Servants were certainly in some senses children in that era. They were young and nearly always unmarried, as we have seen, a fair proportion of them in their early teens and a half or more under 21. They were in some ways treated like children by their masters and mistresses, even when they were rather older, because you had to be married in that society to be accepted as fully grown up. If they went back home to visit their parents, as we have seen them doing at Cogenhoe, or to stay with them, they became resident "children" once again. How many persons called servants were mature in the physiological sense it is difficult to say. It is not improbable that a reason for young persons leaving home and going into service was in fact that they had reached puberty. This makes it obvious that it is impossible to look on servants as children in all senses; they could be men and women in the prime of life, in their 30s or even 40s. Moreover, in their capacity as servants, away from the parental home and perhaps without any connection with it, they were quite independent of their families of origin. This ambiguity about servants will recur as our theme develops. Sometimes we shall have to regard servants as children, children of a particular kind, and sometimes not as children at all.

We may start with such totals for resident orphans as we have been able to recover from the analysis of the lists of inhabitants of settlements in the

TABLE 1.    *Resident orphans, Clayworth, Nottinghamshire, 1676 and 1688*

| | 1676 (Pop. 401) No. | % of all orphans | 1688 (Pop. 412) No. | % of all orphans |
|---|---|---|---|---|
| Orphans living with widowed mother | 32 | 64 | 19 | 34 |
| Orphans living with widowed father | 11 | 22 | 5 | 9 |
| Orphans living with widowed mother and stepfather | 4 | 8 | 14 | 25 |
| Orphans living with widowed father and stepmother | 3 | 6 | 18 | 32 |
| Total | 50 | 100 | 56 | 100 |
| Number of resident children | 154 | – | 162 | – |
| Proportion of all children orphaned | 32% | – | 32% | – |
| Number and proportion of all resident children bereaved of mother | 14 | 9% | 23 | 13% |
| Number and proportion of all resident children bereaved of father | 36 | 23% | 33 | 19% |

*Note*: Servants not taken as 'children' in this table; see text.

seventeenth and eighteenth centuries which has been made by the Cambridge Group. We can construct, for example, a table for orphans on the basis of the two documents written out for his parish by that exceptionally intelligent, well-informed and accurate observer, William Sampson, rector of Clayworth in Nottinghamshire during the 1670s and 80s. Such is table 1 above.

This shows that a third of all resident children present in Clayworth at these two points in time had lost one or other parent by death. It is interesting to see that many more of them were fatherless than motherless, well over double the number in 1676, and that no child was recorded as deprived of both parents. The rector tells us nothing in the lists of his parishioners about the other young unmarried individuals he mentions which would enable us to recognize them as having lost their fathers or their mothers. These others were servants for the most part, of whom there were 67 in 1676, and 65 in 1688. If we look at the evidence of the parish register which Sampson kept so conscientiously over these years, we find that at least 4 of the servants in 1688 were in fact offspring of fathers who had been living in the village in 1676 but who had died.

No doubt there were other orphans amongst the servants in 1688 whom we cannot recognize as such. Coming from outside the village, as we have seen most servants did, they had family histories not accessible in the

Clayworth documents. There may indeed have been a higher proportion of orphans among servants than among resident children everywhere, if the loss of the father or the breakup of the family group by further bereavement led to offspring going into service, as happened in the four cases we know about. Adding these other orphans to the total of 56 at Clayworth in 1688 we arrive at a proportion of well over a third of all unmarried persons there as being bereaved of parents. Even this is a lower limit, for Sampson might have not been able to identify every individual resident offspring of a broken marriage. A closer estimate might be something over 40%, allowing for orphans disguised as resident relative or as lodgers—sometimes billetted on a household by the Poor Law authority—or even as solitaries. A good two-fifths, therefore, of all unmarried dependent young persons had suffered parental deprivation in that village in that year. The death rate had been high in Clayworth over the preceding twelve years, but we cannot regard its situation in 1688 as being at all unusual.

We may notice that quite a number of the orphans at Clayworth, 7 in 1676 and no less than 32 in 1688, were stepchildren living with a remarried parent. Psychologically these children may have been in an even more difficult position than those living with their widowed mothers or fathers, whatever the economic situation, which is always worst for the families of widows.

The inaccessibility of the emotional experience of our ancestors is brought home to us when we realize how little we know, how little we can imagine, of what it can have been like for the young son or daughter of a husbandman or a craftsman to confront the woman whom the father introduced into the home after the death of the mother. The new wife and mother-substitute might have brought children of her own with her, as so frequently happened in Clayworth and Cogenhoe. This would have meant, of course, that there were new brothers and sisters to get used to as well, new rivals for the father's affection. The attention of the mother would be unequally divided, too, between her own boys and girls, those of the man she had married and the ones she might herself have by him.

If we had reliable information on how young children were reared amongst the English peasantry, we might be less baffled, and perhaps less disposed to sentimentality. It seems very likely from such evidence as has been surveyed that the child of peasant parents was brought up with a bevy of other children, caressed and attended to by a knot of other mothers and other adults, too, as is known to be the situation in many "primitive" societies today, rather than being nurtured in the privacy of the cottage, the shack or the boarded-off rooms which the family inhabited. A little boy or a little girl with such a plurality of parental figures would seem likely to have felt the deprivation and the sudden change rather less keenly than the one who, like the children in the supposedly isolated cell of the late-twentieth-century conjugal family, had been exclusively tied to two parents, and especially to the mother.

TABLE 2.    *Resident orphans in 19 English communities, 1599–1811*

|  | No. | % |
|---|---|---|
| Orphans living with widowed mother | 720 | 52.1 |
| Orphans living with widowed father | 333 | 24.1 |
| Orphans living with stepmother only | 0 | 0 |
| Orphans living with stepfather only | 1 | 0.1 |
| Orphans living with father and stepmother | 105 | 7.5 |
| Orphans living with widowed mother and stepfather | 173 | 12.5 |
| Orphans living with two stepparents | 5 | 0.4 |
| Known orphans living with persons other than parents or stepparents | 46 | 3.3 |
| Total orphans | 1,383 | 100% |
| Total children |  | 6,668 |
| Orphans as a proportion of all resident children |  | 20.7% |
| Living with { widowed parents not remarried |  | 76.2% |
| { remarried widowed parents |  | 20.0% |

But we should not exercise our sympathy by thinking of the children alone. There are very large numbers of stepmothers and even of stepfathers represented in table 2, which sets out figures for all 19 of the English places, including Clayworth in 1676 and 1688, for which we have what looks like fairly complete information as to orphanage.

Brenda Maddox has recently demonstrated how difficult and ambiguous is the position of the stepparent in our own society, ambiguous in respect of the law and conventions of marriage, ambiguous in respect of the relatives of the parties to the union contracted, ambiguous above all in respect of the children for whom he or she suddenly becomes responsible. She insists, however, that the difficulties of a man or a woman who marries a spouse whose previous partner has died are worse than those which arise after a divorce, where the former parent is still alive. Let us not forget that the first was the plight, if plight it can be called, of a high proportion of all the married persons at the head of the households in the village of Clayworth in 1688. A long time must go by, once again, before we have much insight into how their situation resembled that of the late-twentieth-century successor to the position of a man's divorced wife. There is a great deal which we do not yet know about family life and illicit love in earlier generations, and much of it may well remain closed to us for ever.

The figures in table 2 put the facts from Clayworth into a somewhat more general context, though they are a poor basis on which to generalize about pre-industrial English society as a whole. In this large sample some circumstances are found which are absent at Clayworth, including the occurrence of full orphans, for children living with two stepparents must have

451

been in this position. There were only five of these out of 1,383 orphans and nearly 7,000 children. It is to be expected that the minimum proportion of resident orphans in these less carefully counted places should be less than at Clayworth, 21% as against 32%. Though we can be certain only that one in five of the children in this larger sample was parentally deprived, we may believe that in fact a much greater number were in this plight. When the names of the settlements are written out in date order, it becomes apparent that the determinable level of resident orphanage must vary quite considerably with the quality of the data. It seems, moreover, to have varied with time as well, which is much more interesting.

As for the quality of data, the documents for Cardington, Puddletown and Ealing are all superior in the detail they contain and in the consistency of their entries. In this they resemble the file for Clayworth, and it must be significant that these places have the highest recorded proportions of resident orphanage, along with St Nicholas-at-Wade. Registration is not particularly good at this last place, and its high figure demonstrates that variation must also have been due to causes other than the quality of the data. The documents for Chilvers Coton and for Harefield are also high in standard, and it would seem that their low levels of resident orphanage represent genuine variation downwards. The modest proportions at Norwich and at Littleover are more likely to have been the result of incomplete identification.

*Family life and illicit love in earlier generations*

TABLE 4.3. *Settlements with recorded proportions of orphans, in date order*

|  | % |
|---|---|
| (1) Ealing, Middx., 1599 | 25 |
| (2) Cogenhoe, Northants., 1624 | 25 |
| (3) Clayworth, Notts., 1676 | 32 |
| (4) Chilvers Coton, War., 1684 | 12 |
| (5) Clayworth, Notts., 1688 | 32 |
| (6) Norwich St Peter Mancroft, 1694 | 7 |
| (7) Lichfield, Staffs., 1695 | 21 |
| (8) Harefield, Middx., 1699 | 16 |
| (9) Stoke-on-Trent, Staffs., 1701 | 25 |
| (10) Monkton, Kent, 1705 | 16 |
| (11) St Nicholas-at-Wade, Kent, 1705 | 36 |
| (12) Puddletown, Dorset, 1724 | 26 |
| (13) Cardington, Beds., 1782 | 34 |
| (14) Corfe Castle, Dorset, 1790 | 17 |
| (15) Ardleigh, Essex, 1796 | 14 |
| (16) Barkway and Reed, Herts., 1801 | 16 |
| (17) Binfield, Berks., 1801 | 13 |
| (18) Littleover, Derby., 1811 | 7 |

(19) Mickleover, Derby., 1811                                    16

This small sample, therefore, can be taken to reveal the expected variability in orphanage from place to place. The impression of variation over time is also conveyed by the listings of proportions according to date. If this effect is a real one, it presumably arose because of shifts in demographic rates, particularly in mortality, by far the strongest influence on orphanage. The mean of mean proportions of identifiable resident orphans for the 19 places is 20.5% or 22% omitting the two lowest figures; the median, a more realistic marker, is 18% (25%). But the first 11 places, which are dated between 1599 and 1705, have a median of 25% (mean of 22.5%), whereas the last eight, dated between 1724 and 1811, have a median of 16.5% (mean of 17.9%). The seventeenth century is becoming known as a period of high mortality over much of England, especially after 1650, and it could be that the effect of this in maintaining higher proportions of orphaned children shows itself in these recordings in spite of variation due to locality and to quality of document. We must remember that all the figures for the 19 places would have to be increased to obtain a total proportion which would include servants and others not being children resident in their families of origin. There must also have been some grandchild orphans in these 19 places, children sent back to the parents of their fathers or their mothers after the death of one or other of them or of both. None happened to be present at Clayworth, but we believe they were not uncommon elsewhere.

This is about as far as it is possible to get with information from lists of inhabitants lacking figures for ages, the usual case, unfortunately, with English materials. Our information can be supplemented, however, with one further set of facts derived from the exceptional entries made during the seven years from 1653 to 1660 in the marriage register for St Mary's, Manchester. Here the names of the fathers of both bride and bridegroom are given, and marked "dec" where appropriate to indicate deceased. Between 52% and 59% of all brides at first marriage were described in this way as fatherless. This proportion which covers all brides, of course, and not simply those resident with their parents or stepparents at the time of the ceremony, is about what we might expect in girls of age to be married, if a fifth of *all* unmarried girls had lost their fathers, and a third had lost either father or mother, or both. The rare recordings of Manchester may accordingly be taken as generally confirming our estimates for the mid and late seventeenth century, and especially Clayworth.

We must recognize, of course, that it is not entirely realistic to compare the class of unmarried, dependent young persons of that generation in England with the class of all persons under 18 years old in the United States

453

in our generation if we want to get an idea of the relative prevalence of parental deprivation then and now. But it is also evident that no direct comparison of like with like would ever be possible, not even one contrasting those of identical age and marital status at the two chosen points in time. Assumptions about maturity, childhood, dependency, subordination were simply different in the earlier society. To discover, however, that a third or considerably more of all unmarried dependents could be parentally deprived in traditional society when mortality was high, and that the figure seldom dropped below one-fifth even at times and in places with more favourable conditions, does make possible the rough comparison which we have in mind. Considering that in our day the very highest proportion of parentally deprived amongst those under 18 is a sixth or somewhat over, it cannot be said that parental deprivation is commoner under the conditions of the late twentieth century in high industrial society than it was in the seventeenth and eighteenth centuries in traditional society. It looks as if the reverse must be true. We are hardly justified, in historical terms, in sympathizing with ourselves for the prevalence of broken marriages in our time and its deplorable effects on our children.

We may complete our note with a glance at such age evidence as we do possess. For England the historical data at present can only be called crude, and not much worked over, but for France the situation is a little better. For the twentieth century we have one very useful set of English statistics, compiled by the Registrar-General from the national Census of 1921-England and Wales. In table 4 will be found proportions of resident orphans in 3

TABLE 4     *Resident orphans: proportions in various age groups*

| Age group | Ealing, 1599 (pop. 427) | % | Lichfield, 1697 (pop. 2,861) | % | Ardleigh, 1796 (pop. 1,145) | % | Census of 1921 % |
|---|---|---|---|---|---|---|---|
| 0−3 | 3/27 | 11.1 | 18/214 | 8.4 | 10/130 | 7.7 | 4.5 |
| 0−5 | 7/43 | 16.3 | 30/348 | 8.6 | 18/190 | 9.5 | 6.1 |
| 0−9 | 17/81 | 21.0 | 79/642 | 12.3 | 31/315 | 9.8 | 8.7 |
| All resident orphans | 33/133 | 24.8 | 268/1,146 | 21.5 | 87/598 | 14.5 | (0−14, 11.3%) |
| Orphans 0−9 as a proportion of all orphans | 17/33 | 51.5 | 79/268 | 29.5 | 31/87 | 35.6 | — |

English settlements up to age 3, up to age 5 and up to age 9, set out alongside the corresponding proportions of orphans recorded in the Census of 1921. The first of these age groups has been used because of the great vulnerability of children in their first 3 or 4 years to parental loss, particularly to the loss of the mother. During the next 2 years of life, ages 4 and

# SPOUSE LOSS

5, infants remain very dependent, and even amongst the very poor in pre-industrial society were extremely unlikely to be sent out of the home, although they might begin to do a little work. By the age of ten, however, the prospect of leaving the family as servants began to be tangible, and we have to reckon with the fact that only up to that age can figures for resident orphans be taken to indicate approximate figures for all orphans. A comparison between the last two rows of the table in the columns for pre-industrial communities gives some idea of how many orphaned children left their families of origin between the age of ten and marriage, since the percentages seem to increase far too little.

Some notion of how much greater the growth in the proportion of orphans would be if we had information on all parental losses after age ten can be gathered from the next table, constructed, of course, on entirely dif-

### Parental deprivation in the past in England

TABLE 5.  *Calculated proportions of orphaned offspring, eighteenth-century France (3 villages) and twentieth-century France[a]*

| Age group | Eighteenth century % | 1960s % |
|---|---|---|
| 0–3 | 4.5 | 0.3 |
| 0–5 | 7.1 | 0.8 |
| 0–9 | 12.5 | 1.9 |
| All orphaned offspring[b] | 32.1 | 8.5 |
| Orphans 0–9 as a proportion of all orphans[b] | 21.1 | 8.5 |

[a]Estimates from Le Bras 1973.  [b]All orphaned offspring taken as those aged 0–25.

ferent principles and for French pre-industrial communities rather than English. Although these figures would seem to imply that fewer children up to age 5 were orphaned in the French eighteenth-century villages concerned than in any of the English, the very different bases of calculation make comparison hazardous. The contrast between the eighteenth century and the 1960s is certainly a startling one, and underlines the enormous difference between ourselves and our ancestors in respect of the risk of death. We may "lose" our parents at a rate comparable to that which they experienced, or at least the Americans may do so, but nearly all of these parents go on living. It should not escape us that the difference between the English census figures of 1921 and estimates for France in the 1960s are considerable, too. Most of the change in orphanage, as in so many other matters of population and social structure, has come recently, within the lifetimes of our older contemporaries. If we knew as much about the history of orphanage in recent times as the history of aging, we might be

455

able to tell a similar story of swift and sudden change taking place within living memory.

In our last table we venture on a direct comparison between orphanage worked out from lists of inhabitants and orphanage worked out from demographic statistics.

These final details serve to draw attention to the instability of the proportions we have been dealing with and warn us against accepting any of them as anything other than a rough estimate. They bring out, however, two points we have stressed more than once in this note. The first is how much more likely you were to lose your father than your mother, and still are, indeed; in this respect the French figures for the eighteenth century seem to be an aberration. The second is how rare it always has been to lose both your parents when a child. In common parlance the word "orphan" seems to mean one who is entirely bereft of the father who begat him and the mother who brought him into the world, and Cinderella is the archetypal orphan. But a Cinderella was a rarity, in the traditional world where the story—that influential piece of mischievous make-believe—is set.

## 6. The Administration Of London's Court Of Orphans

By Charles H. Carlton

During the 16th and 17th centuries the government of London spent much of its time looking after children. If at random one opens a Common Council Journal, a Corporation Letter Book, or a Repertory of the Court of Aldermen, the chances are that one will find at least one reference to the family of a freeman who died leaving minor children. The City assessed freemen's estates, and divided them according to ancient custom. It supervised the marriages of heiresses, and safeguarded orphans' inheritances until their majority. The area of London's government responsible for deceased freeman's children and estates was (by 1529) known as the Court of Orphans.

Surviving records show that the City administered an orphan's estate as early as 1276. On the 12th January Gregory de Rokesle, Mayor, 'and other reputable men of London' granted the wardship and property of John, William, and Matilda, orphans of Allan Godard, to Sarah, his widow, on condition that during their minority Sarah should provide them with 'food, linen, and other woollen clothing, shoes and other necessaries.' During the 14th century London handled 295 cases of orphanage, an average of nearly three a year. With the civil wars of the 15th century the total number of cases declined to 260, though after Bosworth Field the average rose to over five a year. Nonetheless, with so few cases the City could administer orphans informally, and needed no special bureaucratic machinery.

In the 16th century, however, pressure of business greatly increased. Because the surviving records are incomplete we cannot accurately assess the actual number of orphanage cases, but by counting the recognisances in the Letter Books we may discover the rate at which business changed. In the first half of the 16th century the clerks entered an average of 200 recognisances a decade. In the 1550's recognisances increased 257% from 235 to 603, and in the next decade rose a further 51% to 925. This expansion was due partly to the growth of London's population, which between 1510 and 1580 rocketed from 50,000 to 120,000, and principally to the development within the Court of regular administrative procedures. While their creation was needed to deal with the augmented work load, by ensuring that far fewer cases escaped the Court's attention, they increased the business it handled.

When a freeman died leaving minor children, his executors were supposed to come to the Guildhall within fourteen days, and there enter bond with the Chamberlain to produce an inventory of the deceased's personal property within a further three months. In practice they rarely met these deadlines. While it is often hard to discover the day a man died, we do know when he made his will. Usually he wrote it on his death bed, often describing himself as sick in body, but, thanks be to God, perfect in mind. Of a sample of the 24 estates that entered the Court in 1663, the average period between the will and inventory was eighteen months, and in only four was it less than four months.

As London grew and the municipal grape-vine became incapable of learning of every freeman's death, the Court had to develop some mechanism to ensure that every executor gave bond, and so started the administrative cycle. In 1520 the Aldermen ordered the Constables to notify the Common Crier every month of the names and addresses of all freemen who died within their parishes leaving orphans. In 1546 the Aldermen likewise charged the Parish Clerks.

Once the Court had discovered an estate liable to its jurisdiction, it had to assess and inventorise its contents. The Court took great pains to ensure the production of accurate and honest inventories, which it made the responsibility of the Common Crier. He ordered the Beadle of the dead man's ward to forbid the executors to touch the estate, until four freemen appointed by the Common Crier, the deceased's Alderman, or the Lord Mayor, had appraised it. The appraisers made two copies of the inventory, one for the executor, and the other for the City's records, which they signed and swore were "just and true."

If an executor refused to allow the taking of an inventory, the Court could win his goods and throw him in prison. On the 2nd February 1552 a frightened Bartholomew Warner wrote to John Johnson. 'Even now was here with me an officer from my Lorde Mayour, willing my sister to appere tomorrow with th'inventory, and if not that the officer would come into the house and sease upon the goodes.' Abraham Chambers and Philip Owen fared less gently in 1654. When they refused to produce an inventory, the Court incarcerated them in Newgate Jail, there to remain until they complied.

On pain of a fine of eight shillings per pound of her husband's estate the Court forbade the widow to remarry before the Common Serjeant had approved the inventory. Perhaps this restriction stemmed from a sense of propriety—to allow the first husband's side of the bed to cool before being warmed by the second. More likely the rule was intended to prevent the mingling of the two husband's estates, and the chance that the second might defraud the first's children.

Executors could defraud orphans by omitting terms such as jewelry, cash or plate from the inventory, or making a misleading entry. When Charles Morrison died in 1672 he left two thirds of his estate equally among his seven children, and a third to his widow Leonora. His book keeper, Jacob Davies, took this opportunity to ingratiate himself with the widow, whom after concocting a fraudulent inventory, he married. The couple had left out much household stuff, including 'gold and silver of great value,' failed to mention any of Morrison's considerable trading interests abroad, and listed £2,250 face value of East India Company Stock with a market value of £4,950, as an ordinary loan. A more sophisticated opportunity for fraud lay in writing good debts off as bad, in the hope that if the money were repaid months after the Common Serjeant had approved the inventory, it might escape his attention and go straight into a dishonest executor's pocket. To curb this practice the Aldermen in 1568 ordered one of their members in rotation to sit with the Common Serjeant every Friday, to summon executors and ask them on oath how many bad debts they had collected. Next year the Aldermen threatened to imprison any exector who refused to appear, and six months later ordered that when asked an executor had to produce a list of all outstanding debts. Apparently these steps were not very successful. In October 1584 the Common Serjeant reported that in the past seven months alone repaid debts worth £1,058 had escaped the Court's attention. So, in the hope that where exhortation had failed greed might triumph, the Common Council passed an Act letting the Common Serjeant keep, and enjoy for one year, any debts he recovered, and any items he found omitted from the inventory.

In London over two thousand inventories have survived. Written on long rolls of parchment, about seven inches wide, with each sheet sewn to the next, they record every item of a freeman's personal estate: cash, furniture, stock, plate, merchandise and debts. They do not include real property, since Common Law, which took precedence over City custom, determined the inheritance of land.

The Common Serjeant next calculated the deceased's real worth. He abstracted into the Common Serjeant's Books the gross totals listed in the inventory, and from them deducted various claims against the estate. The first, and usually the largest of these claims were all the debts the dead man owed. Then the Common Serjeant subtracted the widow's chamber: 'All her usual apparell belonging to her body, both lynen and wollen and silkes, her usual beds that she and her husband did commonly use during their spousel between them to lie upon, the hangynges of her owne bedchamber, chests wherin she usually kept her said linen and other apparell, and her usual chain, rings of gold & other jewells she was wont to wear upon high festive days.' In addition the widow was allowed to claim one month's housekeeping allowance, and, when necessary, the maternity expenses for a posthumous child. Finally the Common Serjeant deducted the cost of the deceased's funeral. These could be extravagant affairs, with costly mourning clothes, long and expensive sermons, and generous doles of bread and money. At one such handout in 1601 'the number of beggars was so excessive and unreasonable that seventeen of them were thronged and trampled to death.' The Court, in 1544, limited the amount an executor could spend on a funeral according to the dead man's social and financial state. On a Lord Mayor the executor could spend £200, twice as much as on a commoner worth over £2,000. At the other end of the scale a freeman worth between £10 and £20 had to be put away for less than ten shillings.

Daniel Hill's was one of the thousands of estates the Common Serjeant assessed. Hill, a Merchant Taylor, died in 1662, making his will on the 3rd September that year. All his Irish land he left to his eldest son John. Of his personal estate one third plus £50 was to go 'freely to her own use' to his wife Elizabeth, and his five children were to have £300 apiece. An inventory of Hill's estate, taken on the 2nd June 1663 shows a gross total of £3,847. He owed £3,556, his funeral cost £10, the widow's chamber was worth £16, giving him a net estate of only £264. However, when the first inventory was taken sundry debtors owed Hill's estate £3,117. A second inventory, exhibited on 11th November 1675 showed that during the previous thirteen years his debtors had repaid the estate £1,670, leaving £1,447, none of which the executors had much hope of collecting.

Hill was one of the 57 freemen whose estates entered the Court in the mayoral year 1662-63. The total gross value of the 57 estates was £95,933—an average of £1,665 each. Together they owed £44,539, and were owed £99,336.

City custom divided a freeman's net personal estate into thirds. One third, over and above her chamber, went to the widow. Another was divided equally among all children. The remainder, known as the legacy or dead man's portion, was the freeman's to dispose as he willed. If he died intestate, or left no widow, the Court divided his estate in half.

As City custom did not apply to real property, any settlement of land the widow had brought into the marriage could not be counted in her third. On the other hand, the Court included any settlement made specifically to secure her chamber or third—not to have done so would have given them to the widow twice. Since the couple may have been married for many years the Court did not try to separate any settlement of personal property from the husband's estate.

The Common Serjeant divided the orphans' third equally among all the deceased's children. They had to be legitimate. In 1519 Timothy, a child whom his father Thomas Bradshaw coyly confessed had 'been begotten in haste,' failed to gain a part with his legitimate siblings. The surviving brothers and sisters shared the portion of any orphan who died under age. In 1624 some Turkish pirates captured James Kelke, a City orphan, and sold him a slave in Algiers. He lasted less than a year, dying a minor, and his portion passed to his brothers Thomas and Nicholas, who after waiting eleven years in vain for their brother's return came before the Mayor and Alderman and claimed his inheritance. Had all three children died as minors the estate would have left the Court's jurisdiction, to be divided according to the freeman's will or the normal laws of intestacy. During his minority an orphan had no control over his inheritance. He could not make a valid will. Just before his twenty-first birthday Robert Harris died leaving his wife Ann half of his £2,000 portion. In 1628 the Court, citing dozens of precedents, told Chancery that Ann had no claim on her husband's money, which should all go to his brothers and sisters.

Common Council, in October, 1551 passed an Act known as Judd's Law—which let a father disinherit a child who married without permission, or was 'a thefe or fellon or a common whore or common pycher or a common player at unlawful games notoriously known, or. . . comyt any whoredom.' A more usual cause of cutting a child off from his share in the orphan's third was the concept of advancement. A child was considered to have been advanced if his father in advance of his death had given the child his eventual inheritance. The father might make a daughter a marriage settlement, establish a son in business, give him a partnership, lease, annuity, or a commission. If the child could prove that such a gift was only part of what his father had intended for him, then the Court considered that the child had only been partly advanced. Subtle was the definition of an advancement. Basically it was any grant that guaranteed a fairly secure income. Thus the gift of a church living was an advancement; the cost of a university education enabling a son to perform better his pastoral duties was not. The Court—quite properly—did not consider a degree any guarantee of future prosperity.

The division of Sir Abraham Reynardson's estate illustrates the procedures of advancement. The royalist ex-Lord Mayor died in 1661 leaving eight children, three of whom were of age. Before he died Sir Abraham had advanced his eldest son Samuel £6,870. Sir Abraham's estate had a net value of £18,276. The orphans third was £6,092, in which, since it was less than the £6,870 his father had advanced him, Samuel had no claim. Neither had Sir Abraham's eldest daughter. In his will her father had declared that Mary was 'fully advanced and satisfied of her due from my estate by what I have paid and spent in bestowing her in marriage unto Samuel Bernardson as by her account in my book will appear, and his aquitances in full will show.' Since Sir Abraham had given his second son £870, the Common Serjeant considered that Nicolas had been partially advanced, and allowed him £267, bringing his share of the orphan's third up to the £1,145 that each of the five unadvanced children enjoyed.

The system the Common Serjeant used to make these adjustments was known as Hotchpotch. Consider a hypothetical case. A freeman died leaving a net personal estate of £2,400. The orphans third was £800. He has advanced his first child £400, the second £100, the third £60, and the fourth has received not a penny, making a total of £560. Added to the orphan's third this comes to £1,360, which divided among all four children would give them £340 each. But the eldest has already received £400, so only £1,360 less his £400 remains to be shared among the younger three children.

Hotchpotch applied only to the orphan's third. The widow's was hers entirely, and the dead man could do what he willed with his portion. Hotchpotch and the rest of the City's customs were convenient devices for balancing the wishes of the testator with the needs of the widow and orphans—and of society. Many testators, such as Lionel Cranfield and Sir Abraham Reynardson, bequeathed their estates 'according to the laudible customs of London.' Others did not. Some may not have fully understood City custom, or, perhaps, on their death-beds got confused. In 1628 John Broadwater divided his estate into thirds, and left one moiety to his wife, another equally to his seven children, and gave the legacy portion, less deductions for his funeral and debts, to charity. By custom he should have divided the estate after, and not before, deductions. More often executors were ignorant of City customs, and treated the whole of their wealth as a legacy portion. In 1663 John Wetheral left more than two thirds of his estate to his children. He probably overestimated his real worth. The same year Thomas Yates willed his only child £100, which was £106 less than the orphan's third. In this instance the Common Serjeant split the estate into thirds, and divided the dead man's portion in proportion to the legacies he had devised in the will. If, as in Thomas Yates' case, the amount custom guaranteed the widow or orphans was greater than the sum the will gave them, they then had no claim on the legacy portion.

A hypothetical example may clarify this point. A testator treated the whole of his estate as a legacy portion, and left his widow £400, his son £200, his daughter £85, his sister £65, and £50 to charity—a total of £800. In fact his net estate was only worth £600. But the testator had completely ignored City custom, which decreed that £200, a third of his net estate must go to the widow, and the same amount equally to all children. Only the remaining £200, the dead man's third, may be divided according to the proportions laid down in the will. His daughter, however, had no claim in the dead man's third. Custom had already given her £100, half the orphan's third which was £15 more than her father had intended.

The widow and orphans were a little better off than the testator had intended, and his sister and charity slightly poorer. Basically his wishes have been met: he has made provision for his family, and given a little for the good of his soul.

The customs of division were wide. They significantly interfered with the testator's wishes only when he attempted to punish unfairly a wife or child. Immediately after the wedding in 1583 of Alexander Avenon to Clare, daughter of Alderman Sir James Harvey, a bitter quarrel developed over the marriage settlement. Sir James made a deed of gift debarring Clare from the orphanage third. Two months later he died. After 'throwing his sister Clare out and leaving her to the world,' Sebastian, the eldest son and executor, refused to accept City custom, which in 1586 he petitioned the Privy Council to declare void. The Aldermen were appalled. They prophesied dire calamity if the Court of Orphans were abolished: 'Wills and deeds of gift would be forged. . . much perjury would be committed. . . men would defraud their wives.' The Privy Council agreed that it was not meet and proper to continue bitter and unnatural family squabbles beyond the grave.

Once the Court had discovered and assessed an estate, and determined the orphan's share in it, it had to protect the inheritance until the children came of age. The Court allowed executors two options. They could either deposit the money in the City's treasury, or Chamber, where it remained until the children claimed it at majority, or they, or a third party of their choice, could promise to keep the children's portions, and pay it to them when they came of age. Such promises were known as recognisances.

Typical of the tens of thousands of recognisances to be found in the City's records was one given in 1537:

Be it remembered that on the 7th day of July in the 29th year of the reign of King Henry the eight John Odyerne, Roger Will, fishmonger, and John Hoskyn, taylor, citizens of London, came into the court of the said Lord the King in the Chamber of the Guildhall of the City of London, before Sir Ralph Warren, knight, mayor, and the aldermen of the same City and acknowledged that they and everyone of them, by himself severally, and for the whole, did owe unto George Medley, chamberlain of the said City aforesaid £42 sterling payable to the said chamberlain and his successors . . . and unless they, and each of them by himself shall do it, they grant, and each of them doth grant, that the sum aforesaid on the lands, tenements, goods and chattels of them, may be levied by force of this recognisance.

The condition of this recognisance is such that if the above bounden John (Odyerne). . . or any of the recognitors above bounden shall. . . pay. . . to the Chamberlain. . . £39-3-3½ sterling when Albert, Ursula, John and Anne, children and orphans of John Stergyns (whilst he lived citizen and clothworker of London) shall attain their lawful ages. . . this recognisance shall be voided.

Most freemen made their wives their executors. The widow would usually try to keep her children's portions, asking three friends or relatives to stand surety with her. Of the 35 new recognisances taken during the mayoriality of Lionel Ducket (1572-73) the widow guaranteed eight recognisances, another close relative three, and a member of the deceased's company a further eight. In eighteen cases no relationship may be found, though such probably existed in many of them. If the executors were unable to find satisfactory sureties, as were those of one Barwick in 1578, the Court ordered them to surrender the inheritances to the safekeeping of a wealthier and better connected stranger. Sometimes the executors did so voluntarily in the hope that a rich and powerful merchant might provide more security, and, as the child grew older, some useful contacts. In 1611 Lionel Cranfield, a rising merchant whom James I later created Earl of Middlesex, held £150 in inheritances due to the nephews of Richard Perrot, his general factotum.

A recognisance was only as good as its sureties. If they died, left the City, fell on hard times, or were in any way unable to fulfil their promises, then the recognisance became no more than a finely drafted scrap of paper. When a surety became unable to fulfil his obligations his fellows were supposed to produce a satisfactory substitute within three months. It was the Common Serjeant's duty to ensure that this was done. By the late 15th century, as the number of cases increased, the Common Serjeant's informal system of checking on sureties proved inadequate, and, as a chronicler reported, there was much 'mysordering of Orphan's Sureties, the which was so little Runne without callying in of new sureties, that many of them decayed, and that many an orphan thereby was dysapoyntid.' To remedy this, London, in 1492, instituted an annual mid-Lent Monday Court of Orphans, to which the Common Crier summoned at least one surety from each recognisance to certify that he, and his fellows, were all alive, prosperous and within the City.

Holding a child's inheritance was financially an attractive proposition, especially at a time when most merchants were chronically short of capital. When John Isham married Elizabeth, widow of Leonard Barker, an ironmonger, in 1552, he was able to use his stepson's portion of £456 to help launch a successful business career. Isham held the money for eighteen years—twice the average of nine years, which made, nonetheless, a favorable long-term loan. Between its revival in the 1560's and the financial collapse of 1682, the Court provided at least a million pounds to badly needed capital. On their loans, recognitors, of course, had to pay interest, or finding money, the percentage of which the Court determined. In 1532 Common Council established the first table of finding money rates. None was due on the first £10, a shilling per pound on the next ninety, eightpence on the second hundred, fourpence between £200 and £300, and no further interest on inheritances over £300. To keep pace with inflation Common Council revised these schedules in 1561, 1605, 1622 and 1659. Yet they never raised the interest rate above 5%, and usually kept it far lower. For instance a recognitor would have paid 1.56% for £600 according to the 1532 schedule, 3.05% in 1561, 3.87% in 1605, 4.44% in 1622, and 5% in 1659. These rates were less than half those on the open market, where for instance, John Isham in 1564 had to pay 16% for a short loan of £2,000. By City custom he paid his stepson, 3.5% for a long-term loan of £456.

On the other hand executors, like modern trustees, were more concerned with security than income. Almost up to the day it went bankrupt most executors considered no place more secure than the Chamber of the City of London, and during the 17th century the orphans money deposited in the Chamber greatly increased. The City, faced with a mounting deficit, welcomed such loans, and on them became more and more dependent. In 1585 the Chamber owed the orphans £5,593. By 1627 this debt had jumped to £182,795. In 1680 it peaked at £540,989. As the debt increased the Orphans Court became less a social institution and more a crutch for a crumbling and archaic financial system whose collapse was inevitable. In the summer of 1682 the Chamber stopped paying interest on its debts. After a dozen years of petitions, committees, reports, gratuities, and a revolution, Parliament, in 1694, passed 'An Act for the relief of Orphans and other creditors of the City of London.' The Act converted unpaid inheritances into an Orphans' Fund—England's first permanent public debt.

Apart from the unfortunate children who came of age after 1682, and whose inheritances were in the Chamber, when a boy or girl reached twenty-one (or eighteen for a married woman), they came to the Guildhall, where before the Lord Mayor and Aldermen, the recognitor or Chamberlain paid them their inheritances. Then after publically acknowledging satisfaction of all further claims, their dealings with the Court were over, unless, of course, they, in their turn, were unlucky enought to die leaving minor children, and start the whole cycle all over again.

The expansion of orphans' business both fostered and was the result of the formalisation of the Court's procedures. In 1492 the City instituted the annual mid-Lent Monday Court. In 1532 it established the first table of finding money rates, and in 1544 one limiting funeral expenses. The Court, in 1541, laid down a table of fees that each officer should charge for various services. For example, sureties paid the Common Serjeant 6s.8d. and a like fee to the Common Crier for taking or discharging recognisances worth over £100, and 2s. to the Town Clerk for any recognisance he drafted. Like any growing organisation the Court had to adopt standard operating procedures. Yet the City never developed the Court as a separate entity. The Court had no single officer whose sole responsibility was to the orphans: all its officers had duties elsewhere in the City's government. As orphanage business grew in the early 16th century the City grafted responsibility for the various stages of the administrative cycle into the nearest available and most convenient branch of municipal government. And so the Court never developed into anything more concrete than the sum of the various areas of London's government that handled orphans' affairs.

The government of London operated at two levels: through elected deliberative bodies, such as the Courts of Aldermen and Common Council, and through the City's paid permanent officers.

During the 16th century the Common Serjeant was the paid permanent officer most responsible for orphans' affairs. Originally the City's public prosecutor, he is involved with the orphans in 1343 when William de Ilford served as attorney for John le Botoner, an orphan whose mother and step father had seized a brewery his father had left him. Very soon the Common Serjeant became the orphans' administrator as well as their advocate. As the Common Crier's name suggests, his first duty was to summon all with whom the City had business. He opened Common Hall, and the Court of Hustings. He called sureties to the mid-Lent Court and executors to give bond to produce inventories. It was only natural that the Court should make him responsible for taking inventories, and seeing that the Parish Clerks and Constables reported all new cases of orphanage. The Clerks and Constables were local, not City officers, whose main duty—keeping the parish records or the King's Peace—lay elsewhere. In the 17th century with the growth of deposits in the Chamber, the Chamberlain became the Court's busiest officer. He was also the City's chief financial agent, whose responsibility for solving or, at least, postponing, the Chamber's financial collapse, surely encouraged him to dip into the nearest available till—the orphans' money entrusted to his care. The Town Clerk kept all the City's records, including those for orphans. Though the Clerk of Orphans' title might suggest a sole concern with their affairs, this office, charged with writing recognisances, was held by the junior attorney of the Lord Mayor's Court. As one of the few attorneys exclusively privileged to plead before this court, he had business opportunities far more interesting, and lucrative, than the mere drafting of recognisances. The proportion of their total income which City officers derived from the orphans roughly reflected the degree to which orphans' affairs were part of their overall responsibilities. At the end of the 17th century the orphans contributed only about 12% of the Town Clerk's and Common Serjeant's income, and 8% of the Common Crier's.

Common Council had little to do with the orphans. An 18th century list shows that only six of 297 acts Common Council passed between 1342 and 1661 concerned orphans. Four were finding money acts, one was Judd's Law, and the other affirmed the Aldermen's right to determine orphans' affairs. The Aldermen agreed, declaring in 1536 'that from henceforth all orphanages of this City shall be ordered always by this Courte, and not by the executors nor administrators of the freeman so deceased.' The Aldermen operated at three levels. As individuals they reported new cases within their wards and, with the Common Crier, could appoint appraisers. As the Lord Mayor's Court sitting in the Outer Chamber of the Guildhall, they punished those who refused to surrender inheritances or who married heiresses without their license. The much more important function of the Lord Mayor's Court was settling commercial cases through the use of Law Merchant. As the Court of Aldermen meeting in the Inner Chamber of the Guildhall, they acted as the City's chief executive body. Here, often working with their officers, the Aldermen as a whole, or through committees, dealt with every facet of London's government, ranging from great matters of state to petty details of orphanage. For instance, on the 14th November 1626, at a typical meeting of the Court, the Aldermen dealt with 23 items 19 of which concerned orphans.

The administration of London's orphans was a highly complicated business which occupied a surprisingly large proportion of the City's time and energy. First the City had to find estates liable to the Court's jurisdiction. Then the Common Crier had to see that they were appraised. The Common Serjeant assessed and divided the estate, and the Chamberlain ensured that orphans' portions were kept safely until they came of age. The Court of Aldermen exercised overall responsibility for the City's administration of orphans' affairs, as it did for all of London's government. John Stow wrote in 1598 that the government of London consisted of nine courts, of which that of Orphans was but one. Within the *curia* system of government definition of responsibility was at best vaguely defined by areas, and not by departments. Admittedly in the 16th century the Court of Orphans formalised some of its procedures. It introduced tables of funeral rates, finding money and officers' fees. Yet these steps effected the Court's external relations with executors, suitors, recognitors, widows and orphans, and did not define the Court's relationship internally within the City's government. While London, like Whitehall, was confronted in the 16th century with greatly increased demands on its bureaucratic machinery, London did not (to borrow Professor Elton's phrase) enjoy a Tudor Revolution in Government.

# 7. Orphanage In Colonial North Carolina
### By Alan D. Watson

The institution of orphanage in the New World was crucial to developing societies in which formal organizations for the care of the poor and homeless had yet to be established. Children deprived of fathers by reason of death or illegitimacy constituted a potential societal liability as impoverished minors and unskilled and uneducated adults. This paper investigates the nature of orphanage in colonial North Carolina, an area still largely unexplored by social historians, by using Edgecombe County as a test case. Edgecombe was a representative county in North Carolina by virtue of its central geographic location and its predominately agrarian orientation. More importantly, the county records contain the most extensive collection of guardianship accounts, dated 1764 to 1778, to be found among the colonial documents of North Carolina. Finally, the county possesses one of the most complete and descriptive sets of court minutes after 1757 of any county in the province. In order to provide a broader perspective of orphanage in colonial North Carolina, relevant material from other counties has been used intermittently to supplement the discussion of Edgecombe County.

Four extant statutes governed the supervision of orphans in colonial North Carolina. The first, part of the Revisal of 1715, was a brief law bestowing responsibility for the care of orphans upon the precinct, later county, courts. The law directed that orphans with sufficient estates be placed with guardians who would educate and provide for the children "according to their Rank & degree." Otherwise, the orphans were to be apprenticed to learn a handicraft or trade. During the course of the next four decades the lack of more explicit legislation and closer supervision of guardians led to the embezzlement of orphans' estates and the neglect of their education. Governor Gabriel Johnston observed in 1735 that the 1715 law seemed "highly unjust and. . . design[ed] to encourage and protect unjust Guardians who rob their Wards, a practise too common in this country." However, attempts to remedy the defects of that legislation failed until 1755 when a comprehensive measure regulating orphanage passed the assembly.

The 1755 statute reposed authority for taking cognizance of all matters concerning orphans and their estates in the county and superior courts of the province. Through the use of such concurrent jurisdiction the assembly intended to provide a check upon the county courts which had previously exercised virtually independent control over orphan affairs. In practice, however, the county courts continued their dominance. The legislation reiterated the 1715 directive to apprentice impoverished orphans and to place the wealthier children under guardianship. In order to protect the property of the children, the law instructed the courts to bond guardians for

467

good behavior and to require one or more securities to guarantee the responsible conduct of the guardians. If the solvency or integrity of the guardians or securities appeared questionable, the courts could appoint new guardians or demand new securities.

After their appointments guardians were expected to attend the next meeting of the court to submit an inventory of their wards' estates. Thereafter, the guardians were directed by law to attend court once a year to exhibit accounts of the receipts and disbursements of the orphans' estates which were to be entered in books kept expressly for that purpose. The law required the justices of every county to hold an "Orphans Court" on the first day of the first court meeting after January first of each year wherein all business relating to orphans would be transacted. This attempt to systematize orphanage proceedings had antecedents in the proprietary era of North Carolina when the precinct courts convened similar orphans courts. The 1755 legislation followed the customary practice of instructing the churchwardens of the parishes to notify their respective county courts of orphans who did not have guardians or had not been apprenticed as well as to indict those guardians who neglected or violated their trusts.

Apprenticeship was reserved for those orphans whose estates were too small to educate and support them. Boys and girls were bound until they reached the ages of twenty-one and eighteen, respectively, to learn a trade of "Suitable Employment." In turn, their masters or mistresses agreed to provide the orphans with food, clothing, lodging, and the rudiments of an education. At the expiration of the terms of indenture, the apprentices received the customary allowance paid to servants on the occasion of their liberation. The apprentices had recourse to the courts in cases of violations of the terms of their indentures.

The 1755 act remained effective for four years, at which time it was repealed by order of the king in council. According to the chief justice and attorney general of North Carolina, the law gave the county courts unlimited jurisdiction over cases involving questions of equity, that is, the supervision of the disposal of estates of deceased, which was contrary to the laws of Great Britain. Quickly, the assembly in 1760 passed another "Act for the better Care of Orphans" which differed in only one particular from the previous law. The new statute contained a provision for apprenticing free-born illegitimate children and mulatto females to the age of twenty-one. Liable to the same objections as the act of 1755 and linked to the crisis over the inferior and superior court bills of 1760, the orphan act of 1760 was also voided by the crown.

Finally, in 1762, the assembly enacted a satisfactory orphan law in conjunction with inferior and superior court legislation. Other than certain limitations placed upon the jurisdiction of county courts in matters of filial portions, legacies, and the distributions of intestates' estates, the only change of substance was the replacement of the churchwardens by the grand juries of the counties as agencies to inform the courts of unapprenticed children and malfeasance by guardians. Otherwise the provisions of the 1755 law and the addition of the 1760 statute remained effective in the regulation of orphanage in North Carolina.

Although the laws of the province required the county courts to conduct orphans courts at which business affecting orphanage would be transacted,the courts rarely complied. Edgecombe was more strict than most in its observance of the legislation, but even this county called an orphans court only seven times between 1757 and 1775. Usually, proceedings affecting orphans were transacted whenever exigency dictated. The difficulties of travel and the necessity of immediate appointments of masters and guardians to care for orphaned children made impossible the confinement of orphanage matters to a particular day or even to a particular session of the quarterly courts.

In Edgecombe the distribution of orphaned children immediately reflected the economic competency of the populace of the county. Between 1757 and 1775 the county court directed the care of 283 orphans, of whom 188 or two thirds possessed estates sufficient to warrant guardianship. Only one third of the children came from families so poor as to necessitate apprenticeship. Nevertheless, the latter group bears close examination, for they too vividly illustrate the nature of Edgecombe society and the orphanage system.

The apprenticing of impoverished orphans served an indispensable social function in that it relieved the county and parish of the burden of supporting the children, while at the same time it prepared them to enter society as useful adults with the fundamentals of an education and a skill. The indenture of apprenticeship most often contained the agreement of the master or mistress to educate the orphan, teach the orphan a trade, and, of course, supply him with sufficient food, clothing, and lodging. Although the laws of the province merely instructed masters to teach their apprentices to read and write, the courts often took the stricture more seriously. The Edgecombe justices ordered James Ricks to give his apprentice at least one year's schooling as soon as possible. The Rowan court, generally more explicit than most county courts in its instructions, frequently demanded that masters provide apprentices with eighteen months of education during which study the children should learn to read, write legibly, and "cypher to the five common rules." Moreover, the Rowan justices directed that the children be raised "in the Protestant Christian Religion."

The trades to which the children were apprenticed in Edgecombe County not only reflected the agrarian nature of Edgecombe society but also indicated a diversified economy in which specialization of labor was advanced. Almost half of the boys were destined to be planters. Carpentry constituted the next most popular skill; it was followed by a scattering of such trades as shoemaker, blacksmith, wheelwright, tailor, cooper, currier, tanner, saddler, and turner. Three boys were bound to merchant and justice of the peace Aquila Sugg to learn the "art and mystery of sailor," a knowledge of which Sugg must have obtained beyond the limits of the county. While the Tar River was "navigable a considerable part of the year for Boats of a particular construction, carrying from 200 to 400 Barrels; as high as 15 miles above Tarboro," surely it did not form a training ground for mariners. The girls were relegated to the domestic arts of carding, spinning, and weaving, which sufficed to retain them for a future of housewifery.

The inclusion in the 1760 law of a clause for apprenticing illegitimate children might have corrected an oversight in the preceding legislation but more probably reflected a concern for the increasing incidence of children born of illicit unions. Among the apprenticed orphans at least 35, and perhaps 39, of the 95 were illegitimate children. They represented 37 percent of the apprenticed orphans and 12 percent of the total number of orphans included in this study. The figures do not include the number of bastardy cases reported by women whose children for various reasons were not immediately apprenticed by the court. Such children numbered 11 between 1764 and 1775. Although precise birth data cannot be obtained for Edgecombe County, the available evidence does not detract from John Demos's hypothesis that late eighteenth century America may have represented the most free period in the nation's history in terms of sexual behavior.

Illegitimacy was not only a widespread phenomenon in Edgecombe, but several women habitually engaged in sexual relations outside the bonds of marriage. As many as ten women had two or more illegitimate children during the period under study. For example, in 1764 the court apprenticed a daughter of Sabra Revel; two years later the justices had to find a home for a six-month-old daughter of the same woman. Chloe and Ann Worthington, sisters perhaps, were ordered by the court in 1769 to bring "all" their illegitimate children to be apprenticed. The women postponed their appearance for five years but in 1774 produced three children for apprenticeship. The worst offender was Elizabeth Boazman who by 1764 had four illegitimate offspring. Her sixteen-year-old boy was apprenticed in 1765, but three years later when the court summoned her to appear again, she had had another child in the interim. While one hesitates to judge harshly, the county population obviously included men and women of deliberately loose morals.

The justices seemed unconcerned about the incidence of illegitimacy. The usual course of action was to compel the father, if known, to pay the mother £5 for midwife expenses and from £2 10s. 0d. to £5 0s. 0d. annually for three years for maintenance of the child, a rather small sum compared to the £12 to £16 required by the Cumberland court in such cases. If support was not immediately required by the court, then the reputed father produced a £200 bond "saving harmless the Parish of St. Mary for maintaining the child." Occasionally the justices imposed a small fine of £1 5s. 0d. to £2 10s. 0d. on the father. Generally the court viewed illegitimacy as part of the normal course of events in Edgecombe and made little effort to punish sexual offenders. Its only concern was to relieve the county and parish of financial responsibility for the children.

When apprenticing orphans, the Edgecombe court attempted to cushion the shock of the loss of a father and dissolution of the family by finding relatives or friends to care for the children. The court further eased the transition to orphanage by apprenticing siblings to the same master where possible. This was particularly true in the case of illegitimate offspring—the Quin brothers, Faircloth brothers, Johnson sisters, and Revel sisters—and belied a sympathetic understanding on the part of the justices of the more difficult adjustments to be made by those children. The court often bound boys or girls of like age and circumstance to the same master in order that the orphans might enjoy the companionship of peers. Aquila Sugg's three potential sailors were nineteen, eighteen, and sixteen years of age in 1767, while in 1774 illegitimates John Philips Worthington and Dicey Newton, aged six and five respectively, were bound to Jesse Deloach.

The process of apprenticeship was not always routine because the court frequently encountered resistance to binding orphans. Friends or neighbors of the orphan's families kept the children without formal indenture while mothers proved exceptionally reluctant to relinquish their children to the care of others. The maternal desire to maintain the family intact evoked many court summonses for women to produce their children for apprenticeship.

After the signing of an apprenticeship, indenture relations between masters and orphans were not always harmonious. Orphans frequently complained of mistreatment at the hands of their masters. This took the form of physical abuse or neglect by the master to feed, clothe, house, educate, or train the orphans properly. Upon such accusations the court usually summoned the master, and after an investigation either dismissed the complaint, released the orphan from his apprenticeship agreement, or bound the orphan to another master. An intriguing case occurred in Edgecombe when William Clark, one of the justices of the peace, was summoned to show why he "abused" orphans Lucretia and Crawford Johnson. Clark alleged that it was "not in his Power to be of Service to Lucretia & Crawford Johnson. . . [and] that he would Wish & as from Principles of Humanity he would by no Means expose said orphans that he may be discharged from the Trust reposed in him formerly by this Court." The court heeded his plea and remanded the orphans to the care of friends.

The most explicit charges tendered by apprentices, however, are found in the New Hanover County court records. Upon complaint against Mary Gallant for "inordinately beating and abusing" her apprentice, the court

471

required the mistress to enter into bond for her good behavior thereafter. When Jennett Cowan failed to clothe and educate her apprentice, and hired her to Jacob Hook without proper attire, the court placed the orphan under a trustee, widow Hannah Nevin, who received the orphan's wages and purchased the necessary wearing apparel. In another case, the New Hanover justices examined closely William Martindale's complaint that Michael Dyer refused to teach him the trade of shipwright. The court scrutinized the indenture, the orphan law of the province, and relevant sections of a parliamentary statute regarding orphanage in England to determine the best course of action. It finally decided to place Dyer under bond to instruct the orphan properly. Dyer, however, preferred to release Martindale from the indenture, to which the orphan agreed.

At the expiration of the apprenticeship the orphan law directed the masters to provide their charges with the customary "freedom dues" given to indentured servants. A 1741 statute designated freedom dues as a suit of clothes and £5, but in the case of apprenticeship the county courts often exhibited greater liberality. Freedom dues for girls consisted not only of a suit of "freedom clothes" or the equivalent in money but also a cow and calf, supplemented perhaps by a spinning wheel, cards, and knitting needles. Boys received a combination of money, clothes, tools of their trade, and horse, saddle, and bridle. The Rowan court proved exceptionally generous to Thomas Kelly when it ordered the orphan's master to give him a suit of clothes, a set of working tools, and £10 or a horse, saddle, and bridle equivalent in value to £10. Occasionally apprentices had to resort to the courts to compel their masters to liberate and pay them their freedom dues, but they experienced much less difficulty than indentured servants who throughout the counties brought numerous petitions to the courts requesting their freedom.

Guardianship added an extra dimension to the institution of orphanage. The courts placed orphans with sufficient inheritances to pay for their care and tutelage under the supervision of guardians. Of course, the justices made every effort to leave the children, particularly the young children, in the care of their mothers. Where impractical or impossible to rely upon maternal supervision, the courts attempted to place the orphans in homes of relatives and friends. However, custom dictated that once an orphan reached fourteen years of age he should be allowed to choose his guardian. Nevertheless, orphans attaining that age rarely elected to leave their court-appointed guardians. In Edgecombe only seven desired new guardians, of whom three left to lighten the burden of their mother, one to join an uncle, and another, apparently an unruly boy, to find a more satisfactory guardian after three previous attempts by the court had failed.

Upon the designation of a guardian, the Edgecombe court required the appointee to enter into bond with one or more securities for the protection of the orphan's estate. The bond usually amounted to approximately twice the estimated value of the estate, ranging from £25 in the case of Benjamin Mathews to £8,000 proclamation for Micajah Thomas, son of one of the richest merchants in the county. And the idea was meritorious. Josiah Quincy, Jr., noted that executors and administrators of estates in South Carolina made large sums for their services, an observation applicable to North Carolina as well, judging from the numerous complaints made to county courts charging fraud and corruption by executors and administrators. Guardians also stood to gain from their trusts. Not only did they possess the liquid assets which derived from the personal estates of the orphans' fathers, amounting in some cases to more than £1,000 proclamation, but they also controlled such valuable assets as slaves, plantations, gristmills, and stills. No wonder that securities often needed reassurance of the integrity and solvency of the guardians for whom they stood bond. Numerous examples of securities who desired bonded guardians to give counter security or additional security document this anxiety.

The opportunities for financial mismanagement of a minor's estate caused the county courts to attempt a strict supervision of the guardians. The law directed guardians to return immediately to the courts an inventory of their wards' property, after which they were expected to make annual statements of the receipts and disbursements of the orphans' estates. Most counties purchased special books in which to enter those accounts, though, unfortunately, few have survived. If Edgecombe is exemplary, the courts made futile efforts to oversee the guardians and administrators to settle their accounts, but the consequences were rarely gratifying. Edgecombe guardian accounts exist for only 74 of 158 orphans for whom guardians were appointed between 1760 and 1775, and three of these were recorded only at the deaths of the children. Rather than reporting annually to the court as required by law, guardians often chose to skip one to five years before submitting their accounts. James Knight, guardian of Elisha and Hardy Wall, made his first report in 1769, eight years after assuming control of the boys. Justice Aquila Sugg, appointed guardian of Hardy Maund in 1762, and regularly attending court during the subsequent decade, accounted for his charge's estate only after the boy's death in 1772.

The cost of feeding and lodging a child in Edgecombe County in the 1760s ranged from £3 to £5 proclamation per year, the equivalent of the cost of a featherbed and furniture, a cow and calf, or a large desk. These figures obtained for both boys and girls and did not change with increasing age of the children. By way of contrast, the cost of caring for black children amounted to £2 to £3 proclamation annually, and indication of the inferior diet and housing conditions afforded the slaves.

The wearing apparel of the children varied greatly according to their age and especially their wealth. The more fortunate, that is, wealthy, boys received from two to five shirts a year, one or two pairs of breeches or trousers, perhaps a matching waistcoat and breeches, and probably a coat or jacket. However, the accounts often listed only the purchase of cloth, as much as 23½ yards in a year, which the guardians or tailors altered into suitable clothes for the orphans. Rapid growth of the children necessitated at least one pair of shoes per year, which was often supplemented by a pair of boots. Occasionally a pair of yarn stockings accompanied the purchase of shoes. Orphans could expect the acquisition of one hat per year, usually felt or beaver but sometimes raccoon.

Guardian accounts for the girls are not as numerous or explicit as those for their male counterparts. Generally guardians purchased cloth for the girls, as much as 30 yards a year, which the orphans, their families, or tailors converted into finished items of clothing. Sacks, gowns, petticoats, shifts, banyons, and jackets were specifically mentioned. At least one pair of shoes and stockings were expected each year by the girls; a pair of gloves and handkerchiefs were sometimes listed. Caps and hats commonly appeared in the girls' accounts, though less frequently than hats in the boys' listings.

An unrepresentative but highly enlightening example of female dress appears in the account of Paulina Hall, daughter of merchant-planter Thomas Hall, whose estate enabled his children to afford the luxuries of Edgecombe life. At the approximate age of thirteen Paulina's consuming passion for clothes gave her the distinction of being among the best dressed young women in the Edgecombe region. Her first expenditure in 1767 as an orphan was the purchase of a fine cloak, after which followed in quick succession the acquisition of 35 yards of cloth, including the very expensive "mustine," out of which she and a seamstress, one Miss Geddy, fashioned gowns, petticoats, smocks, aprons, and sacks. For those special occasions which demanded a trim figure within the outward cluster of petticoats and bodices, a pair of stays were bought.

To complete her wardrobe Paulina added Barcelona handkerchiefs—the best brand—an average of three pairs of gloves each year (excluding mittens), garters, stockings, and shoes. This last item is engaging. While most orphans and children at that time were fortunate to obtain one pair of shoes per year, Paulina bought six pairs during her first year of orphanage, including the expensive calico and leather variety. Certainly her feet were among the best adorned of any female in the county.

Not only did Paulina's clothes closet not suffer by comparison in 1768, but her purchases bordered on the incredible: in January, 2 yards of fine muslin; February, 4 yards of fine durance, 1 yard of shalloon; March, 6 yards of holland, 1 yard of cambric, 12 yards of striped lutestring, 2 yards of linen, 1 yard of durance, 30 yards of "furriting," and one-half piece of costly chintz. And so the list continued during the course of the year. In addition to the cloth Paulina purchased 19 hanks of silk and 34 yards of ribbon for trimming. Being an industrious young woman, Paulina aided two seamstresses by making some of her clothes. Their efforts required 8 dozen needles, 21½ thousand pins, 4 pairs of scissors, 2 thimbles, and the necessary thread—in one year.

Nevertheless, Paulina's most startling acquisitions were yet to come. On October 14, while pondering the usual array of materials at Uncle James Hall's store in Tarboro, she noticed a capuchin, a hooded cloak, which was a most unusual item of apparel in the area. It would be perfect for the approaching winter season. Money was no object, fortunately, and the purchase was made. But Paulina had shopped too hastily. Two days before Christmas she found a scarlet cardinal, a short hooded cloak, even more expensive than the capuchin, and promptly bought it.

How Uncle James must have delighted to see his niece approaching. Not only did Paulina deplete his stock of clothing goods, but she required the necessary jewelry to accompany them. Included among the jewelry was a "pick tooth" case of combating those irritating pieces of food leftovers after a sumptuous meal at her guardian's house. It should be noted that Edgecombe women seemed to have used little jewelry, and Paulina was unique among the female orphans in her acquisition of four necklaces during her three years as an orphan.

The education of the orphans is especially interesting because it not only indicates the opportunities available for schooling in the county but also reflects the general level of literacy and the importance placed upon the need for education in North Carolina. Historians have consistently belittled the education and educational opportunities of colonial North Carolina; for most, the province ranked last in educational attainments among the English continental colonies. However, recent studies suggest that the North Carolinians were not uncultured boors but probably were versed at least in the rudiments of learning.

An examination of the guardian accounts supports this more favorable interpretation. Nine of 17 girls for whom more than two years of accounts exist received some education. Similar accounts for the boys show that 26 of 36 acquired schooling. Of course, these figures understate the total number of children exposed to formal instruction because some accounts were incomplete or being after the children received their education. Moreover, the omission of expenditures for schooling in records such as those of William Davis means little when the purchase of textbooks and paper obviously denotes exposure to a formal learning process. General compliance with statutory provisions to educate orphans would indicate similar concern for the education of nonorphaned children and, coupled with the observance of apprenticeship regulations, should have provided a satisfactory educational background for the county of Edgecombe.

The means by which North Carolina children received an education were manifold. Instruction by parents, older siblings, or tutors and admission to free and private schools indicate the variety of educational opportunities. Although the records are not always explicit, many Edgecombe orphans must have obtained training in the homes of their guardians. Jacob Fort's guardian paid the orphan's mother to instruct the boy. Guardians also utilized the community school to educate orphans. At least one school served the Edgecombe area in the 1760s, because John Ricks, guardian of David Bunn, was thwarted by the court in his attempt to charge 16 shillings expense "abuilding the Schoolhouse" to his ward's account. However, the court permitted guardians to credit accounts for expenses incurred in boarding itinerant schoolmasters.

Many children were sent to reside at a school or in another's charge for instruction. They constituted approximately half the number of orphans for whom educational expenses were listed. The length of residence varied from one quarter or three months to more than five years in the case of Benjamin Coffield. Their source of instruction is unclear. Perhaps one or two numbered among students at Thomas Tomlinson's school in New Bern; others may have been sent to Virginia with which Edgecombe maintained close ties, particularly through its mercantile establishments. Merchant Henry Irwin instructed his executors to send his sons to Virginia for their later education. Certainly Jeremiah Hilliard did not obtain three months' education at a "Singing School" in Edgecombe County.

School supplies and texts reflected the education received by the children. An inkpot, paper of inkpowder, quill, and quire of paper represented the initial outlay for a student. Sometimes a slate or penknife was purchased. Instruction was based upon hornbooks and primers, which were followed often by spellers. An occasional "cyphering book" indicated a formal course in mathematics, but generally the schoolmasters taught arithmetic from manuscript sum-books from which they dispensed rules and problems to students. The records include payments in one account for a Latin book and dictionary, but the exceptional character of this expenditure shows that little premium was placed on a classical education. Rather, most teachers probably taught English, perhaps exclusively.

Although the schoolmasters were rarely named in the guardian accounts, at least four in the 1760s can be identified. Thomas Bell augmented his carpenter's income with a teaching supplement. Henry Tanton resorted to the classroom when advanced age and infirmities prevented him from active physical work. Reverend Thomas Burgess in neighboring Halifax County extended his services as a teacher to Edgecombe residents who sometimes lacked the benefits of an Anglican minister. James Young seems to have been a transient in the county whose sojourn was too brief to yield information about him. The number of schoolmasters as well as the education afforded the orphans in the Edgecombe area compare favorably with Lawrence Cremin's conclusions about the education of orphans in Virginia.

The deaths of orphans allow further insight into the system of orphanage in Edgecombe County. The records reveal that at least three of the orphans for whom guardians had been appointed died before attaining their majority. Although Mary Coffield possessed a substantial estate of over £150 at her death, her guardian spent only £1 for her "Funeral expenses." Less reserved was Aquila Sugg, guardian of Hardy Maund. According to the guardian account, the orphan remained ill for twelve days before his death during which time £2 8s. 0d. was expended on candles, £3 0s. 0d. "for the Trouble of the House," £4 16s. 0d. for two attendants, and £5 1s. 0d. for Dr. Usher. A £4 0s. 0d. black walnut coffin was ordered and the boy was was dressed in "fine" white silk and linen. Two ministers conducted the service; seven years prior to that time a justice of the peace presided at the funeral of Governor Arthur Dobbs because a clergyman was not available. Of course these examples represent the extremes of funerary behavior, but they reveal the advantages open to the wealthier segment of Edgecombe society.

If Edgecombe County was representative of North Carolina society, most orphans possessed estates sufficient to justify guardianship. From this conclusion may be drawn the inferences that Carolinians generally lived within their incomes and that a semblance of middle class economic status prevailed. Although the apprenticed children composed a minority of the orphans, they presented special problems in that they were completely dependent upon their masters and often suffered the stigma of illegitimate birth. The courts attempted to mitigate these difficulties by binding siblings or children of like age to the same masters. Illegitimate births, many of which were probably never reported to the courts, seemed common in the colony, and the courts accepted illicit sexual practices passively. While apprenticed orphans occasionally complained of harsh treatment by their masters, they were less subject to abuse than indentured servants or slaves.

Orphans accorded guardianship fared better than apprentices because the guardians possessed a source of funds with which to care for the children and at the same time were more closely supervised by the courts. Of course, the wealthier orphans gained greater material advantages than those with smaller legacies, but the size of the estates did not necessarily determine the attention which the children received. Orphans attached to their mothers, brothers, or other relatives enjoyed the inestimable benefits of family affection. Most orphans, including apprentices, probably obtained the fundamentals of an education, and it is reasonable to assume that nonorphaned children also benefited from scholastic instruction. Thus, the educational attainments of colonial North Carolinians may have exceeded previous estimations of their academic competence.

Despite attempts by the courts to supervise guardians closely, North Carolinians evinced their ever-present disdain for the law. Vagaries of the weather and inadequate transportation facilities were partially responsible for the guardians' neglect to abide by orphanage regulations, but the Edgecombe experience demonstrates once again an innate aversion on the part of the colonials for stringent legal restrictions. Of course, such disregard for the law was not peculiar to colonial North Carolinians or even to the colonial era. Moreover, the degree of lawlessness among the provincial populace and the lack of institutional coercions rendered the existing social cohesion in colonial North Carolina all the more remarkable.

REFERENCES

Aries, Philippe. *Centuries of Childhood* (Vintage pbck., 1962).
Beales, Ross W. "In Search of the Historical Child: Miniature Adulthood and Youth in Colonial New England," *American Quarterly*, 27 (1975), 379-98.
Calhoun, Arthur W. *Social History of the American Family*, 3 Vols. (New York, 1917).
Cremin, Lawrence D. *American Education: The Colonial Experience* (New York, 1970).
deMause, Lloyd. "The Evolution of Childhood," in *The History of Childhood*, edited by Lloyd deMause (New York, 1974), 1-73.
Demos, John. *A Little Commonwealth: Family Life in Plymouth Colony* (New York, 1970).
Ebel, Henry. "The Damned," *History of Childhood Quarterly*, 3:3 (1976), 408.
Fox, Vivian C. "Is Adolescence a Modern Phenomenon?" *Journal of Psychohistory*, 5 (1977), 271-290.
Goody, Jack; Joan Thirsk and E.P. Thompson, (eds.), *Family and Inheritance* (Cambridge, 1976).
Greven, Philip J., Jr. *Four Generations* (Ithaca, N.Y., 1970).
Howard, G.E. *History of Matrimonial Institutions*, 3 Vols. (Chicago, 1904).
Laslett, Peter, ed. *Household and Family in Past Time* (Cambridge, 1972).
Macfarlane, Alan. *Witchcraft in Tudor and Stuart England* (New York, 1970).
_____. *The Origins of English Individualism* (Cambridge, 1978).
Mingay, G.E. *English Landed Society in the Eighteenth Century* (London and Toronto, 1963).
Morgan, Edmund S. *The Puritan Family* (Harper Torchbook, 1966).
Murrin, John. Review Essay, *History and Theory*, XI:2 (1972).
Pearson, Lu Emily. *Elizabethans at Home* (Stanford, 1957).
Powell, Chilton L. *English Domestic Relations, 1487-1653* (New York, 1917).
Quitt, Martin, H. From "Elite to Aristocracy: The Psychodynamic Transformation of the Virginia Ruling Class." Paper read at Second Summer Workshop, Institute for Psychohistory. New York, July, 1976.
Shorter, Edward. *The Making of the Modern Family* (New York, 1975).
Spruill, Julia C. *Women's Life and Labor in the Colonial South* (Chapel Hill, N.C., 1938).
Spufford, Margaret. "Peasant Inheritance Customs and Land Distribution in Cambridgeshire from the Sixteenth to the Eighteenth Centuries," in *Family and Inheritance*, edited by J. Goody, J. Thirsk, and E.P. Thompson (Cambridge, 1976), 156-176.
_____. "First Steps in Literacy: The Reading and Writing Experiences of the Humblest Seventeenth-Century Spiritual Autobiographies," *Social History* 4 (1979): 407-435.
Thirsk, Joan. "Younger Sons in the Seventeenth Century," *History*, 14 (1969).
Thomas, Keith. *Religion and the Decline of Magic* (New York, 1971).
_____. "Age and Authority in Early Modern England," *Proceedings of the British Academy*, LXII (1976), 205-248.
Wells, Robert V. "Family History and Demographic Transition," *Journal of Social History* 9 (1975): 1-19.

# ACKNOWLEDGMENTS

Acknowledgments of Copyrighted
Materials Reprinted in
Part or in Whole

Part Two

*Chapter One,* Courtship to Marriage Formation

p. 121  H. J. Habbakuk, "Marriage Settlements in the Eighteenth Century," *Transactions of the Royal Historical Society* XXXII (1950), pp. 15-30. Reprinted by permission.

p. 126  J. D. Chambers, *Population, Economy and Society in Pre-Industrial England,* edited by W. A. Armstrong, (c) Oxford University Press, 1972, pp. 44-55 by permission of the Oxford University Press.

p. 132  Robert V. Wells, "Quaker Marriage Patterns in a Colonial Perspective," *William and Mary Quarterly,* 3rd Series XXIX: 3 (1972), pp. 415-442. Reprinted by permission.

p. 143  J. William Frost, *The Quaker Family in Colonial America* (St. Martin's Press, Inc., Macmillan & Company, Ltd., 1973), from 162-168. Reprinted by permission.

p. 147  Daniel Scott Smith, "Parental Power and Marriage Patterns: An Analysis of Historical Trends in Hingham, Massachusetts," *Journal of Marriage and the Family* (August, 1973), pp. 419-428. Copyrighted 1973 by the National Council on Family Relations. Reprinted by permission.

*Chapter Two,* Preparenthood

p. 163  Lee Emily Pearson, *Elizabethans at Home* (Stanford, 1957), 363-430. Reprinted by permission of the publishers, Stanford University Press. (c) 1957 by the Board of Trustees of the Leland Stanford Junior University.

p. 177  Lawrence Stone, *The Crisis of the Aristocracy,* (c) Oxford University Press, 1965, pp. 660-669, by permission of the Oxford University Press.

p. 182  Julia Cherry Spruill, *Women's Life and Work in the Southern Colonies* (University of North Carolina Press, 1938), 65-84, 163-176. Reprinted by permission.

p. 193   P. E. H. Hair, "Bridal Pregnancy in Rural England in Earlier Centuries," *Population Studies,* XX: 2 (1966), pp. 233-241. Reprinted by permission.

p. 200   Daniel Scott Smith and Michael S. Hindus, "Premarital Pregnancy in America, 1640-1971: An Overview and Interpretation," *The Journal of Interdisciplinary History,* V (1974), 537-560. Reprinted by permission of *The Journal of Interdisciplinary History* and the M.I.T. Press.

*Chapter Three,* Childbearing

p. 215   J. D. Chambers, *Population, Economy, and Society in Pre-Industrial England,* edited by W. A. Armstrong, (c) Oxford University Press, 1972, pp. 62-75, by permission of the Oxford University Press.

p.225   Michael Eshleman, "Diet during Pregnancy in the Sixteenth and Seventeenth Centuries," *Journal of the History of Medicine* (1975), XXX:1, pp. 23-39. Reprinted by permission.

p. 237   R. V. Schnucker, "The English Puritans and Pregnancy, Delivery and Breast Feeding," *History of Childhood Quarterly,* 1:4 (1974), pp. 637-658. Reprinted by permission.

p. 244   Robert V. Wells, "Quaker Marriage Patterns in a Colonial Perspective," *William and Mary Quarterly,* 3rd Series, XXIX:3 (1972), pp. 415-442. Reprinted by permission.

p. 247   Julia Cherry Spruill, *Women's Life and Work in the Southern Colonies,* (University of North Carolina Press, 1938), 48-55. Reprinted by permission.

*Chapter Four,* Childrearing

p. 256   J. D. Chambers, *Population, Economy and Society in Pre-Industrial England,* edited by W. A. Armstrong, (c) Oxford University Press, 1972, pp. 77-80 by permission of the Oxford University Press.

p. 258   Reprinted from *The World We Have Lost* by Peter Laslett by permission of Charles Scribner's Sons, copyright (c) 1965 Peter Laslett.

p. 260   R. V. Schnucker, "The English Puritans and Pregnancy, Delivery and Breast Feeding," *History of Childhood Quarterly,* 1:4 (1974), pp. 637-658. Reprinted by permission.

# ACKNOWLEDGMENTS

p. 267　John F. Walzer, "A Period of Ambivalence: Eighteenth Century American Childhood," *The History of Childhood,* edited by Lloyd deMause (New York: The Psychohistory Press, 1974), pp. 351-382. Reprinted by permission.

p. 277　Joseph E. Illick, "Child-Rearing in Seventeenth Century England and America," *The History of Childhood,* edited by Lloyd deMause (New York: The Psychohistory Press, 1974), pp. 303-350, Reprinted by permission.

p. 289　Lawrence Stone, "The Rise of the Nuclear Family," in *The Family in History,* edited by Charles Rosenberg (University of Pennsylvania Press, 1975), 13-49, 56-57. Reprinted by permission.

p. 297　W. K. Jordan, *The Charities of London, 1480-1660* (George Allen and Unwin, Ltd., 1960), 206-208. Reprinted by permission.

p. 299　J. H. Plumb, "The New World of Children in Eighteenth Century England," *Past and Present,* 67 (1973), 64-93. World Copyright: *The Past and Present Society,* Corpus Christi College, Oxford, England. The extracts from this article are reprinted with the permission of the Society and the author from *Past and Present: A Journal of Historical Studies,* No. 67 (May, 1975.)

p. 312　Elizabeth Schlesinger, "Cotton Mather and His Children," *William and Mary Quarterly,* 3rd Series, X (1953), 181-189. Reprinted by permission.

p. 334　Steven R. Smith, "Religion and the Conception of Youth in Seventeenth Century England," *History of Childhood Quarterly,* 2:4 (1975), pp. 493-516. Reprinted by permission.

p. 353　N. Ray Hiner, "Adolescence in Eighteenth Century America," *History of Childhood Quarterly,* 3:2 (1975), pp. 253-280. Reprinted by permission.

*Chapter Five:* Post-Childrearing

p. 379　Lawrence Stone, "The Rise of the Nuclear Family," in *The Family in History,* edited by Charles Rosenberg (University of Pennsylvania Press, 1975), 13-49. Reprinted by permission.

p. 386　Reprinted from Philip J. Greven, Jr., *Four Generations.* Copyright 1970 by Cornell University. Used by permission of Cornell University Press.

*Chapter Six:* Spouse Loss

p. 407   Lu Emily Pearson, *Elizabethans at Home* (Stanford, 1957), 490-517. Reprinted by permission of the publishers, Stanford University Press. (c) 1957 by the Board of Trustees of the Leland Stanford Junior University.

p. 421   W. K. Jordan, *The Charities of London 1480-1660* (George Allen and Unwin, Ltd., 1960), 28-32. Reprinted by permission.

p. 425   Alexander Keyssar, "Widowhood in Eighteenth Century Massachusetts," *Perspectives in American History,* VIII (1974), 83-172. Reprinted by permission.

p. 446   Reprinted from *Family Life and Illicit Love in the Past* by Peter Laslett by permission of Cambridge University Press. Peter Laslett, *Family Life and Illicit Love in the Past* (New York, 1977), pp. 160-173.

p. 456   Charles H. Carlton, "The Administration of London's Court of the Orphans," *Guildhall Miscellany,* Vol. 4, 1971-1973, pp. 22-35. Reprinted by permission.

p. 467   Alan D. Watson, "Orphanage in Colonial North Carolina: Edgecombe County as a Case Study," *The North Carolina Historical Review,* LII:2 (1975), 105-119. Reprinted by permission.

# INDEX